Fundamentals of the Computing Sciences

Fundamentals
of the Computing Sciences

Kurt Maly
University of Minnesota

Allen R. Hanson
Hampshire College

Prentice-Hall, Inc.
Englewood Cliffs, New Jersey   07632

Library of Congress Cataloging in Publication Data

MALY, KURT, (date)
    Fundamentals of the computing sciences.

    Includes bibliographical references and index.
    1. Electronic data processing. 2. Electronic
digital computers—Programming. 3. Algorithms.
4. Programming languages (Electronic computers)
I. Hanson, Allen R., (date) joint author. II. Title
QA76.M2743   001.6'4   77-12916
ISBN 0-13-335240-4

Printed in the United States of America

10 9 8 7 6 5 4 3 2 1

PRENTICE-HALL INTERNATIONAL, INC., *London*
PRENTICE-HALL OF AUSTRALIA PTY. LIMITED, *Sydney*
PRENTICE-HALL OF CANADA, LTD., *Toronto*
PRENTICE-HALL OF INDIA PRIVATE LIMITED, *New Delhi*
PRENTICE-HALL OF JAPAN, INC., *Tokyo*
PRENTICE-HALL OF SOUTHEAST ASIA PTE. LTD., *Singapore*
WHITEHALL BOOKS LIMITED, *Wellington, New Zealand*

To My Wife

KM

For Joan, Kristine, and David:

"We are not stuff that abides, but patterns that perpetuate themselves."
(Herbert Wiener, in *The Human Use of Human Beings*.)

AH

Contents

Summary of Book by Chapters

Of central importance to computer science and, in fact, any essentially problem-solving discipline is the notion of algorithms. The core concept, around which the entire book revolves, is the construction of algorithms in general and their computer representation in particular. In *Chapter 1* we introduce the concept of an algorithm very informally, namely, as a method for communicating ideas. By imposing an increasing amount of structure on this informal notion, we eventually obtain a formalism for expressing algorithms: the Turing machine. Since the Turing machine is basically an abstract device, the advanced topics section of Chapter 1 (supplement) discusses the limitations of computability and of the halting problem and its relation to the program debugging problem. This discussion in Chapter 1 is intended to set the framework for the development of an informal algorithmic language (AL), developed in the next chapter.

Once the concept of an algorithm has been formalized, the question arises as to how an algorithm is developed. *Chapter 2* begins with a discussion of the techniques of problem formulation and the modular refinement of algorithms. These techniques are amplified throughout the remainder of the book. To facilitate application of these techniques to the types of problems to be developed, we develop the algorithmic language AL in the next section of Chapter 2. This language is based on the concepts developed during the discussion of the Turing machine in Chapter 1 and is the intermediary expository language employed in succeeding chapters. Based on structured programming constructs, AL provides an open-ended approach to algorithm design. As an example, a Turing machine simulator is developed. The chapter concludes with a discussion of the practical aspects of computing languages, their structural properties, and considerations in the choice of language for different types of problems.

The formulation of precise algorithms from imprecise problem descriptions is one of the least understood processes for the novice. *Chapter 3* is devoted to an amplification of these processes given the discussion begun in Chapter 2. Specifically, the concept of a design document is introduced; this document specifies the hierarchical structure of the modules comprising the solution and a description of each module. The design document represents the complete solution to the problem in terms of abstract algorithms. The remainder of the chapter is devoted to the transformation of the ideas embodied in the design document into a working program, including questions relating to the selection of data structures, implementation plans, documentation, test data, etc.

Once some familiarity with the notion of an algorithm is gained, it becomes apparent that for any given problem there exists a plethora of algorithms which in some sense represent the solution to the original problem. In *Chapter 4* we introduce the idea of the complexity of an algorithm: Given several algorithms ostensibly solving the same class of problems, how does one decide which algorithm is the "best"? Various techniques for transforming proposed solutions into "better" algorithms are presented. Several sections of this chapter require some mathematical maturity.

In *Chapter 5* we are concerned with a particular class of algorithms employed to illustrate the techniques developed in Chapter 4. These algorithms are practical algorithms devoted to sorting and searching; analyses of these procedures are carried as far as possible to illustrate the difficulties encountered in the analysis of relatively complex algorithms. The chapter concludes with a practical problem derived from business data processing: maintenance of a collection of records.

Because of the finite nature of the computer and its storage devices, algorithms operating primarily on numbers are subject to error. This fact introduces another variable in the study of constructing algorithms. *Chapter 6* is devoted to the study of the nature of errors and their causes. The types of errors considered include round-off errors and truncation errors. Since some familiarity with calculus is required, it is recommended that this chapter be skipped by those readers without the requisite background. The remainder of the book, with the exception of Chapter 7, does not depend on the concepts developed here except in the most general sense.

In *Chapter 7* we investigate a variety of numerical algorithms, including systems of linear equations (supplement), iterative techniques, root finding, interpolation and integration (supplement), and descriptive statistics. The general idea here is to provide a selection of commonly used algorithms within the framework developed in the first six chapters. Both practical and theoretical aspects of these procedures are discussed.

The first seven chapters of the book are devoted to the nature, structure, and complexity of algorithms with emphasis on numerical calculations. In the remaining chapters we shift the emphasis to algorithms concerned basically with nonnumeric applications. In *Chapter 8* we are concerned with system processes, including the nature of operating systems, file structures, command languages, the structure of processors, and compilers and interpreters. The discussion culminates in two reasonably comprehensive examples: lexical scanning and symbol table maintenance and finally an example simulation of a simple computer system is developed (supplement). The latter example leads into a discussion of multiprogramming and general system processes.

In *Chapter 9* we address the general area of data structures. The distinction among data objects, abstract structures, and physical data structures is made to facilitate the later discussion. The remainder of the chapter is devoted to types of data structures and their implementation, including linear structures and nonlinear structures. The symbol table maintenance problem from Chapter 8 is continued as a forum for the discussion of string operations and the general problem of garbage collection.

The manipulation of symbols representing textual material is considered in *Chapter 10*. In this chapter we discuss the use of the computer in the area of textual analysis. A discussion of nonnumeric processing is followed by several comprehensive examples, including the generation of concordances and the problem of stylistic analysis based on statistical methods and structural properties of the text.

In *Chapter 11* we are concerned with the phenomena of recursion. Using several well-known examples, the concept of a recursive process is developed. Several of the examples from preceding chapters are resurrected and formulated as recursive processes; general procedures for developing recursive solutions to problems are provided. The implementation of recursive procedures in languages not supporting recursion is discussed; this discussion provides a basis for the comparison of iterative and recursive formulations of algorithms. In the final section we approach the problem of measuring the complexity of recursive algorithms, taking into account the overhead of the recursive implementation.

The final chapter is an excursion into some aspects of artificial intelligence. In *Chapter 12* we discuss the use of games as an approach to artificial intelligence and develop the minimax tree-searching procedure and its derivatives. The forum for this discussion is the implementation of a program for playing Kalah. In the final section we present an open-ended robotics example designed to illustrate the range of problems considered in this area of computer science. This chapter represents a synthesis of representation of complex data structures, algorithmic complexity, recursion, and heuristic programming.

We should note that wherever possible actual FORTRAN or SNOBOL programs are provided to illustrate the techniques under discussion. Ample opportunity is left for the reader to improve and extend these programs as he/she sees fit, either through the exercises provided within each chapter or through the exercises at the end of each chapter. The actual programming expertise required for the maximal use of the book is provided by the supplemental volume, containing introductions to FORTRAN and SNOBOL. This volume forms the basis for a concurrent programming laboratory which should accompany the course based on this book. We should further emphasize that it is not our intent in the book to cover topics introduced here in depth; rather, the topics form an introduction into the major problem areas of computer science.

Preface

During the past thirty years, the electronic digital computer has become a force which cannot be lightly dismissed. The industries surrounding this machine may become the single largest industry in this country. Growing in conjunction with this remarkable device and the underlying technological advances has been the field of computer science, devoted to the study of the computer and the processes it supports.

It is the purpose of this book to introduce topics selected from computer science using an approach that is fairly rigorous yet straightforward. The authors feel the time has come to strip away from the cult of computer science many of its ritualistic qualities while leaving intact the basic concepts inherent in the study of the computer: information processing, its applications, and its limitations. The book itself is an outgrowth of two courses offered to freshmen and sophomores in the computer science department of the University of Minnesota. As we see it, the book has a variety of audiences. The major audience is composed of undergraduate computer science majors. As a basic course(s) in computer science, many of the topics covered in detail in advanced courses are introduced here, hopefully with enough basic material to facilitate the transition to the advanced courses yet with enough left out to induce in the reader a yearning for knowledge. If this has been accomplished, the authors are more than satisfied.

The actual audience comprising the courses on which the book is based was an interesting mixture of computer science students, electrical and mechanical engineering students, students from other "hard" sciences, mathematics majors, and humanities students. Many of the students in the last category were particularly interested in the second course dealing with SNOBOL, string and list processing, their applications, and artificial intelligence. By choosing topics contained in the book carefully, it is possible to tailor courses appealing to a wide variety of students, including those outside the sciences.

We have endeavored to keep topics and concepts self-contained wherever possible. While this induces a somewhat fragmented chapter structure, it facilitates the "pick and choose" tailoring which we find very useful once the basic framework has been established in the first four chapters. Little advanced mathematics is required; those topics which require advanced skills are collected into a supplemental volume (*Supplement to Fundamentals of the Computing Sciences*)†; the Advanced Topics section may be skipped without distracting from the basic concepts introduced in each chapter. In addition to the exercises at the end of each chapter we interspersed a number of exercises throughout the text to encourage an active reading of the book. Most of these exercises contribute to the flow of exposition, and we therefore provide solutions in the supplemental volume to those which we believe are important to the understanding of the underlying concepts.

For the reasons discussed at the end of Chapter 2, the expository languages are FORTRAN and SNOBOL. Because FORTRAN is heavily implementation-dependent, illustrative programs are written from the vantage of standard FORTRAN. Nonstandard features are introduced through extensibility mechanisms, even though these features may appear intact in many versions of FORTRAN. It is expected that the development of programming fluency will be accomplished concurrently with the development of topics found in this book.

As we see it, the first course in computer science and hence a book claiming to be an introduction to the computing sciences should possess two major characteristics:

I. First and foremost should be the teaching of a problem-solving methodology. This should include the proper way to state a problem, procedures for finding a solution of a set of solutions, a statement of the solution in a proper algorithmic language, selection of the "best" solution, and *finally* the translation into a well-structured program with subsequent testing and debugging.

II. Second, the above should be achieved in conjunction with an introduction to the major areas of computer science to give the student both preparation for the advanced courses in the curriculum and the possibility of making an early selection of special interest fields.

We note that of the concepts and methods suggested in characteristic I) only the last is dependent on the existence of an actual programming language. In view of this, arguments concerned with the selection of a programming language for classroom use become much less important. Problem solution construction may be done in a simple structured language, amenable to proving the correctness of programs, and only the final step need be accomplished with an implemented language. While many of the algorithms are ultimately written as FORTRAN or SNOBOL programs, these choices are not critical. The concepts of problem-solving are developed using a structured algorithmic language. It is a trivial matter, once the concepts of algorithmic problem

---

†The supplemental volume is broken into four sections; these sections include the introductions to FORTRAN and SNOBOL, the advanced sections of each chapter (retaining the original numbering system of the chapters), and the solutions to the exercises. Those instructors wishing to use their own language materials are granted permission to copy and distribute the solutions to the exercises as they see fit.

solving are firmly developed, to translate solutions in the algorithmic language into solutions in any "real" programming language.

Since we view this book as a textbook for a first course in computer science (B1, according to the ACM Curriculum 68 recommendations), we mainly address the computer science student as a user of the computer. Therefore, we only superficially touch on hardware, computer architecture and design, and machine and assembly language and discuss them only insofar as they concern the user in such areas as assembly, compilation, and operating systems. We feel that this is a reasonable approach since this material is properly covered in separate books; also, the days when a thorough knowledge of assembly language was a requisite for programming are long since gone.

HOW TO USE THE BOOK

We suggest that at least two ten-week quarters are required to adequately cover the material. The concepts introduced may be covered in the course lectures while commensurate programming language skills are being developed in parallel programming laboratories for which the supplement can be used as reference. Or the chapters of this book may be covered directly if the students have obtained a working knowledge of some high-level programming language through a "service" course or through self-study. For a one-semester course, chapters may be selected depending on the known or assumed interests of the audience. For example, a course with a basically numerical flavor may be obtained by eliminating Chapters 9–12. A course with a nonnumerical flavor might include Chapters 1–3 and 8–12.

ACKNOWLEDGMENTS

The authors are deeply indebted to their colleagues for comments, appraisals, and criticisms during the preparation of this manuscript. Special thanks are due Oscar Ibarra for organizational suggestions and his contribution to Chapter 1 in particular and also to Jay Leavitt for a critical analysis of the faults in early drafts of Chapter 7; finally, many thanks are due Edward Riseman for his contributions to the robotics section in Chapter 12. Grateful acknowledgment is made to the patience of the students of computer science who endured the early versions of the courses on which this book is based. Among the many, we particularly wish to mention John Mehaffey, Tom Moher, and Richard Weston for their valuable contributions to the development and running of the programming examples. Last but not least we gratefully acknowledge our debt to Joan Hanson, Judi Matheson, and Anna Moody for the typing of the manuscript, Christiana Maly and Joan Hanson for aid in proofreading and editing and our respective departments for their support.

KURT MALY
ALLEN R. HANSON

Fundamentals of the Computing Sciences

1

Algorithms

1.0 INTRODUCTION

It might be argued that man's very existence depends on his success at problem-solving. If we intuitively define a problem as a discrepancy between a desired situation and the current situation in which we find ourselves, a problem solution becomes a procedure, or method, for transforming the current situation into the desired one. Trivial examples of problems then include getting to work on time in the morning, deciding what to eat for breakfast, etc. We don't normally consider such everyday activities as problems to be solved since their solution is usually rather trivial. We normally reserve the word *problem* to cover more substantial situational discrepancies. The problem-solving process, that is, the method by which one goes about solving a problem, is rather interesting in itself. G. Polya makes the comment†

> A great discovery solves a great problem but there is a grain of discovery
> in the solution of any problem. Your problem may be modest; but if it
> challenges your curiosity and brings into play your inventive faculties,
> and if you solve it by your own means, you may experience the tension and
> enjoy that triumph of discovery.

The solutions to everyday problems such as described above do not normally tax our intellectual capabilities, and their solution is of relatively little importance to anyone except ourselves. On the other hand, the solution of a generally interesting problem involves stating the problem in understandable form and communicating the problem solution to others who may be interested. In those cases in which a computer is the ultimate recipient of the solution, this communication involves transmittal of a *procedure* stating explicitly the steps leading to the solution. It is this concept of prob-

†G. Polya, *How To Solve It: A New Aspect of Mathematical Method*, 2nd Ed., Princeton University Press, Princeton, N.J., 1945, p. v.

1

lem solution and communication which makes the study of algorithms of importance to computer science and the subject to which this first chapter is devoted.

1.1 A BRIEF HISTORICAL PERSPECTIVE

Man's inventiveness in producing labor-saving devices is legend. The second industrial revolution was important not so much for any specific device or "thing" that emerged from it but rather as an intellectual advance. As Alvin Toffler† states,

> ... technological innovation does not merely combine and recombine machines and techniques. Important new machines do more than suggest or compel changes in other machines—they suggest novel solutions to social, philosophical, even personal problems. They alter man's total intellectual environment—the way he thinks and looks at the world.

Just as it would be foolish to attempt to outline and analyze the second industrial revolution in a few pages, it would be presumptuous to attempt to do the same for the information processing revolution currently under way. We leave it for future historians and humanists to assess the importance of what we are currently experiencing and to place it in proper perspective. We shall attempt only to outline selected germane ideas and historical events of primary importance, fully realizing that doing so may result in a biased perspective.

One of the important contributions of the second industrial revolution was the development of the foundations for the machine tool industry. This effectively allowed the mass production of precision mechanical instruments. As we shall see, many of the ideas discussed below, while important conceptually, were well beyond the engineering capabilities of the time. One cannot, therefore, consider the development of the computer (for example) in isolation from the emergent disciplines surrounding it.

The industrial revolution resulted in the development of a technology aimed at relieving the monotony and physical exertion required in hitherto manual tasks. This technology was concerned with (mainly) the efficient transmission, manipulation, and control of power. Intertwined with its development has been the emergence of a parallel technology concerned with the efficient transmission and manipulation of information. The products of the latter technology are designed to relieve the monotony and mental exertion encountered in basically menial tasks.

One of the earliest mechanical aids for a basically menial task was the abacus, known and used by the Greeks (and others), dating from circa 3000 B.C. (although probably not in its present form). While the abacus remains an important computing device in many parts of the world even today, it has all but disappeared in most Western cultures.

Without dwelling on the events of the intervening centuries, the next major conceptual advance occurred in France in 1642. Blaise Pascal, at that time 19 years old, invented a mechanical adding machine (Figure 1.1) which operated on the same prin-

---

†Alvin Toffler, *Future Shock*, Bantam Books, New York, 1970, p. 29.

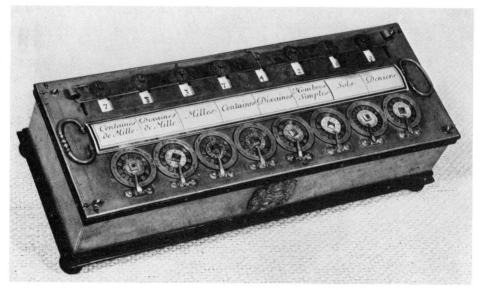

Fig. 1.1   Pascal's adding machine. (*Courtesy of IBM Corporation*)

ciple as the odometer in a car. That is, it implemented the operations of addition and subtraction by counting the number of revolutions of appropriately linked wheels.

Apparently this device was conceived to help his father, Etienne, who was a tax collector in Normandy. This simple device has been improved over the years (Pascal's original machine was unreliable); its direct descendants include present-day mechanical adding machines, cash registers, gas and electric meters, etc. Approximately 30 years later, Gottfried Wilhelm Leibniz extended Pascal's device to include the operations of multiplication and division. Even though Leibniz' device did not work so well as it should have because of engineering difficulties, the advantages inherent in such devices were recognized by him:†

> Also the astronomers surely will not have to continue to exercise the patience which is required for computation. It is this that deters them from computing or correcting tables, ... For it is unworthy of excellent men to lose hours like slaves in the labor of calculation which could safely be relegated to anyone else if machines were used.

It wasn't until 100 years later, in 1773, that Otto Hahn perfected a four-process device (addition, subtraction, multiplication, and division) which was reliable.

During the early 1800s, Joseph Jacquard revolutionized the textile industry by introducing an automatic loom capable of weaving extremely intricate patterns completely automatically, once the loom had been properly set up (Figure 1.2). The control of the loom components was accomplished by a series of cards which passed through a sensing mechanism one at a time. Each card contained holes in appropriate locations

†D. E. Smith, *A Source Book of Mathematics*, Vol. I, Dover, New York, 1959, p. 182.

Fig. 1.2 An example of a Jacquard automatic loom. (*Courtesy of IBM Corporation*)

which controlled the motion of the hooks, the color of thread, etc. Thus, once a particular pattern had been designed and transferred to these cards, the loom could produce as many copies of the pattern as desired. It is interesting to note that a similar loom had been designed in Germany around 1660 but that the inventor was drowned by order of the German government and the idea suppressed. However, Jacquard's invention was to provide a portion of the framework from which emerged the next major development in information processing.

The protagonist is now an eccentric Cambridge mathematician by the name of Charles Babbage, and the year is roughly 1812. As Babbage himself states,†

> The earliest idea that I can trace in my own mind of calculating arithmetical tables by machinery arose in this manner:
>
> One evening I was sitting in the rooms of the Analytical Society at Cambridge, my head leaning forward on the table in a kind of dreamy mood, with a Table of logarithms lying open before me. Another member, coming into the room, and seeing me half asleep, called out, "Well, Babbage, what are you dreaming about?" to which I replied, "I am thinking that all these Tables (pointing to the logarithms) might be calculated by machinery."

†Charles Babbage, *Passages from the Life of a Philosopher*, Longman, Green, Longman, Roberts and Green, London, 1864; reprinted by Dover, New York, 1968, p. 42.

Babbage's accomplishments, interests, and eccentricities were many; we are mainly interested in the two devices whose design and construction were to occupy the remainder of his lifetime. The first of these Babbage called the *difference engine*. It was designed to compute the tables referred to in his statement by evaluating a polynomial (i.e., an expression of the form $a_1 X^n + a_2 X^{n-1} + \cdots + a_n X + a_{n+1}$) using a procedure known as the difference method. Since most mathematical functions can be approximated as closely as is desired by some polynomial, the difference engine would have been capable of producing highly accurate tables of these functions. The latter feat, because of the repetitive nature of the calculations and the accuracy required, is virtually impossible to accomplish by humans; errors are bound to creep in. After a modest amount of support from the British government (which was interested in the device to compute nautical tables) was lost, Babbage terminated work on the partially completed engine (Figure 1.3) in 1833.

Fig. 1.3   Babbage's difference engine. (*Courtesy of IBM Corporation*)

During development of the difference engine (which was a machine for performing a single task), Babbage conceived of a device of far greater generality: the *analytical engine*. If one compares the notion of the four-process machine perfected by Hahn and the difference engine as proposed by Babbage, one extremely important concept emerges. While Hahn's machine was rather limited in the operations it performed, it could be used to perform any computation. That is, a human operator is responsible for determining the sequence of events which are to occur and for using the machine to perform the basic operations. On the other hand, Babbage's difference engine was designed to perform a single task without human intervention. In this sense it was more limited than Hahn's device, even though the task it was designed to carry out was more complex.

We have already seen how Jacquard used a series of punched cards to control the weaving process, one card for each basic operation of the loom. What Babbage saw was that there is no fundamental difference between the weaving operation and the performing of computations. Once the operation to be performed is identified and broken down into a series of basic tasks, it is possible to perform them mechanically given the proper device. Again, as Babbage states,†

> The analogy of the Analytical Engine with this well-known process [the weaving process] is nearly perfect. The Analytical Engine will consist of two parts:
> 1st. The store in which all the variables to be operated upon, as well as all those quantities which have arisen from the results of other operations, are placed.
> 2nd. The mill into which the quantities about to be operated upon are always brought.
>   Every formula which the Analytical Engine can be required to compute consists of certain algebraical operations to be performed upon given letters, and of certain other modifications depending on the numerical value assigned to those letters.
>   There are therefore two sets of cards, the first to direct the nature of the operations to be performed—these are called operation cards; the other to direct the particular variables on which those cards are required to operate—these latter are called variable cards. Now the symbol of each variable or constant is placed at the top of a column capable of containing any required number of digits.
>   Under this arrangement, when any formula is required to be computed a set of operation cards must be strung together, which contain the series of operations in the order in which they occur. Another set of cards must then be strung together, to call in the variables into the mill, in the order in which they are required to be acted upon. Each operation will require three other cards, two to represent the variables and constants and their numerical values upon which the previous operation card is to act, and one to indicate the variable on which the arithmetical result of this operation is to be placed.
>   The Analytical Engine is therefore a machine of the most general nature. Whatever formula it is required to develop, the law of its development must be communicated to it by two sets of cards. When these have been placed, the engine is special for that particular formula.

As we shall see in later chapters, Babbage's analytical engine (Figure 1.4) is identical conceptually to modern computers, except that it was to be of mechanical construction rather than employing electronic circuitry. The construction of the analytical

†Babbage, *ibid*, pp. 117ff.

Fig. 1.4 A portion of Babbage's analytical engine as constructed recently from his plans. (*Courtesy of IBM Corporation*)

engine was doomed to fail for this very reason; technically it could not be built in Babbage's time because of the engineering precision required. It was never completed, and Babbage died a broken man in 1871. With his death, the concept of a truly general-purpose computing engine was laid aside and forgotten. The developments which led up to modern computers were to be spurred by a completely different sequence of events.

The next major crisis in search of a solution occurred during the U.S. census of 1880. Tabulation of the census results was accomplished, for the most part, completely by hand, a task which took approximately 7 years to complete. A projection indicated that the results of the 1890 census would require more than 10 years to prepare using the same method. A young engineer by the name of Herman Hollerith was to rescue the Census Bureau by developing an automated tabulating machine, using punched cards in the tradition of the Jacquard loom. The original idea for the device is attributed to John Billings, who was responsible for the gathering of vital statistics for the 1880 and 1890 censuses. Hollerith developed this idea into a working machine which was used during the 1890 census (Figure 1.5).

Hollerith devised a system in which the census information was represented as a series of holes punched into a card. He realized quite early that these holes could be

Fig. 1.5 Cover of *Scientific American* illustrating Hollerith's tabulating machines in use. (*Courtesy of Scientific American*)

used to automatically sort the cards on the basis of the information punched into the card. Thus, it was fairly easy to determine, for instance, what proportion of the population was female and over the age of 35.

The machines themselves were designed to sense the presence or absence of a hole or holes in the card and to advance the appropriate counters, to indicate that the card was to be placed into an appropriate bin, etc. Using these machines, the results of the 1890 census were tabulated in less than two years, even though the population of the United States had grown from approximately 50 million in 1880 to around 62 million in 1890. In 1896, Hollerith formed the Tabulating Machine Company, which, many years later, was to evolve into the behemoth International Business Machines Corporation. An associate of Hollerith, James Powers, modified and refined the original equipment and later went into competition with Hollerith. In 1911, he formed the Powers Tabulating Machine Co., which was eventually to become another giant: Sperry Rand Corporation.

Tabulating machines and methods continued to be refined and improved over the years, spurred by additional problems in information handling such as those created by the passage of the Social Security Act of 1935. By the late 1930s, these machines were quite powerful, and many businesses depended on them for their routine record-keeping operations. In the meantime, developments in other areas, such as the emergence of the electronics industry, were setting the stage for the development of the first computers as we now know them. During the late 1930s and early 1940s, events occurred rapidly, and the most we shall be able to do here is merely sketch the basic sequence, totally ignoring some major efforts.

There are two very important requirements for the crystallization of an idea and the subsequent realization of that idea as a concrete entity. One is recognition that a problem exists and that a machine with a certain set of characteristics will solve, or at least alleviate, the problem. The second is that whatever technology is required to realize the machine must exist in a sufficiently advanced state. Babbage failed because, although he realized (perhaps prematurely) the need for his analytical engine, the technology did not exist to implement his machine. Hence, Babbage is classified as a genius and dreamer. However, the period from the late 1930s to the early 1940s saw both the need (World War II) and the technology (electronics) reach a critical state. It is not surprising, therefore, that many people realized (almost simultaneously) that the computer's time had come. It is interesting to note that the development of the computer during this time period proceeded from the current situation and did not draw at all on Babbage's remarkable achievements.

Prior to World War II, the need for computational power was evidenced in the fields of astronomy and physics, among others. The preparation of lunar tables is a case in point. In 1937, Howard Aiken, a graduate student in physics at Harvard University, wrote a memorandum laying down the principles for a computer and specified how his design differed from currently available tabulating machines. The most important of these differences was, perhaps, the requirement that the machine be completely automatic in operation. Also, since the machine was to be used for scientific computing, it would have to be much more general than tabulating equipment and, as a result, much more complex. In collaboration with IBM, the project was started in 1939 and completed in 1944. Dubbed the Mark I (Figure 1.6), it was basically electromechanical in nature (i.e., it used relays) and, although it contained many of the features of current machines, was outdated before completion, largely because of other designs based on electronic circuits. A similar machine was also developed at Bell Telephone Laboratories. The fact that they were both outdated before completion in no way reduces their contribution to the growing computer field. They were simply based on a technology which had already been supplanted by one more appropriate to the task.

World War II was to provide yet another impetus for the development of automatic computing machinery. Aberdeen Proving Grounds was experiencing major difficulties in computing ballistic tables for new weaponry being developed there. In 1942, John Mauchly and J. Presper Eckert, both of the Moore School of Electrical Engineering at the University of Pennyslvania, wrote a memo on "The Use of High Speed Vacuum Tube Devices for Calculating." After a series of meetings, the Moore School and the Ballistic Research Laboratory at Aberdeen entered into an agreement to build a computer based on that paper, under the guiding hand of Captain Herman Goldstine. Called the ENIAC, the computer was composed of 18,000 vacuum tubes

Fig. 1.6   The IBM-Harvard Mark I. (*Courtesy of IBM Corporation*)

and weighed over 30 tons. The sequence of numerical calculations it performed was determined by means of a front panel board which was rewired each time a new sequence was required. Thus, although ENIAC was less flexible than the Mark I, it represented one of the first attempts at constructing an all-electronic computer (Figure 1.7).

Note that although both the Mark I and ENIAC were capable of performing the basic arithmetic operations as well as storing the results of these operations for future use, the interface of these facilities to the human user was extremely poor. It was necessary to sit down at the machines and actually rewire the front panel (ENIAC) or manually set up switches (Mark I) in order to use them. The input to the Mark I was eventually changed to paper tape in order to facilitate human interaction with the machine.

During the construction of the ENIAC, Goldstine had a chance encounter with the great mathematician John von Neumann and interested him in the project. By this time, it was clear that one of the greatest failures of the ENIAC was its inability to store any great amount of information. As a result of discussions with the various members of the Moore School group, von Neumann wrote a memo discussing the advantages of storing both the instructions for controlling the sequence of events which were to occur as well as the data upon which the operations were to be performed. Thus, the idea of a stored program machine was born. Concurrently, advances in methods for storing large amounts of information (relative to Mark I and ENIAC) made it feasible to actually construct such a machine. A subsequent paper written by

Fig. 1.7 The ENIAC computer. (*UPI Photo*)

von Neumann outlined the design principles for a new type of machine to be called EDVAC; this report was the first to describe a computer as a logical organization of functional units, abstracted from the engineering details of implementation. He also pointed out that since electronic circuits exhibit two stable states (e.g., "on" and "off") the number system which should be used internally is the binary system. The complete contribution of von Neumann can only be appreciated by reading the original version; it is probably one of the most important documents in the field of computer science.

Several machines based on von Neumann's principles were constructed simultaneously, including the EDSAC machine built in Cambridge, England, by Wilkes, Kilburn, and Williams, completed in 1949. In 1951, Mauchly and Eckert completed the EDVAC; in the meantime, they had formed (in 1946) the first company devoted to commercial computers. Their first machine was known as UNIVAC-I, derived from UNIVersal Automatic Computer. Babbage's dream was now a reality. Further advances in technology, including the introduction of the magnetic core as a storage device and the transistor, resulted in bigger and faster machines.

In 1946, von Neumann and Goldstine returned to the Institute for Advanced Study at Princeton University where they undertook the design and construction of a machine now known as the *von Neumann machine;* it was the forerunner of modern computers.

It would be tempting to continue this discussion into the 1950s and 1960s and beyond, but to do so would serve no purpose. The seminal ideas have been described in their historical context. Although much has been accomplished since 1950, we leave it to the interested reader to consult the appropriate literature should interest in historical details go beyond our modest introduction. Suffice it to say that technology is currently advancing at a truly amazing rate. It is now possible, using integrated circuits, for example (Figure 1.8), to build into less than 1 cubic foot of space a computer with potentials and capabilities far beyond anything dreamed of in the 1950s. For the sake of completeness, a modern computer installation is illustrated in Figure 1.9.

One further point deserves attention. The Mark I required approximately $\frac{1}{3}$ second to perform one addition. Computers currently on the market perform this same operation in less than 100 nanoseconds (10^{-7} second). Thus, the rate at which computers can process information has increased by a factor of 10^7 in the few years since their conception. One way to appreciate the magnitude of this increase is to compare it with the gains registered in other contemporary technologies. For example, it used to

Fig. 1.8   These chips, called integrated circuits, contain most of the circuitry necessary to implement the major part of a computer. (*Courtesy of IBM Corporation*)

Fig. 1.9 A typical computer installation: the IBM 370 Model 155. (*Courtesy of IBM Corporation*)

require an arduous trek of a week or more to cover the approximately 3000 miles from New York to Los Angeles. One can now fly this same distance in approximately 3 hours, which represents an increase in transportation rates by a factor of 50. If these rates had increased by the same factor as computational speeds, we would be able to travel from New York to Los Angeles in .025 second!

This tremendous increase in computational power allows us to consider the solution to problems which were unthinkable just a few years ago. It also allows us to make mistakes faster than we have ever been able to do. In the next section, we shall examine some of the concepts which will allow us to harness this awesome power and direct it toward our own needs.

1.2 INFORMAL NOTIONS CONCERNING ALGORITHMS AND PROCEDURES

In the previous section, we observed the development of a device which could perform any computational process. In this section, we wish to examine the problem of what it means to "describe" a sequence of events in such a way that the carrying out of this sequence results in some accomplishment. In the case of a computer, this description will be in terms of the basic operations of arithmetic, augmented by convenience features.

As a point of departure into this discussion, note that the "description" of a sequence of "events" plays a large part in our everyday life and has to do with our ability to communicate. Assume for the moment that you know how to do something, or have some information, which you feel would be useful to another person or in which another person has expressed interest. It is now up to you to communicate this information as clearly and succinctly as possible. For example, suppose someone asks you if you know how to prepare Chinese egg custard and, if you do, whether you would be willing to share your information. Clearly, an answer like "Well, you mix all the necessary ingredients and cook it" is not particularly useful, since it conveys almost no information. What you might do is to select your favorite recipe and hand it over, perhaps with some tips on preparing it. Figure 1.10 is one such recipe.†

4 extra large eggs, beaten	1 C. small shrimp or lobster flakes
$1\frac{1}{2}$ C. stock	1 t. soy sauce
$\frac{1}{2}$ t. salt	1 T. oil
1 scallion, minced	

Mix all ingredients, except oil, in deep bowl. Put 1″ water in wide pot, then place deep bowl of batter inside. Cover pot tightly and steam 15 min. Heat oil very hot and pour over custard. Steam 5 more min. Serves 4.

Fig. 1.10   Recipe for Chinese egg custard.

This recipe illustrates several of the major aspects of what is called a *procedure* (more about this later), a method of transmitting information about a particular task to be accomplished. The first and most obvious fact is that the recipe is written in English; were it written in any other language, it would be difficult to discern that it was even a recipe (assuming, of course, that it was a language we were unfamiliar with), much less a recipe for Chinese egg custard. Therefore, one of the characteristics of a procedure is that it is written in some form which is understandable by both parties involved. The second immediately observable fact is that it consists of two parts: a list of ingredients (in our jargon, the *input*) and a group of instructions which specify the actions to be performed on the input to obtain the *output* (custard). From this simple example, it is possible to define a procedure slightly more formally:

Definition 1.1: A procedure is a finite sequence of well-defined instructions, each of which can be mechanically carried out in a finite amount of time with a finite amount of effort.

In this case, most of us are familiar enough with the basic operations of cooking so that we would be able to carry out the procedure with sufficient aptitude to ensure an edible product. However, many of the terms used in the recipe have a meaning

†Isabelle C. Chang, *Chinese Cooking Made Easy*, Paperback Library, Inc., New York, 1959, p. 78.

peculiar to the process of cooking: For example, the instruction *mix* carries with it a rather ambiguous interpretation. We know that we are to mix all the ingredients in a deep bowl, but how much are they to be mixed and with what implements? How wide a pot is required? When communicating a process via a procedure, these ambiguities are very often resolved by the recipient, by making use of basic knowledge and skills. However, when the recipient is a mechanical device, similar to the ones discussed in Section 1.1, ambiguities such as these are intolerable since the device has no source of information upon which it can draw to resolve them. Each step in the procedure must then be unambiguous so the device executing the procedure (be it human or computer) is not faced with a variety of possible interpretations for an instruction. In this sense it is mechanical.

It is relatively easy to illustrate the last problem by taking an example with which we might be less familiar. Figure 1.11 (following Example 1.1) is a procedure, the execution of which will result in a useful object. Figure 1.12 is another example. You are invited to try to decipher either or both before they are discussed in later sections.

The whole point of this preliminary discussion is, of course, to illustrate some of the assumptions underlying communication between people. Even in ordinary conversation, each participant (perhaps consciously, perhaps unconsciously) forms hypotheses concerning the conversation and, more importantly, produces a conceptual framework relating his or her internal knowledge and skill structure to that of the other person. By doing so, we have a tendency to tailor our conversations to the assumed characteristics of the other, and we interpret possibly ambiguous statements in terms of our own internal framework, which may include the totality of our experience and knowledge.

Consider a conversation between two people in the context just discussed and observe the differences which must necessarily occur when one is replaced by, say, Babbage's analytical engine. Such a device has essentially no belief structures, is incapable of disambiguating meaning, and has an extremely limited vocabulary. Every instruction must be precisely stated, and it is unreasonable to expect useful results otherwise.

For those cases in which it is difficult to form even the most elementary hypotheses about the other participant in the exchange, much more explicit instructions must be given, even when it is known that this participant is a person sharing our language. For example, many popular magazines publish construction articles for consumption by the general public; it is unreasonable to assume that everyone who will attempt the construction is an accomplished woodworker, seamstress, or craftsman in general. These articles tend to be much more explicit than would be the case if such an assumption could be made. Example 1.1 illustrates this point.

Example 1.1 Construction of an Appliance Cart

The accompanying article originally appeared in the June 1975 issue of *Family Circle* (published monthly by the Family Circle, Inc., Mattoon, Ill.).

PLYWOOD PROJECTS

THE APPLIANCE CART shown on page 92 measures 24"x36"x36" high. Pieces A through H can be cut from a single sheet of ¾" A-B, A-C or MDO APA grade-trademarked plywood. Pieces J, K and L can be cut from an additional quarter sheet, or you can probably find pieces of appropriate sizes in your lumber dealer's odd-size bin. The smaller apartment-size cart measures 24"x24"x36" high; all pieces for this version can be cut from one sheet of plywood.

Photo Courtesy of Family Circle—Bob Strode

FIG. 1 EXPLODED VIEW (LARGE CART)

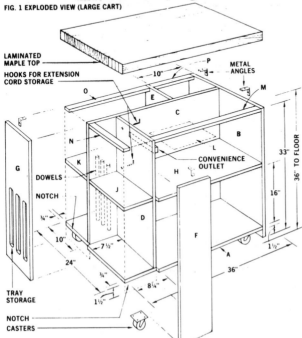

The larger unit is designed to house a toaster, coffee maker, mixer, crock pot, electric fry pan, corn popper, blender, can opener and waffle iron, and includes a spacious tray storage compartment. The compact cart provides no tray storage, but will accommodate all the same appliances except the corn popper. Both units include convenience outlets that are connected to a wall receptacle by an extension cord, allowing the appliances to be used on the cart's butcher block top.

GENERAL DIRECTIONS:

How to Buy Plywood—APA grade-trademarked plywood comes in two types: (1) Exterior for outdoor use. (2) Interior for indoor use. Within each type are grades for every job (*i.e.*, grades with two appearance sides where both sides of the panel will be seen, grades with only one appearance side for applications where only one side will be in view in the finished job). The right grade to use is given in the materials list (*see right*).

Building Hints—*Planning*: Before starting, study the plan carefully to make sure you understand all details.

Making Layout—Following the cutting guide, draw all parts on the plywood panels using a straightedge and a carpenter's square for accuracy. Use a compass to draw corner radii. Be sure to allow for saw kerfs when plotting dimensions; if in doubt, check width of saw cut.

Cutting—For hand-sawing use a 10 to 15 pt. cross-cut. Support panel firmly with face up. Use a fine-toothed coping saw for curves. For inside cuts start hole with drill then use coping or keyhole saw. For power sawing a plywood blade gives best results, but a combination blade may be used. Panel should be face down for hand power sawing and face up for table power sawing. With first cuts reduce panel to pieces small enough for easy handling. Use of scrap lumber underneath panel, clamped or tacked securely in place, prevents splintering on back side. Plan to cut matching parts with same saw setting. If available, you may use a jigsaw, bandsaw, or sabre saw for curved cuts. In any case be sure blade enters face of plane.

Drilling—Support plywood firmly. For larger holes use brace and bit. When point appears through plywood, reverse and complete hole from back. Finish slowly to avoid splintering.

Planing—Remember, edge grain of plywood runs in alternate directions so plane from ends toward center. Use shallow-set blade.

Sanding—Most sanding should be confined to edges with 1-0 or finer sandpaper, before sealer or flat undercoat is applied. You may find it easier to sand cut edges smooth before assembling each unit. Plywood is sanded smooth in manufacture—one of the big timesavers in its use—so only minimum surface sanding is necessary. Use 3-0 sandpaper in direction of grain only, after sealing.

Assembly—Assemble by sections; for example, drawers, cabinet shells, compartments—any part that can be handled as an individual completed unit. Construction by section makes final assembly easier. For strongest possible joints, use a combination of glue and nails (or screws); to nail-glue, check for a good fit by holding the pieces together. Pieces should contact at all points for lasting strength. Mark nail locations along edge of piece to be nailed. In careful work where nails must be very close to an edge, you may wish to predrill using a drill bit slightly smaller than nail size. Always predrill for screws.

MATERIALS: ¾" A-C or MDO APA grade-trademarked plywood (as above); 7' of 1x2 pine (5' for smaller cart); 24"x36" butcher block (24"x24" for smaller cart, see Buyer's Guide on page 140); 13' of ¾" dowel (larger cart only); four 2" spherical casters; 6d finishing nails; white glue; wood putty; four ¾"x¾" metal angles with ¾" wood screws; multiple convenience outlet with extension cord (available at electrical supply stores); two square-bend screw hooks; finishing materials (see below and Buyer's Guide on page 140).

CUTTING DIRECTIONS:

SIZE (inches)			CODE	USE
Large	Both	Small		
Plywood				
24x35¼		24x23¼	A	bottom shelf
	24x33		B	end
30¾x34½		30¾x22½	C	center partition
	30¾x13¼		D	partition
	30¾x 9¼		E	partition
	33x8¼		F	side
	33x10		G	end
14x27¾		14x15¾	H	shelf
	7½x13¼		J	shelf
9¼x24½		9¼x12½	K	shelf
	9¼x 9¼		L	shelf
1x2 pine				
27¾		15¾	M	support
	13¼		N	end support
24½		12½	O	support
	9¼		P	support

FIG. 1 shows the assembly of the larger cart, but it can also apply to apartment-size unit (except for tray compartment). FIGS. 2 and 3 apply to larger unit only. FIG. 4 applies to both carts.

ASSEMBLY: All joints glue-nailed. A ("good") side of plywood should be on outside of cart.

With a sabre saw, stationary saw or hand saw, cut a ¾"-deep, 10"-long notch in one 24" side of piece A to accommodate end G (see FIG. 4). Cut a ¾"-deep by 8¼"-long notch on the front edge of A to accommodate piece F (see FIG. 4). For the large cart only, cut tray slots in piece G as shown in FIG. 2. The openings can be cut with a self-starting sabre saw or by drilling starter holes in the corners, then cutting with a keyhole saw.

Glue-nail ends G and B to bottom shelf A, with G and B hanging 1½" below A (see FIG. 1). Fasten partition C between G and B, flush with the inner edge of G; nail through A into C.

Glue-nail partition D to A and C, 7½" from the open end G and flush with the end of remaining notch in A (see FIG. 1). Fit side F into the notch in A, flush with the top of D, and glue-nail to D and A. Glue-nail partition E to C and A, 9¼" inside end B.

Fasten shelf H to B, C and D, 16" above bottom shelf A. Fasten shelf J at the same level between F and C.

For the large cart only, drill ¾"-diameter, ¼"-deep blind holes in shelf K as shown in FIG. 3. Drill corresponding blind holes in bottom shelf A behind end G (see FIG. 4). Cut nine 16½" lengths of dowel. Glue a dowel length into each blind hole in A, then glue K to the dowels and glue-nail K to G, C and E (see FIG. 1). For the smaller cart, simply fasten K to G, C and E.

Fasten shelf L at the same level as K by gluing, nailing through B and using a nail-set to drive nails at a slight angle through C just below H and through E just below K. Fasten 1x2 supports M, N, O and P flush with the tops and edges of B, F, G and E (see FIG. 1).

Install a strip of convenience outlets (check with your local electrical supply store to see what is available) on the inner side of partition

D, approximately 1" below the top, and about 1" in from the outer edge. Install screw hooks in partition D midway between the convenience strip and partition C, for storage of the extension cord used to connect the outlets to a wall receptacle (see FIG. 1). Unless you have had previous experience in electrical work, it is recommended that you have a professional electrician check this phase of the project.

Install casters approximately 1½" in from each corner on the underside of bottom shelf A. Screw a metal angle to the inside of pieces F and G, and two to piece B, flush with the top. Set the butcher block in place and fasten with wood screws driven through the angles.

Finishing

Remove the butcher block top, and apply a polyurethane or oil finish, following manufacturer's directions. Fill all exposed nail holes in the cart with wood putty and sand smooth. The cart can be finished with latex low-lustre enamel, as seen on page 92. Fill any minor openings in the panel face and sand smooth. Coat with enamel undercoater and then top-coat with latex low-lustre enamel (see Buyer's Guide, page 140) for washable surface. Alternate finishes include high gloss and natural.

For a high gloss finish, first moisten the plywood surface with a damp (not wet) sponge. Coat all surfaces with a wet mix of spackle spread with a broad knife or spatula. Scrape off the excess and allow to dry for at least 15 minutes. Sand smooth with fine production paper. Apply white undercoat and allow to dry. Moisten the surface and sand with wet-or-dry sandpaper, using a circular motion. Wipe dry with a cloth or paper towel. Apply several thin coats of spray enamel, following manufacturer's directions. (Brush-on enamel may also be used; one or two coats should suffice.)

For a natural finish, fill all raw plywood edges, following manufacturer's directions. Sand smooth. Apply a clear oil finish or a plastic finish, again following label directions. ■

FIG. 2 PIECE G

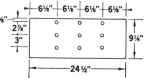

FIG. 3 PIECE K

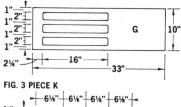

FIG. 4 PIECE A

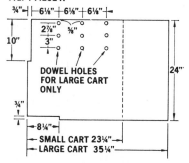

DOWEL HOLES FOR LARGE CART ONLY

SMALL CART 23¼"
LARGE CART 35¼"

Note that the project is broken down into several major sections:

1. An overview of the project, as represented by the original picture and Figure 1.
2. A brief description of the materials used and the design criteria.
3. A statement of the general directions and building hints. Here an attempt is made to provide an overview of the terminology employed and a general outline of the skills required, e.g., making the layout, cutting, drilling, etc. Note also that there is a recommendation to build the unit in easily manipulated subunits.
4. The materials required, the constraints on these materials in terms of their dimensions, and the use to which each piece will eventually be put.
5. The actual assembly instructions in chronological order such that proper execution of the sequence results in a properly constructed cart (hopefully). For those sections requiring more detailed instructions, diagrams are provided (Figures 2–4).
6. And finally, the finishing instructions are given. Notice that these instructions provide alternatives for the final finish; obviously, only one of the final paragraphs is actually executed.

The construction plans as written will permit, simply by selecting the appropriate set of internal parameters, the construction of two distinct carts, one large and one small. Thus, we have one set of instructions which produces one of two distinctly different results. The implications of this example for the specifications of more formal procedures will become clearer in the following discussions. In Chapter 3, we shall discuss the construction of a similar type of document for designing *programs* (sequences of instructions to be executed by a computer); the analogy is quite striking.

■

```
????????????????????????????????????????????
1st row:     p 5, k 8, p 5
2nd row:     p 4, sl next st on a No. 5, k in
             back loop of next st, then p st on
             dp, k 6, sl next st on dp, p next
             st, then k in back of st on dp
3rd & odd:   k the k sts and p the p sts
4th row:     p 3, sbc, p 1, k 6, p 1, sfc, p 3
6th row:     p 2, sbc, p 2, sl next 3 sts on dp
             and hold in front, k next 3 sts, then
             k the 3 sts from dp (front cross—fc—
             made), p 2, sfc, p 2
8th row:     p 1, sbc, p 3, k 6, p 3, sfc, p 1
             .
             .
             .
????????????????????????????????????????????
```

Fig. 1.11   A mystery procedure.

```
                    &DUMP = 1
                    &TRIM = 1
                    VOWELS = 'AEIOU'
        START       WORD = INPUT              :F(END)
                    EQ(SIZE(WORD),1)          :S(ACHCK)
                    END = 'WAY'
        BEGIN       WORD LEN(1) . CH =
                    VOWEL CH                  :S(VOW)
                    WORD = WORD CH
                    END = 'AY'                :(BEGIN)
        VOW         WORD = CH WORD END
        OUT         OUTPUT = WORD             :(START)
        ACHCK       WORD 'A' = 'AN'           :(OUT)
        END
```

Fig. 1.12   Another mystery procedure.

EXERCISE 1.1: If you have never worked with hand tools to any great extent (even if you have, try to pretend you have not), read the construction article carefully and make a list of those terms which have an interpretation peculiar to this type of construction. These are essentially the basic *language* elements which allow us to talk about such a project. This exercise should clearly point out the assumed background on the part of the recipient of these instructions.

The list obtained in Exercise 1.1 can probably be broken into two parts: descriptive terms (e.g., 6d finishing nails) and terms which assume a specific skill (e.g., cut a 3/4″-deep, 10″-long notch in . . .). The descriptive terms are related to what we shall eventually consider the *input* to a procedure; i.e., they describe the form of the materials to be manipulated. The skill-specific terms are related to the assumed basic operations which can be executed with no further explanation. To actually build the cart, we must be fluent in these skills; otherwise the procedure describing the actual construction will be useless to us. Thus, the mystery procedure of Figure 1.11 is absolutely meaningless unless we happen to be familiar with the basic terminology of knitting and have the basic skills required to interpret instructions specified in that terminology. Figure 1.13 lists the definitions of the abbreviations used in Figure 1.11. The mystery algorithm of Figure 1.12 is discussed in Chapter 10.

However, many of these terms actually refer to some physical manipulation of the environment, and unless these manipulations are known and understood, one still cannot produce the end result. For example, the term *purl* refers to a basic action to be performed which is different from the basic action implied by the term *knit*. All this may seem rather obvious, but the important point to remember is that the instructions of Figure 1.11 are actually a shorthand notation for specifying a *sequence* of these

Abbreviations and Terms

Beg—beginning
dec—decrease
dp—double pointed
inc—increase
k—knit
p—purl
psso—pass slipped stitch over
rd—round
sc—single crochet
sl—slip
st—stitch
tog—together
y o—yarn over
*—means to repeat instructions following asterisk
    as many times as specified, in addition to the
    first time
[ ]—brackets—designate changes in size
(,)—parentheses—means to repeat the instructions
    in parentheses as many times as specified

Fig. 1.13 Some of the terms used in Figure 1.11.

basic actions to be performed in a strict order. Any deviation from this sequence will certainly not result in the construction of the correct end product.

EXERCISE 1.2: What would be necessary to add to Figures 1.11 and 1.13 in order that the procedure represented in Figure 1.11 becomes absolutely intelligible and unambiguous?

As already noted in Section 1.1, a computer is essentially a physical device designed to carry out a collection of primitive actions. A procedure is then a sequence of instructions, couched in terms which evoke the proper operation. To learn how to make effective use of the computer, we must learn how to specify the appropriate sequences of actions which are to occur, implying that we must be familiar with the basic "skills" of the machine and how they are expressed. These topics are covered in more detail throughout the remainder of the book; for the time being, let us concentrate on the notion of a procedure as it might apply to a machine, ignoring some of the peripheral problems.

Example 1.2 Summing the First *m* Integers

For the sake of example, let us assume that we wish to "compute" the sum of the first m integers. That is, we wish to determine the value of the sum $1 + 2 + 3 + \cdots + (m - 2) + (m - 1) + m$ for some value of m, which will be fixed when the procedure is actually executed. We might be tempted to write something like the following:

Procedure 1.1 Summing the First m Integers

Step 1. Set the value of *sum* to zero.

Step 2. Set the value of *n* to 1.

Step 3. Replace the value of *sum* by $sum + n$.

Step 4. Replace the value of *n* by $n + 1$.

Step 5. If the value of *n* is zero, display the value of *sum* and stop; otherwise, go to step 3.

Clearly, this sequence of instructions is a procedure; each instruction is well defined under the tacit assumption that the device carrying out the procedure has a basic understanding of the terms set, replace, +, display, stop, go to, etc. Each instruction can certainly be carried out in a finite amount of time and with a finite amount of effort. It is, unfortunately, incorrect in that it does not solve our problem as originally stated. In addition, there is an aesthetically unpleasant quality inherent in this procedure in that although each step is finite (in time and effort) the procedure itself requires infinite time since it will never terminate (*n* will never be zero in step 5). It is easily modified, however, as shown below.

Let *m* be a given positive integer.

Procedure 1.2 Summing the First m Integers

Step 1. Set the value of *sum* to zero.

Step 2. Set the value of *n* to 1.

Step 3. Replace the value of *sum* by $sum + n$.

Step 4. Replace the value of *n* by $n + 1$.

Step 5. If *n* is greater than *m*, display the value of *sum* and stop; otherwise, go to step 3.

Notice that this procedure stops for every value of *m* ($m \geq 1$). The procedure computes the sum of the first *m* positive integers (i.e., after execution of the procedure, the value displayed is $1 + 2 + 3 + 4 + \cdots + m$). We also note that the procedure has an input quantity (*m*) and an output quantity (*sum*). ■

From this informal discussion on the notion of a procedure we may extract the following characteristics of all procedures:

1. *Effectiveness:* Each instruction must be effective; that is, the components of each instruction must be sufficiently basic and well understood so that the instruction may be carried out in a finite length of time with finite effort. An instruction such as

   If 2 is the only integer $n \geq 2$ such that for some integers *x*, *y*, and *z* the relation

   $$x^n + y^n = z^n$$

   holds, then go to step 2; otherwise, go to step 4

is not effective since no one knows at present whether or not 2 is the only integer satisfying the stated property. This statement is actually a rephrasing of an interesting problem in number theory which we shall return to shortly. As another example, suppose an instruction read

While the tire pressure is less than 28 lb, continue pumping in air

in the context of a procedure for fixing a flat automobile or bike tire. Normally, this instruction is effective in that an intact tire will eventually reach the proper pressure, assuming the correct equipment for inserting air is available. On the other hand, if there were another hole in the tire and the instruction were interpreted literally, it would be possible to continue pumping indefinitely.

2. *Definiteness:* Each step of the procedure must be well defined (i.e., unambiguous). For example, "*sum + n*" should not have any interpretation other than ordinary arithmetic addition. Even when the constituent operations are well defined, an instruction may still be ambiguous in interpretation. As an example, consider the instruction

$$6 \div 2 + 1$$

There are two values possible as a result of the evaluation of this instruction: 4 and 2. If the division is done first, the value is 4, while if the addition is done first, the value is 2. In the absence of any external information governing the order of evaluation, the instruction is not well defined. Similarly, the instruction

if *n* is equal to *m*, display *sum* and stop

is not well defined since there is no specification of an action to take for the case when *n* is less than or greater than *m*.

3. *Input/output:* A procedure may have zero or more allowable input quantities obtained from a well-defined set of possible inputs (the input domain) and one or more output quantities. For the examples already considered, the inputs and outputs are well defined:

	Recipe	Cart Construction	Knitting	Addition
Inputs	Eggs, salt, shrimp, ...	Wood, nails, glue, ...	Yarn	*m*
Outputs	Custard	Cart	Sweater	*sum*

Both procedures of Example 1.2 satisfy the conditions for a procedure, but they differ in one important aspect. The first procedure of the example never terminates, while the second terminates for every positive value of *m*. The term *algorithm* is usually reserved for procedures which always terminate. An algorithm may therefore be defined as follows:

Definition 1.2: An algorithm is a procedure which always terminates after a finite number of steps for any allowable set of input quantities (if there are inputs).

The term *algorithm* originally referred to any computation performed via a set of rules applied to numbers written in decimal form. The word itself is derived from the phonetic pronunciation of the last name of Abu Ja'far Mohammed ibn Musa al-Khowarizmi. Al-Khowarizmi was an Arabic mathematician who provided a set of rules for performing the basic arithmetic operations of addition, subtraction, multiplication, and division on decimal numbers during the ninth century A.D.

Usually, an algorithm is formulated and presented as representing a solution to a problem. That is, an algorithm specifies the way in which the inputs are utilized—how they are to be processed—in order to produce the results. It is not the case that the use of an algorithm automatically implies the correct solution; the input/output relationships must also be fulfilled. Indeed, the assertion that an algorithm solves a particular problem implies the fulfillment of this desired relationship between input and output. Clearly, the extent to which this relationship is fulfilled depends not only on the sequence of instructions comprising the algorithm but also on the quality of the inputs. Bad inputs will produce bad results, regardless of the structure of the algorithm; rotten eggs used in the creation of the egg custard will not produce an edible result. Poor-quality construction materials will not produce a functional and/or aesthetically pleasing appliance cart. As summarized in Table 1.1, only "good" inputs, operated upon by a "correct" algorithm, will produce the desired results.

Table 1.1 EFFECTS OF THE QUALITY OF INPUTS AND ALGORITHM STRUCTURE ON THE QUALITY OF OUTPUTS

Input	Algorithm	Output
Good	Good	Good
Bad	Good	Bad
Good	Bad	Bad
Bad	Bad	Bad

We all are familiar with the uses of algorithms and procedures in everyday life. Very often, those things which we do unconsciously, or without much thought, have been formalized into sequences of actions. For example, the problem of locating a word in a dictionary (one without the thumb index) is a case in point. Most of us would use some slight modification of the following procedure.

Procedure 1.3 Finding a Word in a Dictionary

Step 1. Open the dictionary at approximately the halfway point.

Step 2. Compare the given word with the words on top of the pages. If the sought for word is on these pages, locate the word however you wish and stop. Otherwise, go to step 3.

Step 3. If the sought for word is less than (using lexicographical ordering) the word at the top of the left column of the left page, *replace* the dictionary by the first half of the dictionary and go to step 1. Otherwise, replace the dictionary by the last half and go to step 2.

Although it may not be obvious, this procedure will always terminate with the word being sought if it is in the dictionary or by failing to locate the word if it is not in the dictionary. Hence, the procedure is an algorithm. The method being used is called the *binary search* method and is discussed in more detail in Chapter 5; it is also the most efficient method in this case. Most dictionaries have thumb indices for each letter of the alphabet, which the algorithm ignores.

EXERCISE 1.3: Rewrite Procedure 1.3 to make use of the thumb indices while maintaining the general outline begun in the example.

The algorithm is also quite general in that it can be (and is) used for telephone books, thesauri, or any list of items which are in some sorted order.

EXERCISE 1.4: One well-known TV game show has a game in which an item is shown and the contestant is responsible for guessing its retail price within a prescribed time limit. The only response from the moderator is an indication, after each guess, whether the guessed price is higher or lower than the actual retail price. Write an algorithm which a contestant could use to find the price.

Another classic example of an algorithm is one due to Euclid for finding the greatest common divisor (gcd) of two integers. The greatest common divisor of two positive integers m and n is the largest integer (≥ 1) which evenly divides both m and n.

Example 1.3 Euclidean Algorithm

Input: m and n (positive integers).
Output: d, the greatest common divisor of m and n.
Algorithm†:

Step 1. Divide m by n and let r be the remainder.
Step 2. If $r = 0$, let $d \leftarrow n$ and stop; otherwise, go to step 3.
Step 3. Let $m \leftarrow n$, $n \leftarrow r$, and go to step 1. ■

The use of a procedure as the specification of a solution to a problem versus an equivalent algorithm has some practical as well as theoretical importance (as we shall see in the next section). Clearly, when no interpretation of an instruction beyond the "literal" is allowed, procedures are not particularly useful; there is something unappealing about a solution which may never provide the correct answer. This is certainly the case when the device executing the procedure is mechanical; here, no interpretation other than the literal is possible. On the other hand, humans are quite comfortable with procedures because of their ability to seek alternative interpretations or to

†The symbol ⟵ means replace; thus, $d \leftarrow n$ means replace the value of d by the current value of n.

augment the interpretation with additional data. For example, the statement

> While the tire pressure is less than 28 lb, continue pumping

may or may not be effective, as we have seen. Were we to actually execute such an instruction, we would probably note that after pumping for 5 or 10 minutes with no perceptible effect there is something else wrong and would seek the cause of the failure of our efforts to inflate the tire. We would not interpret the instruction literally.

Merely to assert that a sequence of instructions comprises an algorithm is usually not sufficient; it is necessary to show that the conditions of Definition 1.2 are fulfilled and, furthermore, that the input/output relationships implicit in the problem statement are obtained by execution of the sequence of instructions. To show that the instruction sequence of Example 1.3 is an algorithm, we must demonstrate that the execution will always terminate and that after termination d is the gcd of m and n. In this case, the procedure will always terminate with the correct answer and is therefore an algorithm (see Section 1.4.1 in Part C of the supplementary volume).

As a nontrivial example of a procedure that is not an algorithm, let us examine a problem first considered by Fermat in the seventeenth century: Find integers x, y, z, and n such that

$$x^n + y^n = z^n$$

Clearly, for $n = 2$ there are solutions; $x = 3$, $y = 4$, $z = 5$ is one such solution (are there others?). We may therefore consider only $n \geq 3$. The proof that a solution exists (or does not exist) for equations of this type has fascinated mathematicians for many years. Fermat first stated this problem as follows:

> It is impossible to divide a cube into two cubes, a fourth power into two fourth powers, and in general any power except the square into two powers with the same exponents.

Fermat added in the margin of his notebook the cryptic comment

> I have discovered a truly wonderful proof of this, but the margin [of the notebook] is too narrow to hold it.

Nowhere in Fermat's notes does this proof appear. Since then, the greatest mathematicians have been unable to prove or disprove Fermat's Last Theorem (as it has come to be called); only for special cases of n are proofs available.

Instead of trying to prove the general theorem, suppose we look for counterexamples. It may not be at all obvious how to construct a procedure which will systematically search for a solution, particularly if we add the requirement that the procedure find the counterexample (if it exists) in finite time. A useful strategem, when faced with a difficult problem, is to attempt to simplify the problem, solve the simpler one, and then see if this solution provides insight to the solution of the more difficult problem. Let us adopt this strategy and consider the following simpler problem: Are there integers x, y, z, and n such that $x^n + y^n = z^n$ for

$$lower \leq x, y, z, n \leq upper \tag{1}$$

where *upper* and *lower* are given integers? We can construct an algorithm which will solve this problem by systematically varying x, y, z, and n between their respective boundaries.

EXERCISE 1.5: Write an algorithm (use the notation developed in Examples 1.1–1.3) to solve problem (1).

It might be tempting to assume that a procedure of the form

1. Let *lower* ⟵ 1 and *upper* ⟵ 10.
2. {algorithm from Exercise 1.5}.   (2)
3. If the result from step 2 is "solution not found," let *lower* ⟵ *upper* + 1, *upper* ⟵ 2 * *upper*, and go to step 2; otherwise, print x, y, z, and n and stop.

is indeed a solution. But a short analysis of procedure (2) indicates that it will not test all possible combinations of integers; for instance, $x = 2$, $y = 3$, $z = 12$, and $n = 4$ will never be tested (what combinations of integers will not be tested in general?). It would be rather difficult to modify the procedure to generate and test every possible combination of four integers without duplication. In the next section, we shall consider this problem in some detail. Without worrying about duplication of effort, procedure (2) may be modified by replacing step 3 with step 3':

3'. If the result from step 3 is "solution not found," set *upper* ⟵ 2 * *upper* and go to step 2; otherwise, print x, y, z, and n and stop.

The modified procedure may or may not terminate, depending on the disproof or proof of Fermat's Last Theorem. Thus, we have no effective method for determining whether or not a computer program to find a counterexample to the theorem will ever stop with an answer.

As we shall see in later chapters, many different algorithms and procedures may exist which are solutions to a given problem. The selection of one, or several, of these for translation to a computer program depends on many factors. In general, computationally inefficient procedures and algorithms can often be transformed into more efficient ones with a little thought. Of course, one of the major problems consists of finding any solution, to say nothing of the most efficient one. Quite often this process consists of trial and error, guided by whatever intuitions and knowledge one has. In many cases, a full and complete understanding of the problem involved occurs only after several fruitless attempts have been made to solve what was originally thought to be the problem. When this understanding occurs and it is clear what solutions ought to work, then a search for the most efficient might be appropriate, but certainly not before. One only has to watch a child in an intense problem-solving situation run through several plausible solutions before finding a potentially useful one (which then may be modified to become reasonably efficient) to appreciate the frustrations inherent in this process. Problem solutions do not emerge full-blown, complete in every detail, from the mind—to obtain one requires thinking, common sense, practice, and an understanding of the problem domain.

To illustrate this process we shall develop a more efficient procedure to (dis)-prove Fermat's Theorem. The main inefficiency of the above procedure lies in generating many sets of the four integers (x, y, z, n) over and over again. Thus, we should strive to obtain a procedure which will generate all sets of four integers without ever repeating one. Remember the restriction that we have to find the counter-example (if it exists) in finite time; hence, we cannot simply vary each variable from one to infinity. As before, we look first at the simpler problem of generating all pairs of integers. Once we have such a procedure, we can apply it to each integer of the pairs and obtain pairs of pairs (i.e., four integers) of integers.

The problem to be examined here first is that of finding a technique for generating without repetition all pairs of positive integers of the form (n, m), for $n \geq 1$, $m \geq 1$. As we shall see repeatedly throughout the book, the choices of how to represent the essential aspects of a problem have a substantial influence on the ease with which the problem can be solved. Again, the choices of this representation are very often not obvious and require some experimentation to determine a "reasonable" one. The appliance cart construction used the "standard" materials for this type of construction; it would have been much more difficult to design and construct the cart had we been constrained to feathers, or water. Similarly, it is very often much more difficult to "construct" a problem solution if the wrong materials are selected. One aspect of "learning" to solve problems is developing the ability to recognize the form and type of the materials. This question is explored in many places throughout the book, particularly in Chapter 9. In this case, our problem might be stated as follows:

> For each positive integer, develop a technique for assigning a unique *pair* of integers to this integer.

That is, we wish to construct a correspondence (commonly called a function) between an integer, say k, and a pair of integers (m, n) so that, given the value of k, the pair (m, n) may be found. It would be equally useful if the inverse were also true; that is, given a pair (m, n), find the unique integer k. The generation problem, as originally stated, is then solved since it is only necessary to step through the integers, beginning at 1, and generate for each value the pair (m, n). Since each component of the pair (m, n) is itself a positive integer, it might be fruitful to consider the first component by itself and the second component by itself; e.g., consider a checkerboard-like arrangement in which each row is labeled by an integer, as is each column. Such an arrangement is shown in Figure 1.14.

By selecting one of the squares, say the one marked A, the pair of values corresponding to this square may be immediately determined, e.g., (3, 4). Such a structure is known as a *table;* each square is identified by its row and column values, known as the *indices*. Thus, if we name the table *checker*, then "*checker*(3, 4)" refers to the square containing the A. If some value is written here, say A, then we say "*checker*(3, 4)" has the value A. Returning to the original problem, if we examine Figure 1.15, we

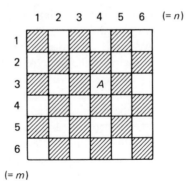

Fig. 1.14   Checkerboard structure.

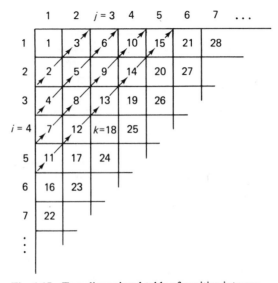

Fig. 1.15   Two-dimensional table of positive integers.

discern an obvious relation between the table indices i and j and the table entries k. We reference the table entry k in the ith row and jth column by "$table(i, j)$" and assign the entries as shown by the arrows [e.g., $table(4, 3) = 18$]. That is, we assign the positive integers from 1 to infinity in such a way that the first integer is in the upper left corner, the next two on the diagonal going from $table(2, 1)$ to $table(1, 2)$, the next three on the diagonal going from $table(3, 1)$ to $table(1, 3)$, etc. Thus, we obtain an exact correspondence between table entries (the positive integers) and table indices (pairs of positive integers). Our problem would be solved if we could find a formula which would enable us to compute the pair (i, j) given the table entry k.

It is very often the case that when attempting to solve a problem of the above nature the inverse problem may in fact be simpler to solve. Let us adopt this stratagem here and attempt to find the value of the table entry given i and j. Examining Figure

1.15, we note that on each diagonal the sum of the indices is constant; for instance, on the diagonal through the points (3, 1), (2, 2), and (1, 3) the sum is always 4. Similarly, on the diagonal through the points (4, 1), (3, 2), (2, 3), and (1, 4) the sum is 5. If we label each diagonal as shown in Figure 1.16, we note that the sum of the indices of points lying on a common diagonal is always one more than the label of the diagonal. Examining Figure 1.16, it is obvious that the nth diagonal passes through exactly n table points. Because of the way we have defined the value of the entry $table(i, j)$, we only have to compute the number of entries preceding and including (i, j) to obtain the value k. This is simply the number of entries on the first $i + j - 2$ diagonals (see Figure 1.16) plus j for the j entries on the $i + j - 1$ diagonal on which the value k is found. Therefore,

$$k = 1 + 2 + 3 + \cdots + (i + j - 2) + j \tag{3}$$

Sir Isaac Newton was allegedly the first to supply the simple relationship

$$1 + 2 + 3 + \cdots + n = \frac{n(n + 1)}{2} \tag{4}$$

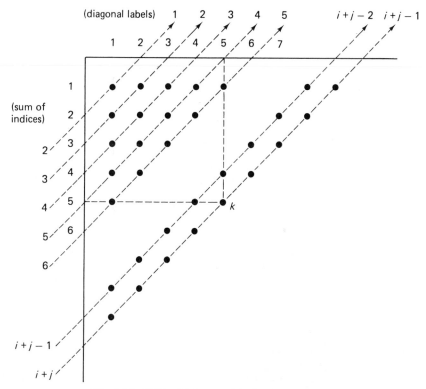

Fig. 1.16   Table of integers with diagonals labelled.

for adding the first n integers. If we let $n = i + j - 2$ [from equation (3)] and substitute this into equation (4) [remembering to add the j term from (3)], we obtain the formula for k:

$$k = \frac{(i + j - 2)(i + j - 1)}{2} + j \tag{5}$$

This completes the solution for the inverse part of the problem. The important point here is not the final equation which was obtained but the process by which it was obtained. We shall have more to say concerning this process in later chapters; for now it is sufficient to note that there is no set procedure which, if followed faithfully, will guarantee finding a solution to a problem. Each problem is unique in itself and requires an understanding of the nature of the problem and the domain in which the problem is posed if it is to be solved.

EXERCISE 1.6 (optional): Find a solution to the original problem of computing the pair (i, j) given a value of k. Using this, write a procedure which will prove or disprove Fermat's theorem by exhaustively examining all values of x, y, z, and n.

Solution: Assume we have already computed from k the number of diagonals which precede the diagonal on which k is located; let us call this number d. From Figure 1.16 we already know that

$$d = i + j - 2 \tag{6}$$

and substituting this result into equation (5) yields

$$k = \frac{d(d + 1)}{2} + j \tag{7}$$

However, from equation (7) the value of j can be obtained immediately:

$$j = k - \frac{d(d + 1)}{2} \tag{8}$$

From equation (6) we have

$$i = d - j + 2 \tag{9}$$

Equations (8) and (9) constitute the solution to the problem; note, however, that (9) can be evaluated only after equation (8) has been evaluated.

EXERCISE 1.7: Given the table entry k (see Figure 1.15), derive an expression for d, the number of complete diagonals preceding k. Hint: The cases in which k lies in the first row or column may be tricky.

Once we have the two functions

$$j = f_2(k) = k - \frac{d(d + 1)}{2}$$

and

$$i = f_1(k) = d - j + 2$$

we can easily generate all possible combinations of four positive integers by repeated application of f_1 and f_2 as shown in Figure 1.17. That is, we choose a value of k and compute i and j from f_1 and f_2. Each i and j is treated as a new k; x and y are computed from i by another application of f_1 and f_2, while z and n are computed from j in a similar way.

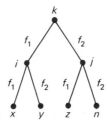

Fig. 1.17 Correspondence between positive integers and sequences of four positive integers.

EXERCISE 1.8: Give an intuitive argument why this method (graphically illustrated in Figure 1.17) when applied consistently from $k = 1$ will generate every possible combination of four positive integers and none will be repeated.

The modified procedure for (dis)proving Fermat's conjecture may easily be constructed. Recall that the problem is to

Find integers x, y, and $z \geq 1$ and $n \geq 3$ such that $x^n + y^n = z^n$.

Procedure 1.4 Fermat's Theorem
Input: None.
Output: x, y, z, and n.

1. $k \leftarrow 1$.
2. $j \leftarrow f_2(k)$, $i \leftarrow f_1(k)$.
3. $y \leftarrow f_2(i)$, $x \leftarrow f_1(i)$, $n \leftarrow f_2(j)$, and $z \leftarrow f_1(j)$.
4. If $n \leq 2$, go to step 6.
5. If $x^n + y^n = z^n$, output x, y, z, n and stop; otherwise, go to step 6.
6. $k \leftarrow k + 1$.
7. Go to step 2.

Note that as k ranges over the values from 1 to an arbitrarily large positive integer, each sequence of four positive numbers is generated exactly once (which implies that each sequence is tested only once), a considerable improvement over the procedure of Exercise 1.5. It is fairly evident now that whether or not Procedure 1.4 constitutes an algorithm is dependent on whether Fermat's Last Theorem is true or false. If the theorem is true, Procedure 1.4 will never terminate with a solution, since there is none.

End of Solution.

Before concluding this section, note that as a consequence of attempting to prove or disprove Fermat's theorem, the concept of a table was introduced. This structure is a fairly common one and will be used repeatedly in subsequent chapters. It represents, for many problems, a fairly natural organization of information. For example, the tic-tac-toe diagram, familiar to all of us, is a 3 × 3 table. Each entry in the table has three possible values: blank, naught, or cross.

Another structure which we shall find useful is known as an *n*-tuple, which is an ordered (there is a first element and a last element) sequence of *n* values. In the above discussion, each sequence of four positive integers would be called a 4-tuple. Furthermore, by providing a name for an *n*-tuple, e.g., *seq*, we allow reference to the *i*th element ($1 \leq i \leq n$) by *seq*(*i*). Thus, to reference the first element in the *n*-tuple called *seq*, we write *seq*(1), to reference the last element, we write *seq*(*n*), etc.

EXERCISE 1.9: Write a procedure which will generate all possible 6-tuples whose elements are positive integers.

This concludes our informal discussion of algorithms and procedures. In the next section, we shall attempt to formalize these notions in terms of an abstract computing device similar to actual computers.

1.3 FORMAL ASPECTS OF PROCEDURES

Of central importance to computer science is the question: Is there a formalism in which the concept of algorithm and procedure may be embedded in order to lend the legitimacy which a science requires? If we consider our informal notion of an algorithm, there are several questions which arise, including

1. What do we mean by "effective"?
2. What sort of instructions are well defined?
3. What language should we use to specify the instructions, particularly in light of the unambiguity requirement?

In the last section, an attempt was made to use standard English to phrase the answers to these questions as well as for the instructions themselves. While this is sufficient in most cases, if the procedures and/or algorithms are to be executed by sentient beings who have a common understanding of the terms involved, English is generally not suited to formal representations of algorithms or procedures because of the unambiguity requirement. We wish to discuss and describe algorithms which are to be executed by machines whose powers to deduce the meaning of an instruction from its context are very limited indeed. The goal of this section is to define a language in which it is reasonably easy to write algorithms consistent with the unambiguity criterion. We are really searching for a formalism in which to express things that are computable. This chapter represents an exploration of the domain of algorithms and procedures; once an understanding of the domain is achieved, it will be possible to explore their conceptual representation as well as their representation on an existing physical device (e.g., a computer).

The exploration of formal systems in which to represent procedures and algorithms has an extremely rich intellectual history. We have already seen how al-Khowarizmi was attempting to formalize the rules of addition as early as the ninth century. In an attempt to come to grips with the underlying questions, mathematicians have proposed several formal (i.e., rigorous) definitions of algorithms. Unfortunately, there is no way to "prove" that these formal definitions are equivalent to our "intuitive" definition (i.e., informal notion) of an algorithm. However, it is satisfying to note that these formal definitions are equivalent to each other and that no one has yet found an algorithm that satisfies the informal notion which cannot be expressed in any of the formal systems. For these reasons, it is generally accepted that any one of the formal definitions corresponds to our intuitive notion of an algorithm.

Note that here we are considering information as a commodity to be manipulated, similar to flour, wood, etc., but with an attendant set of natural manipulations. We must exclude, at least insofar as the scope of this chapter is concerned, discussions of algorithms which require "physical" interaction with the real world (as in baking a cake or assembling an appliance cart). Even though a recipe may represent an algorithm, one could not expect (nor would we particularly want) a computer to actually bake a cake. In essence, a computer can do only one thing: process information. However, since "information" can, in the form of appropriately encoded symbols, "represent" many abstract concepts, a computer is a much more powerful device than might be evident at first glance.

One approach to standardization is to choose a machine (i.e., a computer) **M** which can perform a small collection of simple instructions and say that an algorithm for a particular problem exists if and only if one can write a sequence of instructions for **M** solving the particular problem. This certainly removes all the difficulties surrounding questions 1, 2, and 3 above since the semantics (meaning) of each instruction is defined by what the machine does when it executes the instruction.

So that the class of algorithms representable on **M** is commensurate with the class of algorithms executable on a computer, our hypothetical machine will be modeled after modern machines. From our discussion in Section 1.1, it should be fairly obvious that the basic components of a computer include

1. Memory unit: This device stores the instructions to be executed, any data which are needed, and all intermediate results, including the final results.
2. Control unit: This section selects the appropriate instruction for processing, usually starting at the beginning of a sequence of instructions and selecting instructions in order, unless instructed to do otherwise by the instructions themselves.
3. Arithmetic and logical unit: This device performs simple operations such as addition, subtraction, multiplication, division, etc.
4. Input/output unit: This device allows and provides a means of communication with the outside world. Through the I/O unit, final results.are communicated, special input data are provided, the instructions themselves are input, and so on. Often these units are limited to accepting and displaying symbols; a unit similar to an electric typewriter often performs both functions. However, computers can be and often are connected to special sensors and effectors which allow them to sense their environment and manipulate parts of it. For the purposes of this discussion, such special devices are ignored; this does not limit the usefulness of the discussion, since the end result in either case is a symbol.

The formal model chosen is known as a Turing machine; it is named after Alan Turing, a British mathematician, who first proposed it prior to the development of modern computers. A computer actually represents a highly restricted form of a Turing machine; fortunately, for practical purposes, this restriction is not a serious one, although it does have some interesting theoretical consequences. This formalism retains parts 1 and 2 of the description given above, omits part 3, and has a very limited form of input/output facilities.

Definition 1.3: A Turing machine **M** consists of three parts (see Figure 1.18): a memory unit, a control unit, and a program, each of which are described in more detail below.

1. *Memory unit:* The memory of a Turing machine consists of an infinite *tape* divided into squares, each square capable of containing (i.e., storing) a symbol from a prespecified set of symbols called the *alphabet* of the machine. These are the symbols with which we represent the data, etc. There are two important facts to realize:

   i. The memory capacity of a Turing machine must be conceptually infinite since, as we shall see later, we must allow for the possibility that the computation performed by the machine never terminates. Recall that the termination of computation is the distinction between algorithms and procedures.
   ii. Since by Definition 1.3 we included the program as part of the Turing machine description, each specific algorithm or procedure will be represented by a distinct Turing machine with its own alphabet.

Thus, when formalizing a procedure (i.e., by representing it as a Turing machine), it is important to first specify the alphabet of the Turing machine on which the procedure will execute. For instance, we shall choose a particular representation of the Turing machine which is functionally similar to modern computers†; in this model, the corre-

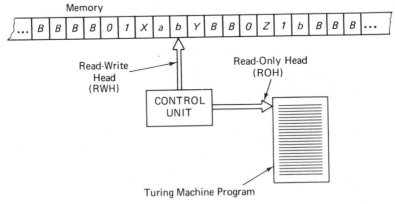

Fig. 1.18 Components of a Turing machine.

†Since the Turing machine was first proposed in 1937, before the first computers were actually built, the situation is actually the other way around: Modern computers can be viewed as being modeled after Turing machines.

sponding alphabet consists of only the two symbols *0* and *1* plus one special symbol, *B*, which represents the blank square. This special symbol is needed since at any stage of the computation only a finite number of squares contain nonblank symbols. We must be able to separate these squares from the infinitely many unused squares. We shall, as it becomes necessary, augment this initial alphabet with other special symbols. A blank tape is one which contains only blank squares; initially, every square of the tape contains the symbol *B*.

Input/output is governed by the following conventions:

i. Before the program starts, the input (strings of symbols from the machine's alphabet) is placed on the tape, and the read-write head is positioned over the first symbol of the input string. The first symbol is defined to be the leftmost symbol on the tape which is not *B*.

ii. After program execution stops, the string under and to the right of the read-write head, up to the first blank, is the output.

2. *Control unit:* This unit determines which instruction is to be executed next and performs the execution. The control unit communicates with the infinite tape by means of a read-write head (RWH) and with the program by means of a read-only head (ROH). The RWH is capable of reading or writing the contents of a single square, while the ROH reads a single Turing machine instruction at a time. A Turing machine halts (that is, stops executing instructions) if and only if a HALT instruction is encountered (see below).

3. *Program:* This is a finite sequence of primitive instructions (any or all of which may be identified by a unique label) that the Turing machine is capable of executing. The primitive instructions and their interpretations are

LEFT . . . . Move the RWH one square left.

RIGHT . . . . Move the RWH one square right.

WRITE *a* . . . . Replace the symbol on the square currently under the RWH by the symbol *a*.

GO TO *n* . . . . Move ROH to the instruction labeled *n*.

IF *a* GO TO *n* . . . . If the symbol under the RWH is *a*, move the ROH to the instruction labeled *n*; otherwise, move the ROH to the next instruction.

HALT . . . . Terminate the computation.

This impoverished instruction set actually represents the minimum set of instructions required to evaluate any "computable" function; that is, one cannot find a richer set of instructions which will increase the "power" of the Turing machine. Because of their inherent simplicity, it is possible to define the semantics of each instruction unambiguously, simply by stating their effect on the Turing machine. Also, because of their small number and basic simplicity, it is an extremely arduous task to actually write any realistic procedure using these instructions. However, in Chapter 1 we are simply laying the groundwork for considering "real" programming languages in the context of "real" computers. In the next chapter, a more useful language, called

AL, is defined. AL instructions are much closer to actual programming languages, and it is much easier to specify algorithms. The semantics of AL instructions are based on the Turing machine model discussed here and, as such, satisfy the unambiguity criterion.

Let us now recapitulate the notion of a Turing machine: An input string to a Turing machine is a finite string $x = a_1 a_2 \ldots a_m$ of symbols from a well-defined alphabet. x may, in fact, contain no symbols at all; in this case x is said to be *null*. Initially, this string is written on the tape with an infinity of blanks to its left and right (see Figure 1.19). (Note that the string x may be an encoding of some input quantity.) The read-write head is then set to scan symbol a_1, and execution of the program begins with the first instruction. The Turing machine may or may not halt with input x.† If

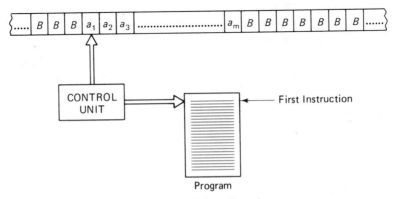

Fig. 1.19   Initial configuration.

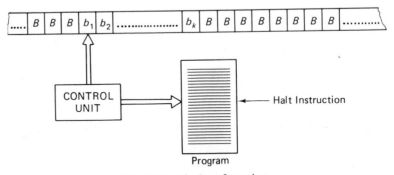

Fig. 1.20   Final configuration.

†As an example of a Turing machine which never halts, consider a machine with input $x = 1$ and the program

$$1 \quad \text{RIGHT}$$
$$\text{IF } B \text{ GO TO } 1$$

Of course, this is a trivial example. However, the Turing machine programmed with the procedure obtained for Fermat's problem may or may not halt with a solution depending on whether Fermat's conjecture was correct.

it halts, then the tape at that time will contain a string $y = b_1 b_2 \ldots b_k$ with an infinity of blanks to its left and right (see Figure 1.20). We say that y is the output of the Turing machine corresponding to x. Therefore, a Turing machine is uniquely specified by providing its alphabet and its program.

Before beginning an example, a few definitions are required. A *binary string* is defined to be an n-tuple each of whose values are either 0 or 1. In this context the value 0 or 1 is called a *binary digit*, abbreviated *bit*. Thus,

$$1$$
$$0$$
$$101$$
$$1101100111$$

are all binary strings, composed of 1, 1, 3, and 10 bits each, respectively.

Example 1.4

Design a Turing machine which, given a nonnull binary string as input, halts with a *0* if the input contains an even number of *1*'s and halts with a *1* otherwise.

Let us define zero as an even number and assume that the first n bits of a given string contain an even number of *1*'s. Then the first $n + 1$ bits will contain an even number of *1*'s only if the $(n + 1)$st bit is zero. Therefore, at the start of the execution of our program it is assumed there is an even number of *1*'s on the tape; the string will then be processed from left to right, one bit at a time. We shall need two nearly identical sections of instructions. One section processes the string under the assumption that the number of *1*'s up to the current symbol is even. For the other section, the assumption is that the number of *1*'s is odd.

The general idea, then, is to start at the left end of the string, assuming that the number of *1*'s is even (this takes care of the blank tape). The next bit is examined, and one of three possibilities occurs:

1. If the symbol is a *B*, write the proper answer (which depends on the section of instructions currently being executed) and stop.
2. If the symbol is *0*, erase it and continue executing the current section of instructions.
3. If the symbol is a *1*, switch to the other process and continue executing.

Thus, as long as the symbol being examined is zero, nothing is done except replacing the symbol by *B*. As *1*'s occur, they cause the program to switch back and forth between two sections of instructions, one signifying that the number of *1*'s is odd and the other that the number is even. The final answer depends on which section the Turing machine is executing when it reaches the right end of the string.

The alphabet for the Turing program below consists of the symbols *0, 1,* and *B*:

The number of *1*'s is even until now

```
10   IF B GO TO 30            end of string?
     IF 1 GO TO 21            switch to other process, number of
                              1's becomes odd

20   WRITE B
     RIGHT                    repeat process by going back
                              to beginning of same process

     GO TO 10
30   WRITE 0                  number of 1's is even
     HALT
```

The number of *1*'s is odd until now

```
11   IF B GO TO 31            end of string?
     IF 1 GO TO 20            switch to other process
21   WRITE B                  erase
     RIGHT
     GO TO 11                 repeat
31   WRITE 1                  number of 1's is odd
     HALT
```

■

EXERCISE 1.10: Design a Turing machine which, given a binary string as input, produces as output the reverse of the string (e.g., input: 1011; output: 1101).

Example 1.5

Design a Turing machine that will add two arbitrary positive integers m and n.

We could try to write a program which simulates the way we commonly add two integers. That is, the representation of the integers is processed from right to left by taking two digits at a time, looking up their sum in an addition table, and propagating any carry to the left. This process assumes, of course, that the integers are represented in a *positional* number system.

EXERCISE 1.11: Discuss the implications for a Turing machine program and data representation designed to add two integers represented in a positional number system in light of the above discussion. Include in your discussion the representation of the addition table (whether embedded in the program or stored on the tape), the method by which carries are handled, and the general complexity of the process involved.

As we shall see repeatedly throughout this book, the choice of data representation is often the most crucial decision one must make; a correct choice (there may be more than one) very often drastically simplifies the program associated with the problem to be solved. It is unfortunate, but in many cases the first choice is not the correct one; however, very often the experience gained in working with the incorrect choice will provide insight into the selection of the correct one.

In this case, one choice of representation is related to the number system in which the integers to be added are defined. When the number 834.28 is written in the number system with which we are most familiar (called a *positional* system), we are actually conforming to a standard accepted long ago. Man's propensity for counting things led to the development of number systems; the earliest of these systems are the *grouping* systems, similar to the system developed by the Romans. This system was originally a simple marking method,

$$\text{NNI NNI NNI NNI NNI NNI NNI NNI NNI NNI NNI III}$$

representing the number 58. The next logical step is the addition of special symbols for groups of symbols:

$$\text{V V V V V V V V V V V III}$$

again representing 58. The inclusion of higher symbols results in the familiar Roman numeral

$$\text{LVIII}$$

An alternative representation of numbers makes use of positional notation to specify the number of groups of objects. The size of each group is known as the *base* of the system; these number systems are known as positional systems. In our ordinary system of writing numbers, the value of any digit depends on its position in the number. The value of a digit in any position is 10 times the value of the same digit one position to the right, or one-tenth the value of the same digit one position to the left. Thus, for example,

$$173.246 = 1 * 10^2 + 7 * 10^1 + 3 * 10^0 + 2 * 10^{-1} + 4 * 10^{-2} + 6 * 10^{-3}$$

where $*$ indicates multiplication. There is no reason that a number other than 10 cannot be used as the base, or *radix*, of the number system. In fact, bases of 2, 8, and 16 are commonly used in conjunction with digital computers (recall von Neumann's observation). Numbers expressed in base 2, base 8, and base 16 are called, respectively, *binary*, *octal*, and *hexadecimal* numbers. When the base used is not clear from the context, it is indicated by a parenthesized subscript. Thus,

$$743_{(8)} = 7 * 8^2 + 4 * 8^1 + 3 * 8^0 = 483_{(10)}$$

$$1011.101_{(2)} = 1 * 2^3 + 0 * 2^2 + 1 * 2^1 + 1 * 2^0 + 1 * 2^{-1} + 0 * 2^{-2} + 1 * 2^{-3}$$
$$= 11.625_{(10)}$$

EXERCISE 1.12: Each of the binary strings introduced earlier may be considered as a number in the base 2 system. For each number, what is its value in the base 10 system?

The simple marking system discussed above (without the inclusion of higher symbols) represents what might be called a unary number system (i.e., a system with only one symbol), or a *tally* system. In this system, there is a direct correspondence between the number of "marks" and the number of things to be added. Addition is particularly easy; if we consider the marks to be toothpicks, then addition is performed by picking up the piles representing the numbers to be added and placing them in one big pile. We shall choose the unary number system and encode an integer *n* as a string of *n* *1*'s.

The justification of this choice is inherent in a thoughtful consideration of the issues raised in Exercise 1.11. Thus, if $m = 4$ and $n = 3$, the initial and final configurations of the tape of the Turing machine should be as shown in Figures 1.21 and 1.22, respectively. In this case, the alphabet of the Turing machine consists of the symbols *1*, +, and *B*. Note that the symbol + does not have any standard arithmetic significance; it is simply another symbol in the Turing machine alphabet. The *meaning* of this symbol is defined in terms of the entire Turing machine.

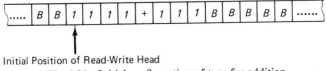

Initial Position of Read-Write Head

Fig. 1.21   Initial configuration of tape for addition.

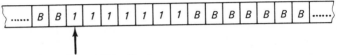

Final Position of Read-Write Head

Fig. 1.22   Final configuration of tape for addition.

Observe that addition can be achieved by replacing the first *1* in the input string by *B* and the + by a *1*. The following Turing machine program will do this for any two positive integers (> 0) written on the input tape under our assumed conventions:

```
      WRITE B
   1  RIGHT
      IF 1 GO TO 1        move right until + is found
      WRITE 1
   2  LEFT
      IF 1 GO TO 2        reposition RWH at beginning of
                          string
      RIGHT
      HALT
```

Note that this program does not work correctly if the first integer is zero (which we carefully excluded). To be consistent with our notation, a zero would be represented by zero *1*'s, e.g.,

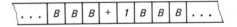

to add 0 and 1. Execution of the program on this input tape would produce

| . . . | B | B | B | 1 | 1 | B | B | B | . . . |

which is clearly incorrect.

EXERCISE 1.13: Write a Turing machine program which will add two nonnegative integers *m* and *n* using the unary number system as encoding for the input; i.e., fix the error in the program given above or rewrite it so that the zero case will give the correct answer. ■

Turing Machines and Algorithms

Using the concept of a Turing machine, we can now propose a formal definition of a procedure. We say that there is a procedure to solve a given problem if we can program a Turing machine to solve the problem (with possible encodings of inputs and outputs). The procedure becomes an algorithm if the Turing machine always halts. Thus, there are algorithms for addition, multiplication, exponentiation, deciding if an integer is prime, etc. In fact, it can be shown that any computation that can be performed by a modern-day computer can be simulated by a Turing machine.

The reverse is not true, however, because of the infinite nature of the Turing machine's tape. By necessity, every device constructed by man must be finite; that is, we have only a finite supply of raw materials. Restricting the tape of the Turing machine to be of fixed length changes rather drastically the class of computations which can be performed (such a restricted Turing machine is known as a *finite state machine*). However, as noted earlier, this restriction usually does not result in any practical difficulties.

Thus, it is believed that Turing machines correspond to a class of devices that can perform exactly those computations that can be algorithmically (in the intuitive sense) carried out. Of course, this statement cannot be proven since we have no way of defining precisely what we mean by the phrase "algorithmically carried out." However, several formal definitions of an algorithm have been considered and have all been shown to be equivalent to computations by Turing machines. Thus, Turing machines are generally accepted as the formal basis of computability.

Algorithms and Procedures

Recall that earlier an algorithm was defined as a procedure which terminated after a finite number of steps, for any allowable input quantities. It is relatively straightforward, then, to relate algorithms to Turing machines which always halt, for any allowable inputs. Let us examine a specific problem in this context. Recall that the first procedure of Example 1.1 never terminated. If translated literally into an actual computer program, it would execute forever (if we let it) without printing anything. It contains what is known as an *infinite loop*, that is, a loop structure which, once entered, can never be exited. Such a loop is illustrated below:

1. $i \leftarrow 1$.
2. ....
                                    : Procedure statements; the value
                                    : of i must not be changed by any
                                    · statement in this group.
   n. ....
$n + 1$. $i \leftarrow i + 1$.
$n + 2$. If $i < 0$, then print "end of computation" and halt; otherwise, go to step 2.

Such a loop is easy to program in any of the actual programming languages considered here and most of the languages currently used anywhere. Representing a very common type of program error, it would be extremely valuable if it were possible to construct an algorithm which would accept as input any algorithm or procedure (say **A**) and determine whether or not **A** contains an infinite loop.† Such an algorithm would be a universal *debugging* algorithm for infinite loops.

Let us assume such an algorithm exists (call it **A'**); **A'** has the following properties:

1. The input to **A'** is any algorithm or procedure (say **A**) and its attendant data (if any).
2. **A'** stops and prints the message

> HALT: if **A** eventually terminates execution

or

> DOES NOT HALT: if **A** contains an infinite loop

Then **A'** is the solution to the debugging problem. However, since it is possible (by assumption) to find algorithm **A'**, it is also possible to modify **A'** to the procedure **A''** with the properties

1. The input to **A''** is any procedure or algorithm (say **B**) whose data is **B** itself. Thus, **B** is a procedure which accepts a copy of itself as input and operates on it.
2. **A''** stops and prints the message

> HALT: if **B** does not halt when its input is **B**

3. **A''** prints the message

> DOES NOT HALT: if **B** eventually stops when its input is **B**

and then goes in an infinite loop (i.e., does not stop).

Now we have an extremely interesting observation: Since **B** may be *any* algorithm or procedure, we may legitimately consider the case in which **B** is identical to **A''**. Then we have the conclusions that

---

†As an obvious solution, we could simply have the algorithm simulate the execution of the suspect algorithm and see if it terminates. However, this will not be sufficient. Why not?

1. **A″** stops and prints HALT only if **A″** does not halt when its input is **A″**, and
2. **A″** does not stop and prints DOES NOT HALT only if **A″** eventually stops when its input is **A″**.

In either case, we are led to a logical contradiction, and consequently, we must conclude that the assumption concerning the existence of algorithm **A′** is false. Thus, there does not exist a *universal debugging* algorithm.

It is quite easy to show, using the same general techniques, that there is no universal *algorithm* which will decide whether or not an arbitrary *procedure* is an algorithm or not. This does not imply, however, that it is impossible to find an algorithm which will decide whether or not a specific procedure is an algorithm or not. It simply says that we cannot find one which can decide for all procedures. This problem is known as the *halting* problem for Turing machines and is discussed in more detail in Section 1.4.1 in Part C of the supplementary volume.

Similarly, the result on the universal debugging algorithm does not imply that all program errors are undetectable. We can, and do, provide very useful error checks for almost all programs written in an actual programming language. It is impossible, however, to provide an infallible error-checking program (or algorithm) for infinite loops. Note that this result does not depend in any way on the assumptions underlying our Turing machine's construction.

1.4 CONCLUSIONS

The idea of using mechanical devices as an aid to human endeavors (both physical and mental) has developed as man has developed. While we have been primarily interested in recent aids to mental processes in this chapter, we would be remiss if we failed to note how old the idea actually is. In the *Iliad*, for instance, we find Hephaestos at his bellows:

> ... twenty tripods beat
> To set for stools about the sides of his well-builded hall,
> To whose feet little wheels of gold he put, to go withal,
> And enter his rich dining-room, alone, their motion free,
> And back again go out alone, miraculous to see.

This is an obvious reference to mobile automata (= computers?). Our main concern has been, however, with what might be called information processing devices and how these machines might be used. The Jacquard loom, for instance, could be "programmed" to weave an infinite variety of patterns. The impact of this loom on the textile industry derived not from the fact that it was a better loom mechanically (it was not) but rather that it was a *general-purpose* machine. By providing it with a program, it became a single-purpose device in that it would weave the same pattern over and over again, without intervention. Another device with similar characteristics is the player piano; again, the "program" is the piano roll, and the piano, when properly "programmed," becomes a machine performing a single action among a class of actions.

In each case, we have a machine with certain characteristics which may be programmed to perform certain actions within the class of actions for which it was designed. This observation immediately led us to a discussion of methods for describing procedures and algorithms, first informally and then formally. Under our conventions, an algorithm becomes a representation of a "problem" solution, in which some of the information is provided by implication. A program is a specific realization of an algorithm which may be executed on a physical device—hence, each step in the algorithm must be specified in the minutest detail. Following the analogy of the piano a little further, a musical score might be likened to an algorithm in that it represents a solution to a "problem" (one of composition); the interpretation of the music and the mood it conveys is obtained by implication. A piano roll is a specific realization of this algorithm, for execution by a type of piano. So it is with computers; we are bound to examine ways for specifying algorithms.

The remainder of this book is concerned with the development and representation of algorithms and procedures of the type suited for execution on digital computers. By restricting ourselves to algorithms of this nature, it is possible to obtain a more satisfactory notion of what we mean by an algorithm by defining an abstract device (in this case a Turing machine) and examining the class of algorithms executable by this abstract formalism. As it turns out, this class is very wide indeed. Since it is convenient to express the essence of these algorithms in special kinds of languages, just as the knitting algorithm was expressed in a special language, in the next chapter we shall turn our attention to the structure of one such language.

References

The references given below are only a small representation of the wealth of material available. Each of the works cited contains substantial numbers of references into the literature.

An interesting book devoted to the art of "discovery" in mathematics but of direct importance to the art of writing programs is

G. POLYA, *How To Solve It*, 2nd ed., Princeton University Press, Princeton, N.J., 1971 (paperback).

A much more complete account of the historical development of the modern computer, by a central figure in the field, may be found in

HERMAN H. GOLDSTINE, *The Computer from Pascal to von Neumann*, Princeton University Press, Princeton, N.J., 1972.

Also of interest is Babbage's autobiography, already cited.

An interesting account of man's fascination with machines fashioned in his own image is provided by

JOHN COHEN, *Human Robots in Myth and Science*, A. S. Barnes, Cranbury, N.J., 1967.

Just for fun, try reading the following in light of our analogy between the player piano and the computer:

KURT VONNEGUT, JR., *Player Piano*, Aron Books, New York, 1970.

A fascinating collection of papers, both historical and current, is

ZENON W. PYLYSHYN (ed.), *Perspectives on the Computer Revolution*, Prentice-Hall, Englewood Cliffs, N.J., 1970.

This collection contains abstracts from some of Babbage's work, portions of von Neumann's original design paper for EDVAC, and others.

Aiken's paper:

H. H. AIKEN, "Proposed Automatic Calculating Machine," edited by A. Oettinger and T. C. Bartree, *IEEE Spectrum* (Aug. 1964), pp. 62–69.

von Neumann's first computer program and the structure of EDVAC is the subject of a paper by Donald Knuth:

D. E. KNUTH, "von Neumann's First Computer Program," *Computing Surveys, 2* (1970), pp. 247–260.

Of particular importance to this chapter as a source of inspiration and many examples is the first volume of a seven-volume work in progress:

D. E. KNUTH, *The Art of Computer Programming: Fundamental Algorithms*, Vol. 1, Addison-Wesley, Reading, Mass., 1969.

A general discussion of interesting mathematical problems in general and of Fermat's theorem in particular is found in

H. DORRIE, *100 Great Problems of Elementary Mathematics*, Dover, New York, 1965.

The formalization of algorithms as Turing machines is found in a variety of sources. A rich book is

B. A. TRAKHTENBROT, *Algorithms and Automatic Computing Machines*, Heath, Lexington, Mass., 1963 (translated from the Russian by J. Kristian et al.).

Exercises

1 Try to think of some examples of procedures and algorithms from everyday life. Some representative samples are
  (a) Instructions for assembling a model car or a stereo receiver.
  (b) A score for a piece of music.
  (c) A recipe for baking cookies or cakes.
  (d) Any situation in which a basically mechanical procedure is implied, e.g., fixing a flat tire, replacing a light bulb, playing a game such as tic-tac-toe, etc.
Formalize these algorithms and procedures by writing down the set of instructions which would enable another person to carry them out. Specify which are algorithms and which are procedures.

2 Can you think of any procedures which are useful even though there are conditions under which they may not terminate or cases for which they may not guarantee the correct results? This is very often the case when the recipient of the set of instructions is a human; we make certain assumptions about the ability of people to interpret ambiguous instructions. The most crucial assumption is that people will think and act intelligently when following the instructions; we therefore tend to be a little sloppy in formalizing them.

3 Using the algorithmic notation developed in Section 1.2 augmented by whatever notation you feel necessary, develop algorithms which solve (or represent the solution to) each of the following problems:

(a) The least common multiple (LCM) of two integers m and n is the smallest integer evenly divisible by both m and n. Find an algorithm which, when given m and n as input, will print the least common multiple of m and n. Examples:

$$LCM(3, 5) = 15$$
$$LCM(2, 4) = 4$$
$$LCM(12, 20) = 60$$

(b) Develop an algorithm which accepts as input an n-tuple and n (the number of elements in the n-tuple) and outputs the n-tuple in reverse order.

(c) Given two tuples, an n-tuple and an m-tuple, provide an algorithm which generates a k-tuple the values of which are those values appearing in both the n-tuple and m-tuple. This list of values is known as the *intersection* of the sets of values represented by the n- and m-tuple. Examples:

Input	Output
(1, 2, 3, 4)	
(3, 5, 2, 0)	2 3 (in any order)
(88, −2, 8, 45, 67, −9)	
(3, 5, 1)	None
(0)	
(0, 34, 8)	0

(d) Given the same inputs as in part (c), generate and output a k-tuple whose values appear in either the m-tuple or the n-tuple. These values represent the *union* of the m- and n-tuple. Using the same examples as above, the outputs should be 0, 1, 2, 3, 4, 5; 3, 5, 1, 88, −2, 8, 45, 67, −9; and 0, 34, 8, respectively. Note that these values appear without repetition; i.e., in the first example, 2 appears in both tuples; however, 2 must appear only once in the output.

(e) A prime integer is defined to be an integer which is divisible only by 1 and the integer itself. Develop an algorithm which, given any integer as input, will output the answer PRIME or NOT PRIME.

(f) π is defined to be the ratio of the circumference to the diameter of a circle ($\pi = C/D$). One method for computing π is to approximate it by a series of n terms:

$$\pi = 4 - \tfrac{4}{3} + \tfrac{4}{5} - \tfrac{4}{7} + \tfrac{4}{9} - \tfrac{4}{11} + \cdots$$

where the dots imply an infinite number of terms. Develop an algorithm which, when given n (the number of terms; six are shown above), will output the approximation.

(g) In or around 1202 A.D., an Italian mathematician named Fibonacci was investigating mathematical models of population growth in rabbits. His assumptions were that it takes rabbits one month to reach maturity after birth and that every month after maturity each pair of rabbits will produce another pair. Furthermore, rabbits never die.

Assuming a rabbit population of one pair of infants at month 1, the number of pairs of rabbits on hand during month n is given by the nth term of the Fibonacci sequence:

$$1 \quad 1 \quad 2 \quad 3 \quad 5 \quad 8 \quad \ldots$$

Each term of this sequence is the sum of the two immediately preceding terms. Develop an algorithm which, when given n as input, will print the first n terms of the sequence.

(h) Write an algorithm which will accept as input an n-tuple and will print out the value of the maximum element in the n-tuple.

(i) Modify part (h) to include the minimum element as well as the maximum element.

(j) Modify part (i) to print out the number of times the maximum and minimum values appear in the n-tuple.

4 Using the Turing machine notation developed in Section 1.2, write Turing machine programs for each of the following. Be sure to specify the initial configuration of the tape, the alphabet, the way in which the data are represented, and the interpretation of the final configuration of the tape.

(a) Given any binary string as input, reverse the string.

(b) Given any binary string as input, the output is *1* if the number of *0*'s in the string is odd and *0* if the number of *0*'s is even.

(c) Given the unary representation of a number on the tape, generate all successive integers (in unary representation) separated by some special symbol.

(d) Design a Turing machine which will multiply two unary numbers.

(e) Given two unary numbers, form the difference between them. You may assume that the first number on the tape is larger than the second, so that the difference will always be positive.

These few problems should convince you of the inefficiency of Turing machine programs that is inherent in repeated passes over portions of the tape and the painstaking nature of Turing machine programming. This should be sufficient to motivate the development of a more expressive programming language, which is the subject of the next chapter.

2

Problem-Solving

2.0 INTRODUCTION

Before we proceed to define an algorithmic language closer to an actual programming language than the Turing machine language introduced in Chapter 1, we shall address ourselves to the question of how to begin thinking about finding an informal algorithm for the solution of a given problem. The ultimate goal is, of course, a computer program which will correctly solve the given problem. It is an unfortunate fact that few people are good problem-solvers; when confronted with a novel problem, many will not develop the solution in any sort of consistent, structured way, if they find a solution at all. Many errors or inefficiencies creep into the solution, and the end result may work but not necessarily well. When the end result is a fairly large computer program, this kind of an approach to problem-solving is doomed to disaster for a variety of reasons. The trial-and-error approach to programming is definitely a one-way road to a program that requires an inordinate amount of time to write, which probably cannot be understood by anyone other than the person who wrote it, and which most likely does not work correctly. On the other hand, a program (problem solution, algorithm) developed in a logically consistent way, starting with the problem statement and systematically refining this statement, has the following characteristics:

1. The resultant program will be easily understood by others since it will not have haphazardly added sections to "patch up" errors; i.e., the overall *structure* of the program will be transparent.
2. The first approach to the program will probably be a correct one; even if problems arise in the construction of the algorithm, they can be easily corrected, *consistent with the structure thus far developed, before* any of the actual program is written.
3. At each step in the development, it is possible to be reasonably certain that the solution being developed will be correct, in the sense that the final algorithm will represent one possible solution to the problem.

4. The amount of time required before the final program works is drastically reduced.

In this chapter, we shall first develop a set of guidelines for approaching problem-solving. Next we shall present a representational framework for formally specifying the algorithm(s) resulting from the problem study. The representation chosen is a language called AL (for Algorithmic Language) whose form is motivated by the proposed problem-solving techniques and whose syntax is close to existing programming languages. AL thus serves as the intermediate step between informal solution specification and the final program. We shall conclude the chapter with two extensive examples illustrating the techniques previously developed for obtaining an algorithmic solution from the original problem statement.

2.1 MODULAR REFINEMENT

In this section, we wish to examine techniques for designing the solution to problems in some sort of systematic way. As mentioned earlier, one of the reasons for systematically designing a solution is so that the end product may be easily understood; therefore, instead of first discussing ways in which construction of a solution proceeds, let us examine the problem of understanding the function of a large complex system. One way of accomplishing this goal is to consider an extant solution; that is, we shall look at a system already constructed in an attempt to discover its working principles. Just as we used the player piano as an aid in conceptualizing algorithms, we shall draw conclusions concerning the understanding of algorithms via the understanding of a complex physical system, e.g., the automobile.

The automobile can be considered a solution to the problem of providing transportation of a certain mass from point *a* to point *b* at varying speeds by means of various routes. The problem we wish to solve is how do we explain the functioning of an automobile to someone who has asked the question, "How does an automobile work?" There are obviously many solutions to this problem; the worst approach would be to take a list of all parts and proceed down the list, trying to explain the functioning of each part as one comes across it. This approach will certainly lead to disaster because the human mind cannot understand the myriad of details without the conceptual framework in which the parts are embedded and from which one can view the interrelationships and functions of each. For example, one of the first parts on the list might be "air filter"; one might describe the function of the air filter as the removal of dirt particles greater than a specified size from the incoming air. Air for what? Where does it go? Who needs it? How much air? . . . These questions obviously cannot be answered without generating a whole new set of questions, ad infinitum.

The proper approach would be to find those components of the system which perform clearly defined functions and which can be viewed independently of each other. Thus, we do not have to consider the automobile as a whole, but rather we can concentrate on a single component, thereby reducing the conceptual complexity of the system to be studied. To satisfy the previously stated criteria for the transportation problem, a car can be viewed as consisting of the following component systems:

1. Engine (provides power to drive train).
2. Drive train (transmits power to wheels).
3. Wheels (provides rolling support of chassis, directional control, and motion).
4. Chassis (provides structural cohesiveness and payload support).
5. Control (of both direction and force).

Although each of the components interacts as stated above, each can be studied in isolation. For example, the engine can be viewed separately as a system which, given fuel and control, will produce the required motive force to the drive train. After precisely describing the ways in which the engine interacts with the rest of the system, we can view the engine as a system by itself and apply the same process in its description. When explaining the engine, it is then not necessary to consider any other portion of the original system; rather, the engine can be decomposed into its major subsystems (e.g., carburetor, block, fuel pump, etc.). When looked at from the point of view of a list of parts, we have effectively grouped a small collection of parts, on the basis of their functional relationships, into a subsystem which can be readily understood. These subsystems can in turn be grouped on the basis of their functional relationships, given a name, and considered as components of a system of greater complexity. Continuing in this way, the entire system is eventually described in a logically consistent way. Note that this approach to the general description of a car provides us not only with a list of the parts necessary for its construction but also with a hierarchy of functional subsystems.

Let us now consider an algorithm as a sequence of instructions. An analogy can be drawn between the understanding of an algorithm as represented by the list of instructions and the understanding of the car from a list of parts. The implication is that we want to group the instructions into functional units, which we shall call *modules*, provide them with names, and specify their interaction with other modules. Similarly, these modules may be grouped to form modules of higher complexity until a hierarchy of modules is formed.

Thus far, we have been concerned only with the understanding of existing systems (algorithms); however, the interesting problem which we want to discuss in this chapter is how to obtain the algorithm and its hierarchical description for a given problem.

The starting point for most problem-solving tasks is generally a vague outline of the problem. It should be clearly understood that problems in the real world are neither well defined nor precisely specified. Potentially, the worst advice one can give to the beginning programmer is to tell him to start writing instructions in some algorithmic language for those parts of the problem which are well specified and to which he knows a solution, the justification for this procedure being that hopefully the rest will come miraculously once we start to write algorithms or programs.

Rather, we should begin the process of problem-solving by trying to understand the problem. After obtaining an initial understanding of the problem statement, we begin by generating the precise formulation of the problem. That is, we have to state precisely what the input, if any, is to the algorithm and what the range of admissible values is. Similarly, we have to clearly describe what it is we wish to compute: ⟩ must generate a precise description of the desired result (output).

Example 2.1

Suppose somebody states to his computer scientist friend, "I have this long list and would like to have it sorted." It is clearly an ill-defined problem, and we have to assert certain facts about input and output before we can even try to solve this problem. What are the relevant facts we need to know? A possible dialogue between the computer scientist and his friend might be as follows:

Question	Answer
a. Concerning input:	
What forms are the items in the list?	Names
What characters are allowed?	A–Z, blank, –
What is the maximum length?	30 characters
How many names?	2560
Are they all different?	Yes
b. Concerning output:	
In what order should the list be sorted?	Lexicographical order
What is the ordering relation between blank, '–', and the alphabetic characters?	Blank smaller than A–Z smaller than –

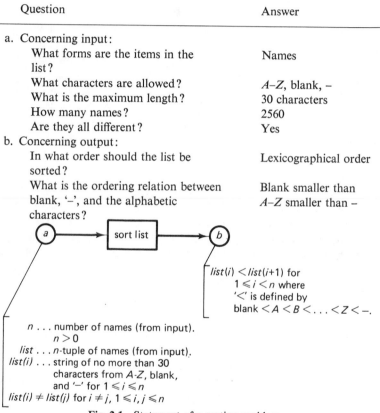

$list(i) < list(i+1)$ for
$1 \leq i < n$ where
'$<$' is defined by
blank $< A < B < \ldots < Z < -$.

n . . . number of names (from input).
$n > 0$
$list$ . . . n-tuple of names (from input).
$list(i)$ . . . string of no more than 30
characters from A-Z, blank,
and '–' for $1 \leq i \leq n$
$list(i) \neq list(j)$ for $i \neq j$, $1 \leq i, j \leq n$

Fig. 2.1 Statement of a sorting problem.

From these answers we may then state a general well-defined problem class which includes the specific problem as an instance, as shown in Figure 2.1. The statements pertaining to ⓐ and ⓑ are assertions about the input to and the output from a computation module. ■

Once we are fairly confident that the initial description and input/output relationship are the ones desired, our next step is a creative one, and as such no "recipe" for it can be provided. The creative step consists of finding an outline of a solution to which we apply the following process. Formulate the outline in such a way that it consists of independent subtasks (modules) which can be executed in sequence. In this decomposition (or refinement) process we do allow repeated execution of a module (or modules) but insist on the linear flow. This serves to impose a structure on the resulting algorithm which will eventually describe the problem solution such that the human mind can grasp its meaning and manipulate its form if necessary. The next step in the refinement of the main module is to develop the communications between the modules. As can be seen from Figure 2.2, we know what we are given, (a), and what our target is, (b). For many problems it is advantageous to start with the target and develop the form of the input from right to left. That is, in Figure 2.2, we would first define the communication at point (n), which is the output of module $n - 1$, proceeding to the left until we have defined the communication at point (1). At this point of the refinement, we may not be able to give a precise definition of the form of all the intermediate results and may have to delay their description until the modules which produce them are completely specified.

When we postulated that a module should be refined into a linear sequence of submodules, we did not explicitly describe what a module is. We view a module as one of the three following items. First, the module describes a task sufficiently complex so as to allow further linear decomposition. In this case, we simply apply the process outlined above again to this module. Second, a module describes a task sufficiently simple so that we can describe how it should be accomplished with a few instructions in the algorithmic language (AL). Third, a module may still represent a highly complex task whose solution we can outline but which cannot be decomposed further into a linear sequence of modules. In this case, we give an algorithmic description of the flow of control for the subtasks, identifying them by name and description only, and apply the process of refinement to each of the modules corresponding to the subtasks.

The major emphasis in this approach is the precise statement of the input/output relationship of each module. This effectively isolates each module and allows us to concentrate on one module at a time. Thus, on the first level of refinement (the original statement: the top line in Figure 2.2) we have the first step in the translation of the original English language statement of the problem into a formal description. At the second level of refinement we describe the general outline of the algorithm and make certain decisions concerning the way information is to be transmitted from module to module. As we continue to progressively refine each module the structure of the algorithm solving the original problem becomes more and more precise until all modules consist only of instructions.

Example 2.1 (continued)

Let us apply the general guidelines developed thus far to the sorting example. The first step is an attempt to formulate a vague outline of the process which will solve the problem. This is essentially a creative process and as such cannot be molded into any formalism. However, in Chapter 4, we shall explore generally useful strategies which aid in the development of problem solutions.

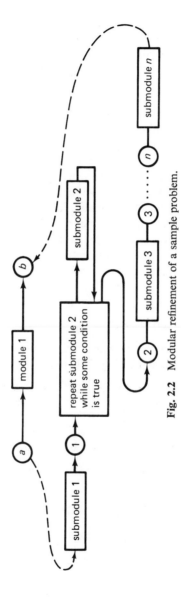

Fig. 2.2 Modular refinement of a sample problem.

```
*********************************
* STOP:   Before reading any further, write down (in any language *
* you wish) at least two general schemes for sorting a list of numbers *
* (say n of them). As we shall see repeatedly throughout this book, *
* there are usually many possible solutions to the same problem, so *
* do not despair if you do not see our solution immediately. Yours *
* is probably just as valid.                                      *
*********************************
```

In this example, we are concerned with sorting strings of alphabetic symbols. However, the basic idea of sorting is the same; as long as we have an effective method for comparing two elements and determining which is the "larger," it does not make any difference whether the elements are numbers or strings of symbols. Of course, at a certain conceptual level, one can consider a number as nothing more than a string of symbols. At any rate, one specific sorting scheme might be the following: Find the largest (in the sense defined in Figure 2.1) element and put it at the end of the list; then repeat the process on the remaining elements. This process is repeated $n - 1$ time (if there are n elements in the list), and then the entire list will be sorted. Implicit in this scheme is the fact that at each step the list which must be searched for the largest element is one element shorter than the list in the previous step; for instance, consider the following sample problem:

Sort the list

$$45 \quad 2 \quad 67 \quad -78 \quad 33 \quad 1$$

using the sorting method described above.

1. The largest element in the list is 67. Place this at the end of the list. This is accomplished by exchanging 67 with 1, so the list becomes

$$45 \quad 2 \quad 1 \quad -78 \quad 33 \quad 67$$

2. The remainder of the list is

$$45 \quad 2 \quad 1 \quad -78 \quad 33$$

The largest element is 45, which must be exchanged with 33 to produce

$$33 \quad 2 \quad 1 \quad -78 \quad 45$$

and thus the entire list is

$$33 \quad 2 \quad 1 \quad -78 \quad 45 \quad 67$$

EXERCISE 2.1: Continue the steps outlined above.

EXERCISE 2.2: Repeat Example 2.1 and Exercise 2.1 on the following list of words separated by blanks:

THIS   ANY   EVERY   ALL   ALWAYS   FOREVER   IS   A

using the standard lexicographic ordering (dictionary ordering).

In Figure 2.3, we illustrate the results of the modular-refinement procedure applied to the module *sort list* with the above outline in mind. In Figure 2.3(a), we formalize the basic idea of iterating over a module which will find the largest element in a *j*-

tuple and place it in the last element of the *j*-tuple. After defining ② it is clear what ①
should be. Figure 2.3(b) is a refinement of submodule 1 into the two tasks of finding

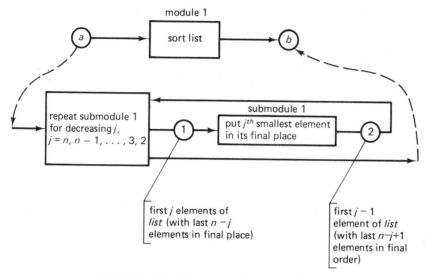

Fig. 2.3(a)   Modular refinement of 'sort' module.

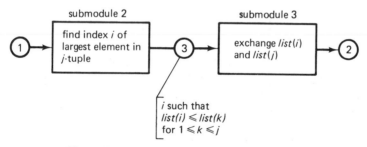

Fig. 2.3(b)   Modular refinement of 'sort' module.

out where the largest element is and then placing it in at the end of the *j*-tuple. We
leave it for later exercises to continue the refinement of submodule 3 since at this
point we are interested only in the general strategy. ■

This approach to problem-solving has two distinct advantages over the trial-and-
error approach mentioned before. First, it reduces the complexity of the problem with
which we must deal at any given time and therefore allows us to solve more complex
problems. A second advantage is that it enables us to verify the correctness of our
algorithm relatively easily since we can prove correctness of the entire algorithm by
proving correctness of each submodule separately. This we are able to do only because
we have required that the flow of control (the order in which the submodules are
executed) be strictly linear. It should not be the case, for instance, that submodule 1 in
Figure 2.2 is executed again after submodule 3 has been executed. If this were to occur,
correctness could not be proved by providing correctness of submodule 3 and sub-

module 1 independently since the execution of submodule 1 would depend on what submodule 3 does.

Another major advantage of program development by modular refinement is the ability to modify the underlying algorithm and/or program structure without a major effort. Even the best laid plans have a habit of going awry; it is much easier to modify a well-designed algorithm than it is to modify actual program code. Discovery of the need for modification in one of the submodules does not cause undue difficulty since only the modules higher up which are directly affected by the proposed changes need be modified. In fact, several up and down refinements might be needed before the algorithm is in its final form.

To outline the general idea of a correctness proof, assume we have already proven that submodule 2 in Figure 2.3(b) will when given a j-tuple of names output the index i of the largest element in this tuple. Then, since at ② we have the last $n - j + 1$ elements in their final order and j is decreased by 1 at the beginning of submodule 1, it must be the case that the stated property holds at ①. Observing that this process terminates when submodule 1 has been executed for $j = 2$, we may obtain the status of the computation at ⓑ by substituting 2 for j in the assertion at ②:

$$\text{Last } n - 1 \text{ elements in final order}$$

which implies the assertion at ⓑ.

Correctness of an algorithm is of particular importance when the final "program," i.e., an algorithm which can be executed by a computer, is produced. During the translation from algorithm to program, errors will undoubtedly occur. Therefore, it is vital that the modular structure of the algorithm be retained during the translation process. This effectively allows us to *debug* (remove errors) from each section of the program completely independently of the other sections simply by simulating the input (whose range we have defined precisely) and determining whether the output has the desired property. The viability of this approach depends a great deal on the structures provided in the programming language chosen as the final vehicle for representation of the algorithm. Some programming languages are more appropriate for this structured approach because they provide primitives very close to the structures inherent in the final refinement. A more complete discussion of this important question is found in Section 2.5. Note, however, that the general approach to problem-solving being developed here is absolutely independent of any particular programming language.

We realize that we have not given any detailed rules to be followed during problem-solving but rather have provided a framework from which to view the problem-solving process. Unfortunately, there are no recipes, no cookbooks, and no magical processes for obtaining the outline of an algorithmic solution to a problem. All we can provide are the guidelines designed to reduce the complexity of the problem-solving process which will help to produce a correct algorithm once the skeletal solution has been conceived. In this respect, problem-solving is an art which requires talent, experience, and an ability to work and think.

2.2 AN INTRODUCTION TO THE ALGORITHMIC LANGUAGE AL

AL, which is an acronym for algorithmic language, is a language very close to an actual programming language in style yet specifically tailored to facilitate the structured problem-solving concepts developed in the last section. This section constitutes a brief introduction to AL; additional features will be introduced in subsequent chapters as necessity dictates. The major focus here is the definition of the structure of AL and its instruction set.

The basic approach will be to define AL instructions and concepts in terms of Turing machine programs which will ultimately fulfill the unambiguity requirements discussed previously. As noted in Chapter 1, Turing machines are notoriously inefficient in their use of the tape. One of the underlying reasons for this inefficiency is the nature of the tape itself: The squares, which represent the Turing machine's storage, are undifferentiated. To find an item on the tape, the Turing machine must search the entire tape under the control of the program, looking for a pattern which represents the item desired. As an example, consider the statement

$$n \longleftarrow 10 \qquad\qquad (1)$$

where n represents a variable whose current value, as a result of this statement, is 10. One of the major drawbacks to the use of a Turing machine as a programming tool is the lack of the concept of a variable; other drawbacks include the requirement of an infinite tape and the ultimate length of most Turing programs. Any real computer can have, at most, a finite number of storage locations. In this case, the idea of a variable as an addressable entity into which data (a value) can be stored or from which data can be retrieved at different times during execution makes sense. It alleviates the need to exhaustively search a large number of storage locations in order to find the value required for a computation. Given the address, one can go directly to the location and either retrieve the value found there or place a value there. For example, after (1) has been executed, a statement such as

$$n \longleftarrow n + 1 \qquad\qquad (2)$$

could be used to change the value of n to 11. Two problems immediately arise:

1. The operator $+$ is not defined in the Turing machine language. However, as we have seen in Example 1.4, $+$ can be represented as a Turing machine program itself. Therefore, at the conceptual level at least, this problem is not insurmountable.
2. What are the semantics of (2); that is, how should it be executed? Intuitively, execution of (2) is not complex and would probably proceed as follows:
   (a) The location containing the value of n [on the right-hand side of (2)] must be found.
   (b) This value must be copied to a blank area on the tape.

(c) The value of 1 must be copied to a contiguous area of the tape; the two values are separated by $+$.

(d) The program of Example 1.4 must be executed on this portion of the tape.

(e) The resultant value must be copied back into the storage area for n [the reference to n on the left-hand side of (2)].

In fact, this sequence could be the first stepwise refinement of the problem

> Write a Turing machine program to execute the statement $n \leftarrow n + 1$ assuming suitable conventions regarding tape structure and representation of the data.

At any rate, the program would clearly require multiple passes over the tape in order to accomplish the execution. In a real computer, using the general structure of the Turing machine, this scheme would require an inordinate amount of time to execute, even for such a simple statement as (2). The problem can be alleviated if we differentiate the squares (cells of the tape) by uniquely numbering each one. This number is known as the *address* of (the storage location of) n. All one has to do, then, is to maintain a rather small table of variable names and their addresses; reference to a variable is relatively simple provided the RWH can be moved directly to a square once the address is known.

For simplicity's sake let us for the moment restrict the variable names in AL to be only one alphabetic character and the values of the variables to be only 0 or 1. We define the alphabet of the Turing machine to consist of $0, 1, B, \$$, and $a, \ldots, z$. A portion of the tape, delimited by squares containing $, is designated as the data area; this area is located to the right of the working area and will consist of a group of pairs of squares. One square will contain the name of the variable, and this will be followed by a square containing the value of the variable. For instance, in Figure 2.4, the tape configuration corresponding to an AL program containing three variables a, b, and c with their current values 0, 1, and 1 is illustrated. There is one problem with this representation. Suppose the Turing machine, representing a given AL program, computes a certain result in a program using the working tape. In this program, execution of a RIGHT instruction might move the read-write head inadvertently into the data area. We should, therefore, replace each RIGHT instruction in the program by a sequence of instructions which check whether the data area has been reached and, if so, moves the whole data area one (or more) squares to the right. Only then can the normal RIGHT instruction be executed.

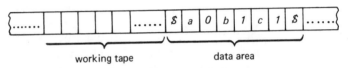

working tape   data area

Fig. 2.4 A Turing machine representation of variables.

EXERCISE 2.3: Write the Turing program for the new RIGHT instruction when there is a data area on the tape.

A reference to a variable x in the AL program can therefore be defined as the Turing program which will move its head to the first $, then to the square containing the symbol x, and finally one square to the right, where the value of x is found.

EXERCISE 2.4: Write a Turing machine program to reference a variable m; that is, it should mark the current location of the read-write head on the working tape, search for the value of m in the data area, and copy it to the marked square.

It is a trivial extension to allow the variable names to become strings of characters and the values of variables to occupy an arbitrary number of squares; the conceptual complexity of the Turing machine program from Exercise 2.4 is not greatly increased. We shall, therefore, assume multicharacter variable names and values other than 0 and 1.

2.2.1 Basic Statements

The core instruction (statement) of AL is the assignment statement,

$$variable \longleftarrow expression \tag{3}$$

where *expression* is a sequence of *operators* (e.g., $+$, $-$, . . .) and *operands* (e.g., variables or constants) which can be evaluated and assigned as the new value of the variable appearing on the left-hand side. We shall be quite unrestrictive in the usage of operators and correspondingly in the type of values we allow variables and constants to have (e.g., the value might be an integer, a string of characters, or bit string, etc.). However, we do require that the arguments to an operator be of the proper type it requires. Whenever an operator is not self-explanatory through its symbol we shall add its intended semantics as a comment. This statement does not differ greatly from the informal assignment statement used extensively in Chapter 1.

We define the semantics of a statement to be the effect of executing that statement. If we consider a simplified form of (3),

$$variable \longleftarrow operand\ operator\ operand$$

then the semantics are particularly simple:

> A reference to a variable (operand) on the right-hand side is defined as the Turing program which copies the value of the variable from the data area to a location which depends on the operator to which this variable is an operand. A reference to an operator activates the corresponding Turing program, which performs the operation required, leaving the result on the working tape. A reference to a variable on the left-hand side copies the result from the working tape to the appropriate value field in the data area.

Example 2.2

Let us analyze the various stages of the contents of the tape during execution of the statement

$$a \longleftarrow b * v$$

where the initial configuration is

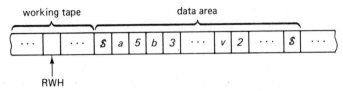

First, the reference to *b* will cause the value 3 to be copied to the working tape:

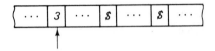

Next, we place the operator next to the first argument, store the value of *v* next to the square containing the operator, and put the read-write head at the beginning of the first argument:

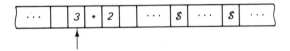

Next to last, we activate the Turing program for multiplication, resulting in

The last step is the reference to *a* on the left side of the ⟵, which causes the value under the read-write head to be copied to the value field of *a*:

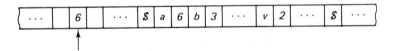

EXERCISE 2.5: Extend the semantics of the simplified version of (3) (above) to include, first,

$$variable \longleftarrow operand_1 \quad operator_1 \quad operand_2 \quad operator_2 \quad operand_3$$

and then to (3) itself.

Since a high level of abstraction is desired, variables are not restricted to a single name; they are considered to be any addressable quantity. Examples of variables then include *n*-tuples, tables, or any arbitrary function. For instance, in the statement

$$list(i) \longleftarrow list(j)$$

where *list* is any *n*-tuple, the value field in the data area actually contains *n* distinct value fields. Reference to *list(j)* on the right side translates into a Turing program which copies the value of the variable j and the name *list* onto its normal tape and computes from these values the address of the value field of the jth element in *list*. In general, we allow any function reference on both sides of the assignment statement. The Turing machine will implement a function by storing the function name in the data area followed by pairs of values for each defined value of the function. The first element of each pair gives the argument of the function and the second provides the value of the function at this point. For instance, consider the function *"telephone-number"* whose argument is a name; the corresponding value is the telephone number of the individual named. The algorithm section (4) would result in the tape configuration in Figure 2.5, assuming all entities are separated by a blank.

$$\begin{aligned}
&\textit{telephone-number}(\text{`Joe'}) \longleftarrow 3289; \\
&\textit{telephone-number}(\text{`Ann'}) \longleftarrow 1243; \\
&X \longleftarrow \textit{telephone-number}(\text{`Joe'})
\end{aligned} \qquad (4)$$

EXERCISE 2.6: Write a Turing program which when given a function name, an argument, and a value on the working tape will store the value in its proper place in the data area. (Caution: The function may not yet be defined for this argument; see also the comments below.)

In solving Exercise 2.6 the reader will realize how much less complex the Turing program would be if all the value fields or name fields were of equal length and some information about the type of a variable (e.g., string, tuple, function) were to be stored together with its name. When we discuss programming languages and their realizations on computers we shall see that this is precisely what is done.

Since our algorithms are intended to be executed by a physical, even if only hypothetical, machine, we have to provide means for communications between the machine and the human being. The two statements in (5) serve this purpose:

$$\begin{aligned}
&\textbf{input } \textit{variable 1, variable 2, } \ldots \textit{, variable n} \\
&\textbf{output } \textit{variable 1, variable 2, } \ldots \textit{, variable m}
\end{aligned} \qquad (5)$$

For instance, executing statement (6),

$$\textbf{output } \textit{telephone-number} \qquad (6)$$

after statements (4) would cause the two pairs (Joe, 3289) and (Ann, 1243) to be printed. We print in bold face those words in AL which have a special meaning so as to distinguish them from variables with the same name.

Any two statements in an AL algorithm are separated by a semicolon, and any number of statements can be made into a single *compound statement* by enclosing them with the words **begin** and **end**. Each such block should be given some proper name by adding a meaningful comment of the form

$$/*\text{this is a comment}*/ \qquad (7)$$

Fig. 2.5 Data area for (4).

after the word **begin** and the same after **end**. For example,

$$
\begin{aligned}
&\cdot\\
&\cdot\\
&\cdot\\
&\textbf{begin } /*\text{max-index}*/\\
&\quad S_1;\\
&\quad S_2;\\
&\quad\cdot\\
&\quad\cdot\\
&\quad\cdot\\
&\quad S_{n-1};\\
&\quad S_n\\
&\textbf{end}; /*\text{max-index}*/\\
&\cdot\\
&\cdot\\
&\cdot
\end{aligned}
\tag{8}
$$

If only a few statements are to be grouped together, we may use brackets as abbreviations for the **begin-end** delimiters:

$$[S_1; S_2] \tag{9}$$

To halt execution of an AL algorithm, we use the same instruction as was used for the Turing machine:

$$\textbf{halt} \tag{10}$$

2.2.2 Control Structures

Control over the flow of execution in Turing machine programs was accomplished by means of the IF statement and the GO TO statement. The use of these statements could seriously degrade the readability of Turing machine programs since they could be used to transfer control to any point within the program. When abused, this violates the principle of modular refinement which requires the isolation of modules from each other and not haphazard interconnection. Since branching capabilities are required in an algorithmic language, we somehow must prevent the unrestricted intertwining of modules.

One method which reduces the potential for unnecessarily complex branching, and which is consistent with the requirement of linear flow, is through the use of what are called single-entry/single-exit structures. That is, if at some point of execution several branches must be provided, execution must resume at a common point in the program independently of the branch chosen.

The Case Construct

Let E be any expression which, during the execution of the algorithm, may evaluate to one of $\alpha_1, \ldots, \alpha_n$ and $S_1, \ldots, S_n$ be AL statements (either simple or compound). Then the structure of the **case** construct is given by the diagram in Figure 2.6 with the following interpretation: If E evaluates to α_1, S_1 is executed, and then control

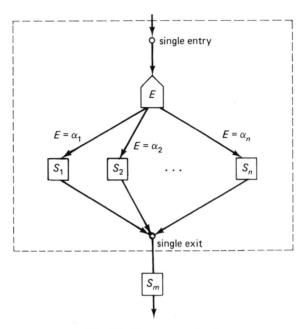

Fig. 2.6   The **case** construct.

is transferred to S_m; if E evaluates to α_2, S_2 is executed with subsequent transfer of control to S_m; etc. In this and subsequent figures, arrows represent flow of control. In AL the **case** construct is written as

$$
\begin{aligned}
&\textbf{case } E \textbf{ of} \\
&\quad \alpha_1 : S_1; \\
&\quad \alpha_2 : S_2; \\
&\quad \alpha_2 : S_3; \\
&\qquad . \\
&\qquad . \\
&\qquad . \\
&\quad \alpha_n : S_n \\
&\textbf{end } /*\text{case name}*/
\end{aligned}
\tag{11}
$$

Example 2.3

Suppose you are sightseeing in a strange city and that you had parked your car on some corner. Unfortunately, after walking around for some time, you have forgotten where the corner is. Since the streets of the city form a rectangular grid, you decide to take a *random walk* in order to find your car. Your random walk consists of throwing a die (which you happen to have in your pocket) at every intersection. You go east, west, north, or south, depending on whether the die shows 1, 2, 3, or 4, respectively; if the die shows 5 or 6, you roll again. See Figure 2.7. Were we to write an algorithm to simulate your progress, we would probably represent the map of the city as a table

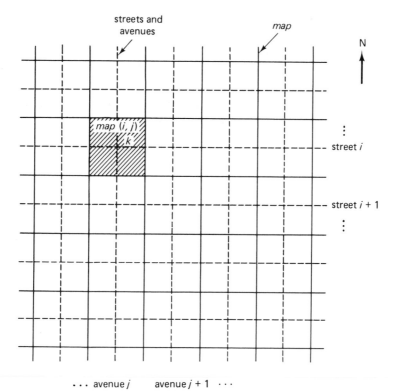

Fig. 2.7 Map for random walk problem.

whose entries are the intersections. Let your current position be the ith street and the jth avenue and assume you have walked k blocks; then $map(i, j)$ should have been set to k to record your progress. Assume that in another portion of the algorithm we have set the value of the variable *die* to a random value between 1 and 4, inclusive. The following **case** statement will properly record your progress:

```
case die of
    1:  j ← j + 1; /*turn east*/
    2:  j ← j − 1; /*turn west*/
    3:  i ← i − 1; /*turn north*/
    4:  i ← i + 1 /*turn south*/
end; /*direction*/
k ← k + 1;
map(i, j) ← k
```

The If-Then-Else Construct

This construct is only a special form of the **case** construct. Let P be a conditional expression which has only two possible values, true or false. The diagram of this con-

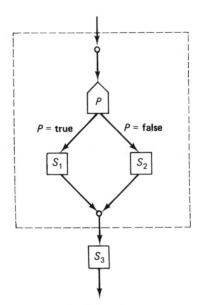

Fig. 2.8   The **if-then-else** construct.

struct (Figure 2.8) has the formalization (12) or (13) depending on whether or not S_2 in Figure 2.8 is the null statement:

$$\text{if } P \text{ then } S_1 \tag{12}$$

$$\text{if } P \text{ then } S_1 \text{ else } S_2 \tag{13}$$

Again control is transferred to a common point after the statement is executed regardless of which branch was chosen.

Example 2.4

Suppose we wish to develop an algorithm to compute a taxpayer's tax due the federal government. At one point in this algorithm we will have to set a flag *standard_deduction* to **t** (true) or **f** (false) depending on whether the *itemized_deductions* exceed a predefined threshold called *deduction_threshold*. Either of the following alternatives will accomplish this:

1. **if** *itemized_deductions* $>$ *deduction_threshold*
            then *standard_deduction* $\leftarrow$ **f**
            else *standard_deduction* $\leftarrow$ **t**

2. *standard_deduction* $\leftarrow$ **t**;
        if *itemized_deductions* $>$ *deduction_threshold*
                then *standard_deduction* $\leftarrow$ **f**

The While Construct

We have already seen the need to repeatedly execute a sequence of statements as long as a certain condition is true. The AL construct which fills this requirement is known as the **while** iteration:

$$\textbf{while } (P) \textit{ statement} \tag{14}$$

where P is a conditional expression (predicate) as before. See Figure 2.9.

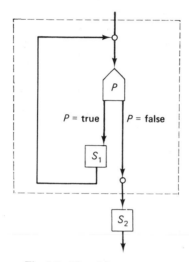

Fig. 2.9 The **while** construct.

Example 2.5

Write an AL algorithm which will sum the first n integers.

```
begin /*sums the first n integers*/
    /*initialize answer and set up temporary variable*/
    integer ← 1;
    answer ← 0;
    while (integer ≤ n)
    begin /*addition loop*/
        answer ← answer + integer;
        integer ← integer + 1
    end /*addition loop*/
end /*sums*/
```

One of the properties of an algorithm is that it terminates with an answer. The last construct introduced is the only one which may cause a violation of this property; we should carefully check that the variables contained in P in the body of the iteration statement are modified so that P eventually becomes false. Otherwise, an infinite loop may occur; for example, the following **while** statement is such a loop:

$$x \leftarrow 1;$$
$$\textbf{while } (x \leq 1) \; y \leftarrow y + 1$$

Procedures

The facilities developed in AL up to this point allow us to group statements (via the **begin-end** delimiters) and to control the flow of execution of statements. These features are not sufficient to impose on the algorithm both the hierarchical structure and the interaction among modules obtained by modular refinement. The feature required is one which enables us to isolate a block of statements, name it, and provide it with input/output parameters. We refer to the isolated block of statements as a *procedure*.

The defining statement (15) for a procedure precedes the group of statements comprising the *procedure body;* these statements are completely independent of other procedures. The only communication is via the list of input and output variables.

$$\textbf{procedure } \textit{name-of-procedure (formal input 1, formal input 2, } \ldots$$
$$\ldots, \textit{formal input j; formal output 1, } \ldots, \textit{formal} \qquad (15)$$
$$\textit{output k)S}$$

In this statement, *name-of-procedure* is a name we provide to identify the group of statements comprising the procedure body.

Example 2.6

Assume that somewhere in the modular refinement of an algorithm it is necessary to compute the value $1 \times 2 \times 3 \times \cdots \times n$ for various values of n. The input value to the procedure will be the value of n and the output value will be the expression as given. Since the stated objective of a procedure is to isolate the block of statements completely from the environment in which the procedure is used, we do not need any more information. The procedure will have one input and one output, as represented by variable names which we are free to pick however we choose; these variables are called the formal input and formal output parameters, respectively. The way in which the procedure is linked to its environment is discussed below. The procedure given below will achieve the desired results:

```
procedure product(n; prod)
begin /*compute product of first n integers*/
    if n < 1 then [output 'error in product; input out of range'; halt];
    i ← 1;
    prod ← 1;
    while (i ≤ n) [prod ← prod * i; i ← i + 1]
end /*compute*/
```

If we assume that at some point in the algorithm we wish to obtain the value of the product of the first m integers in a variable called *res*, then we must provide a correspondence between the formal parameters n and *prod* and the actual parameters m and *res*. This is accomplished through a statement of the form

$$name\text{-}of\text{-}procedure(input\ 1,\ input\ 2,\ \ldots,\ input\ j; \\ output\ 1,\ output\ 2,\ \ldots,\ output\ k) \tag{16}$$

which in this particular instance is

$$product(m;\ res)$$

In Example 2.6, a procedure was defined in order to isolate the statements comprising the computation to be performed in order to develop them independently of the remainder of the algorithm, consistent with the tenets of modular refinement. Another reason for the inclusion of the procedure feature in AL is that the computation represented by the procedure might be required at several places in the algorithm, with a different set of input/output variables. For example, the module computing the index of the largest element in a j-tuple might be used in an algorithm in several places. At one point the input might be a 10-tuple, while at another point the input might be a 250-tuple. To make it possible to activate (call) a procedure from different places with different input variables, we shall define (i.e., write the algorithm for) the procedure in terms of formal input and output variables, e.g., n and *prod* in Example 2.6. When the procedure is called with a particular set of actual input/output variables (m and *res* in Example 2.6), the *addresses* of the actual parameters are transmitted to the procedure. The procedure will use them as the addresses of the corresponding formal parameters. Thus, a reference to a particular formal parameter in the procedure body is equivalent to a reference to the corresponding actual parameter. When a procedure is called with a variable which appears only as an input and not as an output variable, the assumption is made that the value of that variable will not be changed by the procedure.

To illustrate these conventions, let us discuss the algorithm fragment (17) within a module M:

$$\vdots$$

$$find\text{-}max\text{-}index(list, j; i);$$

$$\vdots$$

$$find\text{-}max\text{-}index(cost, k; i);$$

$$\vdots$$

procedure *find-max-index(list, n; index)*   (17)
begin

    .
    .
    .

  procedure body

    .
    .
    .

  cmax ← 0

    .
    .
    .

end /∗procedure find-max-index∗/

The Turing program for the procedure *find-max-index* will have its own data area and working tape but any reference to *list*, *n*, or *index* will be translated to a reference to the actual variables in the data area of module *M* from which the call originated; see Figure 2.10. Thus, if *find-max-index* wants to fetch the value of *n*, it has to move its head either to the value field of *j* or that of *k* depending on whether the call came from the first or second statement in (17). However, during execution of the statement

$$cmax \leftarrow 0$$

in (17) the value should be set in the data area for *find-max-index* since it is a variable local to this procedure.

Although these control structures are sufficient to express any algorithm for any solvable problem, and despite our intention to keep AL simple, we shall introduce two convenience features into the language. Quite often it is desirable to terminate a **while** iteration or a **procedure** execution prematurely. For this purpose, AL contains an instruction (18) which terminates the iteration or **procedure** execution and transfers control to the next statement after the **while** iteration or the **procedure** call. Again, a comment is required to indicate which construct is terminated:

terminate /∗process name∗/   (18)

The second convenience feature is included in recognition of our ability to make mistakes. No matter how well organized our program development is, errors have a distinct tendency to appear at the least expected time and place. It is reasonably easy to "trap" a fairly common error which may occur in conjunction with the **case** statement: It is quite possible that the expression *E* might not evaluate to any of the values $\alpha_1 \ldots \alpha_n$. Therefore, we allow the user to specify a branch, labeled "error," which is taken if *E* does not evaluate to one of the α values. In this branch we may state any corrective action if we wish the algorithm to continue execution or cause some error message to be printed with a subsequent halt.

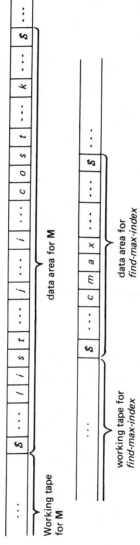

Fig. 2.10 Tape configuration for algorithm with 'procedure'.

$$\textbf{case } E \textbf{ of}$$
$$\alpha_1 : S_1;$$
$$\alpha_i, \alpha_j, \alpha_k : S_m;$$
$$\cdot$$
$$\cdot$$
$$\cdot$$
$$\alpha_n : S_n;$$
$$error : S_{n+1}$$
$$\textbf{end } /*\text{case name}*/$$

In this particular example of the **case** construct, a third convenience feature has been introduced. In many cases, a statement is to be executed for several of the possible values of E. Rather than forcing the programmer to repeat this statement for each value of E for which it is to be executed, one statement may be preceded by several α's separated by commas. Thus,

$$\alpha_a, \alpha_b, \alpha_c : S$$

is a shorthand notation for

$$\alpha_a : S;$$
$$\alpha_b : S;$$
$$\alpha_c : S;$$

This concludes our brief introduction to AL. As stated earlier, additional features will be introduced as the need arises. The intention is to leave AL open-ended so that it may be expanded as required. In this sense, it is much more general than normal programming languages.

Example 2.3 (continued)

To illustrate the features of AL introduced up to this point, we shall complete the random walk problem begun earlier. The algorithm will be written as a procedure whose input parameters are your starting position (*istart, jstart*), the position of the car (*idest, jdest*), and the number of streets and avenues in the city (*nstreet, navenue*). The output from the procedure will be a blank table (*map*) except for those positions corresponding to intersections visited; these will be filled in with a value (k) representing the number of blocks walked from the starting point to reach that point.

```
procedure random_walk(istart, jstart, idest, jdest, nstreet, navenue; map)
begin /*simulate random walk*/
    i ← 1;
    while (i ≤ nstreet)
    begin /*initialize map*/
        j ← 1;
        while (j ≤ navenue) [map(i, j) ← ' '; j ← j + 1];
        i ← i + 1
    end; /*initialize*/
```

```
        map(istart, jstart) ← 0;
        i ← istart;
        j ← jstart;
        k ← 0;
        while (i ≠ idest ∨ j ≠ jdest)
        begin /*walk*/
            /*get random direction*/
            random(4; die);
            case die of
                1:  j ← j + 1; /*turn east*/
                2:  j ← j − 1; /*turn west*/
                3:  i ← i − 1; /*turn north*/
                4:  i ← i + 1 /*turn south*/
            end; /*direction*/
            k ← k + 1;
            map(i, j) ← k
        end /*walk*/
    end /*simulate*/
```

Note that we have assumed the existence of a procedure called *random* which, when activated, will return a random value (between 1 and 4, inclusive) as the value of *die*. When this algorithm is translated to an actual program to be executed, this procedure will have to be provided; many languages provide a library of commonly used procedures which usually contains a random number generator. The output of this routine will have to be modified to provide the values within the proper range. ∎

EXERCISE 2.7: The algorithm presented in Example 2.3 contains several known flaws, including

1. The input parameters have not been checked to make sure they are in the correct ranges, e.g.,

$$nstreet, navenue \geq 1$$
$$1 \leq idest \leq nstreet$$
$$1 \leq jdest \leq navenue$$
   .
   .
   .

2. No provision has been made for checking whether or not a random direction will take you out of the city (i.e., off the defined map).
3. Return to an intersection will overwrite the value of k already there with the new value; this implies that the route through the city will no longer be evident from the map.

Write an algorithm which correctly takes into account these problems. (Hint: For problem 3, you may want to consider printing out the map whenever an overwrite is encountered.)

2.2.3 Summary of AL

1. *Basic statements*

Comments   /*this is an AL comment*/   see (7)

Assignment   *variable ← expression*   see (3)

Variable names: Any string of alphabetic or numeric characters (including-, —), the first of which must be alphabetic.

Expression: Any legal combination of constants, variables, operators, etc.

Operators: They include addition ($+$), multiplication ($*$), subtraction ($-$), division ($/$), etc. The logical operators (which return a truth value) include equal ($=$), not equal ($\neq$), less than ($<$), less than or equal to ($\leq$), greater than ($>$), greater than or equal to ($\geq$), etc. Logical connectives include **and** ($\land$), **or** ($\lor$), etc. Either the symbolic form or the written expression of the operator is allowed.

Input/output   **input** *variable list*   see (5)
                                output *variable list*
Where *variable list* is a list of the variables whose values are to be printed or read. Items in the list are separated by commas.

Compound statement   **begin** /*comment*/   see (8)
                                S_1;
                                S_2;
                                .
                                .
                                .
                                S_n
                                end /*comment*/
                                or [S_1; S_2]   see (9)
Where the S_i are AL statements, either simple or compound.

Halt statement   **halt**   see (10)

2. *Control structures*

If-then-else   **if** P **then** S_1 see (12), (13)
                                if P **then** S_1 **else** S_2
Where P is a predicate which evaluates to true or false.

Case statement

case E **of**
$\quad \alpha_1 : S_1;$ see (11)
$\quad \alpha_2 : S_2;$
$\qquad \cdot$
$\qquad \cdot$
$\quad \alpha_n : S_n;$
$\quad error : S_{n+1}$
end /*case name*/

     Where E is an AL expression which evaluates to one of the α_i. Each α_i is any legitimate value of the expression E. S_i is an AL statement, either simple or compound.

While statement

while (P) S see (14)
     Where P is a predicate and S a statement.

Procedure definition

procedure $name(f_{i_1}, \ldots, f_{i_n}; f_{o_1}, \ldots, f_{o_m})$ S
     Where the f_i's and f_o's represent formal input and output parameters.

Procedure call

$name(a_{i_1}, \ldots, a_{i_n}; a_{o_1}, \ldots, a_{o_m})$
     Where the a_i's and a_o's represent actual input and output parameters.   see (16)

3. *Convenience features*

Terminate statement   **terminate**   see (18)

Error branch in case statement   See case statement above.

2.3 AN EXAMPLE: SIMULATION OF A TURING MACHINE

This example is concerned with the simulation of a Turing machine on a physical device; that is, we wish to write an AL program which when given a Turing program P and an input x will produce the same result as the Turing machine. For simplicity's sake, we assume that instructions in the Turing program are numbered sequentially and that transfer addresses in the GO TO and IF instructions refer to the position of an instruction relative to the first instruction in the program. In addition, assume that the alphabet of the Turing machine consists of the symbols 0, 1, and B.

If we wish to simulate the behavior of a Turing machine on a physical device, it is clear that the size of the Turing tape must be limited to finite size. Unfortunately, this limitation on the tape size effectively limits the class of algorithms which can be programmed. On the other hand, the class of algorithms is now completely consistent with the class representable on an actual computer. It is not our intention here to discuss the effects of these limitations in detail; we leave that for a more advanced course in automata theory. However, in a real sense the limitations alluded to in this discussion are not serious ones. The *finite* Turing machine can actually be thought of as a simplistic model of an actual computer. The tape corresponds to the *memory* of the computer, the control unit to the *central processing unit*, and the read-only head to the *instruction counter*, and the read-write head can be viewed as corresponding to a *register* (storage) which holds temporary results. Viewed in this light, the problem takes on a considerably different dimension: We are effectively asking for the design of an algorithm describing the action of a simple, though real, computer.

In keeping with the tenets of problem-solving developed in this chapter, the first step is the formulation of the problem. This includes precise statements concerning the input and output. The input to "simulation" (the name of the algorithm to be developed) will be a Turing program P and the input x to P; the output of simulation should be y, the output of the Turing program P working on x. Figure 2.11 illustrates the initial statement of the problem. Before it is possible to describe ⓐ and ⓑ in Figure 2.11, a decision must be made concerning the external representation of the description of the Turing machine. As stated in Chapter 1, the initial description of a Turing machine consists of x, a string of input symbols, and P, a sequence of instructions.

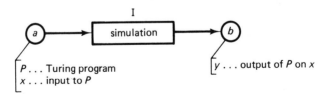

Fig. 2.11   Initial statement of the Turing machine simulation problem.

We are forced to limit the size of the tape while recognizing that different Turing programs will require different limits. Hence, we shall make the size of the tape an input parameter to the problem and define the external communications as follows:

Input	Comments	Example
n	The size of the tape	50
$symbol_1$		*1*
$symbol_2$		*0*
.	The input x to P	*0*
.		
$symbol_j$		*1*

program	Separator of x and P	program
instruction$_1$ ⎫ instruction$_2$ ⎪ . ⎬ . ⎪ instruction$_m$ ⎭	The program P with the operation code, symbol, and transfer address in a fixed position for each instruction	⎧ RIGHT IF *1* GO TO 1 ⎨ WRITE *1* IF *B* GO TO 1 ⎩ HALT
end	End of program and end of input to simulation	end

Output	Comments	Example
message	Message if the Turing program was incorrect	
symbol$_1$ ⎫ symbol$_2$ ⎪ . ⎬ . ⎪ symbol$_k$ ⎭	The output y of P	⎧ *1* ⎨ *0* ⎩ *1*

In the process of modular refinement, the first step is to obtain a vague outline of the solution after we have formulated the problem. For this problem, this stage is not too difficult once we realize that every instance of the Turing machine's execution can be described with a few items. The status of its computation has to account for the contents of the tape and the associated read-write head and also the read-only head associated with the Turing program. This status description changes every time an instruction is executed; the final state of the computation is reached when the instruction executed is a HALT instruction. At this point, the contents of the tape starting at the read-write head up to the first blank form the output symbol. Given this internal representation of a Turing machine execution, we can decompose the problem into three independent tasks. First, initialize the internal description in correspondence to the external input data. Second, as long as the instruction is not a HALT instruction, modify the internal description according to the meaning of the current instruction. And finally, output the result. The resulting refinement is given in Figure 2.12, which also contains the communications to be developed next.

An obvious decision is to represent the tape as an n-tuple of symbols and the read-write head as a variable, *rwh*, whose value is an index into this tuple. At point ② of Figure 2.12 we should be sure that all the symbols are legal, i.e,. either *0*, *1*, or *B*; however, it is quite possible that the simulation resulted in an error. For.instance, the status description might indicate that *rwh* equals n and that the next instruction is RIGHT, in which case we obviously cannot modify the description accordingly. For cases like these, we introduce *fatal*, a variable whose value is "true" or "false" depending on whether or not an error occurred; *message* will contain some comment about the nature of the error.

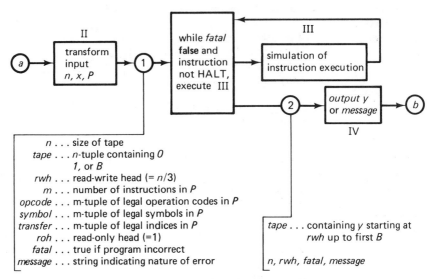

Fig. 2.12   Refined Turing machine simulator problem statement.

A somewhat more difficult decision is how to represent the input to the iteration over module III, ①, which consists of the initial status description of the Turing machine. At this point, we already know how many instructions there are, say *m*, and we could decide to store the program as an *m*-tuple whose elements are strings which represent the instructions. What speaks against this representation is the fact that in module III an instruction may be executed repeatedly (when it occurs as part of an iteration), and we would have to analyze the string every time to decide what kind of instruction it is, what symbols are involved, etc. Instead, we require that module II analyze the instructions (now only once for each instruction) and extract the relevant information. We discover that there are up to three items in each instruction which must be included in the representation. These items are the name of the instruction, which will be called "opcode"; a possible symbol (found in the WRITE and IF instructions); and a possible transfer address (in the GO TO and IF instructions). Let *m* be the number of instructions in *P*; then *P* can be represented as a table with *m* rows and 3 columns. Each row corresponds to one instruction. The first element of each row represents the opcode, the second the possible symbol, and the third the possible transfer address. Remember, we do not have to store the label of an instruction since it is the same as the index of the instruction in the table. To make the algorithm more transparent, each of the three columns will actually be represented by a separate *m*-tuple: *opcode*, *symbol*, and *transfer*.

In a manner analogous to the use of *rwh*, we define the variable *roh* as an index into the various *m*-tuples which describe the program. Again, at this point, we can request that this description represents the initial state of a proper Turing machine. That is, the input symbols have been checked to make sure they are within the alphabet, that instructions have no misspellings and do not use undefined symbols, and that all transfers are within the allowed range, 1 to m. The variables *fatal* and *message* are again used to indicate if this is not true.

We can apply the refinement procedure again to module II since it consists of two discernible independent tasks. One is the initialization of the internal description as it pertains to the tape, and the second is the initialization pertaining to the program description. Figure 2.13 illustrates this refinement and the proper communications.

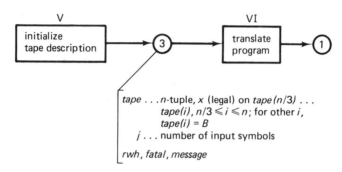

Fig. 2.13 Refinement of module II.

The point we wish to make is that to describe the actions of module V, for instance, we do not have to even think about what all other modules do. All that we are concerned with now is the problem of initializing the tape and *rwh* given n and $symbol_1, \ldots, symbol_j$. Since this task is easily grasped at once, we can write the algorithm for it immediately without further refinement.

Algorithm 2.1 (Initialization of tape description, module V)

```
begin /*tape initialization*/
    input n;
    i ← 1; /*initialize tape to all blanks*/
    while (i ≤ n) [tape(i) ← 'B'; i ← i + 1];
    i ← n/3; /*store y on tape*/
    fatal ← f;
    input symb;
    while (symb ≠ 'program' ∧ i ≤ n)
    begin /*check symbol*/
        case symb of
                '0', '1', 'B':  tape(i) ← symb;
                error    :  [fatal ← t; message ← message +
                            'illegal symbol' + symb + ';']
        end; /*symb*/
```

$$i \leftarrow i + 1;$$
input *symb*
end; /*check*/
if *symb* ≠ 'program' **then** [*fatal* ← **t**; *message* ← *message* + 'input too long;';
        while (*symb* ≠ 'program') **input** *symb*];
$$rwh \leftarrow n/3; j \leftarrow i - 1 - n/3$$
end /*tape*/

EXERCISE 2.8: Give the algorithmic description for module VI in Figure 2.13. Remember that the external input data to this module are the *m* instructions followed by an instruction containing the opcode END; you may use the AL statement

input *op, symb, trans*

to read in on one line the opcode into the variable *op*, the symbol (if any) into *symb*, and the transfer (if any) into *trans*. Your algorithm will have to set the tuples *opcode, symbol*, and *transfer* and compute *m*. At the same time it has to check that the entries are legal. (Hint: The transfers can be checked only after you have computed *m*.)

The only sizable module left to expand is the "simulation" module (III). Its input is the output of "transform *n, x, P*," and it executes instructions as long as no HALT instruction is encountered and *fatal* is false. Algorithm 2.2 simulates the Turing machine by scanning the *roh*[th] instruction and depending on its opcode modifies the status description of the Turing machine accordingly. The line numbers have been added to facilitate references to individual instructions in Example 2.7.

Algorithm 2.2 (Simulate the change in the status description incurred by one instruction)

```
1    begin /*process one instruction*/
        case opcode(roh) of
3        'GO TO':  roh ← transfer(roh);
4        'HALT' :  ;/*iteration stops*/
5        'IF'    :  if tape(rwh) = symbol(roh) then roh ← transfer(roh)
                                              else roh ← roh + 1;
6        'LEFT'  :  if rwh = 1 then [fatal ← t; message ← message +
                       'attempt to move left off tape encountered at instruction'
                       + roh +';']
                                else [rwh ← rwh − 1; roh ← roh + 1];
7        'RIGHT':  if rwh = n then [fatal ← t; message ← message +
                       'attempt to move right off tape encountered at instruction'
                       + roh +';']
                                else [rwh ← rwh + 1; roh ← roh + 1];
8        'WRITE':  [tape(rwh) ← symbol(roh); roh ← roh + 1]
9        end; /*opcode*/
10       if roh > m then [fatal ← t; message ← message + 'no halt encountered']
11   end /*process*/
```

As an exercise, the reader is to specify module IV. We remind the reader that the algorithm will have to check whether *fatal* is true and output the message if this is the case.

EXERCISE 2.9: Give the algorithm of module IV as specified in Figure 2.12.

Example 2.7

Let us trace the execution of Algorithm 2.2 on the following sample Turing machine:

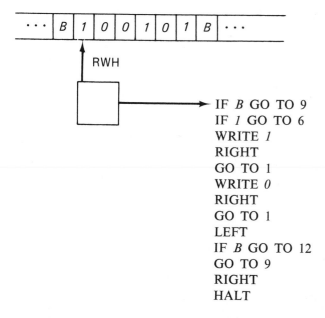

The external description of this Turing machine as required by our algorithm is, according to the specifications,

10
1
0
0
1
0
1
program
IF   *B* GO TO   9
IF   *1* GO TO   6

```
                    WRITE 1
                    RIGHT
                    GO TO              1
                    WRITE 0
                    RIGHT
                    GO TO              1
                    LEFT
                    IF       B GO TO 12
                    GO TO              9
                    RIGHT
                    HALT
                    END
```

Module II should process this input and produce the following internal representation

n	10
tape	('B', 'B', '1', '0', '0', '1', '0', '1', 'B', 'B')
m	13
rwh	3
opcode	('if', 'if', 'write', 'right', 'go to', 'write', 'right', 'go to', 'left', 'if', 'go to', 'right', 'halt')
symbol	('B', '1', '1', *null*, *null*, '0', *null*, *null*, *null*, 'B', *null*, *null*, *null*)
transfer	(9, 6, *null*, *null*, 1, *null*, *null*, 1, *null*, 12, 9, *null*, *null*)
roh	1
fatal	**f**
message	*null*

as input to module III. We shall trace the execution of Algorithm 2.2 by following the changes of the variables *tape*, *rwh*, and *roh*:

tape	*rwh*	*roh*	Comments	Line executed
'B', 'B', '1', '0', '0', '1', '0', '1', 'B', 'B'	3	1	Initial	
'B', 'B', '1', '0', '0', '1', '0', '1', 'B', 'B'	3	2	Since comparison failed, we go to next instruction	5
'B', 'B', '1', '0', '0', '1', '0', '1', 'B', 'B',	3	6	*tape*(3) equals *symbol*(2)	5
'B', 'B', '0', '0', '0', '1', '0', '1', 'B', 'B'	3	7	Set *tape*(3) to *symbol*(6)	8
'B', 'B', '0', '0', '0', '1', '0', '1', 'B', 'B'	4	8	"right" instruction moves read-write head	7
'B', 'B', '0', '0', '0', '1', '0', '1', 'B', 'B'	4	1	Set *roh* to *transfer*(8)	3
'B', 'B', '0', '0', '0', '1', '0', '1', 'B', 'B'	4	2	*tape*(4) ≠ *symbol*(1)	5
'B', 'B', '0', '0', '0', '1', '0', '1', 'B', 'B'	4	3	*tape*(4) ≠ *symbol*(2)	5
'B', 'B', '0', '1', '0', '1', '0', '1', 'B', 'B'	4	4	Set *tape*(4) to *symbol*(3)	8
'B', 'B', '0', '1', '0', '1', '0', '1', 'B', 'B'	5	5		7

⋮ (*a*)

| 'B', 'B', '0', '1', '1, '0', '1', '0', 'B', 'B' | 9 | 1 | | 3 |

'B', 'B', '0', '1', '1', '0', '1', '0', 'B', 'B'	9	9	$tape(9) = symbol(1)$; set roh to $transfer(1)$	5
'B', 'B', '0', '1', '1', '0', '1', '0', 'B', 'B'	8	10	Move read-write head to left	6
		ⓑ		
'B', 'B', '0', '1', '1', '0', '1', '0', 'B', 'B'	2	12		7
'B', 'B', '0', '1', '1', '0', '1', '0', 'B', 'B'	3	13	Halt instruction; execution of module III terminates	4

■

EXERCISE 2.10: Fill in the traces for *a* and *b* in Example 2.7.

As a final comment, we note the discrepancy in the size of the input module and the actual working module. The reason for the input module being actually larger than the working module is that we have to ensure that the input to "simulate" is indeed of the form we set down in the modular refinement. In a real-world environment it cannot be assumed that the input is correct; hence, extensive checking of the input format is mandatory for most problems.

As is apparent in the example, using only the allowable control structures we can with relative ease assert that the desired input/output relation of variables in the module under consideration is achieved. This is possible since backward branches within the module are forbidden (except for the "while" iteration). In addition, all forward branches will eventually merge at the same point. For instance, immediately following the true branch of the **while** iteration in Algorithm 2.1, the following assertions are true:

1. *tape* is an *n*-tuple.
2. $tape(1) = \cdots = tape(n/3 - 1) = $ 'B'.   (19)
3. $i - n/3$ elements of *tape*, beginning at $tape(n/3)$, contain the first $i - n/3$ symbols of *x*, for $n/3 \leq i \leq n$.
4. $tape(i) = \cdots = tape(n) = $ 'B'.

An assertion of the form (19) is known as an *iteration-independent* assertion since it is true independent of the iteration; hence, it will be true after exit from the iteration. Only the iteration control variable will have changed; the range of *i* is now $n/3 \leq i \leq n + 1$. From this fact, the final assertion of the modules follows immediately after passing through the iteration test; this test determines the specific exit taken from the iteration.

Usually, each input variable is defined over a range of values. The values which are the most likely to cause problems during execution are the boundary values (the maximum and minimum values). For this specific example, we find that the assertion is still true even if *x* is the empty string or contains $2n/3$ elements.

From these considerations, it is possible to abstract some general rules for proving correctness of the input/output relations. A module can be viewed as a linear sequence of statements; after each statement we should assert the status of the computation. If the statement passed through was a **while** iteration, we obtain the assertion by taking into account the falseness of the termination condition, the iteration-independent assertion which held true within the iteration, and the assertion true before the iteration. If the statement was a **case** construct, we have to be aware of the assertion before, the value of the **case** expression, and the fact that we could have traversed any of the n branches. That is, the assertion should be independent of whichever branch is taken.

   EXERCISE 2.11: First give the modular refinement of the procedure *find-max-index* (if necessary, see the section on **procedure** definition) and then write its algorithm in AL.

   To conclude this section we remark that many people have made the dejecting discovery that the ability to write algorithms is not linearly proportional to the algorithmic complexity regardless of the choice of the complexity measure, be it number of statements, execution time, or others. There appears to be an exponential relationship effectively creating a barrier of complexity beyond which no problems can be solved. On the other hand, application of the tenets we have postulated in this chapter, which are part of what is often called *structured programming*, does indeed raise the barrier of complexity at least to a higher degree.

2.4 AN EXAMPLE: BREAKING A CODE

   In today's world secrecy in communications is a common occurrence. Clandestine meetings between persons who wish to communicate secretly have proven to be quite unsuccessful in keeping communications secret, mainly due to the advanced stage of technology for "bugging" conversations. The solution most often used to circumvent personal meetings is to send encoded messages. In this case, even if the message gets intercepted, it is difficult to decode it without knowing anything about the code. An entire branch of science has developed to construct "unbreakable" codes on the one hand and to devise algorithms to "break" codes on the other hand. To break a code simply means to find the original text (known as the *clear text*) of the encoded message. Most people have probably never heard of the many ingenious ways of constructing codes but are quite familiar with one set of codes, cryptograms. Cryptograms can be found in the puzzle sections of most newspapers and are messages which are encoded by transposing certain (or all) letters of the alphabet. For instance, the anagram

ZB ZBZVQZE

is decoded into the message . . . . by substituting the letter ? for Z, a ? for B, a ? for E, a ? for V, a ? for Q, and a ? for a blank.

   In general, the person assigned the problem of breaking a code receives only a coded message and very little other information; this obviously makes the problem of decoding very difficult. For the problem we want to solve here, we shall make some simplifying assumptions. Namely, the source text is in English. Second, the code employed is one of the group of codes which use only a single transposition for each letter throughout the text. That is, if an A is to be read as an M at the beginning of the message, it is the case throughout the message. Third, from our informer we know that the messages to be decoded are about a new revolutionary technique to miniaturize computers.

Thus, in this example the problem statement is rather well defined from the beginning and is formalized in Figure 2.14. The next step is to obtain an outline of how to solve the problem. A perhaps obvious idea is to try out all possible transpositions until

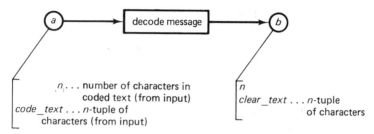

Fig. 2.14   Problem statement for breaking code.

we find one which produces a clear text in English. Before we attempt to formalize this idea by refinement, let us analyze how long the execution of the resulting algorithm would take. The length of the execution is proportional to the number of different transpositions possible; the question to be answered is, How many are there? For the alphabet

$$ABCDE\ldots WXYZ\text{b} \qquad (\text{b represents blank})$$

there are 27 different ways of encoding the letter A. For each of these possibilities, for instance,

$$ABCD\ldots WXYZ\text{b}$$
$$\updownarrow$$
$$A$$

there are 26 ways to encode the letter B, for instance,

$$ABCD\ldots G\ldots WXYZ\text{b}$$
$$\updownarrow \qquad \updownarrow$$
$$A \qquad B$$

Continuing in this manner, we realize that there are

$$27 * 26 * 25 * 24 * \ldots * 3 * 2 * 1 \qquad\qquad (20)$$

possibilities altogether. The number represented by (20) is very large, approximately 10^{27} (see Chapter 5 for a derivation); for all practical purposes it is impossible to implement this first idea. Sometimes a good approach to problem-solving is to investigate how humans solve related problems. In this case, it involves finding out how people, some of whom can decode cryptograms quickly, achieve it. In addition to many tricks, one basic approach consists of computing the frequency of the various letters. (The frequency of a letter is the number of times a particular letter occurs in a text divided by the total number of characters in the text; see Chapter 10.) If the message is long enough (and only then), the frequencies of letters will be similar to frequencies of letters in an English text (we know that the clear text is English), although different letters will be involved. For example, if the letter R is the most common letter in the coded message, it will be likely that the proper transposition is R to E since E is the

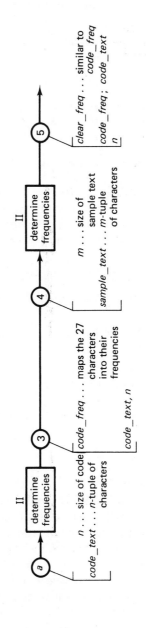

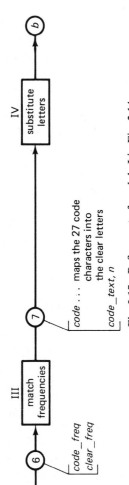

Fig. 2.15 Refinement of module I in Fig. 2.14.

most common letter in an English text. Similarly, if the second most common letter in the code is A, then it probably should be replaced with T, the second most common letter in English, etc.

To utilize the knowledge that the message is about the miniaturizing of computers, we can determine the frequencies of the letters in clear text by analyzing sample texts about this subject. Taking all this information together, we can discern the four separate tasks outlined in Figure 2.15.

We emphasize that the solution outlined in Figure 2.15 does not guarantee that the algorithm will always produce the decoded message. In fact, unless the original transposition code is known, it is possible to decipher a coded message in more than one way. For example, suppose we were to encode the message SEND HELP according to the transposition code shown in Figure 2.16. The resulting message is ARQZP RHS. It is now necessary to decode this message, without reference to the original code. Assume that some algorithm is applied to the message, resulting in the code shown in Figure 2.17. The decoded message is then FINE BIRD, which is obviously

Coded message: ARQZP RHS

Original message: SEND HELP

Coded letters   A B C D E F G H I J K L M N O P Q R S T U V W X Y Z ƀ

Original   S G F A Q C B L O R M Z K J I ƀ N E P Y X W V U T D H
letters

Fig. 2.16   Transposition code for encoding SEND HELP

Coded message: ARQZP RHS

Coded letters A B C D E F G H I J K L M N O P Q R S T U V W X Y Z ƀ

Clear text   F G Q T Z A P R H S O C J L K ƀ N I D M W X Y V U E B
letters

Clear text: FINE BIRD

Fig. 2.17   Transposition code from algorithm.

not the original message, although it is a perfectly reasonable one. Of course, as the length of the original message increases, the chances of this occurring decrease. To investigate all possible decodings of the original message, it would be necessary to use an algorithm similar to the first one proposed. To avoid this impossible task, the solution we have suggested embodies the notion of *heuristic programming* (see Chapter 12). Heuristics are ideas or guidelines which cannot be proven to lead to correct results but which work in a large number of cases. In this example, the heuristics are based on the observation that in longer texts the frequencies of letters tend toward a well-defined pattern. In English this pattern starts with E being the most common, next T, R, N, etc.

To continue our example, we develop the algorithm for module II; this is an example of a procedure invoked at two different places. It expects as input n, an n-tuple of characters, and returns a mapping of characters into frequencies; its AL algorithm is given below.

Algorithm 2.3 (Determine frequencies)

> **procedure** *det_freq(n, text; freq)*
> **begin** /*freq* is assumed to have initially the values 0 for all letters,
>   e.g., *freq*('A') is 0*/
> $i \leftarrow 1$;
>   **while** $(i \leq n)$
>   **begin** /*process one character*/
>   *freq(text(i))* $\leftarrow$ *freq(text(i))* $+ 1$;
> $i \leftarrow i + 1$
>   **end**; /*process*/
> $i \leftarrow 1$; /*alpha* is a tuple of all alphabetic characters*/
>   **while** $(i \leq 27)$
>   **begin** /*divide by size of text*/
>   *freq(alpha(i))* $\leftarrow$ *freq(alpha(i))/n*;
> $i \leftarrow i + 1$
>   **end** /*divide*/
> **end** /*freq*/

We forgo development of the algorithm for module III because it involves the problem of matching frequencies; general solutions are discussed in Chapter 5. Since in Figure 2.15 we have precisely defined its output, this poses no difficulty for the development of the remaining modules. Hopefully, this reinforces the advantages of modular refinement in that we can delay or delegate to somebody else the specification of various modules once we have defined the interfaces between the modules. We shall proceed directly to the algorithm specification of module IV.

Algorithm 2.4 (Substitution of letters)

> **begin** /*substitute letters to obtain clear text*/
> $i \leftarrow 1$;
>   **while** $(i \leq n)$
>   **begin** /*replace one letter*/
>   *clear_text(i)* $\leftarrow$ *code(code_text(i))*;
> $i \leftarrow i + 1$
>   **end** /*replace*/
> **end** /*substitute*/

Finally, the overall structure of the algorithm to solve (heuristically) the cryptogram problem has the following structure:

Algorithm 2.5 (Break a code)

```
begin /*break a code*/
    input n, code_text;
    det_freq(n, code_text; code_freq);
    input m, sample_text;
    det_freq(m, sample_text; clear_freq);
    match_freq(code_freq, clear_freq; code);
    begin /*substitute*/

        ·    Algorithm 2.4

    end; /*substitute*/
    output 'the coded message', code_text;
        output 'is probably the following clear text', clear_text
end; /*break a code*/
procedure det_freq(n, text; freq)
begin /*freq*/

    ·    Algorithm 2.3

end; /*freq*/
procedure match_freq(freq1, freq2; match)
begin

    ·
    ·
    ·

end
```

EXERCISE 2.12: If the output of the above algorithm is not recognizable English, give some methods for completely breaking the code. Specifically, write an algorithm which allows you to change *code*, and using module IV, outline the steps you would take to obtain the final clear text. (Hint: You may have to execute module IV repeatedly.)

2.5 PROGRAMMING LANGUAGES:
WHAT THEY ARE AND HOW THEY SHOULD BE

The last step in obtaining a solution to a problem is the translation of the formally specified algorithm into a form which can be accepted and executed by a modern computer. An algorithm in this form is usually referred to as a program, and the language used to specify the steps in the algorithm is referred to as a *programming language*. Since we wish to minimize the effort involved in this translation process, our major interest lies in the so-called *high-level* programming languages. These are languages which resemble algorithmic languages in form, but perhaps not in detail, yet exhibit a high degree of expressiveness.

As alluded to in the previous sections, and several of the exercises, we have to be much more precise, in general, than we have been for AL. It is necessary to define exactly what the allowable operators are, what type (e.g., integer, string, tuple, . . .) their arguments must be, what data types are allowed, etc. This is necessary because in a computer we wish to represent all values of the same type in a uniform way (i.e., fixed number of bits). For instance, when we say a value i is of type integer we actually mean that i is an integer value between m and n where m, n are computer-dependent constants. In Part A of the supplementary volume we see the "real" effects of considerations such as these for a particular programming language (FORTRAN).

As might be expected, programs written in a high-level programming language are not directly executable by the hardware (i.e., electronic circuitry) comprising a computer. Instructions which are directly executable by the hardware are known as *machine* instructions. Just as we did not want to write complex algorithms in the form of Turing programs, we do not want to write complex programs in machine language. In Section 2.2, we defined a more expressive representational language (AL) and outlined how, in principle, AL algorithms could be translated into an equivalent Turing machine program. We were then free to define algorithms in AL.

Since ultimately, programs will have to be executed as machine language programs, we have to be quite precise in the definition of a high-level programming language so as to enable us to translate a program written in the high-level language mechanically into the equivalent machine language program. In Figure 2.18, a program written in a programming language (here FORTRAN) is translated into a sequence of machine-level instructions. This sequence can be viewed as being equivalent to a Turing machine program; then by analogy the computer represents the Turing machine. The semantics of the instructions comprising the FORTRAN program can

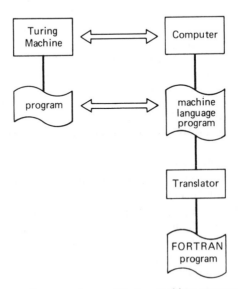

Fig. 2.18   Correspondence of Turing machines to computers.

be defined by the machine language instructions the translator produces, which are in turn defined by the computer which carries them out. By this two-level abstraction, we provide a greater variety of instructions in a more user-oriented format, which facilitates the writing of programs.

In Section 2.2, we discussed the desirable features of a programming language from the vantage point of structuring and verification of algorithms. These features should be available directly as basic constructs in the language. Besides input/output instructions, the basic control structure constructs presented in Section 2.2 are essential to most modern programming languages. The choice of a programming language for a specific application depends not only on the instruction set of the language but also on such practical considerations as general availability and fast translation from the language to machine language. Even though some languages are eminently suitable for a particular problem, translators may not be available for many machines, and if they are available, they might be slow. Another consideration in the choice of a language is the existence of certain convenience features in the language; these include

1. Basic data types and ease of manipulation,
2. Powerful input/output functions, and
3. Generality in procedure calls.

Languages may provide various basic data types, such as integer and real numbers, strings, arrays, and sets together with their attendant operations. The ease with which the data type inherent in the problem under consideration may be manipulated may be a deciding factor in choosing a language. High-level languages are often classified as to the data types they provide and their manipulation. For instance, languages which allow us to write programs efficiently if the main data types used are numerical are useful for *numeric programming* (e.g., FORTRAN). Those which allow for efficient manipulation of strings, mappings in general, and other similar data types are commonly referred to as *nonnumeric* languages (e.g., SNOBOL).

The languages chosen for demonstration purposes in this book are FORTRAN and SNOBOL. Both languages fail in the inclusion of the basic control structures; for this reason, programs written in these languages are both difficult to read and almost impossible to prove correct. However, each has socially redeeming features. FORTRAN is the most widely available language. Fast translators exist for most computers, and the language is quite suitable for the numeric applications discussed in the following chapters. FORTRAN is also suitable for nonnumeric applications, although the primitives required for this general class of problems must be built by the programmer. SNOBOL is not so widely available as FORTRAN, nor is execution of SNOBOL programs particularly fast. Nevertheless, it has been chosen to illustrate a different approach to language design. SNOBOL incorporates powerful data structures as primitives in the language and provides the facilities necessary for manipulating these structures in rather novel ways. These abilities are very useful in the application areas presented in the final chapters. Other redeeming features will become apparent when the language is studied.

2.6 CONCLUSIONS

The first two chapters have been concerned with the notion of procedures and algorithms, beginning with an intuitive definition of procedures and algorithms and advancing to more formal notions of computability, as summarized in the first two columns of Figure 2.19. These issues are central to computer science for a number of reasons: First, the notion of an algorithm is essential to computer programming, and, second, the meeting of mathematics and computer science has provided a framework from which to view the theory of computation, including verification of real programs.

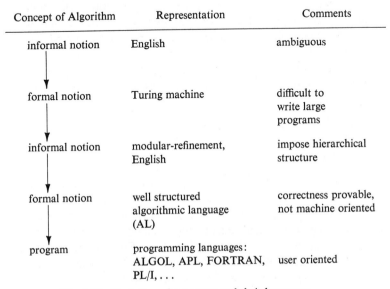

Concept of Algorithm	Representation	Comments
informal notion	English	ambiguous
formal notion	Turing machine	difficult to write large programs
informal notion	modular-refinement, English	impose hierarchical structure
formal notion	well structured algorithmic language (AL)	correctness provable, not machine oriented
program	programming languages: ALGOL, APL, FORTRAN, PL/I, . . .	user oriented

Fig. 2.19 Evolution of programs and their languages.

While Turing machines are valuable for the formal representations of algorithms, the requirement of an infinite tape precludes their use as a practical computing device, irrespective of the fact that it is difficult to write large programs. This problem arises because very few instructions are provided. The power of the Turing machine as a formal model lies in the relationship between an instruction and the physical device carrying out the instruction. In this way, the meaning of the instructions (semantics) is defined unambiguously. The semantics of instructions in programming languages such as FORTRAN can be unambiguously defined in a similar manner.

Perhaps the most important aspect of this chapter is the development of the concept of modular refinement, that is, the process by which one proceeds from the initial problem statement to the final formal specification of the algorithm in AL, including the hierarchical module specifications and their interactions. We believe that the major portion of the effort involved in obtaining a solution should be spent on this phase; only a relatively small effort will be necessary for the translation into a program and its subsequent debugging. This question will be discussed in more detail in the next chapter.

References

Again, the book by Polya is highly relevant to the concepts developed throughout this chapter:

G. POLYA, *How To Solve It*, 2nd ed., Princeton University Press, Princeton, N.J., 1971 (paperback).

An analysis of the various methods for beginning development of the solution to a variety of problems is found in

W. WICKELGREN, *How To Solve Problems: Elements of a Theory of Problems and Problem-Solving*, W. H. Freeman, San Francisco, 1974 (paperback).

The precepts of structured programming and stepwise refinement of problem statements have been elegantly laid out by

O. J. DAHL, E. W. DIJKSTRA, and C. A. R. HOARE, *Structured Programming*, Academic Press, New York, 1972.

and

NIKLAUS WIRTH, *Systematic Programming: An Introduction*, Prentice-Hall, Englewood Cliffs, N.J., 1973.

Wirth's book devotes a considerable amount of space to proving the correctness of programs.

While the algorithmic language AL developed in this chapter is not an actual programming language, it bears a resemblance to a recent programming language called PASCAL. More information on PASCAL may be found in

KATHLEEN JENSEN and NIKLAUS WIRTH, *PASCAL User Manual and Report*, Lecture Notes in Computer Science, Vol. XVIII, Springer, New York, 1974.

and also in Wirth's book *Systematic Programming*, cited above.

Discussion concerning the structure of various languages, their design philosophies, their applicability to various classes of problems, and their internal structure may be found in

J. SAMMET, *Programming Languages: History and Fundamentals*, Prentice-Hall, Englewood Cliffs, N.J., 1969.

M. ELSON, *Concepts of Programming Languages*, Science Research Associates, Inc., Chicago, 1973.

W. PETERSON, *Introduction to Programming Languages*, Prentice-Hall, Englewood Cliffs, N.J., 1974.

T. PRATT, *Programming Languages*, Prentice-Hall, Englewood Cliffs, N.J., 1975.

Sammet's book is a historical treatment of the development of modern languages, while Elson, Peterson, and Pratt are more thorough in their treatment of language structures and facilities.

An interesting discussion of the various methods of cryptanalysis and a historical development of the U.S. effort in this area is presented in

FLETCHER PRATT, *Secret and Urgent*, Bobbs-Merrill, Indianapolis, 1939.

Exercises

1 Assume we wish to remove the restriction to have labels correspond to instruction indices in the Turing machine simulator. How can we effect the change? What module(s) has to be modified? Implement the modification first in the modular refinement and then in the AL algorithm.

2 In a vein similar to Exercise 1, we wish to remove the restriction on the alphabet of the Turing machine; recall that the allowable symbols were *0*, *1*, and *B*. Rather, we would like the alphabet itself to become an input to the program. Answer the questions indicated in Exercise 1.

3 Given the vague problem statement (which is all we usually get in the real world; problems are just not as well defined as they often appear to be in some exercises): "I have a list of students together with all their grades. I want to obtain a ranking of the students according to their grades,"
(a) Formulate a precise problem statement (you may make any reasonable assumption).
(b) Modularly refine the problem.
(c) Write the AL algorithm.

4 Suppose we want to restrict AL so it can be used to describe programs. What restrictions would you impose on the data types and operators if the area for which it is to be used is a field of your choice. (If the exercise is difficult now, redo it after Part A of the supplementary volume has been studied.)

5 Following (a), (b), and (c) of Exercise 3, solve the problem of filling out the federal income tax return so as to minimize your taxes (the algorithm should only be general enough so as to allow all possibilities insofar as it concerns you).

6 Using the techniques developed in this chapter, translate each of the algorithms obtained as solutions to Exercise 3, Chapter 1, into AL programs.

7 In Exercise 4, Chapter 1, several Turing programs were developed. Model these solutions in AL. Can you compare the expressive power of AL versus the Turing machine language on the basis of these algorithms?

8 Develop an AL algorithm which will output the prime numbers between 1 and *n*. Can you think of more than one way to solve this problem? Which method do you think is better? Why? On what analysis is your conclusion based? (Hint: Consider an *n*-tuple containing the numbers from 1 to *n*. Systematically cross out all multiples of 2, then all multiples of 3, etc. What's left?)

9 Write an AL algorithm which will convert any decimal number (less than some maximum value) into Roman numerals. Also write the inverse algorithm (i.e., Roman numerals to decimal).

10 Develop an AL algorithm which, given a string of characters and a text, will count the number of times the string appears in the text. From this algorithm, develop one which will accept as input a given text and which will produce as output a list of all the words in the text, together with the number of times each appears. You will probably have to be careful how you define a word.

3

Implementation of Algorithms

3.0 INTRODUCTION

In the previous two chapters, we have examined the notion of an algorithm in the context of a problem solution and formal procedures for their specification. In this chapter, we shall attempt to provide a general framework from which the problem-solving process can be viewed, from inception to working program, and shall discuss one of the most underrated aspects of programming: the problem of documentation.

At one point in this chapter we shall differentiate various classes of programs. The next six sections of this chapter are devoted to the study of what are often referred to as *production programs*. They usually possess one or more of the following characteristics: They are large, complex programs, are frequently executed, and are widely distributed. We shall distinguish three separate phases in the development of such production programs. The design phase encompasses problem definition, modular refinement, and algorithmic specification in AL. We shall provide a formal framework to collate this information and shall call it the design document. Next comes the selection of the physical data structures to be used in the final program together with the specification of a set of test situations which the program should handle properly. Last, we shall discuss the actual production of the program and the testing required to ensure that it executes as desired. The reason for this concern with proper procedures is that a production program consists of much more than simply a listing of the program statements.

However, the goal of this book is not to give a list of complete production programs each with design document, data and test design, and program listing. Rather we want to identify the various areas of computer science and isolate the local problems common to production problems in these areas. The major emphasis will be our attempt to convey how to develop solutions rather than use them. That is, we wish the reader to learn by experience how to solve problems in computer science so that novel problems which arise can be solved by drawing on this experience. Therefore, in the last section of this chapter we shall discuss the form of documentation used through-out the book. By necessity, since the goals are different, it will diverge slightly from the form presented in the earlier sections, but we conclude with an example to illustrate how the first form can be reconstituted.

3.1 PROBLEM-SOLVING AND THE COMPUTER

At the risk of being slightly repetitious, let us review the salient points from the first two chapters. Since this book is about computer science and programming, let us assume that whenever we write *problem solution* we actually mean a program which will solve the originally stated problem. The inherent assumption in this statement is that the problem which we want solved is amenable to a computer solution. It is probably worth digressing slightly to discuss the latter point. It should be obvious by now that one of the first steps is to recognize that we have a problem, and second, that the computer will be of some aid in its solution. In real life, neither of these two steps is always obvious; indeed, some people earn their livelihood by recognizing the exist-ence of problems and suggesting potential solutions. Assuming that the problem is recognized, and recognized correctly, what characteristics are there to indicate that the computer may be of some aid in solving it?

Obviously, the answer to the latter question depends on a number of factors. Some of them are

1. *The nature of the problem itself.* Since a certain amount of time is invested in solving a problem, the solution, when it is obtained, must be useful. Now, usefulness is often in the mind of the beholder. To some people, the production of a concordance (see Chapter 10) to Poe (for example) is an extremely im-portant endeavor and would be deemed extremely valuable (and presumably worth the considerable effort involved in its production). Others could care less about concordances but would be very interested in the solution to a particularly complex set of linear equations (see Chapter 7). To the student, the solution to any problem which illustrates an educational concept is potentially useful (even though it may not be recognized as such at the time). One there-fore has to judge the utility of the proposed solution based on some rather fuzzy notions. Note that pleasure could be one aspect of this decision; some problems (whose solutions may appear to be absolutely useless) are simply fun to solve. Witness the place of recreational mathematics, crossword puzzles, jigsaw puzzles, murder mysteries, etc., in our pursuit of pleasure and happi-ness.

2. *Economics.* In the marketplace, the use of the computer to solve a problem costs money, from the purchase of the necessary equipment and its sub-sequent upkeep, through the training of personnel who know how to use the machine, to the production and maintenance of the programs necessary to provide the computational power. The last point is one which is often over-looked but, in fact, where very often the highest expenditures occur. It is more

or less to this problem that this chapter is devoted. At some point, someone has to make the decision that the use of the computer is economically justifiable; this decision is often not an easy one to make. For example, let us consider two businesses which are contemplating the acquisition of an entire computer installation to streamline their record-keeping processes (including sales and inventories). One company is very small, employing about 10 people, and sells a single product, let us say aluminum lawn furniture. They sell to a small number of retail outlets and must order aluminum tubing and plastic webbing, issue paychecks once a week, and maintain a stock inventory. It is probable that the use of a computer in this situation would not be economically justified; one person can easily maintain the necessary records using standard office procedures. On the other hand, the second company is a large insurance company with millions of accounts, thousands of employees, and thousands of daily transactions. In this case, standard office procedures would probably not be adequate to maintain records which are up to date and accurate. The use of the computer should certainly be considered and would undoubtedly be economically justified. These are two clear cases; others are not so clear: As one example, what about the company with 100 employees, producing a wide range of products? Only a careful economic analysis would indicate whether the use of the computer is justified. Again, the decisions must be made on all known facts and sometimes rather hazy assumptions. An interesting point to note here is that even if the first company decided to use data processing equipment, the differences in the final solution to its problem and that of the insurance company's would not be differences merely in degree; an entirely different design philosophy would be evident in the two cases. The economic question is intimately tied to the next factor, namely, the existence of a solution.

3. *Solution existence.* Once a problem has been recognized and clearly stated, the question immediately arises as to the existence of the solution. While this might seem to be an obvious point, it is worth elaborating a little. Clearly, some problems have an immediate and obvious solution: Problem: I'm tired. Solution: Get some sleep. (Note that the computer does not help us solve this problem at all.) The implementation of this solution, however, might not be trivial, depending on the circumstances under which the original problem arose (e.g., you are in the middle of a class on programming). At any rate, a solution most definitely does exist. For other problems, the case might not be so obvious; Fermat's Last Theorem (see Chapter 1) is a problem for which there is no known solution. This does not imply that there is no solution but rather that the solution is so elusive that an inordinate amount of time could be spent on searching for one. In other cases, we are luckier. For example, suppose you were faced with the problem of dividing an angle into three equal angles and the only tools you had available were a straightedge and a drawing compass. After reflecting for a moment (and perhaps recalling a little geometry), you

realize that you can't do it with the tools available. Let us remind those whose recollection of geometry is a little fuzzy that it has been proven that an angle cannot be trisected using only a straightedge and compass. The only recourse is to obtain additional tools or forget it. For most problems, however, a solution does exist, and the question really is composed of several questions:

(a) Is the obvious solution the most efficient, in terms of the effort involved in implementing it and/or in terms of how efficiently the tools are used in its implementation? (The answer to this question is really not so simple as it sounds, and we shall return to it later.)

(b) If the answer to (a) is no, do I have any other alternatives? That is, do other solutions exist, and are they more efficient?

(c) Is the problem so universally encountered that other people have spent time solving it, and, if so, are these solutions readily available? In other words, if someone else has tackled the problem and has done a lot of the necessary work, why not use what is available and save yourself some work? There is no point in reinventing the wheel if all you need is something round. On the other hand, if existing solutions are not adequate for your needs, the only recourse is to do it yourself.

Question (a) is a rather interesting one; let us consider it in the context of a computer program as the manifestation of the solution to a particular problem. In its simplest form, the question is really one of trading your time (as designer and implementer of the solution) versus the machine's time (as executer of the program). A classical example is the eight-queens problem. It is rather simply stated: Eight queens are to be placed on a chessboard so that no piece is under attack. The problem is that each piece is considered to act as a queen; i.e., it attacks all pieces in the same row and column and on the two diagonals passing through its position. The last consideration makes it a very difficult problem indeed (try it). The obvious solution is to generate possible positions in some systematic way until eventually a solution is found (one can prove that there are 92 different solutions). A cursory analysis shows, however, that there are an enormous number of different ways to position eight pieces on a chessboard and that even on a modern high-speed computer it would take years of execution time to find a solution according to this simple algorithm. In Chapter 4 we shall develop a rather complex program which can be executed in seconds to find all solutions. But we have to spend considerable time in developing and implementing the solution, whereas the first algorithm could have been implemented with very little effort. This problem illustrates the trade-off between programmer's time and execution time. If a program is to be executed frequently, as production programs are, it does pay to invest in programmers to save on computer costs.

The preceding discussion has been a capsule look at some of the factors which influence the decision to use the computer to solve a problem. In the next section we shall examine the implications of these decisions and look at additional decisions which must be made during the actual implementation process.

3.2 THE RELATIONSHIP BETWEEN ALGORITHMS AND WORKING PROGRAMS

Briefly, the steps we have taken thus far include

1. Recognizing the problem.
2. Analyzing the problem.
3. Selecting the computer as a tool.
4. Designing an algorithm which solves the problem.

The next step is clearly the implementation of the selected algorithm on the computer. The question is: Into what form should we fit the various parts developed to alleviate the task of producing a reliable, working program which does precisely what we want it to do? This part of the design phase, called *program documentation*, is often the most neglected aspect of the problem-solving process. In fact, the documentation of a program is very often viewed as an onerous task to be performed after the program has been written and is running. However, it is our position that by integrating the documentation into the design and implementation phase, both jobs are considerably easier since they complement each other.

EXERCISE 3.1: It is relatively easy to convince yourself of the need for program documentation. Go to the scrap paper bin at your computing center and find a program written in a language you know, preferably one with few comments. Try to decipher the program; that is, determine what the program does, what all the variables stand for, and how to use it.

For more insight, let us again return to the analogy between algorithms and physical systems. The way to determine how a certain "thing" works is to consult the instruction manual; this is particularly true when it malfunctions and must be repaired. Programs are not unlike other tools in this respect; they must be built, maintained, repaired, upgraded, etc. It is much easier to perform these design and upkeep functions if we know how the program works, what each of the parts does, how the parts affect each other, what the level of performance of the program is to be, how it can be tested to ensure it is functioning correctly, and how it is to be used.

As we have suggested in earlier chapters, a problem is rarely stated in precise terms; however, it is expected that the final solution will be stated precisely in terms of a program. It should be recognized, however, that there are different classes of programs with regard to their ultimate use.

1. Some programs are run only once, or at most a few times. Many homework problems, such as the exercises in this book, are in this class. They are designed to illustrate a concept, and, for the most part, that is the limit of their usefulness. One would not expect many pages of documentation describing a 40-line program. On the other hand, sufficient documentation must be included so that someone else could read and understand the program; FORTRAN (or SNOBOL . . .) statements are not sufficient for this purpose.

2. Other programs are designed to be run reasonably often by a small group of basically competent people. For example, the Turing machine simulator begun in the last chapter, and continued in this one, may ultimately be used in a course on automata theory for students to check out their Turing machine programs. One would expect more documentation for a program of this type, in addition to a user's manual and appropriate messages from the program when something goes wrong. How many of you have attempted to use a new language (say FORTRAN) and when something has gone wrong (it will!) have received an error message that was absolutely and utterly incomprehensible?

3. Other programs are designed to be executed many, many times by a wide variety of users. For example, the utility subroutines and functions in FORTRAN fall into this category. Very often these programs are based on rather obscure algorithms in order to increase their efficiency and/or accuracy. Furthermore, they might be distributed from a central point to many computer installations for use on the resident system. This usually entails modification of the program to fit the host machine; good documentation, at all levels, is required here.

4. Finally, there are programs which are extremely large, very complex, and designed to be run many times. The record-keeping systems of an insurance company or an airline reservation system are good examples. One would expect extremely detailed documentation at all levels as well as well-written user's manuals, etc.

If we assume that we are addressing ourselves to these *production* programs, the criteria for the form of a good program (i.e., design, implementation, testing, and documentation) attain a completely different dimension. These programs are often written by teams of people, each of which has a specific responsibility for some aspect of the job; communication in such an environment is absolutely crucial. The tenets of modular refinement, introduced in the last chapter, coupled with the documentation strategy introduced here, are a good start toward providing that communication. Let us, therefore, examine the process of implementing a very large program and then tailor that process to smaller programs. Some of the criteria for production programs include the following:

1. *Correctness:* It is vital that a program is correct and does indeed produce the desired output for all possible values of input parameters. It is unfortunately the case that during the lifetime of a production program everything which can conceivably go wrong will. Hence, it is important that, before delivery, a program has been tested thoroughly to see whether it will work under all circumstances and will "gracefully" stop if any input or intermediate values are not within legal ranges; furthermore, the action taken in response to an error of this type should be understandable to the person using the program at the time. Programs which exhibit these characteristics are called *robust*.

2. *Modifiability and maintenance:* Any program which is used in the "real" world will have to be maintained; that is, when errors occur (and they will occur, regardless of the effectiveness of the testing), they must be corrected. Further-

more, it is a known fact that no matter how carefully the program was designed, after it has been in use those using the program will want extensions and modifications. For example, we may wish to make the Turing machine simulator more general by allowing the Turing program to have labels on instructions instead of references through indices, or the program for the insurance company may have to be modified to allow a more flexible access to clients' records.

3. *Efficiency:* Since the programs we are discussing here will be executed many times, perhaps by many people, it is crucial that they be efficient in their use of computer time, manpower, and memory. Quite often these criteria impose conflicting restraints on the program structure, and it will depend on the circumstances as to how these conflicts are resolved.

3.3 THE DESIGN DOCUMENT

It should be clear by now that the above requirements can be met only if the program was the result of a rather careful design. The design of large programs often does not involve the discovery of new algorithms but instead requires emphasis on the organization and management of the implementation. The task of program design can then be likened to an architectural problem, in that principles of system organization are involved. One does not begin the design and construction of a new home by going to the lumberyard and purchasing boards and nails. There is a logical order in which a home is designed, beginning with a general concept and progressing through sketches, partial models, blueprints, and finally detailed construction plans. During the construction phase, the efforts of the various people responsible for the actual construction have to be carefully coordinated. It would not do to begin construction of the roof before the second-story walls are completed. The necessity of careful design and implementation becomes more important as the complexity of the structure increases. For homes, some of the steps can be eliminated; for high-rise office buildings, none of them can be, and the whole process becomes one of organization and coordination (after the initial concept is settled upon).

The program designer should have a set of tools available which aid in this organizational process. To meet the criterion of correctness and robustness the problem solution has to be developed according to the tenets of modular refinement. The major advantage here resides in the independence of modules so that they can be independently tested and verified. In addition, the module structure and isolation of partial solutions significantly enhance the ease with which a program can be modified.

To maintain a program we clearly need documentation which unambiguously specifies a solution. An obvious, though not very useful, candidate is the program itself. Programs, no matter how well written and commented, contain too many irrelevant details imposed by the language in which they are written to seriously consider them as such documentation; it is extremely difficult to understand the entire solution of any nontrivial problem using only the program itself. It is interesting to note that there is at least one very popular language (COBOL) which was designed so that the final program would be very readable to anyone looking at it. The idea was to embed the documentation in the program itself. In some sense the approach was at least partially successful; probably more than 90% of all programs written in the business world are written in COBOL. The language is, unfortunately, rather cumbersome to use, although this is a matter of opinion and personal preference. The documentation embedded within a program (e.g., COBOL), though, is not sufficient to provide a clear understanding of the overall concept which preceded the program.

One way of achieving the understanding required before attempting to extend or modify a program is to examine the complete modular refinement of the problem statement. Here the complexities of the problem solution are completely laid out; it can be followed to whatever level is necessary. Once the modules in which the errors occurred (or those which we wish to alter or extend) are found, they can be modified rather easily. To satisfy these global requirements, it is necessary to collect all the relevant information into an easily readable format which preserves the logical structure of the program; this we shall do in the design document.

The design document will completely specify the problem's solution in terms of logical structures, names of data structures and algorithms, data flow, organization of modules, variables modified by each module, etc. One of the first things to note is that the process of modular refinement imposes a logical structure on the construction of a program. Each level in the refinement process is essentially a more completely specified representation than the levels which precede it; thus, this process may be represented as in Figure 3.1, using the Turing machine simulator from the last chapter as an example.

Since the result of the modular-refinement process is a hierarchy of modules, as indicated in Figure 3.1, it is trivial to associate with each module a numeric identifier based on Dewey's decimal notation, which provides an organization for the design document. The description of each module should include

1. <u>*d.d.* . . . . *.d* name</u>
2. <u>General description</u>
3. <u>Input parameters</u>
4. <u>Output parameters</u>   (1)
5. <u>Global data referenced</u>
6. <u>Data structures introduced and associated utility routines</u>
7. <u>Module flow</u>
8. <u>AL algorithm</u>

The original problem statement is on the highest level and is denoted by 1 in this classification scheme; modules on the next level are numbered 1.1, 1.2, etc., from left to right. Thus, a module on the ith level will have an identification number $d_1.d_2. \ldots .d_i$ consisting of i digits. For example, the second module from the left on the third level in Figure 3.1 has the three-digit Dewey decimal number 1.1.2. In addition to its numeric identification, each module also has a mnemonic name. For informational purposes we then add a brief verbal description to each module which clearly identifies

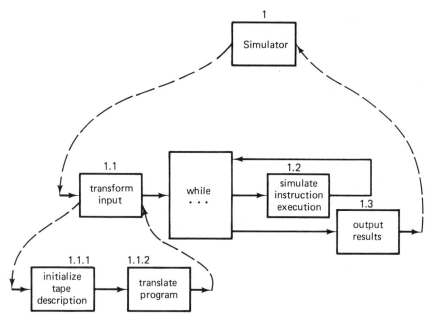

Fig. 3.1 Representation of the modular-refinement process: The Turing machine simulator.

its task. The third and fourth points on the list of items which have to be specified for a module are the formal input and output parameters. Not only do we name them, but we specify the legal ranges for the input parameters, whether they have yet to be checked or have been checked in some previous module, and the range of the output parameters. More specifically, the relations of the values of the output parameters to those of the input parameters are indicated.

The fifth item is a list of variables which have been introduced on a higher level and are to be made available for reference and modification. To clearly delineate those names which may be used in a module, let us say one which has the number $d_1.d_2. \ldots .d_i$, only those items which have been used in module $d_1.d_2. \ldots .d_j$ (with $j < i$) and thus introduced at this level in item 6 of the list are available. This means that a module does not have access to any variables and/or data which have not been explicitly passed down to it through the hierarchy of modules. This does not preclude the possibility that the module itself generates internal names and data, which may in turn be passed on to modules further down in the hierarchy. For example, if we introduce a variable in module 1.1 of Figure 3.1, both modules 1.1.1 and 1.1.2 can reference it and/or modify it. But this variable is not available to modules 1.2 and 1.3. If we had wanted these modules to have access to this variable, it should have been introduced and described as such in module 1. Whenever a data structure is created by a particular module we add its name to item 6. Since at the moment the only physical data structures we know are simple variables, *n*-tuples, and tables, the term *associated utility routines* is for the time being meaningless. In practice, these routines will be used to specify how actual data values are to be retrieved from the structure. Thus, for the trivial case of an n-tuple x, the associated retrieval routine is simply $x(index)$. The module flow is a graphical representation of the refinement of the current module together with a brief description of communications between modules (although this is redundant information; why?).

Each module may be one of the following three objects:

1. Unique, refinable task
2. Unique task   (2)
3. Utility routine

A unique refinable task is one which does not occur anywhere else in the solution and which can be refined still further using only sequencing and iteration over modules. A unique task is one which cannot be directly refined because the flow of control involves branching. In this case, the AL algorithm (item 8) will detail the flow of control and when necessary invoke modules which can be refined. A utility routine is a module which appears in several places of the refinement and may be called with different actual arguments. Its refinement will be given only once (at the location where it is first referenced). In the case where the module flow in (1) is empty, that is, the module is basic enough, the algorithm in item 8 of (1) will specify what the task of the module is. If the modules in item 7 of (1) are all of category 1 and 3 as specified in (2), the algorithm consists simply of a sequence of procedure invocations. That is, we equate each such module with a procedure in AL. For all the modules of category 2, the algorithm will specify the flow of control, invoking procedures which will be refined on the next lower level. To illustrate these points, we shall now initiate a running example based on the Turing machine simulator (Example 3.1).

Example 3.1 Design Document for the Turing Machine Simulation

1. Turing_simulation

General description: This module reads in the description of a Turing machine together with its input, simulates the execution of the Turing machine, and writes out the output of the Turing machine.

Input parameters: None.
Output parameters: None.
Global data referenced: None.
Data structures introduced and associated utilities:

1. Turing tape descriptors (check in module 1.1):

$$n \ldots \text{size of tape}$$
$$tape \ldots n\text{-tuple of symbols ('}0\text{', '}1\text{', or '}B\text{')}$$
$$rwh \ldots \text{tape head } (1 \leq rwh \leq n)$$

2. Turing program descriptors (check in module 1.1):

> *m* . . . number of instructions
> *opcode* . . . *m*-tuple of instruction keywords ('if', 'go to',
>   'write', 'right', 'left', 'halt')
> *symbol* . . . *m*-tuple of symbols ('*0*', '*1*', or '*B*')
> *transfer* . . . *m*-tuple of indices ($1 \leq \cdots \leq m$)
> *roh* . . . instruction counter ($1 \leq roh \leq m$)

3. Error indicators:

> *fatal* . . . **t** if Turing program is syntactically incorrect or
>   its execution causes an illegal situation to occur
> *message* . . . contains error message if fatal is **t**

Module flow:

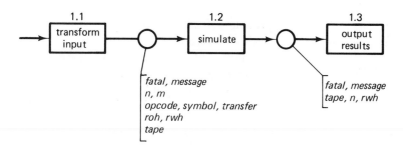

Algorithm:

```
begin
    transform_input;
    if fatal then [output message; halt];
    simulate;
    if fatal then [output message; halt];
    output_result
end
```

****

1.1 Transform_input

General description: Reads in the tape size, the input string to the Turing machine, and the Turing program and translates it into a form which can be efficiently manipulated.
Input parameters: None.

Output parameters: None.
Global data referenced: *fatal*.
Data structures introduced and associated utilities: None.
Module flow:

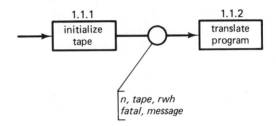

Algorithm:

> **procedure** *transform_input*
> **begin** /∗transform∗/
>   *fatal* ⟵ **f**;
>   *initialize_tape*;
>   *translate_program*
> **end** /∗transform∗/

****

1.2 Simulate

General description: Given the internal form of the Turing machine description, it modifies the description according to the instructions until a halt instruction is encountered.
Input parameters: None.
Output parameters: None.
Global data referenced: *n, m, opcode, symbol, transfer, roh, rwh, tape, fatal, message*.
Data structures introduced and associated utilities: None.
Module flow: None.
Algorithm:

```
procedure simulate
begin /∗process instructions∗/
    while (¬ fatal ∧ opcode(roh) ≠ 'HALT')
    begin /∗execute one instruction∗/
        case opcode(roh) of
             'GO TO':  roh ⟵transfer(roh);
             'HALT':  ;
```

'IF':   **if** *tape(rwh)* = *symbol(roh)* **then** *roh* ← *transfer(roh)*
                                   else *roh* ← *roh* + 1;
'RIGHT':   **if** *rwh* = *n* **then** [*fatal* ← **t**; *message* ← *message* +
             'attempt to move right off tape encountered at instruction'
             + *roh* + ';']
                              else [*rwh* ← *rwh* + 1; *roh* ← *roh* + 1];
'LEFT':   **if** *rwh* = 1 **then** [*fatal* ← **t**; *message* ← *message* +
             'attempt to move left off tape encountered at instruction'
             + *roh* + ';']
                              else [*rwh* ← *rwh* − 1; *roh* ← *roh* + 1];
'WRITE':   [*tape(rwh)* ← *symbol(roh)*; *roh* ← *roh* + 1]
   end; /*opcode*/
   if *roh* > *m* **then** [*fatal* ← **t**; *message* ← *message* + 'no halt encountered;']
  end /*execute*/
end /*process*/

```
********************************************************************
```

EXERCISE 3.2: Give the description of module 1.3.

```
********************************************************************
```

1.1.1 Initialize_tape

General description: Reads in tape size and Turing machine input and prepares tape.
Input parameters: None.
Output parameters: None.
Global data referenced: *n*, *tape*, *rwh*, *fatal*, *message*.
Data structures introduced and associated utilities:

> *symb* . . . contains one symbol of Turing machine input
>   ('*0*', '*1*', '*B*', 'program')
> **input** . . . reads *symb*;

Module flow: None.
Algorithm:

procedure *initialize_tape*
begin /*initial*/
    input *n*; *i* ← 1;
    while (*i* ≤ *n*) [*tape(i)* ← '*B*'; *i* ← *i* + 1];
       /*read input*/
    i ← *n*/3;
    while (*i* ≤ *n*)

begin /*process one symbol*/
    input *symb*;
    case *symb* **of**
            '0', '1', 'B':   *tape(i)* ← *symb*;
          'program':   **terminate**;
              error: [*fatal* ← **t**; *message* ← *message* +
                             'illegal input symbol' + *symb* + ';']
    end; /*symb*/
    i ← *i* + 1
  end;/*process*/
  if *i* > *n* **then** [*fatal* ← **t**; *message* ← *message* + 'too many input symbols;';
              while (*symb* ≠ 'program') **input** *symb*];
  rwh ← *n*/3
end /*initial*/

****

EXERCISE 3.3: Give the description of module 1.1.2; remember to define the utility routines for reading a Turing machine instruction.

****

The above design document is by its definition self-explanatory; we only wish to discuss several features which were not utilized in this example. For instance, assume that in the algorithm for module 1.2 the actions in the case statement are nontrivial and that each action merits further refinement. In this case, we invoke a procedure and provide a comment which identifies the module corresponding to this procedure, e.g.,

              'GO TO': *go to_action*; /*module 1.2.1.*/
              'HALT': *halt_action*; /*module 1.2.2.*/
                    ·
                    ·
                    ·

Similarly, no module in this example was of the utility category. Assume that in the following module flow

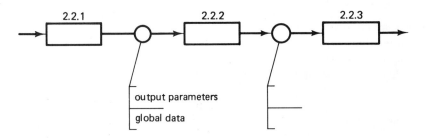

module 2.2.2 is a utility routine which is used in several places. Then we would insert an additional communication node before 2.2.2 indicating the formal input parameters and in parentheses the actual arguments as follows:

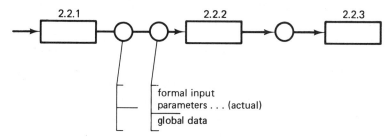

In any other part of the refinement, if the above was the first occurrence, we shall refer to the module by its proper name 2.2.2. ■

3.4 SELECTION OF DATA STRUCTURES

At this stage of obtaining the final product, namely a working program together with its documentation, we have a design document. We emphasize "a" because it may not be the final one. In the course of implementing the access routines for data structures it may prove that the approach detailed in a module is not suitable because it is too inefficient, and we have to redesign it. In the algorithms of the design document we did not use any declarations and, furthermore, did not concern ourselves with the availability of certain data types and operators in the programming language to be used as implementation vehicle. Therefore, we must now provide a mapping between the types assumed in AL and the realities of the actual programming language.

Physical Representation of Data

In most cases, there will be several alternative representations of data structures, identified as variables, tuples, tables, and mappings in AL, within the constraints of the programming language. Their usefulness will be measured in terms of the storage requirements of the structure chosen and the execution time of the routines required to manipulate them. Quite often these two criteria will be conflicting; rarely will there be one choice which is best in both respects. In this chapter, we shall not be concerned with the physical representation of general mappings but only with primitive types. The discussion of the former subject is postponed until Chapter 9.

We have come to realize that the representation of data cannot be viewed in isolation but must be considered in conjunction with the operations performed on them. Data representations should be such that the operations performed most commonly are as efficient as possible (within the constraint of available memory). The issues involved are best illustrated by examples, and for this purpose we shall use the Turing machine simulation to be implemented in FORTRAN. We make the assumption that memory efficiency is not a major concern (if it were, refer to Chapter 9). With this in mind, the representation of *tape* is obvious: an array of fixed dimension in which each word will contain a Hollerith constant representing the tape symbol (it is only used in comparisons, assignment, and input/output); similar considerations hold for *symbol* and *transfer*. The only real problem is *opcode* since it is used in a **case** statement; see module 1.2. In AL the value of *opcode(roh)* was a string of symbols. If we represent these six strings by the integers 1 through 6, the **case** statement may be implemented as a computed GO TO statement (which is certainly more efficient than a series of comparisons of Hollerith strings). Thus, we shall represent *opcode* by an array containing integers from 1 to 6. It is important to note that this conclusion was reached by investigating the statement where it is used and not where it is initially defined. In module 1.1.2 the array is set only once for each entry. In the **case** statement of module 1.2 the entry may be referenced many times, e.g., if the entry corresponds to an instruction which is part of a loop in the Turing program. Hence, it is necessary to make the latter operation efficient. In summary, in FORTRAN we have the following data structures (excluding those needed in modules 1.3 and 1.1.2, if any):

> ROH . . . . integer index into OPCODE, SYMBOL, TRANS
> RWH . . . . integer index into TAPE
> TAPE . . . . array of 100 words containing Hollerith constants
> OPCODE . . . . . . array of $\leq$ 50 integers (1, 2, . . . , 6)
> SYMBOL . . . . . array of $\leq$ 50 words containing Hollerith constants
> TRANS . . . . array of $\leq$ 50 indices into OPCODE, SYMBOL, TRANS
> N . . . . integer, add check for being less than 100
> M . . . . integer, add check for being less than 50

We have omitted in this selection process the representation of *message* because FORTRAN does not provide string catenation as a primitive operator (however, see Section A.10 in the supplementary volume and Chapter 9). Instead of accumulating the messages as done in the algorithm, they are printed as errors are found. This is accomplished through an additional procedure whose input parameters are an index and other parameters if needed; it will have a list of error messages in form of WRITE and FORMAT statements. The index will be used to branch to the proper WRITE statement, which may use some of the other input parameters in producing the message, after which control is returned to the point of call.

Normally the form of the data external to the program is known. For example, some of the data may reside on cards and other parts on magnetic tape, and still others may be input from a terminal (see Chapter 8). If this is not the case, the external form of the data must be specified at this point, and the utility routines which access these data must be defined. Once we have decided upon the physical internal representation of external data, we are in a position to describe the form and position, say on cards, of these data which will enable the utility routine to work as defined.

Implementation of Nonextant Operators

In many cases, it will happen that operators were used in the design of algorithms for which no equivalent operators exist in the programming language. In such cases, it is necessary to define procedures which will achieve the same result, using the primitive operators of the implementation language; see Section A.10 in the supplementary volume. A simple example is the string catenation operator discussed above. At that time we decided not to implement it at all but rather redesigned the algorithm to eliminate the operation altogether. In subsequent chapters, we shall encounter various operators and their implementation in languages such as FORTRAN.

3.5 THE IMPLEMENTATION PLAN

Software projects, i.e., the design and implementation of programs to solve specific problems, may be classified in two groups. The first category comprises the tasks of discovering algorithms which solve a problem hitherto unsolved or for which the solution is not known to the problem-solver. The second category consists of problems where the solutions to the constituent subproblems are all known and the stress is on the organization and management of the implementation. Although the principles espoused in this and the subsequent section apply mainly to the second category, we can and will use them in producing software for problems in the first category (although in abbreviated form), which in general are on a much smaller scale. In the remainder of the book, we shall acquaint the student with the basic problems and their solutions she can expect to encounter in the field of computer science. In developing software for these problems we shall use the same techniques employed for large-scale software projects albeit they may not always be necessary.

As mentioned previously, the production of quality software is really an engineering or, more specifically, an architectural problem. That is, the architect has first to produce a blueprint, which is the design document. The next stage is the evaluation of the blueprint for consistency and efficiency. The blueprint may then be used to estimate construction costs, manpower needs, etc. Finally, a plan has to be drawn up to specify the order in which basic units will be constructed. In the remainder of this section, we shall discuss these principles as they apply to the programmer.

Design Evaluation

For a reasonably large program the design document will certainly not be the result of the work of only one person. Rather, an entire team will be working on it in a hierarchical structure. Thus, before the document is approved for the next stage it has to be evaluated in terms of overall efficiency both for code and data structures. If the criteria set by the user of the program are not met, the solution has to be redesigned. In Chapter 4, we shall develop the tools to measure the efficiency of algorithms, and we delay further discussion on this point until then. Next, the document must be checked for consistency. Are the communications between modules consistent? More specifically, we have to ensure that points 3 through 6 in the module descriptions are not contradictory (points 7 and 8 are used for measuring efficiency).

Cost Estimation

At this point we have a design document which has been evaluated to meet the design criteria and which has been verified insofar as possible without actually executing a program. Although it will rarely matter to the student how long it will take to implement an algorithm, in the world of business we need to know beforehand how much it will cost to complete a product. The main consideration to the software (program) manager will be the question of manpower. How many people are needed to implement the current design for how long? How many people for how long are needed to implement specified future modifications? How many people are needed to maintain the program? To answer these questions we have to analyze the design document, as described below.

Generation of Test Data and Planning

Principally, we distinguish two alternatives for implementing a design. The first alternative is to implement in a top-down fashion. We begin with the modules at the highest level (fewest digits in Dewey's notation), using dummy procedures to test their interfacing; a dummy procedure is one which, when activated, simply returns without doing anything. Next, we implement the modules on the lower level, proceeding downward until all modules are working satisfactorily. In many situations this alternative is the preferred one; nevertheless, we shall not pursue it because in the context of what we wish to attain in this text the following procedure is more applicable. The second alternative is referred to as the bottom-up method since the modules are implemented and tested starting at the lowest level.

Specifically, we take the design document, identify the lowest-level modules, and determine in what order they should be implemented. This order is not necessarily trivial, although the modules should be independent and one should be able to implement and test them in parallel. However, sometimes it is a much more complex task to prepare the input for a module as required by the design than to await completion of the module which produces the requested data. In this case, the latter module would be implemented first and used to provide the test environment. Next, we establish which modules will be tested in depth. For many modules, particularly on the higher levels, item 8 in the design document consists solely of a sequence of invocations of procedures all of category 1 and 3 as defined in (2). In such a situation elaborate tests do not have to be designed, but rather this module is merged, in the implementation, with its parent module by replacing the call to the procedure in the parent module by the corresponding sequence of calls. In all other cases, we have to analyze items 3, 4, 5, and 6 to prepare proper test situations. If the values of the input parameters (and/or global data referenced) are not guaranteed to fall into the defined range, we have to provide a test run with the values outside the range to see whether the module exits gracefully. For each class of values which cause the algorithm to act differently we select a representative value and describe what the output values (or values of data structures introduced) should be. This should include all cases where the program will stop execution and emit an error message.

Example 3.2 Implementation Plan for the Turing Machine Simulator

Assuming that we have only one person available and cannot avail ourselves of parallel implementation, the order of module implementation is self-evident:

$$\text{order of implementation:} \quad \begin{array}{l} 1.1.1 \\ 1.1.2 \\ 1.2 \\ 1.3 \\ \text{merge } 1.1 \text{ into } 1. \end{array}$$

For module 1.1.1 we have to check whether n is less than or equal to 100, whether *symb* is within the defined range, and whether or not there are too many input symbols. In addition, we should check whether the program acts properly in the other extreme case, that is, when the Turing machine has no input. Hence, we have the following test design:

Module 1.1.1

	Input		Expected Output			
	n	*symb*	*fatal*	*tape*	*message*	*rwh*
1.	110		t	—	'too large tape request'	—
2.	80	*0*	t	*B . . . B01B0B . . . B*	'illegal input symbol'	26
		1				
		A				
		0				
		program				
3.	4	*0*	t	*0011*	'too many input symbols'	1
		0				
		1				
		1				
		0				
		program				
4.	50	program	f	*B . . . B*	—	16

EXERCISE 3.4: Give the test design for module 1.1.2.

The input to module 1.2 (item 4 of 1.2) is presumed to be correct insofar as the syntax of Turing programs is concerned. That is, all instructions were of proper form, symbols are within the alphabet, and transfers are within the range of indices. We must, however, test the program's handling of an attempt to move off the tape, the situation where no halt instruction was encountered, in addition to the execution of the six different cases. Thus, the test design is as follows (the source column is for reference purposes only):

Module 1.2

	Input						Output			
source	opcode	sym-bol	trans-fer	tape	other		tape	rwh	fatal	message
1. WRITE B	6	'B'	0	BB1101BBB	rwh = 3		BBB111BBB	4	f	
RIGHT	4	0	0		roh = 1					
IF 1 GO TO 2	3	'1'	2		m = 9					
WRITE 1	6	'1'	0		n = 9					
LEFT	5	0	0							
IF 1 GO TO 5	3	'1'	5							
RIGHT	4	0	0							
GO TO 9	1	0	9							
HALT	2	0	0							
2. RIGHT	4	0	0	BBBBB	rwh = 1		BBBBB	5	t	'attempt to move right off tape encountered at instruction 1;'
GO TO 1	1	0	1		roh = 1					
					m = 2					
					n = 5					
3. LEFT	5	0	0	BBBBB	rwh = 1		BBBBB	1	t	'attempt to move left off tape encountered at instruction 1;'
GO TO 1	1	0	1		roh = 1					
					m = 2					
					n = 5					
4. RIGHT	4	0	0	BBB	rwh = 1		BBB	1	t	'no halt encountered'
					roh = 1					
					m = 1					
					n = 3					

114

EXERCISE 3.5: Give the test design for module 1.3.

As a final comment we add that this algorithm and test design do not take into account infinite loops in the original Turing program. That is, although our program may pass all the designed tests, it still may *abort* due to a time limit because the Turing program is in a loop. The only way to provide a graceful exit in such a situation is to keep a counter for the number of Turing machine instructions executed and to execute at most a predefined number of instructions (which depends on the time limit for program execution). ■

We finally are now able to estimate the cost of implementing the design. Again we shall only outline an approach, which in this case is to use the length of the algorithm specification in a module and the number of test cases (and the time it takes to prepare the input in proper form). Usually it will depend very much on the environment (competency of programmers, quality of design) as to what these figures (number of statements per day implemented, number of tests performed per day) are; they can be assigned only after some experience has been gained. A possible cost estimate for the Turing machine example is given in Figure 3.2, which plots the jobs implemented by whom on a time scale.

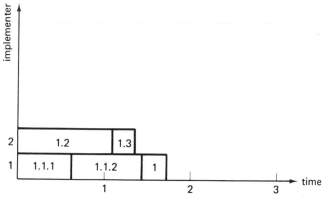

Fig. 3.2 Implementation chart for Example 3.1 using two people.

Similarly, we can answer the question, What will be the cost for certain modifications we may apply to the design? For instance, assume we want the simulator to accept statements with proper labels. First we analyze the design document for all occurrences of references to *transfer*. At the point where *transfer* is input to module 1.2 we wish it to be of the same form as before. Hence, the only candidate for modification is module 1.1.2. Having thus isolated the affected modules, we design the changes and estimate the implementation cost of the modification using the same principles.

3.6 PRODUCTION AND MAINTENANCE OF A PROGRAM

The last, and in general the least, step in the long line of obtaining a working program to solve a given problem is the translation of the design document and implementation plan into an actual program. It is difficult to attach any meaningful figures to the duration of the various phases, but roughly speaking the figure of 70% of the total time for the design phase and 30% for the *coding* is at least in the right range for most problems. The steps involved in this last phase are the following: Take the algorithm from a module description and the physical representation of the data; follow the rather mechanical translation rules outlined below to produce a first draft of the program. Items 3 through 6 are used to establish proper communications, and item 1 together with the control structures of the algorithm are used to establish proper documentation of the program itself. Next is the debugging and testing of the program, and finally, we have to determine what to keep to alleviate the problem of maintenance.

Translation of an Algorithm into a Program

Depending on the programming language to be used this step may prove to be quite straightforward or may involve at least local modifications to the algorithm. For languages which support the control structures of AL, e.g., PASCAL and PL/I, the statements comprising the algorithm may be translated more or less directly to conform to the syntax of the chosen language. For languages not supporting the control structures of AL, e.g., FORTRAN and SNOBOL, we have to simulate these features using only features available in the selected programming language. That this can be done for both FORTRAN and SNOBOL without losing the property of a well-ordered structure—at least in the macroscopic view—is illustrated in Sections A.9 and B.10 of the supplementary volume. In these sections, a rather mechanical procedure is given for translating the AL control structures into those of FORTRAN and SNOBOL.

For either class of languages the production of a program is not completed with the translation of executable statements. In addition, we have to formalize the specifications of the data structures underlying the program. That is, we have to provide the declaration statements required by the compiler and, unless they are trivial, write procedures (e.g., subroutines and functions) which will access these data structures both for retrieving and setting data values.

Debugging and Testing

Although the terms *debugging* and *testing* are sometimes used synonymously, they do convey rather different concepts. Debugging implies the process of obtaining a syntactically correct program so that it executes on the computer. Testing refers to the process of ensuring that the executable program is, on the one hand, semantically correct—that is, it provides the correct answers—and, on the other hand, that it does not suddenly stop execution (*bomb out*) due to an unforseen situation which the program is unable to handle. Thus, we may say that we first *debug* a program to get it to run at all, and then we undertake a thorough *testing* to verify that the program handles all situations properly.

The least troublesome kinds of *bugs*, or errors, are the syntactic errors in the program. By syntactic errors we refer to misspellings, omissions of symbols such as "," or "*", improper forms of statements, etc. When we first submit the program to the computer's translator (compiler) it will give us a list of all the syntactic errors in the program. The form of these messages depends solely on the translator used. Usually, within two rounds of submission and corrections we will have a syntactically correct program. However, when we ask for the program to be executed, in all probability it will not work. Either we encounter an "ungraceful" exit or the results are not as described by the test design. Two possibilities exist: First, we did not translate the algorithm properly, or, second, the algorithm itself is wrong. The first of these two possibilities is the more likely particularly if the programming language is FORTRAN because of the introduction of large numbers of GO TO statements. The remedy for this problem is to take the test cases and trace the execution of the algorithm by hand and compare the flow of control to that of the FORTRAN program. Having ensured the correctness of the translation, we now have to analyze the algorithm itself for logical errors.

Before doing so it usually pays to check whether the input to a module is really in the form required by the test design. For instance, if we were to test the procedure SIMULA before we had module 1.1 available, we would have to set all the arrays as defined in the test design. A simple input error which sets, for instance, TRANS(2) to the value 9 instead of 7 would soon cause an abortive termination of the program if $m = 8$ (why?). The main question remains: How can we locate logical errors in the algorithm? In most computing centers the compilers provide what are called *tracing options*. These options, among others, allow the programmer to

1. Trace assignments to variables.
2. Trace the flow of control.
3. Check and trace array references for being out-of-bounds.

With any or all of these options *turned on*, any occurrence of a specified event will be printed out. We first prepare a trace of the relevant data structures of a module by hand using only the knowledge of what the module is supposed to do. Comparison of this prepared trace with the actual trace of the program should then enable us to pinpoint the error (wherever the two traces start to diverge), and we can then adjust the algorithm and program accordingly.

Example 3.3 Typical Error in Design

Assume we carelessly designed the algorithm in module 1.2 so that the statement for the "left" instruction reads

$$\text{'LEFT':} \quad [rwh \leftarrow rwh - 1; roh \leftarrow roh + 1];$$

and that the corresponding program, when executed, aborted with a cryptic message such as "address reference out of range." Since one of the most common errors in programming concerns an improperly valued index to an array, a decision is made to trace the assignments to *roh* and *rwh* (which are used as indices to arrays). From the problem statement we know that they should always be in the range of 1 to *m* and 1 to *n*, respectively, but in the trace output we shall suddenly see a message such as

ASSIGNMENT OF 0 TO RWH AT STATEMENT 12:

if 12 was the statement number (not label) assigned to the FORTRAN statement

$$RWH=RWH-1.$$

Obviously, TAPE(0) is not defined, and what will happen when we execute such a reference is completely unpredictable (at least insofar as the programmer is concerned). ■

There are some pitfalls when using the tracing options of which one should beware. One of the most paradoxical ones is the case where a program passes one test after the other when the trace is on but refuses to work at all when the trace is turned off. The paradox is resolved when we become aware that by adding the tracing specifications we modify the program. That is, the machine program produced by the compiler and executed by the computer has a structure that differs insofar as the location of instructions and data, in relation to each other, are concerned. Hence, a reference TAPE(0) may create havoc in one case but be completely harmless and actually self-correcting in another case.

EXERCISE 3.6: Familiarize yourself completely with the tracing options available in your compiler. Give the procedure SIMULA to a hostile colleague and ask him to introduce as many subtle errors as he wants. Debug and test this defiled procedure.

For the very rare cases where tracing options are not available the programmer has to simulate them herself. This can be achieved by adding to the program statements (clearly labeled as "*debugging*" statements) which will perform the same actions provided by tracing. For example, before each array reference, add statements which check the range of the index and print out an error message in case the index is not within the range. Clearly, by doing it ourselves we are forced to locate the error by elimination because the "debugging program" would be longer by order of magnitudes were we to add all checking statements at once.

Maintenance and Modifications

If we have designed and implemented a problem's solution according to the rules developed in this and the preceding chapters, maintenance and modification are easy tasks indeed. As for modifications, we first identify the concerned modules as outlined earlier and then proceed forward as if we were designing and implementing new modules. Insofar as maintenance is concerned, we have to keep all the material we developed for testing the modules. This means that we have to store (safely and retrievably) all the procedures used to set up test data and to call modules. Furthermore, we should save those versions of the programs which contained the tracing specifications because they will be useful when tracking down an error which has never occurred before.

EXERCISE 3.7: Deliver a complete product which will solve the Turing machine simulation problem.

EXERCISE 3.8: Have a friend introduce an error into your program of Exercise 3.7 so that it continues to run for most Turing programs but aborts with a cryptic message from the system for a specific Turing program which he will show you. Find the error.

3.7 AN ABBREVIATED APPROACH TO DOCUMENTATION

The first sections of this chapter were devoted to the study of proper design and implementation of production programs. Next we shall discuss the approach to the documentation of problem solutions we have selected for use in the remainder of the book. It differs to some degree from the form discussed earlier due to a difference in emphasis.

In the remainder of the book the emphasis is on an examination of typical areas of computer science, their attendant problem domains, and basic methodologies. We are more concerned with the development of problem solutions than with the formal specification of the final program. Therefore, we shall rarely, if at all, produce the final design document with the test data; rather we shall roughly adhere to the following outline:

1. Verbal problem description
2. Assumptions made
3. Problem statement
4. Modular refinement
5. Algorithms for selected basic modules
6. Exercises
7. Discussion of data representation in program
8. Final programs for selected modules

Lest the reader think that these two approaches are incompatible, the next example represents a comparative study of the two documentation strategies. The first part of the example shows the manner in which sample problems are presented throughout subsequent chapters. The second part of the example gives the solution to the same problem as a production program in the form described in earlier sections of this chapter.

Example 3.4 Text Alignment Problem

The purpose of this example is to illustrate the techniques of solution refinement and program construction as will be done throughout the remainder of the book and to contrast them with the ideas set forth in this chapter. The problem to be considered is one of aligning an arbitrary text so that the right and left columns are justified, much as is done in newspaper typesetting. For example, the final program will accept a text, such as the first few lines of this example, and produce as output the aligned text so that each line contains precisely *nchar* characters (the exact number of characters may vary):

> The purpose of this example is to illustrate the techniques of solution refinement and program construction as will be done throughout the remainder of the book and to contrast them with the ideas set forth in this chapter. The problem to be considered is one of aligning an arbitrary text so that. . . .

While this is certainly a practical problem, and one to which a great deal of attention has been directed, we shall not be concerned so much with the practical aspects of the problem. Rather, we will be concerned with the development and presentation of the solution; thus, some rather strict simplifying assumptions are made.

Example 3.4.1 Text Alignment Problem (as done throughout the book)

The problem we wish to consider is the problem of aligning an arbitrary text so that the first and last characters in each line are nonblank and each line consists of the same number of characters. It is assumed that the text is presented in some machine-readable format, together with the number of characters in the text and the desired width of the resulting output lines. The initial statement of the problem is shown in Figure 3.3. One reasonable approach to this problem might be to eliminate any blanks

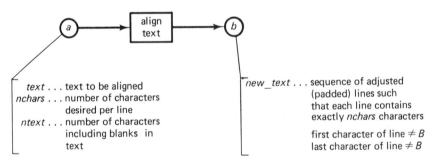

Fig. 3.3 Statement of the Text Alignment Problem.

preceding the first character of the text; then simply count off *nchars* + 1 characters. If the last character in this string is a blank, then we print the line (assuming that each word is separated by exactly one blank and that all punctuation is adjacent to a word and belongs to that word). If the last character is nonblank, then we must back up to the end of the last complete word in the string, counting the number of characters as we back up. This count gives us the number of blanks to be inserted in the line; these blanks are inserted in the interior of the line, the line is printed, and the process repeats from where we left off, with the possible exception of the last line in the text (which we may have to handle as a separate case). Thus, the next level of refinement is as shown in Figure 3.4. Each module is sufficiently simple so that it may be specified completely as an AL algorithm.

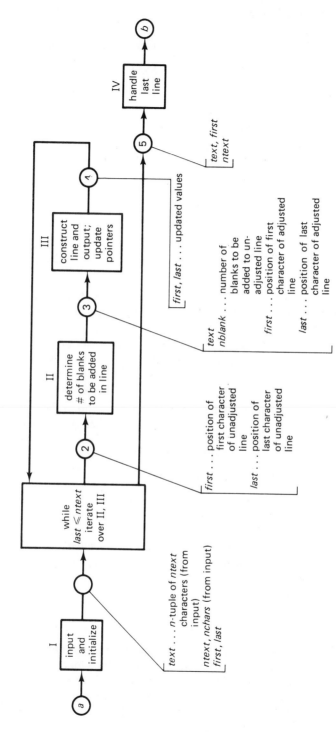

Fig. 3.4 Refinement of the Text Alignment Problem.

121

Algorithm 3.1 (Determine the number of blanks required to pad line of text)

Global data referenced: *text, first, last, nblank*.

begin /*determine number of blanks required*/
    if *text(last)* ≠ ' ' **then**
      if *text(last* + 1) = ' ' **then** *nblank* ⟵ 0
                      else begin /*find end of previous word*/
                              while(*text(last)* ≠ ' ') [*last* ⟵ *last* − 1;
                                          nblank ⟵ *nblank* + 1];
                            last ⟵ *last* − 1;
                            nblank ⟵ *nblank* + 1
                        end /*find*/
             else
      [*last* ⟵ *last* − 1; *nblank* ⟵ 1]
end /*blanks*/

Notice that this module assumes that the values of *first* and *last* are properly initialized, that words are separated by exactly one blank, there are at least two full words per line, and that *text* is not empty.

It is now necessary to add the number of blanks just computed to the line and output it (module III). We shall assume that the blanks to be added are inserted to the right of the first word in the line. This can be accomplished by copying characters, beginning at *first*, until a blank is encountered. At this point the required number of blanks are inserted, and the copying continues until the end of the line is reached. We copy the characters into a new tuple, called *line*, and then output *line*.

Algorithm 3.2 (Insert blanks into line of text)

Global data referenced: *text, nblank, first, last*.

begin /*insert blanks and output line of text*/
    i ⟵ 1; *j* ⟵ *first*;
    while (*text(j)* ≠ ' ') [*line(i)* ⟵ *text(j)*; *i* ⟵ *i* + 1; *j* ⟵ *j* + 1];
    while (*nblank* > 0) [*line(i)* ⟵ ' '; *i* ⟵ *i* + 1; *nblank* ⟵ *nblank* − 1];
    while (*i* ≤ *nchars*) [*line(i)* ⟵ *text(j)*; *i* ⟵ *i* + 1; *j* ⟵ *j* + 1];
    output *line*;
    first ⟵ *last* + 2;
    last ⟵ *first* + *nchars* − 1
end /*insert*/

EXERCISE 3.9: Algorithm 3.2 will add all the necessary blanks immediately after the first word in the current line. This has the effect of producing a lot of "white" space down the left side of the resultant output. Modify this procedure so that the blanks are distributed in some way throughout the line. Note that actual typesetting machines have facilities for inserting partial blanks between single characters, but we have no way of producing this effect. You can, however, do better than Algorithm 3.2.

EXERCISE 3.10: Provide the AL algorithms for modules I and IV.

To translate these modules into FORTRAN code, we must decide as to how to represent the text. For simplicity, let us assume that the text is represented in a FORTRAN array, with one character per word. This is obviously not the most efficient use of memory but will simplify the resulting code. As mentioned several times, the selection of the appropriate data structure is often one of the most crucial decisions which must be made during this final translation phase; see Exercise 3.13. Using this assumption, the translation of module II is relatively straightforward.

Purpose: To count the number of blanks required to align a line of text.
Communication:

variables referenced through blank COMMON:	TEXT . . . an integer array containing the text to be processed; each word contains one character of the text left justified, blank filled; TEXT is not modified; words are separated by exactly one blank;
	FIRST . . . an integer value used as a pointer into TEXT denoting the first character of the unadjusted line; FIRST is not modified;
	LAST . . . an integer value used as a pointer into TEXT denoting the last character of the unadjusted line; LAST is modified;
	NTEXT . . . # of characters in text;
	NCHARS . . . # of characters per output line.

subroutines and functions called: None.
formal parameters: NBLANK . . . (integer) returns the number of blanks which must be added.

Known flaws: No error-checking on parameter values is performed.
Program:

```
C :::::::::::::::::::::::::::::::::::::::::::::::::::::::::::::::::::::::::::::::::::::::::::::::::::::::::::::::::
C               SUBROUTINE COUNTB
C :::::::::::::::::::::::::::::::::::::::::::::::::::::::::::::::::::::::::::::::::::::::::::::::::::::::::::::::::
              SUBROUTINE COUNTB (NBLANK)
C
C      FINDS THE END OF THE ADJUSTED LINE IN THE TEXT AND
C      COUNTS HOW MANY BLANKS HAVE TO BE INSERTED
       INTEGER TEXT(1000), FIRST
       COMMON TEXT, FIRST, LAST, NTEXT, NCHARS
C
C
       IF (TEXT(LAST) .EQ. 1H ) GO TO 40
           IF (TEXT(LAST + 1) .NE. 1H ) GO TO 10
C      NO ADJUSTMENT NECESSARY
               NBLANK = 0
```

```
            GO TO 30
C           FIND END OF PREVIOUS WORD
    10              IF (TEXT(LAST) .EQ. 1H ) GO TO 20
                    LAST = LAST - 1
                    NBLANK = NBLANK + 1
                GO TO 10
    20              LAST = LAST - 1
                    NBLANK = NBLANK + 1
    30      RETURN
    40 LAST = LAST - 1
       NBLANK = 1
       RETURN
       END
```

EXERCISE 3.11: Complete the FORTRAN program for the text alignment problem. Run your program on a set of data which is sufficient to convince yourself that it executes correctly. Then run it on the first paragraph of this example.

EXERCISE 3.12: Incorporate the improvements indicated in Exercise 3.9 into the FORTRAN program and redo Exercise 3.11.

EXERCISE 3.13: It was noted in the text that the selection of the data structure in this example was not the most efficient in terms of memory. One possible alternative would be to pack as many characters as possible into one word, using the techniques discussed in Section 3.8. Redo the text alignment problem using this alternative and compare the resulting programs. ■

```
*******************************
* STOP:  Before proceeding, attempt to produce on your own the *
* design document, data structure, test data, and FORTRAN pro- *
* gram (in that order) for the text alignment problem.         *
*******************************
```

Example 3.4.2 Design Document for the Text Alignment Problem

1. Text_alignment

General description: This program reads a text consisting of a sequence of characters and breaks it into a list of lines of equal length so that both the first and last characters of each line are nonblank, inserting blanks if necessary between words.

Input parameters: None.

Output parameters: None.

Global data referenced: None.

Data structures introduced and associated utility routines:

> *ntext* . . . number of characters of *text* (from input)
> *text* . . . *ntext*-tuple of characters (from input)
> *first* . . . index into *text* indicating position of first character of a line
> *last* . . . index into *text* indicating position of last character of a line
> *nchars* . . . number of characters in the desired line (from input)
> *nblank* . . . number of blanks to be added to line

Module flow:

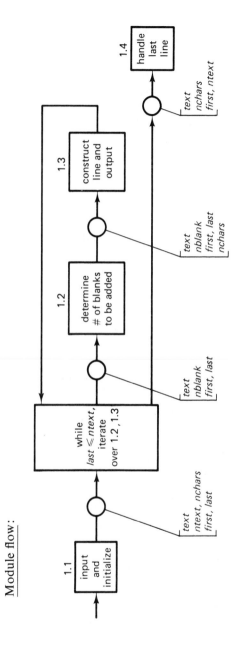

AL algorithm:

```
begin/*text alignment*/
    initialize;
    while (last ≤ ntext)
    begin/*output a line*/
        count_blank;
        pad_line
    end; /*output*/
    last_line
end /*text*/
```

****

1.1 Initialize

General description: Read in text and initialize indices.
Input parameters: None.
Output parameters: None.
Global data referenced:

$$\left.\begin{array}{l} ntext,\ nchars \\ text \end{array}\right\}\text{read from input}$$
$$first,\ last$$

Data structures introduced and associated utility routines: None.
Module flow: None.
AL algorithm:

```
procedure initialize
begin/*read in*/
    input ntext, text, nchars;
    j ← 1;
    while (text(j) = ' ') j ← j + 1; /*eliminate leading blanks*/
    first ← j; last ← first + nchars − 1
end /*read*/
```

****

1.2 Count_blank

General description: Finds the end of the adjusted line in the text and counts how many blanks have to be inserted.
Input parameters: None.
Output parameters: None.
Global data referenced: *text, first, last, nblank*.
Data structures introduced and associated utility routines: None.
Module flow: None.

AL algorithm:

```
procedure count_blank
begin /*determine number of blanks required*/
    if text(last) ≠ ' ' then
        if text(last + 1) = ' ' then nblank ← 0
                                else begin /*find end of previous word*/
                                      while (text(last) ≠ ' ') [last ← last − 1;
                                                                nblank ← nblank + 1];
                                      last ← last − 1;
                                      nblank ← nblank + 1
                                    end /*find*/
                    else
        [last ← last − 1; nblank ← 1]
end /*determine*/
```

****

1.3 Pad_line

General description: Copies proper characters from text into line and inserts a number of blanks after the first word.

Input parameters: None.

Output parameters: None.

Global data referenced: *text, nblank, first, last, nchars*.

Data structures introduced and associated utility routines:

line . . . nchars-tuple of characters (transmitted to output)

Module flow: None.

AL algorithm:

```
procedure pad_line
begin /*insert blanks, and output line*/
    i ← 1; j ← first;
    while (text(j) ≠ ' ') [line(i) ← text(j); i ← i + 1; j ← j + 1];
                /*get first word*/
    while (nblank > 0)[line(i) ← ' '; i ← i + 1; nblank ← nblank − 1];
                /*insert blanks*/
    while (i ≤ nchars)[line(i) ← text(j); i ← i + 1; j ← j + 1];
                /*get remainder of line*/
    output line;
                /*update indices*/
    first ← last + 2;
    last ← first + nchars − 1
end /*insert*/
```

****

1.4 Last_line

General description: The last characters of the text forming an incomplete line are printed unadjusted.

Input parameters: None.

Output parameters: None.

Global data referenced: *text, first, ntext, nchars.*

Data structures introduced and associated utility routines:

$$line \ldots nchars\text{-tuple of characters}$$

Module flow: None.

AL algorithm:

```
procedure last_line
begin /*output last line*/
    i ← 1; j ← first;
    while (j ≤ ntext) [line(i) ← text(j); i ← i + 1; j ← j + 1];
            /*pad with trailing blanks*/
    while (i ≤ nchars) [line(i) ← ' '; i ← i + 1];
    output line
end /*output*/
```

****

FORTRAN data structures and test design:

TEXT . . . an integer array dimensioned at 1000; each word contains one character left justified, blank filled.

LINE . . . an integer array dimensioned at 100; each word contains one character left justified, blank filled.

Test cases for module 1.2:

	INPUT		OUTPUT	
1. FIRST	1			1
LAST	5			5
TEXT	A CAT		NBLANK	0
2. FIRST	1			1
LAST	6			5
TEXT	A CAT		NBLANK	1
3. FIRST	1			1
LAST	7			5
TEXT	A BIG CAT		NBLANK	2

Test cases for module 1.3:

INPUT		OUTPUT		
FIRST	1			
LAST	5			
NBLANK	2			
TEXT	A BIG CAT	LINE	A	BIG

Test cases for module 1:

INPUT		OUTPUT		
TEXT	A BIG CAT AND A SMALL DOG	LINE	A	BIG CAT
			AND	A
			SMALL	DOG
NTEXT	25			
NCHARS	10			

FORTRAN program:

```
      PROGRAM TEXTLI(INPUT, OUTPUT, TAPE5=INPUT, TAPE6=OUTPUT)
C
C         THIS PROGRAM READS A TEXT CONSISTING OF A SEQUENCE OF
C         CHARACTERS AND BREAKS IT INTO A LIST OF LINES OF EQUAL
C         LENGTH SUCH THAT BOTH THE FIRST AND LAST CHARACTERS
C         OF EACH LINE ARE NON-BLANK INSERTING BLANKS IF
C         NECESSARY BETWEEN WORDS
C
      INTEGER TEXT(1000), FIRST
      COMMON TEXT, FIRST, LAST, NTEXT, NCHARS
C
C         READ IN TEXT AND INITIALIZE INDICES
C
      READ (5,11) NCHARS, NTEXT, (TEXT(I), I = 1, NTEXT)
      WRITE(6, 21) NCHARS, NTEXT, (TEXT(J), J=1, NTEXT)
      WRITE(6, 31)
      J = 1
   20 IF (TEXT(J) .NE. 1H ) GO TO 30
          J = J + 1
      GO TO 20
   30 FIRST = J
      LAST = FIRST + NCHARS - 1
C
C         OUTPUT LINES UNTIL NOT ENOUGH CHARACTERS FOR FULL LINE
C
   40 IF (LAST .GT. NTEXT) GO TO 50
          CALL COUNTB(NBLANK)
          CALL PADLIN(NBLANK)
      GO TO 40
   50 CALL LASTLI
```

```
   11 FORMAT (2I5/(80A1))
   21 FORMAT(29H THE LENGTH OF THE NEWLINE IS, I5,
     *36H THE NUMBER OF INPUT TEXT CHARACTERS,I5/////10X,12H INPUT TEXT
     *//////(1H ,80A1))
   31 FORMAT(/////10X,13H OUTPUT TEXT://///)
      STOP
      END
C :::::::::::::::::::::::::::::::::::::::::::::::::::::::::::::::::::::::::::::::::::::
C                 SUBROUTINE COUNTB
C :::::::::::::::::::::::::::::::::::::::::::::::::::::::::::::::::::::::::::::::::::::

               SUBROUTINE COUNTB (NBLANK)
C
C        FINDS THE END OF THE ADJUSTED LINE IN THE TEXT AND
C        COUNTS HOW MANY BLANKS HAVE TO BE INSERTED
C
      INTEGER TEXT (1000), FIRST
      COMMON TEXT, FIRST, LAST, NTEXT, NCHARS
C
C
      IF (TEXT(LAST) .EQ. 1H ) GO TO 40
            IF (TEXT(LAST + 1) .NE. 1H ) GO TO 10
C        NO ADJUSTMENT NECESSARY
                  NBLANK = 0
            GO TO 30
C        FIND END OF PREVIOUS WORD
   10             IF (TEXT(LAST) .EQ. 1H ) GO TO 20
                     LAST = LAST - 1
                     NBLANK = NBLANK + 1
                  GO TO 10
   20             LAST = LAST - 1
                  NBLANK = NBLANK + 1
   30     RETURN
   40 LAST = LAST - 1
      NBLANK = 1
      RETURN
      END
C:::::::::::::::::::::::::::::::::::::::::::::::::::::::::::::::::::::::::::::::::::::
C                 SUBROUTINE PADLIN
C:::::::::::::::::::::::::::::::::::::::::::::::::::::::::::::::::::::::::::::::::::::

               SUBROUTINE PADLIN(NBLANK)
C
C        COPIES PROPER CHARACTERS FROM TEXT INTO
C        LINE AND INSERTS A NUMBER OF BLANKS AFTER
C        THE FIRST WORD
C
      INTEGER TEXT(1000), FIRST
      DIMENSION LINE(100)
      COMMON TEXT, FIRST, LAST, NTEXT, NCHARS
C
C        GET FIRST WORD
C
      I = 1
      J = FIRST
   10 IF (TEXT(J) .EQ. 1H ) GO TO 20
            LINE(I) = TEXT(J)
            I = I + 1
            J = J + 1
      GO TO 10
```

130

```
C
C          INSERT BLANKS
C
   20 IF (NBLANK .EQ. 0) GO TO 30
             LINE(I) = 1H
             I = I + 1
             NBLANK = NBLANK - 1
      GO TO 20
C
C          GET REMAINDER OF LINE
C
   30 DO 40 K = I, NCHARS
             LINE(K) = TEXT(J)
             J = J + 1
   40 CONTINUE
      WRITE (6,51)  (LINE(I), I = 1, NCHARS)
   51 FORMAT (1H , 100A1)
C
C          UPDATE INDICES
C
      FIRST = LAST + 2
      LAST = FIRST + NCHARS - 1
      RETURN
      END
C:::::::::::::::::::::::::::::::::::::::::::::::::::::::::::::::::::::::::::::::::::::::::::::::::::::::
C                   SUBROUTINE LASTLI
C:::::::::::::::::::::::::::::::::::::::::::::::::::::::::::::::::::::::::::::::::::::::::::::::::::::::

            SUBROUTINE LASTLI
C
C        THE LAST CHARACTER OF THE TEXT FORMING
C        AN INCOMPLETE LINE ARE PRINTED UNADJUSTED
C
      INTEGER TEXT(1000), FIRST
      COMMON TEXT, FIRST, LAST, NTEXT, NCHARS
      DIMENSION LINE(100)
C
C
      I = 1
      DO 10 J = FIRST, NTEXT
             LINE(I) = TEXT(J)
             I = I + 1
   10 CONTINUE
C
C          PAD WITH TRAILING BLANKS
      DO 20 K = I, NCHARS
             LINE(K) = 1H
   20 CONTINUE
      WRITE (6,31)  (LINE(I), I = 1, NCHARS)
   31 FORMAT (1H , 100A1)
      RETURN
      END
```

To complete this example, actual output from the FORTRAN program developed above is shown in Figure 3.5. ∎

THE LENGTH OF THE NEWLINE IS   44 THE NUMBER OF INPUT TEXT CHARACTERS   388

        INPUT TEXT

    THE PURPOSE OF THIS EXAMPLE IS TO ILLUSTRATE THE TECHNIQUES OF SOLUTION REFINE
MENT AND PROGRAM CONSTRUCTION AS THEY WILL BE DONE THROUGHOUT THE REMAINDER OF T
HE BOOK AND TO CONTRAST THEM WITH THE IDEAS SET FORTH IN THIS CHAPTER. THE PROBL
EM TO BE CONSIDERED IS ONE OF ALIGNING AN ARBITRARY TEXT SO THAT THE RIGHT AND L
EFT COLUMNS ARE JUSTIFIED, MUCH AS IS DONE IN NEWSPAPER TYPESETTING.

        OUTPUT TEXT:

THE PURPOSE OF THIS EXAMPLE IS TO ILLUSTRATE
THE   TECHNIQUES OF SOLUTION REFINEMENT AND
PROGRAM   CONSTRUCTION AS THEY WILL BE DONE
THROUGHOUT   THE REMAINDER OF THE BOOK AND TO
CONTRAST   THEM WITH THE IDEAS SET FORTH IN
THIS   CHAPTER. THE PROBLEM TO BE CONSIDERED
IS ONE OF ALIGNING AN ARBITRARY TEXT SO THAT
THE   RIGHT AND LEFT COLUMNS ARE JUSTIFIED,
MUCH AS IS DONE IN NEWSPAPER TYPESETTING.

Fig. 3.5   Output from FORTRAN program for Text Alignment Problem.

3.8 CONCLUSIONS

The purpose of this chapter has been twofold: On the one hand, we presented tools to be used in the development of the design of a production program. We formalized the results of this design phase in the framework of a design document and discussed how it serves as an aid in the design of the physical realization of the data structures in the eventual program and in the form and specification of the test cases. The last step was to take the algorithm and data structure specification and to produce the actual program, debug it, and execute the various tests resulting in a final product which can be released to the customer. We further pointed out the usefulness of this documentation for the purpose of maintaining the program and how the modular structure of the product facilitates modification to the program.

In the last part of this chapter we noted that the goals of this book are not to list and explain production programs but rather to elucidate and at the same time present problems in computer science. This goal necessitated a slightly different way of presenting solutions, but as shown in our extensive example, it is not difficult to obtain the documentation explained in the first part of the chapter from the form used throughout the remainder of the book.

One commonsense observation to be made is that the solutions we have presented here and those to be presented later do not represent the initial approach to the solution. The final solution usually does not emerge full-blown from the programmer's mind; it is often evolved over a period of time through several abortive attempts. Very often it is necessary to throw away an almost completed solution and begin again; only after trying several plausible solutions does an understanding of the nature of the problem emerge. At this point, problem solution begins in earnest. Good programming and efficient implementation require imagination, practice, and work.

References

Articles on the range of subjects discussed in this chapter can be found in the journal

Transactions on Software Engineering, published by the Institute for Electrical and Electronic Engineers (IEEE).

Furthermore, the following special issue of *Computing Surveys* [published by the Association for Computing Machinery (ACM)] has become a classic in this field:

Special issue: "Programming," *Computing Surveys*, 6(4) (Dec. 1974) editor: P. J. Denning; contributors: P. J. Brown, B. W. Kernighan, P. J. Plauger, D. E. Knuth, N. Wirth, and J. M. Yohe.)

Contributions to the area of managing large software projects include

R. T. Baker, "Chief Programmer Team Management of Production Programming," *IBM Systems Journal, 11*(1) (1972), pp. 56–73.

G. M. Weinberg, *The Psychology of Computer Programming,* Van Nostrand Reinhold, New York, 1971.

F. P. Brooks, Jr., *The Mythical Man Month and Other Essays on Software Engineering,* Addition-Wesley, Reading, Mass., 1974.

A highly readable discussion of how to write programs to avoid bugs (and how to find them if they are there) is found in

B. W. Kernighan and P. J. Plauger, *The Elements of Programming Style*, McGraw-Hill, New York, 1974.

An exhaustive study of various ways to ensure correctness of a program is given in

W. C. Hetzel, *Program Test Methods*, Prentice-Hall, Englewood Cliffs, N.J., 1973.

Finally, a collection of tips and hints on how to construct and maintain well-structured, readable programs is given in

H. Ledgard, *Programming Proverbs*, Hayden, New York, 1975.

Exercises

1 Assuming that you have a Turing machine simulator, perform the necessary steps to implement the following modification: Turing program instructions should be recognized as *free-format* instructions; i.e., the various constituents are not constrained to start in specified columns. That is, follow the recommended procedure of modifying the design document, test design, and program.

2 The same as Exercise 1 for the following modification: The user should be allowed to specify her own alphabet and use symbols from this alphabet in the Turing program.

3 How would you select your physical data representation for the line-padding example if you were under severe memory constraints?

4 You are given an array MESSAG dimensioned at 100 and an array NEWM dimensioned at 5. MESSAG contains a character string which is stored starting at the first character of the first word of MESSAG and continuing to the last character of the first word, to the first character of the second word, etc. Likewise, NEWM contains a character string. Let LMES and LNEW be the current length of the strings MESSAG and NEWM, respectively; implement the AL catenation operator

$$messag \longleftarrow messag + newm;$$

in FORTRAN using the proper values for word length and number of bits per character on your computer.

5 Take any FORTRAN subroutine from either Exercise 1 or 2 and have some other person introduce random errors; debug and retest it again so that you can ascertain that it works properly.

6 You may have seen that some computer centers take your job identification such as KJM123, enlarge each letter as seen below, and print it on the first page of your job output for easy identification.

```
K   K    JJJJ   M       M    1     2 2      3 3
K  K      J     MM    MM     11    2   2    3    3
KK        J     M  M  M      1       2        33
K  K     J J    M       M    1      2      3    3
K   K    JJJJ   M       M    1111  2222      3 3
```

Implement a program to achieve this. (Hint: For the time being, do not be overly concerned about storage efficiency.)

4

Computational Complexity

4.0 INTRODUCTION

The concept of an algorithm, as developed in the preceding chapters, was constructed from the vantage point of formalization. That is, we were concerned basically with the operational characteristics of algorithms and procedures, with techniques for expressing algorithms, with formal aspects of the representation of algorithms, and with the development of programs from algorithms.

In this chapter we turn our attention to the question of the efficiency of a program, which was largely ignored in Chapter 3. More specifically, the question of optimality is of prime concern; that is, given a variety of algorithms for solving a particular problem, how do we choose the *best* one from the available set?

Clearly, the criteria for *best* must be formulated into a rigorous definition which reflects those quantities which influence the performance of the algorithm. Thus, in this chapter we are concerned with the question of performance. First, we have to establish standards for the measure of the complexity of a particular algorithm which will allow us to search for an optimal algorithm among all those which compute the same function. Second, we shall present certain techniques which have proven helpful in the design of algorithms with relatively low complexities for a given problem. The importance of carefully analyzing an algorithm with regard to its complexity cannot be overemphasized, particularly since intuition in this area is usually wrong, as we shall see in some of the examples later on in this chapter. Consider, for instance, a library function such as SQRT mentioned in Part A of the supplementary volume for a particular computer system. On an average computer system it might be called 5000 times or more each day, and as a result, implementing an algorithm whose execution cost is lower will result in considerable savings in real money over the long run even if the optimization is only minute. In general, any program which is executed repeatedly and often is a prime target for analysis. The strategy we shall employ to find the best algorithm for a given problem involves the following three parts:

1. Selection of a complexity measure and the meaning of optimality. The measure should be sensitive to as many aspects of an algorithm as possible; it should embody the meaning of optimality as appropriate for the problem and the environment in which it will be solved.
2. Analytic derivation of the optimal value of the measure for the particular problem as defined in part 1. In many cases this will not be possible; it is usually possible, however, to derive upper and lower bounds on the complexity measure.
3. Search for an algorithm which achieves the optimal value. Again, we may not be able to find such an algorithm. In this case, we investigate existing algorithms and rank them according to the measure.

4.1 COMPLEXITY MEASURES

For any given problem let

α represent the collection of algorithms solving the problem,

$\mathfrak{D}$ be the domain of input values, and

$T(\mathbf{A}, x)$ represent the amount of work done by a specific algorithm $\mathbf{A}$ in α on the specific input value x in $\mathfrak{D}$.

Thus, α contains all the possible algorithms which solve the problem, and $\mathfrak{D}$ describes the admissible ranges of input values to the problem. Obviously, the main problem is to define T. Several possibilities freely suggest themselves; for instance, we could measure the amount of work done by $\mathbf{A}$ by the amount of time spent by computer $\mathbf{X}$ executing $\mathbf{A}$. However, were we to execute the same program on some computer $\mathbf{Y}$ which is different from $\mathbf{X}$, the time required to execute $\mathbf{A}$ will usually be different. An even worse measure would be to consider the number of instructions in a program as indicative of the amount of work. Quite often the reverse is true; namely, the longer the program, the less time spent in executing it. We already intimated in Chapter 3 with the eight-queens problem that the straightforward solution can be programmed with relatively few statements but requires an inordinate amount of time to find a solution. As we shall see in this chapter, there exists a more complex solution, which requires more instructions to implement but which executes in much less time.

A relatively machine-independent measure is the amount of storage required by the program and how often each instruction in a program is executed. However, to use the latter measure, we have to define what is meant by an instruction. Do we measure in terms of AL instructions, FORTRAN instructions, machine instructions, or other instructions? If we measure, for example, in terms of FORTRAN instructions, we have to be aware of the fact that FORTRAN instructions may be translated into different machine instructions depending on the computer system used. Unfortunately, no unique measure exists which reflects all these situations.

We still have not defined what is meant by the complexity of a particular algorithm since T depends on the value of x. The two most commonly used complexity measures are the *worst-case* measure and the *expected value* measure. The first can be defined as

$$c_w = \max_{x \in \mathfrak{D}} T(\mathbf{A}, x) \qquad (1)$$

and the second as

$$c_e = \operatorname*{average}_{x \in \mathfrak{D}} T(\mathbf{A}, x) \qquad (2)$$

using whatever definition has been chosen for T. These measures are actually quite simple. In both cases, we determine the amount of work done by the algorithm on all possible input values individually. The worst-case measure is obtained by selecting the largest of these values; it thus measures the performance of the algorithm under the worst possible conditions. The expected value measure is obtained by averaging all the values and thus measures the performance of the algorithm under all conditions.

Note that both c_w and c_e might not exist because, on the one hand, the algorithm turns out to be a procedure (cf. Chapter 1) or, on the other hand, $\mathfrak{D}$ contains infinitely many elements. In the latter case, the amount of work required may grow without bound for certain input values. A simple remedy is to express $T(\mathbf{A}, x)$ not as some absolute numerical value but as a function of the size of x (e.g., number of digits, absolute value, number of elements in a set, length of a tuple, etc.). Let the size of x, denoted by $|x|$, be n; then (3) and (4) define the worst-case and expected value measures:

$$c_w(n) = \max_{\substack{x \in \mathfrak{D} \\ |x| = n}} T(\mathbf{A}, x) \qquad (3)$$

$$c_e(n) = \operatorname*{average}_{\substack{x \in \mathfrak{D} \\ |x| = n}} T(\mathbf{A}, x) \qquad (4)$$

All that has been done here is to restrict the computation of the measures to inputs of a fixed size; it is now possible to examine the behavior of an algorithm as a function of the size of the input. If both measures are the same, they are denoted by $c(n)$.

Example 4.1

We wish to define complexity measures for algorithms which solve the following problem. Given a list of names and one additional name, return the value zero if the name is not in the list. Otherwise, the position of the name in the list is returned; if there is more than one instance of the name in the list, any one of their positions is to be returned. Assume that $T(\mathbf{A}, x)$ is the total number of AL instructions executed. In this case, c_w from (1) certainly does not exist since the list of names may be arbitrarily long, but by defining the size of x to be the number of names in the list we can calculate both (3) and (4). Consider the two algorithms $\mathbf{A}_1$ and $\mathbf{A}_2$, which both solve the problem.

/*let *list* be a given *n*-tuple of names and *name* the name
to be searched for*/

| $\mathbf{A_1}$ | $\mathbf{A_2}$ |

```
begin                                      begin
  i ← 1;                                     i ← n;
  while (i ≤ n) if list(i) = name            list(0) ← name;
                then [output i; halt]        while (list(i) ≠ name)i ← i − 1;
                else i ← i + 1;              output i;
  output 0;                                  halt
  halt                                     end
end
```

The worst case for both algorithms obviously occurs when the name is not in the list. If we count the evaluation of the Boolean expressions in the **while** iteration and the **if-then-else** statement in the computation of $T(\mathbf{A}, x)$, then for $\mathbf{A_1}$, $c_w(n)$ has the value $3n + 4$, while for $\mathbf{A_2}$, the corresponding value is $2n + 5$. Thus, for $n > 1$, algorithm $\mathbf{A_2}$ has a lower complexity measure than $\mathbf{A_1}$. ■

As indicated earlier, it is not possible to provide a clear-cut choice for the measure T, although it is possible to define two types of measures of a quite general nature. The first is the *execution analysis* of *dominant* instructions in the algorithm. In this method, those instructions which carry the main burden of work are identified, ignoring such instructions as I/O statements, index operations, iteration control statements, etc. (often referred to as *overhead*); each execution of a dominant instruction is assigned a unit measure of 1. The second type of measure is used if we want to obtain a detailed *cost analysis* for a particular algorithm to be executed on a particular computer. The latter measure is machine-dependent, and it will not be considered in any great detail.

A convenient way to express the dominant behavior measure is by means of the order notation.

Definition 4.1: A function $f(n)$ is said to be of the *order* of $g(n)$, $O(g(n))$, if and only if there exist constants $c_1 > 0$, $c_2 > 0$, and n_0 such that

$$c_1|g(n)| \leq |f(n)| \leq c_2|g(n)| \qquad \text{for } n < n_0$$

Example 4.2

Let $f(n) = 2n^2 + 3n - 5$; then we can state that $f(n)$ is of the order of $g(n) = n^2$, $O(n^2)$, since it is true that for $c_1 = 1$, $c_2 = 3$, and $n_0 = 1$

$$|n^2| \leq |2n^2 + 3n - 5| \leq 3|n^2| \qquad \text{for all } n > 1 \quad ■$$

If we wish to analyze the algorithms for Example 4.1 in terms of this measure, we first have to identify the dominant instruction. Most instructions in both algorithms are simple indexing instructions; the only costly operation is the comparison of two names since they are strings of perhaps many characters. In the worst case, A_1 executes this operation n times, and A_2, $n + 1$ times. Therefore, both algorithms have a complexity measure of $c_w(n) = O(n)$ if we use the order notation. Hence, with respect to this analysis, neither algorithm is superior.

We can develop a general approximating rule for the selection of the dominant instruction(s) in our algorithms by observing that the structure of an algorithm written in AL is essentially a linear sequence of blocks of statements which may contain nested iterations, for example,

> $[A$: straight line code executed once
> ⌜**while** iteration; number of iterations depends on n, the input size
> $[B$: linear sequence of statements
>   ⌜**while** iteration; dependent on n
>   ⌞C
> ⌞ $[D$: linear sequence
> $[E$: linear
> ⌜**while** iteration, independent of input size
> ⌞F

From this structure we can deduce that the blocks of statements contributing most to the work of the above algorithm in terms of order analysis are blocks B, C, and D, since they are part of an iteration which is dependent on the size of n. The reason we do not consider the iteration F is that it is independent of the size n. Notice that the amount of work done by the algorithm can be conveniently broken into two parts. One part depends on the size of the input and is thus a function of n, while the other part is independent of n and remains constant. As n increases, the constant part becomes a smaller and smaller fraction of the total work done and for large enough n can be totally ignored. For example, assume we have two algorithms, B_1 and B_2; the amount of work done by B_1 is $O(n)$ with a large constant part, while B_2 is $O(n^2)$ with a small constant part. In Figure 4.1, we have plotted the amount of work done by each as a function of n.

Unless it is known that the algorithms are to be executed mostly for inputs of a size smaller than n_0, algorithm B_1 is clearly preferable to B_2. Therefore, except for the degenerate cases where the iteration is executed only once or at most a few times, that is, for small values of n, we can neglect the contribution of A, E, and F as well. We count execution of block C, being the innermost block, as one unit of the dominant instruction execution. Then computation of the relevant complexity of the algorithms consists simply of evaluating how often block C is executed in the worst or average case.

In Chapter 5 we shall observe that there exist algorithms for the search problem which have a complexity of $O(\log_2 n)$ under certain restrictions, thus making the distinction between A_1 and A_2 obtained from the previous analysis redundant. In

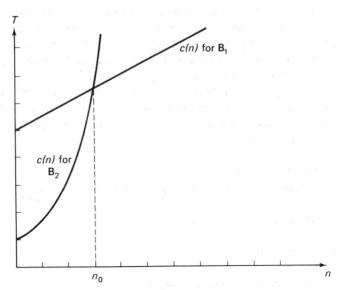

Fig. 4.1   Complexity functions of different orders.

general, it is much more important to attempt to obtain algorithms of a smaller order of complexity than to try to optimize an algorithm without actually achieving a reduction in the order of complexity. To illustrate the importance of this, let us consider the various sizes of a problem which can be handled by algorithms of different orders of complexity. Let $c_w(n) = O(f(n))$ and assume that a complexity measure of 1000 corresponds to an execution time of 1 second on a particular computer; then Table 4.1

Table 4.1   Size of input which can be processed by six different algorithms for the same problem

$f(n)$	time (T)		
	1 second	1 hour	1 year
$\log_2 n$	10^{301}	10^{10^6}	$10^{10^{10}}$
n	1000	10^6	10^{10}
$n \log_2 n$	140	10^5	10^9
n^2	31	1897	10^5
2^n	9	21	34
2^{2^n}	3	4	5

shows for six different algorithms solving the same problem the size of the input each algorithm can process in various time intervals. (When entries are expressed as powers of 10, they are only approximations.) Even if we let the computer run for a whole year, as opposed to one second, we can only process a problem with two more elements if the complexity of the algorithm is $c_w(n) = O(2^{2^n})$ as indicated in the last row of Table 4.1. It matters very little whether $c_w(n)$ was $3 * 2^{2^n}$ or $0.01 * 2^{2^n}$. The relation between the input size processable in 1 second or 1 year will still be not quite twofold.

Example 4.3

Assume that the problem is to search a list of n names for a given name. Further, let the linear algorithm A_1 solve the problem for a list of 1000 names in 1 second of central processor time. If we had an algorithm A_2 of logarithmic complexity, then A_2 could, according to Table 4.1, solve the problem with a list of 10^{301} names in the same time. Likewise, if a third algorithm A_3 were of $O(n \log_2 n)$, only a list with 140 names could be processed by A_3 in 1 second. ■

The question arises as to what we should do if we cannot improve on the order of the measure but have several algorithms of the same order available. It seems appropriate that we perform a careful analysis of the overhead involved in each algorithm. This analysis is known as *cost* analysis; operations are grouped into the following three classes:

1. Reference to a memory location (storing or fetching a value); logical operations (comparisons, shifting, etc); (5)
2. Arithmetic operations such as plus, minus;
3. Arithmetic operations such as multiplication.

We introduce this rather arbitrary separation because on many computers instruction costs are separated along these lines. To distinguish costs on different computers we define the constants c_r, c_p, and c_m to represent the cost of an instruction of class 1, 2, or 3, respectively, for a particular computer. The amount of work an algorithm performs according to these definitions is given in (6). The various n's indicate the number of times an operation is executed.

$$T(A, x) = n_r c_r + n_p c_p + n_m c_m \tag{6}$$

In general, it will be quite difficult to analyze a program written in a high-level language in terms of the basic instructions (5), particularly in the case of references. For instance, the reference *telephone-number*('joe') in an AL program translated into machine language might involve several instructions of various types. One solution is to classify the references possible in a programming language and by analyzing the translation of each type into machine language obtain a measure for each high-level reference. It should be obvious, however, that now T does not depend only on the computer but also on the translator used to obtain the machine language program from the high-level language program. Since we are mainly interested in methodology, we shall avoid the problem by not including references in our analyses.

Example 4.4

Consider the simple problem of evaluating $v^2 + x^2 - y^2 - z^2$. First, we have to realize that exponentiation is not a basic machine instruction; a typical library routine for exponentiation has a complexity measure of

$$T(A_L, x) = 20c_p + 25c_m$$

not counting references. Therefore, were we to use the library exponentiation routine for evaluating the expression (call this algorithm A_1), the total complexity measure would be

$$T(\mathbf{A}_1, x) = 83c_p + 100c_m$$

An improvement to $\mathbf{A}_1$ would be to replace exponentiation by a multiplication (algorithm $\mathbf{A}_2$), which in this case can be done by rewriting the expression as

$$v * v + x * x - y * y - z * z$$

with a measure of

$$T(\mathbf{A}_2, x) = 3c_p + 4c_m$$

Finally, consider the algorithm $\mathbf{A}_3$;

$$(v - y) * (v + y) + (x - z) * (x + z)$$

which has a measure of

$$T(\mathbf{A}_3, x) = 5c_p + 2c_m$$

Which of the algorithms should we choose? The answer to this question is that it depends on the values of c_p and c_m. Quite commonly, $c_m = 2c_p$; then we obtain

$$T(\mathbf{A}_2, x) = 11c_p, \qquad T(\mathbf{A}_3, x) = 9c_p$$

and $\mathbf{A}_3$ should be the algorithm selected. ∎

EXERCISE 4.1: Given two complex numbers $u = (a, b)$ and $v = (c, d)$, let their product be defined as $u \circledast v = (R, I)$, where $R = ac - bd$ is the real part and $I = bc + ad$ is the imaginary part. Compute the measure T for the algorithm which evaluates R and I according to the definition and then for the algorithm:

$$a_1 = (a + b)(c - d)$$
$$a_2 = ad$$
$$a_3 = bc$$
$$R = a_1 - a_3 + a_2, \qquad I = a_3 + a_2$$

not counting references in either case. For what ratios of c_m and c_p would the second algorithm be better?

Another complicating factor in cost analysis is the influence the hardware of a computer has on the measure. For instance, many modern computers can perform several operations in parallel, making it much more difficult to count the number of operations executed in sequence. If we rely solely on cost analysis to compare several algorithms, hardware considerations are not so important since on the average their effects tend to be the same for all the algorithms.

The last item we wish to consider for the cost function T is the amount of storage an algorithm requires. We shall often observe an inverse relationship between amount of work and amount of storage used. In some cases, it is not important how much storage is used (within reason, of course); however, when using small computers, we have to be very conscientious about the way storage is used. Measure (7) reflects the two components (storage and work) in which the weights w_1 and w_2 are assigned values according to the relative importance of the two components:

$$T(\mathbf{A}, x) = w_1(n_r c_r + n_p c_p + n_m c_m) + w_2 n_s \qquad (7)$$

The value of n_s in (7) measures the total amount of storage used by the algorithm (both data and program); its value is either in terms of bits or words, whichever seems appropriate.

We can now define the complexity measure of the optimal algorithm for a problem as

$$C_n = \min_{\mathbf{A} \in \mathfrak{a}} c(n) \tag{8}$$

The optimal algorithm is thus that algorithm which requires the minimum amount of work among all algorithms. Depending on whether $c(n)$ in (8) is the worst-case or the expected value measure, C_n is called the best-worst or best-average measure, respectively.

Example 4.5

Consider the problem of raising an object, say a real number, to an integer power n; this process is commonly called power evaluation. We define a^n to mean $a * a * \cdots * a$, an expression containing n terms. It is obvious that we can evaluate, for example, a^{15} more efficiently than by using 14 multiplications. The sequence of steps shown in (9) actually uses only 5 multiplications:

$$\begin{aligned}
a^1 &= a \\
a^2 &= a^1 * a^1 \\
a^3 &= a^2 * a^1 \\
a^6 &= a^3 * a^3 \\
a^{12} &= a^6 * a^6 \\
a^{15} &= a^{12} * a^3
\end{aligned} \tag{9}$$

Let us restrict the class of algorithms $\mathfrak{a}$ to those algorithms which compute a^n by repeatedly multiplying intermediate powers. Under this restriction the choice of T for the order analysis is, quite obviously, the number of multiplications executed. We should be aware that this choice has implications for $\mathfrak{D}$ (the domain of input values) since the assumption is made that each multiplication has the same cost. This seems to be a trivial assumption if the objects are real numbers, because on a computer the cost of multiplying two real numbers together is independent of the values of the real numbers. But consider the case when the object a is a polynomial. It is clear that the multiplication involved in $(x + 1) * (x + 1)$ is less costly than the multiplication in $(x + 1)^3 * (x + 1)^3$ since many more terms are involved in the latter expression. Therefore, we restrict $\mathfrak{D}$ to those objects for which multiplication is constant, i.e., independent of the values of the operands. The size of the input is then simply the value of n, and both measures $c_w(n)$ and $c_e(n)$ reduce to $T(\mathbf{A}, n)$.

To simplify the discussion we shall describe the various stages in the computation by the $(m + 1)$-tuples $(x_0, x_1, \ldots, x_m)$. The elements of this tuple represent powers which have been calculated. For sequence (9), m equals 5, and each x_i is the exponent of the intermediate power computed. Hence, the 6-tuple $(1, 2, 3, 6, 12, 15)$ completely describes the computational steps involved in calculating a^{15}. In this notation, $T(\mathbf{A}, n)$ is simply m.

EXERCISE 4.2: Find a way to compute a^{21} using only six multiplications and express its execution in terms of a 7-tuple.

Since each line in (9) represents a product of previously calculated powers, the following relations hold among the elements of the tuple:

$$x_0 = 1$$

$$\cdot$$
$$\cdot$$
$$\cdot$$

$$x_i = x_j + x_k \qquad \text{for } 0 < i \leq m, 0 \leq j \leq k < i \qquad (10)$$

$$\cdot$$
$$\cdot$$
$$\cdot$$

$$x_m = n$$

Remembering that $a^x * a^y = a^{x+y}$, it is apparent that each addition in (10) corresponds to the formation of an intermediate power by a multiplication process. A tuple whose elements have the property (10) is called an *addition chain*. Clearly, minimizing the number of multiplications is equivalent to minimizing the length of the addition chain, and therefore, (11) defines the measure of the optimal algorithm:

$$C_n = \min_{A \in \mathcal{Q}} T(A, n) = \min_{A \in \mathcal{Q}} m \quad \blacksquare \qquad (11)$$

4.2 ANALYTIC DERIVATION OF BOUNDS FOR C_n

In deriving bounds for C_n we are really only interested in the case where T measures the dominant instruction. We do not gain much more insight by using cost analysis measures, and it is extremely difficult to account for overhead in a mathematical model of the problem. Thus, once we have established a formal description of the problem and identified the dominant instruction (operation) we shall attempt to derive a bound for C_n without any reference to a particular algorithm. That is, we do not assume that there exists an algorithm with the same measure as the bound. Rather, we are interested in determining the theoretically minimum number of operations which are necessary to solve the problem for any input. We realize that these ideas are rather vague but hope that the various examples, particularly in this and the next chapter, will clarify these notions, and we refer the interested reader to the references.

Example 4.5 (continued)

To obtain the lower bound on the complexity measure for power evaluation, we observe that the elements in the addition chain grow most rapidly if we always add the current element to itself (i.e., multiply the element by 2) to obtain the next element; that is,

$$x_0 = 1$$
$$x_1 = x_0 + x_0 = 2x_0 = 2$$
$$x_2 = x_1 + x_1 = 2x_1 = 4$$
$$x_3 = x_2 + x_2 = 2x_2 = 8$$

$$\cdot$$
$$\cdot$$
$$\cdot$$

$$x_m = x_{m-1} + x_{m-1} = 2x_{m-1} = 2^m = n$$

That means that for every element of an addition chain, equation (12) must hold independently of any particular algorithm:

$$x_i \leq 2^i \qquad \text{for } 0 \leq i \leq m \tag{12}$$

In particular (12) must hold true for $i = m$, which yields

$$x_m = n \leq 2^m \tag{13}$$

Taking the logarithm of both sides of (13) results in

$$\log_2 n \leq m \tag{14}$$

Since (14) holds for any m independent of the algorithm used, we obtain the lower bound (15) on C_n:

$$C_n = \min_{A \in \alpha} m \geq \log_2 n \tag{15}$$

However, let us not forget that this is only a lower bound and it does not guarantee that there exists an algorithm which achieves it. All we can deduce from (15) is that in the event we find an algorithm with $c(n) = O(\log_2 n)$ we cannot hope to improve on the order of complexity since $\log_2 n$ is a lower bound on the complexity of the optimal algorithm. ∎

4.3 TECHNIQUES

You cannot expect us to provide you with a "recipe" for solving any given problem. If such a recipe existed, problem-solving would be a purely mechanical procedure and would cease to be of any interest. However, it has been found that many problems, although completely different on the surface, have yielded to the same basic attack. From these observations certain principles have been extracted. We remind the reader that none of the principles discussed may be applicable to a particular problem. Nonetheless, even if they do not immediately produce a solution, as we attempt to formulate a method of attack, they may provide enough insight to suggest the outline of solution.

4.3.1 Induction

Induction as a mathematical term refers to a proof technique for theorems about integers. Let $T(n)$ be a theorem about the integers; for instance,

$$T(n): \quad \sum_{i=1}^{n} i = \frac{n(n+1)}{2} \tag{16}$$

Then a *proof by induction* consists of the following two steps:

1. Prove that $T(1)$ is true.
2. Prove that if $T(1), \ldots, T(n-1), T(n)$ are all true, then $T(n+1)$ also is true.

Example 4.6

The first part of proving (16) by induction consists merely of stating

$$\sum_{i=1}^{1} i = \frac{1(1+1)}{2}$$

which is indeed true. Second, we assume that for any $k \leq n$, theorem (16) is true. Hence, by assumption it is true that

$$\sum_{i=1}^{n} i = \frac{n(n+1)}{2} \tag{17}$$

and we wish to prove

$$T(n+1): \quad \sum_{i=1}^{n+1} i = \frac{(n+1)(n+2)}{2}$$

Adding $n+1$ to both sides of (17), we obtain

$$\sum_{i=1}^{n} i + (n+1) = \frac{n(n+1)}{2} + (n+1)$$

The left side of this equation is equal to the left side of the equation to be proven. The right-hand side can be transformed into

$$\frac{n(n+1)}{2} + (n+1) = \frac{n^2}{2} + \frac{3n}{2} + \frac{2}{2}$$
$$= \frac{(n+1)(n+2)}{2}$$

which equals the right-hand side of $T(n+1)$, and thus, we have satisfied step 2 in the induction proof and therefore have proven theorem (16). ■

Let us now draw an analogy to algorithm development. We wish to obtain an algorithm **A** which will solve a problem with input x of size n. We postulate that the input can be represented as n individual elements, i.e., $x = (x_1, \ldots, x_n)$; then the induction technique consists of the following steps:

1. Find an algorithm **B** which solves the problem for $n = 1$.
2. Find an algorithm **C** which takes as input $\bar{x}_i$, the solution for $x_1, \ldots, x_i$, and x_{i+1} and produces the solution $\bar{x}_{i+1}$.

Given these two algorithms **B** and **C**, the solution $\bar{x}_n$ to the original problem is found by

Algorithm **A**
```
      begin
          x̄₁ ← B(x₁);
          i ← 1;
          while (i < n)[x̄ᵢ₊₁ ← C(x̄₁, xᵢ₊₁); i ← i + 1]
      end
```

Finding the Maximal Element in a Set

In Chapter 2 we came across this problem as a subtask of the sorting procedure. At that time we did not go beyond the module definition. To repeat: We are given an n-tuple, $n > 1$, say x, of real values, and for simplicity's sake we assume that they are all different. We want to find the location and value of the largest element in the tuple. Subsequently, we require that this largest element be moved so that it is the last element of x [i.e., $x(n) > x(i)$ for $1 \leq i < n$].

Given this problem statement, let us develop an algorithm using the induction technique. First, algorithm **B** is rather trivial since in a 1-tuple the only element is by necessity the maximal element. Thus,

Algorithm **B** (Find maximal element of 1-tuple)
$$\textbf{begin}$$
$$maxval \leftarrow x(1);$$
$$maxind \leftarrow 1$$
$$\textbf{end}$$

Now, the assumption for algorithm **C** is that *maxval* contains the maximum value among the first i values and that *maxind* points to its location; in addition, we are given $x(i + 1)$ for which we do not as yet have an ordering. Two possibilities exist: One, $x(i+1)$ is greater than *maxval*, in which case we would have to update our solution, and two, $x(i + 1)$ is smaller than *maxval*, which means that the old solution is also the new solution. Hence,

Algorithm **C** (Induction part of maximal element)
begin
    if $x(i + 1) >$ *maxval* **then** [*maxval* $\leftarrow x(i + 1)$; *maxind* $\leftarrow i + 1$]
end

Putting these two algorithms into the framework established above results in the following solution (the statements effecting the move to the last position have been added):

Algorithm 4.1 (Finding the maximal element)

```
procedure maxelement (x, n; x)
begin /*find maximal element and exchange it to nth position*/
    maxval ← x(1);
    maxind ← 1;
    i ← 1;
    while (i < n)
    begin /*check i + 1 element*/
        if x(i + 1) > maxval then [maxval ← x(i + 1); maxind ← i + 1];
        i ← i + 1
    end /*check*/
    x(maxind) ← x(n);
    x(n) ← maxval
end /*find*/
```

Consistent with our earlier discussion, the block of statements in the iteration dependent on the size of n is selected as the dominant construction. More specifically, the comparison "$x(i + 1) >$ *maxval*" may be taken as the dominant instruction; this is actually the common selection for such searching algorithms. The comparison is executed exactly $n - 1$ times both in the expected and worst cases, and therefore the algorithm is of $O(n)$.

EXERCISE 4.3: If we remove the restriction that all the elements of the n-tuple are different, which maximal element (in terms of position within the tuple) would algorithm **A** find if there is more than one maximal element.

In performing statistical analyses of data, it is often required to find not only the maximal element of a set of data but also the minimal element. If the minimal element is to be stored in $x(1)$, Algorithm 4.1 may be replicated with only one change in the comparison; that is, the comparison should read $x(i + 1) < maxval$. We shall call this algorithm *minelement*; Algorithm 4.2 finds both the maximum and minimum elements in an n-tuple.

Algorithm 4.2 (Find both maximum and minimum)

> **begin**
>   *maxelement*$(x, n; x)$;
>   *minelement*$(x, n - 1; x)$;
>   **output** 'the minimal element is', $x(1)$, 'the maximal element is', $x(n)$
> **end**

We note that the call to *minelement* involves only the first $n - 1$ elements, since if all elements are different, the maximum cannot also be the minimum value, as long as n is greater than 1. The number of comparisons executed by Algorithm 4.2 is always $2n - 3$ (why?) and therefore still of $O(n)$. In its FORTRAN implementation below, we give only the code for *minelement*, changing the variable names of Algorithm 4.1 to indicate that only the minimum element is sought.

Purpose: Find the minimal and maximal element of the n-tuple LIST.
Communication:

subroutines and functions called:	MAXELT . . . finds maximal element of X (first argument, N its dimension is second argument) and puts it in X(N);
	MINELT . . . like MAXELT, but puts minimal element in X(1);
formal parameters:	LIST . . . . N-tuple; modified such that LIST(1) is minimum and LIST(N) maximum;
	N . . . . size of LIST.

Flaws: Works only for $N > 1$.
Program:

```
C:::::::::::::::::::::::::::::::::::::::::::::::::::::::::::::::::::::::::::::::::::::::::::::::::::::::::::::::::
C                SUBROUTINE MINMA(LIST, N)
C:::::::::::::::::::::::::::::::::::::::::::::::::::::::::::::::::::::::::::::::::::::::::::::::::::::::::::::::::
                 SUBROUTINE MINMA(LIST, N)
C
C
C       THIS PROGRAM FINDS THE MINIMAL AND MAXIMAL
C       ELEMENTS OF THE N-TUPLE LIST
C
        REAL LIST(N)
C
C       FIND THE MAXIMUM ELEMENT
C
        CALL MAXELT(LIST, N)
C
C       FIND THE MINIMUM ELEMENT
C
        CALL MINELT(LIST, N - 1)
        RETURN
        END
C:::::::::::::::::::::::::::::::::::::::::::::::::::::::::::::::::::::::::::::::::::::::::::::::::::::::::::::::::
C                SUBROUTINE MINELT(X, N)
C:::::::::::::::::::::::::::::::::::::::::::::::::::::::::::::::::::::::::::::::::::::::::::::::::::::::::::::::::
                 SUBROUTINE MINELT(X, N)
C
C       THIS ROUTINE FINDS THE NINIMUM VALUE OF THE ARRAY X(N)
C
        DIMENSION X(N)
        REAL MINVAL
C
C       INITIALIZE MINIMUM
C
        MINVAL = X(1)
        MININD = 1
C
C       INDUCTION PART
C
        DO 10 I = 2, N
             IF (X(I) .GT. MINVAL) GO TO 10
C       UPDATE MINIMUM
                  MINVAL = X(I)
                  MININD = I
   10 CONTINUE
C
C       MOVE TO FIRST POSITION
C
        X(MININD) = X(1)
        X(1) = MINVAL
        RETURN
        END
```

```
C::::::::::::::::::::::::::::::::::::::::::::::::::::::::::::::::::::::::::::::::::::::::::::::::::::::::::::::::
C                    SUBROUTINE MAXELT(X, N)
C::::::::::::::::::::::::::::::::::::::::::::::::::::::::::::::::::::::::::::::::::::::::::::::::::::
                     SUBROUTINE MAXELT(X, N)
C
C       THIS ROUTINE FINDS THE MAXIMUM ELEMENT OF THE ARRAY X
C
        DIMENSION X(N)
        REAL MAXVAL
C
C          INITIALIZE MAXIMUM
C
        MAXVAL = X(1)
        MAXIND = 1
C
C          INDUCTION PART
C
        DO 10 I = 2, N
              IF (X(I) .LT. MAXVAL) GO TO 10
C          UPDATE MAXIMUM
                    MAXVAL = X(I)
                    MAXIND = I
     10 CONTINUE
C
C          MOVE TO LAST POSITION
C
        X(MAXIND) = X(N)
        X(N) = MAXVAL
        RETURN
        END
```

Note: In the induction framework the addition $i + 1$ is performed repeatedly; the FORTRAN program is actually a translation of the equivalent framework:

.
.
.

$$i \leftarrow 2;$$
$$\textbf{while } (i \leq n)[\bar{x}_i \leftarrow C(\bar{x}_{i-1}, x_i); \; i \leftarrow i + 1]$$

.
.
.

Polynomial Evaluation

A recurrent minor problem is to implement algorithms for evaluating polynomials. If a specific polynomial is given, for instance,

$$3x^4 - 2x^3 + 5x - 10$$

an expression can be written to evaluate it directly. The problem of interest here is to develop an algorithm to evaluate the general polynomial

$$p(x) = a_0 + a_1 x + a_2 x^2 + \cdots + a_n x^n$$
$$= \sum_{i=0}^{n} a_i x^i$$

In the problem statement in Figure 4.2, we note that the size of the problem is actually $n + 1$. This results from the common mathematical convention of designating the degree of a polynomial by n, the value of the largest exponent. The induction assumption of the algorithm is that *val* contains the value of $\sum_{j=0}^{i} a_j x^j$. To obtain the partial solution $\sum_{j=0}^{i+1} a_j x^j$, the term $a_{i+1} x^{i+1}$ must be added to *val*. If the value of x^i has been saved from the last computation (call it *xpow*), this can be done using two multiplications and one addition.

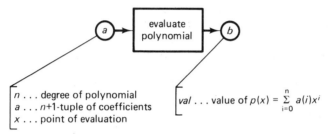

Fig. 4.2   Polynomial evaluation problem.

Algorithm 4.3 (Induction part of polynomial evaluation)

    begin
        xpow ⟵ *xpow* * *x*;
        val ⟵ *val* + *a*(*i* + 1) * *xpow*
    end

EXERCISE 4.4: Complete the algorithm for polynomial evaluation. (Hint: Be careful about initialization; the size is $n + 1$.)

If the number of multiplications executed is selected as the dominant instruction, then $c_w(n)$ is clearly $2n$. This number can be reduced by observing that $p(x)$ may be reformulated as follows:

$$p(x) = \sum_{i=0}^{n} a_i x^i$$
$$= a_0 + x \sum_{i=0}^{n-1} a_{i+1} x^i$$
$$= a_0 + x(a_1 + \sum_{i=0}^{n-2} a_{i+2} x^i)$$
$$= a_0 + x(a_1 + x(a_2 + \sum_{i=0}^{n-3} a_{i+3} x^i))$$
$$\vdots$$
$$= a_0 + x\big(a_1 + x(a_2 + x(a_3 + \cdots + x(a_{n-1} + a_n x) \ldots)))$$

Example 4.7

The polynomial

$$p(x) = 4x^4 + 3x^3 - 7x^2 + 2x - 10$$

can be reformulated as

$$
\begin{aligned}
p(x) &= -10 + x(2 - 7x + 3x^2 + 4x^3) \\
&= -10 + x(2 + x(-7 + 3x + 4x^2)) \\
&= -10 + x(2 + x(-7 + x(3 + 4x)))
\end{aligned}
$$

$$
\underset{a(0)}{\big|} \quad \underset{a(1)}{\big|} \quad \underset{a(2)}{\big|} \quad \underset{a(3)}{\big|} \; \underset{a(4)}{\big|} \quad \blacksquare
$$

Since parenthesized expressions have to be evaluated from the inside out, the induction assumption will be that *val* contains the value of the parenthesized expression involving $a(n), a(n-1), \ldots, a(n-i)$. This observation leads to the algorithm known as Horner's scheme, which has a complexity of n.

Algorithm 4.4 (Horner's scheme for polynomial evaluation)

> **begin**
> $val \leftarrow a(n) * x + a(n-1);$
> $i \leftarrow 1;$
> **while** $(i < n)[val \leftarrow val * x + a(n-i-1); i \leftarrow i + 1];$
> **output** *val*
> **end**

Storage Allocation

Assume the following idealized situation: We define a *file* to be a collection of information requiring a certain number of machine words to store (the size of file). We have files of sizes $r_1 \neq r_2 \neq \cdots \neq r_n$ and a storage area of size m, and no file is larger than m. (Similar problems arise in manufacturing; for instance, suppose you were building a bookcase. You have boards m feet long, you need boards of length $r_1, r_2, \ldots, r_n$, and you wish to minimize the waste. None of the desired boards may be obtained by piecing together boards of shorter length.) The only problem is that m is smaller than the sum of the sizes; that is, there is not enough room to store all of the files. We would like to know which combination of the files produces the smallest waste (i.e., empty space) subject to the restriction that a file cannot be broken up. If several solutions exist, any one will be satisfactory. In this section we shall use the induction technique to obtain a basic algorithm and later return to it for improvement.

The solution to this problem which may come first to mind is to try out all possible combinations and pick that which comes closest to m. If we represent a particular combination as a bit string of length n such that a "1" bit in position i means that file i is part of this combination, we can realize the algorithm fairly straightforwardly. Generate all binary strings of length n in order (by interpreting the strings as numbers); each string represents one possible solution. Each time a new string is generated, the file sizes corresponding to "1" bits in the string are summed. If the sum of the sizes is smaller than m, it is compared to the sum of the current solution. If it is greater, the string becomes the new solution. This is essentially the maximal element algorithm developed earlier, with a few modifications. Since there are 2^n different binary strings of length n, this algorithm will have to perform up to n additions of the file sizes 2^n times. On the other hand, no additional storage, besides $r_1, \ldots, r_n$, will be needed. In many cases, this algorithm will be rather inefficient. For instance, assume that the two sizes r_2 and r_3 together already exceed the limit m; the above algorithm will nevertheless check all combinations which involve r_2 and r_3 although they cannot possibly be solutions.

To alleviate this problem we shall develop an algorithm based on the induction principle which keeps track of only those combinations which are *viable*, i.e., whose sums do not exceed m. Thus, the assumption for the induction part of the algorithm is that we have a set, call it S_i, of all viable combinations of i files with one of them having minimal waste. The question is, How can we obtain a set of *viable* combinations for the first $i + 1$ files given the size of the $(i + 1)$st file? Certainly, S_{i+1} should contain all elements of S_i and in addition those elements which are obtained by setting the $(i + 1)$st bit to 1 in all elements of S_i as long as the new sum does not exceed m. We can save on the computation of the sum if, in addition to the bit string, we store in each element of S_i the sum of the file sizes this combination represents. As we add the new element to S_{i+1} we have to check whether a new solution has been obtained. In Figure 4.3, the problem statement for the induction part of the algorithm has been formalized.

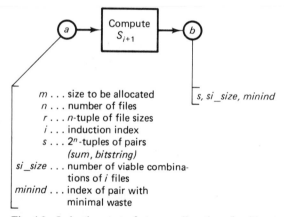

Fig. 4.3 Induction part of storage allocation algorithm.

Algorithm 4.5 (Induction part of storage allocation algorithm)

```
begin /*compute Sᵢ₊₁*/
    new ← (r(i + 1), bit(i + 1)); /*bit is a function which maps i + 1
                                     into a bit string of n zeroes except
                                     a 1 in position i + 1*/
    j ← 1; k ← si_size + 1;
    while (j ≤ si_size)
```

     begin /*if necessary add new viable combination*/
       $old \leftarrow s(j)$;
       $newsum \leftarrow old(1) + new(1)$; $newbit \leftarrow old(2) \lor new(2)$;
       if $newsum = m$ **then** [**output** $newbit$; **halt**];
       if $newsum < m$ **then**
           begin /*found viable combination*/
              $s(k) \leftarrow (newsum, newbit)$;
              if $newsum > s(minind, 1)$ **then** $minind \leftarrow k$;
              $k \leftarrow k + 1$
           end; /*found*/
       $j \leftarrow j + 1$
     end; /*if necessary*/
     $si\_size \leftarrow k - 1$
   end /*compute*/

In Algorithm 4.5, the concept of a **function** (*bit*) has been introduced as a new AL construct. A function is a procedure with no formal output parameters. It returns a single value (here a bit string) associated with the procedure name.

To ensure that the algorithm will find a solution should only one file be selected, *s* must be initialized to $00 \ldots 0$ (why?). We shall assume that *r* has been tested in order to make sure that all file sizes are less than *m*. In the case where r_i, for some *i*, is equal to *m*, a trivial solution has been found, and it is not necessary to search for a solution.

Algorithm 4.6 (Size 1 storage problem)

        begin /*initialization*/
          $s(1) \leftarrow (0, bit(0))$;
          $s(2) \leftarrow (r(1), bit(1))$;
          $si\_size \leftarrow 2$;
          $minind \leftarrow 2$
        end /*initialization*/

This algorithm still generates $O(2^n)$ viable combinations in the worst case; to convince yourself of this fact, count the number of times

$$s(k) \leftarrow (newsum, newbit)$$

is executed in the worst case (give an example of such a situation). On the average, "many" fewer will be generated. However, the new algorithm has only to perform one addition of file sizes for each viable combination in contrast to the *n* possible additions of the brute-force algorithm. The price paid for execution efficiency is the large amount of memory required for the new algorithm, which may make it impractical for large values of *n*.

We select the comparison between *newsum* and *m* as the dominant instruction (i.e., a representative of the innermost iterative block). For *i* equal to 1, the value of si_size is 2, and in general, si_size is at most 2^i after *i* induction steps. Thus, the complexity is

$$c_w(n) = \sum_{i=1}^{n} 2^i$$
$$= 0(2^n)$$

Example 4.8

For $r_1 = 2$, $r_2 = 5$, $r_3 = 3$, $r_4 = 6$, and $m = 12$, let us trace the execution of Algorithm 4.5 in terms of what combinations are added at each induction step and the values of *si_size* and *minind*.

Viable Combinations	*si_size*	*minind*
$i = 1$		
1 (0,0000)		
2 (2,1000)	2	2
$i = 2$		
3 (5,0100)		3
4 (7,1100)	4	4
$i = 3$		
5 (3,0010)		4
6 (5,1010)		4
7 (8,0110)		7
8 (10,1110)	8	8
$i = 4$		
9 (6,0001)		8
10 (8,1001)		8
11 (11,0101)		11
12 (9,0011)		11
13 (11,1011)	13	11

Thus, the combination of the second and fourth files produces the least waste, and 13 out of 16 possible combinations were generated. ∎

Purpose: Compute the combination of files of given sizes with minimal waste.
Communication:

variables referencing input:
    M . . . . available storage size;
    N . . . . # of files;
    R . . . . N-tuple of file sizes;
    WSIZE . . . computer word size (= 60); machine-dependent DATA constant;

subroutine or functions called:
    STRING . . as specified in Section A.10 of the supplementary volume.

Program:

```
C::::::::::::::::::::::::::::::::::::::::::::::::::::::::::::::::::::::::::::::::::::::::::::::::::::::::::::::::
C                 PROGRAM STORAG(INPUT, OUTPUT)
C::::::::::::::::::::::::::::::::::::::::::::::::::::::::::::::::::::::::::::::::::::::::::::::::::::::::::::::::
      PROGRAM STORAG(INPUT, OUTPUT, TAPE5=INPUT, TAPE6=OUTPUT)
C
C        THIS PROGRAM COMPUTES COMBINATIONS OF FILES OF
C        GIVEN SIZES WITH MINIMAL WASTES
C        S...2:::N-TUPLE OF PAIRS (SUM, BITSTRING)
C        R...SIZE OF FILES
C        SISIZE...NUMBER OF VIABLE COMBINATIONS OF FILES
C        WSIZE...THE NUMBER OF BITS OF THE COMPUTER WORD (60)
C
      INTEGER S(1024, 2), R(10), SISIZE, ONE, BITSTR, WSIZE
      DATA  ONE/1/, WSIZE/60/
C
C        INPUT DATA AND CHECK FOR VIOLATIONS AND OR TRIVIAL SOLUTION
C
      SISIZE=0
      READ (5, 11) M, N
      WRITE (6, 12) M, N
      IF (N .LE. 10) GO TO 30
            WRITE (6,21)
            STOP
   30 READ (5, 31)  (R(I), I = 1, N)
      WRITE (6, 32)  (R(I), I = 1, N)
      DO 80 J = 1, N
            IF (R(J) .LT. M) GO TO 80
                IF (R(J) .EQ. M) GO TO 60
C        ILLEGAL INPUT
                    WRITE(6, 51) J, R(J)
                    STOP
C        TRIVIAL SOLUTION
   60               WRITE (6, 61) M, N,(R(I), I = 1, N),J, R(J)
                    STOP
   80 CONTINUE
C
C        INITIALIZE SOLUTION FOR ONE FILE
C
      S(1, 1) = 0
      S(1, 2) = 0
      BITSTR = 0
      CALL STRING(ONE, WSIZE, 1, BITSTR, WSIZE - N + 1)
      S(2, 1) = R(1)
      S(2, 2) = BITSTR
      SISIZE = 2
      MININD = 2
C
C        ITERATE OVER FILES 2 THROUGH N
C
      DO 110 I = 2, N
C        CREATE NEW VIABLE COMBINATIONS
            NEWSIZ = R(I)
            NBITST = 0
            CALL STRING(ONE, WSIZE, 1,NBITST, WSIZE - N + I)
            K = SISIZE + 1
```

```
C
C          FOR ALL OLD VIABLE COMBINATIONS TRY NEW COMBINATION
C
           DO 100 J = 1, SISIZE
                NEWSUM = S(J, 1) + NEWSIZ
                NEWBIT = S(J, 2) .OR. NBITST
                IF (NEWSUM .EQ. M) GO TO 120
                     IF (NEWSUM .GT. M) GO TO 100
C        ADD NEW COMBINATION
                          S(K, 1) = NEWSUM
                          S(K, 2) = NEWBIT
C        CHECK FOR NEW MINIMUM
                          IF (NEWSUM .LE. S(MININD, 1)) GO TO 90
                               MININD = K
  90                           K = K + 1
 100       CONTINUE
           SISIZE = K - 1
 110 CONTINUE
C
C       PREPARE OUTPUT
C
     NEWSUM = S(MININD, 1)
     NEWBIT = S(MININD, 2)
 120 WRITE(6, 121) NEWSUM
     WRITE(6,141)
     DO 130 I = WSIZE-N+1,WSIZE
          J = 0
          CALL STRING(NEWBIT,I,1,J,WSIZE)
          IF(J.EQ.0) GO TO 130
                J = I-WSIZE+N
                WRITE(6,131)J
 130 CONTINUE
  11 FORMAT(
  12 FORMAT(
   "I5/36H
  21 FORMAT(
  31 FORMAT(
  32 FORMAT(
  51 FORMAT(
   "
  61 FORMAT(
   "
   "
 121 FORMAT(
 131 FORMAT(
 141 FORMAT(
     STOP
     END
```

EXERCISE 4.5: The FORMAT statements in the FORTRAN program have not been completed because they are partially machine-dependent. Complete them.

Figure 4.4 shows some sample output from this program.

```
THE SIZE OF MEMORY AVAILABLE IS     12
THE NUMBER OF FILES TO BE STORED IS 4
THE FILE SIZES FROM 1 TO N ARE :

    2    5    3    6
THE SIZE OF THE SELECTED COMBINATION IS:    11
THE FOLLOWING FILES WERE SELECTED
              2
              4
```

Fig. 4.4 Sample output from file storage program.

4.3.2 Backtracking

The technique of backtracking is related to the induction technique at least with regard to the iterative nature of the solution. The technique becomes applicable whenever the solution to a problem requires finding one (or more) elements among many "elements" which satisfies a number of conditions and the element itself consists of several subelements which can be computed separately. If the solution element x has n components, then we construct the components $x(1)$, $x(2)$, ..., $x(i-1)$ iteratively. These components form a *partial solution* if they do not violate any of the conditions attached to the problem. The basic assumption of backtracking is that many possibilities exist from which $x(i)$ may be selected. To obtain an $x(i)$, one of these is selected so that again no condition is violated. It follows that if there is no way to select such an $x(i)$, then $x(1)$, ..., $x(i-1)$ cannot be part of the solution. In this case, we *backtrack* and select another possibility for $x(i-1)$ (if it exists) and again try for $x(i)$. If no possibility exists for $x(i-1)$, we repeat the backtracking step to $x(i-2)$, etc.

To illustrate these rather abstract definitions, let us analyze the following word pattern problem. We are given a set of root words, for example,

$$\text{SERVE}$$
$$\text{SCRIBE} \qquad (18)$$
$$\text{SIGN}$$

a set of prefixes, for example,

$$\text{PRE}$$
$$\text{CON}$$
$$\text{DE} \qquad (19)$$
$$\text{CO}$$

and an arbitrary word which forms the input of the problem. The problem is to determine whether or not the prefix of the word belongs to the set of prefixes and the root of the word to the set of roots. A solution to this problem is to first compute the set of all possible words defined by the prefixes and the roots. Next, the input word is compared to all members of the set. For the above example the set of words is

PRESERVE	CONSERVE	DESERVE	COSERVE	
PRESCRIBE	CONSCRIBE	DESCRIBE	COSCRIBE	(20)
PRESIGN	CONSIGN	DESIGN	COSIGN	

The algorithm would make 12 comparisons in the worst case.

Let us now attempt to formulate the problem into a framework so that it can be solved by backtracking. We define the solution element x to be one of the words in (20). It has two components: $x(1)$ is the prefix which can take on one of the possible values in (19), while $x(2)$ is the root with values in (18). The condition attached to x is that it matches the input word. Informally, the backtracking algorithm can be stated as follows: Iteratively select all the possibilities for $x(1)$; if any of the choices for $x(1)$ satisfies the partial condition that it matches the beginning of the word, we iteratively try all the possibilities for $x(2)$; if a solution is found, we are finished, but if none matches, we backtrack to a different $x(1)$ until none is left, in which case no solution is found. In Algorithm 4.7, the set of prefixes (roots) is named *prefix* (*root*), and *npref* (*nroot*) is its size.

Algorithm 4.7 (Matching words)

```
    begin /*match prefix and root of a word*/
        j ← 1; x(2) ← null;
        while ( j ≤ npref )
        begin /*try a prefix*/
            x(1) ← prefix(j);
            if match(word, x) then
                    begin /*try a root, prefix already matches*/
                        k ← 1;
                        while (k ≤ nroot)
                        begin /*root match*/
                            x(2) ← root(k);
                            if match(word, x) then
                                    [output word, 'matches prefix' + x(1) +
                                            'and root' + x(2); halt];
                            k ← k + 1
                        end /*root*/
                    end /*try a root*/
                        else j ← j + 1
        end; /*try a prefix*/
        output 'no match with' + word
    end /*match*/
```

Before we make a general analysis of the algorithm, its performance on the sample set (20) will be discussed. As the dominant instruction we select the comparison *match*, which occurs in both iterations. Algorithm 4.7 obviously performs best if the given word does not start with any of the prefixes. It takes only four comparisons before the message "no match . . ." is printed; by way of comparison, the initial algorithm would require 12 comparisons. The worst case occurs for a word which starts with CON but whose root is not one in the set since for both prefixes "CO" and "CON" we make three comparisons in the inner iteration, which totals 10 comparisons (still less than 12). In general, if all *npref* prefixes are different (in the sense that none is a prefix of another prefix), the best case is *npref* comparisons and the worst *npref* + *nroot* comparisons, versus *npref* * *nroot* comparisons for the initial algorithm.

EXERCISE 4.6: Compute the worst-case complexity if the assumption of different prefixes is removed.

This example is a special instance of a wide class of problems amenable to *backtracking*. The class is characterized by each component of the solution being selected from a predefined set of possibilities where the order of selection is simply the natural order encountered when representing the set as a tuple. If a problem can be formulated in such a way, Algorithm 4.8 will find a solution if it exists. It thus serves as a framework for backtracking algorithms in a manner analogous to the one developed for induction. Let *x* be an *n*-tuple which represents the solution. Figure 4.5

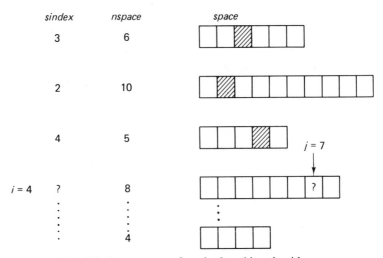

Fig. 4.5 Data structure for a backtracking algorithm.

is a graphical description of the data structure selected for Algorithm 4.8 in the context of a specific example. *space* is an *n*-tuple of tuples containing the possibilities for the solution; that is, *space*(*i*, *j*) is the *j*th possible component for *x*(*i*). The size of each tuple is recorded in the *n*-tuple *nspace*. Thus, in Figure 4.5, there are six potential components for *x*(1) recorded in *space*(1, *k*), $1 \leq k \leq 6$. The actual components comprising the current partial solution are recorded in *sindex*; for this example, the indices of the components already selected for $x(1)$, $x(2)$, and $x(3)$ from *space* are *sindex*(1), *sindex*(2), and *sindex*(3), corresponding to the solution $x(1) = space(1, 3)$, $x(2) = space(2, 2)$, and $x(3) = space(3, 4)$. The iteration variable over the components is the variable i, i.e., $x(1), x(2), \ldots, x(i)$, where $x(i)$ is the component currently being investigated. j indexes the current possibility being considered for the ith component of the solution. The function *violatec* used in Algorithm 4.8 returns the value **t** or **f** depending on whether the conditions attached to the solution are violated or not.

EXERCISE 4.7: Initialize *space*, *nspace*, and *n* to solve the word pattern problem. Complete the algorithm by specifying *violatec* and *write*.

Algorithm 4.8 (Framework for a class of backtracking algorithms)

```
begin /*backtracking algorithm; initialize component
          count i and index j into component space*/
    i ← 1; j ← 1;
    while (i ≤ n)
    begin /*iterate over components*/
        while (j ≤ nspace(i) ∧ violatec(space, sindex, i, j)) j ← j + 1;
        if j ≤ nspace(i) then
            begin /*set new component and advance*/
                sindex(i) ← j;
                i ← i + 1;
                j ← 1
            end /*set*/
                            else
            begin /*backtrack to previously found component and
                      try different one*/
                i ← i − 1;
                if i = 0 then terminate; /*iterate*/
                j ← sindex(i) + 1
            end /*backtrack*/
    end; /*iterate*/
    if i > n then write(space, sindex;) /*output solution x*/
            else output 'no solution found'
end /*backtracking*/
```

The Eight-Queens Problem

The game of chess has given rise to many problems which cannot be considered chess problems per se but which nevertheless rely on the characteristics of the chessboard and pieces. The eight-queens problem has not only interested amateur puzzle-solvers but was investigated by many mathematicians as well. Simply stated, the problem is to place eight queens on a chessboard so that no queen is under attack by another queen. For those unfamiliar with chess, the problem states that we have to place eight pieces on an eight-by-eight board so that no two pieces are either in the same row, in the same column, or on the same diagonal. Figure 4.6 shows two boards; one of them (b) represents a solution, while on the other the diagonal condition is violated for the queen in the rightmost column (among others) and hence it does not constitute a solution. The reader should not presume that we have given away the problem by presenting a possible solution. For a long time it was not known how many solutions existed until 92 was proven to be the proper number. The above solution is only 1 of these 92 different ones, and we challenge the reader to produce other solutions by trial and error.

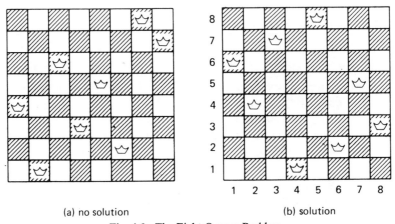

(a) no solution   (b) solution

Fig. 4.6   The Eight-Queens Problem.

Were we to solve the problem by writing an algorithm which generates all possible ways in which eight pieces may be placed on the board and check each for validity, it would take an astronomical amount of time to execute. The number of different ways, n, to select eight positions out of 64 squares is roughly 10^{10}. Before proceeding to the algorithm which finds all solutions, let us first formulate a backtracking algorithm for one solution. The first question to be answered is how to represent the solution as a tuple of components. The answer is obvious if we view the chessboard as an 8-tuple of columns. Then the solution x of Figure 4.6(b) is represented by

$$x = (6, 4, 7, 1, 8, 2, 5, 3)$$

where a component of x, $x(i)$, is the index of the queen in the ith column according to the ordering used in Figure 4.6. This immediately suggests that each component space consists of the integer 1 through 8 (the size of each component is therefore 8) and that 8 identical component spaces make up the solution space. Note that for this problem x and *sindex* are identical. Thus, if we set the following variables,

$$space \leftarrow ((1, 2, 3, 4, 5, 6, 7, 8),$$
$$(1, 2, 3, 4, 5, 6, 7, 8),$$

$$\cdot$$
$$\cdot$$
$$\cdot$$

$$(1, 2, 3, 4, 5, 6, 7, 8))$$
$$nspace \leftarrow (8, 8, 8, 8, 8, 8, 8, 8)$$
$$n \leftarrow 8$$

the Algorithm 4.8 will find a solution after we have written the function *violatec*. When this function is called we can always assume that the first $i - 1$ components of x do not violate any conditions and that therefore it is only necessary to check whether the addition of the ith component will violate the conditions. For the eight-queens problem we have to check the row, the column (this is trivially true since we iterate over the columns), and the diagonal property. We shall not pursue the brute force method for performing the check but shall consider the following refined method.

An auxiliary data structure *row_check* is introduced which is to be used for indicating those rows selected so far. Initially, all the entries in *row_check* are false, indicating that no row is covered by a queen. Before accepting an index j as the value for $x(i)$, we determine whether *row_check*(j) is **t** or **f**. If it is false, the row condition is not violated; otherwise, j is not acceptable for this component. For instance, if the second row is selected while considering the third column and *row_check*(2) is false, then no queen was yet placed in this row, which implies that this is an acceptable component at this point. The same method can be used for checking the diagonal property by observing that the sums of the coordinates (row and column index) of two queens are the same if they are on one of the diagonals going from lower left to upper right. For the diagonals running from lower right to upper left, the differences of the coordinates are the same. For instance, the queens on (4, 3) and (2, 5) are on the same diagonal since the sums of the indices in both cases equal 7. Similarly, (2, 6) and (4, 8) are on one diagonal since the differences of the coordinates are -4. Since the sums of the coordinates vary from 2 to 16, we need a *sums* mapping which maps the integers 2 through 16 into true or false and likewise a *differ* mapping of the integers -7 through 7 into true and false. However, in introducing these data structures we went beyond the framework of Algorithm 4.8 and must modify it slightly. When we backtrack we not only have to restore i and j but also have to restore the auxiliary data structures to their status at the $(i - 1)$st step.

EXERCISE 4.8: Write the function *violatec* using the notation of Algorithm 4.8 assuming that *row_check*, *sums*, and *differ* are global variables to be set in that function.

The solution so far outlined is a classical example of a backtracking situation where the values of the component space equal the component space index. In such a situation, we do not have to define explicitly the solution space but may use the index for the value. In Algorithm 4.9 this feature has been implemented; in addition, i and j have been changed to mnemonics which are more congruent with the problem at hand.

Algorithm 4.9 (Find one solution to the eight-queens problem)

Global data referenced: *sums, differ, row_check*

```
begin /*eight queens*/
    col ← 1; row ← 1;
    while (col ≤ 8)
    begin /*try to place one queen*/
        while (row ≤ 8 ∧ violatec(x, col, row)) row ← row + 1;
        if row ≤ 8 then
            begin /*place one queen*/
                x(col) ← row;
                col ← col + 1; row ← 1
            end /*place*/
                        else
            begin /*backtrack*/
                col ← col − 1;
                if col = 0 then terminate; /*try*/
                row ← x(col) + 1;
                adjust_aux_data(col, row − 1;)
            end /*backtrack*/
    end; /*try*/
    if col > 8 then output x
                else output 'no solution'
end; /*eight*/
procedure adjust_aux_data(i, j;)
begin /*restore status of auxiliary data structure*/
    row_check(j) ← f;
    sums(i + j) ← f;
    differ(i − j) ← f
end /*row*/
```

Algorithm 4.9 obtains a single solution to the eight-queens problem. One way of obtaining all solutions is to make sure that after one solution is found the algorithm continues searching for a solution from the next available alternative. This may be accomplished by beginning the next search given the partial solution $x(1), \ldots, x(n − 1)$ and setting the index j to the next alternative in the nth row of space. Algorithm 4.10 incorporates these modifications into Algorithm 4.8.

Algorithm 4.10 (Framework to obtain all solutions of certain backtracking algorithms)

> **begin** /*backtracking . . .*/
> $i \leftarrow 1; j \leftarrow 1;$
> **while** $(i \geq 1)$
> **begin** /*get one solution*/
>   **while** $(i \leq n)$
>   **begin** /*iterate . . .*/
>
>   ·
>   ·   {as before in Algorithm 4.8
>   ·
>
>   **end**; /*iterate*/
>   **if** $i > n$ **then**
>   **begin** /*output and search further*/
>   *write*(*space, sindex*;);
> $i \leftarrow n;$
> $j \leftarrow sindex(n) + 1$
>   **end** /*output*/
> **end**; /*get*/
> **output** 'no more solutions'
> **end** /*backtracking*/

The only difference between a mechanical translation of Algorithm 4.10 and the FORTRAN program below lies in the realization of the mapping *differ* since we cannot index an array with negative integers in FORTRAN.

Purpose: Print out all solutions to the eight-queens problem.
Communication:

variables referenced through COMMON block AUXDAT:	ROWCHK . . . 8-tuple of logical values; referenced and modified in RDCHEK and ADJAUX;
	SUMS . . . . . . 16-tuple as before;
	DIFFER . . . . 15-tuple as before;
subroutines or functions called:	RDCHEK . . . function returns .TRUE. if queen in Jth (second argument) row and Ith (first argument) column is in violation; modifies AUXDAT;
	ADJAUX . . . subroutine to adjust AUXDAT; same arguments as for RDCHEK.

Program:

```
C::::::::::::::::::::::::::::::::::::::::::::::::::::::::::::::::::::::::::::::::::::::::::::::::::::::::
C                   PROGRAM QUEENS(INPUT, OUTPUT)
C::::::::::::::::::::::::::::::::::::::::::::::::::::::::::::::::::::::::::::::::::::::::::::::::::::::::
      PROGRAM QUEENS(OUTPUT, TAPE6=OUTPUT)
C
C        THIS PROGRAM FINDS AND PRINTS OUT ALL
C        SOLUTIONS TO THE QUEENS PROBLEM
C
      DIMENSION X(8)
      INTEGER X, ROW, COL
      LOGICAL ROWCHK, SUMS, DIFFER, RDCHEK
      COMMON /AUXDAT/ ROWCHK(8), SUMS(16), DIFFER(15)
C
C        INITIALIZE AUXILLARY DATA STRUCTURES
C
      DO 10 I = 1, 8
           ROWCHK(I) = .FALSE.
   10 CONTINUE
      DO 20 I = 1, 15
           SUMS(I) = .FALSE.
   20 CONTINUE
      DO 30 I = 1, 15
           DIFFER(I) = .FALSE.
   30 CONTINUE
      COL = 1
      ROW = 1
C
C        OBTAIN ALL SOLUTIONS
C
   40 IF (COL .LT. 1) GO TO 100
C
C        GET ONE SOLUTION
C
   50      IF (COL .GT. 8) GO TO 90
C          TRY TO PLACE ONE QUEEN
   60           IF (ROW .GT. 8) GO TO 80
                     IF (.NOT. RDCHEK(COL, ROW)) GO TO 70
                          ROW = ROW + 1
                     GO TO 60
C          PLACE ONE QUEEN
   70                     X(COL) = ROW
                          COL = COL + 1
                          ROW = 1
                GO TO 50
C           BACK TRACK
   80                COL = COL - 1
                     IF (COL .LT. 1) GO TO 100
                          ROW = X(COL)
                          CALL ADJAUX(COL, ROW)
                          ROW = ROW + 1
                GO TO 50
```

```
C
C         END OF ONE SOLUTION
C
   90        IF (COL .LT. 1) GO TO 100
C
C         OUTPUT SOLUTION AND FORCE BACKTRACK
C
                 WRITE(6, 91)  (X(I),I = 1, 8)
C        NO OTHER SOLUTION POSSIBLE, IN COLUM 8
                 COL = COL - 1
                 ROW = X(COL)
                 CALL ADJAUX(COL, ROW)
                 ROW = ROW + 1
      GO TO 40
C
C         NO MORE SOLUTIONS
C
  100 WRITE(6, 101)
   91 FORMAT(39H THE SOLUTION TO THE QUEENS PROBLEM IS , /1H , 8I5)
  101 FORMAT(18H NO MORE SOLUTIONS )
      STOP
      END
C::::::::::::::::::::::::::::::::::::::::::::::::::::::::::::::::::::::::::::::::::::::::::::
C               FUNCTION RDCHEK(I, J)
C::::::::::::::::::::::::::::::::::::::::::::::::::::::::::::::::::::::::::::::::::::::::::::
      LOGICAL FUNCTION RDCHEK(I, J)
      LOGICAL ROWCHK, SUMS, DIFFER
      COMMON /AUXDAT/ ROWCHK(8), SUMS(16), DIFFER(15)
C
C         THIS FUNCTION CHECKS TO SEE IF THERE IS
C         ANOTHER QUEEN IN LINE IF SO RDCHEK WILL BE TRUE
C
      RDCHEK = .FALSE.
      RDCHEK = ((ROWCHK(J) .OR. SUMS(I + J)) .OR. DIFFER(I - J + 8))
      IF (RDCHEK) RETURN
C         KEEP TRACK OF SELECTION
            ROWCHK(J) = .TRUE.
            SUMS(I + J) = .TRUE.
            DIFFER(I - J + 8) = .TRUE.
      RETURN
      END
C::::::::::::::::::::::::::::::::::::::::::::::::::::::::::::::::::::::::::::::::::::::::::::
C               SUBROUTINE ADJAUX(I, J)
C::::::::::::::::::::::::::::::::::::::::::::::::::::::::::::::::::::::::::::::::::::::::::::
                 SUBROUTINE ADJAUX(I, J)
C
C         THIS ROUTINE ADJUSTS THE DATA STRUCTURES ROWCHK
C         SUM AND DIFFER TO ALLOW FOR BACKTRACKING
C
      LOGICAL ROWCHK, SUMS, DIFFER
      COMMON /AUXDAT/ ROWCHK(8), SUMS(16), DIFFER(15)
C
C         ADJUST DATA
C
      ROWCHK(J) = .FALSE.
      SUMS(I + J) = .FALSE.
      DIFFER(I - J + 8) = .FALSE.
      RETURN
      END
```

EXERCISE 4.9: Fill in the FORMAT statement labeled 91 so as to approximate the printout to the picture in Figure 4.6.

EXERCISE 4.10: Formulate the storage allocation problem as a backtracking problem, and give the necessary specifications.

4.3.3 Divide-and-Conquer

The *divide-and-conquer* method is very much in the vein of the methodology of structured programming developed in Chapter 2. While in Chapter 2 we were mainly concerned with methods for breaking a task into its constituent subtasks in order to obtain a linear flow of control, we now want to divide the problem in terms of the size of the input. This strategy is based on the observation that twice the half is not always the whole or the whole is sometimes greater than the sum of the parts. If, for instance, we can partition a problem of size n into two independent problems of size $n/2$ for which $c(n) = n^2$ for some algorithm, then solving the two smaller problems separately will yield a complexity measure of $c(n) = c(n/2) + c(n/2) = n^2/4 + n^2/4 = n^2/2$. While this is not an improvement in the order, it at least halves the complexity. However, it may be possible to apply the same procedure to each of the problems of size $n/2$ and solve four problems of size $n/4$; in this case, the measure becomes

$$c(n) = 4c\left(\frac{n}{4}\right) = \frac{4n^2}{16} = \frac{n^2}{4} \tag{21}$$

Ideally (which rarely happens), if n is a power of 2 (e.g., $n = 2^k$ for some k), we could obtain the measure (22) by repeatedly applying the procedure.

$$c_n = nc_n(1) = n \tag{22}$$

In general, it is not easy and often requires considerable effort to structure a problem in such a way that the solution to two identical problems of size $n/2$ will imply a solution to the original problem. Hence, a reduction such as shown in (22) is practically never achieved.

To be more specific, the applicability of the divide-and-conquer technique is based on the assumption that we already have an algorithm, say **A**, which will solve the problem for input x of size n. Given that the complexity of algorithm **A** is $c_A(n)$, we hope to find an algorithm **B** whose complexity $c_B(n)$ is hopefully smaller than $c_A(n)$. When applying this method the input is first divided into two (or more) equal-sized sets (assume that n is even):

$$x = (y, z) \qquad \text{with} \qquad |y| = |z| = \frac{n}{2}$$

Next, **A** is executed first with y and then with z as input; denote by $\bar{y}$ and $\bar{z}$ the output of the respective computations. In general, it is not true that these two partial solutions directly form the solution $\bar{x}$ to the original problem, and we must find an algorithm A_1 to combine the two partial solutions. Thus, algorithm **B** for computing $\bar{x} = A(x)$

can be stated as follows:

> **begin** /*B, divide and conquer for **A** on $x = (y, z)$*/
> $\bar{y} \leftarrow A(y)$;
> $\bar{z} \leftarrow A(z)$;
> $\bar{x} \leftarrow A_1(\bar{y}, \bar{z})$
> **end** /*B, divide*/

The complexity for **B** is

$$c_B(n) = c_A\left(\frac{n}{2}\right) + c_A\left(\frac{n}{2}\right) + c_{A_1}(n) \tag{23}$$

from which we can deduce two necessary conditions which ensure that c_B is smaller than c_A. First, c_A must be of at least linear order. Otherwise, it is not true that

$$c(n) > c\left(\frac{n}{2}\right) + c\left(\frac{n}{2}\right)$$

(e.g., $\sqrt{n} \not> \sqrt{n/2} + \sqrt{n/2} = \sqrt{2n} \approx 1.4\sqrt{n}$). Second, the complexity of the recombination algorithm A_1 has to be smaller than that of **A**.

Maximal Elements, Revisited

The algorithm we developed earlier for finding both the maximal and the minimal element in an n-tuple had a complexity of $2n - 3$ comparisons. Since this is of $O(n)$, we certainly cannot improve on the order of complexity by applying the divide-and-conquer principle to this algorithm, but we may be able to improve on the coefficients in the expression for the number of comparisons. According to the rules, we partition x into halves; let us assume that n is even:

$$x = (x_1, \ldots, x_n), \qquad |x| = n$$

$$y = (x_1, \ldots, x_{\frac{n}{2}}), \qquad |y| = \frac{n}{2}$$

$$z = (x_{\frac{n}{2}+1}, \ldots, x_n), \qquad |z| = \frac{n}{2}$$

Calling Algorithm 4.2 *minimax*, it is executed as follows:

$$minimax(y; y);$$
$$minimax(z; z);$$

After execution, the minimum of the first half of values will be in $x(1)$ and that of the second half in $x(n/2 + 1)$; likewise, the two maxima will be in $x(n/2)$ and $x(n)$, respectively. Clearly, this is not the final solution, and we must specify an algorithm for combining the two partial solutions into the final solution. If $x(1)$ is smaller than $x(n/2 + 1)$, then it is smaller than all elements in the second half and therefore part of the final solution. Similar considerations for the maxima lead us to the recombination algorithm A_1:

Algorithm 4.11 (Recombination for maximal elements problem)

begin /*recombination*/
     if $x(n/2 + 1) < x(1)$ **then** $[t \leftarrow x(1); x(1) \leftarrow x(n/2 + 1); x(n/2 + 1) \leftarrow t]$;
     if $x(n/2) > x(n)$ **then** $[t \leftarrow x(n); x(n) \leftarrow x(n/2); x(n/2) \leftarrow t]$
end /*recombination*/

The complexity of executing minimax twice is

$$2 * c_w\left(\frac{n}{2}\right) = 2 * \left[2\left(\frac{n}{2}\right) - 3\right]$$
$$= 2n - 6$$

Since the recombination algorithm requires two comparisons, the complexity $\bar{c}_w$ of the new algorithm is

$$\bar{c}_w(n) = 2 * c_w\left(\frac{n}{2}\right) + 2 = 2n - 4$$

which is one comparison less than before.

For all practical purposes this reduction in complexity is useless since the reduction does not affect the dependency of the complexity on n but is reflected only in the constant part of the expression. In general, such a reduction does not merit the implementation of the somewhat longer algorithm. However, by continued application of the divide-and-conquer principle we can affect the coefficient of n in the expression for the complexity. As is quite often the case for continued application of the divide-and-conquer method, the final algorithm consists mainly of invocation of the recombination algorithm.

For simplicity we shall assume that n is a power of 2; we break x into $n/2$ sets of two elements and for each of these sets place the minimum in the first and the maximum in the second position:

begin /*solve for sets of 2*/
     $i \leftarrow 1$;
     while $(i < n)$
     begin
         if $x(i) > x(i + 1)$ **then** $[t \leftarrow x(i); x(i) \leftarrow x(i + 1); x(i + 1) \leftarrow t]$;
         $i \leftarrow i + 2$
     end
end /*solve*/

The next problem is to recombine pairwise the $n/2$ subtasks of size 2 into $n/4$ partial solutions of size 4. We introduce the variables *tsize* and *tindex* to indicate the size and the position of the subtasks to be recombined and rewrite the recombination algorithm accordingly.

Example 4.9

Let x and n be

$$x = (5, 12, 3, 11, 9, 4, 16, 2)$$
$$n = 8$$

The first step results in the transformation of x into

$$x = (5, 12, 3, 11, 4, 9, 2, 16)$$

and now we wish to recombine with

$$tindex = 1$$
$$tsize = 2$$
$$x = (5, 12, \ldots)$$

and

$$x = (\text{-}, \text{-}, 3, 11, \ldots)$$

to obtain

$$x = (\circled{3}, 11, 5, \circled{12}, \ldots)$$

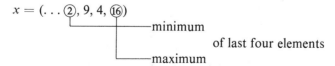

minimum

of first four elements

maximum

The next recombination occurs with:

$$tindex = 5$$
$$tsize = 2$$
$$x = (\text{-} \ldots \text{-}, 4, 9, \text{-}, \text{-})$$

and

$$x = (\text{-} \ldots \text{-}, \text{-}, \text{-}, 2, 16)$$

resulting in

$$x = (\ldots \circled{2}, 9, 4, \circled{16})$$

minimum

of last four elements

maximum

In each recombination step, the task size is doubled. The final solution is obtained when the result of the recombination algorithm is of size n. Algorithm 4.12 is the complete specification of the minimum/maximum selection algorithm formulated according to the divide-and-conquer principle.

Algorithm 4.12 (Multiple recombination of min-max problem)

```
begin /*repeatedly recombine subtasks*/
    tsize ← 2;
    while (tsize ≤ n/2)
    begin    /*combine all tasks into tasks of double size*/
        tindex ← 1;
        while (tindex < n)[combine(x, tindex, tsize; x);
                        tindex ← tindex + 2 * tsize];
        tsize ← 2 * tsize
    end /*combine*/
end; /*repeatedly*/
```

procedure *combine*$(x, i, m; x)$
begin /*combine tasks*/
   if $x(i + m) < x(i)$ **then** $[t \leftarrow x(i); x(i) \leftarrow x(i + m); x(i + m) \leftarrow t]$;
   if $x(i + m - 1) > x(i + 2 * m - 1)$ **then** $[t \leftarrow x(i + m - 1);$
$$x(i + m - 1) \leftarrow x(i + 2 * m - 1);$$
$$x(i + 2 * m - 1) \leftarrow t]$$

end /*combine*/

Example 4.9 (continued)

At the next iteration we have

$$tindex = 1$$
$$tsize = 4$$
$$x = (3, 11, 5, 12, \ldots)$$

and

$$x = (\text{-} \ldots \text{-}, 2, 9, 4, 16)$$

transformed into

$$x = (②, 11, 5, 12, 3, 9, 4, ⑯)$$

                      ——minimum of eight elements
                      ——maximum of eight elements ∎

    We leave it as an exercise to prove that the complexity of Algorithm 4.12 is given by

$$c_w(n) = 1.5n - 2$$

which indeed shows an improvement in the coefficient of n.

    EXERCISE 4.11: Prove that the complexity (in terms of number of comparisons) of Algorithm 4.12 is $1.5n - 2$. [Hint: Use induction to prove that if the relations

$$c_w(n) = 2 * c_w\left(\frac{n}{2}\right) + 2$$
$$c_w(2) = 1$$

are true, it follows that $c_w(n) = 1.5n - 2$.]

    Purpose: Place the minimal element of an n-tuple x into $x(1)$ and the maximal into $x(n)$.
    Communication:

subroutines or functions called: COMBIN . . . subroutine: array X,
                                  its dimension N, an index
                                  I, and a length M are arguments;
                                  X is modified;
formal parameters: X . . . . N-tuple of real numbers;
                                  modified;
                N . . . . size of X.

Flaws: Works only if N is a power of 2.

Program:

```
C:::::::::::::::::::::::::::::::::::::::::::::::::::::::::::::::::::::::::::::::::::::::::::::::::::::::::::::::
C                    SUBROUTINE MINMAX(X, N)
C:::::::::::::::::::::::::::::::::::::::::::::::::::::::::::::::::::::::::::::::::::::::::::::::::::::::::::::::
                     SUBROUTINE MINMAX(X, N)
C
C          THIS ROUTINE FINDS THE MINIMUM AND MAXIMUM
C          ELEMENTS OF THE ARRAY X(N)
C
       INTEGER TSIZE, TIND
       DIMENSION X(N)
C
C          SOLVE FOR SETS OF 2
C
       DO 10 I = 1, N - 1, 2
             IF (X(I) .LE. X(I + 1)) GO TO 10
                 T = X(I)
                 X(I) = X(I + 1)
                 X(I + 1) = T
   10 CONTINUE
C
C          COMBINE ALL TASKS
C
       TSIZE = 2
   20 IF (TSIZE .GT. N/2) GO TO 40
C          COMBINE TASKS INTO ONE OF DOUBLE SIZE
             DO 30 TIND = 1, N - 1, 2 * TSIZE
                 CALL COMBIN(X, N, TIND, TSIZE)
   30        CONTINUE
             TSIZE = 2 * TSIZE
       GO TO 20
   40 RETURN
       END
C:::::::::::::::::::::::::::::::::::::::::::::::::::::::::::::::::::::::::::::::::::::::::::::::::::::::::::::::
C                    SUBROUTINE COMBIN(X, N, I, M)
C:::::::::::::::::::::::::::::::::::::::::::::::::::::::::::::::::::::::::::::::::::::::::::::::::::::::::::::::
                     SUBROUTINE COMBIN(X, N, I, M)
C
C          THIS ROUTINE PLACES THE MINIMUM ELEMENT
C          IN X(1) AND THE MAXIMUM ELEMENT IN X(N)
C
       DIMENSION X(N)
C
C
       IF (X(I + M) .GE. X(I)) GO TO 10
C          REVERSE MINIMA
             T = X(I)
             X(I) = X(I + M)
             X(I + M) = T
C          REVERSE MAXIMA
   10 J1 = I + M - 1
       J2 = I + 2*M - 1
       IF (X(J1) .LE. X(J2)) GO TO 20
             T = X(J1)
             X(J1) = X(J2)
             X(J2) = T
   20 RETURN
       END
```

Integer Multiplication

Given $x = x_1x_2 \ldots x_n$ and $y = y_1y_2 \ldots y_n$, both integers, find an algorithm for computing $x * y$ (multiplication). The dominant instruction is clearly the number of multiplications of digits. The usual school-book algorithm obviously has a measure of complexity of $c_w(n) = n^2$ (the worst case occurs if all the digits are nonzero), thus satisfying the first necessary condition for application of divide-and-conquer. If the size of the input to the algorithm is the number of digits, how can we express the operation of multiplication in terms of the multiplication of two (or more) $n/2$-digit numbers? Note that it is possible to express both x and y as the sum of two $n/2$-digit numbers as shown in (24) (assume for convenience that n is even):

$$x = a * 10^{n/2} + b \qquad \text{(e.g., } 2340 = 23 * 100 + 40\text{)}$$
$$y = c * 10^{n/2} + d \qquad \text{(e.g., } 1235 = 12 * 100 + 35\text{)} \tag{24}$$

By multiplying the two expressions from (24), we obtain (25); clearly, we need three multiplications of $n/2$-digit numbers since two terms occur twice in the product:

$$x * y = ac * 10^n + (bc + ad) * 10^{n/2} + bd$$
$$= ac * 10^n + [(a + b)(c + d) - ac - bd] * 10^{n/2} + bd \tag{25}$$

{e.g., $2340 * 1235 = (23 * 12)10^4 + [(23 + 40) * (12 + 35) - 23 * 12 - 40 * 35]10^2 + 40 * 35$}. Hence, if we designate the school-book algorithm as **A**, then the statements below constitute algorithm **B**:

> **begin** /*compute product of two n-digit integers using divide and
>   conquer*/
>   /*let $x = (a, b)$, $y = (c, d)$ as in (24)*/
>   **A**$(a, c; ac)$; /*compute product of a and c using algorithm **A***/
>   **A**$(a + b, c + d; abcd)$;
>   **A**$(b, d; bd)$;
> $xy \leftarrow ac * 10^n + (abcd - ac - bd) * 10^{n/2} + bd$
> **end**

Taking into account the fact that the expressions $a + b$ and $c + d$ might actually be of length $n/2 + 1$, the bound on the measure $c_w(n)$ for algorithm **B** is (remember, for our choice of dominant instruction, additions of digits do not enter into the complexity measure)

$$_Bc_w(n) = {}_Ac_w\left(\frac{n}{2}\right) + {}_Ac_w\left(\frac{n}{2} + 1\right) + {}_Ac_w\left(\frac{n}{2}\right)$$
$$= 3{}_Ac_w\left(\frac{n}{2}\right) + n + 1$$
$$= \frac{3n^2}{4} + n + 1 \tag{26}$$

from which we conclude that for $n > 4$ algorithm **B** is superior.

If we assume that n is a power of 2, we can indeed apply the divide-and-conquer technique to the above algorithm **B**. Thus, **B** now becomes our given algorithm **A**, and the new **B**, call it $\bar{\text{B}}$, has complexity (26) obtained by replacing ${}_Ac_w(n/2)$ in (26) by

$3_A c_w(n/4) + n/2 + 1$. Hence,

$$_{\bar{B}} c_w(n) = 3\left[3_A c_w\left(\frac{n}{4}\right) + \frac{n}{2} + 1\right] + n + 1 \tag{27}$$

Continuing this process, we eventually arrive at an algorithm $\hat{\mathbf{B}}$ whose complexity is given in (28) using the fact that $_A c_w(1) = 1$:

$$_{\hat{B}} c_w(n) = 3^{\log_2 n} + n\left[\left(\frac{3}{2}\right)^{\log_2 n} + \cdots + \frac{3}{2} + 1\right] + \log_2 n$$

$$\leq 4n^{1.59} \tag{28}$$

Although algorithm $\hat{\mathbf{B}}$ has actually achieved a reduction in order over algorithm $\mathbf{A}$, it is superior to $\mathbf{A}$ only for $n > 16$ because of the coefficient. We shall not attempt at this point to describe explicitly algorithm $\hat{\mathbf{B}}$ since this is best done via techniques to be introduced in Chapter 11.

EXERCISE 4.12: Perform a cost analysis on algorithm $\mathbf{B}$ using $w_1 = 1$, $n_r = 0$, $w_2 = 0$; the interpretation for n_p should be the number of additions of digits. This analysis is quite important here because it may be that the additions we have to perform in (25) may actually cost us more than we gain through the smaller number of multiplications.

It might appear that the assumption that n is a power of 2 in the above problems is essential to the reduction in order. But as we shall see later, this is not the case at all. The only problem is that it becomes more difficult to calculate the measure. The problem of integer multiplication is of particular interest since every computer offers it as a feature, usually as part of the hardware. One reason that numbers are commonly internally represented by strings whose lengths (e.g., 8, 16, 32, . . .) are a power of 2 is that algorithms are used which work on the divide-and-conquer principle. Without going into their details we shall state only that there exist algorithms for integer multiplications whose complexity measure is of $O[n \log_2 n \log_2 (\log_2 n)]$ and that the value of C_n for this problem is not known.

Storage Allocation, Revisited

To apply the divide-and-conquer technique to the storage allocation problem, we assume the algorithms developed earlier. The files are divided into two groups of equal size which are independently solved using the original value of m as shown in Figure 4.7. If either *minind1* or *minind2* represents an optimal solution, no other steps need be performed. To find the best viable combination for all n files we must now check all possible combinations of any two elements, one from $s1$ and one from $s2$. Since both sets have in the worst case $O(2^{n/2})$ elements, this implies that the *recombination* algorithm has a complexity of $O(2^{n/2} * 2^{n/2}) = O(2^n)$, which is of the same order as the original algorithm. Thus, apparently no saving has resulted from the application of divide-and-conquer. However, if we can assume that the original induction algorithm is modified to produce the elements of s ordered on the "sum" part of each element, then the complexity of the recombination algorithm can be reduced.

EXERCISE 4.13: Make the necessary modifications to the induction algorithm such that it produces s ordered on the "sum" part. [Hint 1: Change the induction assumption to

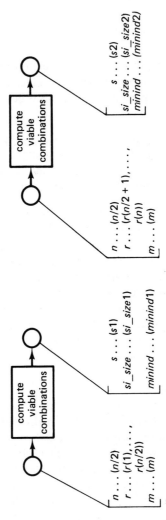

Fig. 4.7 'Divide' on storage allocation problem.

include the fact that S_i is ordered, and have the induction part produce S_{i+1} also ordered; for the initialization part, you should assume that r is already sorted. (Why?)] Take again the comparison of two sums as the unit of complexity and show that the resulting induction algorithm is still of $O(2^n)$. (Hint 2: You may need additional storage; if you cannot find a modified induction algorithm exhibiting the required complexity, look in the index under "merging.")

> *Algorithm 4.13* (Recombination algorithm of divide-and-conquer as applied to algorithm from Exercise 4.13)

```
begin /*s1 and s2 contain viable combinations of the first and
          last files respectively*/
    j ← 1; k ← si_size2; max ← 0;
          /*the current solution is represented by s1(m1) together
              with s2(m2); the size of the current solution is
              recorded in max*/
    while ( j ≤ si_size1 ∧ k ≥ 1)
    begin /*check combination s1(j) and s2(k)*/
        newsum ← s1(j, 1) + s2(k, 1);
        if newsum = m then [m1 ← j; m2 ← k; terminate];
        if newsum < m then
                begin /*possible new optimum*/
                    if newsum > max then
                            begin /*found new optimum*/
                                max ← newsum;
                                m1 ← j;
                                m2 ← k
                            end; /*found*/
                    j ← j + 1
                end /*possible*/
                    else
                        /*newsum too large*/
                    k ← k − 1
    end; /*check*/
    output (s1(m1, 1) + s2(m2, 1), s1(m1, 2) ∨ s2(m2, 2))
end /*s1 and s2*/
```

We leave it to the reader to convince herself that Algorithm 4.13 will indeed find the optimal solution if the stated assumptions are fulfilled.

The worst case for this algorithm occurs if we do not find a solution with no waste. That means that the comparison in the iteration will have been executed $si\_size1 + si\_size2$ times; since both the sizes are of $O(2^{n/2})$, the complexity of the recombination algorithm is $O(2^{n/2} + 2^{n/2})$, which is $O(2^{n/2})$. From Exercise 4.13 we know that there exists an algorithm for producing an ordered set of viable combinations of n files in $O(2^n)$; hence, the complexity of the new algorithm is given by

$$c_w(n) = c_A\left(\frac{n}{2}\right) + c_A\left(\frac{n}{2}\right) + c_{A_1}(n)$$
$$= 0(2^{n/2}) + 0(2^{n/2}) + 0(2^{n/2})$$
$$= 0(2^{n/2})$$

where A is the modified algorithm from Exercise 4.13 and A_1 is the recombination algorithm 4.13. This is clearly an improvement over the original algorithm A. Interestingly enough, no one knows how to repeatedly apply the divide-and-conquer principle to this problem or even if it is possible at all. The main problem is that the recombination of more than two subproblems costs more than is gained by partitioning.

EXERCISE 4.14: Given $n = 6$, $r = (2, 5, 8, 10, 11, 14)$, and $m = 28$, find the optimal solution using both algorithms, and compare their performances on this particular input.

4.4 CONCLUSIONS

In contrast to the first three chapters where we established the basic methodology of problem solution, the emphasis of this chapter has been on providing some answers to the question of how to select the "best" algorithms for a class of problems. The necessary background tools for this task are order and cost analysis, which provide a framework for analyzing and measuring the performance of algorithms. One of the lessons to be learned from order analysis is that whenever we realize an algorithm in a programming language we should concentrate our efforts of optimization on those sections of the algorithm which contribute to the complexity measure in the order analysis; these are usually the tight innermost iteration structures. Second, we use cost analysis to select algorithms only when several solutions exist whose orders of complexity are in the optimal range.

However, there are circumstances under which an algorithm with a higher order of complexity might be chosen over one with a lower order. A cost analysis might indicate that the algorithm with lower complexity is better only for unreasonably large values of n. It may also be the case that the algorithm of lower order, when translated into a program, exhibits undesirable side effects. In Chapters 6 and 7, the nature of some of these side effects (e.g., errors in computed values) will be examined.

In addition, several general techniques were developed to aid in finding solutions to certain classes of problems. In later chapters, additional techniques (e.g., recursion, heuristic search) are developed after the groundwork has been laid for understanding their underlying processes.

References

For a discussion of complexity measures much deeper and more exhaustive than that presented here (and for more examples), see

D. E. Knuth, *The Art of Computer Programming*, Vol. II., Addison-Wesley, Reading, Mass., 1974.

An excellent book on algorithms is

A. Aho, J. E. Hopcroft, and J. D. Ullman, *Theory of Algorithms*, Addison-Wesley, Reading, Mass., 1974.

Here references may be found to the original work of researchers in this area, including V. Strassen and A. Schönhage for their work on multiplication of numbers, S. Winograd and V. Strassen on multiplication of matrices, T. S. Motzkin and V. Pan on polynomial evaluation with preprocessing, A. Borodin and V. Pan on optimality proofs, and S. Sahni on storage allocation.

Exercises

1 The public relations manager of a football team wishes to enhance his team's public image without altering the team's performance record. She has available an ordered list of the results of all games played by the team as well as their dates. The idea is to determine how far to go back in the record such that the won/lost record is best among all possible periods terminating at the current date. For the football team dearest to you, develop a program to find the won/lost record best for its public image. Make the minimum number of games involved an input parameter.

2 See if you can apply the induction technique to the problem of sorting; see Chapter 2. Complete the assignment from problem statement to final working FORTRAN program and analyze its performance.

3 Repeat Exercise 2 using the divide-and-conquer technique instead of induction. (Hint: One solution involves a procedure which merges two sorted sequences.)

4 Formulate the word pattern problem, see (18) and (19) in Section 4.3.2, defined by:

prefix	root	suffix
PRE	SERVE	ED
CON	SIGN	IVE
CO	POSE	S
DE	DUCT	ING
PER		

as a backtracking problem. Initialize *space*, *nspace*, and *n* and specify *violatec* and *write*.

5 Instant insanity: If you wish a taste of it, try the following problem. A set of four cubes is given; the faces of the cubes are colored as shown. The object is to form one row of cubes such that no two faces in a row of faces are the same color. Furthermore, this condition must hold for all rows. Write a backtracking algorithm to solve the instant insanity problem. How many solutions are there?

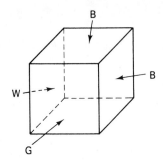

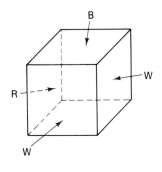

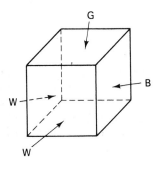

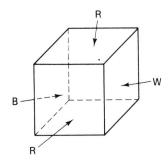

Colors: Red: R
       Blue: B   All rear faces are green.
       White: W   All bottom faces are red.
       Green: G   Other faces are colored as shown.

5

Analysis of Algorithms:
Searching and Sorting

5.0 INTRODUCTION

In this chapter we shall study the classes of algorithms concerned with the maintenance of data bases and the retrieval of information from these data bases. For the purposes of this chapter a *data base* is simply a collection of records, often called a *file*, in which each *record* might consist of a simple number (e.g., a student's score on an examination) or a reasonably complex set of information similar to that which a credit company might record for each of its customers. The emphasis will be on the development and analysis of algorithms for retrieving specific records from the data base and algorithms for structuring the data base; this structure will in turn reduce the complexity of searching algorithms. The data structures involved in the representation of a data base are discussed in more detail in Chapter 9.

Although the problem domain is rather narrow, it is one which has been extensively studied because of its importance to data processing. The class of algorithms is a particularly rich one, and, as we shall see, the goal of finding an optimal solution is overly optimistic in this case. The best we can do is illustrate conditions under which the given algorithm is better (or worse) than other algorithms designed to solve the same class of problems. It remains the responsibility of the person who wishes to make use of the algorithms to decide, given some a priori knowledge of the problem domain, which of the algorithms best suits his current needs, using the techniques of cost analysis as postulated in the previous chapter. To gain some insight into the nature of the operations in this problem domain, let us examine a data base as it might be maintained by the Friendly Finance Company (FFC), a private lending institution. This company might keep the following information on customers to whom it has lent money:

1. Customer identification number
2. Name [last name, first name, middle initial (if any)]
3. Total amount of loan

4. Outstanding portion of loan
5. Payment record; number of months in arrears
6. Extra information (address, credit rating, etc.)

A typical FFC record might then be as shown in Figure 5.1. The list of all FFC's customer records constitutes a data base upon which FFC must perform operations. In

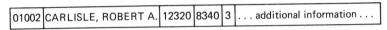

| 01002 | CARLISLE, ROBERT A. | 12320 | 8340 | 3 | . . . additional information . . . |

Fig. 5.1   A typical FFC record.

the normal course of business activities, FFC may wish to perform operations such as

I. Produce an alphabetical list of customers;
II. Produce a list of deadbeats and print their records in decreasing order of months in arrears;
III. Find the record of Carlisle, Robert A.;
IV. Insert the record of a new customer into an alphabetic list of customers;
V. Produce a list in decreasing order of amount of outstanding loan.

The list is not meant to be all-inclusive but rather illustrates some of the processes to be discussed later.

The information item used in these operations to identify a record is called the *key*; thus, operation III represents the problem of locating a record whose key matches the given key (the name Carlisle, Robert A.). In operation V we wish to rearrange the records of customers in such a way that the values of the keys (item 4 of the record) decrease as we print the list. It should be apparent from these examples that the item selected as the key depends on the operation to be performed. Any information item can be considered a key in certain contexts; furthermore, several keys may be employed:

> Produce a list of customers in Chicago whose payments are three or more months in arrears. Print the list in descending value of outstanding portion of loan.

In this example, a complex search key has been defined based on city and number of months in arrears. The key defining the order of the desired list (size of outstanding portion of the loan) is different from either of the search keys.

More formally, let X be a collection of n records. X_i may represent a single quantity as in the case of a student's grade, or it may represent an aggregate of information as in the case of FFC records. That portion of the record which is currently the key will be denoted by k_i.

Let us now return to the main purpose of this chapter, that is, the examination of the classes of algorithms for performing the operations which have been implicitly defined above. In the discussion that follows, we shall use the comparison of keys as the dominant instruction. Whenever a cost analysis of a particular algorithm is presented, c_m and c_p will be assumed to be zero for simplicity's sake; c_r will, however, be split into two constants c_a and c_k. The first, c_a, represents the cost of moving an array element [i.e., $t \leftarrow x(i)$], while the latter, c_k, represents the cost of comparing two keys [i.e., $k(i) < k(j)$].

The reason for differentiating between these two costs is because they are particularly relevant to the class of algorithms under consideration. The movement of records in the data base and the comparison of keys may be complex algorithms in themselves. Records might be quite long and their movement quite costly. Key comparisons may entail manipulation of long character strings.

5.1 SEARCHING

The searching problem may be rather simply stated: Given a collection of records and a key for one of those records, locate (and retrieve) that record whose key matches the given one. Formally, given a collection X and a key k', locate that X_i for which $k_i = k'$, or give an indication that the record is not in the collection if it cannot be located. We assume here, and in the remainder of this chapter, that each k_i is unique. The class of algorithms $\mathcal{C}$ we wish to consider are those which locate a record by comparing keys; algorithms utilizing other methods are discussed in Chapter 9.

In principle, the domain of inputs, $\mathfrak{D}$, contains all possible collections of n records. Note that for the searching problem the only germane part of the record is the key. Therefore, we set $\mathfrak{D}$ to all possible n-tuples of keys together with the search key. Once a key has been located and its position in the n-tuple determined, the associated record may be recovered from the data base.

Algorithm 5.1 is a restatement of an earlier solution (Algorithm $\mathbf{A}_2$ in Example 4.1) to the search problem; the notation has been modified to conform to the current problem description.

Algorithm 5.1 (Search for a given record)

Global data referenced: n, k (an n-tuple of keys), and k' (the given key)

```
begin /*search*/
    i ← n;
    k(0) ← k';
    while (k(i) ≠ k') i ← i − 1;
    output i
end /*search*/
```

EXERCISE 5.1: Let k be an n-tuple of randomly selected unique integer-valued keys.

1. Write a FORTRAN program for generating such a k.
2. Implement Algorithm 5.1 in FORTRAN. Select several keys within the range of values in the tuple k. For $n = 100$, measure the central processor time required to find the value of i for the selected keys (translate the **while** construct as suggested in Section A.9 of the supplementary volume).

3. Repeat the process for algorithm A_1 from Example 4.1 using the FORTRAN "DO" statement and compare the processor times obtained to verify the results of the cost analysis from Chapter 4.

We have already shown that for these search algorithms

$$c_w(n) = O(n) \tag{1}$$

and it is quite obvious that C_n is the same since in order to determine that a record with a particular key is not in the collection we have to check all n keys.

The problem of finding a person's telephone number is certainly one which can be solved by an algorithm similar to 5.1. An interesting problem is the following: If the order of complexity is n, how is anyone able to find any number in a collection of, say, 100,000 such numbers. The answer to this question is quite simple: Someone has preprocessed the input and transformed it into a form which lowers the complexity of the searching algorithm. In the case of a telephone book, application of the pre-processing technique (here, alphabetization; for general techniques, see Section C.4 of the supplementary volume) is certainly merited, and its cost can be neglected when the complexity of the searching algorithm is computed. In fact, for most data base applications the cost of preprocessing can be ignored. Since the records in a telephone book are arranged in lexicographical order, let us modify $\mathfrak{D}$ to include only sorted n-tuples of keys (together with the search) and analyze the effect of this modification on the searching algorithm.

Binary Search

Consider the problem of looking up a word in a dictionary, assuming it is of the type which does not have thumb indices for the letters of the alphabet. We observe the obvious: Dictionaries have entries arranged in alphabetic order. The procedure many people use, either consciously or unconsciously, to locate a given word (the key) can be loosely described as follows (c.f. Procedure 1.3):

> Open the dictionary at the page which you estimate contains the word; if the word is on the page you are done. Otherwise, determine whether the word falls before the page or after the page you are looking at. If it falls before (after) replace the dictionary by all the pages preceding (succeeding) the page you are on and repeat the process. Eventually, you will find the page containing the sought for word.

The generalization of this method is known as *binary search*. Informally, the binary search method proceeds by deciding (on the basis of a key comparison) at each step whether the record is in the lower or upper portion of the collection of records; the portion of the collection not containing the record is discarded, and the process repeats on the portion retained. The binary search method assumes that the collection of records is sorted and clearly will not work if it is not. Figure 5.2 graphically illustrates the decisions made during binary search for k' (the key being sought). In Figure 5.2, the subscript on k represents the upper boundary of the portion of the collection

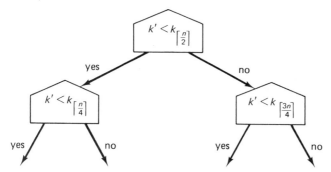

Fig. 5.2   Decision procedure for searching a sorted collection of records.

which must be searched after the decision has been made. Performing the comparison step $\lfloor \log_2 n \rfloor + 1$ times will leave only one entry remaining, which must be the desired record if it is in the table at all. The number of comparisons required, $\lfloor \log_2 n \rfloor + 1$, may most easily be derived for the case in which $n = 2^j$ for some j. After the ith comparison has been made, the size of the candidate area in which the record may occur has been reduced to at most $(n/2^i) + 1$; furthermore, after the jth comparison, the size has been reduced to at most $(n/2^j) + 1$, which evaluates to 2. Hence, only $j + 1$ comparisons, $j = \log_2 n$, must be made. For any other n, we note that

$$2^{j-1} < n < 2^j$$

for some j. We know that

$$\log_2 n = j - 1 + \alpha$$

for some $\alpha < 1$; hence, the number of comparisons required is

$$\lfloor \log_2 n \rfloor + 1$$

From this we conclude that both $c_w(n)$ and $c_e(n)$ have the value $\lfloor \log_2 n \rfloor + 1$ since the number of comparisons depends only on n and not the particular values of the keys.

Without proving it, we state a key result: For any search algorithm **A** based on comparison of keys,

$$C_n = c(n) = O(\log_2 n)$$

This result states that at least $O(\log_2 n)$ comparisons of keys are required (for some inputs) to search a sorted collection for a particular record, regardless of the search algorithm employed.

We turn now to the implementation of the binary search algorithm in AL. The algorithm makes use of, but is not dependent on, the fact that in AL it costs no more to determine which of the three relations "smaller than," "equal to," or "greater than" is satisfied than it does to determine whether "less than or equal to" is satisfied. That is, at each midpoint in the collection we shall not only ask in what portion the key may be but also whether the key is at the midpoint. Therefore, as long as we have a viable region, i.e., the upper bound is not smaller than the lower bound, we keep checking the middle record of the region.

Algorithm 5.2 (Binary search)

```
procedure binsearch(n, k, key; location)
begin /*search n-tuple k for location of the key key
          and point to this location (0 if not found)*/
    low ← 1; high ← n; location ← 0;
    while (low ≤ high)
    begin /*check middle key of region [low, high]*/
        mid ← ⌊(high + low)⌋/2;
        case compare(key, k(mid)) of
                lt:  high ← mid − 1;
                eq:  [location ← mid; terminate];
                gt:  low ← mid + 1
        end /*compare*/
    end /*check*/
end /*search*/
```

Example 5.1

Let k be the 9-tuple (2, 6, 7, 10, 12, 15, 17, 25, 26) and assume *key* has the value 15; then a trace of Algorithm 5.2 will produce the following table:

key	low	high	mid	output
15	1	9	5	
	6		7	
		7	6	6

Under the same assumptions, if *key* has the value 8, we shall obtain

key	low	high	mid	output
8	1	9	5	
		4	2	
	3		3	
	4		4	
		3	0	■

It should be clear that introducing the three-way comparison does not improve the worst-case complexity [$c_w(n)$ is still $O(\log_2 n)$], but the expected complexity of a successful search is now roughly

$$\lfloor \log_2 n \rfloor - 1$$

The reason for this reduction is that the location of the key may be found after only one comparison; i.e., the location may be found while the size of the candidate area is larger than 1.

The FORTRAN program below implements the original search procedure based on a two-way branch; namely, "Is the key in the lower or upper portion?"

Purpose: Locate the integer key KEY in a sorted table K of N integer keys.
Communication:

subroutines or functions called: None.
formal parameters: K ..... sorted N-tuple of integer keys;
                                                      N ..... size of K;
                                                      KEY ... integer key to be searched for in K; loca-
                                                               tion of the key is returned as the value of
                                                               the function.

Flaws: No provisions are made for the key not being present.
Program:

```
C::::::::::::::::::::::::::::::::::::::::::::::::::::::::::::::::::::::::::::::::::::::::::::::::::::::::::::::::::::
C                         FUNCTION SEARCH (K,N,KEY)
C::::::::::::::::::::::::::::::::::::::::::::::::::::::::::::::::::::::::::::::::::::::::::::::::::::::::::::::::::::
           INTEGER FUNCTION SEARCH (K,N,KEY)
C               THIS FUNCTION LOCATES THE INTEGER KEY IN THE ARRAY K(N)
           INTEGER K(N), HIGH
C               INITIALIZE BOUNDARIES OF CANIDATE AREA
           HIGH = N
           LOW = 1
C               TEST FOR END OF SEARCH
       10 IF (HIGH.LE.LOW+1) GO TO 30
                 I= (HIGH+LOW)/2
                 IF (KEY.LT.K(I)) GO TO 20
C          RESET BOUNDARIES TO UPPER HALF
                     LOW=I
           GO TO 10
C          RESET BOUNDARIES TO LOWER HALF
       20              HIGH=I-1
           GO TO 10
C          LOW (OR HIGH) ELEMENT IS ONLY ONE REMAINING
       30 SEARCH=LOW
           IF (KEY.NE.K(LOW)) SEARCH=HIGH
           RETURN
           END
```

EXERCISE 5.2: Rewrite the above program to alleviate the known flaw.

5.2 SORTING

Sorting can be viewed as a task per se or perhaps even more importantly as a task which, when applied to a collection of records, makes it possible to retrieve information from a large file in a reasonable time. As we shall see, there is a variety of algorithms for sorting n keys, but all can be roughly partitioned into two groups: one group with a complexity of $O(n \log_2 n)$ (called fast sorting algorithms) and one group with a complexity of $O(n^2)$. Only an exhaustive cost analysis will show which algorithm is best suited for a given environment. Due to the nature of the problem we shall encounter cases where cost analysis shows that a slow sorting algorithm is actually better than a fast one.

First, let us abstract a problem definition from the application-oriented sorting problems of the previous section. The domain of inputs, $\mathfrak{D}$, is the set of all n-tuples

$$K = (k_1, k_2, \ldots, k_n)$$

of keys which might be numbers, strings, etc., and an ordering relation. The ordering relation, denoted by "$<$", defines the meaning of $k_i < k_j$. For integer-valued keys, $<$ may represent the usual numeric ordering; for alphabetic keys, $<$ may represent the standard lexicographical order, although in some cases the order relation may be considerably more complex. Using this notation the sorting problem is reduced to one of finding a *permutation*, $i_1, i_2, \ldots, i_n$, of the indices such that the n-tuple

$$K' = (k_{i_1}, k_{i_2}, \ldots, k_{i_n})$$

satisfies the property

$$k_{i_1} < k_{i_2} < \cdots < k_{i_n}$$

assuming no two keys are equal. Throughout this section we shall make the assumption that a file does not contain equal keys because the loss of generality is minor.

Example 5.2

Let K be the 5-tuple

$$(k_1 = \text{PIG}, k_2 = \text{DOG}, k_3 = \text{DUCK}, k_4 = \text{COW}, k_5 = \text{STEER})$$

for which the ordering relation is the standard lexicographical order. Then the permutation of the indices (4, 2, 3, 1, 5), that is,

$$K' = (k_4, k_2, k_3, k_1, k_5)$$

satisfies the property that

$$\text{COW} < \text{DOG} < \text{DUCK} < \text{PIG} < \text{STEER} \quad \blacksquare$$

Again only those algorithms which find the permutation by comparing individual keys are considered.

After a mathematical model for the problem has been established, the next step is to derive values or bounds for the complexity of the optimal algorithm. As before, let $T(\mathbf{A}, x)$ be the number of comparisons executed by algorithm $\mathbf{A}$ on input x (the n-tuple K); then one can show that for

$$C_n = \min_{\mathbf{A} \in \mathfrak{a}} c_w(n)$$

we can obtain the lower bound

$$C_n \geq n \log_2 n - 1.443n \tag{2}$$

The bound (2) is often called the $n \log n$ rule; it implies that any sorting algorithm based on comparison of keys will require at least $n \log_2 n$ comparisons for some input K. An expanded discussion of this rule may be found in Section 5.4.2 of Part C in the supplementary volume.

For the derivation of an optimal complexity value one generally assumes a somewhat simplified model in which the records are neglected. For practical purposes, however, they do have to be handled in any final algorithm. Principally, there are two situations; in the first, it is not necessary to physically rearrange the records but only to determine in what order they should be accessed. In the second case, we wish to physically rearrange the records in such a way that their keys are ordered; usually, there is the restraint that we cannot use temporary storage to create a new ordered file. To appreciate the problem we should realize that a record might take anywhere from ten to hundreds of computer words to store, whereas the key is usually not longer than a few computer words. Thus, we may be able to use an additional n locations for the purpose of rearranging the keys only, but we may not have enough space to create a whole new file while maintaining the old file in memory.

The first problem is solved by using a temporary n-tuple T for storing the indices of records. Initially, T_i is set equal to i, and whenever an exchange $k_i \leftarrow k_j$ is executed by the sorting algorithm, the corresponding values of T, $T_i \leftrightarrow T_j$, are exchanged. After K has been sorted, T_1 will be the index of the record with the smallest key, T_2 the index of the record with the next smallest key, etc.

Example 5.3

Let K, R, and T be the following 4-tuple:

K	R	T
5	JOHN DOE; 25; M; 6000	1
2	MARY DOE; 18; F; 8000	2
8	ALLAN SMITH; 48; M; 18000	3
3	JANE SMITH; 36; F; 28000	4

After we have sorted K we obtain:

K	T
2	2
3	4
5	1
8	3

Iterating over T, we reference first Mary's record $R(T(1))$; next Jane's, $R(T(2))$; then John's, $R(T(3))$; and finally Allan's, $R(T(4))$. ■

If it is the case that we wish to physically rearrange the keys and the associated data in the file, we can achieve this reordering by creating a new n-tuple R'; records are copied from R to R' according to the indices stored in T. R is then set equal to R', resulting in a sorted version of R. Unfortunately, this algorithm requires a temporary storage as large as the file being sorted. If this is not possible, an algorithm is needed which will rearrange the records in R *in place;* such an algorithm is discussed in Section 5.4.3 of Part C in the supplementary volume.

Thus, in the discussion of the sorting problem to follow, we may safely neglect the actual location of the records and concentrate only on the keys. Then the statement of the actual sorting problem may be reformulated as follows: Given an unsorted n-tuple K of keys and an ordering relation, modify K so that consecutive elements satisfy the ordering relation. Of all the techniques developed in Chapter 4, induction and the divide-and-conquer method will prove the most applicable to the sorting problem.

Induction leads us to the following observations. One element is sorted, which certainly is true. Assume j elements are sorted; then it remains to ensure that $j + 1$ elements of the tuple are sorted. As depicted in Figure 5.3, this idea leads to the *straight*

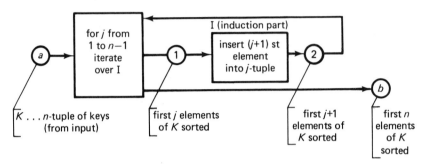

Fig. 5.3   Outline of insertion sorts.

and *binary insertion sorts*. *Backward* induction leads to the sorting method shown in Figure 5.4. The initial hypothesis is that n elements are unsorted, and the inductive step consists of asking, If j elements are unsorted, how can we make $j - 1$ elements unsorted?

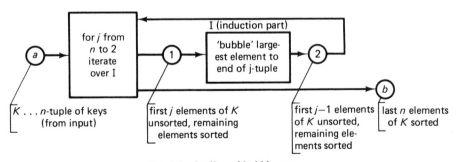

Fig. 5.4   Outline of bubble sorts.

As we shall see, all the basic sorting procedures derived from these ideas will be slow $[O(n^2)]$ sorts, but by refining the techniques fast $[O(n \log_2 n)]$ sorts may be obtained. In contrast, the divide-and-conquer method leads immediately to a fast sort due to the fact that we can keep dividing until the tuple considered is of length 1 and the complexity of the recombination algorithm is linear.

Insertion Sorts

From Figure 5.3 we deduce that insertion sorts are based on the principle of inserting an element into a progressively larger sorted list. The insertion sort to be discussed first is normally used as an *internal* sort for relatively small values of n. A sort is called internal if no storage other than main memory is used. For the sake of discussion, let us assume throughout this chapter that we wish to sort a given list of keys into ascending order and, furthermore, that $<$ denotes the proper comparison operator. Note that for the refinement of module I in Figure 5.3, one solution is to compare the $(j + 1)$st element to $k_j, k_{j-1} \ldots$ until a key is found which is smaller. If we shift the keys larger than k_{j+1} one to the right during this process, all that is left to do is to insert the (hopefully saved) key at the location of the element last shifted. However, this is not the only reason the sorted j-tuple is searched from the jth element toward the first element. If it turns out that the $(j + 1)$-tuple is already sorted, then the number of comparisons executed is minimized using this order.

In the search Algorithm A_2 of Example 4.1, the concept of a fence was introduced for the first time. A *fence* is a properly selected element, added at either or both ends of a list to ensure that the search terminates. Since the induction part of the insertion sort is essentially a search, Algorithm 5.3 for the insertion sort includes the concept of a fence.

Algorithm 5.3 (Induction part of insertion sort)

Global data referenced: K

```
begin /*insert (j + 1)st element; assume that K(0) is −∞ (the fence);
          j is the induction variable*/
      safe ← K(j + 1); i ← j;
      while (safe < K(i)) [K(i + 1) ← K(i); i ← i − 1]; /*find proper place*/
      K(i + 1) ← safe;
      j ← j + 1
end /*insert*/
```

Example 5.4

Let $n = 4$ and $K = (28, 13, 45, 5)$; then repeated execution of Algorithm 5.3 will produce the following trace table:

K	j	$safe$	i	Comments
$-\infty$, 28, 13, 45, 5	1	13	1	
$-\infty$, 28, 28, 45, 5			0	Proper index for *safe* is 1
$-\infty$, 13, 28, 45, 5	2	45	2	Proper index for *safe* is 3
$-\infty$, 13, 28, 45, 5	3	5	3	
$-\infty$, 13, 28, 45, 45			2	
$-\infty$, 13, 28, 28, 45			1	
$-\infty$, 13, 13, 28, 45			0	Proper index for *safe* is 1
$-\infty$, 5, 13, 28, 45				

Analysis of this algorithm shows that the iteration to find the proper place for k_{j+1} takes in the worst case $j + 1$ comparisons which occur if k_{j+1} is smaller than $k_j, \ldots, k_1$. Since this innermost iteration is executed for j with values from 1 to $n - 1$, it follows that

$$c_w(n) = \sum_{j=1}^{n-1} (j + 1) = \frac{n^2}{2} + O(n) \tag{3}$$

Without proof we note that the average behavior of Algorithm 5.3 is given by

$$c_e(n) = \frac{n^2}{4} + O(n) \tag{4}$$

To provide the flavor of a cost analysis we shall, as indicated earlier, use

$$T(\mathbf{A}, x) = w_1(n_a c_a + n_k c_k) + w_2 n_s$$

where c_a is the cost of moving a key ($k_i \leftarrow k_j$) and c_k is the cost of comparing two keys. In the worst case, j keys are moved during each search iteration, and therefore,

$$n_a = \sum_{j=1}^{n-1} (j + 2) = \frac{n^2}{2} + O(n)$$

n_k is given by (3), and thus, we obtain

$$c_w(n) = w_1 \left(c_a \left(\frac{n^2}{2} + O(n) \right) + c_k \left(\frac{n^2}{2} + O(n) \right) \right) + w_2(n + 2) \tag{5}$$

It should be apparent from this discussion that the straight insertion sort is far from optional for large n; furthermore, the algorithm requires keys to be moved quite a number of times. If, instead of using the sequential search algorithm to locate the position of the $(j + 1)$ st key, a binary search were used, the value of (3) would prove to be optimal, but a cost analysis (5) would show that n_a is still of $O(n^2)$.

EXERCISE 5.3: Provide the complete algorithm for the binary insertion sort [i.e., to locate the proper index for the $(j + 1)$st element, use the binary search algorithm] and find its complexity according to order analysis.

Nevertheless, the insertion sort does have advantages and many uses. We note that Algorithm 5.3 will need only $n - 1$ comparisons to find out whether a list is already sorted, which is not a feature of most fast sorting algorithms. Also, the number of comparisons decreases drastically from (3) in relation to the *sortedness* of the list; i.e., the closer the list is to being sorted, the fewer comparisons are needed. Another advantage is its utter simplicity; very little overhead is involved, which is particularly beneficial when n is small ($n < 20$).

To obtain the effect of a 0th element of an array in FORTRAN we have to resort to a special requirement noted in the communications section of the FORTRAN program below.

Purpose: Sort the list KEY of N elements.
Communication:

subroutines or functions called: None.

formal parameters: KEY ... N-tuple of integer keys;
                                                                    modified such that KEY will
                                                                      be sorted;
                                N ..... size of KEY.

special provisions: To ensure proper referencing we require the following statements in the calling program (let K be the name of the list of keys and n its actual dimension):

                  DIMENSION $K(n)$, $KO(n + 1)$
                  EQUIVALENCE $(KO(2), K(1))$
                  DATA $KO(1)/-999999/$

     Program:

```
C:::::::::::::::::::::::::::::::::::::::::::::::::::::::::::::::::::::::::::::::::::::::::::::::::::::::::::::::::::
C                 SUBROUTINE INSORT (KEY,N)
C:::::::::::::::::::::::::::::::::::::::::::::::::::::::::::::::::::::::::::::::::::::::::::::::::::::::::::::::::::
                  SUBROUTINE INSORT (KEY,N)
C           THIS ROUTINE SORTS THE LIST KEY OF N ELEMENTS
            DIMENSION KEY(N)
            INTEGER SAFE
C
C           BEGIN SORT
C
            LIM=N-1
            DO 10 J=1, LIM
                  SAFE=KEY(J+1)
                  I=J
C           TEST FOR END OF SEARCH ITERATION
      20          IF (SAFE.GT.KEY(I)) GO TO 30
                        KEY(I + 1) = KEY(I)
                        I=I-1
                  GO TO 20
      30          KEY (I+1)=SAFE
      10 CONTINUE
            RETURN
            END
```

EXERCISE 5.4: Add statements to INSORT so that you can compute n_a and n_k in (5) and compare your results for various test runs with (3), (4), and (5).

Bubble Sorts

The bubble sort is based on the premise that if we make repetitive sweeps through the table of keys, interchanging elements whenever a comparison fails, eventually the table will be in sorted order. The simplest sort of this type performs $n - 1$ sweeps, each time bubbling the currently largest element to its proper place. A simple refinement of module I of Figure 5.4 leads to the following algorithm:

Algorithm 5.4 (Refinement of module I for bubble sort)

Global data referenced: K

    begin /*first j elements of K unsorted*/
        $i \leftarrow 1$;

while $(i < j)$
begin /*check if two consecutive elements out of order*/
    if $K(i + 1) < K(i)$ **then** $[t \leftarrow K(i); K(i) \leftarrow K(i + 1); K(i + 1) \leftarrow t]$;
    $i \leftarrow i + 1$
end /*check*/
end /*first; $j - 1$ elements of K unsorted*/

EXERCISE 5.5: Write a FORTRAN subroutine which implements the bubble sort. Using the data generated in Exercise 5.1, validate the theoretical cost values derived below. What effect (if any) does a partial ordering of the list have on the performance of the program?

For each execution of module I the comparison will be executed $j - 1$ times independent of the values of the keys; hence, both the worst-case and average complexity measures are

$$c(n) = \sum_{j=2}^{n} (j - 1)$$

$$= \sum_{j=1}^{n-1} j = \frac{n^2}{2} + O(n) \tag{6}$$

which is slightly worse than the straight insertion sort. The difference is even more accentuated in terms of cost analysis since in Algorithm 5.4 elements are swapped whenever a comparison fails:

$$c_w(n) = w_1\left(c_a\frac{3n^2}{2} + c_k\frac{n^2}{2}\right) + w_2(n + 1)$$

$$c_e(n) = w_1\left(c_a\frac{3n^2}{4} + c_k\frac{n^2}{2}\right) + w_2(n + 1) \tag{7}$$

Certain obvious improvements may be made to the bubble sort. For example, a pointer may be kept whose value is the position of the last interchange of elements during the current pass. On the next pass, there is no reason to check elements past the value of the pointer, since they are known to be in sorted order already. Furthermore, the algorithm should terminate when a pass is made which does not require any interchanges, since then the elements are in order. While these improvements reduce the number of comparisons that must be made, they do not reduce the number of interchanges that are required. But we reiterate here a point made earlier that we should not try to optimize an algorithm if it does not lead to a reduction in the order of complexity. A detailed cost analysis will show that for most computers the additional overhead (i.e., pointers, flags which must be changed every time we compare, etc.) will, on the average, actually increase the complexity.

EXERCISE 5.6: Modify the program from Exercise 5.5 to include these improvements. On the average, is the performance of the bubble sort better than, worse than, or about the same as the insertion sort or the simple bubble sort for lists of various sizes? What about lists which are partially ordered?

In keeping with our philosophy, rather than discuss all kinds of tricks to locally improve the bubble sort, we shall strive to obtain a reduction in order by applying the divide-and-conquer technique.

The variation of the bubble sort to be described is known as the *quicksort*, first proposed by C. A. R. Hoare. The theme is not to bubble the largest element in a tuple to the right but to bubble k_1 into its final position, m, such that all elements to its left are smaller than the new k_m and all elements to the right of m are larger than k_m. Assuming such a procedure has been found (call it *final-pos*), the divide-and-conquer technique may be applied by partitioning at m rather than the usual $n/2$. In this case, the recombination part of the divide-and-conquer algorithm is trivial because once the left part and the right part are sorted the entire tuple is sorted. Instead of using a known algorithm for sorting these parts, the same process is applied to each of them. That is, after we have executed *final-pos* on the original n-tuple, we save the right tuple $(k_{m+1}, \ldots, k_n)$ for later processing. The left tuple $(k_1, \ldots, k_{m-1})$ becomes the new input to which *final-pos* is applied. Whenever an input tuple is of size 1, no sorting is necessary, and the tuple last saved is restored and processed in the same way.

Example 5.5

Let K be a 16-tuple; a subproblem is saved for later processing by recording in the consecutive elements of a tuple a pair of pointers which delineate the tuple yet to be processed. In the figure below, a straight line represents a tuple to which we apply *final-pos* with its result circled (an element is also circled if the subproblem it represents is of size 1).

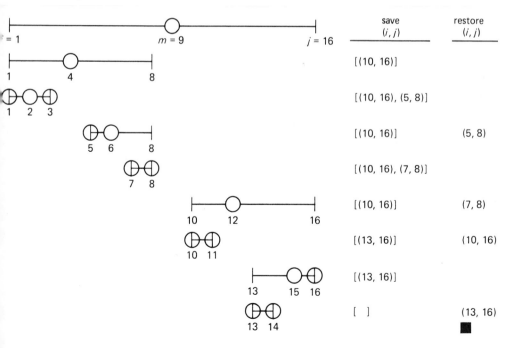

Since this problem is somewhat complicated we proceed via modular refinement. Figure 5.5 details the first level of abstraction, while Figure 5.6 is a refinement of module I of Figure 5.5.

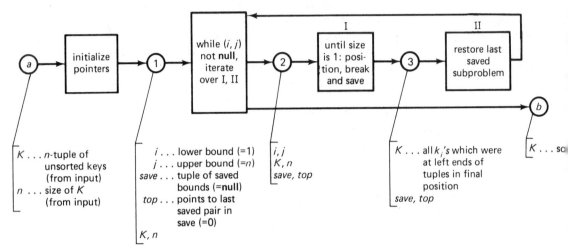

Fig. 5.5   First level of refinements for quicksort.

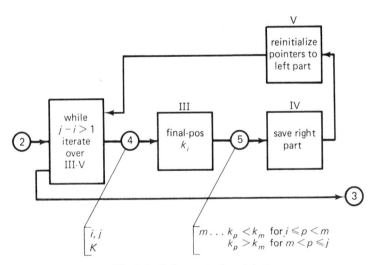

Fig. 5.6   Refinement of module I.

All the modules, with exception of *final-pos* (module IV in Figure 5.6), are sufficiently simple to be described in a few statements. We leave it as an exercise to write the AL algorithm for it; only an informal outline will be given here. Given the subtuple

$(k_i, \ldots, k_j)$, we wish to bubble k_i, call it *key*, into its final location *m*. To accomplish this, two pointers are maintained (*smaller* and *bigger*) which, together with *i* and *j*, delineate the two areas in which all the elements are either smaller or bigger than *key*. Initially, their values are *i* and *j*, indicating empty regions; starting with k_{bigger}, we compare it to *key*, and as long as the value of k_{bigger} is greater than *key* we keep decrementing *bigger*. When we encounter an element less than *key*, we move it to $k_{smaller}$ and increment *smaller* as long as $k_{smaller}$ is less than *key*. The process of switching between incrementing and decrementing continues until the two pointers finally meet; this is the desired location (*m*), and we can insert *key*. Since *key* is compared exactly once with each of the remaining $j - i$ elements, the complexity of *final-pos* as applied to the tuple $(k_i, \ldots, k_j)$ is $j - i$.

Example 5.6

Let $K = (7, 9, 1, 5, 8, 3)$, $i = 1$, $j = 6$, and $k = 7$; upward arrows in the lines below indicate the value of *smaller* and *bigger*.

		Comments
7 9 1 5 8 3		Move k_6 to 1
↑ ↑		
3 9 1 5 8 3		Move k_2 to 6
↑ ↑		
3 9 1 5 8 9		
↑ ↑		
3 9 1 5 8 9		Move k_4 to 2
↑ ↑		
3 5 1 5 8 9		
↑ ↑		
3 5 1 5 8 9		
↑↑		
3 5 1 ⑦ 8 9		Insert *key* at 4

EXERCISE 5.7: Give the AL algorithm for the procedure *final-pos*(K, i, j; m, K).

The only remaining task is to write the AL algorithm according to the refinements of Figures 5.5 and 5.6.

Algorithm 5.5 (Quicksort)

```
procedure quicksort(K, n; K)
begin /*quick*/
    i ← 1; j ← n; top ← 0; save(0) ← null;
    while ((i, j) ≠ null)
```

begin /*subproblem iteration*/
   while $(j - i \geq 1)$
   begin /*solve one subproblem, save other*/
     final-pos$(K, i, j; m, K)$;
     if $j - m \geq 2$ **then** $[top \leftarrow top + 1; save(top) \leftarrow (m + 1, j)]$;
     $j \leftarrow m - 1$ /*position to solve left problem*/
   end; /*solve*/
     $(i, j) \leftarrow save(top); top \leftarrow top - 1$ /*restore saved subproblem*/
   end /*subproblem*/
end /*quick*/

One conclusion reached in the discussion of the divide-and-conquer technique is that it will produce rather poor results when the division is not balanced. It is quite clear that the division is most unbalanced when each k_i is already in its final place (i.e., the left part is of size 0 and the right part of size $j - 1$). Since *final-pos* always takes $j - 1$ comparisons and since in this case $n - 1$ subproblems of decreasing (by 1) size are generated, we have

$$c_w(n) = \sum_{j=1}^{n} j$$
$$= \frac{n^2}{2} + O(n) \tag{8}$$

It is fairly easy to provide an intuitive justification for the expected complexity measure:

$$c_e(n) = O(n \log_2 n) \tag{9}$$

Let us count the number of comparisons when quicksort works best: Assume n is of the form $2^k - 1$ (for the sake of an example, let $n = 15$). The best case is when the final position of k_1 is 8; we need 14 comparisons to go from

```
            |—————————————— 15 ——————————————|
            1                                15
```

to

```
            |——— 7 ———|—O—|——————————|
            1          7 8 9          15
```

12 comparisons in the best case to

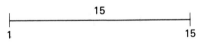
```
     |—3—|—O—|——|—O—|——3——|—O—|—3—|
     1    3 4 5   7 8 9    11 12 13   15
```

and 8 to

```
 |1|—O—|1|—O—|1|—O—|1|—O—|1|—O—|1|—O—|1|—O—|1|
 1   2   3   4   5   6   7   8   9   10   11   12   13   14   15
```

In general, at the ith step, $n - (2^i - 1)$ comparisons are required to generate the next level. Since there are $\log_2 n$ levels, the number of comparisons (N) will be

$$\begin{aligned} N &= \sum_{i=1}^{\log_2 n} n - 2^i + 1 \\ &= (n + 1)(\log_2 n) - 2^{\log_2 n + 1} + 2 \\ &\simeq n \log_2 n - 2n \end{aligned}$$

The figures corresponding to the average complexity for the cost analysis are

$$\begin{aligned} n_a &= O(n \log_2 n) \\ n_k &= O(n \log_2 n) \\ n_s &= n + O(\log_2 n) \end{aligned} \qquad (10)$$

In (10), n_s reflects the storage requirements for the pointers which must be saved.

EXERCISE 5.8: Provide an argument why there are never more than $\log_2 n$ pairs of pointers saved at any one point during execution.

One conclusion to be drawn from (8), (9), and (10) is that quicksort should not be used for data which are nearly or already sorted. In these situations, quicksort is at its worst $(O(n^2))$; in comparison, a straight insertion sort takes only $O(n)$ comparisons. In addition, analysis of Algorithm 5.5 indicates that for short sequences the amount of overhead involved (saving and restoring) is exorbitant. On the other hand, for short sequences, the insertion sort requires almost no overhead and only a few comparisons to sort the sequence. For this reason quicksort is never used for small sequences (the cutoff point is determined by the values of c_a, c_k, etc., but usually lies somewhere between 10 and 20). We can make excellent use of these characteristics in the following way: Whenever the length of a sequence to be sorted is less than the value implied by the cutoff considerations, a straight insertion sort is invoked to sort this sequence. As a matter of fact, this rule applies to any fast sorting algorithm.

EXERCISE 5.9: Modify Algorithm 5.5 according to the small-sequence rule above.

The quicksort has been used to illustrate how a complete divide-and-conquer algorithm (divide until size is 1) can be implemented. In Chapter 11 we shall consider similar algorithms from a different point of view, namely, as a *recursive* process, which will lead to a much simplified form of Algorithm 5.5.

Merge Sorts

Our discussion of sorting is concluded by examining a second algorithm based on the divide-and-conquer technique. First, we divide the input tuple K into halves, $(k_1, \ldots, k_{n/2})$ and $(k_{n/2+1}, \ldots, k_n)$. Next, one of the known algorithms, say the straight insertion sort, is executed on both the $n/2$-tuples, and we obtain two tuples, each of which is sorted. Clearly, we cannot simply append the second tuple to the first

tuple and proclaim it the solution. In Figure 5.7 the recombination part of the algorithm is stated in such a way that the result is produced in the temporary *n*-tuple
called *K′*. The procedure *merge* is parameterized (using a little foresight) in such a
way that it can be used by an algorithm based on repeated application of divide-and-
conquer.

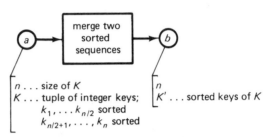

$$n \dots \text{size of } K$$
$$K \dots \text{tuple of integer keys;} \quad K' \dots \text{sorted keys of } K$$
$$k_1, \dots k_{n/2} \text{ sorted}$$
$$k_{n/2+1}, \dots, k_n \text{ sorted}$$

Fig. 5.7   Recombination part of merge sort.

Algorithm 5.6 (Merge two sorted sequences)

procedure *merge(from, first, sec, end, to, start; to)*
begin /*merge the sequences *from(first)*, *from(first + 1)*, ... , *from(sec − 1)*;
                              from(sec), ... , *from(end)*
          into the tuple *to(start)*, *to(start + 1)*, ...*/
    $i \leftarrow first$; $j \leftarrow sec$; $k \leftarrow start$;
    while$(i < sec \land j \leq end)$
    begin /*move the smaller element as long as both sequences
                are not exhausted*/
          if *from(i) < from(j)* **then** $[to(k) \leftarrow from(i); i \leftarrow i + 1]$
                              else $[to(k) \leftarrow from(j); j \leftarrow j + 1]$;
      $k \leftarrow k + 1$
    end; /*move*/
    if $i < sec$ **then** *copy(from, i, sec − 1, to, k; to)*
                else *copy(from, j, end, to, k; to)*
end /*merge*/

The procedure *copy* in the above algorithm copies the remaining elements of one
of the sequences into the target tuple.

Example 5.7

Let *K* be the tuple

$$(1, 4, 6, 10, 15, 2, 8, 9, 16, 18, 20)$$

let the call to merge be of the form

$$merge(K, 1, 6, 11, K', 1; K')$$

and let the values of the variables i, j, k be represented by arrows:

K   K'

1, 4, 6, 10, 15, 2, 8, 9, 16, 18, 20
↑   ↑   ↑

1, 4, 6, 10, 15, 2, 8, 9, 16, 18, 20   1,
   ↑   ↑   ↑

                                1, 2,
  ↑   ↑   ↑

                                1, 2, 4,
    ↑   ↑   ↑

1, 4, 6, 10, 15, 2, 8, 9, 16, 18, 20   1, 2, 4, 6,
      ↑   ↑   ↑

                                1, 2, 4, 6, 8,
     ↑   ↑   ↑

                                1, 2, 4, 6, 8, 9,
   ↑   ↑   ↑

                                1, 2, 4, 6, 8, 9, 10,
     ↑   ↑   ↑

1, 4, 6, 10, 15, 2, 8, 9, 16, 18, 20   1, 2, 4, 6, 8, 9, 10, 15,
         ↑   ↑   (invocation of *copy*)   ↑
1, 4, 6, 10, 15, 2, 8, 9, 16, 18, 20   1, 2, 4, 6, 8, 9, 10, 15, 16, 18, 20   ■

Following is the FORTRAN implementation of Algorithm 5.6.

Purpose: Merge two sorted sequences into one sorted sequence.
Communication:

subroutines or functions called:	COPY	subroutine with arguments X, I, J, Y, K, N; copies X(I), . . . , X(J) into Y(K), . . . , Y(N); Y is modified;
formal parameters:	FROM ...	integer N-tuple;
	FIRST ⎫	indices such that FROM(FIRST),
	SEC ⎬ ...	. . . , FROM(SEC-1) is sorted and so
	END ⎭	is FROM(SEC), . . . , FROM(END);
	TO	integer N-tuple; modified;
	START ...	index such that elements FROM-(FIRST), . . . , FROM(END) are moved to TO(START), . . . in sorted order;
	N	size of FROM and TO.

Program:

```
C::::::::::::::::::::::::::::::::::::::::::::::::::::::::::::::::::::::::::::::::::::::::::::::
C                    SUBROUTINE MERGE (FROM,FIRST,SEC,END,TO,START,N)
C::::::::::::::::::::::::::::::::::::::::::::::::::::::::::::::::::::::::::::::::::::::::::::::
                     SUBROUTINE MERGE (FROM,FIRST,SEC,END,TO,START,N)
C           THIS ROUTINE MERGES TWO SORTED SEQUENCES INTO ONE SORTED
C           SEQUENCE. THE MERGED LIST IS TO(START)
            INTEGER FROM(N),TO(N),FIRST,SEC,END,START
C
C           INITIALIZE POINTERS
C
      I=FIRST
      J= SEC
      K=START
C           MERGE UNTIL ONE SEQUENCE IS EXHAUSTED
   10 IF ((I.GE.SEC).OR.(J.GT.END)) GO TO 40
            IF (FROM(I).LT.FROM(J)) GO TO 20
C           MOVE FROM SECOND SEQUENCE
                   TO(K)=FROM(J)
                   J=J+1
            GO TO 30
C           MOVE FROM FIRST SEQUENCE
   20              TO(K)=FROM(I)
                   I=I+1
   30         K=K+1
      GO TO 10
   40 IF (I.GE.SEC) GO TO 50
C
C           COPY REMAINING ELEMENTS OF SECOND SEQUENCE
C
            CALL COPY (FROM,I,SEC-1,TO,K,N)
            RETURN
C           COPY REMAINING ELEMENTS OF FIRST SEQUENCE
   50 CALL COPY (FROM,J,END,TO,K,N)
      RETURN
      END
```

EXERCISE 5.10: Specify the procedure *copy* and implement it in FORTRAN.

The question is, How often is the dominant instruction in the while iteration ["from(i) < from(j)"] of Algorithm 5.6 executed in the worst case? Let us investigate this number for the tuple

$$K = (2, \ldots, 90, 200,$$
$$100, \ldots, 180)$$

Observe that the first element of the second sequence, 100, is greater than the first $n/2 - 1$ elements of the first sequence. As these $n/2 - 1$ elements are moved, $n/2 - 1$ comparisons will be executed. Next, we move the elements 100, ..., 180, taking $n/2$ comparisons, and finally, we copy the element 200. In general, the comparison cannot be executed more than $i + j - 1$ times without violating the iteration condition; thus, the complexity of the recombination algorithm is given by

$$c_w(n) = n - 1$$
$$= O(n)$$

The total algorithm using the merging procedure once is therefore as follows:

> **begin** /*sorting, with one application of divide-and-conquer*/
>   **input** n, K;
>   *insort*$(K(1), n/2; K)$
>   *insort*$(K(n/2 + 1), n/2; K)$
>   *merge*$(K, 1, n/2 + 1, n, K', 1; K')$
>   *copy*$(K', 1, n, K, 1; K)$
> **end** /*sorting*/

with its complexity

$$c_w(n) = \frac{(n/2)^2}{2} + \frac{(n/2)^2}{2} + O(n)$$

$$= \frac{n^2}{4} + O(n)$$

which is an improvement only in the coefficient of n^2.

Following steps similar to those involved in finding a good algorithm for the minimal and maximal element, we shall now proceed to apply repeatedly divide-and-conquer. As expected, the resulting algorithm will be a fast sort. Hence, according to the small-sequence rule, we shall stop partitioning the input when the problem size (length of the tuple) has reached 16.

Let us compare the structure of two algorithms obtained from application of the divide-and-conquer technique. The structure of the quicksort algorithm actually parallels the process of divide-and-conquer in that quicksort accepts a tuple, splits it into two parts, and repeats the process on each part. In contrast, the minmax algorithm was obtained by first conceptually applying the divide-and-conquer technique to the input data and subsequently developing the structure of the algorithm from the resulting form of the data. In this situation, the structure obtained is one which consists mainly of continued invocation of the recombination part after n problems of size 1 have been solved.

The structure of the merge sort algorithm is similar to that of the minmax algorithm, only now we start with problems of size 16 because of the small-sequence rule. In the modular refinements in Figures 5.8 and 5.9 we use the term "run" to indicate a sorted subsequence and note that n does not have to be a power of 2.

Module V of Figure 5.9 has to be executed whenever n is not a multiple of $2m$ and has to deal with two cases. In the first case, only one run remains, and we only wish to copy these elements into the target n-tuple. The other possibility is that we have one complete run of length m and one run of length smaller than m; in which case we wish to perform a merge with appropriate boundaries.

Algorithm 5.7 (Merge runs of length m into runs of length $2m$; modules I, II of Figure 5.8)

procedure *merge_run*(*orig, targ, m, n; targ*)
begin /*sweep*/
    $i \leftarrow 1; j \leftarrow m + 1; k \leftarrow 2 * m; l \leftarrow 1;$

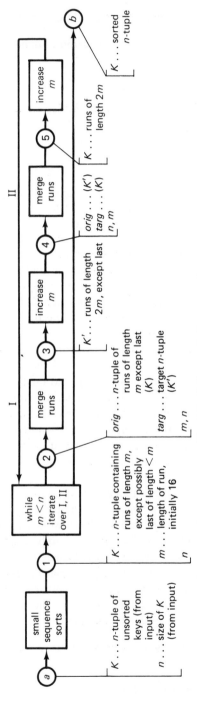

Fig. 5.8 Refinement of merge sort.

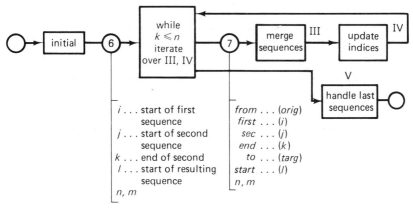

Fig. 5.9 Refinement of module I (or II) of Figure 5.8.

while $(k \leq n)$
begin /*merge consecutive runs*/
    merge(orig, i, j, k, targ, l; targ);
    $i \leftarrow i + 2 * m; j \leftarrow j + 2 * m; k \leftarrow k + 2 * m; l \leftarrow l + 2 * m$
end; /*merge*/
if $i > n$ **then terminate**;
if $j > n$ **then** *copy(orig, i, n, targ, k; targ)*
       else *merge(orig, i, j, n, targ, l; targ)*
end /*sweep*/

EXERCISE 5.11: Add the necessary AL statements according to Figure 5.8 to obtain a complete merge-sort algorithm.

Order analysis is understood best by visualizing the sequence of merges done by the merge sort; see Figure 5.10.

The cost of applying the insertion sort to the $n/16$ sequences of length 16 is

$$\left(\frac{n}{16}\right)\left(\frac{16^2}{2}\right) = 8n$$

For large enough values of n, the number of levels in Figure 5.10 is roughly $\log_2 n$, and since at each level n comparisons are performed, the total complexity of the merge sort is

$$c_w(n) = n \log_2 n + O(n) \qquad (11)$$

The cost analysis for the merge sort is performed in a manner similar to the order analysis; $\log_2 n$ sweeps are executed, and during each sweep we move each element exactly once; thus,

$$c_w(n) = w_1(c_a n \log_2 n + c_k n \log_2 n) + w_2 2n \qquad (12)$$

The merge sort is a particularly good example for pointing out the weakness of the dominant instruction chosen. Inspection of the algorithm from Exercise 5.11 and of

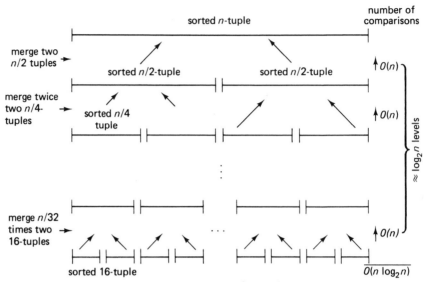

Fig. 5.10   Sequence of merges performed by merge sort.

Algorithms 5.6 and 5.7 reveals that around a core statement which does the actual comparison of keys are a large number of statements devoted solely to bookkeeping functions. These functions include updating pointers and indices, testing for boundaries, etc. However, the effort expended in performing these functions is not reflected in the measure; were they to be included in some way (e.g., see Exercise 5.12), rather different comparative results might be obtained. However, it should be noted that by using a tailor-made merge procedure for the call in the iteration of Algorithm 5.7 most of the pointers and their updating become redundant because they are clearly related to each other by m.

EXERCISE 5.12: Perform cost analysis for the worst case which includes for n_a updating of pointers and indices (1 unit each) and for n_k comparison of indices (1 unit each) on the merge and insertion sort. For $w_1 = 2$, $w_2 = 3$, $c_a = 6$, and $c_k = 4$, compute the values of n for which insertion sort is better (has a lower complexity) than merge sort. (Hint: Use a tailor-made merge procedure.)

A variation on the merge sort as described above is the natural merge sort. This merge sort is called natural because it makes use of naturally occurring sequences in the input. The overall structure of the algorithm as outlined in Figure 5.8 remains the same, but module IV disappears, and module III has to be modified so that such merging does not end at predetermined points but rather the iteration is terminated when a run ends (i.e., $x_i > x_{i+1}$ or $y_j > y_{j+1}$). The advantage of this sort is that it will perform rather well on (nearly) sorted inputs for which the binary merge sort will still take $O(n \log_2 n)$. But on the average the two sorts behave nearly identically due to the additional overhead required by the natural merge sort for determining the boundaries of the natural runs.

In the next section we shall attempt to solve a specific problem for the Friendly Finance Company. However, the few algorithms developed in the preceding sections are not sufficient to obtain a solution which is as efficient as possible. Normally, the programmer's repertoire would also include those searching and sorting algorithms included in Section 5.4 of Part C in the supplementary volume. Understanding the following example does not require detailed knowledge of the structure of these algorithms; rather, only the complexity results, as summarized in Table 5.1.

5.3 A BUSINESS PROBLEM

The FFC has recently acquired a medium-sized computer and wishes to computerize its record-keeping system. To this end it poses to its program development section the problem outlined in Figure 5.11. Obviously, this task does not form a complete data management information system, but its solution will at least indicate how the algorithms discussed in this chapter may be incorporated and how the analyses performed may be used to advantage. We shall make several assumptions which if not true may change the course of our development completely. First, the master file and any other files concurrently in use will fit into main memory; second, though all files fit into memory, it is at a premium, and as a first approximation we select $w_1 = 1$ and $w_2 = \log_2 n$; third, there will be sufficient temporary storage available that any

---

MEMO

To: Software Development Group
From: System Development Manager
Subject: Conversion to Computerized Data Base

As you may be aware, FFC is converting its internal record-keeping system to a computer-based system. Your function during this conversion will be to supply the necessary software systems for a smooth transition. The immediate problem will be the development of one master program which will be available to both headquarters and district offices which have access to the computer. The basic data structure will be a master file, sorted on the customer's name, whose records have the form given in Figure 5.1. The following three tasks should be accomplished within the program:

a)   Input a small (10–40) unordered collection of new customers' records and output a file sorted on the name.

b)   Input the master file and a number of small files (output of (a)) already sorted on name; update the master file by incorporating these small files.

c)   Implement a query system for the master file which allows a user to perform the following:

       WHAT IS THE RECORD OF   customer name?

       CHANGE FIELD __ OF __ TO __ .

       PRINT A LIST OF RECORDS SORTED ON FIELD __ .

Fig. 5.11 Hypothetical business problem.

Table 5.1 SUMMARY OF ANALYSIS OF SORTING ALGORITHMS

Name	Order analysis ($n > 20$)		Cost analysis ($n < 20$)					
	worst case	average	worst case			average		
			n_a	n_k	n_s	n_a	n_k	n_s
Straight insertion	$n^2/2 + O(n)$	$n^2/4 + O(n)$	$n^2/2 + O(n)$	$n^2/2 + O(n)$	$n + 2$	$n^2/4 + O(n)$	$n^2/4 + O(n)$	$n + 2$
Binary insertion	$n\log_2 n + O(n)$	$n\log_2 n + O(n)$	$n^2/2 + O(n)$	$n\log_2 n + O(n)$	$n + 1$	$n^2/4 + O(n)$	$n\log_2 n + O(n)$	$n + 1$
Shell	$O(n^{1.5})$	$O(n(\ln n)^2)$	$O(n^{1.5})$	$O(n^{1.5})$	$n + 1$	$1.2n^{1.3} + O(n)$	$O(n^{1.5})$	$n + 1$
Bubble	$n^2/2 + O(n)$	$n^2/2 + O(n)$	$3n^2/2 + O(n)$	$n^2/2 + O(n)$	$n + 1$	$3n^2/4 + O(n)$	$3n^2/2 + O(n)$	$n + 1$
Quick	$n^2/2 + O(n)$	$O(n\log_2 n)$	$n^2/2 + O(n)$	$n^2/2 + O(n)$	$n + \log_2 n$	$O(n\log_2 n)$	$O(n\log_2 n)$	$n + 0\,(\log_2 n)$
Selection	$n^2/2 + O(n)$	$n^2/2 + O(n)$	n	$n^2/2 + O(n)$	$n + 1$	n	$n^2/2 + O(n)$	$n + 1$
Heap	$O(n\log_2 n)$	$O(n\log_2 n)$	$O(n\log_2 n)$	$O(n\log_2 n)$	$n + 1$	$O(n\log_2 n)$	$O(n\log_2 n)$	$n + 1$
Merge binary/natural	$n\log_2 n$	$n\log_2 n$	$n\log_2 n$	$n\log_2 n$	$2n$	$n\log_2 n$	$n\log_2 n$	$2n$

sorting algorithm under consideration might need (in particular, the number of records in the master file will be less than 2000). If the last assumption were not justified, w_2 would have to be increased. Decisions in terms of cost analysis will be based solely on formulas derived in this chapter. The values of the machine-dependent coefficients, c_a and c_k, are selected to be the number of machine cycles required to execute the corresponding instructions, which in this case are 10 and 6, respectively. In a real-world situation these formulas would have to take into account more than key movements, key comparisons, and storage.

The overall structure of the problem is shown in Algorithm 5.8; we shall solve each submodule separately but not necessarily independently of the others.

Algorithm 5.8 (Business problem)

Global data referenced:　　M (table representing master file) and
　　　　　　　　　　　　　　n (number of records in M)

```
begin /*business*/
    input mode;
    while (mode ≠ 'stop')
    begin /*select node*/
        case mode of
            'sort':    sort_small; /*module I*/
            'update':  update_master; /*module II*/
            'query':   query_system /*module III*/
            end; /*mode*/
        input mode
    end /*select*/
end /*business*/
```

For module I we shall for the moment conform to the small-sequence rule and consider only slow sorts, although the limit is slightly smaller than the expected size of the input files. Since this module will be executed most frequently, we consider the average case columns in Table 5.1 and come to the conclusion that, according to our formulas, selection sort with a complexity of

$$c_e(40) = \underset{\underset{\approx\,5420}{\underset{\uparrow}{w_1}}}{1(10 * 40 + 6 * 800)} + \underset{\underset{w_2}{\uparrow}}{(\log_2 40) * 41}$$

is the most suitable one. As discussed in Section 5.4 of Part C in the supplementary volume, since the selection sort moves each key only once, we do not have to rearrange the records; rather the algorithm is modified to move the whole record with each key, as shown in Figure 5.12. For the second subproblem, module II, a quick look in the order analysis column shows that the complexity is in the range of $2400 * 12 \approx 29{,}000$ to $2400 * 1200 \approx 3 * 10^6$ if the small files S_i, $1 \le i \le k$, are simply added to the master

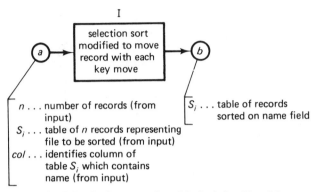

Fig. 5.12   Refinement of module I of algorithm 5.8.

file M, which is then resorted. It is quite clear that we can do much better by exploiting the fact that all files are already sorted. Let us break the problem into two parts: First, obtain a medium-size sorted file, S, containing all small files, and second, incorporate S into M (see Figure 5.13). The only fast sort listed in Table 5.1 which can accom-

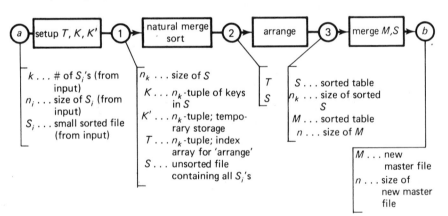

Fig. 5.13   Refinement of module II of algorithm 5.8.

modate a priori sorted subfiles of varying length is the natural merge sort with a complexity (order analysis) of

$$c(n) = n \log_2 \left(\frac{n}{n_k} \right)$$

where n is the size of S and n_k is the average length of the small files. The second problem is solved by merging the two files S and M with a complexity

$$c(n) = n$$

where n is the size of the new M. Thus, the total complexity of module II in terms of order analysis is

$$c(2400) = 400 * \log_2 \left(\frac{400}{20}\right) + 2400$$
$$\approx 4130$$

which certainly is much better than the initial range of 10^4–10^6; it is not necessary to perform any cost analysis. Module III of Algorithm 5.8 cannot be linearly decomposed, and its structure is given by Algorithm 5.9.

Algorithm 5.9 (Query system, action module)

Global data referenced: M (table representing master file) and
  n (number of records in M)

```
begin /*query*/
   input qmode;
   case qmode of
      'retrieve':  input field, key; retrieve(field, key;); /*module IV*/
      'modify':    input field, key, value; modify(field, key, value;); /*module V*/
         'sort':   input field; sort(field;) /*module VI*/
   end /*qmode*/
end /*query*/
```

Modules IV and V in Algorithm 5.9 require no discussion since the retrieval problem was seen to have been optimally solved by the binary search algorithm. However, module VI of Algorithm 5.9 does need some consideration. This time the size of the file is in the range of 2000 records, and virtually nothing is known about the ordering of the keys, with one exception. In the event that sorting is to be performed on the *name* field, the file is already sorted, and we only need to print it out. For any other situation we cannot make any assumption about the distribution of the keys. (In practical circumstances we may have some a priori knowledge about the distribution and should incorporate it into our analysis.) Thus, the first decision is to eliminate all slow sorts from contention. From order analysis we also eliminate quicksort because of its worst-case behavior, which, for all we know, might happen frequently. That leaves binary insertion, Shell, heap, and merge sorts. Computing the complexity in terms of cost analysis for these sorts implies the selection of the heapsort since it has the smallest value of all in both the worst and average cases. Hence, module VI will consist of a heapsort whose input is K, the key tuple, and T, the index tuple; the output T will be used by an output module which prints the records of M in the order specified by T.

This completes the refinement of the original problem, and, as can be seen from these refinements, once the various algorithms have been implemented, we need very little additional control structure to realize a management information system. The only work lies in the design of the interfaces and the selection of the appropriate algorithms according to the tenets of order and cost analysis.

5.4 CONCLUSIONS

In this chapter we have been concerned mainly with searching and sorting. The methods presented are suitable for internal searches and sorts; that is, they are suitable when the entire table (file) to be searched or sorted fits completely into central memory. Most large-scale business data processing applications are, in fact, operations on very large files of information. It is unlikely that the file of customers for the Friendly Finance Company would fit entirely into main memory. The need for auxiliary storage of the file to be sorted imposes some complications on the sorting methods employed. We have not discussed methods for which this is the case, the only exception being the merge sort, which, with suitable modifications, may be used to sort information stored on magnetic tape (for example). However, this chapter is not meant to be a survey of available searching and sorting techniques. We leave it to the reader with an interest in external sorting and in the various other sorting methods available to consult the references and available literature.

References

The primary reference for this chapter must be

D. E. KNUTH, *The Art of Computer Programming*, Vol. 3: Sorting and Searching, Addison-Wesley, Reading, Mass., 1973.

since this reference contains algorithms, discussions, and analyses of all the major sorting and searching methods in use, including external sorting algorithms.

For historical interest, the quicksort algorithm was first proposed in:

C. A. R. HOARE, 'Quicksort,' *Computer Journal, Vol. 5* (1962), pp. 10–15.

Exercises

1 Given a tape containing 250,000 records which are to be sorted on a key (one word long) and a maximum of 40,000 words of core memory available for data, write (and implement) an algorithm to produce a sorted tape.

2 Complete the algorithmic specification of the business problem in Section 5.3 (i.e., add control structures and have argument lists correspond to those of the appropriate algorithms in Sections 5.1 and 5.2) and implement it for sample data of your choice.

3 What sorting algorithm would you use if the only information you have is
   (a) $n = 10,000$; X is nearly sorted.
   (b) $n = 10,000$; keys uniformly distributed (i.e., each permutation of keys is equally likely).

4 In the binary search method we compute the midpoint of the candidate area. If we interpret the key as an integer, we can simulate the human procedure when looking up a word in a dictionary by multiplying the number of points in the interval $(high - low + 1)$ by the fraction $[key - K(low)]/[K(high) - K(low)]$ and add the integer portion of the result to the beginning of the interval, *low*. Discuss advantages and disadvantages of this modification to the binary search algorithm. Implement the modification and compare its performance to the binary search.

5 Similarly to the development in Section 5.1, establish, first, operational criteria for a system to handle departmental records in your college and, second, implement it.

6 Write a program for testing sorting algorithms which will measure performance in terms of central processing time and output for various values of n average time, worst-case time (and for which case the algorithm was worst), and best case.

7 What sorting algorithms would you consider for use in a minicomputer (core memory is at a premium)?

8 In realistic situations we have to admit the possibility that records with identical keys are present in the data base. In such a situation we wish a sorting algorithm not to move identical records in relation to each other. Which of the algorithms discussed have this property?

9 At the end of each tax year the IRS will receive the following two lists:
    (a) From employers, a list of persons together with their wages earned and the amounts withheld for taxes.
    (b) From employees, a statement of wages earned and taxes paid by an employer.
    Let n be the size of the larger list; implement an algorithm of a complexity of $O(n \log_2 n)$ which will output the following information:
    (a) A list of employees who have not filed a tax return.
    (b) A list of employers who have not filed their withholding returns.
    (c) A list of employees whose tax returns do not agree with the withholding statements of their employers.

6

Errors: Their Causes and Effects

6.0 INTRODUCTION

The development of a final program has been analyzed through various stages in the previous chapters, culminating in the quest for optimality. A point not to be overlooked is that the program which is finally obtained must be executed on real data to produce usable results. The last factor which enters into our discussion of program development is concerned with the actual execution of programs. The fundamental limitation of digital computers lies in their finitude; it rests with us to examine the implications of this limitation.

Since the underlying number system of a computer is different from the one we are accustomed to, we shall address the question of how to map one system into the other, and what the differences (*representation error*) are. Once we realize that the input data a program operates on may not be as expected, it is not surprising that further errors are introduced during execution (*round-off error*). Furthermore, there exists a class of problems whose underlying nature can be considered, in the widest sense, a continuous process. Realizing the solution to problems of this class on a basically discrete device (the computer) introduces yet another possibility for errors (*truncation error*).

If we want a program to produce results which differ from the "correct" results by not more than a specified amount, optimality analysis performed on algorithms alone may lead to an improper selection. It may be the case that an algorithm of low complexity, once realized as a program and executed, produces results with unacceptable errors, whereas an inferior algorithm may produce acceptable results. Accordingly, the optimal algorithm should be the best (in terms of complexity analysis) algorithm among those which produce the results within an acceptable range.

6.1 FINITE REPRESENTATION OF NUMBERS AND ITS IMPLICATIONS

When the semantics of AL operations and constructs were explained in Chapter 2, we did so by means of Turing machines. This allowed us to ignore the problem of representing the result of an operation, such as 4/3, as a real number because an infinite tape was available. On this tape the only requirement was that a value had to be surrounded by blanks. Since a computer's memory is finite, the number of bits required to represent a single value must obviously be restricted. We also observed at that time that the semantics of AL operations could have been stated much more simply had we imposed a uniform structure on the values.

The limitations of a finite memory and the desirability of uniformity leads to a discrete number system of the following form. In a computer each number is, in general, represented by a fixed number of bits, say s. This restriction does not pose any problems for the representation of integer values, with one exception. Integers whose absolute value is greater than some constant (which depends on s) cannot be represented. For real numbers, a fraction of the s bits is reserved for the mantissa and the remainder for the exponent and the signs of both. The resulting generalized form,

$$x = \pm p^q(.b_1 b_2 \ldots b_t), \qquad b_1 \geq 1 \tag{1}$$

is called the *normalized floating-point* representation. In (1), p represents the base of the discrete number system used (often 2 for computers), q is a signed integer representing the exponent, and the b_i's are the relevant digits of x; i.e., the leading digit is nonzero (the values of the other digits may vary between 0 and $p - 1$).

Example 6.1

The following table gives normalized floating-point numbers and their customary representation:

Customary Representation	Normalized Representation				
	Sign	Base	Exponent	Mantissa	t
12.56	+	10	+2	1256	4
−3.678	−	10	+1	3678	4
0.0038	+	10	−2	38	2
−0.02006	−	10	−1	2006	4
120.625	+	2	+111	1111000101	10

Thus, any discrete number system may be characterized by the following set of descriptors:

$$p \ldots \text{base (e.g., 2, 10, 16)}$$
$$m, M \ldots \text{lower and upper limit of exponent, i.e., all}$$
$$\text{integers } g \text{ such that } m \leq g \leq M$$
$$t \ldots \text{number of digits constituting the mantissa}$$

Since the first digit in (1) can take on $p - 1$ different values and each of the remaining $t - 1$ digits p different values, a discrete number system contains only

$$N = 2(p - 1)p^{t-1}(M - m + 1)$$

different numbers. The number (represented by x_s) smallest in absolute value expressible in this number system is

$$x_s = p^m \overbrace{(.1000 \ldots 0)}^{t \text{ digits}}$$

and the largest is

$$x_b = p^M \overbrace{(.(p-1)(p-1)\ldots(p-1))}^{t \text{ digits}}$$

To complete the number system a representation of zero is added in which all the digits of the exponent and the mantissa are zero.

As an example, consider a hypothetical computer whose number system is described by

$$\begin{aligned} p &= 2, & M &= +3 \\ m &= 0, & t &= 2 \end{aligned} \tag{2}$$

As shown in Figure 6.1, only $2 * 1 * 2 * 4 + 1 = 17$ numbers are available to represent all real numbers. The circles in Figure 6.1 represent all the numbers representable in this system.

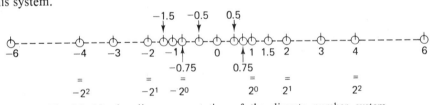

Fig. 6.1 Number line representation of the discrete number system defined in (2).

The number system which we are accustomed to, i.e., the real number system, consists of a continuum of numbers. Any member of this system can be put into the form

$$x = \pm p^q(.b_1 b_2 b_3 \ldots), \qquad b_1 \geq 1, 0 \leq b_i < p \tag{3}$$

The question now is, How can the numbers in the real number system be mapped onto the numbers in the discrete number system? There are two mappings commonly employed: *chopping* and *rounding*. In Figure 6.2, the real number line has been overlaid with the elements of a discrete number system. In chopping, all real numbers lying between two adjacent positive (negative) discrete numbers are mapped into the left (right) discrete number. For rounding, we have to consider the midpoint between adjacent discrete numbers. All real numbers between two such adjacent midpoints are mapped into the discrete number they surround.

As a notational convention, we use **float**(x) to represent the discrete representation of the real number x, regardless of the mapping used. For example, for

$$x = 2^{10}(.1011)$$

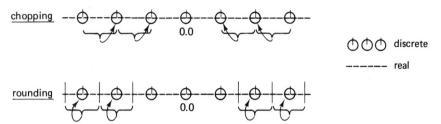

Fig. 6.2 Mappings of real number system onto a discrete number system.

in the system of Figure 6.1, we have

$$\mathbf{float}(x) = 2^{10}(.10)$$

if chopping is used. In general, for any

$$x = \pm p^q(.b_1 b_2 b_3 \ldots b_t b_{t+1} \ldots)$$

mapped onto a discrete system by chopping, the result is

$$x = \pm p^q(.b_1 b_2 b_3 \ldots b_t)$$

Rounding can be implemented by retaining $t + 1$ digits for the mantissa, adding $p/2$ (1 for $p = 2$) to the $(t + 1)$st digit, and truncating the result to t digits. Numbers larger in absolute value than $\mathbf{float}(x_b)$ [6 in the system of (2)] are not approximated at all but cause an *overflow* error; numbers smaller in absolute value than $\mathbf{float}(x_s)$ [.5 in system (2)], except zero, are not approximated either and cause an *underflow* error. Throughout this chapter we shall assume that chopping is used since it is cheaper to implement and actually is the selected method for most computers. The derivations of results in this chapter are quite similar for rounding, and no major difficulties should be encountered in obtaining them.

Example 6.2

The following table displays rounding into system (2):

| | Floating-Point Representation | |
Real Number	With Enlarged Mantissa	Result
$2^{10}(.1011)$	$2^{10}(.101)$	
	$+$	
	$2^{10}(.001)$	$2^{10}(.11)$
$2^{00}(.11101)$	$2^{00}(.111)$	
	$+$	
	$2^{00}(.001)$	$2^{01}(.10)$
$2^{01}(.10011)$	$2^{01}(.100)$	
	$+$	
	$2^{01}(.001)$	$2^{01}(.10)$

■

EXERCISE 6.1: Analogous to Figure 6.1, give a geometric representation of the number system

$$p = 3, \qquad M = +3$$

chopping

$$m = -3, \qquad t = 2$$

Since the computer's number system contains only finitely many points, we introduce an error into our computation in most cases just by converting a number into its floating point form; this error is commonly called the *representation* error. We emphasize that though a number may be represented in the floating-point format (1) without error in one number system, it is possible that the same number will not be represented in another system without error. For instance, $10^0(.8)$ cannot be represented exactly in the number system (2) since the representation of the number in base 2 is $2^0(.11001100 \dots)$; i.e., the mantissa is an infinitely repeating sequence of the group 1100.

The representation error is a specific instance of a class of errors known as *round-off errors*. The term *representation error* is usually restricted to the errors incurred when mapping from a value in the real number system to a value in a discrete number system. The term *round-off error* includes not only the representation error but, as we shall see in Section 6.2, those errors introduced as a computation proceeds.

Definition 6.1: The absolute round-off error of a number x is defined as the difference between x and its floating-point representation:

$$A(x) = x - \mathbf{float}(x) \tag{4}$$

The relative round-off error of a number x is defined as the quotient of the absolute values of the absolute round-off error over the floating-point representation of x:

$$R(x) = \frac{|A(x)|}{|\mathbf{float}(x)|} \tag{5}$$

For the relative round-off error we use as the divisor the floating-point representation because usually we do not know the true value x. We shall devote most of our efforts toward the analysis of relative error (5) because the absolute error (4) is often quite misleading. Consider, for example, the number 56,238,921 with the floating-point representation

$$\mathbf{float}(x) = 10^8(.5623)$$

Then the absolute error

$$A(x) = x - \mathbf{float}(x)$$
$$\simeq 9000$$

sounds quite large, whereas the relative error

$$R(x) = \frac{|A(x)|}{|\mathbf{float}(x)|}$$
$$= \frac{10^4(.8921)}{10^8(.5623)}$$
$$\simeq 10^{-3}(.2)$$

seems to be intuitively a more accurate statement of the error. On the other hand, for

$x = .002983$ with

$$\textbf{float}(x) = 10^{-2}(.2)$$

the absolute error is $10^{-3}(.983)$, but the relative error is about 50%.

We shall not be able to give explicit formulas for the magnitude of the round-off error which is rather characteristic of the whole study of the effects of errors. We shall provide upper bounds on the magnitude of the error, often based on the values actually computed. That is, after the computation is completed we shall be able to state that the error is certainly not greater than this bound but that it may be much smaller. Actually, most of the results derived will be on the pessimistic side because of simplifications.

To obtain a bound on the representation error induced by the conversion of x to the computer's number system it is only necessary to rewrite x as

$$x = p^q(\pm.d_1d_2 \ldots d_t) + p^{q-t}(\pm.d_{t+1}d_{t+2} \ldots) \tag{6}$$

Clearly, the first operand in (6) is **float**(x), and the second represents $A(x)$. The latter term is largest if all the digits $d_{t+1}, d_{t+2}, \ldots$ are $p - 1$; hence, the bound

$$|A(x)| \leq p^{q-t}(1.) = p^{q-t} \tag{7}$$

can actually never be reached. We estimate the relative error by assuming the smallest value for **float**(x),

$$R(x) \leq \frac{p^{q-t}}{p^q(.1)}$$
$$= p^{-t+1} = r$$

and conclude that the bound on the relative round-off error is independent of x and depends only on the base and the number of digits in the mantissa; we denote this constant value by r.

EXERCISE 6.2: Find numbers which upon conversion to the number system (2) will exhibit maximal (minimal) round-off errors. What acceptable (no under- or overflow) number exhibits the largest absolute error?

6.2 ROUND-OFF ERRORS

6.2.1 Propagation Error Due to One Arithmetic Operation

The next question to be considered is how the representation errors are propagated and/or compounded when the floating-point values are used as arguments to arithmetic operations. In addition, arithmetic operations themselves will introduce errors into the resultant value even if the representation errors in the arguments are zero.

For the moment, let us assume that currently the floating-point representations x' and y' deviate from the true values (i.e., those values which would have been obtained had the computation been performed in the real number system) x and y by the amounts a_x and a_y, respectively, that is,

$$x = x' + a_x$$
$$y = y' + a_y \tag{9}$$

In this case the current relative round-off errors are

$$r_x = \frac{|a_x|}{|x'|}$$

$$r_y = \frac{|a_y|}{|y'|}$$

(10)

Summation of the two equations (9) yields

$$x + y = x' + y' + a_x + a_y$$

Before we can state how much the computed sum $(x + y)'$ differs from the true sum $x + y$, we have to know how the computer performs the arithmetic operation $+$ on the two numbers it uses as approximations for x and y. To minimize the propagated error, most machines perform addition using $2t$ digits during the computation and chop the result back to t digits.

Example 6.3

Computer addition of the two numbers

$$x' = 10^2(.1256), \quad y' = 10^2(.9263)$$

produces the result (assuming $t = 4$)

$$(x + y)' = 10^3(.1051)$$

which differs from the "true" sum $x' + y'$ by .09. Thus, addition, and in general all arithmetic operations, does not yield the result which we would expect. Even if x' and y' were equal to x and y, respectively, $(x + y)'$ would not equal $x + y$. Another important difference from normal addition is seen if, for instance, $y' = 10^{-2}(.9263)$. In this case the computed sum is actually x' because for addition we have to adjust the mantissa of y' such that the two exponents are the same:

$$\begin{array}{r} x' = 10^2(.1256) \\ y' = 10^2(.00009263) \\ \hline (x + y)' = 10^2(.1256) \end{array}$$

Furthermore, the order in which addition of several numbers is performed matters very much; if the order is changed, the result may be different; e.g.,

$$\begin{array}{ll} x' = 10^1(.365) & x' = 10^1(.365) \\ y' = 10^1(.369) & z' = 10^2(.125) \\ (x + y)' = 10^1(.734) & (x + z)' = 10^2(.161) \\ z' = 10^2(.125) & y' = 10^1(.369) \\ (x + y + z)' = 10^2(.198) \neq & (x + z + y)' = 10^2(.197) \quad \blacksquare \end{array}$$

Given this method of adding numbers, the bound for the relative error is

$$r_{x+y} \leq \frac{1}{|(x + y)'|}(r_x|x'| + r_y|y'|) + r$$

(11)

The bound (11) shows some startling implications: If x' and y' are both positive numbers, then it merely states that the relative error in $x + y$ is roughly the sum of the errors r_x and r_y and an additional round-off error, r, induced by the addition. The situation is considerably different if x' is positive and y' is negative; in this case the process is the subtraction of two positive numbers. If x' and y' are as described, the bound on the relative error,

$$r_{x-y} \leq \frac{1}{|(x-y)'|}(r_x|x'| + r_y|y'|) + r \tag{12}$$

may be very large if x' and y' are close together because of the term $1/|(x-y)'|$. This effect is often referred to as *catastrophic cancellation*.

Example 6.4

Let

$$x = 5.70986, \qquad y = 5.69012$$

and the current computer representation be

$$x' = 10^1(.570), \qquad y' = 10^1(.569)$$

Then the true difference is

$$x - y = 0.01974$$

and the computed difference is

$$(x - y)' = 10^{-1}(.1)$$

which leads to a relative error of

$$r_{x-y} = \frac{.00974}{.01}$$
$$= .974$$

or, in other words, an answer which is nearly 100% incorrect. ■

The bounds on the propagation errors in multiplication and division are

$$r_{xy} \leq r_x + r_y + r$$
$$r_{x/y} \leq r_x + r_y + r \tag{13}$$

They indicate that the operations of multiplication and division are relatively harmless compared to addition in terms of error propagation. Intuitively, this statement is quite obvious because we do not have to adjust the exponents (shift the mantissa) when performing multiplication (division) but only have to add (subtract) the exponents and multiply (divide) the mantissas.

6.2.2 Propagation in Compound Operations

Once the bounds for the four basic arithmetic operations have been obtained it is relatively easy to derive error bounds for some common numeric algorithms. First, let us discuss the process of summing n numbers (14); throughout this section we use *unprimed* symbols to indicate computed values:

$$S_n = \sum_{i=1}^{n} a_i \tag{14}$$

As innocent as this problem appears, it is one of the major causes of erroneous results in many numerical algorithms. In such algorithms it is quite common to have iterations of the form (in an actual program it may "look" different):

$$
\begin{aligned}
&sum \leftarrow 0;\ i \leftarrow 1; \\
&\textbf{while}\ (i \le n) \\
&\textbf{begin} \\
&\qquad \cdot \\
&\qquad \cdot \\
&\qquad \cdot \\
&\qquad sum \leftarrow sum + a(i); \\
&\qquad \cdot \\
&\qquad \cdot \\
&\qquad \cdot \\
&\textbf{end}
\end{aligned}
\tag{15}
$$

where n may be very large (e.g., 1000 to 1,000,000). If S_n is computed according to the framework (15), then the error bound for the sum is

$$r_{S_n} \le \frac{1}{|S_n|} \left(\sum_{i=1}^{n} r_{a_i} |a_i| + r \sum_{i=2}^{n-1} |S_i| \right) + r \tag{16}$$

Example 6.5

Let us estimate the relative round-off error induced by calculating the sum of n equal positive numbers, i.e., $a_i = a$; let the current error be r. According to (16), the error bound

$$
\begin{aligned}
r_{S_n} &\le \frac{1}{na} \left(\sum_{i=1}^{n} ra + r \sum_{i=2}^{n-1} ia \right) + r \\
&= \frac{r}{n} \left[n + \frac{n(n-1) - 2}{2} \right] + r \\
&= r \left(\frac{n-1}{2} - \frac{2}{n} \right) + 2r
\end{aligned}
$$

is linear in n. It should be noted that in establishing the bound the "true" values for the partial sums were used instead of the computed values S_i because we wanted a priori knowledge about the magnitude of the error. It certainly is a good approximation as long as rn is small compared to any of the S_i's. ∎

The bound (16) sheds some light on how to actually implement a summation algorithm. For instance, if the numbers are of the same (or nearly the same) absolute value but have alternate signs, then the relative error can be quite large depending on whether n is even or odd because of the term $1/|S_n|$. Another algorithm with a much better error bound is to calculate separately the sums of the positive and negative terms and then subtract the latter value from the former.

EXERCISE 6.3: Establish a bound (see Section C.6 of the supplementary volume) on the relative error in the computation of

$$I_n = \sum_{i=1}^{n} a_i b_i$$

similar to (16). Simulate by hand the computer's execution on the numbers

a_i: $10^{-1}(.2368)$ $10^1(.5126)$ $-10^1(.1293)$ $10^{-1}(.9286)$ $10^0(.8164)$ $-10^0(.4173)$
b_i: $10^1(.1986)$ $-10^0(.4812)$ $10^1(.9252)$ $10^{-1}(.3186)$ $-10^1(.7201)$ $-10^0(.1908)$

and compute an error bound from your simulation results and the formulas developed. Select numbers for which the a_i's and b_i's are approximations, and compute the actual relative round-off error.

Another common part of numerical algorithms is of the form

$$
\begin{aligned}
&prod \leftarrow 1; \ i \leftarrow 1; \\
&\textbf{while} \ (i \leq n) \\
&\textbf{begin} \\
&\qquad . \\
&\qquad . \\
&\qquad . \\
&\qquad prod \leftarrow prod * a(i); \\
&\qquad . \\
&\qquad . \\
&\qquad . \\
&\textbf{end}
\end{aligned}
\tag{17}
$$

and involves the computation of the product of n numbers:

$$P_n = \prod_{i=1}^{n} a_i$$

The relative round-off error in computing this product according to (17) is bound by

$$r_{P_n} \leq \sum_{i=1}^{n} r_{a_i} + (n-1)r \tag{18}$$

Let us now apply the tools we have developed in this section to a specific problem, namely, the computation of e^x by means of the approximation formula†

$$e^x \simeq 1 + \sum_{i=1}^{n} \frac{x^i}{i!}$$

The approximation becomes better as n gets larger. The "natural" algorithm may be

†The term $i!$ is read as "i-factorial" and is defined as $i! = i(i-1) \cdot (i-2) \ldots 3 \cdot 2 \cdot 1$.

stated as follows:

$$e^x = 1 + \sum_{i=1}^{n} a_i$$

$$a_i = P_i = \prod_{j=1}^{i} b_j$$

$$b_j = \frac{x}{j}$$

According to (13), the relative error in each b_j is bound by

$$r_{b_j} \leq r_x + r_j + r$$

and if we assume no error in the representation of an integer, the error in b_j is bound by twice the error r. Substituting this error into (18) yields

$$r_{a_i} = r_{P_i} \leq \sum_{j=1}^{i} r_{b_j} + (i - 1)r$$

$$= \sum_{j=1}^{i} 2r + (i - 1)r$$

$$= (3i - 1)r$$

And finally, from (16) the error incurred when computing $e^x - 1$ may be obtained:

$$r_{e^x-1} \leq \frac{1}{|S_n|} \left[\sum_{i=1}^{n} (3i - 1)r \left| \frac{x^i}{i!} \right| + r \sum_{i=2}^{n} |S_i| \right] + r \tag{19}$$

The question arises as to what to do with the bound (19); essentially, two options are open. First, we can compute e^x according to the algorithm and use the intermediate results to compute (19). This allows us to give an a posteriori estimate of the error, but often we wish to use the error bound as a selection criterion for determining (before execution) which of several algorithms is the best. To that effect, we can try to estimate the values to be computed and thus arrive at an a priori estimate of the bound (19). To illustrate the latter approach, assume that x is positive; an upper bound for the term $|x^i/i!|/|S_n|$ is certainly 1; similarly, the bound for $|S_i|/|S_n|$ is also 1. If we use these rather crude estimates for the terms in (19), we obtain

$$r_{e^x-1} \leq \sum_{i=1}^{n} (3i - 1)r + r \sum_{i=2}^{n} 1 + r$$

$$= r[1.5n(n + 1) - n + (n - 1) + 1]$$

$$= 1.5n^2 r + 0(nr)$$

However, if x is negative, these estimates are no longer true, and we have to devise other means to estimate the computed terms. Consider, for example, the case for $x = -5.5$; some hand calculations show that the terms a_i are bound by

$$|a_i| = \left| \frac{x^i}{i!} \right| \leq 45$$

the partial sums by

$$|S_i| \leq 25$$

and, last, the disastrous (for the end result) lower bound for S_n,

$$|S_n| \geq 10^{-3}$$

Substituting these bounds into their corresponding terms in (19) yields

$$r_{ex-1} \leq 10^3 \left[\sum_{i=1}^{n} (3i - 1)45r + r \sum_{i=2}^{n} 25 \right] + r$$

$$= r \left[45 * 10^3 \left(\frac{3n(n+1)}{2} - n \right) + 25n + 1 \right]$$

$$= 7.25 * 10^4 n^2 r + 0(nr)$$

Even if we computed the actual values of a_i and S_i instead of using rough estimates, the bound would still be disastrously large. This indicates that the algorithm is not a good one. For this particular problem, note that the error for positive values is relatively small. The relationship

$$e^{-x} = \frac{1}{e^x}$$

suggests that an alternative algorithm is to evaluate e^{-x} for negative values of x and to take the reciprocal of the result.

EXERCISE 6.4: Analyze the error in the computation of sin x using the formula

$$\sin x = \sum_{i=1}^{n} (-1)^{i+1} \frac{x^{2i-1}}{(2i-1)!}$$

Discuss the error in terms of the "natural" algorithm, an algorithm with reordering of terms, and the algorithm as outlined in Section 4.4.2 of Part C in the supplementary volume. Use both hand-calculated and computer-calculated estimates for the terms in your bound.

6.3 TRUNCATION ERRORS

In principle, three different kinds of procedures are normally used to solve numerical problems (as defined in Chapter 2). In one case, an explicit analytic formula is given for calculating a value (or values) which may then be expressed directly as an algorithm. When realizing the algorithm by a program on a computer we only have to take the effects of the round-off errors into account. Using the tools developed in the previous section, we may estimate the "correctness" of the computed value x'.

In the second case, an explicit mathematical expression is given for the value α, but it cannot be translated into an equivalent algorithm. For instance, consider the mathematical formulation

$$\alpha = \int_{1}^{2} \frac{\sin x}{\ln x} dx$$

We may be able to derive an explicit algorithm (formula) for this definite integral through mathematical manipulations or we may not, depending on our ingenuity and knowledge of mathematics. But, in general, we cannot hope to express all formulations as algorithms. For those instances in which an algorithm is not obtainable, we try to find a formulation which approximates the original one and which can be realized by an algorithm. For the above example we could, for instance, approximate sin $x/\ln x$ by a polynomial because we do know an algorithm for computing the definite integral of a polynomial. The error introduced by employing an approximative method for computing α is called the *truncation error*, or, more specifically, the *static* truncation error.

Finally, an approach which is often employed and which is applicable in both the previous situations is as follows: Assume an explicit formulation of the problem is given which may or may not be realizable as an algorithm. We attempt to find a transformation (function) $\mathbf{T}$ which takes as its argument an approximation x_i to α and returns a value x_{i+1} which hopefully is closer to α than x_i. Starting with a user-supplied initial guess x_0, we repeatedly apply $\mathbf{T}$ to the last result of the application of $\mathbf{T}$ until, for some n, x_n is close enough to α for our purpose. The difference between the true value α and the computed approximations x_i is called the *dynamic* truncation error, and it measures the "goodness" of the transformation $\mathbf{T}$.

It should be clear that the truncation error and the round-off error will show some degree of interdependence, which implies they should not be viewed in isolation. This is particularly true in those cases where the solution to a numerical problem involves a mixture of all three basic approaches.

Static Truncation Error

Let α be the value of a function F (we use here the term function in a broader sense so as to include functionals or, in general, any explicit mathematical procedure) and let $\bar{F}$ denote the approximate function. The static truncation error is then simply

$$T = |F - \bar{F}|$$

For instance, consider the problem of finding the area F of the shaded portion of Figure 6.3.

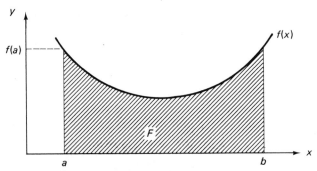

Fig. 6.3   Area bounded by the curve $y = f(x)$, from $x = a$ to $x = b$.

The analytical solution to this problem is, of course,

$$F = \int_a^b f(x)\, dx$$

However, for the sake of discussion, let us assume that the integration cannot be done analytically, so that we are forced to look for other alternatives. A geometric approach to finding the approximate area under the curve would be to approximate f by a sequence of straight-line segments. Let us designate this approximation to f by $\bar{f}$. The area under each line segment is determined by the area of the trapezoid so formed. The actual area F may then be approximated by the area $\bar{F}$, which is the sum of the areas of the trapezoids. In Figure 6.4 the width of all the trapezoids has been chosen

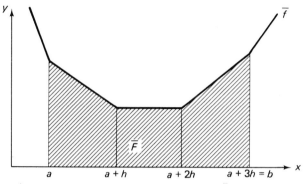

Fig. 6.4 Approximate area $\bar{F}$.

to be $h = (b - a)/n$ with $n = 3$. We note the fact that at the points $a, a + h, a + 2h$, and $a + 3h$, $\bar{f}$ equals f, and thus the area $\bar{F}$ in Figure 6.4 is

$$\bar{F} = [f(a) + f(a + h)]\frac{h}{2} + [f(a + h) + f(a + 2h)]\frac{h}{2}$$

$$+ [f(a + 2h) + f(a + 3h)]\frac{h}{2} \qquad (20)$$

It should be clear from Figure 6.4 that $\bar{f}$ will be a better approximation to f if the partition of the interval between a and b is refined (i.e., made smaller). The procedure outlined above is readily generalized to involve a variable number, n, of partitions (trapezoids). Let

$$a = x_0, x_1 = x_0 + h, \ldots, x_i = x_0 + ih, \ldots, x_n = b \quad \text{and} \quad f_i = f(x_i)$$

Then we can generalize equation (20) to

$$\bar{F} = \left(\frac{f_0 + f_n}{2} + \sum_{i=1}^{n-1} f_i\right)h \qquad (21)$$

The truncation error is in many cases more tractable to mathematical analysis than the round-off error, and quite often we can obtain a closed expression for its value. It is common to express the approximation $\bar{F}$ in terms of a parameter, which in the above example is the width, h, of the partitioning interval. In the case where the function f of this example has a second derivative, it can be shown that the value of the static truncation error is

$$T(h) = \frac{b - a}{12}h^2 f''(g) \qquad \text{for } a < g < b$$

from which we see that T decreases as h decreases. One might conclude that any degree of accuracy is obtainable simply by making h sufficiently small. However, the smaller

h gets, the bigger the round-off error becomes since h is inversely proportional to n, the number of evaluations of f. A typical behavior of the truncation error T as a function of h, the round-off error R as a function of h, and the total error is depicted in Figure 6.5. The best choice of h is often quite difficult to determine analytically. An

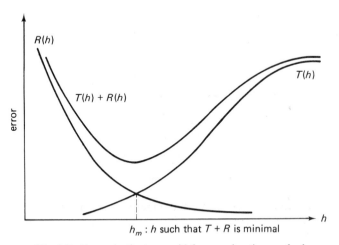

Fig. 6.5   Errors in the trapezoidal approximation method.

empirical approach would be to start out with some large h (< 1) and successively halve this value. The values of $\bar{F}$ should smoothly converge to a certain value for a time until they start diverging or randomly oscillate. When this happens we know that the round-off error is becoming predominant and is eliminating any gain made by reducing the value of h; then the optimal value for h has just been passed. The FORTRAN program given below will evaluate $\bar{F}$ using the trapezoidal method; it is left as an exercise to write a driver routine which will determine the optimal n.

> *Purpose:* Evaluation of an approximation to a given area.
> *Communication:*

subroutines or functions called:	FUN ... user-supplied function;
formal parameters:	FUN ... name of function partially delineating an area; must be declared external in calling program;
	N ..... # of trapezoids to be used; has to be > 1;
	$\left.\begin{matrix} A \\ B \end{matrix}\right\}$ ..... boundaries of interval; value of function INTEGR is real.

Program:

```
C::::::::::::::::::::::::::::::::::::::::::::::::::::::::::::::::::::::::::::::::::::::::::::::::::::::::::::::::::::::::::::::::::::::::::::::::::::::::::::::::::
C                    FUNCTION INTEGR (FUN, N, A, B)
C::::::::::::::::::::::::::::::::::::::::::::::::::::::::::::::::::::::::::::::::::::::::::::::::::::::::::::::::::::::::::::::::::::::::::::::::::::::::::::::::::
      REAL FUNCTION INTEGR(FUN, N, A, B)
C         THIS FUNCTION DETERMINES AN APPROXIMATION FOR A FUNCTION TO
C         A GIVEN AREA
C         DETERMINE SIZE OF PARTITION
      H=(B-A)/N
C         INITIALIZE INTEGRAL
      INTEGR=(FUN(A)+FUN(B))/2.
      ARG=A+H
C         ADD VALVES OF FUN AT INTERMEDIATE POINTS
      DO 10 I=1,N-1
          INTEGR=INTEGR+FUN(ARG)
          ARG=ARG+H
   10 CONTINUE
      INTEGR=INTEGR*H
      RETURN
      END
```

EXERCISE 6.5: Write a program which will calculate the best attainable $\bar{F}$ using the trapezoidal method (function INTEGR) and the procedure outlined above.

This FORTRAN program exposes an interesting fact concerning the round-off error. To minimize the cost of evaluation, the calculation of the partitioning point

$$x_i = x_0 + ih$$

was replaced by

$$x_i = x_{i-1} + h$$

thus saving n multiplications. However, by doing so we have introduced into x_i a cumulative error whose bound is given by (16); for the original case each x_i is calculated from original data, and the error is the one incurred by representation, one addition, and one multiplication. As long as the calculated values stay within the interval $[a, b]$ no detrimental effect is incurred because only the size of the trapezoids is changed. But if x_i becomes greater than b, which may occur for i close to n, we actually change the area under consideration from $[a, b]$ to $[a', b']$. Thus, if n is large, the second method of calculating the partitioning points should definitely be chosen to reduce the corresponding round-off error, although it is more costly to do so. This example shows that algorithm optimization sometimes runs counter to error minimization and that to minimize the number of arithmetic operations does not imply that the error is minimized. Fortunately, as we shall see, this increase in error usually results from the kind of optimization which we do not encourage: local optimization which does not change the order of magnitude of the algorithm's complexity.

EXERCISE 6.6: Write a FORTRAN program with the same specification as above to evaluate $\bar{F}$ using the *midpoint* rule. (Let $a = x_0, x_1 = x_0 + h, \ldots, x_n = b$, and replace f by the step function $\bar{f}$ such that $\bar{f}(x) = f(x_i + (h/2))$ for all x in the interval $[x_i, x_{i+1}], 0 \leq i < n$.)

Dynamic Truncation Error

The dynamic truncation error is that error inherent in *iterative methods* designed to solve numerical problems. It measures the rapidity of the *convergence* of the calculated values x_n to the solution α:

$$E_n = |x_n - \alpha|$$

The smaller E_n is for a fixed n and a given transformation $\mathbf{T}$,

$$x_n = \mathbf{T}(x_{n-1})$$

the better the method. An obvious criterion for the iterative method to work at all is that after some initial oscillation the error continues to decrease:

$$E_i \leq E_{i-1} \qquad \text{for } i > n_0$$

Let us first consider as an example the problem of computing α such that

$$f(\alpha) = 0$$

for some function f. If we assume that the function is given as a discrete sequence (see Figure 6.6) of m pairs of values $\langle x_k, f(x_k) \rangle$, where the x_k's are in ascending order and for only one value j is $f(x_j)$ zero, the problem is reduced to a searching problem for which we can use the optimal binary search algorithm from Chapter 5 [as long as $f(x_1) \cdot f(x_m) < 0$; why?].

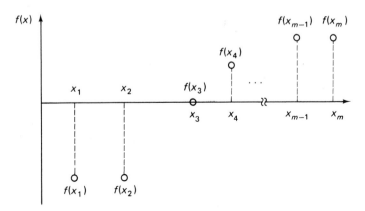

Fig. 6.6 Function given as a sequence of points.

The discrete method illustrated in Figure 6.6 may be generalized, and an iterative scheme called the *bisection method* can be obtained. The assumption for the binary search algorithm (only one zero between x_1 and x_m and $f(x_1) \cdot f(x_m) < 0$) carry over to the bisection method as follows: We have to find two points $P_1 = a$ and $P_2 = b$ such that $f(a) \cdot f(b) < 0$ with only one zero between them.

We select the midpoint of the interval $[a, b]$ as the initial guess x_0 and define the computed values x_i as the midpoints of candidate intervals, which are computed in a manner similar to that employed by the binary search algorithm. Initially, the candidate interval [*left, right*] is equal to the interval $[a, b]$; the left or right boundary is replaced by the midpoint x_i depending on whether $f(x_i) \cdot f(left)$ is greater or smaller than zero. Algorithm 6.1 defines the transformation $\mathbf{T}$ whose geometric interpretation is shown in Figure 6.7.

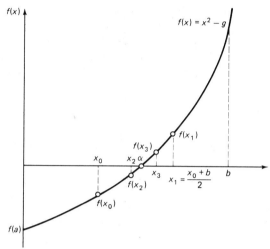

Fig. 6.7 Bisection method for $f(x) = x^2 - g$.

Algorithm 6.1 (Bisection transformation)

Global data referenced: the candidate interval limits *left* and *right*, its midpoint x_i, and the function f

```
begin /*bisection*/
    if f(x_i) * f(left) > 0 then left ⟵ x_i
                            else right ⟵ x_i;
        x_{i+1} ⟵ (left + right)/2
end /*bisection*/
```

Neglecting for the moment the round-off error, repeated execution of Algorithm 6.1 will produce a sequence of points which will converge to α if the stated assumptions hold. Since the true solution always lies within the candidate interval, the midpoint x_i cannot be farther away from α then half the size of the interval. At each iteration step we halve the size of the interval, and hence, the truncation error is certainly bound by

$$E_n \leq 2^{-n}|b - a| \tag{22}$$

We might be tempted to choose the number of iterations so that

$$E_n \leq |\mathbf{float}(x_s)|$$

to obtain the best possible approximation to α. However, the fallacy in this argument is that we disregarded the effects of the round-off errors induced by the execution of Algorithm 6.1. A phenomenon occurs in iterative methods similar to the one we have already observed in specific instances of the static truncation error. For most of the execution the round-off error has for all practical purposes no effect as long as it is small compared to the difference between successive approximations. But when this difference (in the example it equals the size of the current candidate interval) is of the same magnitude as the round-off error accumulated in one execution of the transformation **T**, we should stop the iteration since nothing can be gained from proceeding further. At the start of each iteration all values should therefore be assumed to be exact; i.e., they have no round-off error. In the example the size of the candidate interval should thus be greater than the accumulated absolute round-off error,

$$E_n \le r_{x_n} |x_n| \tag{23}$$

with the assumption that

$$r_{x_{n-1}} = 0$$

To determine beforehand how many iterations will be needed to obtain the best obtainable approximation x_n, we have to estimate both sides of (23) in terms of n and solve the inequality for n.

   EXERCISE 6.7: Determine the number of iterations needed to find the best approximation on your computer for α such that $\alpha^2 = 12$, using the bisection method.

   To summarize the bisection method we may say that its advantage is that it will guarantee a root to be of a desired precision within certain limits and that we can determine beforehand the maximum number of cycles that are required to achieve this precision. The disadvantages are that it might be difficult and/or expensive to determine the initial points a and b satisfying our assumptions for a general function $f(x)$. Furthermore, the number of cycles is large and fixed compared to other methods derived later.
   Algorithms whose behavior is dominated by the dynamic truncation error are more properly referred to as *fixed-point iteration methods*. The fixed point of a transformation is defined as that value for which the argument equals the result of applying the transformation:

$$x = T(x)$$

In the iterative scheme discussed thus far, the sequence of values x_0, $x_1 = T(x_0)$, $x_2 = T(x_1), \ldots, x_n = T(x_{n-1})$ converges toward the true value α [which should not be changed by the application of **T**, that is, $\alpha = T(\alpha)$]. Hence, we require from the transformation **T** that

   1. Its fixed point coincide with the value α we wish to compute, and
   2. The iteration scheme

$$x_i \leftarrow T(x_{i-1})$$

   converge to the fixed point of **T**.

For instance, let α be defined as the value of x for which

$$f(x) = 0$$

for some function f. We can choose **T** to be

$$T(x) = x - f(x)$$

since the fixed point of **T** will be a zero of f, i.e.,

$$\mathbf{T}(\alpha) = \alpha - f(\alpha) = \alpha \qquad [\text{since } f(\alpha) = 0]$$

which fulfills condition (1). Whether the iteration scheme

$$x_i \leftarrow x_{i-1} - f(x_{i-1})$$

will converge (i.e., the truncation error decreases) or not depends mainly on the form of f and the initial guess. Commonly, a variety of possibilities exists for the choice of **T** to satisfy condition 1, and the problem is to establish a bound on the truncation error to see whether it decreases (condition 2). The last step is to derive from that bound the number of iterations needed to obtain a given acceptable error in the end result.

Example 6.6

Let α be defined as the positive zero of $f(x) = .1x^2 - 2.5$, and let us prove whether or not the simple selection of $\mathbf{T}(x) = x - f(x)$ will satisfy condition 2. To illustrate the process geometrically, we first construct the graph for $\mathbf{T}(x)$ (see Figure 6.8).

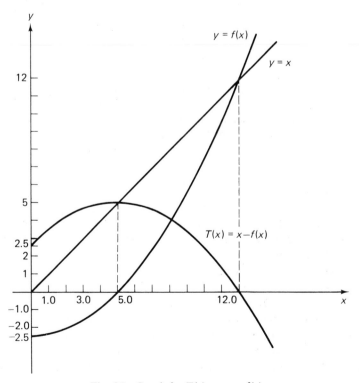

Fig. 6.8 Graph for $\mathbf{T}(x) = x - f(x)$.

The fixed point of **T** is found by intersecting $y = T(x)$ from Figure 6.8 with the line $y = x$; we conclude from the graphical representation of the iteration scheme

$$x_n \leftarrow x_{n-1} - (.1x_{n-1}^2 - 2.5)$$

in Figure 6.9 that the scheme will definitely converge as long as x_0 is in the interval $[-5, 15]$. ∎

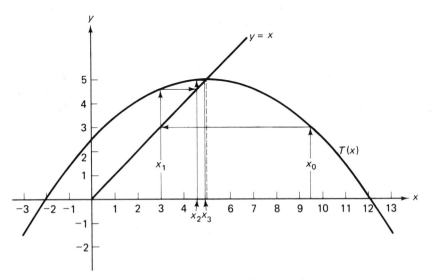

Fig. 6.9 Convergent fixed-point iteration scheme.

EXERCISE 6.8: Let α be defined as the zero of $f(x)$. Does the choice of $T(x) = x - cf(x)$ lead to a convergent fixed-point iteration scheme, and for what values (if any) of x_0 and c will it converge for $f(x) = x^2 - 2$? (Hint: Draw your conclusions from a geometrical representation of the scheme.)

6.4 CONCLUSIONS

In this chapter, we have introduced yet another vantage from which to evaluate the performance of an algorithm that has been realized as a computer program. It has been shown that an algorithm, in its abstract form, might be a perfectly reasonable solution to some problem. It may be the optimal algorithm, in the sense of Chapter 4, and yet be absolutely unusable when translated into a working program because of errors in the final result. These errors are not inherent in the algorithm itself but rather are a function of the nature and structure of the device chosen to execute the algorithm. The computer is, by its very nature, a finite device. The very translation of a number from the real number system to a computer representation may introduce a fairly large initial error into the data on which the final result depends. This error can be compounded and propagated by the performance of arithmetic operations until the final result is nowhere near the correct and/or expected value. Thus, the selection of an algorithm depends not only on a careful construction and analysis of the abstract formulation but must also take into account the physical characteristics of the computer.

In the next chapter, we shall continue our investigation into the analysis of algorithms in the context of generally usable mathematical and computer techniques for solving wide classes of problems. Here we shall see the tension which develops when searching for optimal solutions with minimal error.

References

An easy-to-read essay on errors can be found in

T. E. HULL and D. D. F. DAY, *Computers and Problem Solving*, Addison-Wesley, Reading, Mass., 1970.

A somewhat more advanced discussion better aligned to the presentation in this chapter is provided in

J. A. JACQUEZ, *A First Course in Computing and Numerical Methods*, Addison-Wesley, Reading, Mass., 1970.

For a wealth of examples and case studies with emphasis on error effects, see

W. S. DORN and D. D. McCRACKEN, *Numerical Methods for Fortran IV Case Studies*, Wiley, New York, 1972.

Exercises

1 Describe the number system your computer uses; specifically, give the smallest, x_s, and the biggest, x_b, number in absolute value and the number of points in the system.

2 What can you say about the size of the interval between successive points on the line representing the discrete number system of a computer? Is it constant? Does it vary? If so, how does it vary?

3 Give the floating-point representation (on your computer) of the numbers

$$x_1 = \tfrac{1}{3}, \qquad x_2 = \tfrac{5}{8}, \qquad x_3 = \pi, \qquad x_4 = e, \qquad x_5 = 12.6781498734$$

using chopping and rounding.

4 For the numbers of Exercise 3, compute the absolute and relative errors and compare them to bounds (7) and (8).

5 Compute the actual relative error in the results of the operations $x_1 + x_5$, $x_2 - x_5$, $x_3 * x_4$, and x_4/x_1 (numbers from Exercise 3) and compare them to bounds (11), (12), and (13).

6 Write a program which, for $n = 10$, 100, 1000, 10,000, and 100,000, will compute $\alpha = \sum_{i=1}^{n} x_5$ using formulation (15). Compute the actual relative error by comparing the result of (15) to the result of the single operation algorithm $\alpha = n * x_5$. In addition, compute the error bound (16) and compare it to the real error.

7 Give the bounds for r_{e^x} using the bounds established for r_{e^x-1}.

8 Write a program which will plot the graphs of $T(h)$, $R(h)$, and $T(h) + R(h)$ for a function f such that you can give an explicit expression for T and R using the trapezoidal rule to find an area $\bar{F}$.

9 The function $f(x) = x^3 + 2x^2 - 9x - 18$ has one zero in the interval $[0, 5]$. Implement an iterative scheme which will find the zero within an error of $E_n \leq 10^{-5}$.

10 Given the quadratic equation

$$ax^2 + bx + c = 0$$

compute the error bounds for x_1 and x_2 using the two following algorithms:
(a) $x_1 = (-b + \sqrt{b^2 - 4ac})/(2a)$
   $x_2 = (-b - \sqrt{b^2 - 4ac})/(2a)$.
(b) $x_1 = 2c/(-b + \sqrt{b^2 - 4ac})$
   $x_2 = -2c/(b + \sqrt{b^2 - 4ac})$.
Assume that the square root operation does not produce any round-off error. Compare your results for $a = 1$, $b = 10^5$, $c = 1$.

11 During one phase in the construction of a house, it is necessary to lay the floor joists (the beams supporting the floor) on 16-inch centers. Assume that the house is to be 40 feet long and that you have a 50-foot tape measure, which can be read to $\frac{1}{8}$ inch (that is, the actual distance is within $\frac{1}{8}$ inch of the read distance). If the joists are laid out starting at one end and working toward the other, comment on the error incurred in the position of the last joist using each of the following measuring techniques:
(a) The position of the center of the first joist is marked and 16 inches are measured. This marks the center of the second joist. From this mark, another 16 inches are measured, marking the center of the third joist, and so on.
(b) The tape is extended to 40 feet, and the center of each joist is marked directly from the tape.
Note: The joints of the 4×8 sheets of plywood which form the subfloor of the house must be approximately over the center of every third joist. Which measuring method (if any) will ensure that this occurs?

12 The trapezoidal rule was the result of approximating the graph of the function $y = f(x)$ by means of a straight line (i.e., $y = ax + b$) joining the end points of each subinterval. Develop an algorithm which uses a polynomial of degree 2 (i.e., $y = ax^2 + bx + c$) to approximate the function using three points (i.e., two equal subintervals). This rule is known as Simpson's rule. Compare its performance to the trapezoidal rule.

7

Numerical Applications

7.0 INTRODUCTION

In Chapter 4 we defined as "best" that algorithm which was of lowest complexity. This definition still holds true if the algorithm under consideration is of a nonnumerical nature. We arbitrarily define a nonnumerical algorithm as one whose execution does not involve any of the errors mentioned in Chapter 6. However, if the algorithm under consideration is of a numerical nature, i.e., one which does involve one of the errors discussed in Chapter 6, the above statement is not necessarily true, as we have seen in some of the previous examples.

If the execution of the algorithm involves either round-off or truncation errors, we have to change our definition of "best" in order to take into account the correctness of the output. The generally accepted method is to establish an error bound ϵ and require that an algorithm produce an output x which differs from the true solution α by an amount less than ϵ:

$$|x - \alpha| \leq \epsilon \tag{1}$$

That algorithm is considered "best" whose complexity is lowest with the added restriction that its output x satisfies condition (1).

In this chapter we shall consider some representative numerical algorithms which have been proven to be of practical usefulness in a wide variety of situations. It is our intention to provide the structure of these algorithms while simultaneously studying their performance.

7.1 DESCRIPTIVE STATISTICS

Thus far we have been concerned with algorithms and procedures as entities for study and have not really considered the data to which the algorithms are to be applied. There are, however, very important classes of algorithms whose sole purpose is the *description* of the actual data and/or the reduction of large amounts of data to tractable form. In the latter classes fall most of the procedures and methods of statistics. It is not our purpose in this section to provide a general introduction to this area but rather to point out that these methods are amenable to the same kinds of analyses as described earlier.

Descriptive statistics are used to characterize large sets of data by a few carefully selected parameters which capture vital aspects of the data. Viewed in this light, they are one solution to the problem of data reduction. Consider an experiment which consists of measuring the heights of adults in a city. The result of this experiment will be a table of heights which, if unprocessed, yields very little information to the peruser. The two most common statistics used to characterize a data set are the *mean* and the *standard deviation*. The first measures more or less where the values of the experiment aggregate (central tendency), and the latter is a measure of the dispersion of the data around the mean taken as a clustering point. For the above example the mean therefore indicates the average height, and the standard deviation measures how much variation from this average occurs in the population. The mean μ is formally defined as

$$\mu = \frac{\sum_{i=1}^{n} x_i}{n} \tag{2}$$

and the standard deviation as

$$\sigma = \left[\frac{\sum_{i=1}^{n} (x_i - \mu)^2}{n - 1} \right]^{1/2} \tag{3}$$

where the x_i are the data points and n is the number of points.

Example 7.1

Let the data set be the collection of grades of a student (using the standard four-point system, i.e., A $= 4$, B $= 3$, C $= 2$, D $= 1$, N $= 0$); e.g.,

$$\text{student } A: \quad X_A = \{2, 1, 2, 2, 3, 2, 1, 2, 2\}, \qquad n_A = 9$$
$$\text{student } B: \quad X_B = \{0, 1, 4, 1, 3, 2, 4, 1, 0, 2, 3\}, \qquad n_B = 11$$

Then

$$\mu_A = \tfrac{1}{9}(2 + 1 + 2 + 2 + 3 + 2 + 1 + 2 + 2) = 1.91$$
$$\mu_B = \tfrac{1}{11}(0 + 1 + 4 + 1 + 3 + 2 + 4 + 1 + 0 + 2 + 3) = 1.82$$

and

$$\sigma_A^2 = \tfrac{1}{8}[.11^2 + (-.89)^2 + .11^2 + .11^2 + 1.11^2 + .11^2 + (-.89)^2 + .11^2 + .11^2]$$
$$= .36$$

$$\sigma_B^2 = \tfrac{1}{10}[(-1.91)^2 + (-.91)^2 + 2.09^2 + (-.91)^2 + (1.09)^2 + .09^2 + 2.09^2$$
$$+ (-.91)^2 + (-.91)^2 + .09^2 + 1.09^2] = 2.09 \quad \blacksquare$$

Example 7.1 points out the danger of basing one's conclusion on only one of the statistics. Both students have a comparable grade point average, but their respective standard deviations show that while student A is a rather consistent "C" student with little variation in her grades, student B (whose standard deviation of the grades is relatively large) is a rather inconsistent student with wild variations in his grades. More generally speaking, it should be clear that the results of any data reduction might be quite misleading, and one should refrain from drawing conclusions from descriptive statistics which are not warranted. For instance, consider a small company consisting of a "director" with a salary of $100,000 and nine clerks each with a salary of $4000. It certainly would be somewhat misleading to state that the average salary in this company is $13,600. The problems with this example are, first, the sample size n is too small to draw *statistically significant* conclusions, and, second, the mean is not very descriptive of samples which are heavily *biased*. That is, one or more values are disproportionally large (small) if compared to the rest. A commonly used solution to this problem is to use the *median* instead of the mean. The median m is defined as that value that is smaller than half the data points and larger than the other half.

EXERCISE 7.1: Find out as many salaries as you can of faculty members at your university. Compute the mean, median, and standard deviation. (If the mean is very much different from the median, you know that the sample is heavily biased.)

A way to graphically depict the data set together with its descriptive statistics is to plot a *histogram*. To obtain the histogram we usually partition the range of the data into equal-sized bins and plot the number of data items in each bin. In the event we have a large sample we can normalize the histogram by dividing the number of points in each bin by the sample size.

Example 7.2

Assume we have performed the experiment of measuring the heights (in meters) of adults in the two regions A and B with the following results ($n = 20$):

Heights in Region A (in meters)		Heights in Region B (in meters)	
1.68	1.78	1.58	1.91
1.85	1.69	1.92	1.85
1.73	1.75	1.84	1.85
1.79	1.79	1.97	1.73
1.88	1.63	1.88	1.78
1.93	1.58	1.91	1.62
1.75	1.82	1.74	1.78
1.74	1.64	1.86	1.69
1.68	1.71	1.73	1.86
1.82	1.96	1.68	1.74

First we have to determine the range of the data sets, namely, $1.58 - 1.96$ for the first and $1.58 - 1.97$ for the second. Next we decide on the bin size, say .1, and count the number of data points falling into each range. The resulting histogram is shown in

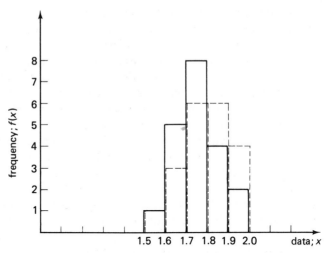

Fig. 7.1   Histogram of two samples.

Figure 7.1, with the unbroken line indicating sample A and dashed lines indicating the histogram of sample B.   ∎

EXERCISE 7.2: Compute the mean and standard deviation for the two samples of Example 7.2 and add them to the histogram.

EXERCISE 7.3: Write an AL algorithm for computing the plot $f(x)$ of the histogram for a set of data x of size n.

Computation of descriptive statistics plays a major role in data processing, and it is vital that we develop efficient algorithms which are stable (insensitive to round-off errors) for their computation. If the data are all given at once as an n-tuple, we can view definitions (2) and (3) as the "natural" algorithms (note they have to be executed in sequence). If we set c_r for the cost analysis to zero and let n_p be the number of additions (subtractions) of data and n_m the number of multiplications (divisions), the complexity of this algorithm is

$$c(n) = w_1[(n-1)c_p + c_m + (n + (n-1) + 1)c_p + (n+1)c_m] + w_2 nc_s$$
$$= w_1[(3n-1)c_p + (n+2)c_m] + w_2 nc_s$$

plus the complexity of the square root operation.

We can reduce the complexity of this algorithm by noting that (3) can be reformulated into

$$\sigma^2 = \frac{\displaystyle\sum_{i=1}^{n} (x_i - \mu)^2}{n-1}$$

$$= \frac{\displaystyle\sum_{i=1}^{n} x_i^2 - 2\mu \sum_{i=1}^{n} x_i + \sum_{i=1}^{n} \mu^2}{n-1}$$

$$= \frac{\sum\limits_{i=1}^{n} x_i^2 - 2\mu n\mu + n\mu^2}{n-1}$$

$$= \frac{\sum x_i^2 - n\mu^2}{n-1} \qquad (4)$$

Using formulation (4) we can write an algorithm which will compute σ and μ concurrently.

Algorithm 7.1 (Computation of the mean and the square of the standard deviation)

procedure *statist*$(x, n; sigmas, mu)$
begin /*statist*/
    sum $\leftarrow x(1)$; *squares* $\leftarrow x(1) ** 2$; $i \leftarrow 2$;
    while $(i \leq n)$ [*sum* $\leftarrow$ *sum* $+ x(i)$; *squares* $\leftarrow$ *squares* $+ x(i) ** 2$; $i \leftarrow i + 1$];
    mu $\leftarrow$ *sum*/*n*; *sigmas* $\leftarrow$ (*squares* $- n * mu ** 2)/(n-1)$
end /*statist*/

It should be noted that Algorithm 7.1 does not need to store all the data but can be modified to read one datum at a time; thus, $n_s = 1$. From Algorithm 7.1 we derive its complexity

$$c(n) = w_1[2nc_p + (n+4)c_m] + w_2 c_s$$

which is better than before but not in terms of order analysis.

To answer the question as to which is the more stable algorithm we have to go back to bound (16) of Chapter 6. One of the main terms which dominate the bound is the term

$$r \sum_{i=2}^{n} |S_i|$$

which indicates that the bound is proportional to the sum of the partial sums. In both algorithms the terms in the partial sums of the standard deviation are all positive, but in the second algorithm these terms will be much larger. The reason is obvious, since for the "natural" algorithm the mean is first subtracted from the data; the more closely the data are clustered around the mean, the smaller the terms involved become. Thus, in cases of centralized data we definitely should select the natural algorithm.

However, as suggested before, Algorithm 7.1 can be modified in such a way that the data do not have to be stored; in the case of a large data set this can be of crucial importance. Moreover, it is often the case that the data are computed one at a time and we wish to update the mean and the standard deviation to adjust for the extra sample point. That is, given μ_n (the mean of n sample points), σ_n (the standard deviation of n sample points), n, and a new point x_{n+1}, we wish to calculate the updated μ_{n+1} and σ_{n+1}. A simple modification to Algorithm 7.1 will achieve this goal.

An algorithm which combines the updating capability of the modified Algorithm 7.1 with the stable behavior of the natural algorithm is given below. The derivation of this algorithm is rather involved, and it will not be presented; only the result is cited.

Algorithm 7.2 (Stable computation of μ and σ^2 without storing data)

procedure *statist*(*c, mu, sigmas, n, x; c, mu, sigmas, n*);
begin /*since σ^2 is defined only for $n \geq 2$ we have to initialize
      $c \leftarrow 0$; mu $\leftarrow x_1$; sigmas $\leftarrow 0$; $n \leftarrow 1$; in the main program before
      calling *statist* with the second, third, etc., data value*/
  $c \leftarrow c + n * (x - mu) ** 2/(n + 1)$;
  $mu \leftarrow (n * mu + x)/(n + 1)$;
  $sigmas \leftarrow c/n$;
  $n \leftarrow n + 1$
end /*since*/

Example 7.3

Let us execute Algorithm 7.2 with the sample points $x_1 = 3$, $x_2 = 5$, and $x_3 = 7$.
First we initialize the variables to

$$c = 0, \quad mu = 3, \quad sigmas = 0, \quad n = 1$$

Next we call *statist* with these values and $x = 5$, which will result in

$$c = 2, \quad mu = 4, \quad sigmas = 2, \quad n = 2$$

Calling *statist* with the above values and $x = 7$ yields the final result

$$c = 8, \quad mu = 5, \quad sigmas = 4, \quad n = 3$$

To verify the result we compute

$$\mu = \tfrac{1}{3}(3 + 5 + 7)$$
$$= 5$$

and

$$\sigma^2 = \tfrac{1}{2}(4 + 0 + 4)$$
$$= 4 \quad \blacksquare$$

EXERCISE 7.4: Implement both Algorithms 7.1 and 7.2 as FORTRAN programs. Run
both of them on a set of 10,000 centralized data. Compare run times (CPU time) and accuracy
(use double precision runs for comparison).

7.2 SOME BASIC ALGORITHMS IN NUMERICAL MATHEMATICS

7.2.1 Root Finding

One of the most important mathematical manipulations is that of finding the
root(s) of an equation. This problem occurs so frequently that a considerable amount
of effort has gone into finding efficient solutions. One interesting application occurs in
the implementation of a square root library function (cf. Part A of the supplemental
volume), e.g., finding x such that

$$f(x) = x^2 - a$$

is equal to zero. Of course, the solution implies that $x^2 - a = 0$ or $x = \sqrt{a}$. It is clear that the procedure for solving this problem must be as efficient (in terms of speed and accuracy) as possible since it may be called thousands of times during the execution of a program (recall our discussion in Chapter 4). It should be clear that for only a few functions f can the problem of finding its root(s) be solved directly; examples are polynomials of degree less than 4. However, in many cases the round-off error can be quite catastrophic (see the quadratic equations in Chapter 6), and they are rarely used in any application. One of the better known iteration schemes is the *Newton-Raphson* method, which utilizes the following transformation [$f'(x)$ denotes the derivative of $f(x)$]:

$$\mathbf{T}(x) = x - \frac{f(x)}{f'(x)} \tag{5}$$

leading to the iteration scheme

$$x_n \longleftarrow x_{n-1} - \frac{f(x_{n-1})}{f'(x_{n-1})}$$

The Newton-Raphson method has a simple geometric interpretation, which is illustrated in Figure 7.2. To obtain x_n, find the intersection of the x-axis and the tangent of $f(x)$ at the point $(x_{n-1}, f(x_{n-1}))$.

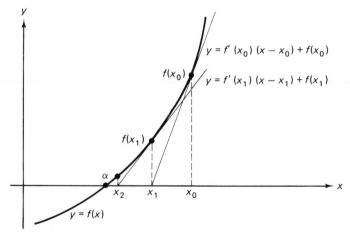

Fig. 7.2   Geometric interpretation of the Newton-Raphson Method.

Example 7.4

Let $f(x) = x^2 - q$. According to equation (5), the transformation $\mathbf{T}$ is given by

$$\mathbf{T}(x) = x - \frac{x^2 - q}{2x} = \frac{1}{2}\left(x + \frac{q}{x}\right)$$

and the Newton-Raphson method is

$$x_n \longleftarrow x_{n-1} - \frac{x_{n-1}^2 - q}{2x_{n-1}}$$

From the graph of f, given in Figure 7.3, we note that choosing $x_0 > \sqrt{q}$ has the

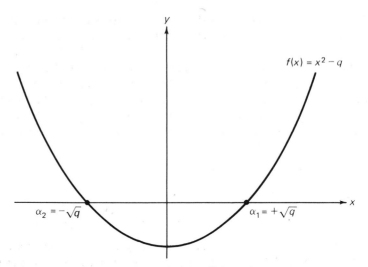

Fig. 7.3 Graph of the function $f(x) = x^2 - q$.

effect of guaranteeing that the points $x_1, x_2, \ldots$ will lie in the interval between x_0 and $\sqrt{q}$ since $\alpha = \sqrt{q} \leq x_{m+1} < x_m$ for all m. ∎

Lest the reader assume that all we can do with the Newton-Raphson method is to find roots of polynomials, we shall now give examples of problems which can be transformed into root-finding problems. It should be clear that this method can be applied to the finding of roots of any function, not just polynomials.

A related yet different problem is to find that value of x for which $g(x)$ takes on a given value c. In other words, find α such that

$$g(\alpha) = c$$

for a given g and c. For instance, for what value of x does sin (x) have the value .6? The proper formulation as a root-finding problem is to select f as the function

$$f(x) = g(x) - c$$

because if $f(\alpha) = 0$, then $g(\alpha)$ equals c. For the above example the iteration scheme

$$x_n \longleftarrow x_{n-1} - \frac{\sin (x_{n-1}) - .6}{\cos (x_{n-1})}$$

will converge to α such that sin $(\alpha) = .6$.

Another problem which can be easily formulated as a root-finding problem is that of finding the point(s) of intersection of two curves in a plane. Consider the two curves in Figure 7.4, which represent a quarter circle given by $f_1(x) = \sqrt{r^2 - x^2}$ and the straight line $f_2(x) = k_1 x + k_2$. We wish to compute α, the value of the x-coordinate of the point of intersection. At this point it must be true that

$$f_1(\alpha) = f_2(\alpha)$$

Hence, if we select $f(x)$ as

$$f(x) = f_1(x) - f_2(x)$$

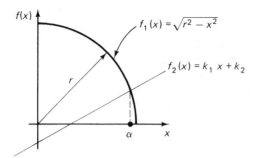

Fig. 7.4 Intersection of two curves in a plane.

then the root of $f(x)$ will be the desired point. For example, consider the circle $f_1(x) = \sqrt{4 - x^2}$ and the straight line $f_2(x) = 2x - 1$; then $f(x)$ is given by

$$f(x) = \sqrt{4 - x^2} - 2x + 1$$

and the Newton-Raphson algorithm by

$$x_n \longleftarrow x_{n-1} + \frac{\sqrt{4 - x_{n-1}^2} - 2x_{n-1} + 1}{2 + x_{n-1}/\sqrt{4 - x_{n-1}^2}}$$

7.2.2 Interpolation

The example we used in Chapter 6 to illustrate the truncation error is only an instance of a wide class of problems. The class we wish to consider can be characterized as follows: Given a function $f(x)$ and a mathematical procedure **P**, apply **P** to f to obtain a value F. Whereas equation (6) may define a perfectly reasonable procedure (integration)

$$F = \int_a^b f(x)\, dx \qquad \left(\text{e.g., } F = \int_0^1 \frac{\sin x}{x^2}\, dx \right) \qquad (6)$$

there may not exist a corresponding algorithm to calculate F which can be implemented on a computer. Rather, we may be forced to replace f by a function $\bar{f}$ for which there exists an algorithm to compute $\bar{F}$ (here the integral of $\bar{f}$) and so that $\bar{F}$ approximates F as closely as possible. Obviously, we can only broach the problem as defined above, and we restrict ourselves to the class of problems where an explicit algorithm exists for the mathematical procedure **P** if $f(x)$ is a polynomial. For instance, if **P** represents differentiation, then there exists an algorithm if $f(x)$ is a polynomial:

$$f(x) = \sum_{i=1}^{n} a_i x^i$$

$$f'(x) = \sum_{i=0}^{n-1} (i + 1)a_{i+1} x^i$$

Given this restriction, we face two problems: first, how to approximate f with a polynomial $\bar{f}$ so as to minimize $|F - \bar{F}|$ and, second, how to formulate computationally efficient algorithms to evaluate $\bar{F}$. The latter point is discussed in more detail in Section 7.3.1 of Part C of the supplementary volume (Newton-Cotes formulas for integration). The first problem is the choice of $\bar{f}$. If we define a function dist$(f, \bar{f})$ as representing the distance between f and $\bar{f}$ according to some definition of *distance*, then we obviously want to select $\bar{f}$ so that dist$(f, \bar{f})$ is a minimum. Depending on the definition of "distance," several approaches to the selection of $\bar{f}$ are open. Since in many cases f is to be approximated only over a given interval $[a, b]$, we shall interpret dist$(f, \bar{f})$ as the distance between f and $\bar{f}$ over the interval $[a, b]$.

Our choice of the meaning of "distance" is the sum of the differences (absolute value) between the two function values at $n + 1$ selected points in the interval $[a, b]$. More formally,

$$\text{dist}(f, \bar{f}) = \sum_{i=0}^{n} |f(x_i) - \bar{f}(x_i)| \qquad \text{for} \qquad x_i \in [a, b], 0 \le i \le n \qquad (7)$$

Example 7.5

Let $f(x)$ be 2^x, the approximation interval be $[0, 2]$, and the selected points be $x_1 = 0$, $x_2 = 1$, and $x_3 = 2$. As can be seen from Figure 7.5, the function

$$\bar{f}(x) = \tfrac{1}{2}(x^2 + x + 2)$$

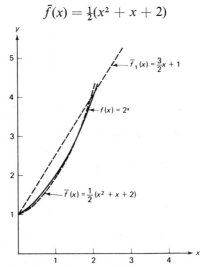

Fig. 7.5 Various approximations to a function.

has distance zero. On the other hand, the function

$$\bar{f}_1(x) = \tfrac{3}{2}x + 1$$

has the distance $|\bar{f}_1(1) - f(1)| = .5$ from the function f. ■

EXERCISE 7.5: Compute the distance of $\bar{f}$ and $\bar{f}_1$ to the function f as given in Example 7.5 where distance is interpreted as the sum of the areas in each interval $[x_{i-1}, x_i]$ between the function and its approximation.

Given this definition of distance and assuming that the function f is given at the $n + 1$ points,

$$x_0 < x_1 < x_2 < \cdots < x_n$$

then there is a unique polynomial $p(x)$ of degree n which satisfies

$$\text{dist}(f(x), p(x)) = 0, \qquad x \in [a, b] \tag{8}$$

Although the polynomial is unique, it may be written in many different ways. The form

$$p(x) = \sum_{i=0}^{n} f(x_i) l_i(x) \qquad \text{with } l_i(x) = \prod_{\substack{k=0 \\ k \neq i}}^{n} \frac{x - x_k}{x_i - x_k} \tag{9}$$

is called the Lagrange interpolation polynomial, and we leave it to the reader to verify that it satisfies condition (8).

Example 7.6

Given $f(x) = 2^x/x$, what is the interpolation polynomial over $[2, 8]$ for $n = 2$ and $x_0 = 2$, $x_1 = 4$, and $x_2 = 8$? First we have to calculate the various l_i's:

$$l_0(x) = \frac{(x - 4)(x - 8)}{(2 - 4)(2 - 8)} = \frac{1}{12}(x^2 - 12x + 32)$$

$$l_1(x) = \frac{(x - 2)(x - 8)}{(4 - 2)(4 - 8)} = -\frac{1}{8}(x^2 - 10x + 16)$$

$$l_2(x) = \frac{(x - 2)(x - 4)}{(8 - 2)(8 - 4)} = \frac{1}{24}(x^2 - 6x + 8)$$

whose graphs are shown in Figure 7.6. Since $f(2) = 2$, $f(4) = 4$, and $f(8) = 32$, we

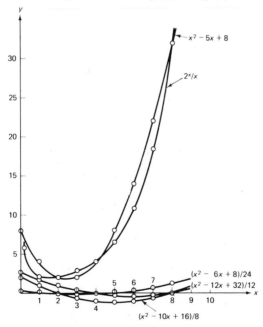

Fig. 7.6   The Lagrange interpolation polynomial for $f(x) = 2^x/x$.

then obtain

$$p(x) = \tfrac{2}{12}(x^2 - 12x + 32) - \tfrac{4}{8}(x^2 - 10x + 16) + \tfrac{32}{24}(x^2 - 6x + 8)$$
$$= \tfrac{1}{6}(x^2 - 12x + 32 - 3x^2 + 30x - 48 + 8x^2 - 48x + 64)$$
$$= \tfrac{1}{6}(6x^2 - 30x + 48)$$
$$= x^2 - 5x + 8$$

To check that the distance

$$\text{dist}\left(\frac{2^x}{x}, p(x)\right) = 0$$

is zero we verify that

$$p(2) = 2$$
$$p(4) = 4$$
$$p(8) = 32 \quad \blacksquare$$

EXERCISE 7.6: Find the interpolation polynomial for the function $f(x) = x^2 \log_2 x$ over the interval [1, 4] with $n = 2$, and $x_0 = 1$, $x_1 = 2$, $x_2 = 4$.

An application of the Lagrange interpolation polynomial is the plotting of a function given only as a sequence of discrete value points. For instance, we may have given a function f as a sequence of seven pairs of the form (x-coordinate, y-coordinate), as shown in Figure 7.7. We want to plot a function which approximates f. If no plotter

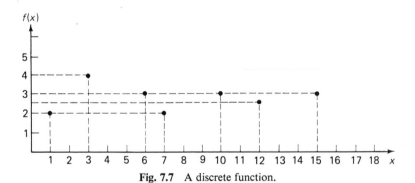

Fig. 7.7   A discrete function.

is available, then the approximation curve shown in Figure 7.8 would have to be represented as a sequence of symbols. Nevertheless, many more points could be printed than were originally given. We might be tempted to simply calculate the interpolation polynomial of degree 6 and use it to plot the approximation function. But we should realize that the round-off error in calculating the interpolation polynomial would be rather great since for $x = 15$ the numbers involved would be of a magnitude of $15^6 \approx 10^{10}$. Instead, we group the interpolation points and calculate for the two groups of four points (one point overlapping) separate interpolation polynomials. Doing so, we can generalize this method to a function given by n points: Divide the n

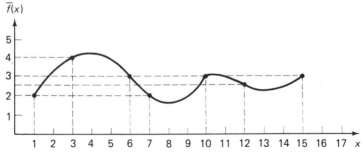

Fig. 7.8 Approximation by a group of polynomials.

points into overlapping groups of m points, and compute for each group the interpolation polynomial of degree $m - 1$. The resulting function will be continuous and pass through all points, but at the overlapping points the curve may have *corners*. That is, the transition from one polynomial to the next may not be smooth.

To return to our example, we compute two polynomials passing through the following points:

$$p_1(x): \quad x \quad \begin{vmatrix} 1\ 3\ 6\ 7 \end{vmatrix} \qquad p_2(x): \quad x \quad \begin{vmatrix} 7\ 10\ 12\ 15 \end{vmatrix}$$
$$f(x) \quad \begin{vmatrix} 2\ 4\ 3\ 2 \end{vmatrix} \qquad\qquad f(x) \quad \begin{vmatrix} 2\ \ 3\ 2.5\ \ 3 \end{vmatrix}$$

and the approximation function $\bar{f}$ is then given by

$$\bar{f}(x) = \begin{cases} p_1(x) & \text{for } 1 \leq x \leq 7 \\ p_2(x) & \text{for } 7 \leq x \leq 15 \end{cases}$$

It is of no great difficulty to write an algorithm to evaluate $\bar{f}(x)$ at, say, $x = 1.0, 1.1,$ $1.2, \ldots, 14.8, 14.9, 15.0$. Therefore, we go on and develop an algorithm for plotting a discrete function using a sequence of $(m-1)$th-degree interpolation polynomials as stated in Figure 7.9. Module I of Figure 7.9 consists basically of an iteration over the

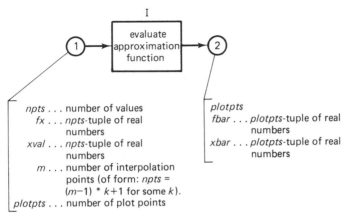

Fig. 7.9 Evaluation of plot-function.

evaluation of different polynomials of which there are $k = \lfloor npts/(m-1) \rfloor$. In each iteration we have to evaluate one polynomial, determined by a set of m consecutive points of *xval* and *fx*, a certain number of times. We assume that the plot points are to be roughly equally spaced, with the difference between any two points being $h = (xval(npts) - xval(1))/plotpts$. If *beg* and *end* are indices delineating the interval for an interpolation polynomial, then the basic block consists of evaluating

$$p(x): \quad \begin{vmatrix} xval(beg), \, xval(beg+1), \, \ldots, \, xval(end) \\ fx(beg), \, \ldots \quad\quad\quad\quad\quad , fx(end) \end{vmatrix}$$

at the points

$$xval(beg), \, xval(beg) + h, \, xval(beg) + 2*h, \, \ldots, \, xval(end)$$

Algorithm 7.3 (Computing the approximate plot of a function)

```
begin /*plot*/
    if mod(npts, m − 1) ≠ 1 then[output 'incorrect number of points';
                                terminate];
            /*initialization*/
    h ⟵ (xval(npts) − xval(1))/plotpts;
    degr ⟵ m − 1; beg ⟵ 1; i ⟵ 1; end ⟵ beg + degr:
    while(beg < npts)
    begin /*evaluate for one interval*/
        x ⟵ xval(beg);
        while (x ≤ xval(end))
        begin /*one point of interval*/
            xbar(i) ⟵ x;
            fbar(i) ⟵ lagrange( fx, xval, beg, end, x);
            i ⟵ i + 1;
            x ⟵ x + h
        end; /*one*/
        beg ⟵ beg + degr;
        end ⟵ end + degr
    end /*evaluate*/
end /*plot*/
```

In the following FORTRAN implementation of Algorithm 7.3 we took advantage of FORTRAN conventions for argument correspondence (i.e., call by reference) to indicate to the function LAGRAN the starting point of the data to be used. We have not attempted to optimize the function LAGRAN and have implemented the "natural" algorithm specified by (9).

Purpose: Compute the approximate plot of a function.
Communication:

subroutines or functions called: LAGRAN . . . real function with
arguments FUNC, XCORD,
X, MP; FUNC and XCORD
being arrays of dimension
MP;

$\left.\begin{array}{l} \text{FX} \\ \text{XVAL} \\ \text{NPTS} \end{array}\right\} \ldots$ NPTS-tuples of function
to be plotted;

$\left.\begin{array}{l} \text{FBAR} \\ \text{XBAR} \\ \text{PLOTPT} \end{array}\right\} \ldots$ PLOTPT-tuples representing
function to be computed;
FBAR, XBAR modified;

M . . . . number of interpolation
points; NPTS should be
of form:
$k * (M - 1) + 1$ for some k.

Program:

```
C:::::::::::::::::::::::::::::::::::::::::::::::::::::::::::::::::::::::::::::::::::::::::::::::::
C            SUBROUTINE PLOT (FX,XVAL,NPTS,FBAR,XBAR,PLOTPT,M)
C:::::::::::::::::::::::::::::::::::::::::::::::::::::::::::::::::::::::::::::::::::::::::::::::::
             SUBROUTINE PLOT (FX,XVAL,NPTS,FBAR,XBAR,PLOTPT,M)
C       THIS ROUTINE COMPUTES THE APPROXIMATE PLOT OF A FUNCTION
     DIMENSION FX(NPTS),XVAL(NPTS),FBAR(PLOTPT),XBAR(PLOTPT)
     INTEGER PLOTPT,BEG,DEGR
     REAL LAGRAN
C
C        INITIALIZE INTERVAL INDICES AND INCREMENT SIZE
C
     H=(XVAL(NPTS)-XVAL(1))/PLOTPT
     DEGR=M-1
     I=1
C        ITERATE OVER INTERVALS
     DO 20 BEG=1,NPTS-DEGR,DEGR
           X=XVAL(BEG)
  10       IF (X.GT.XVAL(BEG+DEGR)) GO TO 20
C          EVALUATE A POINT
                 XBAR(I)=X
                 FBAR(I)=LAGRAN(FX(BEG),XVAL(BEG),X,M)
                 I=I+1
                 IF (I.GT.PLOTPT) GO TO 30
                     X=X+H
           GO TO 10
  20 CONTINUE
  30 RETURN
     END
```

```
C:::::::::::::::::::::::::::::::::::::::::::::::::::::::::::::::::::::::::::::::::::::::::::::::::::::::::::
C                    FUNCTION LAGRAN (FUNC,XCORD,X,MP)
C:::::::::::::::::::::::::::::::::::::::::::::::::::::::::::::::::::::::::::::::::::::::::::::::::::::::::::
       REAL FUNCTION LAGRAN(FUNC, XCORD, X, MP)
       DIMENSION. FUNC(MP),XCORD(MP)
C
C          INITIALIZE
C
       LAGRAN = 0.0
C          ADD MP WEIGHTED POLYNOMIALS
       DO 20 I=1,MP
              PROD =1.0
              DO 10 K=1,MP
C             OMIT I-TH TERM
                    IF (K.EQ.I) GO TO 10
                         PROD =PROD*(X-XCORD(K))/(XCORD(I)-XCORD(K))
    10        CONTINUE
              LAGRAN=LAGRAN+FUNC(I)*PROD
    20 CONTINUE
       RETURN
       END
```

In the subroutine PLOT we have the seemingly superfluous test for checking I against the total number of plot points. However, remembering the comments we made during the discussion of the static truncation we realize that the statement

$$X = X + H$$

may lead to a marked round-off error in X. Thus, the number of computed interpolation points may not agree with the predicted number PLOTPT.

7.3 CONCLUSIONS

In this chapter we have examined rather cursorily several of the important applications of the computer for what might be called *numerical* applications. For problems in this class, it is important to find algorithms for their solution which are simultaneously of a low order of complexity and highly accurate. Many of these are characterized by a large number of repetitive calculations, which leads us to the low-complexity requirement. The nature of the repetitive calculations is such that there is a potential for the propagation of the types of errors discussed in Chapter 6; hence, we look for those algorithms in which this tendency is minimized.

This chapter essentially concludes our discussion of what might be called *numerical* algorithms. These algorithms may be characterized as those for which the question of error propagation is of prime importance. The following chapters are mainly devoted to discussions of algorithms for which this property is not of major importance; these algorithms are commonly called *nonnumerical*. Nonnumerical algorithms operate, for the most part, on *symbols*, and the standard error analyses do not apply to any great extent. This does not imply, however, that there are no problems with errors when working with algorithms of this type but merely that the considerations are different.

We conclude this discussion by repeating a maxim first formulated by Richard Hamming:

THE PURPOSE OF COMPUTING IS UNDERSTANDING, NOT NUMBERS

References

A comprehensive introduction to numerical analysis is

A. RALSTON, *A First Course in Numerical Analysis*, McGraw-Hill, New York, 1965.

For more information on statistics, see

P. L. MEYER, *Introductory Probability and Statistical Applications*, Addison-Wesley, Reading, Mass., 1970.

Algorithm 7.2 is due to R. J. Hanson and is based on material in

C. L. LAWSON and R. J. HANSON, *Solving Least Squares Problems*, Prentice-Hall, Englewood Cliffs, N.J., 1974.

Exercises

1 Draw a function $f(x)$ for which Newton-Raphson's method will not converge for some initial guess.

2 The equation

$$ax + bx \log_2 x = c$$

occurs in scheduling processors for parallel sorting. Using the Newton-Raphson method, find an x that satisfies the above equation for $a = 100$, $b = 10$, $c = 800$.

3 Compute a fifth-degree interpolation polynomial for sin (x) between $[-\pi, \pi]$ and compare its graph to the graph of Taylor's fifth-degree approximation polynomial.

4 Give an algorithm for computing the median of a sample. [Hint: In the literature you will find algorithms whose complexity is of $0(n)$.]

5 Write a program to simulate the game of roulette. Establish typical values of input parameters (i.e., how many plays per evening, how many players, amounts of bets, etc.) and compute μ and σ for the amount the bank wins each day.

8

System Processes

8.0 INTRODUCTION

The first seven chapters of this book have been concerned with the nature and representation of algorithms, their analysis, and their implementation on a computer. The emphasis in these chapters, particularly the last four, has been on numeric algorithms which have proven useful to a wide variety of users. In this chapter the emphasis shifts to a different class, namely, nonnumeric algorithms. The distinction between numeric and nonnumeric algorithms is vague; very often an algorithm will exhibit characteristics of both. Specifically, in this chapter we shall consider those processes which provide the facilities normally associated with general-purpose computing systems designed to provide problem-solving capabilities to users such as students in a university computing center, engineers, data processors, etc. As a general disclaimer for this chapter we emphasize that we shall not depict any one particular system but rather will concentrate on concepts with examples typical of many systems.

To this end, let us reconsider the structure of a typical computer configuration, as introduced in Figure A.5 of the supplementary volume. In Part A of the supplementary volume the focus is with the variety of input/output devices available and the manner in which FORTRAN allows control of these devices. In this chapter the emphasis is on the totality of *resources* constituting such a system. Figure 8.1 represents a block diagram of a functional computer with examples of several devices given in Figure 8.2. A computer system, when viewed at the level of Figure 8.1, is seen as a collection of *hardware* which has been designed to perform a basic set of functions. On the other hand, the existence of a collection of hardware does not imply that the system will be of general use. To be of service to the user the hardware facilities must be made accessible without requiring detailed knowledge of the hardware structure. That is, a computer system consists not only of the hardware but also of a collection of *software* (= programs) which allows the hardware to be utilized in useful and efficient ways.

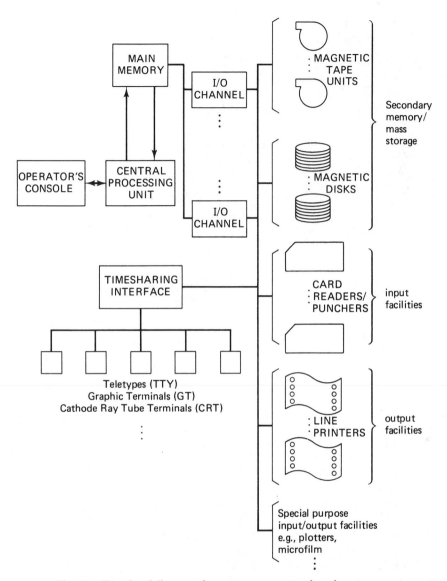

Fig. 8.1 Functional diagram of a computer system; selected components shown in Fig. 8.2.

We have already seen examples of the type of software which might be available on such a system: the translator discussed in Chapter 2 and the FORTRAN compiler mentioned in Part A of the supplementary volume. One can then conceive of a software *system* whose sole concern is the efficient utilization of the various resources (both hardware and software) which constitute the entire system. This software system

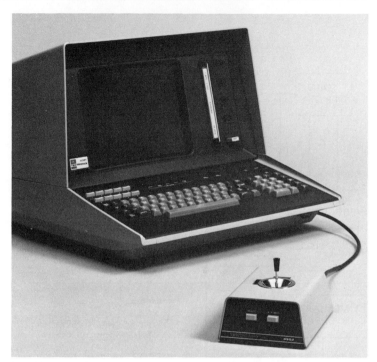

(top: Courtesy of Tektronix, Inc., bottom: Courtesy of California Computer Products, Inc.)

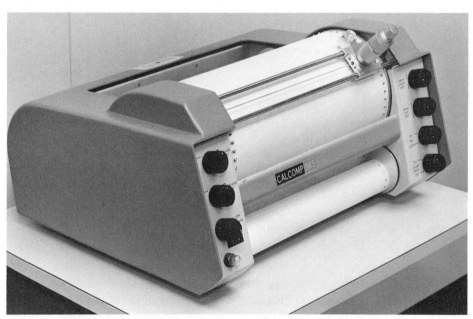

Fig. 8.2 Illustration of selected devices from Fig. 8.1: (*top*) Tektronix 4051 graphics terminal with joystick input device (user terminal), (*bottom*) Calcom 565 Plotter (special purpose output device for plotting).

is often termed an *operating system* and is also called a *monitor, control program, supervisor,* or *executive.* We shall consider the terms to be synonymous (which is not precisely correct) and shall select *operating system* (OS) as the generic name. Operating systems are designed according to two major constraints:

1. The functional capabilities of the hardware, and
2. Generality from the user's point of view.

These two design constraints are very often in conflict, and most operating systems represent a compromise between these and other conflicting design goals. The system shown in Figure 8.1 is intended to have *multiprogramming* capabilities; i.e., several jobs (user programs) may reside concurrently in memory and compete for the various resources.

For instance, since the hardware provides only a limited number of input/output channels, a user requesting control of one may have to wait if they are all currently in use. It is not the intent here to discuss the various factors which play a role in the design of such a system or to go into much detail as to the structure of an actual operating system. Rather, we must be content with a sparse overview of the function of the system and defer details to later courses.

8.1 THE NATURE OF OPERATING SYSTEMS

As already discussed, one of the major functions of an operating system is the allocation of the various resources of a computer system to a user or to other parts of the system. A second function is the facilitation of the sharing of these resources among a group of users who have simultaneous access to the computer. Very few users have sole access to any large installation; such access would be uneconomical for a variety of reasons. Hence, it is desirable to have as many users as possible using the system at the same time, although each should appear to have sole access. This implies that one aspect of an operating system is the protection of one user from the actions of another and managing the overhead involved in the concurrent execution of diverse processes (which clearly puts a limit on the number of users who can be accommodated at the same time).

Let us consider the nature of the resources available with which the operating system must work and the functions it might perform. The functional characteristics of typical input/output devices and secondary storage devices are summarized in Table 8.1. The manner in which data are accessed is one of the main differences between main memory and secondary memory. Due to the structure of main memory (see Section 8.3.1) the time required to access any given location in memory is constant. Most secondary storage devices, however, require the mechanical positioning of a read-write head over the beginning of the data (or moving the data to the read-write head), which implies that the access time is not the same for all data but depends on the relative locations of the data and the read-write head.

EXERCISE 8.1: For your installation, identify the complete range of input/output and secondary storage devices available. Prepare a table similar to Table 8.1 containing the devices, the number of each, what they are primarily used for, data exchange rates, storage capacities, etc.

Table 8.1   TYPICAL CHARACTERISTICS OF INPUT/OUTPUT DEVICES AND SECONDARY STORAGE DEVICES

Device	Physical Medium	Capacity	Data Transfer Rate	Function
Card reader	Card	80 chars/card	10 cards/sec	Input
Card puncher	Card	80 chars/card	3 cards/sec	Output
Line printer	Paper (page)	120 chars/line 55 lines/page	15 lines/sec	Output
TTY	User, paper	80 chars/line	10 chars/sec	Input, output
CRT	User, TV screen	80 chars/line 24 lines/screen	30 chars/sec	Input, output
Magnetic tape unit	Magnetic tape	Up to 10^7 chars/reel	$4 * 10^5$ chars/sec	Secondary storage
Disk unit	Magnetic disk	Up to $3 * 10^8$ chars/unit	10^6 chars/sec	Secondary storage
Main memory	Magnetic core†	Up to $8 * 10^6$ characters	1 word/$(.75 * 10^{-6}$ sec)	Main memory

†One alternative.

An operating system must allocate these resources to users so that the utilization of the system and its resources is maximized and the inconvenience (i.e., waiting time for requests to be filled) to the user is minimized. To illustrate the problem of under-utilization, let us first consider the minimal system shown in Figure 8.3 and the nature of the demands placed on such a system by a user. We emphasize that this system represents an oversimplification of existing systems.

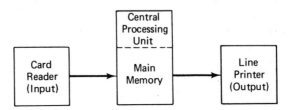

Fig. 8.3   Minimal system configuration.

A typical *job* may consist of reading in, compiling, and executing a FORTRAN program such as one of those developed in the preceding chapters. The four important steps which must be performed in order to complete the job are

1. The deck of cards is read into main memory; this implies that there are resi-dent system routines which control the card reader and which translate the information found on the cards into an internal form, placing this information into some reserved area of main memory.

2. Assuming the FORTRAN compiler is already resident in main memory, it must be activated and take its input from the area of main memory containing

the internal representation of the program obtained from step 1. The resultant code must also be stored in a known section of memory.

3. Beginning at the first instruction, the program must be executed.
4. Any output produced must be sent to the line printer.

Steps 1 and 2 may actually be overlapped in that the compiler may execute as the program is read in. Similarly, steps 3 and 4 may be intermingled in that output is produced as the program is executed.

User access to such a system consists of submission of a deck of cards to the input device and the subsequent recovery of the output from the output device. The total period of time for which any given job is tying up the system is the sum of

1. The time it takes to read the deck of cards,
2. The compile time,
3. The execution time, and
4. The time required to print the output.

Assuming a job consists of 600 cards and produces 900 lines (approximately 17 pages) of output, the total time in the system is approximately

$$60 \text{ sec (input)} + n \text{ sec (execution)} + 60 \text{ sec (output)} = 120 + n \text{ sec}$$

using the figures from Table 8.1. If n is 2 seconds (not an unreasonable assumption), then the total time is 122 seconds. Out of this total time, the central processing unit (CPU) is computing for only 2 seconds, or approximately 1.6% of the time. Since the CPU is usually the most expensive resource in the system, it is highly desirable to avoid such a low utilization factor.

In this example, the function of the operating system is particularly simple and includes the following:

1. Recognize that an input to the system is about to be made;
2. Oversee the input of the program and maintain pertinent system information concerning the program;
3. Recognize that the input represents a FORTRAN program to be compiled and executed;
4. Activate the FORTRAN compiler and oversee the compilation process;
5. When compilation is complete, notify the CPU to begin executing the machine language program produced by the compiler;
6. Direct any output produced to the line printer;
7. When execution is complete, look for another job on the card reader.

Additional functions may include accounting (i.e., charging the appropriate user for the resources used) and various other system maintenance duties.

The reason that the CPU utilization is so low in this example is the disparity in speed between the CPU and the peripheral devices. One obvious method for increasing the CPU utilization is to use I/O devices whose data transfer speeds are more consistent with CPU speeds. From Table 8.1, we note that disks have higher transfer rates than any other device listed. The system shown in Figure 8.4 illustrates a configuration

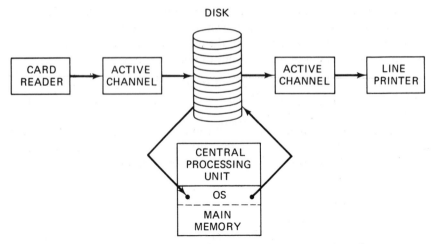

Fig. 8.4 System utilizing secondary storage and active channels.

using secondary storage and *active channels*. An active channel may be a separate processor whose sole task is the handling of peripheral devices, in which case it may be referred to as a *peripheral processor* and can be viewed as a special-purpose computer. At the other end of the spectrum it may be integrated into the central processing unit so that it is possible to route data through the main memory to their target; however, the remainder of the CPU is so constructed that a program can execute concurrently.

In this system, jobs are read in from the input device in a continuous stream (i.e., the jobs are *batched* together on the input device) and are placed on the disk. When one job is finished with the CPU, the operating system goes to the disk, selects the next job to be run (perhaps a simple first-in–first-out selection†), and initiates the sequence of events from the previous example, except that now output is also written to the disk. Thus, the card reader and line printer are continuously reading and printing, while the disk acts as a buffer for all I/O operations. This technique is commonly called *spooling*.

If we assume a 600-card FORTRAN program producing 900 lines of output, that is,

600 cards × 60 characters/card (average) = 36,000 characters from disk

900 lines × 111 characters/line (average) ≃ 100,000 characters to disk

then a total of 136,000 characters are to be read or written. Assuming an average disk data transfer rate of 100,000 characters per second, the total time for the job is

1.4 sec of I/O + 2 sec of execution = 3.4 sec

and the CPU utilization becomes

$$\text{CPU utilization} = 100 * \frac{2}{3.4} \% \simeq 59\%$$

†Compare this with the discussion in Chapter 9 on queues.

which is a considerable improvement over the previous example. But we have to realize that this utilization factor is probably too high due to our neglect of overhead (e.g., the time to properly position a read head of the disk at the start of the FOR-TRAN program).

Two additional features of an operating system have been introduced here. The first is the idea of job scheduling, that is, the selection of the next job to be initiated from the disk. Short jobs (say less than 500 cards) which produce little or no output will obviously increase the CPU utilization, while large jobs which produce an abundance of output will reduce this factor (assuming approximately constant execution time). The criteria by which the operating system selects the next job to be initiated may include

1. The amount of time in the input queue (i.e., how long the job has awaited execution), and
2. The total amount of resources requested by the job, including
    (a) Estimated CPU time,
    (b) Estimated length of output,
    (c) Nature and expense of peripheral devices requested, and
    (d) Amount of main memory requested,

among others. The selection of an actual *scheduling algorithm* is often quite complicated and often counterintuitive, and we defer any further discussion until Chapter 9.

The second feature introduced concerns system I/O handling. The operating system must constantly monitor the operations of the card reader, line printer, disks, and other peripherals to ensure that they are initiated at the proper time. In the system of Figure 8.4, part of this monitoring is provided by *peripheral processors;* these processors perform some of the function which the operating system would normally be required to perform. For example, the card reader has been connected directly to the disk, and the operating system simply initiates the read function; the processor itself performs the input functions to the disk, relieving the operating system of this task. Similarly, the line printer may be connected to the disk. However, since only one device can access the disk at any given time, the operating system must coordinate the requests from the processors for the use of the disk. Conflicting requests can be resolved through a system of *interrupts.* When a device (say the card reader) wishes to access the disk, it *enables* an interrupt, which is a hardware signal (or flag) monitored by the operating system. Enabling an interrupt is a way to notify the operating system that a device wishes an access; the OS then schedules this access, signals the device when the access is granted, disables the interrupt, and returns to monitoring status.

Communications between the user and an OS is provided by means of a *system command* (or *job control*) *language* which specifies a set of commands to the operating system. These directives specify the accounting information necessary for billing purposes, the type of job (e.g., FORTRAN, SNOBOL, AL), the estimated time of execution, the resources required (amount of main memory, peripheral devices, additional system programs required, etc.), the disposition of the job (e.g., compiled, compiled and executed, listed), the disposition of the output (if any), and others. System command languages (SCL's) are often very expressive languages and should be considered high-level programming languages in their own right. The basic difference between SCL's and other languages such as FORTRAN is that the SCL is operating on programs and resources as data.

8.2 FILE STRUCTURES
AND SYSTEM COMMAND LANGUAGES

8.2.1 Files

For reasons of system efficiency, peripheral storage devices such as disks are used as semipermanent storage for both programs and data. They are particularly useful for storing those programs and data which are used frequently, such as the various compilers and interpreters supported by the system, various system programs, and general user programs if space permits. When used in this manner, peripheral devices (particularly disks) may be considered as extensions to main memory, although much slower. Various trade-offs may be made between main memory and these devices as to what information resides where.

For the operating system to manipulate the user's information, it must be structured in a consistent manner. The basic global unit of information is called a *file*, or *data set;* each file has a name, called the *permanent file name*, by which the file is referenced. Each file is composed of a collection of *records*, which may be of variable size and which comprise the basic units of information in a file (compare the discussion in Section 9.0). A file may represent a collection of data, a program and/or related subprograms, combinations of both, or any collection of information which may be represented on the device. Figure 8.5 represents a hypothetical file structure for the

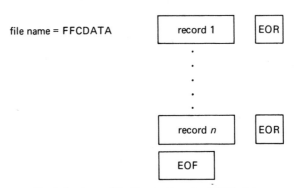

Fig. 8.5   A possible file structure for FFC's data.

Friendly Finance Company's data presented in Chapter 5. Such a structure is known as a *sequential access file* since each record is accessed sequentially, beginning with record 1. In Figure 8.5, each record is of the form given in Figure 5.1. Since records may be of varying lengths, each record is terminated by a special symbol known as the EOR (end of record) marker. Similarly, EOF (for end of file) is a special symbol which marks the physical end of the collection of records constituting the file.

Many physical devices maintain a *directory* of file names currently residing on the device along with the location of the first record of each file (see Figure 8.6); within a device a file is accessed by first looking up its name in the directory and, assuming it exists, setting the *file pointer* to the address of the first record. All manipulations on the

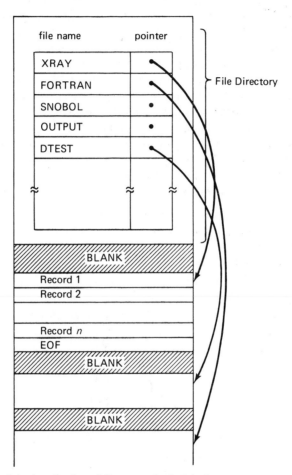

Fig. 8.6   A collection of files on a physical device.

file are then performed relative to this pointer. We shall assume the directory is of a fixed maximum length, although other schemes are also used [e.g., singly linked list(s); see Chapter 9]. Most computer systems provide extensive facilities for manipulating these files, including creation, deletion, modification, and read/write operations. Allocation of file space and directory revisions are done by a portion of the operating system known as the *file supervisor*. Seen in this light, files become a resource to be manipulated by the operating system.

The file structure described above is called the *logical file structure* since it exists independently of the device upon which the file actually resides. This is the structure that the user is aware of. The *physical file structure* may be completely different and depends solely on the physical characteristics of the hardware device upon which the file exists. The operating system will not only have to provide means to implement the mapping of logical files into physical files but also must ensure the integrity and security of each user's files (protect user A's files from unauthorized access by user B). We shall ignore the physical structure and concentrate on the logical structure; only in rare instances will a user be concerned with the physical structure.

It is convenient to distinguish between sequential access files, in which records are read or written contiguously, and *random access files*, in which records are written and read in random order. Each record in a random access file must contain information identifying the record, i.e., the *key*, which is written when the record is written (compare this with the discussion of sorting and searching in Chapter 5 and the discussion on hash coding in Section 8.4.3.2 of this chapter). Information is read from a random (or *direct*) access file by specifying the key associated with the record desired. This key is then used to find the record in the file.

Assuming a sequential access file, typical file operations include

1. Read/write a record or group of records.
2. Access the ith record of a file or the jth file in a collection of files.
3. Rewind the file (i.e., set the file pointer at the first location in the file).
4. Create/destroy files.

Note that it is difficult to add or destroy individual records within a sequential file except at the end of the file (why?).

A program or job which is submitted to a batch system may be considered to be a collection of files, as shown in Figure 8.7. When a program is configured in this way,

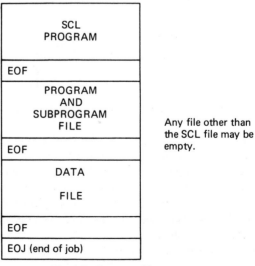

Fig. 8.7   Program file structure.

it is essentially independent of the physical representation of the program; the actual program may reside in memory, on a deck of cards, on a disk, or generally on any peripheral input device. However, the operating system is aware only of the logical file structure described in Figure 8.7. This commonality of representation greatly simplifies the structure of the operating system.

8.2.2 A System Command Language

Considering the array of devices, language processors, system functions, and the like which are available as resources, the operating system represents an attempt to both fully utilize these resources and to facilitate access to them. As indicated earlier, communication to the operating system is accomplished through a specialized language known as the system command language. The function of this language as introduced includes the following:

1. Accounting: user identification, accounting number, estimated central processor time needed, estimated number of lines of output, etc.
2. Specification of the sequence of events to occur, including assignment of system resources.
3. Job termination.

To distinguish job control statements from other information, we shall precede each statement by a /. We select as the general format of these commands

/command name, parameters

Thus, the accounting command, which is normally the first command issued, might be represented as

		estimated	estimated no.	estimated no. of	
/JOB,	account number, user name,	CPU time , in sec	of pages of output	, punched cards of output	, . . .

e.g.,

/JOB, H25V281, WILLIAM FRANTA, 3, 100, 0 . . .

Every system command program entered into the system is terminated by

/ENDJOB

which is the last command issued in a sequence. When this command is encountered, the sequence of events specified by the system command program is complete, and the job is terminated.

Control commands fall into several broad categories, which include

1. File manipulation commands: The file commands supported by the system file structure usually appear intact in the command language. Thus, files may be rewound, accessed, destroyed, written to and read from, etc.

2. Device/file assignment: A specific device must be assigned to a given file so that the operating system may keep track of the resources consumed by the job.

3. System requests: Requests for specific system resources (software) such as language processors, library programs, loaders, etc., must be made so that the operating system may schedule these resources in the correct chronological order.

Let us follow the sequence of events which occur when a simple FORTRAN program, which uses some of the FORTRAN system library routines and which reads from or writes to a magnetic tape, is submitted as a job. The deck structure of this job might appear as in Figure 8.8; numbers down the left side are for reference only.

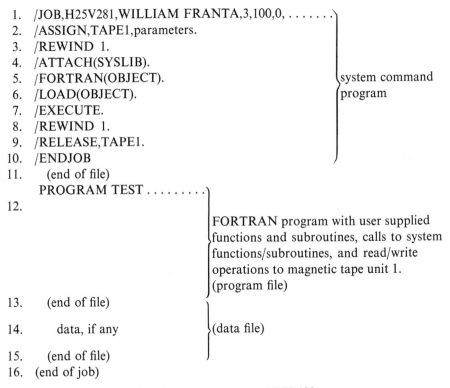

    1.   /JOB,H25V281,WILLIAM FRANTA,3,100,0, ...
    2.   /ASSIGN,TAPE1,parameters.
    3.   /REWIND 1.
    4.   /ATTACH(SYSLIB).
    5.   /FORTRAN(OBJECT).   system command
    6.   /LOAD(OBJECT).   program
    7.   /EXECUTE.
    8.   /REWIND 1.
    9.   /RELEASE,TAPE1.
    10.   /ENDJOB
    11.   (end of file)
             PROGRAM TEST . . . .
    12.
                                             FORTRAN program with user supplied
                                             functions and subroutines, calls to system
                                             functions/subroutines, and read/write
                                             operations to magnetic tape unit 1.
                                             (program file)
    13.   (end of file)
    14.   data, if any   (data file)
    15.   (end of file)
    16.   (end of job)

Fig. 8.8 Typical deck structure of a FORTRAN program.

One can think of the job control records as representing a program to be executed such that once execution is complete, the FORTRAN program has been executed. Line 1 represents the accounting information and job time estimates, as already discussed. Line 2 assigns a magnetic tape unit, identified as logical unit 1, to the FORTRAN program. The parameters indicate the physical characteristics of the tape, the name under which the tape is stored, and how information was recorded. Any statement of the form

$$WRITE(1,n)list$$

or

$$READ(1,n)list$$

in the FORTRAN program will initiate a read/write operation to this unit. Statement 3 ensures that the tape will be rewound to the beginning before any operation is performed on it. Statement 4 attaches the file containing the precompiled FORTRAN system routines (e.g., SQRT) to this job. These routines will now be available to the job, and the programmer may use them in the program as if he had written them. The next statement indicates that the program to be executed is a FORTRAN program; the FORTRAN compiler is loaded into core, and compilation of the program (the second file) is initiated. OBJECT is the name of a file onto which the *relocatable* version of the compiled program is written. Relocatable implies that all addresses in the program are assigned relative to a given address independently of the actual machine address marking the beginning of the program. This address is known only when the program is actually loaded into main memory. Statement 6 represents the actual loading of the program into main memory; the loader is responsible for recomputing all addresses in the program, given the (now) known address of the first instruction in the program. The loader is also responsible for *linking* subprogram calls to the actual locations of these subprograms in memory; for this reason, this kind of loader is often referred to as a *linking loader* (for more information, see the following section). Statement 7 begins execution of the program as it resides in main memory; data are read from the data file according to FORTRAN read/write statements, printed, punched, read and/or written from/to the magnetic tape unit associated with the job, etc. When statement 8 is finally executed, the FORTRAN program's execution has been completed. This statement causes the magnetic tape unit to be rewound, and the following statement causes this tape unit to be released to the system. Since the next statement is /ENDJOB, the job is completed and leaves the system. Statements 11, 13, and 15 separate the files representing the SCL file, the program file, and the data file. Statement 16 marks the physical end of the job.

In most cases, the SCL is a much richer language than has been indicated in this simple example. Many SCL's contain looping and branching facilities similar to those introduced in AL; these facilities allow alternative sections of the SCL program to be executed depending on the state of the system and/or data as well as the repetitive execution of blocks of SCL code.

EXERCISE 8.2: For your particular installation, determine the nature of the system command language. Write a sequence of SCL statements which allow the execution of a simple FORTRAN program, much as was done in Figure 8.8.

Many of the SCL statements above should (and do, in practice) contain specification fields well beyond those indicated. For example, the FORTRAN statement might contain additional information such as

1. The kinds of error messages to be generated, their format, where they are to appear, etc.
2. Whether any kind of program optimization is to take place (see Section 8.4.1).
3. How extensive a cross-reference map that is to be produced should be (the cross-reference map lists variables, their addresses, data locations, and the like; it is extremely valuable for debugging a program but is usually suppressed after the debugging is complete).
4. Execution may be initiated from the FORTRAN control card by setting a parameter.
5. To what file the listable output is to be written; default is usually the output file, which is eventually listed on the line printer.
6. The type of arithmetic rounding/truncation to be performed for all arithmetic operations in the program (see Chapter 6).

Many of the other control cards have extensive options available to the user who wishes to make use of them. In most cases, a complete set of system defaults is specified for the average user. For those jobs which fall into this category, the sequence of SCL commands is particularly simple. At the other extreme is the user who must do extensive file manipulation and data manipulation, assemble programs from various files, compile some programs, and load others. For this category of user, a rich system command language is mandatory; the length of the SCL program required to perform the desired operations may in some cases exceed the length of the programs actually performing the computations.

In the next several sections of this chapter, we shall examine in more detail some of the processors, processes, and algorithms implicit in the discussions of the preceding sections.

8.3 THE STRUCTURE OF PROCESSES AND PROCESSORS

In this section, the emphasis is on the hardware structure of the central processing unit and main memory of a small computer. Based on the structures developed here, in succeeding sections we shall discuss the software interface between the hardware and user, particularly language compilers and system software.

In Chapters 1 and 2 we have seen that the structure of programming languages may be far removed from the actual machine instruction format and even farther removed from the electronic circuitry constituting the system. In Chapter 2, the algorithmic language AL was defined in terms of a machine language based on the Turing machine. However, the translation of an AL program into an executable Turing machine program is nontrivial, even though much of it can be programmed. It is clear that a large amount of processing must be performed in order to achieve the translation of an AL program into its equivalent Turing machine program. Similarly, we can expect that an equally complex process will be needed to translate a FORTRAN program into the equivalent machine language program. To develop an algorithm (e.g., a compiler) for translating from source code (a FORTRAN program, for instance) into a machine language program, it is necessary to define more rigorously the concept of a machine language program in relation to the underlying hardware. In the next section, a realistic, though highly simplified, model of a modern computer is developed from the hardware up. Using this model, the essence of the translation process will be illustrated.

8.3.1 The Structure of Main Memory

The main objection to the Turing machine as a model for a real computer was its inability to directly address a memory cell. The lack of this facility posed great difficulty in implementing storage for the values of individual variables. Here, we may think of memory as organized into words, each of which contains n bits (recall the discussion in Chapter 6), as indicated in Figure 8.9. Each word may be addressed

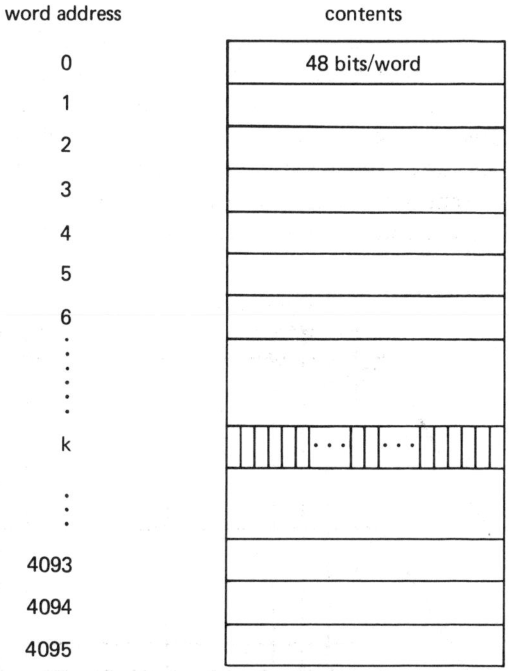

word address	contents
0	48 bits/word
1	
2	
3	
4	
5	
6	
⋮	
k	‖‖‖‖‖ · · ‖‖ · · · ‖‖‖‖
⋮	
4093	
4094	
4095	

Fig. 8.9　The logical structure of main memory.

individually in order to write information into the word or read information from the word. The number of words contained in main memory is variable, but commonly, blocks of 4096 ($= 2^{12}$) words are used. Let us assume that main memory consists of 4096 words of 48 bits each, as shown in Figure 8.9.

The traditional implementation of main storage has been in the form of *magnetic cores;* these are composed of a magnetic material known as *ferrite* in the form of small doughnuts or rings. These cores are capable of being magnetized in one direction or the other (see Figure 8.10); furthermore, the direction of the magnetization is stable

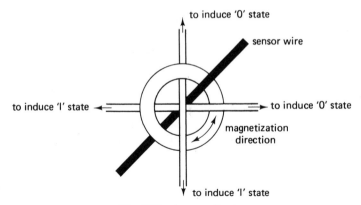

Fig. 8.10   A magnetic core.

and can be switched by sending a suitable signal to the core. The two stable states of such a core are used to represent the bits 0 and 1. Assuming that each word is only 1 bit long, then the diagram in Figure 8.11 shows a common arrangement of the cores. The words are arranged as a 64 × 64 table, and therefore each word is uniquely identified by two numbers each of which can be represented with 6 bits. The lines connecting the cores represent paths along which an electric current flows. By sending one unit of current (less than a unit will not affect the core) through the core (say, ←, ↓),

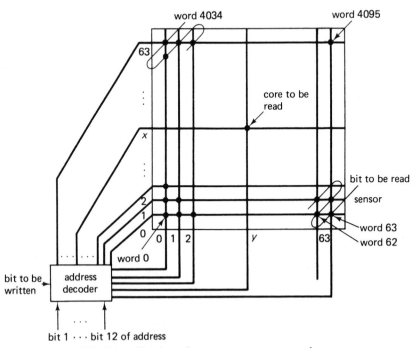

Fig. 8.11   Circuitry of core memory: one core plane.

the core is forced to enter one of the stable states (say 1), while if the current is sent in the directions ($\rightarrow$, $\uparrow$), the core will assume the other stable state (i.e., 0). This property of the core may be used to write information into a word as follows:

> Given the 12-bit address of the word to be written in, compute two indices which will identify the word in the table, say (x, y). Send one-half unit of current in the proper direction through the x and y paths as shown in Figure 8.11. All the cores in row x and column y will receive one-half unit of current, except core x, y, which receives a full unit. Thus, none of the cores are affected except the desired one.

Example 8.1

Assume a 0 is to be written into word 126. The binary address for 126 is

$$000001111110$$

which is translated by the decoder into the two indices

$$(000001, 111110)$$

A current of one-half unit in the directions ($\rightarrow$, $\uparrow$) induces the 0 stable state in the correct core. ■

To retrieve the information in a word, an additional path (the sensor) is required which connects all the cores as shown in Figure 8.11. Whenever a core changes state, the magnetic flux produced induces a current in the sensor, which passes through it. Thus, if a 0 is written into a word which contains a zero, no current will be induced in the sensor; this condition of the sensor may be interpreted as a 0 bit. On the other hand, if the word contains a 1, it will change state when the 0 is written, and a current will be induced in the sensor; this current may be interpreted as a 1. Thus, the information contained in the core has effectively been read. The only problem with this scheme is that the information contained in the word is lost since it has been over-written by zero. This problem may be solved by writing the information back into the word. Thus, a read operation is actually implemented by two successive write operations.

To construct a core memory for 48-bit words, 48 identical *core planes* are stacked together. Each plane will then contribute 1 bit to the 48-bit word, as shown in Figure 8.12. In this scheme a data *latch* or *buffer* has been used as a temporary storage location for the data obtained from the read operation. Once in this buffer the data word may be transmitted to other parts of the system. Inherent in this model of memory is the notion of timing; for instance, one must not try to use the data in the buffer until they have been actually deposited there. Such timing operations are critical to the proper performance of the system but are ignored here.

Most computers use core memory as main memory since cores are fast, reliable, and nonvolatile (information is not lost if power is lost). A word in core memory may

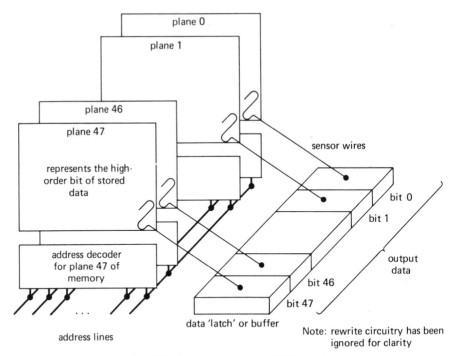

Fig. 8.12 Core memory for a 48 bit word.

be accessed in from 1 to 10 microseconds or less, and the mode of access is random (i.e., each word is accessed individually). Unfortunately, magnetic cores are one of the most expensive magnetic devices used for memory. A typical core has a diameter of about .02 inches; thus, they may be packed relatively tightly, which leads to compact memory. Core memories may contain as few as 1000 words and as many as 1 million words of storage; these are nominal figures.

Recently, *monolithic integrated circuit* memories have supplanted core memories, particularly in mini- and microcomputer systems. Some advantages of these memories are that they are typically faster, cheaper, and smaller than core memory. Disadvantages include the volatile nature of the memory in some cases. A large variety of integrated circuit memories is available at this time; they promise to become increasingly more important as cost- and performance-effective alternatives to core memory.

8.3.2 The Structure of the Arithmetic Unit and Assembly Languages

In addition to the core memory, most computers provide at least one special-purpose storage element which is used to hold temporary values resulting from arithmetic operations or as a buffer to and from memory (see Figure 8.12). This element is called an *accumulator*, or more generally, a *register*.

For the information in memory to be useful, facilities must be provided for the manipulation of this information. The question is, then, What instructions are necessary to provide these facilities? Since it is convenient to transfer data to and from memory via the accumulator, it will be necessary to provide instructions which alter its contents. The two instructions we choose, in mnemonics, are

> LOAD X   the contents of memory location X (X=0 to 4095)
> are loaded into the accumulator

and

> STORE X   the contents of the accumulator are
> stored into memory location X

In the first case, the contents of location X are left unchanged, while in the second, the contents of location X are overwritten by the contents of the accumulator. To these two instructions, a third is added:

$$\text{SHIFT } k$$

where k (base 10) specifies the number of bit positions to shift the accumulator. This instruction is identical in performance to the one defined in Section A.10 of the supplementary volume.

The Arithmetic Unit

A second glaring fault of the Turing machine was that it had no facilities for performing the basic arithmetic instructions. Each operation had to be laboriously implemented in software; however, these operations are so basic that they should be implemented in hardware. The arithmetic unit will perform the four basic arithmetic operations of $+$, $-$, $*$, and $/$, in addition to the three logical operations NOT, AND, and OR.

The arithmetic unit contains a second storage register which holds one operand obtained from memory, while the accumulator holds the other operand. Each of the seven operations is performed by special circuitry using the contents of these two registers. The result of the operation is stored in the accumulator, as shown in Figure 8.13.

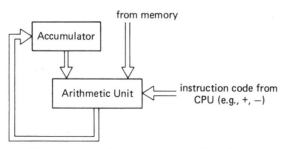

Fig. 8.13   Logical structure of the arithmetic unit.

Example 8.2 Logical Design of Circuitry for Adding Two Binary Numbers

As indicated in Figure 8.13, the arithmetic unit will have circuitry for adding two numbers. Assume that each of the two numbers consists of only four digits; then the task is essentially to design circuitry for the following problem:

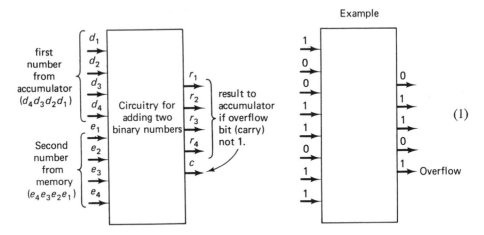

In the logical sense, the circuitry of a computer is a collection of connected *gates*. These gates are implementations of the logical functions AND, OR, and NOT operating on bits. They can be realized on the physical level by transistors, resistors, and the like by interpreting a high voltage as the bit 1 and a low voltage as the bit 0. Let us recall the definition of these logical functions:

$$C = A \cdot B \text{ (AND)} \qquad C = A + B \text{ (OR)} \qquad C = \bar{A} \text{ (NOT)}$$

A	B	C
0	0	0
0	1	0
1	0	0
1	1	1

A	B	C
0	0	0
0	1	1
1	0	1
1	1	1

A	C
0	1
1	0

For designing circuitry one commonly uses the following symbols:

Operation	Symbol
$C = A \cdot B$	A, B → (AND gate) → C
$C = A + B$	A, B → (OR gate) → C
$C = \bar{A}$	A → (NOT gate) → C

As it turns out, the logical function EXCLUSIVE-OR occurs in many circuits; its definition and implementation using the other gates is given below:

$$C = A \oplus B \text{ (EXCLUSIVE-OR)}$$

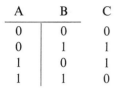

A	B	C
0	0	0
0	1	1
1	0	1
1	1	0

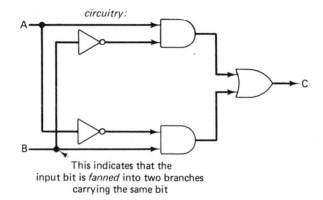

circuitry:

This indicates that the input bit is *fanned* into two branches carrying the same bit

Before we design the complete *adder* as stated in (1), let us consider the simpler problem of designing the circuitry for the binary addition of 2 bits with the result on the output line and its carry on the other line, e.g.,

Examples:

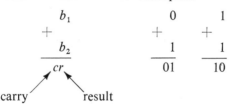

In terms of the truth function we can specify this problem by

b_1	b_2	c	r
0	0	0	0
0	1	0	1
1	0	0	1
1	1	1	0

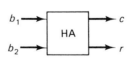

Since the above function is referred to as a *half-adder*, we use the denotation HA. From the definition of the logical functions it is clear that

$$c = b_1 \cdot b_2$$
$$r = b_1 \oplus b_2$$

Hence, the circuitry for the half-adder is given by

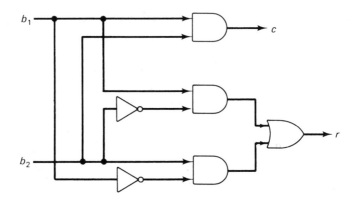

Given this circuitry for the half-adder, we can decompose problem (1) into four iden-tical subproblems whose solutions are called *full adders*. In the normal notation, binary addition is written as

$$
\begin{array}{ccccccc}
c_4\searrow & & c_3\searrow & & c_2\searrow & & 0 \\
d_4 & & d_3 & & d_2 & & d_1 \\
+ & & & & & & \\
e_4 & & e_3 & & e_2 & & e_1 \\
c\ r_4 & & r_3 & & r_2 & & r_1 \\
\text{subproblem:} \quad 4 & & 3 & & 2 & & 1
\end{array}
$$

from which we deduce that a full adder takes three inputs (for instance, the full adder for subproblem 2 takes c_2, d_2, and e_2 as input) and produces one result and one carry bit (for the example these are r_2 and c_3). The definition of these two output bits accord-ing to the rules of binary addition is

A bit of the first number
Corresponding bit in second number
Input carry bit
Output carry bit

b_1	b_2	c_i	c_o	r←—Result bit of $b_1 + b_2$
0	0	0	0	0
0	0	1	0	1
0	1	0	0	1
0	1	1	1	0
1	0	0	0	1
1	0	1	1	0
1	1	0	1	0
1	1	1	1	1

Symbol

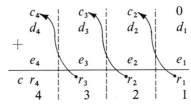

Without proving them, we shall simply state the logical expressions for r and c_o:

$$r = b_1 \oplus (b_2 \oplus c_i)$$
$$c_o = b_2 \cdot c_i + b_1 \cdot (b_2 \oplus c_i)$$

which leads to the following circuitry for a full adder:

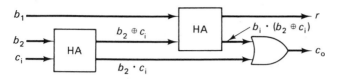

An adder for the two 4-bit numbers in (1) may be constructed from four full adders as follows:

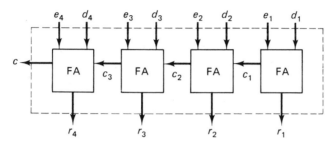

EXERCISE 8.3: Discuss the question of timing for the complete adder circuit developed in Example 8.2. That is, how should the digits of the two numbers be presented to the circuit to ensure correct values on the output lines?

According to the operations supported by the arithmetic unit, we define the following assembly language instructions:

$$\begin{array}{l} \text{ADD X} \\ \text{SUBTRACT X} \\ \text{MULTIPLY X} \\ \text{DIVIDE X} \\ \text{AND X} \\ \text{OR X} \\ \text{NOT} \end{array}$$

The semantics of each instruction are self-explanatory; the contents of the accumulator after an operation are defined as the contents of the accumulator prior to the operation modified by the contents of X as defined by the operator. If (reg) is defined as a shorthand notation for the contents of a specific register or memory location (A = accumulator) and $\leftarrow$ the assignment operator, then the semantics of these instructions may be represented as

$$\begin{array}{ll} \text{ADD X} & (A) \leftarrow (A) + (X) \\ \text{SUBTRACT X} & (A) \leftarrow (A) - (X) \\ \text{MULTIPLY X} & (A) \leftarrow (A) * (X) \\ \text{DIVIDE X} & (A) \leftarrow (A) / (X) \\ \text{AND X} & (A) \leftarrow (A) \text{ .AND. } (X) \\ \text{OR X} & (A) \leftarrow (A) \text{ .OR. } (X) \\ \text{NOT} & (A) \leftarrow \neg(A) \end{array}$$

Input/Output

Normally, the specification of input/output functions is an important aspect of an instruction set. However, in this case, only two simple I/O instructions for transmitting bit strings are provided. These two instructions are

| INPUT X | $(X) \leftarrow$ input from teletype |
| OUTPUT X | teletype $\leftarrow (X)$ |

where we have assumed a simple teletype (TTY) communication.

Program Control

The instructions forming a program reside in main memory in sequential order. The task of the central processing unit (CPU) is to execute these instructions, one at a time, beginning at the first instruction. To maintain its position in the execution sequence, the CPU contains a special register, called the program counter, which is large enough to store the address of any word in memory. When a program is loaded into memory, this register is set to contain the memory address of the first instruction in the program. The instruction indicated by the current value of the program counter is executed, and the value of the program counter is increased by 1 (except in special cases; see below). The CPU decodes this instruction and sends appropriate signals to the remainder of the circuitry.

In many cases, the logical flow of control within a program is not sequential, and instructions must be provided which alter the normal sequential flow. To this end, two instructions are added to the instruction set; PC refers to the program counter:

| TRA X | $(PC) \leftarrow X$ |
| TZR X | $(PC) \leftarrow X$ if $(A) = 0$ |

The first instruction causes the CPU to replace the current value of the program counter with the value X; the second is similar, but the replacement is done only if the value currently in the accumulator is zero. To complete the instruction set, the instruction

HALT

is added; this instruction causes the CPU to stop execution of the program.

The instruction set has been defined in terms of mnemonics since it is easier for us to remember them in this form. As presented here, this language is an extremely simple example of what are commonly called *assembly languages*. These languages are intermediate between expressive high-level languages and machine languages composed of bit strings. In this case there is a one-to-one correspondence between *assembly* instructions and *machine* instructions, although in general this is not the case. Altogether, there are 15 instructions, and therefore a field of 4 bits is sufficient to identify a particular instruction. Table 8.2 assigns a bit representation to each mnemonic instruction. This assignment is completely arbitrary. The address might refer to any of the 4096 words, and we need a 12-bit field to represent it; this leaves 32 bits

Table 8.2   BIT STRING CODE ASSIGNMENT TO INSTRUCTION SET

LOAD	0000	SUBTRACT	0100	OR	1000	TRA	1100
STORE	0001	MULTIPLY	0101	NOT	1001	TZR	1101
SHIFT	0010	DIVIDE	0110	INPUT	1010	HALT	1110
ADD	0011	AND	0011	OUTPUT	0111	1011	

of the word unused. If we were efficiency-minded, we should pack 3 instructions to a word.

Example 8.3

Assume that the program below resides in word 100 through word 106 and the data area is assigned word 107 through word 109 (in the comments we shall refer to location 107 as A, to 108 as B, and to 109 as C):

Line #	op-code	address	unused	Comments
1	1010	1101011	0--0	INPUT A
2	1010	1101100	0--0	INPUT B
3	0000	1101011	0--0	LOAD A
4	0011	1101100	0--0	ADD B
5	0001	1101101	0--0	STORE C
6	1011	1101101	0--0	OUTPUT C
7	1110	0--------0		HALT

As explained in the previous section, the operating system will load the above words in the proper part of core, set the program counter of the CPU to 100, and give it a signal to start executing. Assuming we type in the binary numbers 100 and 11 at the two requests stemming from lines 1 and 2, the contents of locations 107 through 109, after line 5 has been executed, will be

Location	Contents
107	0------0100
108	0------0011
109	0------0111

EXERCISE 8.4: Write an assembly language program for computing the first n Fibonacci numbers [see Exercise 3(g) at the end of Chapter 1].

In many real computers, the arithmetic unit will contain several accumulators plus other special-purpose registers. The circuitry will be expanded to contain comparators, hardware floating-point operations, and the like. However, these additions do not really change the fundamental ideas presented in this section. One can abstract the key ideas into a simple model, as done here. In the next section, we shall discuss the problem of translating from a high-level programming language into assembly language and then into binary machine language.

8.4 COMPILERS AND INTERPRETERS

Computers are designed to (and do!) execute sequences of bit strings which are coded representations of programs. These programs are typically first written in a completely different language which is easier for humans to use. Recall that a *source program* is the program as the programmer wrote it, perhaps in FORTRAN or some other appropriate language. The *object program* is an equivalent program written in machine language ready for execution on the computer. It is readily seen that the function of a *compiler* is to accept a source program and translate it into the object program (a sequence of machine instructions), as illustrated in Figure 8.14.

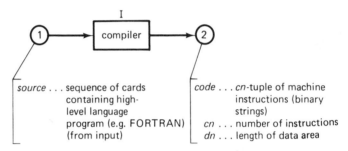

Fig. 8.14   Problem statement for compiler.

8.4.1 Compilers

It should be emphasized that in this section only the very general principles of compiler design will be considered. Actual implementations vary considerably from installation to installation and from language to language. As explained in Section 8.2, a "loader" will take the compiler output, assign some actual part of core as the data area, adjust the addresses in the instructions (which at that point are expressed in terms of location 1, 2, . . . , *dn*), load the program into core, set the program counter, and initiate the CPU.

The machine language program from Example 8.2, together with $cn = 7$ and $dn = 3$, could be considered the output of a compiler whose input was Algorithm 8.1.

Algorithm 8.1 (Sum two values)

```
begin /*sum*/
    input a;
    input b;
    c ← a + b;
    output c;
    halt
end /*sum*/
```

Let us approach the solution of the compilation problem by analyzing a similar task: translation from one natural language (e.g., English) into another (e.g., French). The analogy between programming language and natural language translation, however, is valid only if we assume natural language translation as performed by a novice.

Given a string of characters which represent an English text, the novice translator will probably perform the following three tasks:

1. Recognize the English words involved (= lexically scan the text) and classify them insofar as possible into grammatical categories (e.g., noun, adverb, etc.).
2. Ascertain the grammatical structure of each sentence (= parse the sentence).
3. Look up the translation of the words in a dictionary, and, according to certain rules, transform the grammatical structure into the equivalent French structure to generate the translated sentences and output the new string of characters which represents the French text.

Equivalently, the process of compilation can be broken into three separate processes, as shown in Figure 8.15. First, the characters of the source string must be

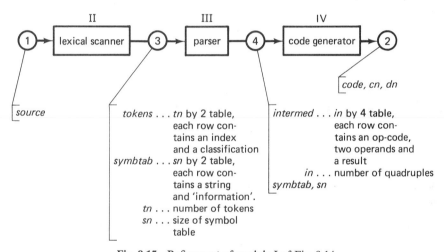

Fig. 8.15 Refinement of module I of Fig. 8.14.

grouped into *tokens*, which are the lexical constituents (e.g., variable names, constants, operators, etc.) of the programming language (i.e., compare to "words" of English). The lexical scanner further has to classify the tokens in accordance with the requirements of the parser. For instance, to ascertain the structure of a statement (= sentence in English) the parser will not want to know the actual names of variables but only that certain tokens are "names"; similarly, integer constants should be classified as "integers". Since it is inefficient to carry the string representation of the token along throughout the entire compilation process, the token is placed in a table called the *symbol table*, and all references to the token are replaced by a fixed-length integer which gives the address of the token within that table. In addition, this table serves to store information about the token, gathered at various times during the translation process, which will be needed by the code generator (e.g., the type of a variable, the location in the data area, etc.). Thus, the output of the first processor, the lexical scanner, is a table of tokens together with their classifications and the symbol table. In actual practice, several symbol tables are produced, one for the variable names, one for operators, etc.; only one will be considered here. The second part of translation, parsing, involves the recognition of the order in which operations are to be performed and representation of the program in a structure for which machine instructions exist. One of the many possible ways to represent this *intermediate code* is by means of a sequence of quadruples. All the elements in each quadruple are actually addresses within the symbol table. The first represents an operator, the second and third operands, and the fourth the name of the result.

The third module, generation of machine code, must first assign locations within the data area to all variables and then store this information in the symbol table. Next, each quadruple is translated into the appropriate sequence of machine instructions, and the resulting sequence constitutes the output of the compiler.

Before we illustrate this process for the computer developed in Section 8.3, let us make some remarks about actual compilers. In reality, most compilers do not execute the three modules in sequence but rather in an interlocked fashion similar to natural language translation. Thus, the parser might analyze one statement at a time, requesting from the lexical scanner a token whenever it needs one. For some languages it is not necessary to produce intermediate code; machine code can be generated directly. Many compilers include a phase during which an attempt is made to improve, or *optimize*, the intermediate code produced by the parser. For instance, the source statements

$$a \leftarrow b * d + c;$$
$$e \leftarrow f/(b * d);$$

might have been represented by the parser as

Operator
First operand
Second operand
Result

	Operator	First operand	Second operand	Result
1	$*$	b	d	$t1$
2	$+$	$t1$	c	$t2$
3	$\leftarrow$	a	$t2$	
4	$*$	b	d	$t3$
5	$/$	f	$t3$	$t4$
6	$\leftarrow$	e	$t4$	

where *ti* are variable names generated by the parser; we can see that quadruple 4 is actually redundant because the operation is performed by quadruple 1. An *optimizer* might produce the equivalent intermediate code

1	$*$	b	d	$t1$
2	$+$	$t1$	c	$t2$
3	$\leftarrow$	a	$t2$	
4	$/$	f	$t1$	$t4$
5	$\leftarrow$	e	$t4$	

which is a representation of the following AL statements:

$$t1 \leftarrow b + d;$$
$$a \leftarrow t1 + c;$$
$$e \leftarrow f/t1;$$

Example 8.4

Execution of modules II–IV of Figure 8.15 will be illustrated using Algorithm 8.1 as the source code. Assuming the variables take on integer values, it can certainly be viewed as a program; the problems with real values are ignored here. To simplify the classification task of the lexical scanner, assume that only the following classes are recognized:

Classification	Code	Example
Operator	1	$+$, $\leftarrow$, **input**, . . .
Variable	2	a, b, . . .
Delimiter	3	;, **begin**, . . .

In addition, the symbol table is filled on a *first-come–first-entry* basis (for better algorithms, see Section 8.4.3.2). Under these assumptions, the lexical scanner will output the following two tables (comments in the source program are simply dropped):

	String Information			Address of String		Classification
symbtab: 1	**begin**		tokens:	1	1	3
2	**input**			2	2	1
3	*a*			3	3	2
4	;			4	4	3
5	*b*			5	2	1
6	*c*			6	5	2
7	←			7	4	3
8	+			8	6	2
9	**output**			9	7	1
10	**halt**			10	3	2
sn = 11	**end**			11	8	1
				12	5	2
				13	4	3
				14	9	1
				15	6	2
				16	4	3
				17	10	1
			tn =	18	11	3

The parser processes these tables by determining which operands belong to which operators and in what sequence the operations are to be performed. If we assume the quadruple form explained before, it might produce the sequence

	Operator	First operand	Second operand	Result
intermed: 1	2	3	—	—
2	2	5	—	—
3	8	3	5	6
4	9	6	—	—
in = 5	10	—	—	—

(All entries are addresses to the symbol table.)

Up to this point, the process of translation has been rather independent of the computer on which the program is to execute. However, this is not quite true because the intermediate form has to be such that it can be easily translated into the machine instructions of the particular computer. To be consistent with previous sections, the target computer will be the machine designed in Section 8.3.

Storage locations are assigned to variable names in order of occurrence of the variable named in the program, namely,

$$a: 1$$
$$b: 2$$
$$c: 3$$

This information is stored in the symbol table entries for a, b, and c. Module III processes each quadruple in turn; for each different operator a different procedure is involved, but each is relatively simple. In principle, the procedure must first load the first operand (its address is found in the corresponding symbol table entry) into the accumulator, then "operate" the second into it, and finally emit a store operation to the target address. Thus, for the above example the output might be

	Op-code	Address	Unused
code: 1	1010	0 ----- 01	0 ----- 0
2	1010	0 ----- 10	0 ----- 0
3	0000	— ----- 01	0 ----- 0
4	0011	— ----- 10	0 ----- 0
5	0001	— ----- 11	0 ----- 0
6	1011	— ----- 11	0 ----- 0
in = 7	1110	— --------------- 0	

Finally, should the "loader" decide to put the program into locations 0 through 6 and have the data area start at word 7, it would have to add 6 to all the address fields of the program (not to instructions which do not use the address field). The resulting memory layout before execution starts is then

Unused Bits

Word 0	1010000000000111	0 ----- 0
1	1010000000001000	0 ----- 0
2	0000000000000111	0 ----- 0
3	0011000000001000	0 ----- 0
4	0001000000001001	0 ----- 0
5	1011000000001001	0 ----- 0
6	1110000000000000	0 ----- 0
7	Unpredictable	
8	Unpredictable	
9	Unpredictable	

After execution of instructions 0 through 6, word 9 will contain the binary string

$$0 \text{ ------- } 101 \ (5 = 2 + 3)$$

if the two input values were 10 and 11, respectively; the value 101 would also have been printed on the TTY. ■

EXERCISE 8.5: Write a FORTRAN subroutine which will generate machine code for the computer of Section 8.3 for the arithmetic quadruples (both binary and unary operators). Assume that each quadruple is stored in one word containing four integers (if the word size is ≥ 32; if larger, two words); otherwise, communications are as indicated in Figure 8.15.

8.4.2 Interpreters

The essential difference between an interpreter and a compiler lies in the fact that the interpreter actually executes the source program. Thus, the output of the interpreter is not a machine program but rather the output of the source program which is the input to the interpreter (as indicated in Figure 8.16). The following analogy might clarify the difference between compilers and interpreters. Assume that a cutting

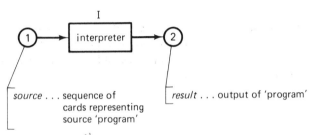

Fig. 8.16   Problem statement for interpreter.

machine (e.g., a machine to cut material for a suit) can be controlled either manually or by a punched paper tape. Further, we are given a set of commands (= program) such as

cut   20 inches

turn   cutter 45°

cut   5 inches

.

.

.

The equivalent of a compiler could then be used to produce a paper tape which can be fed to the machine whenever we need this particular pattern. The equivalent of an interpreter would be a human who takes one instruction at a time, "interprets" it by setting the proper controls on the machine, and then executes it.

The first two modules in the refinement of module I of Figure 8.16 are identical to those of a compiler; only the third module will be different. Since the third module actually executes the intermediate code, it has to be able to act somewhat like a CPU. That is, it must keep track of which instruction to execute next and maintain the status of the computation (i.e., data area). The latter problem can be solved, at least conceptually, by adding a value field to each entry in the symbol table in lieu of a storage location field. (For illustrations of the above concepts, we refer the reader to the Turing machine *simulator* in Chapter 2, which, as we now realize, is a prime example of an interpreter.)

One obvious question is, Why should one use a compiler versus an interpreter to process a particular language, or, in other words, what are the disadvantages and advantages of an interpreter? Probably the foremost advantage of an interpreter is that it allows for easy implementation of delaying the binding time (the time at which type and/or storage location are associated with variable names) to execution time. For example, every variable in a FORTRAN program has either an explicit or implicit type associated with it. The statements

DIMENSION A(50,20)

INTEGER A

specify to the FORTRAN compiler that A is an integer array of size 50 by 20. Therefore, the compiler is able to associate 1000 words of storage for this array in memory; this data area is fixed during execution since no more storage will ever be required for A. This allocation is done at compile time. On the other hand, no such statements exist in SNOBOL; at one point in a SNOBOL program a variable may have a single integer value, while at another it may represent an array requiring 5000 locations, etc. Furthermore, there is no a priori way of determining the precise amount of storage to be assigned prior to execution. It is reasonable, therefore, to expect SNOBOL to be interpreted (which it is).

An interpreter is usually written in a high-level language in an effort to achieve

some measure of machine independence. For each different operator of the intermediate code, a procedure is supplied which specifies how the description of the
status of the computation is changed by this instruction. The interpreter needs only
one copy of this procedure, although it may be quite long due to the extensive type
checking and error checking performed at execution time, among other reasons.

Example 8.5

In Example 8.3, the compiler emitted a sequence of three machine instructions for
a + quadruple. In an interpreted language, the statement $C \leftarrow A + B$ (or the quadruple $+, A, B, C$) might have several meanings depending on of what type the
variables A and B are at the time this statement is executed. For instance, if the types
are "integer," the "plus" procedure might simply add the value fields of the symbol
table entries A and B and place the result in the value field of C. But if the types are
currently "string," it must execute a concatenation of two strings.   ■

This approach is not really appropriate for a compiler since the machine language
equivalent to this procedure may have to be inserted wherever the operator appeared
in the source program. This would tend to produce an unrealistically long code array.
Some assembly languages (and higher-level languages) provide a similar feature, called
macro facilities, which allow the programmer to define an operator as a call to a procedure known as a *macro*. Subsequent use of this operator in the program results in
the substitution of the call with the statements comprising the macro body.

The greatest disadvantage of the interpreter is its slow execution time; execution
time is often on an order of magnitude slower than the execution time of an equivalent
program which was compiled, although such timing comparisons are shaky at best.
Example 8.5 actually points out the raison d'être for interpreting a programming
language. If by definition the language requires that variables may change their type
during execution, one usually employs an interpreter at the cost of increased time (see
Part B of the supplementary volume).

Yet another language processor, the assembler, will not be discussed in any
detail because its structure essentially parallels that of a compiler. The basic difference
lies in the level of the language used for the source program. A compiler denotes the
translation process for high-level language (e.g., FORTRAN, PASCAL) programs,
whereas low-level language (e.g., the assembly language for the computer of Section
8.3.1) programs form the input to the assembler. The nature of all the subproblems is
the same for compilers as for assemblers except that the complexity is much lower for
assemblers. For instance, the grammatical structure of assembly language statements
is in general much less varied than for high-level language statements.

8.4.3 Examples

8.4.3.1 An Example: The Lexical Scanner

In this section we shall consider the construction of the lexical scanner, derived
from the discussion on compilers, in more detail. The emphasis is on the scanning of a
simplified version of FORTRAN, although the principles involved have wide-ranging

applicability, including processing of English text, processing of free-formatted data, etc.

The problem statement shown in Figure 8.17 has been extracted from the general discussion of the preceding sections. To define the relation between the source ① and

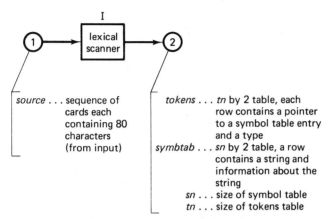

Fig. 8.17   Problem statement for the lexical scanner.

the tokens ② we shall consider the following simplified FORTRAN whose lexical constituent items are

1. names: string of alphanumeric characters starting with a letter;
2. integers: string of digits;
3. reals: string of digits (nonempty) followed by a period followed by a string of digits (possibly empty);   (2)
4. delimiters: single-character operators, parentheses, and blanks; however, blanks are not returned as tokens but are skipped.

Tokens are not to be continued over the next line or card. Before beginning the construction of the scanning algorithm, inspection of (2) yields some simplifications. The definition does not make any distinction among the digits 0 through 9, for instance. Hence, it is not necessary to distinguish between any of these characters, and they may be treated as a single group whose generic name will be "digits." We are assured that no matter what algorithm is devised it will not have to perform different actions for different numbers in the group "digits." Close inspection of (2) reveals that the lexical scanner will only have to deal with the six groups:

$$\begin{aligned}
alpha: &\quad A, B, C, \ldots, Z \\
digit: &\quad 0, 1, 2, \ldots, 9 \\
period: &\quad . \\
delimiter: &\quad +, /, *, (, \ldots \\
blank: &\quad \\
eof: &\quad \text{end of file marker}
\end{aligned}$$

The sixth group is actually included for convenience; it signifies the end of the source text and will be used to terminate the scanning process.

Obviously, the lexical scanner will have to process one character (i.e., group) at a time; therefore, instead of providing the entire source text at once as indicated in ① of Figure 8.17, a utility procedure for providing a character at a time will be used. Each time the procedure is called, it will return the next character in sequence, together with its group classification. As indicated in Figure 8.18, it will read in a new card

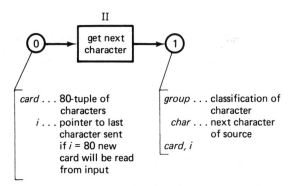

Fig. 8.18 Problem statement for obtaining next source character.

whenever necessary and then return the next character of the source. If the input text is exhausted, the procedure will return a blank character with the group classification "*eof.*"

Since tokens may not be continued over card (line) boundaries, the procedure will emit a blank when it has exhausted a card, which in turn will terminate any token. Because this procedure is quite simple, we immediately proceed to specify it in AL:

Algorithm 8.2 (Obtain next character of source)

```
procedure next(card, i; group, char, card, i)
begin /*next char*/
    if i = 80 then
                begin /*read new card*/
                    char ← ' ';
                    input card;
                    if eof then group ← 'eof'
                            else [group ← 'blank'; i ← 0]
                end /*read*/
    else
                begin /*new character*/
                    i ← i + 1;
                    char ← card(i);
```

case *char* **of**

$$\begin{array}{rl}
\text{`}A\text{', `}B\text{', `}C\text{', } \ldots, \text{`}Z\text{':} & group \leftarrow \text{`}alpha\text{';}\\
\text{`}0\text{', `}1\text{', } \ldots, \text{`}9\text{':} & group \leftarrow \text{`}digit\text{';}\\
\text{`.':} & group \leftarrow \text{`}period\text{';}\\
\text{`}+\text{', `}/\text{', } \ldots, \text{`)':} & group \leftarrow \text{`}delimiter\text{';}\\
\text{` ':} & group \leftarrow \text{`}blank\text{'}
\end{array}$$

end /∗*char*∗/

end /∗new∗/

end /∗next∗/

Consider the original problem; clearly, it can be decomposed into repeated execution of the modules which will obtain one token from the input, as shown in Figure 8.19.

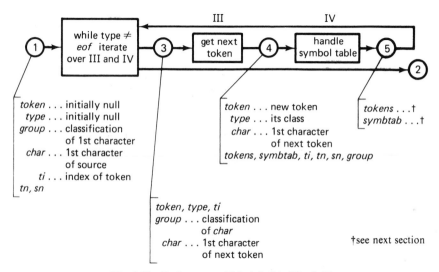

Fig. 8.19 Refinement of Module I in Fig. 8.17.

Module IV and its output will be discussed in the next section. Let us consider the structure of module III. Recall that the goal of the lexical scanning process is to separate the incoming source into a sequence of tokens together with their type. Once the type of the token is known, the action to be performed with each incoming character (or group) is uniquely determined. Furthermore, the first character of a token very often determines the type of that token. Thus, with each token type will be associated a *state*, whose name is identical to the type of token being recognized. For those cases in which the first character does not uniquely identify the type, an ambiguous state is introduced in which the scanner will stay until a character is encountered which enables it to differentiate the states. For instance, a digit at the beginning of a token may lead to a token of type real or integer. Hence, the state "number" is introduced in which the scanner stays as long as the incoming characters are digits. If the next character is a period, the state is switched to "real"; any other character (other than a digit) will terminate the process and tag the token as an integer.

A process as outlined above, where each action performed is uniquely determined by a "state" of the computation and the next input symbol, is called a *finite state automaton*. It is best described by a table indexed by the state and the next input symbol whose entries define the particular action to be taken. Since the action is the same in many cases, only the name of the action is stored in the table; the semantics of these actions are described in Table 8.4. Table 8.3 shows the action table for this particular problem.

Table 8.3 ACTION TABLE FOR LEXICAL SCANNER

group state	alpha	digit	period	delimiter	blank	eof
name	cont	cont	end	end	end	end
number	end	cont	go real	end	end	end
real	end	cont	end	end	end	end
delimiter	end	end	end	end	end	end
initial	go name	go number	go delimiter	go delimiter	skip	end

Table 8.4 ACTION SEMANTICS FOR TABLE 8.3

1) go: change state to second part of table entry; add the character to the current token and loop back for next character
2) cont: add character to token; loop back
3) skip: do nothing; loop back
4) end: set type of token (depends only on state) and return current token.

The size of Table 8.3 can be reduced by noting that all the entries for the state "delimiter" are the same. This action may be performed at the time the state would otherwise be changed to "delimiter," e.g., in the last row of the table. If this action is called "end1" with the following semantics

5) end1: add character, obtain next character; set type to delimiter and return token

a refined action table may be obtained, as indicated in Table 8.5.

Table 8.5 REFINED ACTION TABLE FOR LEXICAL SCANNER

group state	alpha	digit	period	delimiter	blank	eof
name	cont	cont	end	end	end	end
number	end	cont	go real	end	end	end
real	end	cont	end	end	end	end
initial	go name	go number	end1	end1	skip	end

Module III of Figure 8.19 may be refined as shown in Figure 8.20 and Algorithm

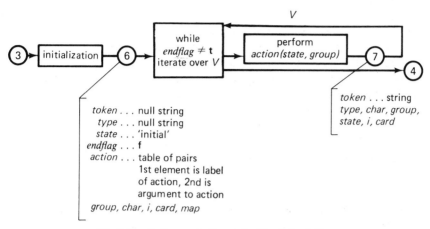

Fig. 8.20   Refinement of module III of Fig. 8.19.

8.3, assuming that the end actions will set a flag (*endflag*) to **true** in order to terminate the iteration. Finally, the mapping of states, *map*, into types is as follows:

map:	state $\longrightarrow$ type	comments
	initial eof	The end1 action should set its own type.
	real real	
	number integer	
	name name	

Algorithm 8.3 (Module V of Figure 8.20)

Global data referenced: *endflag, action, token, type, group, state, char, i, card*

```
begin /*get next token*/
    while (endflag ≠ t)
    begin /*perform action*/
        act ← action(state, group);
        case act(1) of
            'go':    state ← act(2); token ← token + char;
            'cont':  token ← token + char;
            'skip':  ;
            'end':   type ← map(state); terminate; /*perform*/
            'end1':  token ← token + char; type ← 'delimiter'; endflag ← t
        end; /*act*/
        next(card, i; group, char, card, i)
    end /*perform*/
end /*get*/
```

It may be noted that no error-checking facilities have been provided in the implementation of the lexical scanner. The reason for this is that definition (2) leaves practically no room for errors. It is very difficult to conceive of any sequence of characters which will not produce a sequence of legal tokens. However, it is known that the tokens presumably represent the lexical analysis of statements written in a simplified version of FORTRAN. From this additional information (i.e., the semantics of FORTRAN), it is possible to state rules governing the allowable juxtaposition of tokens. For example, if FORMAT statements are excluded, it is impossible to find a real number delimited by a period. Such a construction violates the syntax of FORTRAN. Using this information, the corresponding entry in the action table should be modified to include this information, producing an error message when the situation occurs. Should such an error occur, some corrective action can be taken (e.g., end the token).

EXERCISE 8.6: For your choice of a simplified FORTRAN (you probably will want to omit FORMAT statements and most of the esoteric features of the language), formulate adjacency rules governing allowable sequences of tokens. Incorporate error actions into the action table and Algorithm 8.3.

EXERCISE 8.7: Complete the AL description of the solution of the problem as stated in Figure 8.19. Assuming *tokens* represents a table, module IV should add the token and its type into the next row of the table.

To illustrate the translation process into FORTRAN, module III will be implemented as a FORTRAN subroutine. The first question to answer concerns the representation of the data structures. The action table can be represented by a two-dimensional array if integer codes are assigned to each state and integer-valued groups are defined. Clearly, we cannot use string-valued labels as entries to the table, but by assigning proper integers to the different actions we can use these values as an index to a computed GO TO statement. We can avoid the difficulty of having pairs of values as entries into the action table if we number the action in such a way that the number itself represents the state which is to be attained by a "go" action. To fulfill these requirements we make the following correspondences:

	State			Type	
AL	FORTRAN		AL	FORTRAN	
name	1		name	1	
number	2		number	2	
real	3		real	3	
initial	4		eof	4	
			delimiter	5	

Group		Action	
AL	FORTRAN	AL	FORTRAN
alpha	1	go name	1
digit	2	go number	2
period	3	go real	3
delimiter	4	cont	4
blank	5	skip	5
eof	6	end	6
		end1	7

If we assume that the action table has been set in some initialization procedure and the first character is available, the FORTRAN program below is an implementation of module III.

Purpose: Get next token from source.
Communication:

variables referenced through
blank COMMON:
TOKEN ... string, left justified and zero filled, 1jzf; will be set by ADDC;
TYPE ..... integer($1 \leq \cdots \leq 5$); will be set;

variables referenced through
COMMON block CHAR:
CHAR .... contains one character (A1 format) set by subroutine NEXT;
GROUP ... integer ($1 \leq \cdots \leq 6$) set by NEXT;

variables referenced through
COMMON block TAB:
ACTAB ... 4 by 6 table set by initialization procedure, not changed;

subroutines and functions
called:
ADDC .... subroutine with no arguments; adds current character to current token;
NEXT .... subroutine with no arguments, obtains next character from the source and sets GROUP; when necessary a new card is read in.

Flaws: No provisions have been made for the case in which a token contains more characters than can be stored in one word.

Program:

```
              SUBROUTINE LEX
              INTEGER CHAR,GROUP,ACTAB,TOKEN,TYPE,STATE,ACT
              LOGICAL ENDFL
              COMMON TOKEN,TYPE /CHAR/ CHAR,GROUP   /TAB/ ACTAB(4,6)
       C
       C         INITIALIZATION
       C
              TOKEN = 0
              TYPE = 0
              STATE = 4
              ENDFL = .FALSE.
       C
       C         GET NEXT TOKEN
       C
       10  IF(ENDFL)GO TO 80
       C
       C         PERFORM ONE ACTION
       C
                  ACT = ACTAB(STATE,GROUP)
                  GO TO(20,20,20,30,40,50,60),ACT
       C         GO ACTION
           20              STATE = ACT
                           CALL ADDC
                           GO TO 70
       C         CONT ACTION
           30              CALL ADDC
                           GO TO 70
       C         SKIP ACTION
           40              GO TO 70
       C         END ACTION
           50              TYPE = STATE
                           RETURN
       C         END1 ACTION
           60              CALL ADDC
                           TYPE = 5
                           ENDFL = .TRUE.
       C
       C         OBTAIN NEXT CHARACTER AND LOOP BACK
       C
           70          CALL NEXT
                       GO TO 10
       C
       C         TOKEN IS FINISHED AND NEXT CHARACTER AVAILABLE
       C
       80  RETURN
              END
```

EXERCISE 8.8: Complete the FORTRAN implementation of the lexical scanner as discussed, using the constraints outlined in Exercise 8.7. (Hint: For the procedures NEXT and ADDC, use the STRING routine and a character classification routine similar to the function MAP of Sections A.9 and A.10 of the supplementary volume.)

8.4.3.2 Symbol Table Construction and Maintenance

The processes inherent in the implementation of module IV in Figure 8.19 have been delayed until this section since they are a specific instance of a much more general problem: the efficient storage and retrieval of nonnumeric information. In Chapter 5, several solutions for this problem were proposed, but the techniques to be discussed in this section (address calculations on keys) were specifically excluded. The specific problem of concern here is the maintenance of a symbol table; the TABLE feature of SNOBOL is a highly similar problem in which items of information are to be stored with an associated key and retrieved at some later time using the key. These problems share one property which makes the use of the algorithms developed in Chapter 5 relatively inefficient. In each case, usually only a few ($\sim$ 100) tokens exist, but they must be stored and/or retrieved relatively often. For example, in a medium-sized FORTRAN program, we may expect between 1000 to 5000 occurrences of between 50 to 200 different tokens. We recall that the optimal searching algorithms developed in Chapter 5 had a complexity of $O(\log_2 n)$ under the assumption that the n tokens were sorted. To sort n tokens, the complexity of the optimal algorithm is $O(n \log_2 n)$. Application of these algorithms to the current problem proves rather expensive.

Returning to the discussion surrounding module IV, there are two distinct problems to be considered:

1. Given a fixed, a priori known set of data, find an algorithm to determine whether an item belongs to the set and if so to return its location.
2. Construct and maintain a table of a priori unknown data.

As an example of the first case, consider the problem which arises if a separate symbol table is maintained for FORTRAN delimiters and key words (e.g., READ, WRITE, etc.) and we wish to determine whether a token of type "name" is a key word. The second problem arises when processing FORTRAN variable names; in this case, the token should be entered into the table if it has not yet been encountered and its location returned; otherwise, its location in the table should be returned.

Hash Table for Known Data

The goal to be attained in the solutions of these problems are algorithms with a complexity of $O(1)$, that is, a complexity which is hopefully a small constant independent of the number of tokens involved. As will become evident, this complexity can (sometimes) be achieved if n is relatively small.

Let us consider problem 1 first. In Chapter 5, algorithms were considered whose only operations on keys were comparisons. Now we wish to broaden the range of operations on keys to include, for example, the interpretation of the key (token) as an address into a table. This has the effect of widening the domain of admissible algorithms considerably as compared to the domain involved in Chapter 5; consequently, the optimality results obtained there no longer apply. Accordingly, we store each key in *table(key)*; the statement

$$\textbf{if } table(search\_item) = \textbf{null then}[answer \leftarrow \textbf{f}; \ index \leftarrow 0]$$
$$\textbf{else}[answer \leftarrow \textbf{t}; index \leftarrow search\_item]$$

certainly solves the problem, assuming all keys have been stored in an otherwise empty table. The complexity of this algorithm is certainly of $O(1)$, but a cost analysis indicates a prohibitively large factor due to the storage component. If we assume that the key is stored in m bits (for the FORTRAN problem, m is usually 36 or 48), then this scheme will require a table of size 2^m, which obviously makes it unrealistic.

However, we wish to retain the idea of direct addressing but somehow compress the size of the table. To accomplish this, we need a function which takes the key as argument and returns a unique value which falls within a manageable range. The optimum range, obviously, is from 1 to n because no table entry would be wasted. Functions of this type, which scatter items into a table, are called *hashing* functions (this term is actually more general in that it is also applied to functions for which the uniqueness of values is not required), and the associated tables are often referred to as *hash* tables. So as not to raise any false hopes, we immediately state that no algorithm is known for finding an optimal hashing function for a given set of n keys, and it is still a matter of trial and error, depending heavily on the experience of the designer. The complexity of the algorithm

$$index \longleftarrow hash\_function(key);$$
$$\textbf{if } table(index) = \textbf{null then}[answer \longleftarrow \textbf{f}; index \longleftarrow 0]$$
$$\textbf{else } answer \longleftarrow \textbf{t}$$

is still of $O(1)$, but the constant depends now on the complexity of the function evaluation. The problem of finding a good (minimal range of index values) hashing function reduces to finding one of low complexity; the larger n is, the more difficult it is to find one at all.

Example 8.6

Given the following eight FORTRAN key words,

PRINT	CONTINUE	FORMAT
IF	DATA	WRITE
READ	END	

find a hashing function which will scatter these keys into a table of size 8.

A first guess might be based on the observation that all the first characters are different; therefore, the hashing function may be defined as the function

token $\longrightarrow$ value of first character interpreted as an integer

If we assume that the encoding scheme is A-000001, B-000010, . . . , the mapping

HASH:	ARGUMENT	→	VALUE
	PRINT		16
	IF		9
	READ		18
	CONTINUE		3
	DATA		4
	END		5
	FORMAT		6
	WRITE		23

has a range from 3 to 23. This could be transformed into the range 1–21 by subtracting 2 from *hash*(*key*), i.e.,

$$hash1(key) = firstc(key) - 2$$

A technique which often leads to good results is to actually write down the binary strings representing the keys and to find some combination of columns which yields different integers for different keys. Analyzing the encoding (blank-101101),

PRINT	010000 010010 001001 001110 010100 101101 . . .
IF	001001 000110 101101 . . .
READ	010010 000101 000001 000100 101101 . . .
CONTINUE	000011 001111 001110 010100 001001 001110 . . .
DATA	000100 000001 010100 000001 101101 . . .
END	000101 001110 000100 101101 . . .
FORMAT	000110 001111 010010 001101 000001 010100 . . .
WRITE	010111 010010 001001 010100 000101 101101 . . .

we observe that the fourth, fifth, and sixth bits (from the left), if catenated, always yield different strings (integers). Thus, the calls to the string routine (*m* is the number of bits per word)

$$\text{CALL STRING(KEY,4,3,HASH2,M-2)}$$

with the above eight strings will produce eight different values. Again, the range, 0 to 7, is not 1 to *n* (which is necessary for the index to be used for a FORTRAN array reference), but we can easily remedy the situation by adding one to HASH2. The program fragment below will serve to illustrate this process.

Purpose: Initialize the hash table.
Communication:

variables referenced through
COMMON block HASH: HTAB .... integer of 8 character strings;
                                      array will be set (from input);

subroutines or functions called: STRING . . .as defined in A.10 of the supplementary volume.

Program:

```
      SUBROUTINE INITHA
      INTEGER HTAB(8),HASHCO
      COMMON /HASH/ HTAB
      DATA M/60/,HASHCO/0/
C
C          M DEPENDS ON COMPUTER (WORD SIZE IN BITS)
C          ZERO OUT TABLE FOR ERROR CHECK
C
      DO 10 I = 1,8
           HTAB(I) = 0
   10 CONTINUE
      DO 20 I = 1,8
C          PROCESS ONE KEY
           READ(5,11)KEY
   11      FORMAT(A10)
           CALL STRING(KEY,4,3,HASHCO,M-2)
           IF(HTAB(HASHCO+1).NE.0)GO TO 30
           HTAB(HASHCO+1) = KEY
   20 CONTINUE
      RETURN
C
C          ERROR ON INPUT
C
   30 WRITE(6,31)KEY
   31 FORMAT(1X,A10,20H PROBABLY MISPUNCHED)
      RETURN
      END
```

Hash Table for Unknown Data

When considering the problem of constructing and maintaining an a priori unknown set of data, an even more serious problem than just finding a good hashing function arises. No matter what hashing function is chosen to scatter the incoming elements into the table, it is very likely that sooner or later a collision will occur; i.e., the values of the hash function for two distinct data items will be the same. Methods for handling such collisions will be discussed below. For the moment, we observe that one criterion for the goodness of a hashing function is its ability to scatter elements uniformly throughout the table so as not to produce clusters in the table. Most hashing functions belong to one of the classes shown below; we assume the size of the table is $M = 2^m - 1$:

1. Logical methods: An m-bit binary number is produced from the token by masking out certain bits and/or applying logical operations, e.g., exclusive OR.
2. Multiplicative methods: An m-bit binary number is extracted from the result of multiplying the token by a constant or itself.

3. Division methods: If M is a prime, the remainder after division of the token by M is taken as the value of the function.
4. Additive methods: Add several sections of the token and use the lower order *m* bits.

The construction of a symbol table as specified in module IV of Figure 8.19 is an example, par excellence, of the problems encountered in attempting to store and maintain a set of unknown data. In general, manipulation of these data involves two steps:

1. search: Look up a name in the table in order to determine whether the name has been previously entered in the table.
   retrieve: Obtain any associated information.
2. insert: Add a name not already present in the table along with any associated information.

For simplicity's sake we shall not, as is done in most actual compilers, construct separate symbol tables for variable names, delimiters, key words, and constants but rather shall store all tokens in one table.

First, it is necessary to determine the expected size of the symbol table (the largest number of different tokens we can expect). Assuming that any FORTRAN subroutine (or main program) will not have more than 100 different variable names, adding the number of key words, delimiters, etc., we arrive at an estimate of 255 (i.e., $2^8 - 1$) locations. Thus, a hashing function is required whose values can be represented by 8 bits.

EXERCISE 8.9: Construct a hashing function which takes a FORTRAN token as an argument and returns an integer between 1 and 255. (Hint: Look at various FORTRAN programs and find out what variable names are used; e.g., nearly every program will contain the names I, J, K, . . . ; further, write down the key words, operators, and delimiters most often used.)

Since we do not know what tokens will actually have to be processed, it is inevitable that at some point two different tokens will produce the same value. For this example, such *collisions* will be handled using a rather simple algorithm (for a better solution, see Chapter 9). Whenever collisions occur, all colliding tokens will be placed in an overflow table [which actually will be the lower part of the symbol table, say *symbtab*(256)–*symbtab*(350)]; the searching algorithm for an unsorted collection of records from Chapter 5 is applied to this portion of the table. Since at the moment we are not interested in how to collect information about the tokens needed by the parser, the second column of the symbol table is left empty. Algorithm 8.4 is a specification of module IV with some modifications concerning the input/output relations resulting from the above discussion (i.e., overflow table).

EXERCISE 8.10: Add the specification concerning the overflow table to module IV.

Algorithm 8.4 (Symbol table maintenance, module IV of Figure 8.19)

Global data referenced: *token, symbtab, overpt, ti, tn, tokens, type*

begin /*symbol table; *symbtab* is initially assumed to be all zero*/
    hash(token; hashco);
    lookup(token, symbtab, hashco, overpt; index);
    if *index* = 0 **then** *insert(token, symbtab, hashco, overpt; symbtab, overpt, index)*;
    tokens(ti, 1) ⟵ *index*;
    tokens(ti, 2) ⟵ *type*;
    ti ⟵ *ti* + 1;
    if *ti* > *tn* **then** [**output** 'overflow in token table'; **halt**]
end /*symbol table*/

The procedure *hash* called from Algorithm 8.4 is the solution to Exercise 8.9. The procedure *lookup* determines whether or not a token is in the symbol table. The value returned is the location of the token if it is in the table; otherwise, it is 0. The FORTRAN implementation of *lookup* is given below. The procedure *insert* is called whenever a new token is encountered; it will enter the token in its proper place and return the location (if no more space is available, it prints a message and stops).

    Purpose: Check for presence of token in symbol table.
    Communication:

variables referenced through COMMON block SYMTAB:	SYMTAB . . . 350 by 2 table; 1st element of row a string, 2nd not used here; assumed to be zero at first entry; modified;
	OVERPT . . . index to next free location in overflow portion of SYMTAB; $(256 \leq \cdots \leq 350)$; assumed to be 256 at first entry; modified;
	HASHCO . . . the hashcode of TOKEN;

subroutines and functions called: none.

formal parameters:	TOKEN . . . . string (ljzf) not modified; value returned is 0 if no entry has been found; otherwise, the location of TOKEN in SYMTAB.

Program:

```
        FUNCTION LOOKUP(TOKEN)
        COMMON /SYMTAB/ SYMTAB(350,2),OVERPT,HASHCO
        INTEGER SYMTAB,OVERPT,HASHCO,TOKEN
C
C          INITIALIZE
C
        LOOKUP = 0
C          IS SLOT OCCUPIED
        IF(SYMTAB(HASHCO,1).EQ.0)RETURN
C          DOES IT MATCH
        IF(SYMTAB(HASHCO,1).NE.TOKEN)GO TO 10
C          TOKEN FOUND
             LOOKUP = HASHCO
             RETURN
C
C          SEARCH OVERFLOW PORTION
C
     10 LOOKUP = 256
     20 IF(LOOKUP.GE.OVERPT)GO TO 30
             IF(SYMTAB(LOOKUP,1).EQ.TOKEN)RETURN
             LOOKUP = LOOKUP+1
        GO TO 20
C
C          TOKEN NOT FOUND
C
     30 LOOKUP = 0
        RETURN
        END
```

EXERCISE 8.11: Write the AL specification for the procedure *insert* and implement it as a FORTRAN program, assuming the same communication as for **LOOKUP**. (Hint: Do not forget to check for overflow of the symbol table.)

Obviously, this scheme is not the most efficient way of handling collisions. Since the possibility exists that the overflow table must be searched, the complexity of the overall algorithm is no longer of $O(1)$. As a general rule, no hashing scheme designed to maintain a table of a priori unknown data has a complexity of $O(1)$. Analysis of their performance is left for advanced texts because of the mathematical complexities involved. Suffice it to say that for any range-reducing hashing function, a set of input data can be constructed for which the worst case is of $O(n)$.

EXERCISE 8.12: For the hashing function of Exercise 8.9, construct a set of tokens for which the complexity of *lookup* is of $O(n)$.

8.5 CONCLUSIONS

Most of computer science can be classified as belonging to one of two areas:

1. Application: solving problems using the computer as a tool.
2. System design: designing the tools.

The tools considered throughout this book are general-purpose computing systems.

As such, certain constraints are placed on their design. In particular, such a system must be able to accommodate a variety of users with a variety of problems. Based on these observations, we have suggested in this chapter that a computer should not be viewed as a collection of hardware but rather as a system composed of hardware and software. To expound the relationship between the hardware and the software, we have examined the components comprising a computing system. On the one hand, we investigated the hardware, which ultimately has to execute the user's requested tasks, and discussed the nature of the instructions directly executable by the hardware. On the other hand, the user wants to specify these tasks in a high-level programming language without having to know the details of the hardware. Therefore, a software system (operating system) is required which maps the user's tasks onto the hardware system and coordinates the sequence of events executing on the various hardware elements. One conclusion arising from the discussion in this chapter is that a computing system should allow multiple-user access for reasons of efficiency. However, this constraint required that the additional problems of protection and privacy be considered.

References

Although oriented to one particular computing system, the following book provides an excellent introduction to computer organization:

C. W. GEAR, *Computer Organization and Programming*, McGraw-Hill, New York, 1974.

A rather complete coverage of the principles and structures of operating systems is found in

D. C. TSICHRITZIS and P. A. BERNSTEIN, *Operating Systems*, Academic Press, New York, 1974.

Readers with interest in time-sharing systems, which we did not cover at all, are referred to

R. W. WATSON, *Timesharing System Design Concepts*, McGraw-Hill, New York, 1970.

A detailed discussion of the structure and implementation of system processors and processes is found in

J. J. DONOVAN, *Systems Programming*, McGraw-Hill, New York, 1972.

Comprehensive coverage of compiler (and related resource) construction is provided by

D. GRIES, *Compiler Construction for Digital Computers*, Wiley, New York, 1971.

A survey of all the areas covered in this chapter is found in

P. FREEMAN, *Software Systems Principles*, Science Research Associates, Chicago, 1975.

Exercises

1 Given the assembly language developed in Section 8.3 with the following modifications,

    columns   1–4   contain an integer-valued label
    columns   5–12   contain the mnemonic operation code
    columns 13–16   contain a variable name or label

implement an assembler which will produce relocatable binary code.

2 Implement a lexical scanner for the system command language of your computing system.

3 Find out all you can about the accounting system used by your computing center (e.g., charges for CPU time, paper costs, etc.), and in conjunction with Exercise 2 write the necessary procedures to update an account after a job has been executed. Assume that all the necessary information will be provided by calls to system routines.

4 With the exception of the IF, DO, and assignment statements, all statements in FORTRAN can be classified as to their type (i.e., FORMAT, WRITE, etc.) by their first token (excepting labels). Develop and implement a program which will read in a FORTRAN program and output each statement together with its classification or an error message. You may make simplifying assumptions, e.g., no continuation cards, no declarations, etc.

5 Develop and implement a lexical scanner for a subset of English of your choice.

6 Describe the process of translating

$$ALPHA = ALPHA + (BETA - GAMMA)/(DELTA * EPS)$$

into machine language, including construction of symbol table(s) with actual hashing function(s).

7 Assuming you were to write a processor of English text, discuss how and where you would solve the problem of performing some special action for the following words:

    exercise   example   program
    table   equation   formula
    figure   algorithm   quotation

8 You are given the algorithms for finding (and inserting) an element in(to) a hash table using the following strategy: If a location is occupied, place the element into the next available (empty) location in sequential order. Discuss the advantages and disadvantages of this scheme.

9 Give first a general discussion of the issue of privacy, i.e., what data should be private, who should have access to them, etc., from the point of view of society's right to information versus the individual's right to privacy. Second, develop procedures such that an operating system can provide the degree of privacy desired by a user. That is, design the form of system commands to enable the user to specify varying degrees of privacy and explain what the operating system has to do to implement them.

10 Determine how negative numbers are represented on your computer. Using this representation, design a circuit for subtracting two 4-bit integer numbers.

9

Information Structures

9.0 INTRODUCTION:
CONCEPTS OF STRUCTURAL INFORMATION

The information processed by a computer consists not only of a mass of data but also, and perhaps even more importantly, the structural relationships between separate data items. In preceding chapters we have dealt with quite simple data structures (such as arrays of numeric or nonnumeric data) where the only relevant structural information was the relative position of an item within an array. A more complex problem, for instance, would be the representation of a molecule such as the one shown in Figure 9.1. Here the form of the bonds is as important as the elements involved. Operations on the molecule may involve not only changes in the elements but also changes of structure, such as replacing an atom by an entire structure (Figure 9.2), resulting in a structurally different molecule.

The emphasis in this chapter is on the criteria for the selection of the representa-

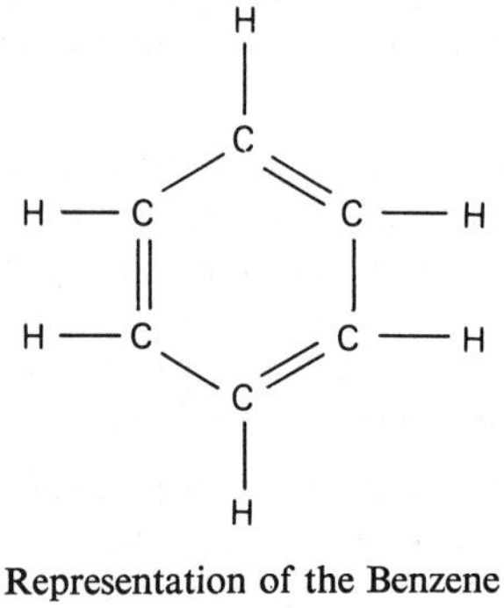

Fig. 9.1 Representation of the Benzene molecule.

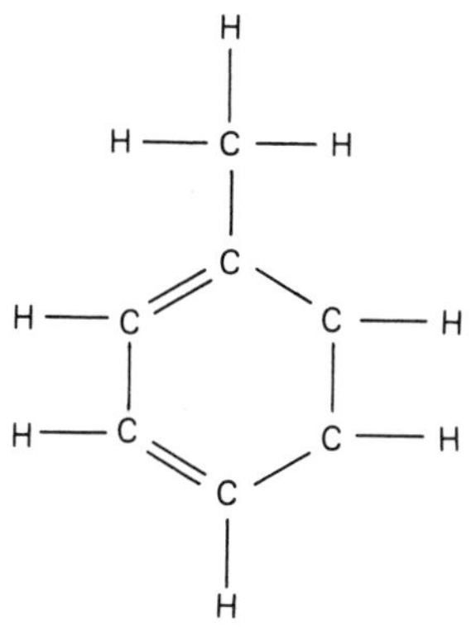

Fig. 9.2   Benzene molecule changed to Toluene.

tion of structural information as well as on the design and implementation of tools to perform the necessary manipulations of the structures.

As an example, consider the processing of a student file, perhaps for a computer-based central records facility. Each record of the file contains an ID number, name of student, address, and various other salient information. All these records are contained in some table (or file) and constitute the "mass of data" referred to in the opening sentence of this chapter; note the similarity to the "record" introduced in Chapters 5 and 8. Suppose the administration requests a list of all freshmen. A program can be written which looks at each record in the appropriate field (the key) and prints the requested names. Every time this information is requested, the entire table must be searched and each record examined. The reason for this inefficient search lies in the fact that the data are a mass of undifferentiated records; there is no structure imposed on the organization of the records relative to each other. In Chapters 5 and 8 methods were considered in which the structure was implicit in the ordering relation. In this chapter more general procedures are considered for imposing structure on the data. To obtain the records of all freshmen, their records can be *chained* together by adding to each record a field containing the structural information, as shown in Figure 9.3, to form a *linked list* of records which share a common property. In this case the structural information takes the form of a *pointer* which is the index of the next freshman record within an array. If the need exists, records could obviously be chained together on the basis of any attribute(s) (keys, in the nomenclature of Chapter 5) within the record, e.g., female students, male students, sophomores, etc. However, each pointer requires that additional space be allocated in the record.

In the terminology of Chapter 4 the molecules and records are *data objects* which form the domain of an algorithm, i.e., the elements which the algorithm manipulates. These data objects may possess an *inherent* structure, or a structure may be imposed upon them to facilitate the performance of the algorithm. In this chapter we shall be concerned with *abstract* and *physical* data structures. Again (see also Chapter 8)

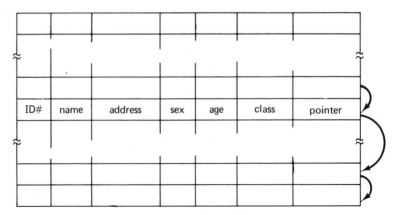

Fig. 9.3   Representation of student records.

physical refers to the actual representation of a data structure in memory together with a definition of the access and retrieval procedures.

9.1 LINEAR STRUCTURES

The simplest abstract data structure is the *list*. The structural information is provided by the linear ordering of the data objects.

Definition 9.1: A list is an ordered collection, X, (possibly empty) of n nodes so that the predecessor of the successor of a node is always the node itself; the first node, $X(1)$, does not have a predecessor, and the last, $X(n)$, has no successor.

We are already quite familiar with one of the physical structures implied by Definition 9.1. The sequential representation of a list is simply the n-tuple. It proved to be quite cumbersome to insert a node into the list because elements had to be moved.

An alternative physical data structure representing a list is the *linked list*. A node in a linked list contains two separate items of information:

1. The *unit of information*, e.g., the student record.
2. The explicit structural information linking one node to the next.

Given this definition of a node, it is not necessary to require nodes, which are in the abstract sense contiguous, to be contiguous in memory.

The unit of information contained in a node may, in some cases, be very simple, as in the case of the carbon ring, while in other cases it may contain several *fields* of information, as in the case of student records. In general, there is no distinction made between the fields containing structural and nonstructural information: A node is considered to be a sequence of contiguous fields. We distinguish linked lists by the number of fields containing the structural information, e.g., *singly* linked lists and *doubly* linked lists. To simplify the implementation we assume that the structure of the nodes comprising a linked list is homogeneous in that the number, location, and type of fields are the same for each, with the possible exception of the first node in the list, as discussed in Section 9.1.1. This does not imply that each field must contain information; fields can be empty.

Definition 9.1 obviously excludes structures capable of representing organic molecules; their representation will be discussed in Section 9.2, which concerns nonlinear structures. Quite often the technical term *list* is reserved for the linked list representation, and unless explicitly modified we shall use the two terms synonymously.

9.1.1 Singly Linked Lists

As the name implies, singly linked lists have only one field for structural information, and Figure 9.4 graphically illustrates such a singly linked list. The node at the beginning of the list is distinguished as the *head* of the list. This node contains information concerning the list as a whole, such as the name associated with the list, the number of elements (nodes) in the list, etc. The end of the list is signified by an empty link field, which in Figure 9.4 is indicated by a /.

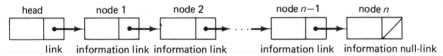

Fig. 9.4   Representation of a singly-linked list.

The question then is why one would use a list instead of the "natural" linear representation of an *n*-tuple or array. Although in a list a linear order is imposed on the nodes which conceptually is identical to that of an array, it does not at all imply that the nodes reside in physically contiguous locations. Rather, the order is defined only by the pointers. Any operation which involves physical movements of records in an array representation (e.g., insertion of an element between two neighboring elements) can be performed in a list representation usually by changing a few pointers.

Specific operations on list structures depend, of course, on the problem under consideration; however, many problems involve *traversing* a list. Specifically, a list may be traversed in order to find the *k*th node or a node containing a specific value. This node may subsequently have its value changed or be deleted from the list altogether, or a new node may be inserted at this point (or any combination of the above). Additional common list operations include combining two or more lists into one, splitting one list into two or more lists, copying a list, and possibly sorting the elements of a list.

It is worthwhile to digress for a moment and ponder the complexity of the operations described above. The seemingly simple operation of accessing the *k*th node in a list is potentially more difficult to perform than the apparently complex operation of joining two lists. The former operation entails a counting procedure, beginning at the head of the list and following the chain of pointers down to the kth node. Thus, if the act of visiting a node is used as the dominant instruction, the complexity of this operation is of $O(k)$. The second operation involves only a change in the link field of the last node in the first list (to point to the beginning of the second list). This operation is particularly easy if one knows the location of the last node (for this reason, this information is often stored in the head of the list); under these circumstances the complexity is of $O(1)$. If the same data were stored in array form, accessing the kth element is an operation with complexity $O(1)$, which involves only the addition of k to the base address of the array, whereas joining two arrays would at least require copying one array into another and thus is of $O(n)$, where n is the number of elements in one of the arrays. We conclude that an important factor to consider in implementing an algorithm to solve a particular problem is not only the representation of the data but also the operations performed on the data. One tries to strike a balance between the conceptual clarity of the representation and the efficiency of operations performed on the representation.

Before discussing the representation and implementation of lists in general, we shall present an introductory example of list processing. In particular, we wish to reconsider the methods for handling collisions generated by the hashing scheme used in the construction of the symbol table in the preceding chapter. The solution proposed there had an $O(n)$ worst-case complexity, where n was the number of elements in the overflow section. For this problem only two operations are necessary: one, finding an element, and two, inserting an element. The latter operation is trivial once the first has been performed. In finding an element in a hash table the efficiency of the algorithms given in Section 8.4.3.2 cannot be improved for those cases where the elements are in the hash location. In the cases of collisions the algorithms had to search the overflow portion of the table. We shall attempt to improve the efficiency of the hashing algorithm by imposing structure on the elements in the overflow table. One may discern a similarity between this problem and the problem of locating all freshmen records in a student file; all elements with a common property are chained together. The only property some elements in the hash table have in common is that they hash into the same value. Hence, each hash value will be forced to correspond to a head of a list which contains all names hashing into this value. To determine whether a name is already in the symbol table only the appropriate list is searched instead of all elements in the overflow section. To complete the structure of the list it is necessary to design the form of the head. In light of the operations required, should any further information be stored in the list head? The only other operation to be performed is to insert a new name. Can it be performed efficiently with the structure as we have it now? If the element is inserted at the end of the list of colliding elements, the answer must be no, unless we kept track of the pointer to the last node during the unsuccessful search. Otherwise, to access the last node in the list we have to traverse the whole list again; if this operation is done repeatedly, a pointer to the last node is normally included in the head to make it directly accessible. But a price has to be paid for this convenience: Every time a node is added to the end of the list the corresponding pointer in the head has to be updated.

However, in this special case it is actually to our advantage to insert a new name at the beginning of the list. This is due to the way names occur in programs; very often references to a name are clustered, as in the statement

$$x \leftarrow x + 1$$

The *find* operation for the second occurrence of x will be very efficient if x was inserted in the beginning. Hence, no pointer to the last element is necessary.

Finally, a decision must be made on how to allocate space for the nodes. Since nodes are never deleted from the symbol table, initially the entire table is considered to be available. A pointer is set to the next available location (initially 1) in the symbol table, and whenever a node is requested this location is used and the pointer incremented to the next location. A separate table is kept for the heads of the lists which are referenced by the values of the hash function. The resulting physical information structure is graphically depicted in Figure 9.5. For an actual symbol table each node will have one additional information field to store information about the name.

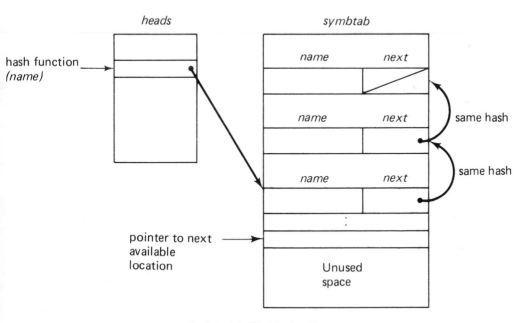

Fig. 9.5   Modified hash table.

Example 9.1

Assume the simple hashing function

name $\longrightarrow$ 1st character (i.e., A–1, B–2, C–3, . . . , Z–26)

which gives rise to a *heads* table of 26 entries. Further, let *symtab* be a 100-tuple;
then after the names

1.	CURRENT	4.	LENGTH
2.	LEFT	5.	MAX
3.	MODE	6.	MIN

have been processed in that order the structure of Figure 9.5 will be of the following
form:

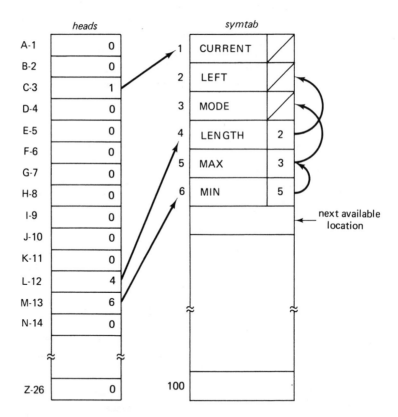

Note that all pointers are indices with respect to the 100-tuple *symtab*. Assume that
the next name encountered is COSINE; then the C list will be fruitlessly searched;
COSINE will then be added as the new first element of this list, resulting in the structure shown on the next page:

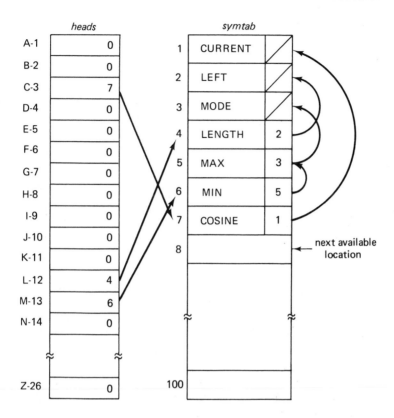

Functional notation will be used in the algorithms presented to indicate fields of a given node; for instance, the statements

$$name(symtab(p)) \leftarrow token;$$
$$next(symtab(p)) \leftarrow p1;$$

will set the name field of the node pointed to by *p* to *token* and the link field to the pointer *p1*.

Algorithm 9.1 (Return a pointer to the location of *token* in *symtab; p* should be zero if not found)

Global data referenced: *heads, symtab*

procedure *find(token; p, hashco)*
begin /*find location*/
    hash(token; hashco);
   p ← *heads(hashco);*
      /*traverse list*/

> **while** $(p \neq 0)$ **if** $name(symbtab(p)) = token$ **then terminate**
>   **else** $p \leftarrow next(symbtab(p))$

end /∗find∗/

Applying an order analysis to Algorithm 9.1 using the comparison in the iteration as the dominant instruction, we find that, unfortunately, the worst-case complexity of the equivalent function (LOOKUP) from Chapter 8 has not been improved.

EXERCISE 9.1: Give an example where the worst-case measure of Algorithm 9.1 is the same as for LOOKUP of Chapter 8.

Let n_{max} be the length of the longest list in the symbol table; then the worst-case complexity of Algorithm 9.1 is of $O(n_{max})$. For any reasonably good hashing function, n_{max} should be considerably smaller than n (the total number of colliding elements). In particular, the measure of any unsuccessful search (i.e., whenever a new token is to be added) is bounded by n_{max} for Algorithm 9.1, whereas it is always of $O(n)$ for the previous algorithm.

A FORTRAN realization of the hash coding example will illustrate the implementation of efficient list processing facilities in a language which normally does not support them directly. In this example, as well as in later ones, a node will be stored so that a minimum number of computer words are used. Each word will be viewed as a continuous bit string, whose maximum size depends on the word length of the host machine, which represents the various fields.

The hash table (HEADS) will be represented by an array of size 64, implying a maximum of 64 distinct hash codes. The symbol table proper (SYMTAB) will contain space for 127 different tokens, implying a link field of 7 ($2^7 = 128$) bits. It is assumed that the name of the token will fit into the remaining (word-size $-$ 7) bits. To retrieve information from the fields of the nodes, user-supplied functions will be used to perform the necessary manipulations of the bit string constituting the node. This allows the FORTRAN realization to closely approximate the AL algorithm. Similar procedures will be used to store information into a field.

Purpose: Determine whether or not a token is in the symbol table.
Communication:

variables referenced through
COMMON block HASH: HASHCO . . . integer to be set;
                            HEADS . . . . integer array; elements are indices into SYMTAB; not modified;
                            SYMTAB . . . integer array; elements are nodes with fields NAME and NEXT; not modified;
                            NEXTAV . . . pointer to next available node in SYMTAB; not modified; assumed to be 1 at first entry;
                            ERROR . . . . logical; not used;

variables referenced through
COMMON block WORD (used
in functions NAME and NEXT): N. . . . . word size; set by main program;
subroutines and functions
called: HASHF . . . . function returns hash code of argu-
                                                  ment string;
                                      NAME . . . . . function returns name field ljzf of
                                                  node in SYMTAB pointed to by
                                                  argument;
                                      NEXT . . . . . . function returns next field rjzf of node
                                                  in SYMTAB pointed to by argument;
                                      STRING . . . . as before;
formal parameters: TOKEN . . . . string (ljzf) not modified; value
                                                  returned is 0 if no entry has been
                                                  found; otherwise a pointer to the
                                                  node containing TOKEN.

Program:

```
          INTEGER FUNCTION FIND(TOKEN)
          COMMON /HASH/ HASHCO,HEADS(64),SYMTAB(127),NEXTAV,ERROR
          INTEGER HASHCO,HEADS,SYMTAB,TOKEN,P,HASHF
          LOGICAL ERROR
    C
    C         GET HEAD OF LIST AND POINTER TO FIRST ELEMENT
    C
          HASHCO = HASHF(TOKEN)
          P = HEADS(HASHCO)
    C
    C         ITERATE OVER LIST
    C
       10 IF(P.EQ.0)GO TO 20
              IF(NAME(P).EQ.TOKEN)GO TO 20
              P = NEXT(P)
          GO TO 10
       20 FIND = P
          RETURN
          END




          FUNCTION NAME(P)
          COMMON /HASH/ DUMMY(65),NODES(127),DUM2(2)
          COMMON /WORD/ N
          INTEGER DUMMY,P,DUM2
    C
    C
          NAME = 0
          CALL STRING(NODES(P),1,N-7,NAME,1)
          RETURN
          END
```

```
FUNCTION NEXT(P)
COMMON /HASH/ DUMMY(65),NODES(127),DUM2(2)
COMMON /WORD/ N
INTEGER DUMMY,P,DUM2
C
C
NEXT = 0
CALL STRING(NODES(P),N-6,7,NEXT,N-6)
RETURN
END
```

Separate functions were used to retrieve the fields of a node in this FORTRAN example, even though it might seem wasteful for this rather simple problem. On the other hand, such segmentation improves the readability of the program immeasurably. As the problem domain becomes more complex, as it will with the general list processing scheme developed below, one is willing to pay the price of the additional overhead due to the function calling sequence. If it is absolutely necessary for production runs, the calls can be replaced by in-line code.

EXERCISE 9.2: Develop and implement (in FORTRAN) an algorithm for inserting a new name into the symbol table. If the symbol table overflows, set the error flag to "true" and return. Use subroutines SETNAM and SETNEX to store information into the appropriate fields.

Drawing on the example of the construction of a symbol table, it is now possible to abstract the features of a general list processing scheme. Commensurate with the level of this book, various simplifications will be made. First, it is assumed that all the nodes of the lists will be of the same size (for some indication of how to handle variable-sized nodes, see the discussion raised in Example 9.4), and second, for the moment it is assumed that the two fields fit into one word. Two problems remain to be resolved. In this example nodes were never deleted from any list; hence, a very simple scheme for allocating nodes was sufficient. In a general-purpose system deletion of nodes will certainly be performed, in which case the allocation mechanism from the example will not suffice. Furthermore, we have to decide what information to keep in the head of a list.

A delete operation results in a node to which nothing points, thus freeing the space occupied by the node for later use, e.g., when a new node is to be created. To reallocate these nodes at a later time it is only necessary to remember where the unused nodes are located. These nodes share the property of being unused; hence, they may be chained together to form a *free-space* list. Whenever a node is freed it is added to the list, and whenever a node is to be created it is detached from the list.

To determine what information to store in the head of the list we need to know what operations will be performed most frequently. The trade-off between speed of operation and cost of maintaining up-to-date information in the head must be considered. For illustrative purposes, each head node will contain, in addition to the pointer to the first node, a pointer to the last node in the list and a field containing the number of nodes in the list. Figure 9.6 illustrates the initial configuration of the system in which only one list, *freesp*, is present and space is available for 1000 nodes.

nodes
info
next
1
2
3
2
3
4
freesp
1
999
1000
1000

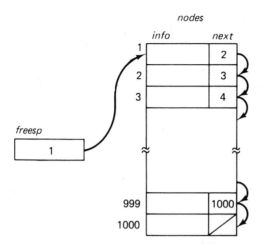

Fig. 9.6 Initial form of list system.

As indicated in Figure 9.6, the head of the free-space list contains only a pointer to the first free node. In a manner analogous to the maintenance of the lists in the symbol table we can insert freed nodes at the beginning, obviating the need for a "last" pointer. The only reason for maintaining the number field could be to allow for checking whether enough nodes remain whenever several are requested. This case will only occur once, since in the event not enough nodes are available, we shall terminate the program. Therefore, this possible use of the number field does not warrant the time needed to maintain it.

It is a trivial matter to initialize the variable *freesp* and the array *nodes* to the form given in Figure 9.6 both in AL and FORTRAN; hence, the details are omitted. However, we shall provide a package of FORTRAN procedures to set and retrieve fields. Since all fields except *info* contain integers in the range between 0 and 1000, a field width of 10 bits is sufficient. Again we assume the word size is greater than max(30, 10 + size(*info*)). This leads to the word structures shown in Figure 9.7.

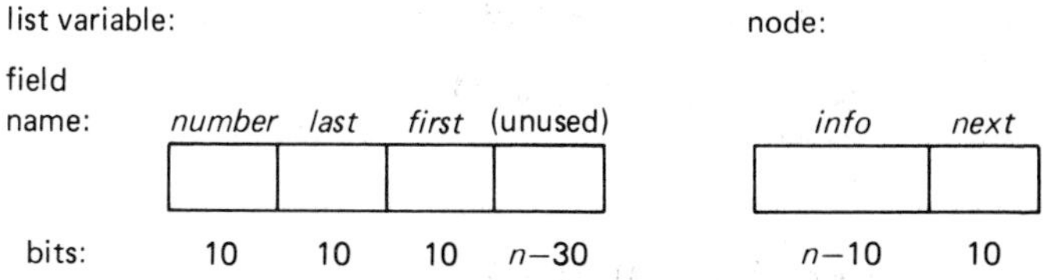

list variable:
node:
field name:
number last first (unused)
info next
bits:
10 10 10 n−30
n−10 10

Fig. 9.7 Word structure in FORTRAN list system (n = *wordsize*).

Purpose: Set of routines to set information in fields of heads and nodes.
Communication:

variables referenced through COMMON block WORD: N .... word size;

variables referenced through
COMMON block LIST:

subroutines and functions called:
formal parameters:

FREESP ... special list head; integer index into NODES;

NODES.... integer array; elements are nodes with fields INFO, NEXT; modified in SINFO, SNEXT;

STRING ... as before;

HEAD .... list head; modified;

I .... integer;

P, P1 ...... pointer to node in NODES;

VAL ...... integer; leftmost N–10 bits contain information.

Program:

```
SUBROUTINE SNUMB(HEAD,I)
COMMON/WORD/N
INTEGER HEAD
C
C      SETS NUMBER FIELD OF LIST VARIABLE HEAD TO I
C
CALL STRING(I,N-9,10,HEAD,1)
RETURN
END
```

```
SUBROUTINE SLAST(HEAD,P)
COMMON/WORD/N
INTEGER HEAD,P
C
C      SETS LAST FIELD OF LIST VARIABLE HEAD TO P
C
CALL STRING(P,N-9,10,HEAD,11)
RETURN
END
```

```
SUBROUTINE SFIRST(HEAD,P)
COMMON/WORD/N
INTEGER HEAD,P
C
C      SETS FIRST FIELD OF LIST VARIABLE HEAD TO P
C
CALL STRING(P,N-9,10,HEAD,21)
RETURN
END
```

```
SUBROUTINE SINFO(P,VAL)
COMMON /LIST/ FREESP,NODES(1000)
COMMON /WORD/N
INTEGER P,VAL,FREESP
C
C      SETS INFO FIELD OF NODE POINTED BY P TO VAL
C
CALL STRING(VAL,1,N-10,NODES(P),1)
RETURN
END
```

```
        SUBROUTINE SNEXT(P,P1)
        COMMON /LIST/FREESP,NODES(1000)
        COMMON /WORD/N
        INTEGER P,P1,FREESP
C
C          SETS NEXT FIELD OF NODE POINTED BY P TO P1
C
        CALL STRING(P1,N-9,10,NODES(P),N-9)
        RETURN
        END
```

EXERCISE 9.3: Write the FORTRAN functions equivalent to these subroutines which will retrieve information from the various fields [e.g., NEXT(P)].

What basic operations should a general-purpose list system provide? Clearly, a procedure is required which will handle storage, that is, a procedure which will obtain a new node from the free-space list and one which will return a node to the free-space list. The first of these procedures may cause an error termination to occur because no nodes are available. The algorithm for this routine (Figure 9.8) involves obtaining the

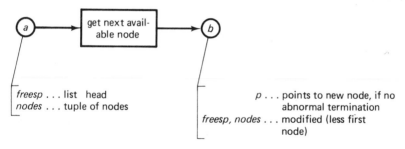

freesp ... list head
nodes ... tuple of nodes

p ... points to new node, if no abnormal termination
freesp, nodes ... modified (less first node)

Fig. 9.8 Problem statement of *get* routine.

pointer to the new node and updating the information in the list. As in all list processing routines (and many others as well) particular attention must be paid to the boundary conditions; in this case, what happens when there are no elements on the list? What happens when there is only one element on the list?

Algorithm 9.2 (Get next available node)

Global data referenced: *freesp, nodes*

> **procedure** *get*(;*p*)
> **begin** /∗get a node∗/
>   **if** *freesp* = 0 **then** [**output** 'freespace list exhausted'; **halt**];
>   *p* ← *freesp*;
>   /∗update∗/
>   *freesp* ← *next*(*nodes*(*p*))
> **end** /∗get∗/

EXERCISE 9.4: Write the AL procedure

$$free(p;)$$

along the same lines as Algorithm 9.2 and implement it in FORTRAN.

The following FORTRAN program is a translation of Algorithm 9.2; it makes use of the general field manipulation routines developed previously.

Purpose: Get next available node from free-space list.
Communication:

variables referenced through
COMMON block LIST: as before;
subroutines and functions called: NEXT . . . as before;
formal parameters: P . . . . pointer to new node set
                                                  by GET.

Program:

```
      SUBROUTINE GET(P)
      COMMON /LIST/FREESP,NODES(1000)
      INTEGER FREESP,P
C
C        CHECK FOR OVERFLOW
C
      IF(FREESP.NE.0)GO TO 10
         WRITE(6,1)
    1    FORMAT(25H FREESPACE LIST EXHAUSTED)
         STOP
C
C        SET POINTER, UPDATE FREESP
C
   10 P = FREESP
      FREESP = NEXT(FREESP)
      RETURN
      END
```

To complete our physical data structure we have to define access and manipulation procedures. These procedures are problem dependent. In Section C.9.4 of the supplementary volume a problem is presented whose solution requires extensive list processing. Therefore, we have selected a representative procedure which will be useful in that context where access and retrieval are somewhat restricted. Specifically, nodes are only added at the end of a list, and deletions are made only at the beginning of the list. Data structures thus characterized include the special class of lists known as FIFO (first-in–first-out) *queues*. A note of caution: If the algorithm uses only one such queue, a quite efficient sequential representation exists.

EXERCISE 9.5: Design a *sequential* representation of *one* queue and provide the *add* and *delete* procedure. (Hint: Use "modulo" computation.)

Assuming that the algorithm has to manipulate several queues, we wish to design a routine which will add a node to a list whose head is an input parameter. The modular refinement of the problem statement in Figure 9.9 is given directly in

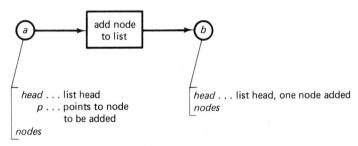

Fig. 9.9 Statement of *add* procedure.

Algorithm 9.3. Since the problem to be presented in Section C.9.4 of the supplementary volume does not require the number field in the list head, all references to it are omitted.

Algorithm 9.3 (Add a node to a FIFO queue)

Global data referenced: *nodes, freesp*

> **procedure** *add(head, p; head)*
> **begin** /*add a node*/
>   *next(nodes(p))* ← 0;
>   **if** *first(head)* = 0 **then** *first(head)* ← *p*
>   **else** *next(nodes(last(head)))* ← *p*;
>   *last(head)* ← *p*
> **end** /*add*/

Purpose: Add a node to a FIFO queue.
Communication:

variables referenced through
COMMON block LIST: as before;
subroutines and functions called: SNEXT
                                    SFIRST   as before;
                                    SLAST
                                    FIRST   from Exercise 9.3;
                                    LAST
formal parameters: HEAD .... list variable; modified;
                                    P .... pointer to node (modified) in
                                                      NODES.

Program:

```
          SUBROUTINE ADD(HEAD,P)
          COMMON /LIST/FREESP,NODES(1000)
          INTEGER HEAD,FREESP,P,FIRST
          CALL SNEXT(P,0)
    C
    C         HANDLE EMPTY LIST
    C
          IF(FIRST(HEAD).NE.0)GO TO 10
                CALL SFIRST(HEAD,P)
          GO TO 20
    C
    C         UPDATE LIST
    C
    10        CALL SNEXT(LAST(HEAD),P)
    C
    C         UPDATE HEADER
    C
    20 CALL SLAST(HEAD,P)
          RETURN
          END
```

EXERCISE 9.6: Write a FORTRAN function TAKEF(HEAD) which removes the first node of the list HEAD and returns a pointer to this node as the value of the function.

Example 9.2 Traffic Simulation

You may have had the unpleasant experience of driving in congested traffic situations where every traffic light turns red as soon as you approach it. In fact, you may also have entertained the notion that it should be possible to coordinate the traffic lights in such a way that traffic flow is made as efficient as possible under any given condition. One of the functions of the *city planner* is to find ways to improve traffic flow in and through the city.

The approach that the city planner might take is to simulate the traffic flow on a computer. Given a city map on which the controlled intersections are marked, she has to determine the pattern of red-yellow-green cycles for each intersection at various times during a 24-hour period. To do so she first must collect statistics on various aspects of the traffic flow. An example of such a statistic is the traffic density at the controlled intersections at the selected times. (Have you noticed the little rubber hoses across some streets?) The next step is to construct a model of traffic flow whose parameters are determined from the statistics gathered. The efficiency of traffic flow is usually measured in terms of average waiting time at an intersection, average time to travel from A to B, and average length of the queues at an intersection, among others. The model can be incorporated into a program which will compute these terms for various patterns of red-yellow-green cycles at all the intersections from which we can select the best patterns.

In general, simulation is an extremely valuable tool to many "system" designers. Because of the complexities involved in many systems, it is very often next to impossible to obtain any sort of analytic results on the performance of a proposed system. If results concerning the performance are required, a *simulation* program may be written which captures the essence of the system under various conditions. It is in the nature of a model that it is a simplified representation of the system, and the results derived from the simulation cannot be taken as absolute statements regarding the performance of the system. On the other hand, if the model is carefully constructed and great attention is paid to extracting the important features of the system, then a simulation model can tell us a great deal about the average performance of the system. In many cases it is certainly more expedient to write a simulation program to find out that a proposed system probably will not work than to construct one and then find out that it actually does not work.

After this slight digression on the nature of simulation programs, let us now return to the traffic flow problem—more specifically, to that aspect of the simulation program concerned with the representation of traffic patterns. Figure 9.10 illustrates a typical

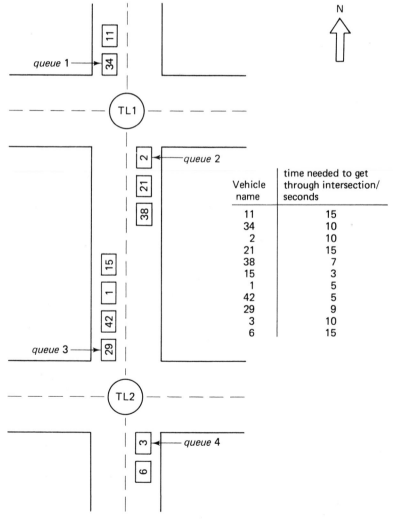

Vehicle name	time needed to get through intersection/ seconds
11	15
34	10
2	10
21	15
38	7
15	3
1	5
42	5
29	9
3	10
6	15

Fig. 9.10   A configuration of vehicles at two intersections.

configuration of vehicles at two representative intersections. The situation is highly simplified since we are at the moment not interested in all the details of the full simulation program but only in the underlying data structures. It should be apparent that the flow of traffic at an intersection corresponds to a FIFO discipline (assuming "civilized" drivers). In Figure 9.10 each car has been given an identifying number (name). Associated with this name is the time needed by the car to pass an intersection (which depends on the length of the car, the temperament of the driver, etc.).

Given the list-processing techniques developed earlier, it is relatively easy to represent the queues in the form of Figure 9.6. The reason for selecting this linked list representation over the sequential representation should be fairly obvious. The main operations on the nodes (cars) are moving a node from one queue to another as the car passes through an intersection or deleting (creating) a node altogether if it leaves (enters) the area under consideration. These operations are done most efficiently if a linked representation is chosen. A possible form of the list system (Figure 9.6) for the situation in Figure 9.10 is given in Figure 9.11. Assume now that the first vehicle of *queue4* has moved to the end of *queue2* and that the first two vehicles of *queue3* have

	number	last	first
queue 1	2	7	2
queue 2	3	8	12
queue 3	4	15	14
queue 4	2	13	9
freesp			1

	name	time	link
1	0	0	5
2	34	10	7
3	21	15	8
4	1	5	15
5	0	0	6
6	0	0	11
7	11	15	
8	38	7	
9	3	10	13
10	42	5	4
11	0	0	16
12	2	10	3
13	6	15	
14	29	9	10
15	15	3	
	⋮		
999	0	0	1000
1000	0	0	

Fig. 9.11   One possible representation of the traffic configuration of Figure 9.10.

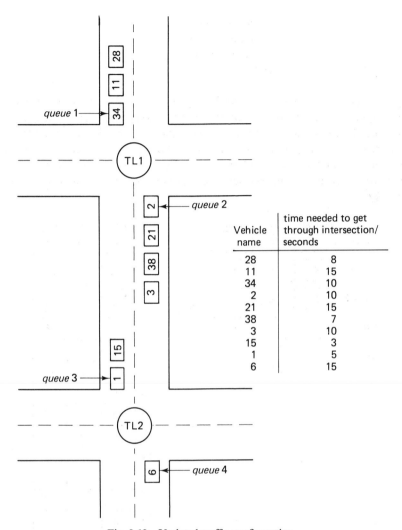

Vehicle name	time needed to get through intersection/ seconds
28	8
11	15
34	10
2	10
21	15
38	7
3	10
15	3
1	5
6	15

Fig. 9.12 Updated traffic configuration.

left the area. In addition, a new vehicle has arrived at the end of *queue*1. The simulation program may have effected these changes by executing the following sequence of calls:

$$
\begin{aligned}
&\textbf{begin} \\
&\quad p \leftarrow takef\,(queue4); \\
&\quad add(queue2, p; queue2); \\
&\quad p \leftarrow takef\,(queue3); \\
&\quad free(p;); \\
&\quad p \leftarrow takef\,(queue3); \\
&\quad free(p;); \\
&\quad get(;p);
\end{aligned}
$$

$$name(node(p)) \leftarrow 28;$$
$$time(node(p)) \rightarrow 8;$$
$$add(queue1, p; queue1)$$

   end

The resulting configurations are shown in Figures 9.12 and 9.13. We emphasize again that the simulation aspects of our discussion have been highly simplified in order to focus on the data structures involved. Nevertheless, it should be apparent how the data required by the city planner may be obtained using these structures. For example, the number of vehicles waiting at any given intersection at any given time can be obtained directly from the number fields of the queue heads associated with that intersection. ■

	number	last	first
queue 1	3	10	2
queue 2	4	9	12
queue 3	2	15	4
queue 4	1	13	13
freesp			14

	name	time	link
1	0	0	5
2	34	10	7
3	21	15	8
4	1	5	15
5	0	0	6
6	0	0	11
7	11	15	10
8	38	7	9
9	3	10	
10	28	8	
11	0	0	16
12	2	10	3
13	6	15	
14	0	0	1
15	15	3	
16	0	0	17
17	0	0	18
	⋮		
999	0	0	1000
1000	0	0	

Fig. 9.13   Representation of configuration of Figure 9.12.

EXERCISE 9.7: Assume that the vehicles in Example 9.2 are completely undifferentiated, i.e., no name or time associated with them. The only result required is the average length of each queue. Describe an alternative data structure which allows this information to be obtained efficiently.

EXERCISE 9.8: In Example 9.2 we used list variables to designate queues. In a realistic traffic flow model hundreds of queues may be involved, making this scheme awkward to use. Discuss an alternative method. (Hint: Look again at Figure 9.5.)

Multilists

The problem of maintaining the records of students at a college or university was considered in the introduction to this chapter. It was suggested there that the problem could be solved by chaining the selected records together to form a singly linked list and, furthermore, that this could be done for several groups of records by generating several singly linked lists. However, were this to be done, the resulting structure would not conform precisely to the definition since each node would actually contain several pointer fields. This divergence occurs because several lists might share the same node. To conform to the definition, as many copies of a record as there were lists in which it resided would have to be created. This is rather inefficient since very often the information field is quite lengthy. Instead, the definition of a node is relaxed slightly to allow it to be shared by as many lists as desired. Thus, if there were 10 lists contained in the student file, a node would be constructed which contained 1 information field and 10 link fields. However, this node would be viewed as representing 10 nodes which are contained in 10 singly linked lists; each node would have an identical information field since there is only one copy stored. The resulting structure is referred to as a *multilist*.

Example 9.3 Multilist Structure for Student Records

Assume we are given the following three singly linked lists of student records (the number of information fields has been reduced to two):

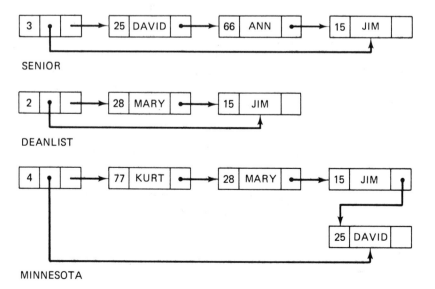

SENIOR

DEANLIST

MINNESOTA

The corresponding multilist structure according to the form given in Figure 9.6 is (the free-space list uses the *minnesota* link)

		id	name	senior	deanlist	minnesota
FREESPACE	6	1	77	KURT	0	0	3
		2	0	0	0	0	12
SENIOR	3 | 5 | 4	3	28	MARY	0	5	5
		4	25	DAVID	7	0	
DEANLIST	2 | 5 | 3	5	15	JIM			4
		6	0	0	0	0	2
MINNESOTA	4 | 4 | 1	7	66	ANN	5	0	0
		⋮	⋮	⋮			
		999	0	0	0	0	1000
		1000	0	0	0	0	

FREESPACE: 6
SENIOR: 3 | 5 | 4
DEANLIST: 2 | 5 | 3
MINNESOTA: 4 | 4 | 1

9.1.2 Doubly Linked Lists

An obvious extension to the concept of singly linked lists is to have the nodes chained in two directions while still retaining the linearity of the nodes. Consider the following problem: In a student file we have a linked list of students ordered by their grade point average (GPA), and we are given a pointer to the node of student JOHN DOE, find and print out the records of the k students with higher GPA's and of the k_1 students with lower GPA's in order. If a second link field is added to each node which contains a pointer to the predecessor, we can, starting at a random node, traverse the list in both directions. Or consider the problem of inserting a new node before a node whose information field has a given property. Obviously, there is no real need for the second link because as we traverse the list in search of the node we can keep track of the last node visited in, say, $p1$. Once we find the node p with the desired property we let the new node point to p and change the *next* field of node $p1$

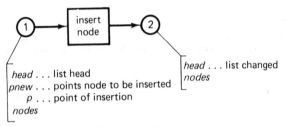

head . . . list head
pnew . . . points node to be inserted
p . . . point of insertion
nodes

head . . . list changed
nodes

Fig. 9.14   Statement of *insert* procedure.

to point to the new node. However, if the list to be searched is very long, the cost of maintaining $p1$ may outweigh the cost of the additional space required for the second link.

We assume that the nodes are stored in the tuple *nodes* with two link fields called *suc* and *pred*, respectively. List heads and the free-space list are as before. The statement in Figure 9.14 is the problem statement of a procedure which will insert a new node, *pnew*, into the list *head* before the node *p*.

Algorithm 9.4 (Insert a node in doubly linked list)

Global data referenced: *nodes*

```
procedure insert(head, pnew, p; head)
begin /*insert*/
    pbef ← pred(nodes(p));
        /*change left side*/
    if pbef = 0 then [pred(nodes(pnew)) ← 0; first(head) ← pnew]
                else [pred(nodes(pnew)) ← pbef; suc(nodes(pref)) ← pnew];
        /*change right side*/
    suc(nodes(pnew)) ← p;
    pred(nodes(p)) ← pnew
end /*insert*/
```

The two parts of Figure 9.15 show how a doubly linked list is modified when a new node is inserted.

list before insertion of node containing TOO

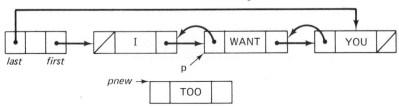

list after insertion:

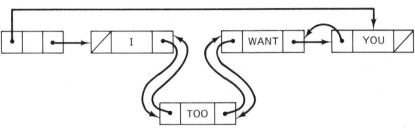

Fig. 9.15 Example of a doubly-linked list.

EXERCISE 9.9: Write the supporting FORTRAN subroutines and functions for a doubly linked list system. Use as many words for one node as are necessary so that you have an information field of 30 bits, and implement Algorithm 9.4. In addition, give an algorithm (FORTRAN program) for adding a node to the end of a doubly linked list.

EXERCISE 9.10: Can you insert a new node into a given singly linked list knowing the point *p* before which it should be inserted? If the answer is no, why not? If the answer is yes, how?

Example 9.4 Storage Allocation for Large Blocks

SNOBOL (see Part B of the supplementary volume) provides the facility for defining arrays at execution time; recall the discussion in Section 8.4.2 on interpreters. This implies that the SNOBOL system must be able to dynamically allocate possibly large blocks of memory during the execution of a program. One method for providing this capability is as follows:

1. The memory from which the allocation is to be made is viewed as one large tuple.
2. This block is initially the only block on a free-space list.
3. When a request for a block of memory of a given size is made, the blocks (initially only one) on the free-space list are traversed until a block is found of a size larger than that requested.
4. The portion of the block not required remains in the free-space list, while the remainder is allocated to the system.

Up to this point, the operations required could be supported using the concept of a singly linked free-space list as developed earlier. However, were we to use the same method for returning a block as developed there, the free-space list would eventually contain many small blocks (why?), without any practical way of collapsing those small blocks which are adjacent to each other. This problem arises because blocks that are adjacent in memory might be widely separated in the free-space list. To remedy this problem, we propose the following:

(a) Each block is delimited by two words, one at the beginning of the block and one at the end of the block. Each word contains the size of the block and a flag indicating whether it is an available block or a block currently being used.
(b) The free-space list is made a doubly linked list; the *pred* and *suc* links are maintained in the first delimiter word of a block.

With these changes, the allocation scheme can now be completed:

5. To return a used block to the free-space list, the flag of the immediately adjacent blocks in memory are checked to determine if they are currently free. If not, the block is returned to the free-space list as before. Otherwise, if one or

both adjacent blocks are free, they are collapsed with the current block. Using the two link fields, the free-space list is updated.

To illustrate this scheme, let us assume that we currently have the following memory configuration:

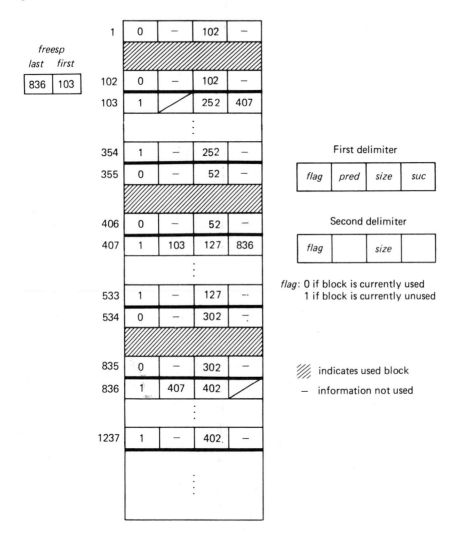

Suppose that the block beginning at location 355 is to be returned to the free-space list. Then the *return* procedure, called with this location as an argument, should modify this memory configuration to

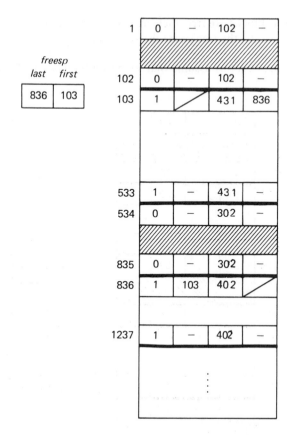

The information in all the locations between 103 and 533 is exactly the same as before, unless the *return* procedure zeroes the values in these locations. Normally, this is not done in the *return* procedure; it is up to the user to zero the block if necessary.

Note that it is absolutely necessary for the proper operation of this allocation scheme that both forward and backward links in the free space be available. The node(s) in the free-space list to be modified (i.e., collapsed with the block to be returned) is not found by traversing the free-space list. Rather, it is found by examining the information contained in the blocks adjacent in memory to the block to be returned. ■

EXERCISE 9.11: Develop algorithms for procedures to return a block (*return(p;)*) and to obtain a block of a given size (*get(size; p)*) as discussed in Example 9.4.

9.2 NONLINEAR STRUCTURES

A structure is called nonlinear when the restriction that the nodes must be linearly ordered is removed. That is, wherever a node may point to nodes other than its successor and/or predecessor, the resulting data structure is nonlinear.

9.2.1 Multilinked "Lists"

The term "list" has been placed in quotation marks since the structures to be discussed bear little resemblance to lists as they are commonly understood. The definition of a node is retained with the understanding that the number of link fields is k (≥ 1). The directions of the pointers are not restricted at all so long as all the nodes in one list are homogeneous in the number and interpretation of the link fields.

To be truly useful, a general-purpose list processing system must be able to cope with different lists (i.e., variable node size). Discussion of such a system is beyond the scope of this book since storage management becomes somewhat more complex (although the techniques presented in Example 9.4 could serve as the starting point of the discussion). Hence, in Example 9.5 we shall assume that all nodes have the same structure.

Example 9.5 Representation and Manipulation of Noncyclic Organic Molecules

One of the problems encountered in organic chemistry is the synthesis and analysis of organic compounds. To provide the reader with some insight into the concepts involved in such research, we shall study a relatively simple and well-understood problem: automatic generation of two-dimensional structural representations of hydrocarbon molecules† and their isomers. The structure of the first few hydrocarbons is given in Figure 9.16; note that the chemical formulas for these compounds is C_nH_{2n+2},

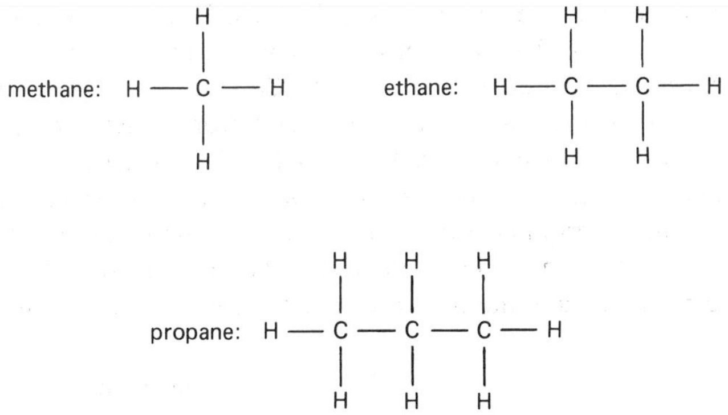

Fig. 9.16 Structure of some saturated hydrocarbons.

where n gives the number of carbon atoms in the molecule. An isomer is a compound whose formula is identical to a normal compound but whose structure is different. For example, Figure 9.17 shows an isomer (actually the only one) of butane which has the same formula, C_4H_{10}. The operation of generating all isomers of a hydrocarbon is complex because it involves structural changes in the bonds of the atoms. We shall

†Hydrocarbon molecules are molecules whose constituents are only hydrogen and/or carbon atoms.

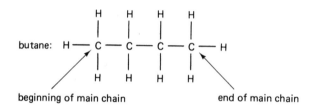

beginning of main chain   end of main chain

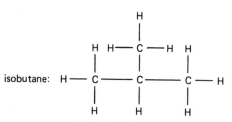

Fig. 9.17 Isomer of a compound.

bypass most of the difficulties and discuss only one way of generating isomers: Delete a CH_2 group from the central chain of carbon atoms and one hydrogen atom from another carbon atom; form a methyl group (CH_3), and attach its free bond to the carbon atom from which the hydrogen atom was removed.

Given these constraints, we can design a data structure most suitable to the operations. Unfortunately, we do not have any choice for this rather complex problem and must select multilinked lists. Alternative representations such as graphs can be found in advanced texts on data structures. We design the node to contain four link fields corresponding to the four bonds of a carbon atom which are designated *north, east, south,* and *west.* This node structure leads to a considerable waste for nodes representing hydrogen atoms since they have only one bond each. The information field need only contain an indicator as to which atom the node represents. It will be useful to store in the head both the number of carbon atoms (n) in the compound and pointers to the beginning and the end of the main carbon chain (see Figure 9.18).

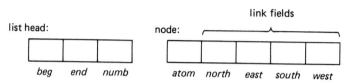

Fig. 9.18 List structure for some organic molecules.

Assume that the list CH4 has been initialized (see Figure 9.19) and that procedures are available to get and free the CH2, CH3 structures. These structures are represented by a pointer to the carbon atom. To generate new hydrocarbons we only have to call a procedure which, when given one molecule, will insert a CH2 structure after the first carbon atom.

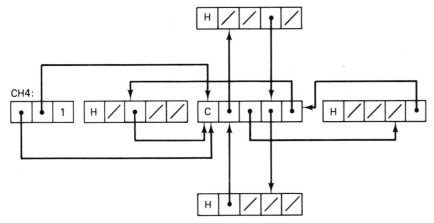

Fig. 9.19 Structure of methane.

Algorithm 9.5 (Generate next hydrocarbon)

Global data referenced: *nodes*

> **procedure** *newhydro(hydroc; hydroc)*
> **begin** /∗new hydrocarbon by inserting CH2 into *hydroc*∗/
>   *get CH2(;p)*;
>   /∗link CH2 to chain∗/
>   *pbef ← beg(hydroc)*; *paft ← east(nodes(pbef))*;
>   *west(nodes(p)) ← pbef*; *east(nodes(p)) ← paft*;
>   /∗change pointers in chain∗/
>   *east(nodes(pbef)) ← p*; *west(nodes(paft)) ← p*;
>   /∗update head∗/
>   *numb(hydroc) ← numb(hydroc) + 1*
> **end** /∗new∗/

We leave it as an exercise to design an algorithm to generate all isomers within the restrictions detailed above. Let us consider the problem of generating a specific isomer given the structure of the molecule and the two pointers to the carbon atoms involved in the change. Note that it is not necessary to consider the addition of methyl groups to the first or last atom in the chain because they do not result in true isomers (why?); hence, the list heads never have to be updated.

Algorithm 9.6 (Create one isomer)

Global data referenced: *nodes*

> **procedure** *isomer(hydroc, pdel, pin; hydroc)*
> **begin** /∗isomer, detach CH2∗/
>   *east(nodes(west(nodes(pdel)))) ← east(nodes(pdel))*;
>   *west(nodes(east(nodes(pdel)))) ← west(nodes(pdel))*;

    getCH3(;pnew);
     /*release old nodes*/
    freeCH2(pdel;); *free(north(nodes(pin)));)*;
     /*attach methyl group*/
    north(nodes(pin)) ← *pnew*; *south(nodes(pnew))* ← *pin*
   end /*isomer*/   ■

EXERCISE 9.12: Develop the algorithms for the various supporting procedures (i.e., *free*, *freeCH2*, etc.). Implement the free-space list as a singly linked list using the *north* fields of nodes.

EXERCISE 9.13: Develop an algorithm to generate all isomers within the framework discussed above.

9.2.2 Trees

  A natural extension to the concept of multilinked lists is the notion of a tree. One characteristic of multilinked lists is that each node contains the same fixed number of pointers. Removing this restriction while introducing further restrictions on the direction of the pointers leads to an abstract data structure called a *tree*.

  Definition 9.2: A *tree* is a set of nodes with one and only one distinguished node, called the *root* node. The remaining nodes are partitioned into disjoint sets which may be empty and which form trees themselves (also called subtrees).

  Trees are the natural representation of many quite familiar structures, such as the hierarchical organization of government and business. A portion of the organization of a hypothetical university will be used to explain the rather abstract definition given above. The tree in Figure 9.20 is the set of nodes

$$\{U, \ CA, \ CLA, \ CM, \ IT, \ ME, \ EE, \ CS\}$$

The root is the node labeled U (underlined below), and the remaining nodes form four disjoint subsets:

$$\underline{U}, \ \{CA\}, \ \{CLA\}, \ \{CM\}, \ \{IT, \ ME, \ EE, \ CS\}$$

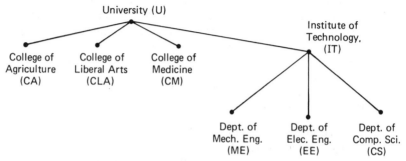

Fig. 9.20 The organizational structure of a university represented as a tree.

The first three sets (subtrees) contain only a root, whereas the last set consists of the root IT and three additional subtrees which in turn consist only of roots:

$$\underline{IT}, \{ME\}, \{EE\}, \{CS\}$$

Since trees are such important concepts, a whole nomenclature has evolved around them. Descendants of a node are called *sons* (also *successors, daughters, descendants*, etc.), all the immediate descendants of a parent node are called *brothers*, (*sisters, siblings*), and the parent node is referred to as *father* (*mother*). The root of a tree has no father. Nodes which have at least one descendant are called *intermediate*, or *nonterminal*, nodes, and those which do not have any descendants, *leaves*, or *terminal* nodes. Implicit in this nomenclature is that the tree expands downward; i.e., the root node is drawn on top with the leaves at the bottom.

A particularly important tree structure is the one commonly known as the *binary tree*.

Definition 9.3: A *binary tree* is a set of nodes either empty or with one and only one distinguished node, called the root node. The remaining nodes are partitioned into two disjoint sets which form binary trees themselves and are called the left and the right subtree of the root node.

There exist effective procedures for transforming a general tree into a binary tree (however, the reverse is not true, as, for instance, no equivalent trees exist for the two different binary trees $_B\!\diagup^A$ and $^A\!\diagdown_B$). Since at most two link fields are required in the node structure, we can represent such a tree as a multilinked list, for which we have already discussed methods of representation and manipulation.

We illustrate one such procedure by transforming the tree shown in Figure 9.21 into a binary tree.

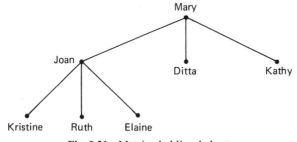

Fig. 9.21   Matriarchal lineal chart.

Informally, the algorithm may be stated as follows:

Link together all immediate descendants (brothers) of a node. Let the parent node point to the leftmost son. Repeat this process for all subtrees.

Applying this procedure to the tree in Figure 9.21 results in the binary tree shown in Figure 9.22.

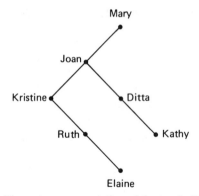

Fig. 9.22   Binary tree representation of the tree in Figure 9.21.

If the tree structure is relatively static, that is, deletions and insertions are rare, it might be more advantageous to use a mixture of sequential and linked representation for the physical data structure. Instead of linking brothers together, they are stored in consecutive storage locations preceded by a word containing the number of brothers following. Figure 9.23 illustrates this storage method using the tree of Figure 9.21; the tree name is MLC (matriarchal lineal chart).

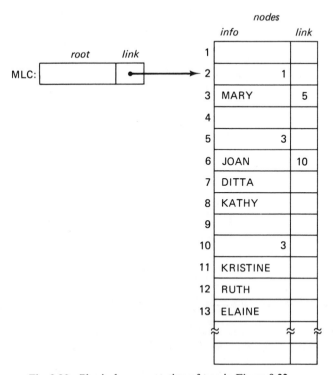

Fig. 9.23   Physical representation of tree in Figure 9.22.

Tree structures may be considered to be a data base containing information relative to the structural characteristics of the data (in addition to the information contained in the nodes); as such, one can query this data base for information such as, What is the name of the second daughter of MARY? For this purpose we may add structural information to the physical data structure to alleviate the problem of locating a node with a given name. Each node is identified by an integer between 1 and the number of nodes in the tree. This integer serves as an index to an array. This array contains the location of the node in the array *nodes*. Assuming the code MARY—1, JOAN—2, DITTA—3, etc., the address array for the tree in Figure 9.23 would then be as shown in Figure 9.24.

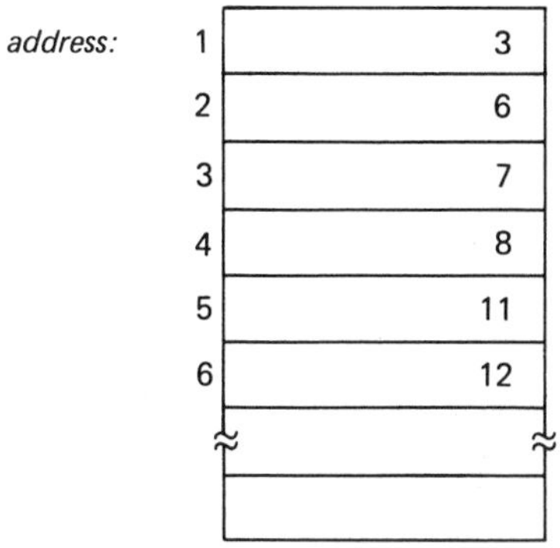

address:

1	3
2	6
3	7
4	8
5	11
6	12

Fig. 9.24 Address array for nodes in Figure 9.23.

Given this additional structural information, the complexity of algorithms which answer questions such as, "What is the kth daughter (from left to right) of a given name?" are clearly of $O(1)$, as the algorithm below shows.

Algorithm 9.7 (Find kth descendant of given node)

Global data referenced: *nodes*

```
procedure daughter(name, k; descend)
begin /*daughter; descend will be null if no kth daughter exists*/
    descend ← 0; p ← link(nodes(address(name)));
    if k > info(nodes(p)) then terminate;
    descend ← info(nodes(p + k))
end /*daughter*/
```

On the other hand, we emphasize that were the address array not available (it is quite wasteful in terms of storage utilization), the complexity of the search algorithm would be greatly increased since we first would have to search the tree for the node containing the name. This is essentially equivalent to a traversal of the tree. For lists, traversing was mentioned only in passing since it did not impose any particular difficulties. In the case of tree structures the algorithms are conceptually more difficult. Since tree traversal is usually described in terms of *recursive procedures*, we delay its discussion to Chapter 11, where we shall return to this problem.

9.3 AN EXAMPLE: STRING PROCESSING

It was a characteristic to the preceding discussion that the information items were stored in fixed-size information fields. For the applications discussed earlier, the average size of each information item was not very much different from the maximum size; hence, this scheme was efficient enough in terms of memory utilization so as not to warrant more elaborate mechanisms. However, in Chapter 10 we shall see applications concerning the processing of English text in which these assumptions are not valid simply because English words vary from 1 to 40 characters (or more), although the average size is around 5 characters. In this section we shall discuss the problems connected with processing of strings of varying size.

9.3.1 String Representation

First, we shall consider the *linear representation* in which the characters of a string are stored in consecutive storage locations. The string is named by providing a pointer to the location of the first character. This pointer can be considered to be the value of a string variable. As an alternative method to the simple variable concept used in Section 9.1, the heads of all strings will be stored in a tuple *heads*; any particular string can be accessed through *heads*(i). To delimit a string we may either record the length of the string in the string "head" or add a special character which does not appear in any string after the last character of the string. In the examples to follow, we choose the first method. Figure 9.25 illustrates how the string THIS IS A STRING is stored using the linear representation.

One method of comparing the efficiency of various string representations is through the use of a *memory utilization factor*. This is defined to be the ratio of the number of bits used to store information (n_s) over the total number of bits allocated for the encoding of characters. Assuming a word size of n bits and an encoding scheme using m bits per character, the memory utilization factor u for the linear representation is

$$n_s = cn * m$$

$$u = \frac{n_s}{cn * n} = \frac{m}{n} \tag{1}$$

Depending on the computer used, this ratio may range from as low as 10% to as much as 100%, implying, in most cases, a waste of memory space. Another disadvantage of this representation is the difficulty of adding characters to the string since in general it will involve copying the string to a block large enough to contain the new string. To delete characters, all characters following the deleted characters must be moved up in storage by a corresponding amount. Therefore, the worst-case complexity of algo-

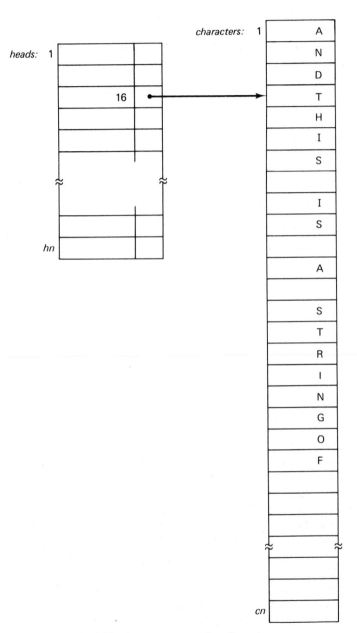

Fig. 9.25 *Linear representation* of a string.

rithms performing the last two operations is of $O(slength)$ if we take a reference to a character as the dominant instruction and let *slength* be the length of the string being operated on. On the other hand, retrieval of the *i*th character in a string can be done quite efficiently simply by adding *i* to the base address of the string given by the pointer variable; the complexity of this operation is therefore of $O(1)$.

The problems of adding elements to and deleting elements from the string may be alleviated by storing the string as a *linked list*, as shown in Figure 9.26. The memory

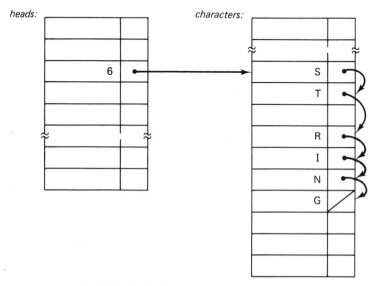

Fig. 9.26   *Linked list representation* of a string.

utilization ratio is somewhat improved for machines for which *u* from (1) is less than 1, assuming both a character and its pointer can be stored in one word. Retrieval of the *i*th character is now clearly of $O(i)$ since it requires that the list be traversed until the *i*th element is encountered.

Whenever a large number of strings must be stored and processed, these two methods are hardly appropriate for many computers because of the low memory utilization ratio. To increase the memory utilization, as many characters as possible may be packed into one computer word. Storing the string in consecutive words in memory leads to the *packed linear representation* shown in Figure 9.27. Since commonly the unused characters in the last word of a string are wasted, the memory utilization is not quite 100 %. Retrieval of the *i*th element in the string requires calculation of the word address and the position of the character within the word. With this information the character can be masked out of the word and shifted to any desired position. Addition and deletion operations are the same as the operations for the

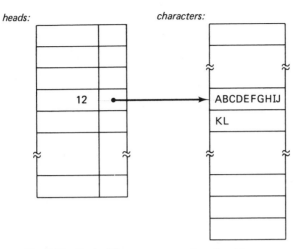

Fig. 9.27 *Packed linear representation* of a string.

linear representation with the additional burden introduced by the packing of characters.

Again, we can speed up add/delete operations by imposing a list structure on equal-length character blocks, as shown in Figure 9.28. Memory utilization is comparable to the packed linear representation. Other operations are similar to the operations for the linked list representation, but again additional overhead is incurred because of the packing of characters.

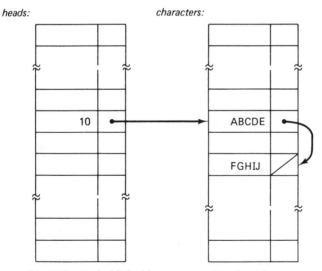

Fig. 9.28 *Packed linked list representation* of a string.

9.3.2 String Operations

In general, one might classify string operations as follows:

1. Retrieval: Get the ith character of a given string; get the substring, k characters long, of a string starting at its ith character.
2. Add/delete: Given a string, add/delete a substring, k characters long, starting at the ith character.
3. Memory management: Allocation of storage locations and reclamation of used storage.

The problem of memory management can be solved in several ways. For instance, a free-space list may be introduced to keep track of all locations which have been freed during execution time. No problems are encountered if we use it for the two list representations. For the linear representations the problem is that blocks of words, which are of varying length, will be released and requested. This results in a fragmentation of memory as discussed in Example 9.4. The techniques presented there are directly applicable to the current problem, and we shall not discuss them any further. Rather, a different approach called *garbage collection* is taken. Upon memory requests (e.g., for a new string) space is allocated, in this case, from the bottom of the array without looking for previously freed blocks in the array. Only when no more space is available is a *garbage collector* invoked. The garbage collector then removes freed blocks (those which are not pointed to by any string variable) by compacting used blocks up toward the top of the array. The pointers associated with each string are modified accordingly, as illustrated in Figure 9.29.

Comparison of the two approaches yields the observation that a small amount of work, each time a request for free space is made, has been traded against one rather large amount of work whenever space is exhausted using the simple bottom of the array allocation process. From the above description of the garbage collector we can deduce three rather distinct components of the process:

marking . . . mark the used blocks in the character array
compaction . . . move the blocks up
adjustment . . . adjust pointers in the *heads* array

If the underlying computer has a machine instruction to count the number of 1's in a word (or conversely the number of 0's) an ingenious way to solve the problem efficiently is to use bit tables. Bit tables, as referred to in this context, are arrays of words in which each bit corresponds to an entire word in another array. In this specific case we can interpret a bit setting of 1 to mean that the corresponding word in *characters* is used. If *characters* is a cn-tuple, then the corresponding bit table will be an array of cn/n words. For the compaction phase we need to know how many unused words precede each block in *characters* since this will be exactly the number of words by which we have to move this block. Given a bit table, we can compute this number by counting the number of 0's which precede the 1's corresponding to this block.

Before Garbage Collection

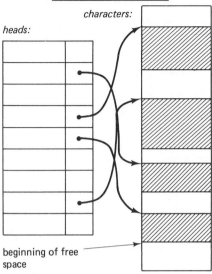

characters:

heads:

beginning of free
space

After Garbage Collection

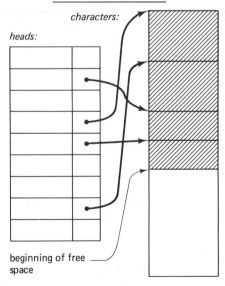

characters:

heads:

beginning of free
space

Fig. 9.29 Garbage collection process.

This operation can be greatly expedited if we reserve in each word of the bit table a field for the cumulative number of 0's so far seen.

Example 9.6 Illustration of Garbage Collection

For illustrative purposes, assume the following situation holds before garbage collection.

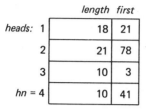

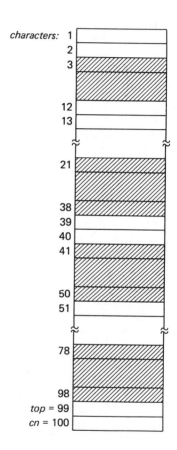

The marking phase, assuming a bit table initially zero, will then traverse the *heads* tuple and set the appropriate bits to 1, resulting in the following bit table (let $n = 48$):

Bit number: 123456789...   41 *cumulative*

bittable:		
1	0011111111110000000011111111111111111111001	12
2	1111111110000000000000000000000000000011111	39
3	111111111111111100———————————————0	—

In the above table we have assumed a 7-bit field for the cumulative number of used words since *cn* is 100. The compaction phase takes the bit table and the character array as input. It traverses the bit table, and for a block of 1's starting at the *j*th bit of *bittable(i)*, it moves the corresponding block in *characters* by

$$cumulative(bittable(i - 1)) + number\_zero(bittable(i), j) \qquad (2)$$

In (2) the function *number_zero* returns the number of zeroes preceding the *j*th bit of bittable(*i*); bittable(0) is assumed to be zero. Applying this procedure results in the following *characters* array:

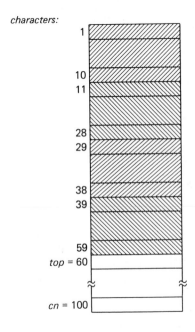

characters:

The adjustment phase is similar to the compaction phase but now the *heads* table is traversed. For each entry in the *first* fields we compute *i* and *j* and subtract the term (2) from the values in these fields, resulting in

heads:	1	18	11
	2	21	39
	3	10	1
$h_n = 4$		10	29

Let us develop a sample procedure for string processing using the packed linear representation in which the number of characters in each string is stored in the string head. Specifically, we wish to design a procedure which will add a copy of the *i*th character of one string to the end of a second string. For example, assume an initial configuration of *heads* and *characters* as shown in Figure 9.30(a) and a call to the procedure *add* with *heads*(2), *heads*(5), and 12 as arguments. Then the changes will be as indicated in Figure 9.30(b). In the modular refinement for this procedure (Figure 9.31) and the algorithm below, characters are assumed to reside in a table with *cn* rows and *nm* columns, where *nm* is the number of characters which can be stored in a word. The most interesting module in Figure 9.31 is module II since it may have to invoke the garbage collector. Whenever a new word has to be started for the second string to accommodate the additional character it is necessary to copy the string into unused space because there is no (easy) way of determining whether the next word is available or not. In case not enough space is available the garbage collector is invoked, and only after successful return can the string be copied into the free space (and the head adjusted).

   Algorithm 9.8 (Module II in Figure 9.31)

   Global data referenced: *heads, characters, top*

```
begin /*check*/
    if number(string1) < i then [error ← t; terminate]; error ← f;
    j ← number(string2);
    if mod(j, nm) = 0 then begin /*new word to be started*/
                            if j/nm + 1 + top > cn then garbage(j/nm + 1;);
                            /*the garbage collector will terminate
                              execution if it does not recover as many
                              words as indicated in the argument*/
                            relocate(string2; string2)
                        end /*new*/
end /*check*/
```

   The procedure *relocate* in Algorithm 9.8 simply copies the string into the unused space and updates the *top* pointer so that the next word is also available. In the FORTRAN implementation below we presume the existence of the necessary field retrieval and setting procedures.

   EXERCISE 9.14: Write the algorithms for modules II and IV of Figure 9.31.

   Purpose: Add the *i*th character of a string to the end of a second string.
   Communication:

variables referenced through
COMMON block STRING: HEADS . . . . . integer array of string heads;
                                fields are retrieved by functions
                                NUMBER and FIRST; modi-
                                fied;

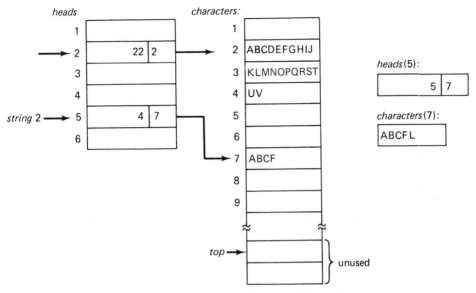

Fig. 9.30 String system before and after call.

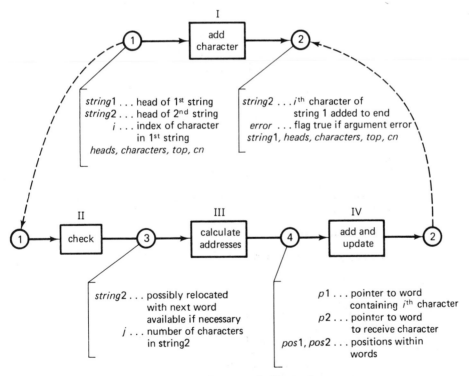

Fig. 9.31 Refinement of *add* procedure.

CHARAC.... integer array of character strings; modified;

TOP .... index into CHARAC; points to first available words; modified; assumed to be 1 at first entry!;

ERROR ..... is set to 1 if improper argument;

variables referenced through
COMMON block COMPU:

N .... word size;

M .... number of bits/character;

NM........ number of characters/word;

subroutines and functions called
    (none of them are given here):

GARBCO.... subroutine reclaims at least as many words as given in argument; otherwise it aborts; modifies COMMON block STRING;

RELOCA .... subroutine copies argument string to unused space and updates TOP;

NUMBER⎫ .. functions to retrieve informations
FIRST ⎬   from string head;
SNUM ...... subroutine sets information in head;

STRING..... as before;

formal parameters:

ST1 .... word in HEADS;

ST2 .... word in HEADS;

I .... integer index.

Program:

```
          SUBROUTINE ADD(ST1,I,ST2)
          COMMON /STRING/HEADS(100),CHARAC(1000),TOP,ERROR
          COMMON /COMPU/ N,M,NM
          INTEGER HEADS,CHARAC,TOP,ERROR,P1,POS1,P2,POS2,CN,ST1,ST2,FIRST
          DATA CN/1000/
    C
    C         CHECKING MODULE
    C
          IF(NUMBER(ST1).GE.I)GO TO 10
                ERROR = 1
                RETURN
       10 ERROR = 0
          J = NUMBER(ST2)
    C         IF NO NEW WORD TO BE STARTED GO TO NEXT MODULE
          IF(MOD(J,NM).NE.0)GO TO 30
    C         IF SPACE AVAILABLE JUST COPY
                IF(J/NM+1+TOP.LE.CN)GO TO 20
                      CALL GARBCO(J/NM+1)
       20       CALL RELOCA(ST2)
```

```
C
C            ADDRESS CALCULATION MODULE
C
   30 P1 = FIRST(ST1) + (I-1)/NM
      POS1 = MOD((I-1)::M,N)+1
      P2 = FIRST(ST2)+J/NM
      POS2 = MOD(J::M,N)+1
C
C            ADD AND UPDATE MODULE
C
      CALL STRING(CHARAC(P1),POS1,M,CHARAC(P2),POS2)
      CALL SNUM(ST2,J+1)
      RETURN
      END
```

EXERCISE 9.15: Using the structures developed in this example, develop and implement an algorithm which returns a substring k characters long, beginning at the ith character of a given string. The procedure should return this substring as a new string in the *heads* table.

9.4 CONCLUSIONS

Probably the most important conclusion that can be drawn from this chapter is that data structures do not exist in a vacuum. They must be considered in the context of both the problem and the language in which the solution is to be implemented.

As we have seen in numerous examples, a solution to a given problem very often dictates a class of data structures which are appropriate to the solution. As the solution is designed, the operations to be performed on the data become apparent. The next step involves an analysis of the algorithms involved in order to pinpoint those operations which contribute the most to the complexity. Finally, the data structures are designed so that these operations may be performed most efficiently. In Chapter 3, we were concerned with the development of algorithms in an orderly way. It should be apparent that the development of the data structures for a given problem solution progresses concurrently with, and is an integral part of, the process of modular refinement.

Much as the form of the final solution was dictated by the choice of an implementation language (e.g., FORTRAN, SNOBOL), so is the form of the underlying data structures influenced by this choice. In this chapter, we have touched on several special problem areas, and it should be noted that for each of these areas a special-purpose programming language exists. For instance, for list processing per se, the special-purpose language LISP (among others) is applicable; for discrete event simulation, one language is SIMULA; while for string processing, one such language is SNOBOL. These languages, although often general-purpose in their own right, are particularly suitable for special classes of problems. Although these languages may not always be available, we have shown in this chapter that a general-purpose language (such as FORTRAN) can be adapted to provide special features.

References

Probably the definitive work on data structures, albeit on a rather sophisticated mathematical level, is:

DONALD KNUTH, *The Art of Computer Programming*, Vol. I, Addison-Wesley, Reading, Mass., 1969.

An excellent introduction on a level for undergraduate students is

E. HOROWITZ and S. SAHNI, *Fundamentals of Data Structures*, Computer Science Press, Woodland Hills, Calif., 1976.

An introduction to the terminology and basic concepts of organic chemistry is given by

M. J. SIENKO and R. A. PLANE, *Chemistry*, McGraw-Hill, New York, 1971.

Exercises

1 In Fortran compilers one often finds keywords and operators plus delimiters in separate tables which are not part of the symbol tables. Why? In addition, implement the retrieval of such tokens for FORTRAN.

2 Design data structures for handling departmental student records which are to be used as follows:
   (a) For the development of a one-year plan of studies for a particular student.
   (b) For the development of graduation requirement checks of a student.
   (c) For the computation of the grade point average of a student.
   (d) Departmental statistics (course enrollment, etc.).
   (e) Listing of all advisees of a faculty member.
   (f) Find the adviser of a student.

3 Assume we wish to represent and store a full binary tree (each intermediate node has two descendants); the only operations required are
   (a) Find the father of a node.
   (b) Find the sons of a node.
   That is, there are no insertions or deletions, etc. Find an efficient (space-wise) representation so that operations (a) and (b) are of a complexity of $O(1)$.

4 Implement the garbage collector for a string-processing system as outlined in Section 9.3.2.

5 Extend the traffic simulation model from Example 9.2 to a more realistic case. Your discussion should include
   (a) The form of the data structures.
   (b) Operations on the structures.
   (c) What statistics have to be gathered.
   (d) A parameterized probabilistic model analogous to the one in Figure 8.21 in Part C of the supplementary volume.
   (e) Specifically, what data the simulation program should produce.

6 Discuss methods to manage memory for multilists. In particular, resolve the problems caused by a node being part of several singly linked lists. These problems include the following: When can we return a node to the free-space list, and when can the garbage collector reclaim a node?

10

Problems in Textual Analysis

10.0 INTRODUCTION

The concepts and techniques introduced in the first nine chapters are of primary interest mainly to computer scientists, to those who would aspire to be computer scientists, or to those who intend to become intimately familiar with the computer and its attendant systems. Clearly, the potential applicability of the computer is so enormous that virtually any scholarly, business, or research endeavor has those aspects which could be considered as a candidate for computer-based solutions and/or analysis. The use of the computer in areas outside pure computer science has led to new methodologies in those areas. In this chapter, we shall consider some of these applications in areas well outside the established realm of the sciences and engineering. Our intent is to establish the applicability of computer-based systems and approaches in these areas.

In 1949, Warren Weaver prepared a memo (unpublished) in which he suggested that a computer should be able to translate between two languages. This suggestion is remarkable in a historical sense; at that time, commercially available computers were almost nonexistent. Coupled with Shannon's proposal concerning the applicability of computers to game playing, it was the impetus for investigations into the nonnumerical aspects of computing. These two ideas, wedded with cybernetics and psychology, laid the foundation for artificial intelligence (Chapter 12). The early language translation projects, because of the infancy of computer science and naive notions concerning the structure of languages, were largely unsuccessful and soon abandoned. This unfortunate circumstance led many scholars, to whom the computer could have been of immense value, to turn away from machine-assisted studies. Consequently, it has not been until relatively recently that interest in the application of the symbol processing capabilities of the computer has been revived to the point where important research (e.g., literary research in the humanities) is being carried out with the aid of the computer. The translation problem is still unsolved, but smaller, more well-defined problems have been successfully solved in many of these areas.

10.1 NONNUMERIC PROCESSING

10.1.1 On the Nature of Nonnumeric Processing

As was intimated in the preceding section, nonnumeric processing is an area of computer science which has been receiving increasing attention. Unfortunately, a great deal of confusion has arisen over the nature of nonnumeric processing and the differences between it and the more established area of numeric processing. In some sense, the distinction is artificial since both types of processing result in the manipulation of symbols to produce a result. In one case (numeric processing), the symbols represent numbers, and the manipulation of these quantities consists of applying the well-known operations of arithmetic. From these basic operations, complex algorithms are constructed in which the final result may be in error because of the inherent limitations of both the algorithm and the computer. Recall our discussion in Chapter 6. Much effort has gone into the development of efficient numeric algorithms.

In the second case (nonnumeric processing), the symbols themselves and their structure (including the relations between them) become the object of processing. There is no numeric error as such in the production of an alphabetized list of names from an unordered list (for example). In fact, many of the list processing algorithms discussed in previous chapters may be considered nonnumeric algorithms. A classic example of a nonnumeric algorithm is the lexical scanner and code generator example developed in Chapter 8. In that example, the symbols representing the source program were translated into an equivalent set of symbols representing the intermediate code. Although a considerable amount of processing occurred, there was very little which could be construed as "numeric."

The distinction is also a fuzzy one, in the sense that many algorithms exhibit characteristics reminiscent of both numeric and nonnumeric processes. The sparse matrix example developed in Section C.9.4.2 of the supplementary volume is an excellent representative of this type of algorithm. On the surface, it is a nonnumeric algorithm since the items of interest are the nodes and their arrangement in the intersecting list structures. On the other hand, the contents of the nodes are the matrix elements themselves, which are subject to numeric algorithms, e.g., finding the inverse of the matrix. Thus, one would normally expect to find the sparse matrix algorithm being used in conjunction with a numeric algorithm.

10.1.2 On the Range of Nonnumeric Processing

In the first seven chapters of this book, we were concerned with the basically numerical calculations performed by a computer. It is important to note that the computer is more than just an ultra-high-speed calculator working solely on numbers. The last two chapters have illustrated that the computer is basically a symbol-manipulator. For example, the compilation process is an example of a symbol-manipulation problem, par excellence. The data which the compiler program operates on are a string of symbols representing some function to be performed. The end result of the compilation process is another string of symbols which represents the same function but which is closer to the format required by the machine.

As an analogy, a section of prose by Hemingway may be thought of as a string of symbols which may be manipulated by the computer. Some people believe this implies that a computer can be programmed to create prose in the style of Hemingway and see this use of the computer as a dehumanizing influence. The argument is blatantly ridiculous since it is people who understand and appreciate Hemingway's way with words, not computers. For those who wish to study Hemingway's use of words and structures, there is no reason they should not use every tool available. Instead of spending years gathering the data upon which their analyses are built, why not take advantage of the immense speed and symbol-manipulating capabilities of the computer? To deny its validity simply because of some misdirected loyalties seems inappropriate. Furthermore, the use of computers in a variety of studies opens the door for trying techniques which would be unthinkable using traditional methods.

The range of applications of the computer in which the processing of symbols in the traditional sense is the central issue is staggering. The following list, although by no means complete, provides a few examples:

I. Computer system processes: translators, compilers, interpreters, accounting systems, operating systems, command language processors. . . . We have already seen many of these applications in the preceding chapters.

II. Algebraic mathematics: symbolic mathematics, theorem proving. . . . The general idea here is to manipulate the symbols representing algebraic expressions; for example, find the first derivative of the expression $x^2 - 3x + 4$, or find the value (symbolic) of $\int \sin x\, dx$. In theorem proving, one attempts to represent facts and relationships concerning objects in a particular domain and then to prove theorems using these quantities; for example,

Facts	Theorem To Be Proved
Turing is human.	There is a fallible Greek.
Socrates is human.	
Socrates is Greek.	
All humans are fallible.	

Of course, this is a rather trivial example, although the general techniques developed for its solution are applicable to a wide range of problems.

III. Text manipulation systems:

1. Editing and composition: editors, formatting, typesetting. . . .

2. Indices: verbal indices, concordances, bibliography construction, dictionaries. . . .

3. Stylistic analysis and authorship studies: Here, the printed word and its representation on the page is the item to be manipulated. This may run from the production of a book, paper, etc., by computer editing and composition, through analysis of works by various authors, to the gen-

eral problem of ascribing a work to one of a group of authors. Many of the examples in this chapter are drawn from this group.

IV. Cryptanalysis: ciphering and deciphering. The concern here is with the protection of the contents of a message by scrambling its form in some way. Computers have been used at both ends of this process: the encoding of information using complex ciphering processes and the decoding of messages when the coding method is unknown (Chapter 2, Section 2.4).

V. Information retrieval: storage, retrieval, and maintenance. The computer has the capability of storing vast quantities of information on secondary storage devices; for example, library catalogues, medical records, criminal files, and the like. Information retrieval refers to the general problem of retrieving information from files in an efficient way, maintaining the integrity and accuracy of the contents of files, and the like.

VI. Linguistics: syntax and semantics. At one level, a sentence may be considered as a string of symbols, assembled according to some rules (the syntax), used to transmit ideas or meaning (the semantics) to someone else. See the discussion of syntax and grammars in Section C.9.4.3 of the supplementary volume. Computers may be used to parse sentences according to some grammar, construct sentences according to a grammar, or to attempt to extract the meaning of a group of symbols representing the sentence.

VII. Business data processing: accounting, inventory control, report generation, management systems, quality control. . . . One of the currently most important uses of computers is in this area. The basic difference between the use of computers in scientific endeavors and business is the amount and nature of the input/output. Business applications are often heavily intertwined with information retrieval systems operating on large data bases, while the actual amount of computing in the strict sense of the word is small (Chapter 5).

VIII. Games and puzzles: board games, word puzzles, crossword puzzles. . . . Often considered one of the recreational areas of computing, the potential applications to education by providing guided tours through complex problem-solving situations is staggering.

IX. System analysis: critical path analysis, simulation, modeling. . . . By providing a means by which complex systems may be simulated, the computer has the potential of streamlining the development of these systems. Much wasted effort and money may be saved by detecting flaws in the proposed design before anything material is involved. One does not actually have to build a bridge in order to analyze its structure to the minutest detail (Sections 8 and 9 of Part C of the supplementary volume).

Although the gross organization of this list may be questioned, it does provide some insight into the use of the computer as a symbol-manipulator. Figure 10.1 illustrates the range of these applications as seen by the Association for Computing Machinery (ACM) for use in their categorization of the computing literature for *Computing*

CATEGORIES OF THE COMPUTING SCIENCES

GENERAL TOPICS AND EDUCATION
1.0 GENERAL
1.1 TEXTS; HANDBOOKS
1.2 HISTORY; BIOGRAPHIES
1.3 INTRODUCTORY AND SURVEY ARTICLES
1.4 GLOSSARIES
1.5 EDUCATION
  1.50 General
  1.51 High School Courses and Programs
  1.52 University Courses and Programs
  1.53 Certification; Degrees; Diplomas
  1.59 Miscellaneous
1.9 MISCELLANEOUS

COMPUTING MILIEU
2.0 GENERAL
2.1 PHILOSOPHICAL AND SOCIAL IMPLICATIONS
  2.10 General
  2.11 Economic and Sociological Effects
  2.12 The Public and Computers
  2.19 Miscellaneous
2.2 PROFESSIONAL ASPECTS
2.3 LEGISLATION; REGULATIONS
2.4 ADMINISTRATION OF COMPUTING CENTERS
  2.40 General
  2.41 Administrative Policies
  2.42 Personnel Training
  2.43 Operating Procedures
  2.44 Equipment Evaluation
  2.45 Surveys of Computing Centers
  2.49 Miscellaneous
2.9 MISCELLANEOUS

APPLICATIONS
3.1 NATURAL SCIENCES
  3.10 General
  3.11 Astronomy; Space
  3.12 Biology
  3.13 Chemistry
  3.14 Earth Sciences
  3.15 Mathematics; Number Theory
  3.16 Meteorology
  3.17 Physics; Nuclear Sciences
  3.19 Miscellaneous
3.2 ENGINEERING
  3.20 General
  3.21 Aeronautical; Space
  3.22 Chemical
  3.23 Civil
  3.24 Electrical; Electronic
  3.25 Engineering Science
  3.26 Mechanical
  3.29 Miscellaneous
3.3 SOCIAL AND BEHAVIORAL SCIENCES
  3.30 General
  3.31 Economics
  3.32 Education; Welfare

3.33 Law
3.34 Medicine; Health
3.35 Political Science
3.36 Psychology; Anthropology
3.37 Sociology
3.39 Miscellaneous
3.4 HUMANITIES
  3.40 General
  3.41 Art
  3.42 Language Translation and Linguistics
  3.43 Literature
  3.44 Music
  3.49 Miscellaneous
3.5 MANAGEMENT DATA PROCESSING
  3.50 General
  3.51 Education; Research
  3.52 Financial
  3.53 Government
  3.54 Manufacturing; Distribution
  3.55 Marketing; Merchandising
  3.56 Military
  3.57 Transportation; Communication
  3.59 Miscellaneous

3.6 ARTIFICIAL INTELLIGENCE
  3.60 General
  3.61 Induction and Hypothesis-Formation
  3.62 Learning and Adaptive Systems
  3.63 Pattern Recognition
  3.64 Problem-Solving
  3.65 Simulation of Natural Systems
  3.66 Theory of Heuristic Methods
  3.69 Miscellaneous
3.7 INFORMATION RETRIEVAL
  3.70 General
  3.71 Content Analysis
  3.72 Evaluation of Systems
  3.73 File Maintenance
  3.74 Searching
  3.75 Vocabulary
  3.79 Miscellaneous
3.8 REAL-TIME SYSTEMS
  3.80 General
  3.81 Communications
  3.82 Industrial Process Control
  3.83 Telemetry; Missiles; Space
  3.89 Miscellaneous
3.9 MISCELLANEOUS

4. SOFTWARE
4.0 GENERAL
4.1 PROCESSORS
  4.10 General
  4.11 Assemblers
  4.12 Compilers and Generators
  4.13 Interpreters
  4.19 Miscellaneous

4.2 PROGRAMMING LANGUAGES
  4.20 General
  4.21 Machine-Oriented Languages
  4.22 Procedure- and Problem-Oriented Languages
  4.29 Miscellaneous
4.3 SUPERVISORY SYSTEMS
  4.30 General
  4.31 Basic Monitors
  4.32 Multiprogramming; Multiprocessing
  4.33 Data Base
  4.34 Data Structures
  4.35 Operating Systems
  4.39 Miscellaneous
4.4 UTILITY PROGRAMS
  4.40 General
  4.41 Input/Output
  4.42 Debugging
  4.43 Program Maintenance
  4.49 Miscellaneous
4.5 PATENTS, SOFTWARE
4.6 SOFTWARE EVALUATION, TESTS, AND MEASUREMENTS
4.9 MISCELLANEOUS

5. MATHEMATICS OF COMPUTATION
5.0 GENERAL
5.1 NUMERICAL ANALYSIS
  5.10 General
  5.11 Error Analysis; Computer Arithmetic
  5.12 Function Evaluation
  5.13 Interpolation; Functional Approximation
  5.14 Linear Algebra
  5.15 Nonlinear and Functional Equations
  5.16 Numerical Integration and Differentiation
  5.17 Ordinary and Partial Differential Equations
  5.18 Integral Equations
  5.19 Miscellaneous
5.2 METATHEORY
  5.20 General
  5.21 Logic; Formal Systems [includes: Boolean algebras, theorem proving; excludes: switching, ternary logic, etc.]
  5.22 Automata: finate-state; celular; stochastic; sequential machines
  5.23 Formal Languages: nondeterministic processors; grammars; parsing and translation; abstract families of languages
  5.24 Analysis of Programs: schemata; semantics; correctness
  5.25 Computational Complexity: machine-based; machine-independent; efficiency of algorithms

5.26 Turing Machines; Abstract Processors
5.27 Computability Theory: unsolvability; recursive functions
5.29 Miscellaneous
5.3 COMBINATORIAL AND DESCRETE MATHEMATICS
  5.30 General
  5.31 Sorting
  5.32 Graph Theory
  5.39 Miscellaneous
5.4 MATHEMATICAL PROGRAMMING
  5.40 General
  5.41 Linear and Nonlinear Programing
  5.42 Dynamic Programming
  5.49 Miscellaneous
5.5 MATHEMATICAL STATISTICS; PROBABILITY
5.6 INFORMATION THEORY
5.7 SYMBOLIC ALGEBRAIC COMPUTATION
5.9 MISCELLANEOUS

6. HARDWARE
6.0 GENERAL
6.1 LOGICAL DESIGN, SWITCHING THEORY
6.2 COMPUTER SYSTEMS
  6.20 General
  6.21 General-Purpose Computers
  6.22 Special-Purpose Computers
  6.29 Miscellaneous
6.3 COMPONENTS AND CIRCUITS
  6.30 General
  6.31 Circuit Elements
  6.32 Arithmetic Units
  6.33 Control Units
  6.34 Storage Units
  6.35 Input/Output Equipment
  6.36 Auxilary Equipment
  6.39 Miscellaneous
6.4 PATENTS, HARDWARE
6.5 MISCELLANEOUS

7. ANALOG COMPUTERS
7.0 GENERAL
7.1 APPLICATIONS
7.2 DESIGN; CONSTRUCTION
7.3 HYBRID SYSTEMS
7.4 PROGRAMMING; TECHNIQUES
7.9 MISCELLANEOUS

8. FUNCTIONS
8.0 GENERAL
8.1 SIMULATION AND MODELING
8.2 GRAPHICS
8.3 OPERATIONS RESEARCH/ DECISION TABLES
8.4 MISCELLANEOUS

Fig. 10.4 Range of applications. *(Courtesy of the Association for Computing Machinery (ACM))*

Reviews, a publication devoted to critical reviews of the literature on computing and computer applications.

10.1.3 About the Chapter

This chapter represents an attempt to outline approaches that might be used in some of the above areas. Since the range of application is so great, it is impossible to cover all areas. We shall limit ourselves to representative algorithms and procedures which might be used in the analysis of textual data since this area seems to be the most ill-understood of the potential application areas. The techniques to be discussed will draw upon the principles developed in the preceding chapters to a certain extent.

The rather large applications area of business data processing will be almost completely ignored, not because it is not an important subject, but because the scope of this book precludes its thorough treatment beyond the basic outline in Chapter 5.

In the next section, we shall discuss the string as a data type, which in some sense duplicates part of the discussion in earlier chapters, although in a different context. The remaining sections illustrate particular problem domains which assume a string of symbols as the basic data item to be manipulated.

10.2 THE STRING AS A DATA ITEM

10.2.1 Operations on Strings

In Chapter 9 we discussed the possible representations of strings and their computer implementations. There, a set of string operation was defined which was sufficient for the purposes of that chapter. The operations were retrieval, additions and deletions of substrings, and garbage collection. Since the intent of Chapter 9 was to consider the data structures involved in the manipulation of arbitrary items, these operations were not developed to any degree. In this section, these operations will be reconsidered from the vantage of strings as an object to be manipulated.

A string may be defined as an ordered sequence of alphanumeric characters such that the smallest manipulatable quantity is a single character. Following the conventions of the SNOBOL language, strings will be defined by enclosing the sequence of characters in single quotes, e.g., 'this is a string'. Thus, any sequence of single characters becomes a string when enclosed in quotes. Every string has the attribute of length, which is determined simply by counting the characters comprising the string, including blanks. The above sample string has a length of 16. The empty string (the string composed of no characters) is also called the null string and has a length of zero. This string is represented as ''.

Every string may be assigned a name. In AL, this is accomplished in the same manner as every other assignment statement:

$$string1 \leftarrow \text{'this is a string'}$$
$$token \leftarrow \text{''}$$

etc. Thus, strings may be referred to by their names (e.g., *token*) or by their contents (e.g., 'this is a string'). These conventions are entirely consistent with SNOBOL, and it might be appropriate for the reader to review the string conventions in SNOBOL as discussed in Part B of the supplementary volume.

The operations to be performed on strings are quite natural and fall into one of three general categories:

1. Decomposition: Decompose a given string into two or more distinct strings.
2. Alteration: Modify the contents of a string without decomposing it.
3. Pattern matching: Search a given string for an occurrence of a given string; perform unconditional matches, such as match the first n characters of the string.

Representative operations from each of these categories are discussed below.

In the algorithms of this and the remaining chapters, we shall include operators equivalent to those in SNOBOL; they will be either bold-faced function calls or procedure invocations to indicate that they are primitive operations and part of AL. We violate the spirit of AL somewhat in modeling its operators on an existing language. It is very difficult to enforce the structured development of a SNOBOL program because of the rather different branching facilities SNOBOL offers. Hence, we shall continue to specify solutions first in AL with its limited control structures and then translate them into SNOBOL. In the discussion to follow, $s_1, \ldots, s_n$ are to be assumed string-valued variables, and p will refer to a pattern.

Basic String Operations

1. Decomposition
   (a) **substring**(s_1, n, m):   Given the string s_1, a substring m characters long is extracted, beginning at the nth character of s_1, and returned as the value of the function. If n is greater than the length of s_1, the null string is returned. If there are not enough characters in s_1, then the returned value is padded with trailing blanks so that its length will always be m.
   (b) **decomp**$(s_1, n; s_2, s_3)$:   String s_1 is decomposed into two strings, s_2 and s_3; s_2 contains the first n characters of s_1, while s_3 contains characters $n + 1$ through the end of s_1. If n is greater than or equal to the length of s_1, s_3 is assigned the null string, and $s_2 = s_1$.
   (c) **first**(s_1):   The first character of s_1 is returned as the value of the function.
   (d) **last**(s_1):   The last character of s_1 is returned as the value of the function.
   In both (c) and (d), if s_1 is **null**, the null string is returned.
2. Alteration
   (a) **substitute**$(s_1, s_2, s_3; s_1)$: s_2 and s_3 are strings of the same length and are ordered by position. Every character of s_1 which is found in s_2 is replaced by the corresponding character from s_3.
3. Pattern matching
   (a) **search**(s_1, p):   The string s_1 is searched from the left for the first occur-

rence of any string defined by p. When a match is found, the position of the first character in s_1 that matches is returned as value. If no match is found, the value of the function is 0.

(b) **replace**($s_1, p, s_2; s_1, flag$):   The string s_1 is searched from the left for the first occurrence of any string defined by p. When a match is found, the string is replaced by s_2 and *flag* is set to **t**. If no match is found, the *flag* is set to **f**.

4. Miscellaneous

(a) **length**(s_1):   Returns the length of s_1; if s_1 is **null**, then the value is 0.

(b) **span**(s_1):   Returns a pattern which will match the longest string consisting only of characters contained in s_1; the match will fail if no character is found.

(c) **break**(s_1):   Returns a pattern which matches the longest string consisting only of characters not contained in s_1; the match fails if no character of s_1 is found.

(d) | and ' ':   Pattern construction operators as defined in SNOBOL.

(e) . and $:   Assignment operator as defined in SNOBOL.

As noted above, these are only representative samples of the operations that may be performed on strings. They do, however, form a basically complete subset of operations which may be used for string-oriented problems. The astute reader will note that many of them are directly translatable into their equivalent SNOBOL operations in a rather straightforward way.

EXERCISE 10.1: Assuming the representation of strings as in Section 9.3, develop AL procedures for each of the string operations developed here. What other operations are convenient?

EXERCISE 10.2: Review the string and pattern matching structure of SNOBOL (Part B of the supplementary volume) and indicate how each of the above operations appear in SNOBOL.

In the next section, we shall provide an example of a string-oriented problem and its solution using these primitives.

10.2.2 An Example: Translation from English to Pig Latin

A very naive approach to mechanical language translation is the direct word-for-word substitution, leaving sentence structure unchanged. Of course, this method fails miserably for natural languages for obvious reasons. However, English may be translated into an artificial language (Pig latin) rather easily using such a procedure. Asway emonstratedday erehay, igpay atinlay earsbay an arkedmay imilaritysay otay Englishway. The translation rules are rather straightforward:

1. The word "a" becomes "an".
2. Other one-letter words and numbers remain unchanged.
3. Words beginning with vowels are given the suffix "way".
4. Words beginning with a consonant string are altered by rotating the consonant string to the end of the word and adding the suffix "ay".
5. A "q" moved in application of rule 4 carries its "u" along with it.
6. "y" may have either vowel or consonant value. We shall assume "y" is a consonant and not worry about words like "yclad," "yclept," and "yttrium."

The problem statement for this example and its first-level refinement are shown in Figure 10.2.

One of the first decisions which must be made prior to the implementation of this

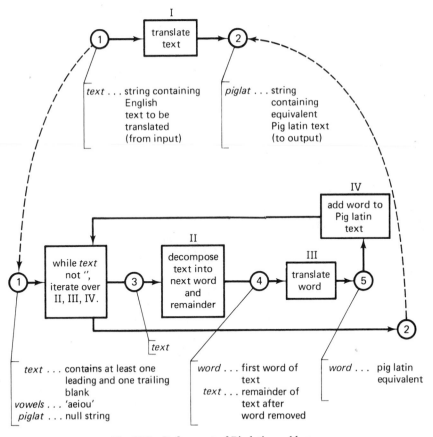

Fig. 10.2 Refinement of Pig latin problem.

solution is, How do we define a word? In this case, we shall assume that a word is any sequence of characters surrounded by blanks. This, of course, includes numbers, abbreviations, etc. Given this definition of a word and the pattern

$$wordp \longleftarrow \textbf{span}(\text{`   '}) \textbf{ break}(\text{`   '}) \, . \, word$$

module II simply consists of the call

$$\textbf{replace}(text, wordp, \text{`'}; text, flag)$$

The process of translating a word from English to its Pig latin equivalent is then quite simple and follows the rules as given above. Algorithm 10.1 is the AL representation of this process, assuming the basic string manipulation procedures discussed in Section 10.2.1.

Algorithm 10.1 (Translate one word, module III of Figure 10.2)

Global data referenced: *consp*-a global pattern which will match the leading consonant string (except q) and assign it to *prefix*; *vowel*-a global variable whose value is 'AEIOU'

```
procedure translate(word; word)
begin /*translate a word*/
      /*one letter rule*/
    if length(word) = 1 then
        [if word = 'a' then word ← 'an'; terminate];
    if search(vowel, first(word)) ≠ 0 then
                            /*vowel rule*/
                        word ← word + 'way'
                                else
                        begin /*consonant rule*/
                            replace(word, consp, ''; word, flag);
                            word ← word + prefix;
                            if first(word) = 'q' then
                                /*q rule*/
                                [decomp(word, 2; qu, word);
                                 word ← word + qu];
                            word ← word + 'ay'
                        end /*consonant*/
end /*translate*/
```

In the SNOBOL implementation of the translation problem to follow, we shall utilize the special features SNOBOL provides but adhere to the structure of Algorithm 10.1; a sample output is shown in Figure 10.3.

INPUT TEXT

IN 1949, WARREN WEAVER PREPARED A MEMO(UNPUBLISHED) IN WHICH HE SUGGESTED THAT A COMPUTER SHOULD BE ABLE TO TRANSLATE BETWEEN TWO LANGUAGES. THIS SUGGESTION I S REMARKABLE IN A HISTORICAL SENSE; AT THIS TIME, COMMERCIALLY AVAILABLE COMPUTE RS WERE ALMOST NON-EXISTENT. COUPLED WITH SHANNON'S PROPOSAL CONCERNING THE APP LICABILITY OF COMPUTERS TO GAME PLAYING, IT WAS THE IMPETUS FOR INVESTIGATIONS I NTO THE NON-NUMERICAL ASPECTS OF COMPUTING. THESE TWO IDEAS, WEDDED WITH CYBERN ETICS AND PSYCHOLOGY, LAID THE FOUNDATION FOR ARTIFICIAL INTELLIGENCE (CHAPTER 1 2). THE EARLY LANGUAGE TRANSLATION PROJECTS, BECAUSE OF THE INFANCY OF COMPUTER SCIENCE AND NAIVE NOTIONS CONCERNING THE STRUCTURE OF LANGUAGES, WERE LARGELY U NSUCCESSFUL AND SOON ABANDONED.

TRANSLATED TEXT

INWAY 1949,AY ARRENWAY EAVERWAY EPAREDPRAY AN EMO(UNPUBLISHED)MAY INWAY ICHWHAY EHAY UGGESTEDSAY ATTHAY AN OMPUTERCAY OULDSHAY EBAY ABLEWAY OTAY ANSLATETRAY ET WEENBAY OTWAY ANGUAGES.LAY ISTHAY UGGESTIONSAY ISWAY EMARKABLERAY INWAY AN ISTOR ICALHAY ENSE;SAY ATWAY ISTHAY IME,TAY OMMERCIALLYCAY AVAILABLEWAY OMPUTERSCAY ER EWAY ALMOSTWAY ON-EXISTENT.NAY OUPLEDCAY ITHWAY ANNON'SSHAY OPOSALPRAY ONCERNIN CAY ETHAY APPLICABILITYWAY OFWAY OMPUTERSCAY OTAY AMEGAY AYING,PLAY ITWAY ASWAY ETHAY IMPETUSWAY ORFAY INVESTIGATIONSWAY INTOWAY ETHAY ON-NUMERICALNAY ASPECTSWA Y OFWAY OMPUTING.CAY ESETHAY OTWAY IDEAS,WAY EDDEDWAY ITHWAY ERNETICSCYBAY ANDWA Y OLOGY,PSYCHAY AIDLAY ETHAY OUNDATIONFAY ORFAY ARTIFICIALWAY INTELLIGENCEWAY (A PTERCHAY 12).CHAY ETHAY EARLYWAY ANGUAGELAY ANSLATIONTRAY OJECTS,PRAY ECAUSEBAY OFWAY ETHAY INFANCYWAY OFWAY OMPUTERCAY IENCESCAY ANDWAY AIVENAY OTIONSNAY ONCER NINGCAY ETHAY UCTURESTRAY OFWAY ANGUAGES,LAY EREWAY ARGELYLAY UNSUCCESSFULWAY AN DWAY OONSAY ABANDONED.WAY

Fig. 10.3   Sample output from Pig latin program.

Purpose: Translate a given English text to its Pig latin equivalent.
Communication:

global variables referenced: TEXT.......... English text; modified;
VOWEL........ string of vowels;
CONSP }   (—consonant string,
FIRSTP } ...... patterns for{—first character,
WORDP}   (—word;
PREFIX }
FIRSTCHAR} ... conditional result of above patterns;
WORD }

functions called: PIGWORD ..... obtains new word from text, translates it; modifies TEXT, WORD.

Program:

```
        DEFINE('PIGWORD()','TRANSLATE')                               1
        VOWEL = 'AEIOU'                                               2
        CONSP = SPAN('BCDFGHJKLMNPQRSTVWXYZ') . PREFIX                3
        WORDP = SPAN(' ') BREAK(' ') . WORD                          4
        FIRSTP = LEN(1) . FIRSTCHAR                                   5
        &TRIM = 1                                                     6
        OUTPUT('OUTPUT',6,'(1X,80A1)')                               7
IN      TEXT = TEXT ' ' INPUT                    :S(IN)               8
        TEXT = TEXT ' '                                              9
        OUTPUT = TEXT                                               10
        OUTPUT =                                                    11
BEGIN   PIGLAT = PIGLAT ' ' PIGWORD()           :S(BEGIN)           12
        OUTPUT = PIGLAT                          :(END)             13
▓▓▓▓▓▓▓▓▓▓▓▓▓▓▓▓▓▓▓▓▓▓▓▓▓▓▓BEGIN FUNCTION PIGWORD▓▓▓▓▓▓▓▓▓▓▓▓▓▓▓▓▓▓▓▓
TRANSLATE TEXT WORDP =                          :F(FRETURN)         14
::.............ONE WORD RULE.....................................
        EQ(SIZE(WORD),1)                        :F(VOWCONS)         15
            WORD 'A' = 'AN'                                         16
            PIGWORD = WORD                      :(RETURN)           17
VOWCONS WORD FIRSTP                                                18
::..............VOWEL RULE.......................................
        VOWEL FIRSTCHAR                         :F(CONS)           19
            PIGWORD = WORD 'WAY'                :(RETURN)           20
::..............CONSONANT RULE...................................
CONS    WORD CONSP =                                               21
        WORD = WORD PREFIX                                         22
        WORD 'QU' =                             :F(CONS1)          23
::..............Q RULE...........................................
        WORD = WORD 'QU'                                           24
CONS1   PIGWORD = WORD 'AY'                      :(RETURN)          25
▓▓▓▓▓▓▓▓▓▓▓▓▓▓▓▓▓▓▓▓▓▓▓▓▓▓▓END OF PIGWORD▓▓▓▓▓▓▓▓▓▓▓▓▓▓▓▓▓▓▓▓▓▓▓▓▓▓
▓▓▓▓▓▓▓▓▓▓▓▓▓▓▓▓▓▓▓▓▓▓▓▓▓▓▓END OF PROGRAM▓▓▓▓▓▓▓▓▓▓▓▓▓▓▓▓▓▓▓▓▓▓▓▓▓▓
END                                                                26
```

There are several known faults with this version of the translation program. Words have been defined as sequences of characters between blanks; however, real sentences are often heavily punctuated and may contain sequences between blanks which are not words, e.g., numbers. The program as written will try to translate punctuation marks and numbers as words.

EXERCISE 10.3: The pattern used to match the next word from TEXT is

SPAN(BLANK) BREAK(BLANK) . WORD

Consider alternatives to this pattern which will alleviate (at least partially) the problems caused by our rather simplistic definition of a word and the problem of punctuation. If an English sentence is punctuated, the Pig latin equivalent of that sentence should also be punctuated. How would you handle numbers appearing in the English text?

In general, the construction of a pattern to match what is normally thought of as a "word" is not a trivial task. In fact, it is an unsolved problem in the area of literary analysis. For any general pattern, there will almost always be words which will not be matched by the pattern. Usually, the specific problem domain will dictate the level of precision required in the construction of the pattern. This problem will become particularly acute in the next section, where techniques for manipulating textual material are considered.

10.3 CONCORDANCES

The most well-established application of computers in humanistic research is in the preparation of concordances or word indices. A concordance in its simplest form is called a word index; it is a listing of significant words in a text together with statistical information (e.g., frequency of occurrence) and the location of the item in the text (e.g., referenced by line numbers). If the actual passages containing each word are shown, it is called a concordance. An example is shown in Figure 10.4.

Since the problem requires the categorization of pieces of information derived from a text, it appears to be particularly suited to machine implementation. In fact, concordances have been produced by computer for 15 years or more. One of the earliest known hand-produced concordances is a concordance to the *Vulgate* (Latin version of the *Bible*), finished in 1244 by Hugo de Sancto Caro. Perhaps the best known of all concordances is Cruden's concordance for the authorized English version of the *Bible*, published in the eighteenth century, requiring more than 30 years of effort to produce. By comparison, a modern computer can produce a concordance in minutes, once the document is in machine-readable form. The production of the machine-readable version of a document is now one of the most time-consuming processes involved in the development of a concordance. However, many modern publishing houses are turning to computer-controlled photocomposition of books, texts, etc. One of the interesting side effects of this trend is that the source document must be prepared in machine-readable form anyway and thus should be available to scholars. In the next section, we shall consider some of the problems involved in source document handling by computer.

10.3.1 Machine Manipulation of Documents: Problems

Many concordance programs will be run on computers whose main function is numeric problem-solving and whose designers have not really considered the problems inherent in processing documents. One of the major problems encountered therein is that of input and output of extended alphabets and graphic embellishments to text. This includes the sometimes subtle distinctions between words in foreign alphabets caused by small variations in the characters, etc. For example, the æ in old English, the special mathematical symbols such as $\sum$, $\int$, Ω, etc., diacritical marks, and the acute accent in Spanish all cause problems when preparing a document in machine-readable form and when producing the final concordance or index. These problems are particularly acute when the final composition of a page of text (perhaps by computer-

750   hraðe inwitþancum ond wið earm gesæt. Sona ðæt onfunde   fyrena hyrde ðæt he ne mette middangeardes,
809   ellorgast on feonda geweald feor siðian. Da ðæt onfunde   se ðe fela æror modes myrðe manna cynne,
1497 ær he ðone grundwong ongytan mehte. Sona ðæt onfunde   se ðe floda begong heorogifre beheold hund

2300 on beorh æthwearf, sincfæt sohte. He ðæt sona onfand   ðæt hæfde gumena sum goldes gefandod,
2713 ær geworhte, swelan ond swellan: he ðæt sona onfand,   ðæt him on breostum bealoniðe weoll

1605 hie heora winedrihten selfne gesawon. Da ðæt sweord ongan   æfter heaðoswate hildegicelum, wigbil
1696 rihte gemearcod, geseted ond gesæd hwam ðæt sweord geworht,   irena cyst, ærest wære, wreoðenhilt
2700 niððor hwene sloh, secg on searwum, ðæt ðæt sweord gedeaf,   fah ond fæted, ðæt ðæt fyr ongon

567   be yðlafe uppe lægon, sweordum aswefede,   ðæt syððan na ymb brontne ford brimliðende lade ne letton.
2217 horde, hond *** , since fahne. He syððan *** , ðeah ðe he slæpende besyred wurde

890   ne wæs him Fitela mid. Hwæðre him gesælde ðæt ðæt swurd ðurhwod wrætlicne wyrm,   ðæt hit on wealle
2700 niðgast nioðor hwene sloh, secg on searwum,   ðæt ðæt sweord gedeaf, fah ond fæted,   ðæt ðæt fyr ongon

1458 Hroðgares: wæs ðæm haftmece Hrunting nama.   Ðæt wæs an foran ealdgestreona: ecg wæs iren, atertanum
1885 wæs on gange gifu Hroðgares oft geæhted: Ðæt wæs an cyning, æghwæs orleahtre, oððæt hine yldo

765   wiste his fingra geweald on grames grapum.   Ðæt wæs geocor sið ðæt se hearmscaða   to Heorute ateah.
1075 broðrum: hie on gebyrd hruron, gare wunde.   Ðæt wæs geomuru ides! Nalles holinga Hoces dohtor

11   ofer hronrade hyran scolde, gomban gyldan.   Ðæt wæs god cyning! Ðæm eafera wæs æfter cenned, geong in
863   wiht ne logon, glædne Hroðgar, ac   Ðæt wæs god cyning! Hwilum heaðorofe hleapan leton, on
2390 bregostol Biowulf healdan, Geatum wealdan.   Ðæt wæs god cyning! Se ðæs leodhryres lean gemunde

654   ond him hæl abead, winærnes geweald,   ond ðæt word acwæð: "Næfre ic ænegum men ær alyfde, siððan ic
2046 gehygd higes cunnian, wigbealu weccean,   ond ðæt word acwyð: 'Meaht ðu, min wine,   mece gecnawan ðone

1700 spræc sunu Healfdenes (swigedon ealle):   "Ðæt, la, mæg secgan   se ðe soð ond riht fremeð on folce,
2864 sunu, sec, sarigferð (seah on unleofe):   "Ðæt, la, mæg secgan   se ðe wyle soð specan ðæt se

2520 beran, wæpen to wyrme,   gif ic wiste hu wið ðam aglæcean elles meahte gylpe wiðgripan,   swa ic gio wið
2905 sexbennum seoc: sweorde ne meahte on ðam aglæcean ænige ðinga wunde gewyrcean. Wiglaf siteð

2163 breostgewædu. Bruc ealles well!" Hyrde ic ðæt ðam fratwum feower mearas lungre, gelice,   last weardode,
2989 helm somod, hares hyrste Higelace bær. He ðam fratwum feng ond him fagre gehet leana mid leodum,

2010 facne bifongen. Ic ðær furðum cwom to ðam hringsele Hroðgar gretan: sona me se mæra mago
3053 lumonna gold galdre bewunden,   ðæt ðam hringsele hrinan ne moste gumena ænig, nefne god

1073 treowe: unsynnum wearð beloren leofum æt ðam lindplegan bearnum ond broðrum: hie on gebyrd hruron,
2039 wealdan moston, oððæt hie forlædan to ðam lindplegan swase gesiðas ond hyra sylfra feorh. Ðonne

Fig. 10.4 Sample page from a concordance. (Reprinted from A Concordance to Beowulf, edited by J.B. Bessinger, Jr., programmed by Philip H. Smith, Jr., p. 329. Copyright 1969 by Cornell University. Used by permission of Cornell University Press.)

controlled composition machines) is desired. We should point out, however, that many modern graphic displays may be programmed to produce virtually any font style, which at least alleviates somewhat the problems of output.

A quick glance at a page of any document will illustrate some of the problems to be considered. For example, this page contains both upper- and lowercase letters, punctuation, and special characters. To prepare a page such as this for machine consumption, certain conventions must be established for encoding special symbols which do not appear in the character set of the machine upon which the analysis is to be performed. Recall that the character sets for several machines appear in Appendix 1 of the supplementary volume; the one notable feature of all these sets is the lack of a variety of special symbols. The problem of limited character sets is being eased somewhat with the widespread introduction of graphics terminals, which may be used to display a wide range of symbols.

10.3.2 The Word Index

The word index is perhaps the simplest version of a concordance. It is the listing of the words in a given text together with a cross reference to the locations of the word in the text (perhaps by means of line numbers). In addition, some simple statistical information is often collected, such as the number of occurrences of each word in the text. Very often, the construction of a word index is a prelude to the construction of a general concordance. We shall consider the problems encountered in the construction of a word index using SNOBOL.

The basic steps which must be taken to produce the index might be summarized as

1. A careful analysis of the characteristics of the text and the definition of the conventions to be followed as the text is translated into machine-readable form.
2. Transcription and verification of the text into machine-readable form. Since most texts are rather lengthy, the assumption is usually made that the text will reside on some secondary storage device, such as a disk.
3. Generation of the word index.

Steps 1 and 2 are the preprogramming aspects of document preparation which very often will simplify the design of the program when thoroughly explored. For the sake of this example, we shall assume that the text does not contain any special symbols which do not appear in the character set of the machine for which the text is prepared. Furthermore, we shall assume that the translated text resides on secondary storage, from which appropriate sections of the text are read when necessary. Since it is inefficient to read single words from a disk, a buffer area will be reserved to contain as large a section of the text (in core) as possible. Only when this buffer is exhausted will an access to the disk be made. Because the word index maintains a cross reference to the original text via line numbers, we shall assume that appearance of the special character "#" in the buffer indicates the beginning of a line. The top-level refinement for the word index problem is shown in Figure 10.5. It might be noted that the construction of the word index is very similar to the construction and maintenance of a symbol table, as discussed in Chapter 8. However, there is one major difference between the two tasks. The number of distinct names in a computer program is usually small, and the symbol table does not become very large. However, in the case of a word index to the *Bible* (for example), the number of distinct symbols (e.g., words) is very large indeed.

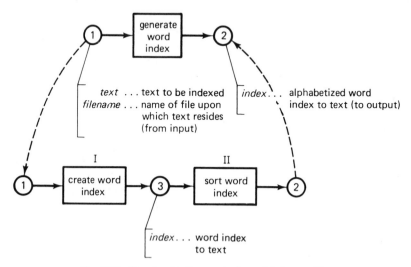

Fig. 10.5   Top level refinement of word index problem.

In many cases, the size of the symbol table (word index) will exceed available core, in which case the table itself must reside on a secondary storage device. This difference points out the distinction between what might be called "toy" computer problems and "real-world" computer problems. In the toy problem domain, every assumption is made to simplify the construction of the program, sometimes even to the point of reducing the program to triviality (in that it can no longer be used to solve any "real" problems). Implementations of solutions to real-world problems often must overcome core limitations and peculiarities of the particular computer system utilized. Therefore, real-world problems require considerably more effort in program design than is evident from a cursory glance at the problem. For the concordance problem, a general program to construct a word index, for example, must work independently of the size of the input text. This implies that a method must be employed to utilize secondary storage devices for the large tables which are constructed.

Expansion of module I in Figure 10.5 results in the top-level refinement for the word index part, as shown in Figure 10.6. Both modules III and V in Figure 10.6 require input from a file. In keeping with our philosophy of ignoring machine-dependent issues, we presume the existence of a procedure which performs the input function. Using this procedure, module V is relatively straightforward; the main problem is the removal of characters which are not part of words.

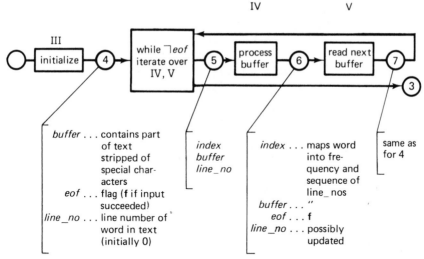

Fig. 10.6 Top level refinement of module I in Figure 10.5.

Algorithm 10.2 (Read and preprocess buffer)

Global data referenced: *nonletters* contains all *n* special (except #) characters;
                          nblank contains *n* blanks; *buffer*

```
procedure read_buf(filename;)
begin /*read*/
    bufferin(filename; buffer, eof); /*machine-dependent operation*/
    if eof then terminate;
    buffer ← ' ' + buffer + ' ';
    substitute(buffer, nonletters, nblank; buffer)
end /*read*/
```

The basic steps in module IV are to update (if necessary) the line number, to obtain the next word, and to enter it in the index. The steps are repeated as long as there are nonblank characters in the buffer. Since all special characters have been removed by *read_buf*, hyphenated words will be returned as two words, and numbers will be ignored.

Algorithm 10.3 (Process the buffer)

Global data referenced: *wordp* as defined in Algorithm 10.1; *index, buffer,*
                          line_no

```
procedure buf_proc()
begin /*process buffer*/
    replace(buffer, wordp, ''; buffer, buf_flag);
```

> **while** (*buf_flag*)
> **begin** /∗process next word∗/
>   **if first**(*word*) = '#' **then** *line_no* ← *line_no* + 1
>   **else begin**
>   *index*(*word*, 1) ← *index*(*word*, 1) + 1;
>   *index*(*word*, 2) ← *index*(*word*, 2) + *line_no* + ',’
>   **end**;
>   **replace**(*buffer*, *wordp*, ''; *buffer*, *buf_flag*)
>   **end** /∗process word∗/
> **end** /∗process buffer∗/

The SNOBOL version of the index problem is relatively straightforward.

Purpose: Produce a word index to a given text residing on a secondary storage device under the name FILENAME.
Communication:

global variables referenced:	NONLETTERS	string of nonalphabetic characters;
	NBLANK	string of blanks, same length as NONLETTERS;
	INDEX	table; maps WORD into the pair (number of occurrences, line locations separated by commas);
	LINENO	current line number;
	BUFFER..........	contains next portion of text from file;
	WORDP, WORD ...	as in program for Algorithm 10.1;
	FILENAME	name of file containing text; "#" occurs at the beginning of every line;
functions called:	BUFFERIN	system-dependent function reads from argument file into BUFFER; final length of BUFFER may be 5000 plus length of 1 record;
	READBUF	calls BUFFERIN with file name; edits BUFFER;
	BUFPROC	no arguments; local variables— FIRST, TEMP; modifies INDEX, LINENO.

Program:

```
        DEFINE('READBUF()')                                        1
        DEFINE('BUFPROC()FIRST,TEMP')                              2
        DEFINE('BUFFERIN()')                                       3
        &ANCHOR = 1                                                4
        &TRIM = 1                                                  5
        NONLETTERS = '0123456789+-";/()$,.[]:="<>|&;'              6
        NBLANK = DUPL(' ',SIZE(NONLETTERS))                        7
        WORDP = SPAN(' ') BREAK(' ') . WORD                        8
        DELIMIT = ' '                                              9
        INDEX = TABLE(20,10)                                       10
        LINENO = 0                                                 11
        INPUT('FILENAME',8,120)                                    12
        OUTPUT('OUTPUT',6,'(1X,80A1)')                             13
BEGIN   READBUF()                               :F(OUT)           14
        BUFPROC()                               :(BEGIN)          15
OUT     INDEX = CONVERT(INDEX,'ARRAY')                            16
        OUTPUT =                                                  17
        I = 1                                                     18
PUT     TEMP = INDEX<I,2>                                         19
        TEMP<2> LEN(SIZE(TEMP<2>) - 1) . LINENOS                  20
        N = 30 - SIZE(INDEX<I,1>)                                 21
        OUTPUT = INDEX<I,1> DUPL(' ',N) '(' TEMP<1> ')'           22
                                                :F(END)           22
        OUTPUT = '          APPEARS IN LINES ' LINENOS            23
        I = I + 1                               :(PUT)            24
::::::::::::::::::::::::::::::::::FUNCTION READBUF::::::::::::::::::::::::::
READBUF BUFFERIN()                              :F(FRETURN)       25
        BUFFER = ' ' BUFFER ' '                                  26
        OUTPUT = BUFFER                                          27
        BUFFER = REPLACE(BUFFER,NONLETTERS,NBLANK)  :(RETURN)    28
::::::::::::::::::::::::::::::::::END READBUF::::::::::::::::::::::::::::::::
::::::::::::::::::::::::::::::::::FUNCTION BUFPROC:::::::::::::::::::::::::::
BUFPROC BUFFER WORDP =                          :F(RETURN)        29
        WORD LEN(1) . FIRST                                      30
        IDENT('#',FIRST)                        :S(UPDATE)        31
        IDENT(INDEX<WORD>,NULL)                 :F(PROCESS)       32
        INDEX<WORD> = ARRAY('2')                                 33
PROCESS TEMP = INDEX<WORD>                                       34
        TEMP<1> = TEMP<1> + 1                                   35
        TEMP<2> = TEMP<2> LINENO ','            :(BUFPROC)        36
UPDATE  LINENO = LINENO + 1                     :(BUFPROC)        37
::::::::::::::::::::::::::::::::::END BUFPROC::::::::::::::::::::::::::::::::
::::::::::::::::::::::::::::::::::FUNCTION BUFFERIN::::::::::::::::::::::::::
:: IF FIRST CHARACTER IN THE FILE IS NOT '#', BUFFERIN ASSUMES THAT
:: YOU HAVE LEFT THEM OUT, AND APPENDS '#' TO THE BEGINNING OF EACH LINE
BUFFERIN DEFINE('BUFFERIN()','NEW')                              38
        BUFFER = FILENAME                       :F(END)           39
        BUFFER '#'                              :S(AGAIN)         40
        DELIMIT = ' # '                                          41
        BUFFER = DELIMIT BUFFER                 :(AGAIN)          42
NEW     BUFFER = DELIMIT FILENAME               :F(FRETURN)       43
AGAIN   GT(SIZE(BUFFER),5000)                   :S(RETURN)        44
        BUFFER = BUFFER ' ' DELIMIT FILENAME    :S(AGAIN)F(RETURN) 45
::::::::::::::::::::::::::::::::::END BUFFERIN::::::::::::::::::::::::::::::
::::::::::::::::::::::::::::::::::END OF PROGRAM:::::::::::::::::::::::::::::
END                                                              46
```

The major objection to the indexing program just developed is that even though the text resides on secondary storage, the index itself remains in core. Therefore, a reasonably sized text will undoubtedly cause problems.

EXERCISE 10.4: Examine the methods by which the memory problems can be alleviated. This would imply secondary storage for the index as well. Provide an intuitive analysis of the increased time required for your solution vis-à-vis the number of disk accesses required, etc. Try to be careful in designing your management scheme. Note that it may require a complete restructuring of the problem solution.

Several additional objections may be raised concerning the final form of the index and its length. For example the index generated by the program contains the words as they were encountered in the text. A more pleasing index would have the words arranged in alphabetical order. Unfortunately, SNOBOL is not a particularly efficient language in which to write a sorting algorithm (why?). Furthermore, it is very often not necessary to return *noise* words such as "and," "is," "it," etc.

EXERCISE 10.5: In light of the considerations raised in Excercise 10.4, how would you restructure the problem so as to include an efficient sorting algorithm? Note that, in general, the solutions to these kinds of problems are usually not trivial and may require an extensive rethinking of the whole problem, taking into consideration the nature of the secondary storage devices.

EXERCISE 10.6: Modify module IV so that noise words are not entered into the index. Rewrite the SNOBOL program to include this modification.

EXERCISE 10.7: The indexing program assumes that the text is already properly structured on a file. Develop a program which will allow a user with minimal background to create such a file. Include modest text-editing capabilities in this program.

Figure 10.7 illustrates a portion of the output of the index program on a small sample of text.

INPUT TEXT

```
 # IN 1949, WARREN WEAVER PREPARED A MEMO(UNPUBLISHED) IN WHICH HE SUGGESTED TH
AT  # A COMPUTER SHOULD BE ABLE TO TRANSLATE BETWEEN TWO LANGUAGES.   THIS SUGGES
TION  # IS REMARKABLE IN A HISTORICAL SENSE; AT THIS TIME, COMMERCIALLY AVAILABL
E  # COMPUTERS WERE ALMOST NON-EXISTENT.   COUPLED WITH SHANNON'S PROPOSAL CONCER
NING  # THE APPLICABILITY OF COMPUTERS TO GAME PLAYING, IT WAS THE IMPETUS FOR
 # INVESTIGATIONS INTO THE NON-NUMERICAL ASPECTS OF COMPUTING.   THESE TWO IDEAS,
 # WEDDED WITH CYBERNETICS AND PSYCHOLOGY, LAID THE FOUNDATION FOR ARTIFICIAL  #
 INTELLIGENCE (CHAPTER 12).   THE EARLY LANGUAGE TRANSLATION PROJECTS, BECAUSE  #
 OF THE INFANCY OF COMPUTER SCIENCE AND NAIVE NOTIONS CONCERNING THE STRUCTURE
 # OF LANGUAGES, WERE LARGELY UNSUCCESSFUL AND SOON ABANDONED.
```

Fig. 10.7a   A part of a sample output from the index program.

WORD INDEX

```
              AT                        (1)
                    APPEARS IN LINES 3
              TIME                      (1)
                    APPEARS IN LINES 3
              COMMERCIALLY              (1)
                    APPEARS IN LINES 3
              AVAILABLE                 (1)
                    APPEARS IN LINES 3
              COMPUTERS                 (2)
                    APPEARS IN LINES 4,5
              WERE                      (2)
                    APPEARS IN LINES 4,10
              ALMOST                    (1)
                    APPEARS IN LINES 4
              NON                       (2)
                    APPEARS IN LINES 4,6
              EXISTENT                  (1)
                    APPEARS IN LINES 4
              COUPLED                   (1)
                    APPEARS IN LINES 4
              WITH                      (2)
                    APPEARS IN LINES 4,7
              SHANNON'S                 (1)
                    APPEARS IN LINES 4
              PROPOSAL                  (1)
                    APPEARS IN LINES 4
              CONCERNING                (2)
                    APPEARS IN LINES 4,9
              THE                       (7)
                    APPEARS IN LINES 5,5,6,7,8,9,9
              APPLICABILITY             (1)
                    APPEARS IN LINES 5
              OF                        (5)
                    APPEARS IN LINES 5,6,9,9,10
              GAME                      (1)
                    APPEARS IN LINES 5
              PLAYING                   (1)
                    APPEARS IN LINES 5
              IT                        (1)
                    APPEARS IN LINES 5
              WAS                       (1)
                    APPEARS IN LINES 5

              .
              .
              .
```

Fig. 10.7b A part of a sample output from the index program.

10.3.3 The General Concordance

As discussed in Section 10.3.1, a concordance is essentially a word index in which the environment of each word is listed in addition to the information obtained in the word-indexing program. Very often the environment will be the entire line; in other cases, it will consist of a given number of words to the left and right of the target word. In fact, the first step in the construction of a concordance is often the generation of the word index. This implies that the concordance must manipulate two files: one containing the original text and the other containing the word index. One could conceive of an algorithm which proceeded as follows: Get the next word in the word index, print the word and its frequency, find the lines containing the word in the text file, and print these lines. The major programming problem here is the following: Find the lines in the text file. The remainder of the process is relatively easy to implement. Therefore, let us consider the problem of finding specified lines in the text file.

The solution to the problem hinges on two factors: the nature of the file containing the text and the format of this file. We have not been overly concerned with the types of files which may reside on secondary storage and, in fact, have assumed that all files were *sequential access* files. For these files, reading (and writing) starts at the beginning of the file and progresses, one record at a time, to the end of the file. If we assume that each record in such a file corresponds to a given line of the original text, then it is easy to see how our problem can be solved. That is, given a word from the index and a line number, say n, the line can be accessed by skipping $n - 1$ records from the beginning of the file and then reading the nth record. This record is printed as the environment of the given word. In those cases where a line exceeds the system-dependent record size, special software conventions may be employed for continuation purposes (across record boundaries). The disadvantage to this approach lies in the number of file operations which must be performed. For each word in the word index, the file pointer must be reset to the beginning of the file; records are then skipped according to the information recorded with each word in the index. This assumes, of course, that facilities exist within the language for manipulating the file pointer.

Recall that during our discussion in Chapter 8 a second type of file structure, *direct access* files, was briefly mentioned. For this type of file, each record is written with a *key*. This record may be subsequently read by requesting a read operation in conjunction with the appropriate key. With this type of file structure, retrieval of a line of text is very simple, since the line number may be used as the key when the file is originally written.

Unfortunately, the file-handling capabilities of SNOBOL are rather primitive. The language does not directly support direct access files, nor does it contain primitives for skipping records in a file. Many installations do, however, support a facility for linking FORTRAN functions or assembly language routines to SNOBOL. These can make use of the file facilities supported by the computer installation, and hence, the situation is not so bleak as it appears.

It should be apparent that the complexity (in an intuitive sense) of the final concordance program depends on a number of factors, including the assumed format of the original text file. Careful thought should be given to the structure of this file before the program is designed. For the word index, the assumed form of the text file was reasonable. Recall that text lines were separated by # and there was no correlation between file records and lines of text. For the concordance program, however, this format is probably not the most efficient one, since some software overhead is required to find the appropriate line given the line number. On the other hand, this format is very efficient in terms of file space. Each record, with the possible exception of the last one in the file, is packed; that is, there are no partially empty records. Thus, file space is minimized. This may not be, as we have seen, the correct parameter to minimize. It is perfectly reasonable to waste space in the file if doing so greatly increases programming efficiency; clearly, one should not carry this to extremes.

Returning to the concordance problem, let us make the following assumptions:

1. The text file is organized as a direct access file. Each record contains one line of the text. The key to each line is the line number. Therefore, to retrieve a line of text, one merely provides the correct key and reads the line. In those cases in which one record is not sufficient to contain a complete line, a software convention will be provided to continue lines over file records.
2. The word file is organized as a sequential access file. The word file contains the alphabetized list of words, the frequency of occurrence of each word, and a string containing the pointers into the text file (i.e., the line numbers on which the word appeared).

Given these assumptions, the top-level refinement for the concordance problem is shown in Figure 10.8. Each of the modules in Figure 10.8 may in fact be separate programs, implying at least four different runs to complete the concordance, or they may be configured as functions, etc., if space permits.

Module I creates the word index; with minor modifications, the program developed in the last section may be used here.

EXERCISE 10.8: Modify the indexing program from the last section to conform to the specifications of Figure 10.8.

Module II sorts the word index; as mentioned previously, this module may in fact be written in another language (perhaps FORTRAN).

EXERCISE 10.9: Given the structure of the word index file, which of the sorting algorithms discussed in Chapter 5 would be a reasonable choice for this problem? Why?

In Section 10.3.2, we suggested that the removal of noise words might take place during the construction of the word index. By performing the removal in this module, the noise words do not appear in the index; however, it might be required that the frequency of these words be determined even though they should not appear in the final concordance. By structuring the series of programs correctly, noise words may be removed or not, depending on the situation. Therefore, we shall leave it as a separate module. Module IV creates the final concordance as described above.

EXERCISE 10.10: Develop a SNOBOL program, consistent with the assumed structure of the word index file, which will create a new word index with the noise words removed.

The structure of module IV is relatively straightforward, and we proceed with the SNOBOL implementation. (See Figure 10.9 for a sample output.)

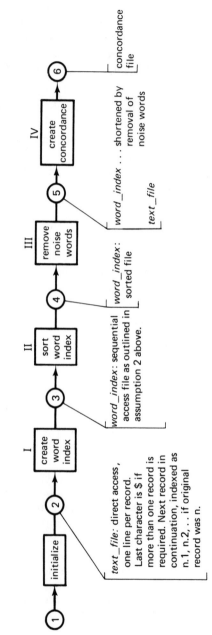

Fig. 10.8 Top-level refinement of concordance program.

text_file: direct access, one line per record. Last character is $ if more than one record is required. Next record in continuation, indexed as n.1, n.2, . . . if original record was n.

word_index: sequential access file as outlined in assumption 2 above.

word_index: sorted file

word_index . . . shortened by removal of noise words

text_file

concordance file

CONCORDANCE

A   3
    IN 1949, WARREN WEAVER PREPARED A MEMO(UNPUBLISHED) IN WHICH HE SUGGESTED THAT
    A COMPUTER SHOULD BE ABLE TO TRANSLATE BETWEEN TWO LANGUAGES. THIS SUGGESTION
    IS REMARKABLE IN A HISTORICAL SENSE; AT THIS TIME, COMMERCIALLY AVAILABLE

AND   3
    WEDDED WITH CYBERNETICS AND PSYCHOLOGY, LAID THE FOUNDATION FOR ARTIFICIAL
    OF THE INFANCY OF COMPUTER SCIENCE AND NAIVE NOTIONS CONCERNING THE STRUCTURE
    OF LANGUAGES, WERE LARGELY UNSUCCESSFUL AND SOON ABANDONED.

COMPUTER   2
    A COMPUTER SHOULD BE ABLE TO TRANSLATE BETWEEN TWO LANGUAGES. THIS SUGGESTION
    OF THE INFANCY OF COMPUTER SCIENCE AND NAIVE NOTIONS CONCERNING THE STRUCTURE

COMPUTERS   2
    COMPUTERS WERE ALMOST NON-EXISTENT. COUPLED WITH SHANNON'S PROPOSAL CONCERNING
    THE APPLICABILITY OF COMPUTERS TO GAME PLAYING, IT WAS THE IMPETUS FOR

CONCERNING   2
    COMPUTERS WERE ALMOST NON-EXISTENT. COUPLED WITH SHANNON'S PROPOSAL CONCERNING
    OF THE INFANCY OF COMPUTER SCIENCE AND NAIVE NOTIONS CONCERNING THE STRUCTURE

OF   4
    THE APPLICABILITY OF COMPUTERS TO GAME PLAYING, IT WAS THE IMPETUS FOR
    INVESTIGATIONS INTO THE NON-NUMERICAL ASPECTS OF COMPUTING. THESE TWO IDEAS,
    OF THE INFANCY OF COMPUTER SCIENCE AND NAIVE NOTIONS CONCERNING THE STRUCTURE
    OF LANGUAGES, WERE LARGELY UNSUCCESSFUL AND SOON ABANDONED.

WITH   2
    COMPUTERS WERE ALMOST NON-EXISTENT. COUPLED WITH SHANNON'S PROPOSAL CONCERNING
    WEDDED WITH CYBERNETICS AND PSYCHOLOGY, LAID THE FOUNDATION FOR ARTIFICIAL

Fig. 10.9 Partial output of concordance program.

Purpose: Create a concordance from the text file and the word index file.
Communication:

global variables referenced: READWORD .... reference causes record to be read from word file;

READTEXT .... reference causes record to be read from text file;

WORD $\Big\rangle$
FREQ $\Big\}$ .... $\Big\{$ a word, its frequency, where it occurred in terms of line numbers separated by commas;
PTRS $\Big\rangle$

PTRPAT............ patterns to match line number in PTRS;

BLNKS5 .... a string of 5 blanks;

LINE .... a line of text;

POINTER .... result of applying PTRPAT to PTRS;

functions called: GETLINE .... obtains LINE from direct access file with argument as key (in the program below a sequential access file was used because of lack of facilities);

CONTINUCHECK .... checks line for continuation and obtains, if necessary, additional records and catenates them to LINE; local variables: I, INDEX.

Program:

```
          DEFINE('GETLINE(POINTER)')                                        1
          DEFINE('CONTINUCHECK(POINTER)I,INDEX')                            2
          &ANCHOR = 1                                                        3
          &TRIM = 1                                                          4
::::::::::::::::::::::::::::::::::::PROVIDE INPUT ASSOCIATIONS::::::::::::::::::::::::::::::::::
          INPUT('READWORD',5)                                               5
          INPUT('READTEXT',8)                                               6
          OUTPUT('SCRATCH',8,'(80A1)')                                      7
LOOP      TEMP = INPUT                              :F(END)                  8
          TEMP '$'                                  :S(NEXT)                 9
          SCRATCH = TEMP                            :(LOOP)                 10
NEXT      BLNKS5 = '    '                                                  11
          PTRPAT = SPAN('0123456789') . POINTER                           12
BEGIN     WORD = READWORD                           :F(END)                13
          FREQ = READWORD                                                  14
          PTRS = READWORD                                                  15
::::::::::::::::::::::::::::::::OUTPUT WORD AND FREQUENCY OF OCCURENCE:::::::::::::::::::::::
          OUTPUT =                                                         16
          OUTPUT =                                                         17
          OUTPUT = WORD BLNKS5 FREQ                                        18
::::::::::::::::::::::::::::GET NEXT POINTER, LINE OF TEXT, AND OUTPUT:::::::::::::::::::
NEXTL     PTRS PTRPAT =                             :F(BEGIN)              19
          PTRS ',' =                                                      20
          LINE = GETLINE(POINTER)                                         21
          CONTINUCHECK(POINTER)                                           22
          OUTPUT = BLNKS5 LINE                      :(NEXTL)               23
::::::::::::::::::::::::::::::::::::END CONCORDANCE PROGRAM:::::::::::::::::::::::::::::::::::
::::::::::::::::::::::::::::::::::::BEGIN FUNCTION CONTINUCHECK:::::::::::::::::::::::::::::::
CONTINUCHECK  I = 0                                                        24
CONT      LINE RTAB(1) '$' =                        :F(RETURN)             25
          I = I + 1                                                        26
          LINE = TRIM(LINE)                                               27
          INDEX = POINTER '.' I                                           28
          LINE = LINE GETLINE(INDEX)                :(CONT)               29
::::::::::::::::::::::::::::::::::::END OF CONTINUCHECK:::::::::::::::::::::::::::::::::::::::::
GETLINE   REWIND(8)                                                       30
NLINE     GETLINE = GT(POINTER,0) READTEXT          :F(RETURN)             31
          POINTER = POINTER - 1                     :(NLINE)               32
END                                                                       33
```

The concordance program as developed in this section is open-ended. To obtain a working program, many problems remain to be solved. We have not even begun to consider the generation of concordances in foreign languages, etc. Note that the function GETLINE could be written to read directly from the original text file as defined for the word index program; it would, however, be very inefficient (why?).

EXERCISE 10.11: Drawing upon the considerations of this and the previous section, redesign the general concordance program to make use of the facilities available at your installation. Given the discussion in Chapter 3, provide a detailed design document for your proposed program(s).

10.3.4 The KWIC Index

Both the word index and concordance developed in the previous sections are used primarily for scholarly research. One variation of the concordance is the KWIC (for key word in context) index. It is a listing of all the lines in a text containing any of a list of prespecified key words. If a line contains several key words, it will appear several times in the listing, once for each key word it contains. A line is printed so that the key word is aligned with the middle of the page. The left context of the key word is printed toward the left margin and the right context toward the right margin. Several blanks are inserted between the key word and the left context. The lines of the text are usually rearranged so that the key words appear in alphabetical order. A sample KWIC index is shown in Figure 10.10.

A modified version of the KWIC index is often used in an information retrieval environment. In this application, a data base of information on a particular subject or group of subjects is maintained. The problem is then one of retrieving specific information from this data base. For example, the data base might contain the titles of recent papers in the area of computer science, say for the last 5 years. A person with an interest in a specialized research area could then query this data base for the titles relevant to this area. As the number of technical articles increases, easy access to the literature is a necessity; much research effort is wasted by reinventing the wheel. The general problem of information retrieval from a large data base is formidable and will not be considered here. Rather, we shall examine a simplified problem: retrieval of those titles from a data base of titles containing specified key words.

In this section, we shall develop a rather comprehensive KWIC index program, written in SNOBOL, which might be useful for the maintenance of personal libraries and the like.

There are two general approaches for generating a KWIC index:

1. A list of key words is supplied, and the data base is searched for occurrences of these terms. The relevant items are then output.
2. A list of noise words is provided, and each data item is output once for each word in the title which is not a noise word.

The first approach is a simplification of the general information retrieval problem, while the second is almost identical with the construction of a concordance. The first is more usable in those situations where it is desired to obtain specific information iuratores iussi; item mancipia minora annis uiginti, quae post proximum | **lustrum** | decem milibus aeris aut pluris eo uenissent, uti ea quoque deciens | 39 44 3

mixtam ex aedilciis et consularibus comitiis, conuenientem errori. et | **lustrum** | eo anno conditum a P. Sempronio Sopho et P. Sulpicio Sauerrione | 10 9 14

auxilio uetiti causam in magistratu dicere dimissique [fuerant]. ne | **lustrum** | perficerent, mors prohibuit P. Furii. M. Atilius magistratu se | 24 43 4

Vibulanus tertium et L. Cornelius Maluginensis. census actus eo anno: | **lustrum** | propter Capitolium captum, consulem occisum condi religiosum | 3 22 1

duo trecenta uiginti unum. censores uicesimi sexti a primis censoribus, | **lustrum** | undeuicesimum fuit. eodem anno coronati primum ob res bello | 10 47 2

et in quinquennium uouerat; tum dictator et fecit ludos et in insequens | **lustrum** | uouit. ceterum cum duo consulares exercitus tam prope hostem sine | 27 33 9

consulis in urbem fecit. census deinde actus et conditum ab Quinctio | **lustrum.** | censa ciuium capita centum quattuor milia septingenta | 3 3 9

largiore uino sum usus. tu quoque uelim inquiras, qua laetitia, quo | **lusu** | apud me celebratum hesternum conuiuium sit, illo etiam – prauo | 40 14 2

quod me ac meos uinci passus sum. ab hostili proelio, tamquam fraterno | **lusu,** | pertrahere me ad cenam uoluisti; credis me, pater, inter inermes | 40 9 11

[dum] modo breuioribus modo longioribus spatiis trahendo eos a porta, | **lusu** | sermonibusque uariatis, longius solito ubi res dedit progressus, inter | 1 5 5

ex Arcadia instituisse ut nudi iuuenes Lycaeum Pana uenerantes per | **lusum** | atque lasciuiam currerent, quem Romani deinde uocarunt Inuum. | 1 5 4

rapit: belli necessitatibus eam patientiam non adhibebimus quam uel | **lusus** | ac uoluptas elicere solet? adeone effeminata corpora militum | 5 6 4

consulentium de caede ruptura ius gentium, non auersum ab intentione | **lusus** | animum nec deinde in errorem uersum facinus. propius est fidem | 4 17 4

ferro interficere. tempora quidem qualia sint ad parricidium electa, undes: | **lusus** | ipse, conuiuii, comisationis. quid? dies qualis? quo lustratus exercitus, quo | 40 13 4

praecellere erudiebat. is cum in pace instituisset pueros ante urbem | **lusus** | exercendique causa producere, nihil eo more per belli tempus | 5 27 2

relictis dilapsi ceteri sparserant se toto passim campo, pars in iuuenales | **lusus** | lasciuiamque uersi, pars uescentes sub umbra, quidam somno etiam | 37 20 5

quibus(dam) honoratis magnoque aestimantibus se puerilia, ut escae aut | **lusus,** | munera dare, alios nihil expectantes ditare. itaque nescire, quid sibi | 41 20 5

peruenerunt. ibi seditio orta est; ad uiginti milia hominum cum l.onorio ac | **Lutario** | regulis secessione facta a Brenno in Thraeciam iter auertunt. ubi | 38 16 2

retro, unde uenerat, cum maiore parte hominum repetit Byzantium: | **Lutarius** | Macedonibus per speciem legationis ab Antipatro ad speculandum | 38 16 6

cum Lutati priore foedere, quod mutatum est, comparandum erat, cum in | **Lutati** | foedere diserte additum esset ita id ratum fore si populus censsuisset, | 21 19 3

moenibus Mutinam confugerint, C. Lutatius, C. Serullius, M. Annius. – | **Lutati** | nomen haud dubium est; pro Annio Serullioque M'. Acilium et C. | 21 25 4

nam si uerborum disceptationis res esset, quid foedus Hasdrubalis cum | **Lutati** | priore foedere, quod mutatum est, comparandum erat, cum in Lutati | 21 19 2

annis ante quadraginta pax cum Carthaginiensibus postremo facta erat, Q. | **Lutatio** | A. Manlio consulibus. bellum initum annis post tribus et uiginti, P. | 30 44 2

inter l. Metellum et Postumium Albinum fuerat. consulem illum cum C. | **Lutatio** | collega in Siciliam ad classem proficiscentem ad sacra retinuerat | 37 51 2

quid sua sponte imperatores faciant, nobis uobiscum foedus est a C. | **Lutatio** | consule ictum in quo, cum cauerretur utorumque sociis, nihil de | 21 18 8

uisae sunt quam ante consules C. Lutatium et A. Postumium fuerunt: | **Lutatio** | et Postumio consulibus deuicti ad Aegates insulas sumus. quod si, | 23 13 4

Galliaque – nam eo quoque processerat – gesta, patre C. Serullio et C. | **Lutatio** | ex seruitute post sextum decimum annum receptis qui ad uicum | 30 19 7

sibi mandatum esse uti peterent quanam ut in ea pace quae postremo cum | **Lutatio** | facta esset manere liceret. cum more tradito [a] patribus potestatem | 30 22 4

l. Paulo magis eripere decus perfecti belli Macedonici potest quam | **Lutatio** | primi Punici belli, quam P. Cornelio secundi, *** quam illi, qui | 45 38 4

ab Romanis ceruicibus iugum superbo Sammiti imposuit? modo | **Lutatio** | quae alia res quam celeritas uictoriam dedit, quod postero die quam | 22 14 13

terra marique magis prosperae res nostrae uisae sunt quam ante consules C. | **Lutatium** | et A. Postumium fuerunt; Lutatio et Postumio consulibus deuicti | 23 13 3

tot cladium nobis causa fuit tu consul Italia expuleris et, sicut penes C. | **Lutatium** | prioris Punici perpetrati belli titulus fuit, ita penes te huius fueri? | 28 41 1

adsignandum, diffisi Placentiae moenibus Mutinam confugerint, | **Lutatius,** | C. Serullius, M. Annius. – l.utati nomen haud dubium est; pro | 21 25 5

renouandae amicitiae causa proficisci uisi. legati erant hi: C. Valerius | **Lutatius** | Cerco Q. Bachius Sulca M. Cornelius Mammula M. Caecilius | 42 6 5

quod ego nihil dicturus sum nisi quod a uobis didici. uos enim, quod C. | **Lutatius** | consul primo nobiscum foedus icit, quia neque auctoritate patrum | 21 18 10

bubus uotis in Hispania Ioui sacrificaret; spondebantque animis, sicut C. | **Lutatius** | superius bellum Punicum finisset, ita id quod instaret P. Cornelium | 28 38 9

a. d. quintum idus Quinctiles caelo sereno interdiu obscurata | **lux** | cum luna sub orbem sol¹⁵ subisset, et l. Aemilius Regillus, cui | 37 4 4

nec erat difficile opus, quod caementa non calce durata erant sed interlita | **luto,** | structurae antiquae genere. itaque latius quam qua caederetur ruebat | 21 11 8

aut nocte faciamus oportet. ecce autem aliud minus dubium; quippe, si | **lux** | exspectetur, quae spes est non uallo perpetuo fossaque nos saepturum | 37 35 10

bellum sunt ab repentina oppugnatione castrorum Romanorum. prima | **lux** | ferme erat, cum uigiles in uallo quique in portarum stationibus erant, | 41 26 2

Hannibal silentio mouit castra et in Apuliam abiit. Marcellus, ubi | **lux** | fugam hostium aperuit, saucis cum praesidio modico Numistrone | 27 2 10

diei magna utrimque caede; nox incertis qua data uictoria esset interuenit. | **lux** | insequens uictorem uictumque ostendit: nam Etrusci silentio noctis | 10 12 5

uelut ab inferis extracti tum primum lucem aspicere uisi sunt, tamen ipsa | **lux** | ita deforme intuentibus agmen omni morte tristior fuit. itaque cum ante | 6 3 6

uirorum qui circa eum cumulati iacent ciues estis. sed antequam opprimit | **lux** | maioraque hostium agmina obsaepiunt iter, per hos, qui inordinati | 22 50 8

ad arma fci et portae stationibus murique praesidiis firmati, et ubi prima | **lux** | mediocrem multitudinem ante moenia neque alium quam Tiburtem | 7 12 3

expellunt extra portam uallumque. inde pergere ac persequi, quia turbida | **lux** | metum circa insidiarum faciebat, non ausi, liberatis castris contenti | 10 33 5

fama Romam perlata est Postumium exercitumque occisum. qui ubi prima | **lux** | metum insidiarum effuse sequentibus sustulit, cum perequitasset aciem | 5 28 12

Fig. 10.10 Sample KWIC index. *(Reprinted from David W. Packard, A Concordance to Livy, p. 130. Copyright 1968. Used by courtesy of Harvard University Press.)*

from the data base, while the second is useful for indexing the entire data base. Since we have essentially provided the skeletal structure required for implementing the latter alternative, let us develop a program for the former, so that the output developed is in the form of an unalphabetized KWIC index.

We make several assumptions concerning the format of the input and output:

1. The title input is assumed to consist of one 80-column card record with no provision for continuation. Only alphabetic and numeric characters are allowed in the title.
2. Any additional data, such as author, source, date, etc., are assumed to immediately follow the title data, again as one 80-column card record, with no provision for continuation.
3. The output will consist of two lines for each key word found in the title. The first line will consist of the title rotated end around to the left so that the key word is left justified. A "*" will indicate the logical end of the title. The second line will be indented 10 spaces and will consist of the data card, printed intact, with no modifications.
4. The list of key words is assumed to reside on as many 80-column card records as necessary. Each key word is separated by at least one blank, and the end of the key words is indicated by a "$", separated from the last key word by at least one blank. The 80-column card records are assumed to be contiguous across card boundaries.

With these assumptions in mind, the top-level refinement of the KWIC information retrieval system is shown in Figure 10.11. Module II is the only nontrivial module in Figure 10.11; this module is responsible for matching the list of key words to the title, rotating the title, and outputting the results when appropriate.

Algorithm 10.4 (Process title; module II of Figure 10.11)

Global data referenced: *keypat*, a pattern which will match any word in the list of key words; *wordp*, a pattern which will match any word in the title string and assign it to *title_word*

```
procedure process_title(title, data;)
begin /*process a title*/
    title ← title + '*';
    replace(title, wordp, ''; title, flag);
    if title_word = '*' then [output 'null title, data ignored'; terminate];
    title ← title + title_word;
    while (title_word ≠ '*')
    begin /*process title*/
        if search(title_word, keypat) ≠ 0 then output title_word + '   ' + title, data;
        title ← title + '   ' + title_word;
        replace(title, wordp, ''; title, flag)
    end /*process title*/
end /*process a title*/
```

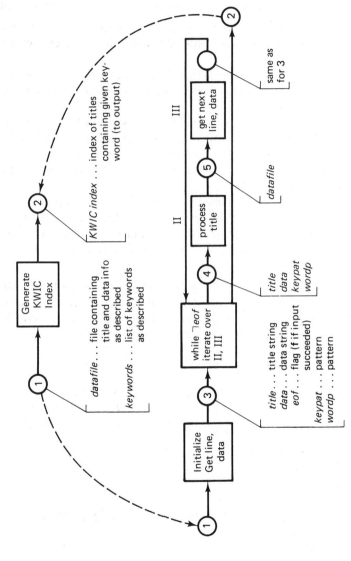

Fig. 10.11 First and second level refinements for KWIC index problem.

The SNOBOL implementation is given below.

Purpose: Given a data base of titles, create a KWIC index for provided key words.

Communication:

global variables referenced: WORDP .... word pattern;
                                     PATT .... word pattern;
                                     BLNKS10 ...... string of 10 blanks;
                                     TITLE .... contains title string;
                                     DATA .... contains data string;
                                     TEMP .... temporary string of key words;
                                     KEY .... assigned in pattern PATT;
                                     TITLEWORD ... assigned in pattern WORDP;
                                     KEYWORDS ....string of key words;
                                     KEYPAT .... pattern of key words;

functions called: PROCESTITL ... processes a title with its data.

Program:

```
        DEFINE('PROCESTITL()')                                         1
        WORDP = SPAN(' ') BREAK(' ') . TITLEWORD                       2
        BLNKS10 = '          '                                         3
        PATT = SPAN(' ') BREAK(' ') . KEY                              4
        &ANCHOR = 1                                                    5
        &TRIM = 1                                                      6
::::::::::::::::::::::::::::::::::::GET LIST OF KEYWORDS AND CONVERT TO PATTERN::::::::::::::
BEGIN   KEYWORDS = ' ' KEYWORDS INPUT              :F(ERROR)          7
        KEYWORDS RTAB(1) . TEMP '$'               :F(BEGIN)          8
        KEYWORDS = TEMP                                               9
:::::::::::::::::::::::::::::::::::::::CREATE PATTERN:::::::::::::::::::::::::::::::::::::::::::
        KEYWORDS PATT =                           :F(KEYERROR)        10
        KEYPAT = KEY                                                  11
START   KEYWORDS PATT =                           :F(OUT)            12
        KEYPAT = KEYPAT | KEY                     :(START)           13
ERROR   OUTPUT = 'ERROR IN KEYWORD INPUT, PROGRAM TERMINATES'         14
                                                  :(END)             14
KEYERROR OUTPUT = 'NO KEYWORDS, PROGRAM TERMINATES'  :(END)          15
::::::::::::::::::::::::::::::::::::::OUTPUT PRELIMINARY INFORMATION::::::::::::::::::::::::::
OUT     OUTPUT = DUPL('-',35) 'KWIC INDEX' DUPL('-',35)               16
        OUTPUT =                                                      17
        OUTPUT = 'KEYWORDS REQUESTED: ' TEMP                          18
        OUTPUT =                                                      19
:::::::::::::::::::::::::::::::::::BEGIN TO PROCESS TITLES AND DATA:::::::::::::::::::::::::::
PROCESS TITLE = ' ' INPUT                         :F(END)            20
        DATA = INPUT                                                  21
        PROCESTITL()                              :(PROCESS)         22
::::::::::::::::::::::::::::::::::::::END MAIN PROGRAM: PROCESS::::::::::::::::::::::::::::::::
```

```
:::::::::::::::::::::::::::::::::::::::::::::::::BEGIN PROCESTITL::::::::::::::::::::::::::::::::::::::::::::::::::
PROCESTITL   TITLE = TITLE ' :: '                                                      23
AGAIN        TITLE WORDP =                                                             24
             TITLEWORD ':: '                                      :S(RETURN)           25
             TITLEWORD KEYPAT                                     :F(CONTINU)          26
             OUTPUT =                                                                  27
             OUTPUT = TITLEWORD ' ' TITLE                                              28
             OUTPUT = BLNKS10 DATA                                                     29
CONTINU      TITLE = TITLE ' ' TITLEWORD                          :(AGAIN)             30
:::::::::::::::::::::::::::::::::::::::::::::::::END PROCESTITL::::::::::::::::::::::::::::::::::::::::::::::::::
END                                                                                   31
```

A sample output from this program is shown in Figure 10.12. There is a variety of modifications which would make this program more useful. They are discussed in the following exercises.

```
---------------------------------KWIC INDEX---------------------------------

KEYWORDS REQUESTED:   COMPUTERS HUMANITIES LITERARY SNOBOL


LITERARY   AND LINGUISTIC RESEARCH ::  THE COMPUTER IN
           R. WISBY(ED.), CAMBRIDGE UNIVERSITY PRESS, N.Y., 1972.

COMPUTERS  IN THE HUMANITIES ::  PROCEEDINGS OF THE INTERNATIONAL JOINT CONFERENCE ON
           L.MITCHELL, MINNEAPOLIS, MINNESOTA, JULY 1973. IN PREPARATION.

HUMANITIES  ::  PROCEEDINGS OF THE INTERNATIONAL JOINT CONFERENCE ON COMPUTERS IN THE
           L.MITCHELL, MINNEAPOLIS, MINNESOTA, JULY 1973. IN PREPARATION.

SNOBOL4:   TECHNIQUES AND APPLICATIONS ::  STRING AND LIST PROCESSING IN
           GRISWOLD, RALPH E., PRENTICE-HALL, INC., INGLEWOOD CLIFFS, N.J., 1975.

COMPUTERS  AND THE CLASSICS ::
           WAITE,STEPHEN V.F., COMPUTERS AND THE HUMANITIES, V.3, NO.1,SEP.1968.

HUMANITIES,  AND IBM ::  HOMER, THE
           MCDONOUGH,J.T.,PROC. OF THE LITERARY DATA PROCESSING CONF.,IBM,1964.
```

Fig. 10.12   Sample output from the KWIC program.

EXERCISE 10.12: The program is reasonably efficient for a small number of key words. For larger numbers, discuss various ways for improving the efficiency, particularly with regard to the methods for detecting a key word in the title.

EXERCISE 10.13: Develop a SNOBOL program for maintaining and editing the data base of titles which forms the input to the program.

EXERCISE 10.14: Improve the error responses of the program and add instructions so that it may be used by someone without prior knowledge of the program structure and data formats.

10.4 STYLISTIC ANALYSIS

style (stil), n. [ME. stil, stile; OFr. stile, style; L. stilus], ...

> 3. a) manner or mode of expression in language; way of putting thoughts into words. b) specific or characteristic manner of expression, execution, construction, or design, in any art, period, work, employment, etc.: as, the Byzantine style, modern style. 4. distinction, excellence, originality, and character in any form of artistic or literary expression: as, this author lacks style. 5. the way in which anything is made or done; manner. . . .†

Stylistic analysis is the study of an author's use of language in an attempt to detect regularities of word usage, function, and structure. As Vinton Dearing‡ has suggested,

> Style is choice between alternatives. Therefore the study of style is the identification of choices and particularly the investigation of consistency over a series of repetitions of the same choice.

If we restrict ourselves to literary style, then these choices may be composed of many aspects—some conscious, others unconscious—including choice of alternative words, syntactic choices, phraseology, semantic choices, and the like.

10.4.1 Goals

If we accept the definition of style as a forced choice among possible alternatives, then the study of style is concerned with the consistency of these choices over large passages of text, i.e., the repetition of choice. What, then, are some of the simpler aspects of style which may be studied with the aid of the computer? In the following section, we shall examine some of these possibilities.

One of the earliest computer-assisted studies of style was the admirable study by F. Mosteller and D. Wallace of the Federalist papers. The Federalist papers were written between 1787 and 1788 by Alexander Hamilton, James Madison, and John Jay. The essays were on the proposed new Constitution of the United States and the system of representative government. They were written primarily to persuade the voters of New York State to ratify the Constitution. A total of 85 essays were written and published in New York newspapers over the signature "Publius." Of the 85 essays, the authorship of at least 12 has been in doubt. Several early attempts to ascribe the authorship of these 12 essays were fruitless. The Mosteller and Wallace study is interesting because it was one of the first to use the computer in gathering the data for a

---

†*Webster's New World Dictionary*, college ed., 1959. G. & C. Merriam Company, Springfield, Mass.

‡Vinton Dearing, "Literary Data Processing," *Proceedings of the Modern Language Association of America, 80* (1965), pp. 3–6.

literary authorship problem and because of the advanced statistical techniques employed. They were able to establish, with a very high probability, that most of the disputed essays had in fact been written by Madison.

This, then, is one of the goals of stylistic analysis: the assignment of a work to one or another of a group of authors when the identity of the author is in doubt. There are, of course, other goals of stylistic analysis. It is not necessary that a particular authorship be doubtful to study the style of an individual author. Once a stylistic trait has been uncovered, scholars may then study this author from a fresh vantage point and attempt to assess the peculiarities in the author's background which led to this trait. We all have peculiarities of style in writing, very often manifested in the overuse of a particular word or phrase.

Studies have been made of the sound of language: alliteration, assonance, and consonance. Using special coding schemes, these studies are aided by computer analysis. The development of language and influences of regional characteristics on style have been studied by use of the computer. Unfortunately, studies reaching toward the syntactic and semantic levels—such as sound and stress, use of homonyms, synonyms, metaphors, and meaning—have not been particularly successful, for a variety of reasons. Our knowledge of the syntactic structure of English, i.e., the grammar of the language, is not sufficiently developed to allow automatic parsing of complex sentences; we would be remiss if we did not note that complex grammars, used for parsing, also cause problems from the computer's point of view. The semantics of language are an entirely different matter; only recently have efforts been made to represent concepts, which would be obtained from a fragment of prose, on the computer.

There is a variety of fascinating studies on the analysis of various aspects of well-known works, for example, the Federalist papers (as noted above), Dylan Thomas' poetry, *The Rime of the Ancient Mariner*, and the works of Dryden, Homer, and Jonathan Swift, to name just a few. In addition, music has been equally well explored. The interested reader is urged to consult the references at the end of the chapter.

10.4.2 Statistical Analysis

We shall consider the analysis of a single author's work or a single piece of text. The general goal will be to provide information which might be useful for comparing this author with another or which might reveal some peculiarities of word and sentence structure.

At the letter level, various statistics can be collected, for example, the average number of vowels per word or sentence, the frequency of one-letter words, etc. At the word level, we can consider average word length, number of words beginning with a vowel, etc. Also, at the sentence level, we can consider average number of words per sentence, average distance between selected marker words (such as "and"), number of commas per sentence, etc. We could continue, clearly, to the paragraph, chapter or verse, and entire text level. However, let us consider the development of a program which will compute the following statistics:

1. Average word and sentence length;
2. Number of words of 1, 2, 3, 4, 5, 6, 7, 8, 9, and greater than 9 letters;
3. Individual letter frequencies; and
4. Average distance between selected marker words.

We shall assume the same input format as for the word index program; in fact, the program to be developed might be incorporated into the word index to provide more extensive information on the nature of the text. The general approach will be to traverse the text word by word, gathering the statistics as we go. The program will determine the following information:

1. Total number of words and sentences in the text. It is assumed that each sentence is terminated by a /; although this is a slight departure from the assumed format utilized in previous examples, it neatly circumvents the problems of trying to decide where a sentence ends. For example, "." is not a reliable marker since it precludes the use of abbreviations in the text. (See also the discussion on lexical scanners in Chapter 8.)
2. Number of letters, i.e., number of A's, B's, etc.
3. Word lengths as described above.
4. Accumulated distances between specified marker words and their numbers of occurrence.

From this information, the statistics we wish to collect can be computed. The program will be configured as a sequence of function calls so that it will be highly modular and easily modified. Since we have discussed much of the essential nature of the program in preceding sections, we proceed directly to the SNOBOL implementation. (See Figures 10.13 and 10.14 for sample input and output.)

```
# IN 1949, WARREN WEAVER PREPARED A MEMO (UNPUBLISHED) IN WHICH HE SUGGESTED #
THAT A COMPUTER SHOULD BE ABLE TO TRANSLATE BETWEEN TWO LANGUAGES. / # THIS SUG
GESTION IS REMARKABLE IN A HISTORICAL SENSE; AT THIS TIME, # COMMERCIALLY AVAILA
BLE COMPUTERS WERE ALMOST NON-EXISTENT. / COUPLED WITH # SHANNON'S PROPOSAL CONC
ERNING THE APPLICABILITY OF COMPUTERS TO GAME # PLAYING, IT WAS THE IMPETUS FOR
INVESTIGATIONS INTO THE NON-NUMERICAL ASPECTS # OF COMPUTING. / THESE TWO IDEAS,
WEDDED WITH CYBERNETICS AND PSYCHOLOGY, # LAID THE FOUNDATION FOR ARTIFICIAL IN
TELLIGENCE (CHAPTER 12). / # THE EARLY LANGUAGE TRANSLATION PROJECTS, BECAUSE OF
THE INFANCY OF # COMPUTER SCIENCE AND NAIVE NOTIONS CONCERNING THE STRUCTURE OF
LANGUAGES, # WERE LARGELY UNSUCCESSFUL AND SOON ABANDONED. / THIS UNFORTUNATE #
CIRCUMSTANCE LED MANY SCHOLARS, TO WHOM THE COMPUTER COULD HAVE BEEN OF # IMMEN
SE VALUE, TO TURN AWAY FROM MACHINE-ASSISTED STUDIES. / CONSEQUENTLY, # IT HAS N
OT BEEN UNTIL RELATIVELY RECENTLY THAT INTEREST IN THE APPLICATION # OF THE SYMB
OL PROCESSING CAPABILITIES OF THE COMPUTER HAS BEEN REVIVED # TO THE POINT WHERE
IMPORTANT RESEARCH (E.G. LITERARY RESEARCH IN # THE HUMANITIES) IS BEING CARRIE
D OUT WITH THE AID OF THE COMPUTER. / # THE TRANSLATION PROBLEM IS STILL UNSOLVE
D BUT SMALLER, MORE WELL-DEFINED # PROBLEMS HAVE BEEN SUCCESSFULLY SOLVED IN MAN
Y OF THESE AREAS. /
```

Fig. 10.13 Text for statistical analysis program.

```
---------------------------STATISTICAL SUMMARY OF TEXT-------------------------

AVERAGE WORD LENGTH = 5 CHARACTERS
AVERAGE SENTENCE LENGTH = 24 WORDS


-----LENGTH       NUMBER OF WORDS
      1           5
      2           29
      3           33
      4           31
      5           15
      6           7
      7           19
      8           19
      9           13
      10           26


-----LETTER        FREQUENCY
      A           85    /1092
      B           20    /1092
      C           50    /1092
      D           27    /1092
      E           141   /1092
      F           20    /1092
      G           22    /1092
      H           46    /1092
      I           79    /1092
      J           1     /1092
      K           1     /1092
      L           56    /1092
      M           33    /1092
      N           83    /1092
      O           73    /1092
      P           30    /1092
      Q           1     /1092
      R           60    /1092
      S           76    /1092
      T           98    /1092
      U           41    /1092
      V           12    /1092
      W           17    /1092
      X           1     /1092
      Y           18    /1092
      Z                 /1092


---------------DISTANCES BETWEEN MARKER WORDS---------------
WORD      AVERAGE DISTANCE BETWEEN OCCURRENCES
COMPUTER              40
TO                    34
IS                    77
COMPUTERS             13
THE                   8
OF                    16
THESE                 130
AND                   16
```

Fig. 10.14 Output from statistical analysis program.

Purpose: Compute the statistics of a text (as described above).
Communication:

global variables referenced:

ALPHBT	string of alphabetic characters;
NONLETTERS	string of nonletters except / and #;
NBLANK	string of blanks; size of NONLETTERS;
WORDP	word pattern;
FIRSTP	pattern for first character;
LETTEROCC	table: character → number of occurrences;

FIRSTOCC
LASTOCC . . . . table: WORD→ {first occurrence, last occurrence, # of occurrences;
NOCC

WLENGTH	array: length of word → how many of that length;

WORD
FIRST . . . . result from pattern {WORDP, FIRSTP;

MARKER	pattern of marker words;
BUFFER	string from file;

AVWORDL
AVSENTL . . . . . . average {word sentence} length;

WORDND
SENTENCENO . . . number of {words sentences letters} in text;
NLETTERS

FILENAME	reference to it causes line to be read from text file;

functions called:

READBUF	calls BUFFERIN with FILENAME as argument and edits BUFFER;
BUFFERIN	fills BUFFER from argument file; length of BUFFER may be 5000 plus length of 1 record;
BUFPROC	processes BUFFER, sets WORDNO, SENTENCENO;
LETTERS	sets NLETTERS and LETTEROCC for argument word;
WORDLENGTH . . .	sets WLENGTH of argument word; local variable: LENGTH;
MARKERCHK	sets NOCC, FIRSTOCC, LASTOCC for argument word.

Program:

```
          DEFINE('READBUF()')                                      1
          DEFINE('BUFFERIN()')                                     2
          DEFINE('BUFPROC()')                                      3
          DEFINE('LETTERS(WORD)')                                  4
          DEFINE('WORDLENGTH(WORD)LENGTH')                         5
          DEFINE('MARKERCHK(WORD)')                                6
          &TRIM = 1                                                7
          &ANCHOR = 1                                              8
          ALPHBT = 'ABCDEFGHIJKLMNOPQRSTUVWXYZ'                    9
          NONLETTERS = '0123456789+-"/()$,.[]:=<>&|;'              10
          NBLANK = DUPL(' ',SIZE(NONLETTERS))                      11
          WORDP = SPAN(' ') BREAK(' ') . WORD                      12
          FIRSTP = LEN(1) . FIRST                                  13
          LETTEROCC = TABLE(26)                                    14
          WLENGTH = ARRAY('10',0)                                  15
          FIRSTOCC = TABLE(20,10)                                  16
          LASTOCC = TABLE(20,10)                                   17
          NOCC = TABLE(20,10)                                      18
          INPUT('FILENAME',8,120)                                  19
          OUTPUT('OUTPUT',6,'(1X,80A1)')                           20
```
* INPUT MARKER WORDS, ONE PER RECORD, AND CREATE PATTERN:MARKER *
```
          MARKER = INPUT                            :S(AGAIN)      21
          MARKER = FAIL                             :(BEGIN)       22
AGAIN     MARKER = MARKER | INPUT                   :S(AGAIN)      23
```
* BEGIN PROCESSING TEXT *
```
BEGIN     READBUF()                                 :F(OUT)        24
START     BUFPROC()                                 :F(BEGIN)      25
          LETTERS(WORD)                                            26
          WORDLENGTH(WORD)                                         27
          MARKERCHK(WORD)                           :(START)       28
```
* BEGIN OUTPUT *
```
OUT       FIRSTOCC = CONVERT(FIRSTOCC,'ARRAY')                     29
          LASTOCC = CONVERT(LASTOCC,'ARRAY')                       30
          NOCC = CONVERT(NOCC,'ARRAY')                             31
          OUTPUT = DUPL('-',27)  'STATISTICAL SUMMARY OF TEXT'     32
          DUPL('-',26)                                             32
          OUTPUT =                                                 33
          OUTPUT =                                                 34
```
* COMPUTE AVERAGE WORD AND SENTENCE LENGTH AND OUTPUT *
```
          AVWORDL = NLETTERS / WORDNO                              35
          AVSENTL = WORDNO / SENTENCENO                            36
          OUTPUT = 'AVERAGE WORD LENGTH = ' AVWORDL ' CHARACTERS'  37
          OUTPUT = 'AVERAGE SENTENCE LENGTH = ' AVSENTL ' WORDS'   38
          OUTPUT =                                                 39
          OUTPUT =                                                 40
```
* COMPUTE WORD LENGTHS AND OUTPUT THEM *
```
          OUTPUT = DUPL('-',5) 'LENGTH     NUMBER OF WORDS'         41
          I = 1                                                    42
PRINT     OUTPUT = DUPL(' ',7) I DUPL(' ',8) WLENGTH<I>            43
                                                  :F(DONE)         43
          I = I + 1                               :(PRINT)         44
```
* COMPUTE LETTER FREQUENCIES *
```
DONE      OUTPUT =                                                 45
          OUTPUT =                                                 46
          OUTPUT = DUPL('-',5) 'LETTER     FREQUENCY'              47
PRINTF    ALPHBT FIRSTP =                          :F(OUTP)        48
```

```
         OUTPUT = DUPL(' ',7) FIRST DUPL(' ',8) LETTEROCC<FIRST>              49
.        DUPL(' ',5 - SIZE(LETTEROCC<FIRST>))  '/' NLETTERS                   49
.                                                    :(PRINTF)                49
::::::::::::::::COMPUTE DISTANCES BETWEEN MARKER WORD AND OUTPUT::::::::::::::::::::::::::::::
OUTP     OUTPUT =                                                             50
         OUTPUT =                                                             51
         OUTPUT = DUPL('-',15) 'DISTANCES BETWEEN MARKER WORDS'               52
.        DUPL('-',15)                                                         52
         OUTPUT = 'WORD     AVERAGE DISTANCE BETWEEN OCCURRENCES'             53
         I = 1                                                                54
REPEAT   EQ(NOCC<I,2>,0)                              :S(INC)                 55
         OUTPUT = FIRSTOCC<I,1> DUPL(' ',20 - SIZE(FIRSTOCC<I,1>))            56
.        ((LASTOCC<I,2> - FIRSTOCC<I,2>) / NOCC<I,2>)                         56
.                                                    :F(END)                  56
INC      I = I + 1                                    :(REPEAT)               57
::::::::::::::::END OF PROGRAM::::::::::::::::::::::::::::::::::::::::::::::::::::::::::::::::::
::::::::::::::::BEGIN BUFPROC:::::::::::::::::::::::::::::::::::::::::::::::::::::::::::::::::::::
BUFPROC  BUFFER WORDP =                               :F(FRETURN)            58
         WORD FIRSTP                                                         59
         IDENT('/',FIRST)                            :S(UPDATE)             60
         IDENT('#',FIRST)                            :S(BUFPROC)            61
         WORDNO = WORDNO + 1                         :(RETURN)              62
UPDATE   SENTENCENO = SENTENCENO + 1                 :(BUFPROC)             63
::::::::::::::::END BUFPROC:::::::::::::::::::::::::::::::::::::::::::::::::::::::::::::::::::::
::::::::::::::::BEGIN LETTERS:::::::::::::::::::::::::::::::::::::::::::::::::::::::::::::::::::
LETTERS  WORD FIRSTP =                               :F(RETURN)             64
         NLETTERS = NLETTERS + 1                                            65
         LETTEROCC<FIRST> = LETTEROCC<FIRST> + 1     :(LETTERS)             66
::::::::::::::::END LETTERS::::::::::::::::::::::::::::::::::::::::::::::::::::::::::::::::::::
::::::::::::::::BEGIN WORDLENGTH:::::::::::::::::::::::::::::::::::::::::::::::::::::::::::::::::
WORDLENGTH  LENGTH = SIZE(WORD)                                             67
         LENGTH = GT(LENGTH,9) 10                                           68
         WLENGTH<LENGTH> = WLENGTH<LENGTH> + 1       :(RETURN)             69
::::::::::::::::END WORDLENGTH::::::::::::::::::::::::::::::::::::::::::::::::::::::::::::::::::
::::::::::::::::BEGIN MARKERCHK:::::::::::::::::::::::::::::::::::::::::::::::::::::::::::::::::
MARKERCHK  WORD MARKER                               :F(RETURN)             70
         IDENT(FIRSTOCC<WORD>,NULL)                  :F(NEXT)               71
         NOCC<WORD> = -1                                                    72
         FIRSTOCC<WORD> = WORDNO                                            73
NEXT     LASTOCC<WORD> = WORDNO                                             74
         NOCC<WORD> = NOCC<WORD> + 1                 :(RETURN)              75
::::::::::::::::END MARKERCHK:::::::::::::::::::::::::::::::::::::::::::::::::::::::::::::::::::
::::::::::::::::FUNCTION READBUF::::::::::::::::::::::::::::::::::::::::::::::::::::::::::::::::
READBUF  BUFFERIN()                                  :F(FRETURN)            76
         BUFFER = ' ' BUFFER ' '                                            77
         OUTPUT = BUFFER                                                    78
         BUFFER = REPLACE(BUFFER,NONLETTERS,NBLANK)                         79
         BUFFER = REPLACE(BUFFER,NONLETTERS,NBLANK)  :(RETURN)              80
::::::::::::::::END READBUF::::::::::::::::::::::::::::::::::::::::::::::::::::::::::::::::::::
::::::::::::::::FUNCTION BUFFERIN:::::::::::::::::::::::::::::::::::::::::::::::::::::::::::::::
BUFFERIN  BUFFER = FILENAME                          :F(FRETURN)            81
READ     GT(SIZE(BUFFER),5000)                       :S(RETURN)            82
         BUFFER = BUFFER ' ' FILENAME                :S(READ)F(RETURN)     83
::::::::::::::::END BUFFERIN:::::::::::::::::::::::::::::::::::::::::::::::::::::::::::::::::::
END                                                                        84
```

The program itself is relatively straightforward, although in order to be genuinely useful, the same sort of cosmetic surgery necessary in the preceding section is required.

10.4.3 Authorship Studies

As we have pointed out in the introduction, one of the most exciting uses of the computer in the study of literary data is in the area of authorship studies, also called attribution studies. The work of Mosteller and Wallace in their analysis of the Federalist papers has already been discussed. It is not our intention here to attempt to duplicate any of these studies but rather to point out some of the basic ideas and orient the reader to the literature.

Authorship studies take a variety of forms which depend, obviously, on the scholarly questions involved. In the Mosteller and Wallace study, for example, the question asked was whether Hamilton or Madison authored the disputed essays. As it turns out, with a very high probability Madison was the author of all 12. The study was based on the occurrence of common words, such as *on, of, enough, also, while,* etc. These are the words which are often used unconsciously and, as such, provide stronger evidence than more uncommon words. Hamilton, it was discovered, used the preposition *upon* five times more frequently than Madison.

In other cases, the question may well be whether a single author was responsible for a particular work. In another classic study, it was determined that Homer's *Iliad* exhibits sufficient consistency throughout that it could be concluded that it was the work of a single poet rather than a montage of ballads by different authors which were strung together. The general idea here was to determine the distribution of high-frequency words throughout the work. If these words appear to be uniformly distributed, or approximately so, then one can conclude that it was the work of one person, since multiple authors would undoubtedly have shown strong fluctuations in the distribution. Again, rather sophisticated statistical analyses are required to lend credence to the results.

At another level of analysis, one might try to determine the semantic content of a work, that is, the meaning embedded in the symbols that constitute the work. In a sense, we are asking, What is the conceptual content of this work? This might involve the construction of a fairly complex structure which in some sense contains the meaning of the work. One could, of course, begin to ask the same kinds of questions outlined above for the syntactic structures developed there. The final extension of such an effort would be the understanding of a work by the computer, in the sense that the structure developed embodies the concepts developed in the work. Such efforts now properly belong to the area of computer science known as *artificial intelligence;* presumably, they will eventually yield a rich storehouse of new techniques.

10.5 CONCLUSIONS

In this chapter, we have attempted to point out the important applications of the computer in areas generally considered to be the domain of the literary scholar. In contrast to the theoretical treatments provided for the algorithms and techniques developed in earlier chapters, when the data were basically numerical in nature, this chapter contains no proofs, no complexity analyses, etc. This omission is intentional; complexity analyses could have been provided for the algorithms developed here, but to do so would obscure the major focus: How can the computer be used in language studies? In this context, the user is generally not a computer scientist who has to produce a production program of optimal efficiency. Rather, we are in the position of, say, a linguist who wants to use the power of SNOBOL to write a program to analyze one text. Whereas we, as computer scientists, spent entire chapters on data base management techniques for efficient storage and retrieval of information, SNOBOL provides the concept of a "TABLE," which solves the problem admirably for the user, even though the complexity of a reference *table⟨word⟩* may be great. Similarly, the operation of pattern matching allows the user to solve complex problems, such as lexical scanning, with a few statements in SNOBOL. Thus, complexity analysis of algorithms for the problems discussed in this chapter are not only not very meaningful but would be rather difficult to obtain because we would first have to analyze the complexity of basic SNOBOL operators.

We have barely scratched the surface of this fascinating area, yet it should be evident that the computer can be of as much value here as in mathematics. Indeed, the essence of the problems developed here is not that much different from the problems considered earlier. The seeming ease with which we can program the computer to digest and manipulate vast amounts of data bodes well for a rapid increase in our understanding of our literary works and provides the scholar with techniques much more powerful than those available only a few years ago.

In this chapter, we have omitted many of the recent attempts at studies in the humanities in general. To completely cover the range of activities in this area would require a treatise well beyond the scope of this one. We can only show the interested reader the right direction.

References

Some early approaches to automatic language translation appear in

H. P. EDMUNSON (ed.), *Proceedings of the National Symposium on Machine Translation*, Prentice-Hall, Englewood Cliffs, N.J., 1961.

Interesting comments on the probability of successful machine translation are found in

Y. BAR-HILLEL, *Language and Information*, Addison-Wesley, Reading, Mass., 1964.

The classic paper on disputed authorship is

F. MOSTELLER and D. WALLACE, *Inference and Disputed Authorship: The Federalist*, Addison-Wesley, Reading, Mass., 1964.

There is a vast literature on the application of computers in the humanities. A journal, *Computers and the Humanities* (Joseph Raben, ed.), is devoted exclusively to this area. IBM offers at least three booklets on this subject, under their Data Processing Application Series:

GE 20–0382–0, *Introduction to Computers in the Humanities.*
GE 20–0383–0, *Literary Data Processing.*
GE 20–0390–0, *Computers in History and Political Science.*

Each of these has an extensive bibliography.

Several conferences have been held on the topic of computers, the humanities, and literary research:

R. WISBEY (ed.), *The Computer in Literary and Linguistic Research*, Cambridge University Press, New York, 1972

and

L. MITCHELL, *Computers in the Humanities*, University of Minnesota Press, Minneapolis, 1974.

For a comprehensive overview of the utility of SNOBOL and an advanced text on techniques, see

RALPH E. GRISWOLD, *String and List Processing in SNOBOL4: Techniques and Applications*, Prentice-Hall, Englewood Cliffs, N.J., 1975.

This reference contains a wealth of ideas for programming projects. Griswold also discusses at length the problems encountered in the machine manipulation of documents.

The journal *Review of the International Organization for Ancient Languages Analysis by Computer* (commonly abbreviated *REVUE*) contains interesting articles limited to the domain implied by its title.

A comprehensive analysis of Jonathan Swift's works, including the computer aspects of the study, is found in

LOUIS T. MILIC, *A Quantitative Approach to the Style of Jonathan Swift*, Humanities Press, New York, 1966.

An overview of the projects involving computer analysis of the classics is provided by

STEPHEN V. F. WAITE, "Computers and the Classics," *Computers and the Humanities*, *3*(1) (Sept. 1968), pp. 25–29.

SIGLASH, the ACM Special Interest Group on Language Analysis and Studies in the Humanities, publishes a newsletter containing timely articles, reviews of books, announcements of works in progress, etc.

The computer-assisted study of Homer's *Iliad* may be found in

JAMES T. McDONOUGH, "Homer, the Humanities, and IBM," *Proceedings of the Literary Data Processing Conference*, IBM, Yorktown Heights, N.Y., 1964, pp. 25–36.

The general idea of a conceptual approach to the analysis of literary data is explored by

JULIUS LAFFAL, "Toward a Conceptual Grammar and Lexicon," *Computers and the Humanities*, *4*(3) (Jan. 1970), pp. 173–186.

The reference to Shannon's proposal is

C. E. Shannon, "Programming a Computer for Playing Chess," *Philosophical Magazine, 41* (March 1950), pp. 256–275.

Exercises

1 The first part of this chapter extends AL to include string-oriented operations in terms of built-in primitive functions. Discuss the appropriateness of the structures developed in terms of the kind of problems considered in later sections. What primitives should a language contain for these kinds of problems? Compare this with the structure of SNOBOL and comment on its utility as a programming language for these problems.

2 Develop AL procedures for the primitive functions **substring, decomp, first, last, substitute, length, span,** and **break**. Discuss the problems involved (in terms of operations required, data structures, etc.) in implementing a general pattern matching structure, such as the structure implied in the **search** and **replace** operations. *Note:* The solution to this exercise implies the solution to Exercises 10.1 and 10.2 and more.

3 Develop an AL algorithm for translating from Pig latin to English. What problems arise here that do not arise in the inverse translation?

4 Develop an AL algorithm which will translate an integer number into its Roman numeral equivalent and vice versa. Implement this algorithm in SNOBOL and provide adequate test values so that you are sure that it is correct.

5 Develop a SNOBOL program which will generate a KWIC index to a given data base. Make any assumptions you wish about the form of the input, etc., but keep in mind that the program must be easy to use.

6 Indicate how you would include a sorting function into the KWIC indexing program developed above. Justify your choice.

7 The way in which punctuation was handled in the word index problem is not particularly satisfactory. For example, "it's" would be replaced by "it s", and "s" would be counted as a word. On the other hand, if the blank were squeezed out, "it's" would become "its", which is indistinguishable from "its". Modify this algorithm to minimize the errors caused by this problem.

8 Assuming that a word index is available for two works (possibly by the same author), how would you compare the resulting indices in order to determine whether or not the works match in some sense? Develop an algorithm which will point out differences in the indices which may be significant. *Note:* The resulting algorithm may not be trivial. What special cases have to be handled?

9 As mentioned throughout the chapter, analysis of syntactic structure is a rather difficult task. On the other hand, generation of random sentences from a simple grammar is considerably easier. Develop a SNOBOL program which will accept as input a grammar, perhaps a BNF grammar as in Section 9 of Part C of the supplementary volume, which will output sentences generated at random from this grammar. Try to tune your grammar so that the number of meaningful sentences is fairly high. You may even want to try to develop a grammar which imitates the style of a particular author or poet.

10 Modify the statistical analysis program developed in Section 10.4.2 to include computation of the variance of the measures computed as well as their means. Try the program on two different texts and analyze the results.

11

Recursive Processes

11.0 INTRODUCTION

In several of the foregoing chapters, we have developed algorithms and procedures for specific problems only up to a point even though there appeared to be a logical continuation of that development. A case in point is the discussion of the balanced division technique (i.e., divide-and-conquer) for producing efficient algorithms from Section 4.3. In some cases, the division could be performed repeatedly using the same subprocesses, changing only the input parameters. Quite often, this technique leads naturally to a formulation of what is called a *recursive* process; the reason for dropping this formulation at that time was a practical one. However, we have now developed the tools and techniques required to pursue this rather interesting methodology.

11.1 PRINCIPLES OF RECURSION

11.1.1 Iteration versus Recursion

It is with apologies to the reader that this next example is represented. It appears in almost every book which touches on the concept of recursion and in many that do not. However, it possesses one quality which makes it an ideal pedagogic tool: simplicity.

Consider the following problem: We have n distinct items and want to know the number of ways in which these items can be arranged. Suppose $n = 3$ and the items are integers; then the number of ways these integers can be arranged is

$$
\begin{array}{ccc}
1 & 2 & 3 \\
1 & 3 & 2 \\
2 & 1 & 3 \\
2 & 3 & 1 \\
3 & 1 & 2 \\
3 & 2 & 1 \\
\end{array}
$$

for a total of 6 distinct combinations. Problems of this type, which have to do with the number of combinations of things, or *combinatorics*, occur quite frequently in probability and statistics. The solution is

$$f(n) = 1 * 2 * 3 * 4 * 5 * 6 * \cdots * (n-1) * n, \qquad n > 0 \qquad (1)$$

where $f(n)$ represents the number of arrangements of n distinct items; this function is usually written as $n!$.

It is very easy to write an AL procedure for computing $f(n)$:

```
procedure factorial(n; f)
begin /*factorial*/
    if n ≤ 0 then output 'argument less than 1'
            else begin /*compute factorial*/
                    f ← 1; i ← 1;
                    while (i ≤ n) [f ← i * f; i ← i + 1]
                 end /*compute factorial*/
end /*factorial*/
```

The FORTRAN realization is also simple:

```
        INTEGER FUNCTION F(N)
        IF(N.GT.0)GO TO 20
C              ERROR CHECK
               WRITE(6,10)
    10         FORMAT(22H ARGUMENT NOT POSITIVE)
               RETURN
C              COMPUTE FACTORIAL
C
    20  F=1
        DO 40 I=1,N
           F=I*F
    40  CONTINUE
C              END COMPUTE
        RETURN
        END
```

and follows the structure of the AL procedure rather closely. There is a point to all this, of course; namely, both the AL procedure and the FORTRAN implementation embody a programming technique known as *iteration*. This is manifested in the manner in which control is obtained over the repetitive calculation F=I*F. In each case, a loop is provided in which the repeated calculation is performed. In the case of the AL procedure, the loop is implicitly defined by the **while** statement and its attendant termination conditions. In the FORTRAN case, the loop is explicitly provided by the DO statement. Most of the algorithms which we have considered up to this point have utilized iterative solutions in those cases where repeated calculations have been required.

However, there is an alternative interpretation of (1) which implies a radically different form of solution. Equation (1) may be rewritten as

$$f(n) = n * f(n - 1) \qquad \text{for } n > 0$$

and

$$f(0) = 1$$

(2)

For f to have values for all nonnegative integers, $f(0)$ is normally defined as 1. Computation of $f(3)$ using this interpretation would proceed as follows:

$$f(3) = 3 * f(2) = 3 * 2 = 6$$
$$f(2) = 2 * f(1) = 2 * 1 = 2$$
$$f(1) = 1 * f(0) = 1 * 1 = 1$$

EXERCISE 11.1: Write out the steps in the computation of $f(5)$ using the above notation.

In this case, the factorial function $f(n)$ has been defined in terms of calls to itself with modified arguments. Again, it is reasonably easy to write the AL procedure for this interpretation:

procedure *factorial*$(n; f)$
begin /*factorial*/
    if $n = 0$ **then** $f \leftarrow 1$
             else $f \leftarrow n * factorial(n - 1; f)$
end /*factorial*/

(3)

ignoring for the moment the initial error check on n. The FORTRAN equivalent is

```
          INTEGER FUNCTION F(N)
          IF(N. GT. 0)GO TO 10
C              TERMINAL VALUE
          F=1
          RETURN
C              NONTERMINAL CALL
    10    F=N*F(N−1)
          RETURN
          END
```

provided FORTRAN allowed this type of call. However, in the discussion of the function and subroutine in Part A of the supplementary volume, it is explicitly stated that a FORTRAN subroutine (or function) cannot contain a call to itself, nor can it call itself indirectly through a sequence of procedure calls. The reason for this restriction is that FORTRAN does not support the mechanism necessary to implement "self-calling" or *recursive* procedures. SNOBOL, on the other hand, does allow recursive functions, and the SNOBOL equivalent to (3) is

$$\text{DEFINE('F(N)')}$$

$$\cdot$$
$$\cdot$$
$$\cdot$$

F   F = EQ(N,0) 1   :S(RETURN)
    F = N * F(N − 1)   :(RETURN)

EXERCISE 11.2: Modify the SNOBOL function for $n!$ to include an error check on the initial value of N. Execute the function for various values of N, using the TRACE functions to watch the progress of the computation.

EXERCISE 11.3: The number of different ways m distinct items can be selected (regardless of the order) from n items is given by

$$\binom{n}{m} = \frac{n!}{(n-m)!m!}, \quad n > m$$

For example, the number of distinct hands (the two hands $1,2,3,4,5\diamondsuit$. and $2,1,3,4,5\diamondsuit$ are counted only once) of stud poker is given by

$$\binom{52}{5} = \frac{52!}{47! \cdot 5!} = \frac{48 \cdot 49 \cdot 50 \cdot 51 \cdot 52}{1 \cdot 2 \cdot 3 \cdot 4 \cdot 5}$$

which computes to a very large number. This relationship also arises in the expansion of $(x + c)^n$:

$$(x + c)^n = \sum_m \binom{n}{m} x^{n-m} c^m, \quad 0 \le m \le n$$

It is easy to show that the *binomial coefficient* $b_{ij} = \binom{j}{i}$ has the property

$$b_{ij} = b_{i-1, j-1} + b_{i, j-1}, \quad j \ge 1, i \ne 0, j$$

which is graphically depicted in *Pascal's triangle:*

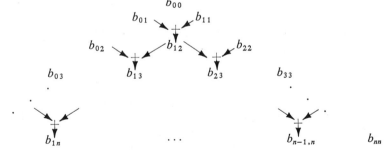

where $b_{00} = b_{0j} = b_{jj} = 1, j \ge 0$. Thus, for $n = 4$, the triangle is

```
                1
             1     1
          1     2     1
       1     3     3     1
    1     4     6     4     1
```

Note that this implies that $(x + c)^4 = x^4 + 4xc^3 + 6c^2x^2 + 4c^3x + c^4$, and the number of different combinations of four items taken two at a time is $b_{24} = \begin{pmatrix} 4 \\ 2 \end{pmatrix} = 6$. Write a recursive SNOBOL program which will print out Pascal's triangle for any given value of n; test your program on some hopefully small values of n. Why do we stress that n should be small?

We have, in fact, already seen several examples of recursion in the preceding chapters, although we did not label them as such. Let us review those instances were no difficulties arose in understanding a process even though it may have been defined in terms of itself.

1. In Part C of the supplementary volume (Section 9.4.3) a BNF grammar is presented for a "subset" of English. In that example, the definition of the nonterminal $\langle subject \rangle$ was

$$\langle subject \rangle : : = \langle simpsub \rangle \,|\, \langle simpsub \rangle \text{ and } \langle subject \rangle$$

The nonterminal $\langle subject \rangle$ appears on both sides of this definition, leading to the generation of strings of the form

dinner and grammar and sentence and dinner and . . .

which is one of the reasons that the grammar was not a particularly realistic one. On the other hand, the same construction is used in the definition of identifiers (e.g., variable names, arrays, labels, etc.) in the formal definition of the programming language ALGOL:

$\langle letter \rangle ::= a\,|\,b\,|\,c\,|\,d\,|\,e\,|\,f\,|\,g\,|\,h\,|\,i\,|\,j\,|\,k\,|\,l\,|\,m\,|\,n\,|\,o\,|\,p\,|\,q\,|\,r\,|\,s\,|\,t\,|\,u\,|\,v\,|\,w\,|\,x\,|\,y\,|\,z\,|\,A\,|\,B\,|\,C\,|\,D\,|$
$\qquad\quad E\,|\,F\,|\,G\,|\,H\,|\,I\,|\,J\,|\,K\,|\,L\,|\,M\,|\,N\,|\,O\,|\,P\,|\,Q\,|\,R\,|\,S\,|\,T\,|\,U\,|\,V\,|\,W\,|\,X\,|\,Y\,|\,Z$
$\langle digit \rangle ~~::= 0\,|\,1\,|\,2\,|\,3\,|\,4\,|\,5\,|\,6\,|\,7\,|\,8\,|\,9$
$\langle identifier \rangle ::= \langle letter \rangle\,|\,\langle identifier \rangle \langle letter \rangle\,|\,\langle identifier \rangle \langle digit \rangle$

Again, this definition allows the formulation of identifiers as simple as A or as long as one wishes, including strings of infinite length. Clearly, practical use of definitions with these characteristics implies some outside control over unlimited application of the recursive rules. The advantage of using these definitions is, of course, that they are concise even for very large sets of items (possibly infinite).

2. The only time we completed application of the divide-and-conquer technique was in the development of the quicksort algorithm in Chapter 5.

3. The definition of a binary tree in Chapter 9 was essentially

A binary tree is a finite set of nodes, possibly empty, with one and only one distinguished node called the root node. The remaining nodes are partitioned into two disjoint sets which themselves form binary trees and are called the left and the right subtree.

Note that in this definition, a binary tree is defined in terms of itself. Since this definition does not allow infinite binary trees, the definition is self-limiting in that it can be applied only a finite number of times before the set of available nodes is empty. At this point, the correct structure has been imposed on the set of nodes.

Finally, we have the recursive definition of functions themselves, such as the factorial function defined earlier. These examples share a common characteristic: They all define something in terms of itself. In some cases, this characteristic is convenient, such as in the BNF definition of large sets; in some cases, it is almost necessary, as in the definition of a binary tree; and in other cases, it is misused, as in the definition of the factorial function. This misuse is not based on theoretical grounds, since the recursive definition of the factorial function is equally as valid as the iterative one, but rather on practical considerations of computing: The overhead involved in supporting recursion in programming languages is very high, as we shall see in succeeding sections. Does this imply that recursion should never be used? The answer to this question is clearly negative and is based on the following observations concerning recursion.

When formulating an algorithm for the solution to a particular problem, the final structure of the algorithm is a function of the type of problem to be solved as well as the underlying data structure involved. Some data structures appear to have a natural iterative component, and others appear to lead naturally to recursive algorithms. Multiplication of two matrices would certainly not be formulated recursively, yet traversal of a binary tree most probably would. Matrices are linear structures in which iteration over the rows and columns is performed easily and naturally. A binary tree is, intuitively, not a linear structure, and an iterative algorithm for visiting every node in the tree might appear unnecessarily complicated, obscuring the essence of the problem. On the other hand, a recursive algorithm, as we shall see, is an elegant and concise representation of the solution to this particular problem. The choice of iteration or recursion depends as much on the structure of the data as on anything else and requires experience and common sense. Since lists and trees are the most commonly used inherently recursive structures, it is not surprising that most of the examples to be presented, and the most widespread use of recursion, are given in conjunction with these structures. In the next section, the formulation of recursive routines to solve a variety of problems is discussed.

11.1.2 Formulation of Recursive Algorithms

As a result of the preceding discussion, the following definition should be self-evident:

Definition 11.1: A *recursive algorithm* is any algorithm which uses itself in the definition of the algorithm. *Recursion* is a concept whose use allows us to specify a function or process in terms of itself.

Taken at its face value, Definition 11.1 seems to be circular; certain implicit assumptions will have to be made in order to make it a workable definition. The most important of these assumptions is that the recursive definition of an algorithm will be structured in a logically consistent manner (much as the factorial definition) such that the actual definition is not circular.

In this section, we shall attempt to provide some practical guidelines for finding a recursive formulation of an algorithm and try to convince the reader that such a definition does indeed completely specify the algorithm. For the moment, the technique of balanced division will provide the necessary example since the resulting algorithms often lend themselves to recursive formulations.

The first stage in obtaining such a formulation is to *identify* the process and its parameters, particularly those parameters which determine the size of the problem upon which the subsequent partitioning of the problem is founded. For example, consider the problem of sorting; one way of applying the balanced division technique resulted in quicksort. After placing the first element of the n-tuple in its final location, j, we stated informally

> Apply the same process to the remaining parts to the left of
> x_j and the right of x_j. (4)

Note that the parameters involved here are the name of the tuple, x, the left (right) boundary of the subtuple to be sorted, *left* (*right*), and the size is the number of elements to be sorted.

The second and perhaps most important stage in the development of a recursive algorithm is to find a *relation* between the process of a given size n and identical processes of sizes which are smaller than n. The emphasis here is on identical; that is, when the original process is divided into smaller processes, they must be the same as the original. This is indeed the case for (4). Thus, given a module (procedure) which will sort an n-tuple (called quicksort), it can be expressed in terms of the same module with different values of the parameters, as shown in Figure 11.1. Recall our conventions for the communication part of a utility module (Section 3.3). Unfortunately, the procedure illustrated in Figure 11.1 suffers from the circularity alluded to earlier. Although quicksort has been expressed in terms of itself, there are no provisions, either explicit or implicit, to terminate the process. This leads us to the third stage in the formulation of a recursive algorithm: the *termination criteria*. At the beginning of any recursive algorithm, it is necessary to test whether the problem has been sufficiently reduced in size so that the explicit statements for its solution can be given. In the case of the factorial example, when the value of n becomes zero, we know by definition that the value of the factorial function is 1. In practice, one usually tests for those values of the actual arguments for which the least amount of work has to be done to solve the problem; this very often occurs when the size of the problem has been reduced to 0 (factorial) or 1 (quicksort). In the above example, a test is inserted to detect when the size of a subtuple to be sorted is 1, since in this case no action need be performed (any tuple of one element is sorted). The AL representation of quicksort is given below. The line numbers are for reference only.

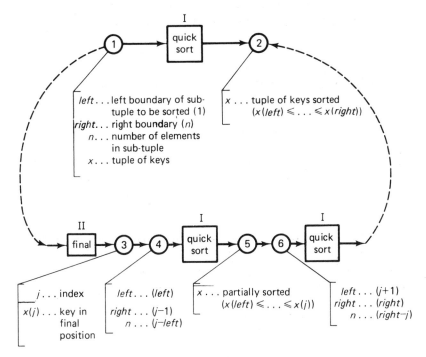

Fig. 11.1   Recursive formulation of quicksort.

Algorithm 11.1 (Recursive formulation of quicksort)

Global data referenced: x

	Line No.
procedure *quicksort* (*left, right, n;*)	
begin /∗sort *n*-tuple x, which is a global variable∗/	
if $n \leq 1$ **then terminate**;	1
final-pos(*left, right; j*);	2
quicksort(*left, j* − 1, *j* − *left;*);	3
quicksort(*j* + 1, *right, right* − *j;*)	4
end /∗sort∗/	

    The reason why Algorithm 11.1 does indeed completely specify a solution is best elucidated by example. Assume that there is an infinite number of copies of Algorithm

11.1 available and that every call to quicksort uses a new copy. Let the global variable x have the value (12, 2, 8, 5, 3); assume quicksort is invoked as

$$quicksort(1, 5, 5;) \qquad \text{original call}$$

The test in line 1 will fail; the procedure call to *final-pos* in line 2 will modify x to (3, 2, 8, 5, 12) and return $j = 5$. Copy 1 of quicksort is called in line 3 as

$$quicksort(1, 4, 4;) \qquad \text{call of first copy}$$

When a return is accomplished from this procedure, $x(1)$ through $x(5)$ will be sorted (why?), and the call to quicksort in line 4 is

$$quicksort(6, 5, 0;) \qquad \text{call of second copy}$$

The value of n here causes copy 2 to return immediately without changing x. Let us now return to trace execution of copy 1. The test in line 1 will fail; *final-pos* will modify the subtuple (3, 2, 8, 5) to (2, 3, 8, 5) and set $j = 2$. The following two calls to quicksort occur at lines 3 and 4:

$$quicksort(1, 1, 1;) \qquad \text{copy 3}$$
$$quicksort(3, 4, 2;) \qquad \text{copy 4}$$

Copy 3 of the algorithm returns immediately to copy 1 after executing line 1; copy 4 will have to sort the subtuple (8, 5). Copy 4 will therefore issue two calls to quicksort (copies 5 and 6); after copy 4 is finished, it will return to copy 1, which will therefore have $x(1)$ through $x(4)$ sorted to (2, 3, 5, 8). Thus, under the assumption that as many copies of the procedure exist as is necessary, Algorithm 11.1 indeed specifies the solution to the sorting problem. In the next section, we shall discuss the implementation of recursive calls where only one copy of the procedure is available; for the time being, an analysis of the algorithm is not considered here since the cost of the overhead necessary for recursive solutions depends on the particular system on which the algorithm is implemented.

   In general, recursive formulations are quite concise and elegant, although it requires some experience to find them. This experience is best gained through examples. Before proceeding to the examples, we shall summarize the salient points in the production of a recursive formulation of an algorithm:

1. Identify the process, parameters, and size.
2. Determine the relation between the original process and identical processes of smaller size.
3. Provide a termination condition and a corresponding action to perform when this condition is satisfied.

11.1.3 Traversal of Binary Trees

In Chapter 9, we omitted discussion of one of the most important operations on trees: tree traversal. This was done for reasons mentioned there; tree traversal is a classic example of the power of a recursive formulation versus an iterative one. The recursive formulation is elegant and natural, whereas the iterative traversal algorithm is forced. Of course, in most cases we would not have the freedom to choose one solution or the other; most likely, we would be forced into the iterative solution because of language choice (recursion not permitted) or efficiency considerations (overhead too high).

Tree traversal is the operation in which all the nodes of a tree are visited in a systematic way to perform some action. For instance, one method of representing the syntax of a statement in a programming language (see Chapter 8) which reflects the precedence relations of the language is via a tree, as shown in Figure 11.2. Given this

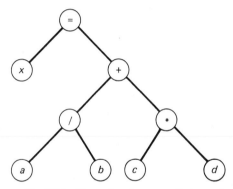

Fig. 11.2   Binary tree for $x = a/b + c * d$.

tree, the *infix*, *prefix*, or *postfix* operator notation for the statement may be obtained by traversing the tree in the appropriate order. Before the traversal procedures are presented, it might be helpful to digress for a moment and discuss the various forms of operator notation mentioned above.

The operator notation which is most familiar to us is the infix notation in which operators appear between their respective operands. This is the notation which has been used throughout this book; some examples are

$$A+B \qquad G \leftarrow H**F*J+2 \qquad R \leftarrow -B+(B**2-4*A*C)**.5$$
$$C*D-F+G \qquad AREA \leftarrow PI*R**2 \qquad SUM \leftarrow X+Y*C+D**2$$

These examples point up some of the common difficulties with infix notation, particularly insofar as its use in computing is concerned. These include the need for precedence relations among the operators and the use of parentheses; e.g., the expression

C∗D−F+G may be computed as

$$(((C*D)-F)+G)$$
$$(C*(D-F))+G$$
or $$(C*(D-F+G))$$

The precedence relations in FORTRAN specify that the first interpretation represents the actual computation to be performed. Expressions can be stated unambiguously and the need for parentheses eliminated by using a representation known as Polish notation. The relations between these forms are (note that the variable names appear always in the same order)

Infix	Reverse Polish (suffix or postfix notation)	Forward Polish (prefix notation)
X←A+B−C	XAB+C−←	←X−+ABC

Both of the Polish forms eliminate the need for parentheses and reflect the precedence rules inherent in the original infix representation. Both forms also simplify the conversion from source string to target code in interpreters and compilers. There is a simple algorithm for converting from infix to Polish; however, it will not be considered here. Our main concern is with the representation of these forms in a tree structure. Given the tree of Figure 11.2, it is easy to obtain the prefix and/or postfix representation of $x = a/b + c * d$ by traversing the tree in the appropriate order. In this example, conversion from infix to postfix will be considered.

The procedure *traversal* has a pointer, *top*, to the root of the tree as its argument. The number of nodes in the tree represents the "size" of the data, although this will not be utilized in the example. The division point is self-evident: It is the root of the binary tree so that its two subtrees form the smaller problems. Thus, we obtain the by now familiar recursive formulation based on balanced division as shown in Figure 11.3. In the diagram of Figure 11.3, we have assumed *tree* and *postfix* to be global variables; the terminal condition can be made particularly simple if we test for the empty tree (i.e., root = **null**); in which case we return without doing anything.

Algorithm 11.2 (Binary tree traversal in postorder)

Global data referenced: *tree, postfix*

```
procedure postfix(top;)
begin /*postfix traverses tree in postorder*/
    if top = null then terminate;
    postfix(left(node(top)););
    postfix(right(node(top)););
        postfix ← postfix + value(node(top))
end /*postfix*/
```

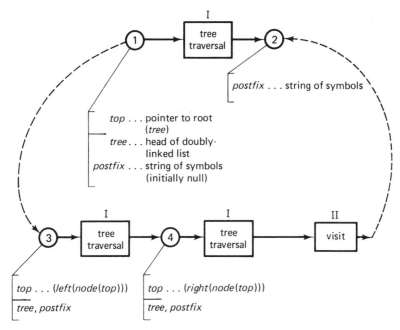

Fig. 11.3   Recursive formulation of tree traversal.

EXERCISE 11.4: Assume that you are given a tree whose nodes contain keys with the following property,

> The values of all nodes in the left (right) subtree are smaller (greater) than the value of the root node

and that all subtrees share this property. Develop a recursive procedure to traverse this tree in such a way that the output consists of a list of keys which is sorted. For example, the output of your procedure for the tree

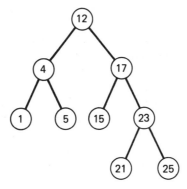

should be the list 1, 4, 5, 12, 15, 17, 21, 23, 25; see Chapter 5 on binary searching and sorting.

Balanced division is not the only technique which leads to recursive solutions, as is illustrated in the next two examples. The technique used in these examples may be viewed as the inverse of the induction (iterative) technique developed in Section 4.3.1. Rather than trying to divide a problem of size n into equal-sized subproblems, we attempt to find a relation between problems of size $n - 1$ and the original problem.

11.1.4 Number of Lattice Points in a Sphere

Consider an n-dimensional sphere of radius $r > 1$, i.e., all the points $(x_1, \ldots, x_n)$ for which $\sum_{i=1}^{n} x_i^2 \leq r^2$, being centered on the origin. How many lattice points (a lattice point is one which has all-integer coordinates) are contained (strictly) within the sphere? It is extremely difficult to visualize a sphere beyond $n = 3$; let us therefore restrict our initial analysis to $n = 3$. The parameters of the procedure *lattice* are the radius r and the dimension n. For $n = 3$, Figure 11.4 illustrates the sphere with some

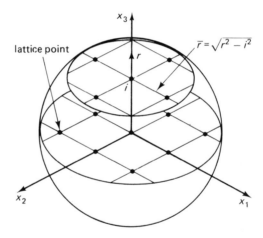

Fig. 11.4 Lattice points of 3-dimensional sphere.

of its lattice points; a relationship is discernible between the number of lattice points of the three-dimensional sphere and the number of lattice points of the two-dimensional spheres (e.g., circles) at the integer points of the third axis. The lattice points of the $(n - 1)$-dimensional spheres centered around the points $(0, 0, \ldots, -\lfloor r \rfloor), \ldots,$ $(0, 0, \ldots, 0), \ldots, (0, 0, \ldots, \lfloor r \rfloor)$ together will cover all the lattice points of the n-dimensional sphere around $(0, 0, \ldots, 0)$. Thus, the relation between $lattice(r, n)$ and $lattice(r, n - 1)$, when *lattice* is viewed as a function, is given by

$$lattice(r, n) := lattice(r, n - 1) + 2 \sum_{i=1}^{\lfloor r \rfloor} lattice(\sqrt{r^2 - i^2}, n - 1)$$

If the termination criterion selected is $n = 0$ (a point), a rather inefficient algorithm is obtained (why?). However, if the termination criterion is $n = 1$, then the computation

$$lattice(r, 1) := 2\lfloor r \rfloor + 1$$

provides the correct result more efficiently. Algorithm 11.3 is the AL representation of the solution to this problem.

Algorithm 11.3 (Number of lattice points in an *n*-dimensional sphere)

```
procedure lattice(r, n; res)
begin /*lattice*/
    if n = 1 then [res ← 2 * ⌊r⌋ + 1; terminate];
    lattice(r, n − 1; res); i ← 1; t ← 0;
    while (i ≤ ⌊r⌋)
    begin /*process (n − 1)-dimensional sphere*/
        lattice((r ** 2 − i ** 2) ** .5, n − 1; t1);
        t ← t1 + t; i ← i + 1
    end; /*process*/
    res ← res + 2 * t1
end /*lattice*/
```

EXERCISE 11.5: Given an *n*-tuple *string* of symbols, write a recursive procedure which will reverse this string. For example, if string = (*r*, *a*, *t*), then the output should be (*t*, *a*, *r*). [Hint: Both techniques (i.e., balanced division, inverse induction) discussed previously will work.] Is this a reasonable way of reversing a string? Would an iterative algorithm be reasonable? What is one major disadvantage of the recursive formulation of this problem; wait until reading Section 11.2 before attempting to answer this last question.

11.1.5 The Tower of Hanoi

The next example has a rather interesting legend surrounding it; the puzzle itself has appeared from time to time in popular form. According to ancient manuscripts, a particular sect of monks in a remote corner of Tibet were set to solving this puzzle on the day of creation. When they finally achieve the solution, the world will end with a clap of thunder. Simply stated, the puzzle is this: Three diamond needles are arranged as shown in Figure 11.5, and the object is to move 64 golden disks from needle *A* to needle *C* subject to a set of rules. These rules are

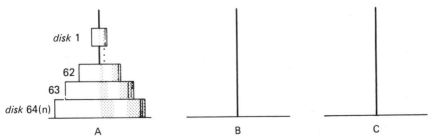

Fig. 11.5   Initial configuration of the Tower of Hanoi problem.

1. Initially, the 64 disks of descending size are located on needle *A*.
2. Any one top disk may be moved from its needle to any of the remaining two needles except that at no time may a larger disk rest on a smaller one.
3. All disks must eventually wind up on needle *C* in descending order, as shown in Figure 11.6.

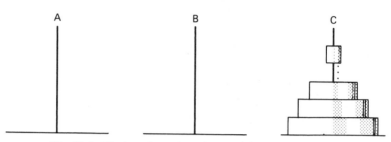

Fig. 11.6 Final configuration of the Tower of Hanoi problem.

To hasten the cataclysmic end, we shall provide the monks with a list of moves which specifies exactly how the disks are to be manipulated to obtain the objective. For example, if only two disks were to be moved ($n = 2$), then the list of moves would be

MOVE DISK 1 FROM A TO B

MOVE DISK 2 FROM A TO C

MOVE DISK 1 FROM B TO C

The parameters of the procedure *hanoi* are the number of disks involved, *n*, and some identification of the needles, say *from*, *to*, and *use*. In the case for $n = 2$, the top disk was moved from needle *A* to the *use* needle (*B*); then the *n*th disk was moved from needle *A* to *C*, followed by the move from *B* to *C*. If the term *top* in the last sentence is replaced by top $n - 1$, the recursive formulation practically falls into our hands, as indicated in Figure 11.7. Again, the termination criterion is the test for $n = 0$, in which case no move is made. The AL implementation of this solution follows.

Algorithm 11.4 (Tower of Hanoi)

Global data referenced: *moves*

```
procedure hanoi(from, to, use, n;)
begin /*tower of Hanoi*/
    if n = 0 then terminate;
    hanoi(from, use, to, n − 1;);
    moves ← moves + 'move disk' + n + 'from' + from + 'to' + to + ';';
    hanoi(use, to, from, n − 1;)
end /*tower*/
```

EXERCISE 11.6: Trace the execution of Algorithm 11.4 with the call *hanoi*('*A*', '*C*', '*B*', 3;)

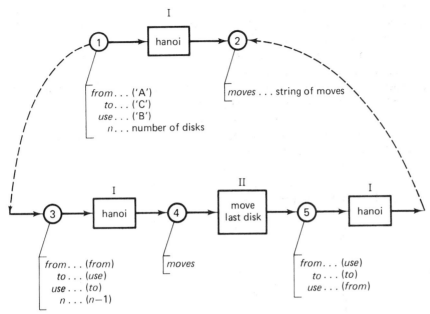

Fig. 11.7   Recursive formulation of the Tower of Hanoi problem.

Before leaving the example, an interesting question is, Exactly how much did we do to hasten the end of the world? Assuming that the initial number of disks is 64 and we have provided the monks with a list of moves, as stated earlier, how long would it take to solve the problem if a move could now be accomplished in 1 second? The total number of moves required is $2^{64} \simeq 10^{19}$ (see Section 11.3). Now, the number of seconds in a year is approximately 31.5×10^6, so the total number of years required is approximately 3×10^{11}. Even if a move could be made every microsecond ($= 10^{-6}$ second), it would still take approximately 3×10^5 years or about 300,000 years. What this all points out, of course, is that when you test Algorithm 11.4, n should be a great deal smaller than 64.

11.2 IMPLEMENTATION OF RECURSIVE PROCEDURES

The assumption made in the last section concerning the number of copies of a procedure which are available at any given time is clearly not a reasonable one (why?) from the point of view of a real implementation; it was made only for pedagogic reasons. For a realistic implementation, it must be assumed that only one copy of the procedure is in memory. The question to be addressed in this section is directed at the mechanism necessary to support recursion given this one copy. It will be instructive to understand exactly why the assumption of multiple copies was made; it effectively allowed us to ignore the interference between variable values when a procedure called itself. The only real difference between these copies lies in the different values for their arguments and their local variables; in addition, the extent of execution in each copy may vary, i.e., how far execution has proceeded in any given copy. In other words, the differences among copies lie in the dynamic aspects of the execution sequence utilizing the copy. It is possible to collect all the dynamic aspects of an instance of execution of a copy into a record, called the *activation record*, which is created whenever a procedure is called. All references to variables, etc., are made relative to this activation record; it is maintained as long as the procedure has not returned control to the calling procedure. Since SNOBOL supports only function-type procedures, we shall not consider subroutine-type procedures in the following discussion, although the mechanisms are virtually the same. A function-type procedure returns a value associated with the function name; hence, the function name will be treated as a local variable. A typical activation record structure is shown in Figure 11.8. In this structure, the current execution point is a pointer to the next instruction in the procedure body which is to be executed when control returns to the procedure.

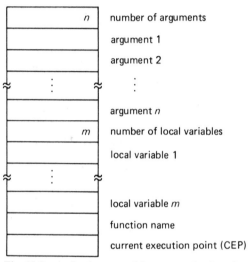

Fig. 11.8   Activation record for a recursive function.

It might appear that an additional item of information is required in the activation record: the location of the activation record of the procedure to which control is returned when the currently active procedure terminates. However, by tracing the utilization of the activation records during recursive calls, it will be seen that this information is not necessary. The first time a procedure is called, an activation record for this invocation is created. Assuming the procedure calls itself recursively, when the second call is encountered the current activation record is saved and a new one created, corresponding to the second invocation. The saved record will only be used again when the called procedure returns. Thus, the first record to be saved is the last one to be reused. In general, the sequence of saving and restoring activation records during recursive calls is the same as the dynamic control aspects of the program in which they are embedded. That is, the activation record saved just prior to the creation of the current activation record is the one which will be used when the current invocation of the procedure terminates. Hence, the data structure most suitable for the activation record operations just described is the last-in–first-out (or LIFO) queue, often referred to as a push-down stack. Activation records are saved by placing them on top of the stack, pushing other entries down. Records are restored from the top of the stack, popping up other entries. One physical data structure representation of such a stack is an array of consecutive storage locations with one end open, as illustrated in Figure ·11.9.

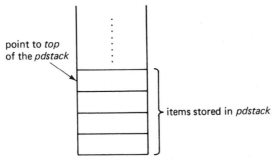

point to *top*
of the *pdstack*

items stored in *pdstack*

Fig. 11.9   Example of a push-down stack.

Access to the top element of the stack is through the stack pointer (*top*), e.g., *pdstack(top)*, where *pdstack* is the name of the array and the value of *top* is the index of the last element stacked. Figures 11.10 and 11.11 illustrate stacking and unstacking operations, giving the status of the stack before and after the operations and the corresponding code for performing them.

Therefore, it is not necessary to maintain any pointer to the calling procedure in the activation record; it is implicit in the order of the records on the stack. Whenever a potentially recursive function is called, the activation record to be saved is stacked; if this invocation of the function causes another call to itself, the current activation record is stacked on top of the old one. Whenever a return is encountered, the activa-

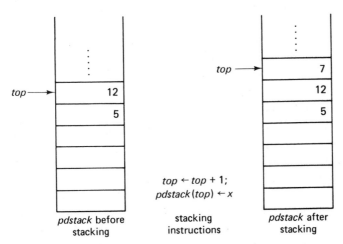

top ──▶ 12

5

top ──▶ 7

12

5

top ← *top* + 1;
pdstack (*top*) ← *x*

pdstack before
stacking

stacking
instructions

pdstack after
stacking

Fig. 11.10   Stacking the values of the variable *x*.

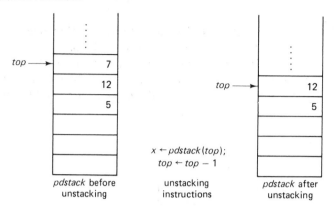

Fig. 11.11   Unstacking the value of the variable *x*.

tion record on top of the stack is popped up, leaving the previous one on the stack. There is no need for a more complex structure.

To illustrate how a real programming language supports recursion, we shall recapitulate the way SNOBOL implements function calls:

1. Within the calling function (the main program is considered to be a function having neither arguments nor local variables)
   (a) The current value of the function [i.e., the value of the function name variable (FN)] is copied into the activation record.
   (b) The current values of the formal arguments are copied into the activation record.
   (c) The current values of all local variables are copied into the activation record.
   (d) Set the current environment pointer (CEP) in activation record to the next instruction to be executed.
   (e) The activation record is stacked.
2. Upon entering the called function (which might be the same as the calling function)
   (a) Assign NULL to FN.
   (b) Assign NULL to all local variables.
   (c) Assign values of actual arguments to formal arguments.

When execution of the function is terminated by a transfer to RETURN or FRETURN the following actions are performed:

3. The function value returned is the current value of the variable FN.
4. Within the function to which we return
   (a) Unstack activation record.
   (b) Restore CEP from activation record.
   (c) Restore values of local variables from activation record.
   (d) Restore values of formal arguments from activation record.
   (e) Restore value of the function from activation record.

Action 2 implies that in SNOBOL the correspondence between formal and actual parameters is by *call by value*. That is, values may be returned from a function only through the function name and the effect of the function on global variables; it is impossible to effect any changes in the calling procedure through the arguments.

EXERCISE 11.7: Compare the correspondence between formal and actual parameters in SNOBOL and FORTRAN. How can call by value be obtained in FORTRAN?

Example 11.1 traces the internal configuration of the push-down stack for Algorithm 11.3; the SNOBOL program for this problem is given below. Remember that in SNOBOL, functions are defined by executing the DEFINE function and that the code for functions may be intermingled with the code representing the main program. However, the code representing the function should not be executed by flowing into it.

Purpose: Compute the number of lattice points in an *n*-dimensional sphere of radius $r > 1$.
Communication:

global variables referenced: None.
functions called: LATTICE ... returns number of lattice points in sphere
                                                  of radius R, 1st argument, and dimension
                                                  N, 2nd argument; recursive; local vari-
                                                  able—I; entry point—LAT.

Program:

```
        DEFINE('LATTICE(R,N)I','LAT')                                    1
        &TRIM = 1 ;   R = INPUT ;   N = INPUT      :F(END)               2
        OUTPUT = 'THE NUMBER OF LATTICE POINTS IN THE '                  5
        OUTPUT = N ' DIMENSIONAL SPHERE OF RADIUS ' R ' EQUALS '         6
        LATTICE(R,N)                              :(END)                 6
:::::::::::::::::::BEGIN FUNCTION LATTICE::::::::::::::::::::::::::::::::::::::::::::::::
LAT     GT(N,1)                                   :S(RECURSE)            7
        LATTICE = 2 :: CONVERT(R, 'INTEGER') + 1  :(RETURN)             8
::::::::::::::::RECURSIVELY COMPUTE SUB-SPHERES AROUND (0,0,...,1):::::::::::::::::::::::
RECURSE     I = 1                                                        9
ITERATE     GT(I,R)                               :S(DOUBLE)            10
        LATTICE = LATTICE + LATTICE((R :::: 2 - I :::: 2) :::: 0.5, N - 1)  11
        I = I + 1                                 :(ITERATE)            12
DOUBLE     LATTICE = 2 :: LATTICE                                       13
::::::::::::::ADD CENTER SUB-SPHERE::::::::::::::::::::::::::::::::::::::::::::::::::::::
        LATTICE = LATTICE + LATTICE(R,N - 1)      :(RETURN)            14
::::::::::::::END OF LATTICE::::::::::::::::::::::::::::::::::::::::::::::::::::::::::::::
::::::::::::::END OF PROGRAM:::::::::::::::::::::::::::::::::::::::::::::::::::::::::::::::
END                                                                    15
```

Example 11.1 Trace of Function LATTICE

From the discussion preceding the program, and the form of the DEFINE function for LATTICE, it is possible to deduce the form of the activation record in this particular case. For convenience, it is presented as a node, where the fields correspond to the structure developed in Figure 11.8. This structure is shown in Figure 11.12,

#ARGS   R   N   #LOCAL   I   LATTICE   CEP

Fig. 11.12   Structure of the activation record for the function LATTICE.

where CEP refers to the current execution point of the program. The CEP is expressed not in terms of the SNOBOL source program but rather in terms of position within the intermediate code generated by the SNOBOL interpreter. Therefore, it is necessary to construct the intermediate text for LATTICE; in the interests of clarity, the triples† corresponding to the transmission of argument values have been elided. Note that this intermediate text is only for LATTICE and does not include the driving program. In Figure 11.13, values in parentheses refer to the result of the indicated triple.

1	>,N,1	8 >,I,R	15 go,8
2	true,(1),7	9 true,(8),16	16 *,2,LATTICE
3	*,2,⌊R⌋	10 call ($\sqrt{r^2 - i^2}, n - 1$)	17 =,LATTICE,(16)
4	+,(3),1	11 +,LATTICE,(10)	18 call($r,n - 1$)
5	=,LATTICE,(4)	12 =,LATTICE,(11)	19 +,LATTICE,(18)
6	RETURN,	13 +,I,1	20 =,LATTICE,(19)
7	=,I,1	14 =,I,(13)	21 RETURN,

Fig. 11.13   Intermediate text for the function LATTICE.

Assuming input values of R=1.5 and N=3, the function LATTICE is called from the main program; the activation record for the main program is ignored for clarity. In LATTICE, execution begins at triple 1, resulting in the execution of triples 1, 2, 7, 8, and 9. At this point, the call in triple 10 is executed, and the current activation record must be stacked:

pdstack:

top = 1 | 2 | 1.5 | 3 | 1 | 1 | ‘ ’ | 10 |

Execution then proceeds from triple 1, except that LATTICE and I have been assigned the null string and R=1.12 and N=2. Again, triples 1, 2, 7, 8, and 9 are executed, and the recursive call in triple 10 is encountered; the stack is now pushed again, resulting in the configuration shown below. The values of the actual arguments are ≈ .5 for R and 1 for N.

pdstack:

top = 2 | 2 | 1.12 | 2 | 1 | 1 | ‘ ’ | 10 |
1 | 2 | 1.5 | 3 | 1 | 1 | ‘ ’ | 10 |

This time, triples 1, 2, 3, 4, and 5 are executed; triple 5 assigns to LATTICE the value 1 (=2 * ⌊0.5⌋ + 1). Triple 6 is now executed, returning the value 1 just computed as the value of the function; however, the return involves popping (unstacking) the top

†Triples are similar to quadruples as used in the compiler of Chapter 8. They do not have a result field; references to results previously computed are accomplished by using the index of the triple which produced this result.

element of the push-down stack and restoring the values of the variables found there, in this case I, R, N, LATTICE, and CEP. CEP is incremented by 1, and execution proceeds with the triples 11, 12, 13, 14, 15, 8, 9, 16, 17, and 18, which involves another call to LATTICE. The values of the actual arguments are 1.12 and 1, respectively. This gives rise to the following stack configuration:

pdstack:

top = 2	2	1.12	2	1	2	2	18
1	2	1.5	3	1	1	' '	10

EXERCISE 11.8: Assuming a stack configuration as shown above, CEP = 1, and that the values of R and N are 1.12 and 1, respectively, continue the trace of LATTICE in the style illustrated. Check your answer by drawing the sphere and counting the lattice points.

11.3 ON THE COMPLEXITY OF RECURSIVE ALGORITHMS

As can be seen from the exercises at the end of the chapter, many of the sorting algorithms discussed in Chapter 5 and many of the list and tree manipulation algorithms from Chapter 9 can be expressed quite elegantly and concisely as recursive procedures. However, the price paid for this elegance is the system overhead necessary to support recursion; this is the major reason recursive techniques are not widely used in production programs. Two related factors contribute to the overhead:

1. Since the implementation is standardized, all parameters pertaining to the dynamic aspects of a program have to be copied into the activation record, even though not all of them are always necessary in any given program. Thus, the time complexity is increased.
2. The parameters which must be copied require storage on the activation record stack, in addition to the system information required to support the recursion. Hence, the space complexity is increased.

Finally, one must consider the overhead involved in implementing the procedure call itself. For instance, it would be quite inefficient to write the selection sort as the following recursive procedure,

```
procedure select_sort(n;)
begin /*select*/
    if n = 1 then terminate;
    select(n; j);
    exchange(j, n);
    select_sort(n − 1;)
end /*select*/
```

since it is quite simple in this case to replace the recursive call in the last statement by an iteration over the two preceding it. In general, whenever a recursive call is the last statement in the procedure, the procedure can be simply written using iteration in place of recursion.

It is possible to partially eliminate the first two inefficiencies introduced by the system by writing algorithms which *simulate* recursion and which keep an explicit push-down stack to save only the necessary parameters. This is essentially what was done in the algorithm for quicksort developed in Chapter 5. Close inspection of the algorithm now will reveal the simulated recursion and the way in which it was embedded in the algorithm. However, one should not try to force a recursive solution to a problem when the natural solution is iterative in nature. The multiplication of two matrices, for example, is basically an iterative process; the data structures themselves are iterative in nature, and one would clearly like to match the features of the structure to the features of the solution. On the other hand, as pointed out in Section 11.1, some structures are essentially recursive, and it shows in the definition of the structures: trees, for example. In this case, the recursive algorithm matches very closely the essential structure of the data, and one would expect very elegant and concise algorithms for manipulating the structure. In the latter case, the recursive formulation is natural and is usually the one thought of first, at least by experienced programmers. After the recursive formulation is obtained, and is understood as a solution, then one can attempt to improve the efficiency by converting it into an iterative algorithm. In many cases, trying to force a recursive algorithm into an iterative mold is just as unnatural as forcing in the other direction, and the resultant procedure is often obscure.

To analyze the complexity of recursive procedures, two constants (c_1 and c_2) are introduced into the order analysis. The first will measure the amount of work pertaining to the procedure call and associated action. The second measures the amount of storage for one activation record. As an example, consider the analysis for the (slightly modified) SNOBOL implementation of the solution to the Tower of Hanoi problem discussed earlier:

```
       DEFINE('HANOI(FROM,TO,USE,N)')                                             1
                                                            :(END)                 2
::::::::::::::::::::::::::::::BEGIN HANOI::::::::::::::::::::::::::::::::::::::::::::::::
HANOI     EQ(N,0)                                           :S(RETURN)             3
          HANOI(FROM,USE,TO,N - 1)                                                 4
          OUTPUT = 'MOVE DISK ' N ' FROM ' FROM ' TO ' TO                          5
          HANOI(USE,TO,FROM,N - 1)                          :(RETURN)              6
::::::::::::::::::::::::::::END HANOI::::::::::::::::::::::::::::::::::::::::::::::::::::
::::::::::::::::::::::::::::END PROGRAM::::::::::::::::::::::::::::::::::::::::::::::::::
END                                                                                7
```

The complexity of the program is clearly

$$c(n) = c(n - 1) + c(n - 1) + d$$

(which reflects the recursive structure), where d includes both c_1 and the cost of executing the dominant instruction, here EQ(N,0). This yields

$$c(n) = 2^{n+1}c(0) + \sum_{i=0}^{n} 2^i d$$

From this we can conclude that the complexity of the program is

$$c(n) = O(2^n)$$

which excludes storage requirements. To determine the storage requirement, it is necessary to compute the number of activation records which can be on the stack at any one time. The procedure HANOI will call itself recursively n times (at the second statement) before EQ fails for the first time. Hence, at least n activation records will be on the push-down stack. At no time will there be more activation records on the stack because the second recursive call in the procedure (from the fourth statement) is executed only after control has returned from the first, which implies that the activation records from the first recursion have been removed before the second recursion begins. Therefore, the total amount of storage required is $c_1 * n$, and the storage complexity is of $O(n)$.

11.4 CONCLUSIONS

The concept of recursion has been introduced relatively late in this book for several reasons. It requires a certain degree of maturity and experience in problem-solving and programming to formulate a recursive solution. Most people are able to comprehend an iterative solution to a problem because it parallels the "natural" way of thinking, which apparently is a sequence of discrete steps. Given an equivalent recursive formulation of the solution, the same people may have great difficulties in convincing themselves that it is equivalent, to say nothing of creating the recursive solution. Although the class of problems amenable to "natural" recursive solutions is limited mainly to those involving operations on inherently recursive data structures such as trees and lists, recursion remains a powerful computational technique.

References

For practical details concerning recursion in SNOBOL, an excellent introduction to the language, and a book to which we are indebted for many of the examples used here, see

R. E. GRISWOLD, J. F. POAGE, and I. P. POLONSKY, *The SNOBOL4 Programming Language*, Prentice-Hall, Englewood Cliffs, N.J., 1971.

Implementation details of SNOBOL in general and recursion in particular may be found in

R. E. GRISWOLD, *The Macro Implementation of SNOBOL4: A Case Study of Machine Independent Software Development*, W. H. Freeman, San Francisco, 1972.

Additional examples of the use of the recursive capabilities of SNOBOL, in addition to valuable ideas on programming in the language, may be found in

R. E. GRISWOLD, *String and List Processing in SNOBOL4: Techniques and Applications*, Prentice-Hall, Englewood Cliffs, N.J., 1975.

The general concept of recursion and its various applications are discussed in

D. E. KNUTH, *The Art of Computer Programming*, Vol. 1: Fundamental Algorithms, Addison-Wesley, Reading, Mass., 1969.

Exercises

1 Given an unsorted n-tuple x, write a recursive procedure to generate a tree which has the following property:

> Given a node N, the values of all nodes in the left (right) subtree are smaller (greater) than the value of the root node (N). Furthermore, all subtrees share this property.

Note that this is the property introduced in Exercise 11.4. What is the complexity (worst-case and best-case order analysis) of the sorting procedure resulting from combining the two algorithms? How does this compare with the optimal algorithms developed in Chapter 5?

2 Write a recursive procedure which will reverse a binary tree. That is, all left nodes become right nodes and vice versa. Implement your solution in SNOBOL and FORTRAN. Which is conceptually simpler? Easier to program? More efficient? What can you conclude?

3 For those sorting algorithms in Chapter 5 which can be formulated more clearly and concisely as a recursive algorithm, give the algorithm. For those which cannot, describe the mismatch in data structure and algorithm which precludes the recursive formulation.

4 The traveling salesman problem is one of those problems for which the complexity of the optimal algorithm is unknown. Simply stated, the problem is this:

> Given n cities and their locations on a map, find a path which, beginning at a designated city, will visit every other city exactly once, returning to the initial city. Furthermore, this path must be of minimal length.

One approach is to generate permutations of the integers $1, 2, \ldots, n$, representing the visiting order of the cities, until a "reasonable" path has been found. For this exercise, write a recursive procedure to generate all permutations of n integers. Before actually running your program, do some preliminary calculations on how many permutations of n integers there are, the maximum recursion level required, and an estimate of the time required to find all permutations. Is this a reasonable approach to a solution for this problem?

5 Given a binary tree, implement a recursive procedure to obtain a copy of the tree.

6 Given a binary tree, define the *depth* of a node as the number of ancestors of the node. Thus, the depth of the root node is 0, the depth of the immediate descendants of the root node is 1, etc. Write an algorithm to traverse this tree such that all nodes at depth k are visited before any node at depth $k + 1$, for $k = 0, \ldots, M$, where M is the maximum depth of the tree. (Hint: Not all tree traversals are naturally recursive.)

7 Simulate the activation record push-down stack for the SNOBOL implementation of the algorithm of Exercise 1 for the input (12, 5, 20, 3, 7, 23), using the general scheme followed in Example 11.1 and continued in Exercise 11.8.

8 In Chapter 8, we discussed the problem of symbol table maintenance, including the operations normally performed on symbol tables. Usually, when a program is executed, a listing of the symbol table is provided for debugging purposes, including pertinent information on each variable (e.g., a cross reference to the source code where the variable appeared, address of the variable, etc.). This output is usually alphabetized on the symbol name. Develop a set of recursive procedures for symbol table maintenance, including an alphabetized dump of the table. (Hint: See Exercise 1.)

9 Representing a symbol table as a binary tree carries with it the search advantages of a binary search but also poses a problem. The table maintenance routines utilizing a binary search in a tree are most efficient if the tree is *balanced*, that is, if the number of nodes in the left subtree of a given node is the same (± 1) as the number of nodes in the right subtree of the node. Furthermore, this condition should hold for all subtrees. However, whether or not this condition holds depends completely on the order in which the variables are encountered in the program. For example, consider a program which contains the variable names LATTICE, S, N, I, AREA, CIRCUM, ROOT, X, and J. If these variables are encountered in alphabetic order, the tree becomes

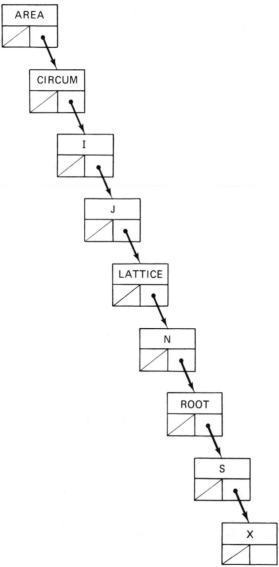

and the search is no better than linear. On the other hand, the balanced tree form would be

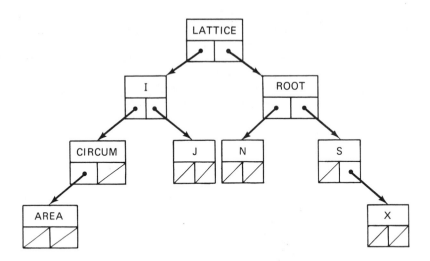

and search is maximally efficient. Develop an algorithm which will take an arbitrary binary tree as its argument and will produce a balanced copy of this tree. What is the complexity of the resulting search algorithm? Is the inclusion of such a balancing procedure in a general sorting algorithm a sensible idea? Can the idea of balancing be included in the routine which creates the tree in the first place? How?

10 Write a recursive procedure which will accept two binary trees as input and will return a value **true** if the structure of the trees is identical and a value **false** if not. To be structurally identical, the two trees, if superimposed, must match, node for node and pointer for pointer.

11 Develop a recursive formulation for the integer multiplication algorithm developed in Chapter 4.

12 Write a recursive procedure for reversing the order of the nodes in a singly linked list and compare it with its iterative counterpart. What are the advantages and disadvantages of the recursive formulation versus the iterative one?

13 *Generalized list structures:* In Chapter 9, the concept of a singly linked list was developed as a relatively efficient way of storing information that was to be accessed in odd ways. This concept becomes more general if we allow the data field of the node in a list to contain either a data element or a list pointer. Thus, the value of any given node may be another list. For example, the expression A*B, in forward Polish notation, may be represented in a list as

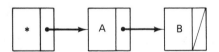

while the expression A∗(B + C) may be represented as

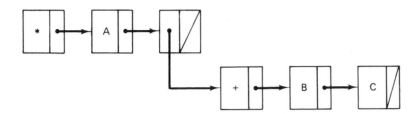

The second list may be formed from the first by replacing the node containing B with another list: the representation of B+C. The expression A∗((C+D)−E) becomes

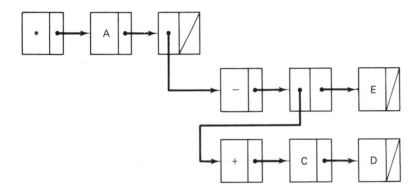

and so on. The only modification to the storage scheme discussed in Chapter 9 is the inclusion of a flag in the node indicating whether the data field contains data or a pointer; thus, the node structure might be

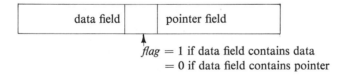

$flag = 1$ if data field contains data
$= 0$ if data field contains pointer

A very powerful language known as LISP† has been built around this generalized list structure. Objects which appear in the data field that are not pointers are known as *atoms*. These are the primitive, *atomic* symbols out of which all lists are built. We can immediately list several operations on these types of lists, in terms of their functional representation:

atom(x): This function returns the value **true** if x is an atom and **false** if not.
head(x): Returns as its value the first part of the argument, i.e., the head of the list x.
tail(x): Returns as its value the second part of the argument, i.e., the tail of the list x.

---

†A good introduction to the LISP language with numerous examples of its utility may be found in Clark Weissman, *LISP 1.5 Primer*, Dickinson Publishing Company, Inc., Encino, Calif., 1967.

To illustrate these two operations on list, assume the list L has the following form:

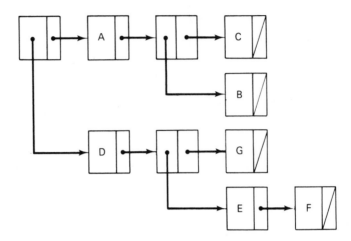

Then **head**(L) is the list

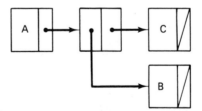

and **tail**(L) is the list

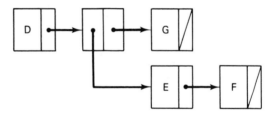

Thus, **head** and **tail** are used to dissect lists into their constituent parts. Both operations are undefined on atoms; the **tail** of a list of one element is defined to be **null**. These operations may be compounded; i.e., **head(tail(head(L)))** is the list

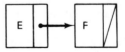

cons(x,y):   Used to construct lists. If x is an atom or a list and y is a list, then **cons**(x,y) is a new list, say L, so that **head**(L) = x and **tail**(L) = y. A list of one element is formed from an atom by setting the second argument of **cons** to 0.

Using these few primitive operations, it is possible to write very powerful list manipulation programs. For example, to create a copy of any given list, no matter what its structure, we write

```
procedure copy(x;)
begin /*copy list*/
    if atom(x) then copy ⟵ x
                  else copy ⟵ cons (copy(head(x)), copy (tail(x)))
end /*copy*/
```

Implement a general list-handling system based on the structures and primitives discussed above; make any assumptions you need concerning limitations on the atoms, and define a slightly extended set of primitive functions which will allow you to write the solutions to Exercises 1–12 of this chapter in your system. (Hint: This is clearly not a simple project.)

12

Artificial Intelligence

12.0 INTRODUCTION

After spending 11 chapters investigating the structure of computers, the techniques of programming, and many well-defined problem and application areas, we turn our attention in this, the final chapter, to a much more elusive, emotionally charged subject, which is rooted in controversies revolving around the question, What are the inherent limitations of the computer? In almost any discussion concerning the capabilities of computers, the question invariably arises as to whether a properly programmed machine is capable of acting in an *intelligent* way. Or, to put it another way, "Can a machine think?" Questions such as these are fraught with difficulties which stem partially from a lack of suitable operational definitions of "intelligence" and "thought," among others. Similar questions, although stated in different terms, predate the advent of modern computers and have occupied psychologists for hundreds of years and philosophers for much longer. It would be presumptuous to attempt any protracted discussion on this particular question, and we shall have to be content with a few comments on the nature of the area in computer science known as *artificial intelligence.*

What is Artificial Intelligence?

In light of the definitional problems mentioned above, it is not surprising that there is little agreement on the question posed. If one were to ask n people associated with the field "What is artificial intelligence?" one would likely get n different answers, although all would most likely agree that there is such a field. Furthermore, most would agree that it is, in some way, concerned with endowing the computer with behavior which would be called "intelligent" were it observed in human activities. Perhaps the best definition would be that artificial intelligence is what people in the area do, that it is a collection of knowledge and investigations designed to increase that knowledge, all of which is held together by a set of unifying principles that are difficult to pinpoint precisely. The question is, then, What is it that workers in artificial intelligence do? Let us briefly examine some representative problem areas and consider some of the issues addressed in these areas. The reader should be forewarned, however, that the domains are not independent in any sense and that similar questions are addressed in many of them.

12.1 ASPECTS OF ARTIFICIAL INTELLIGENCE

Pattern Recognition

Historically, one of the earliest areas to receive attention was the general problem of automatically recognizing *patterns* of information, typically the patterns of individual handprinted or typewritten characters as they appear on a page. The motivation for this investigation is clear; given the time consumed in transforming data to machine-readable form, a system which could scan a page of a document and recognize the individual characters would be a facility worth pursuing and of great economic importance. One could then conceive of a system, for example, that automatically reads and sorts the voluminous amount of mail handled by the postal system each day. Coupled with a voice synthesizer, one would obtain a reading machine for the blind, and so on. Thus, the problem was (and still is) as follows: Given an unknown (to the machine) character, such as the one shown in Figure 12.1a, determine to which of the 26 classes A through Z (restricting ourselves for the moment to alphabetic characters) the character belongs. Once this is done, the character has been recognized, and the result can be used internally within the machine.

The first problem is how the information about the character's structure may be obtained in machine-digestible form. Actually, this is quite easy to do using special equipment; the general approach is something like that shown in Figure 12.1b–d. If a grid (here 15×10) is laid over the character, as shown in Figure 12.1b, and those squares which contain a portion of the character (let's say those which are at least $\frac{1}{3}$ filled) are darkened completely (as in Figure 12.1c), then it is possible to code the information in a matrix of 0's and 1's, as shown in Figure 12.1d. The actual mechanism by which this is accomplished varies, but a common one is to scan the page with a very small dot of light (about the size of one of the grid squares) and measure the amount of light reflected from the page at various points (the grid squares). If the measurement is less than some threshold, then a 1 is output; otherwise, a 0 is output. The end result is the matrix shown in Figure 12.1d for a single character; typically, entire lines and/or pages are obtained as very large matrices. Note that this does not represent the solution to the recognition problem since we still have no idea what the character is. It remains to analyze the resultant data in order to classify them.

The pattern recognition literature abounds with a variety of techniques for classification; let us sketch how one of them might proceed. Usually, the first step consists of the extraction of a set of *features* from the data matrix. The basic idea is to define this set of features so that the values obtained for characters which we call A's (for

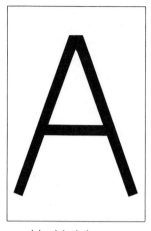

(a) original character

(b) character superimposed
on a grid

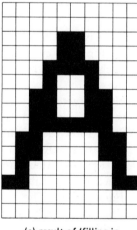

(c) result of 'filling in
the squares'

```
0000000000
0000000000
0000110000
0000110000
0001111000
0001001000
0011001100
0011001100
0011111100
0110000110
0110000110
0100000010
1100000011
0000000000
0000000000
```

(d) completely digitized
character: the resultant
data matrix

Fig. 12.1   Transformation of printed character to machine form.

example) are different from the remaining letters. Using this information, a decision
can be made, perhaps using statistical methods, as to the identity of the character; i.e.,
it can be classified. The selection of a set of features to be used is an important part of
the recognition problem, one for which no general techniques are known; features are
typically chosen on an ad hoc basis. For the character recognition problem, features
such as the number of straight lines, number of enclosed areas, number of downward
(left, right, upward) concavities, number of acute (obtuse, right) angles, number of
end points of lines, and so on are often used.

EXERCISE 12.1: Can you describe a feature set which adequately characterizes each alphabetic character? Assume perfectly printed characters with no gaps, smudges, etc.

EXERCISE 12.2: Write an AL algorithm which when given a data matrix such as the one shown in Figure 12.1d will return a second matrix in which only the areas totally enclosed by the character are marked (e.g., a matrix the same size as the original filled with 0's except for those points which are enclosed by the figure; these should contain a 1). Make the algorithm independent of the size of the data matrix, since typically greater resolution is employed; in the example, only 150 points (15 × 10) were used.

Character recognition systems vary considerably in their ability to recognize characters, ranging from relatively low recognition rates for sloppily written characters on dirty pages to fairly high rates ($> 90\%$) for typed characters on clean pages. On the other hand, people read very sloppily written pages quite easily; we do, of course, make use of additional knowledge beyond the identity of individual characters. This knowledge is the context in which the characters appear as well as wider knowledge derived from a comprehension of the message. In addition, constraints are imposed on these contexts by the language in which the source is written. For example, the character

A

is ambiguous in isolation. However, given the proper context we have no problem at all:

TAE CAT

Those character recognition systems which have incorporated contextual constraints into the recognition process have shown marked improvement over similar systems which do not. This observation has arisen time and again in artificial intelligence. Those structures which are ambiguous in isolation are very often resolvable when knowledge of the constraints imposed by the physical world are incorporated into the system.

The domain of pattern recognition embraces not only the recognition of characters on the printed page but has expanded to include analyses of the patterns found in biomedical images (chromosomes, cellular structures, chest x-rays, and the like), patterns in radar and sonar data, as well as those found in weather data, particle physics images obtained from bubble and spark chambers, etc. Many of these applications have commercial importance, and many others show promise. A particularly interesting example is the analysis of data obtained from the ERTS (Earth Resources Technology Satellite) project; some typical results are shown in Figure 12.2.

An extension of the investigations from pattern recognition into very complex pictorial domains, verging on the development of comprehensive perceptual systems,

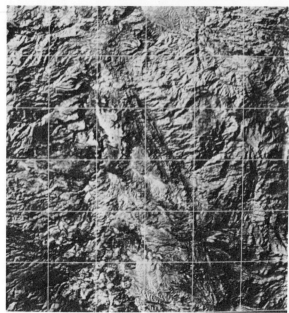

Figure 12.2 An example of computer processed satellite data. (a) is a 768 by 768 point gray level image of an area of Arizona. This figure contains a number of long parallel structures, called lineaments, which are of interest to geologists. These structures are often not recognizable from the ground and can indicate the presence of mineral deposits, fault lines, and the like. They can provide valuable information related to the building of mountain ranges and continental motion. (b) shows possible lineaments detected by computer analysis of (a); the information thus obtained would be interpreted by trained geologists. Proper use of a combination of computer analysis and people trained in a given discipline (e.g. geology) can add much to the understanding of our world.

Reprinted from IEEE Transactions on Computers with permission of the Institute of Electrical and Electronics Engineers. Photos courtesy of Dr. Roger Ehrich.

is now termed *scene analysis*. This line of investigation combines techniques from pattern recognition and artificial intelligence. The general idea is to analyze a scene into its components through the construction of an internal *model* of the world as it appears in the scene. The process should result in the identification of major objects in the scene, the relationships which exist between them, and characteristics of the three-dimensional world evident in the image. The task has proven to be extremely difficult, and many of the investigations have restricted the visual domain to simple scenes, such as those which can be constructed from children's blocks on a flat surface or images derived from cartoon characterizations. Several recent efforts have attempted to analyze "real" scenes, in color, obtained from our everyday surroundings (e.g., outdoor scenes). The problems encountered are formidable, for obvious reasons.

Natural Language Processing

Natural languages are those languages with which people communicate; they are different in both form and substance from artificial programming languages. As we have seen in previous chapters, the computer is reasonably adept at translating from one highly artificial language to another via a compiler or assembler. We have also seen the steps which must precede the actual writing of a program in any language. Generally, the steps are designed to remove the ambiguity in the informally stated problem and include the choice of data representation and a specification of the "organization" of the processing steps, among others.

Early interest in natural language processing arose from two rather diverse applications. One was a desire to construct programs which were, in essence, natural language compilers, i.e., programs which would accept a problem statement in a natural language (e.g., English) and produce as output a program in some artificial language (e.g., FORTRAN) which solves the problem. Such efforts are far from fruition since they require an understanding of both natural language and problem-solving capabilities. The second area of interest was the automatic translation from one natural language to another, for example, from English to French. Again, the commercial applications are obvious. It soon became apparent, after several completely unsuccessful efforts, that there was a host of common problems underlying both areas of investigation.

The first approaches to machine translation were, in retrospect, rather naive, for example, a one-for-one substitution of words from the source language statement to the target language by means of a dictionary lookup. This produces translation of the quality obtained by a neophyte translator with little knowledge of the target language, using a pocket dictionary of the type found on bookstands. Slightly more sophisticated approaches utilized a syntactic analysis of source language statements, which resulted in a parsed sentence (see Part C Section 9 of the supplementary volume). The parsed sentence is translated to the target language using equivalent syntactic rules in the target language, followed by a dictionary lookup of the words. Again, the quality of the resulting translation is far from useful (why?). While the latter approach may preserve the syntactic structure, it completely ignores the meaning of the sentence, or the *semantics*. Perhaps the most useful result from these attempts was that they highlighted the lack of understanding of linguistic structures and an equivalent lack of understanding of computer structures.

The emphasis of investigations into natural language processing shifted to studies in natural language *understanding* by computers. The general idea was to restrict the domain of discourse to one which was reasonably well understood (e.g., algebra word problems stated in English) and to restrict the complexity of the input sentences so that it was not necessary to construct a grammar of the entire language (which still has not been accomplished). These restrictions would then allow investigations to proceed, focusing on the important questions of semantics, disambiguation, the use of large complex structures, and the development of adequate formal internal representations.

One example of a natural language understanding system was the STUDENT program, written by Daniel Bobrow at the Massachusetts Institute of Technology. The program accepts as input a restricted subset of English which is used to express algebra word problems. Note that the input to the program was known to be derived from a particular problem domain. The following problem statement is typical of the type accepted by the program:

> THE SUM OF TWO NUMBERS IS 111. ONE OF THE NUMBERS IS CONSECUTIVE TO THE OTHER NUMBER. FIND THE TWO NUMBERS.

Furthermore, the problem statement contains all the necessary information for its solution, so the amount of deduction required is minimal. STUDENT utilized only a limited amount of world knowledge, such as the fact that 1 foot is 12 inches, and the like. It attempted to relate phrases in the problem statement to the operations which had to be performed in order to solve the problem. Thus, in this example problem, STUDENT might rewrite the problem as (paraphrasing the internal structure of the problem as represented within the program)

$$X = \text{one of the numbers}$$
$$Y = \text{other number}$$
$$Y = X + 1 \qquad \text{(i.e., the two numbers are consecutive)}$$
$$\text{sum of two numbers} = 111$$

so that the equations to be solved are

$$X + Y = 111$$
$$Y = X + 1$$

The solution is then $Y = 55$ and $X = 56$. STUDENT would accept (and solve) quite complex algebra word problems, such as

> BILL'S FATHER'S UNCLE IS TWICE AS OLD AS BILL'S FATHER. 2 YEARS FROM NOW BILL'S FATHER WILL BE 3 TIMES AS OLD AS BILL. THE SUM OF THEIR AGES IS 92. FIND BILL'S AGE.

Similar systems were developed for a variety of restricted domains including baseball data, calculus problems, airline scheduling data, geographical data, chemical data, and so on. Although these systems were the beginning of investigations into problems concerning the representation of knowledge within a program, how that knowledge might be used, and how linguistic constructs might be processed, they were, in most cases, so highly specialized that it was difficult to transfer what was learned in one domain into another. Worse yet, it was unclear whether any general principles were being formulated. They did, however, serve to lay the groundwork for more sophisticated efforts.

The next example is a recent one; the program was written by Terry Winograd at M.I.T. The intention was to demonstrate the feasibility of building a program which has a comparatively unrestricted subset of English in which to phrase the input. The domain of discourse is still restricted, in this case to a robot arm which can move simple objects (e.g., blocks) on a flat surface. The arm and its environment are simulated within the program and displayed on a graphics terminal. The system's performance is impressive; Figures 12.3 and 12.4 illustrate the initial and final state of the system as a result of the following dialogue. Statements in small letters are the input, and statements in capital letters are the system's response.

pick up a big red block.
=====OK.
grasp the pyramid.
=====I DON'T UNDERSTAND WHICH PYRAMID YOU MEAN.
find a block which is taller than the one you are holding and put it into the box.
=====BY "IT", I ASSUME YOU MEAN THE BLOCK WHICH IS TALLER
      THAN THE ONE I AM HOLDING.
=====OK.
what does the box contain?
=====THE BLUE PYRAMID AND THE BLUE BLOCK.
will you please stack up both of the red blocks and either a green cube or a pyramid?
=====OK.
is there a large block behind a pyramid?
=====YES, THREE OF THEM: A LARGE RED ONE, A LARGE GREEN
      CUBE, AND THE BLUE ONE.
put a small one onto the green cube which supports a pyramid.
=====OK.
put the littlest pyramid on top of it.
=====OK.
had you touched any pyramid before you put the green on the little cube?
=====YES, THE GREEN ONE.
when did you pick it up?
=====WHILE I WAS STACKING UP THE RED CUBE, A LARGE RED
      BLOCK, AND A LARGE GREEN CUBE.

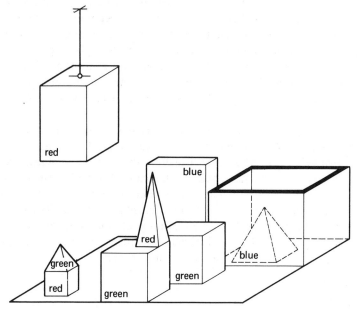

Fig. 12.3 Initial state of Winograd's system prior to dialogue.

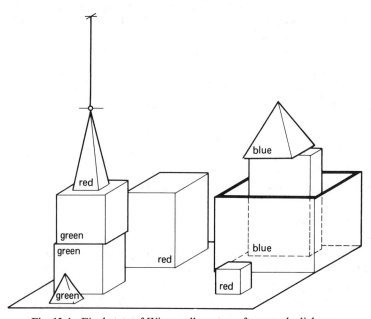

Fig. 12.4 Final state of Winograd's system after sample dialogue.

why?
=====TO GET RID OF IT.
why did you do that?
=====TO CLEAR OFF THE RED CUBE.
why did you clear off that cube?
=====TO PUT ON A LARGE GREEN CUBE.
why did you do that?
=====TO STACK UP THE RED CUBE, A LARGE RED BLOCK, AND A
       LARGE GREEN CUBE.
why did you do that?
=====BECAUSE YOU ASKED ME TO.
does a steeple
SORRY, I DON'T KNOW THE WORD "STEEPLE".
a "steeple" is a stack which contains two green cubes and a pyramid.
=====I UNDERSTAND.
are there any steeples now?
=====NO.
build one.
=====OK.
thank you.
=====YOU'RE WELCOME.

Winograd's system is novel in several respects. It is a complete working system which can carry out reasonably interesting conversations within its domain. It is perhaps the most general approach to linguistic competence to date, combining syntactic and semantic information in a dynamic way. The net result is what has been termed a *conceptual parse* of the input sentence, which is added to the system's data base, where powerful deductive mechanisms are available to resolve ambiguities and to deduce the meaning of the statement. The system is extremely powerful and is probably extensible to other domains, although to date this has not been attempted. It is also an extremely complex system, as its performance implies. Rather than using static data structures to represent knowledge, such as linked lists, the system uses a combination of static and dynamic structures (i.e., procedures or programs). For example, the syntactic processing portion of the system contains separate programs for each of the syntactic units involved. These programs are invoked whenever the system needs to recognize or manipulate them; syntactic and semantic processing are intertwined, each making use of the results of the other.

Before leaving the subject of natural language processing, it might be appropriate to point out that reasonable dialogues can be supported by relatively unsophisticated systems, although the degree to which one can ascribe "understanding" to such a system (in the sense that Winograd's system can be said to "understand"), is minimal. Such a program, called ELIZA, was written some time ago by Joseph Weizenbaum, also at M.I.T.; it was done to illustrate just such a point. A sample dialogue with

ELIZA is given below; again, capitalized statements are the system's response to the input.

men are all alike.
IN WHAT WAY
they're always bugging us about something or other.
CAN YOU THINK OF A SPECIFIC EXAMPLE
well, my boyfriend made me come here.
YOUR BOYFRIEND MADE YOU COME HERE
he says I'm depressed much of the time.
I AM SORRY TO HEAR YOU ARE DEPRESSED
it's true. I am unhappy.
DO YOU THINK COMING HERE WILL HELP YOU NOT TO BE UNHAPPY
i need some help, that much is certain.
WHAT WOULD IT MEAN TO YOU IF YOU GOT SOME HELP
perhaps I could learn to get along with my mother.
TELL ME MORE ABOUT YOUR FAMILY
my father.
YOUR FATHER
you are like my father in some ways.
WHAT RESEMBLANCE DO YOU SEE
you are not very aggressive, but I think you don't want me to notice that.
WHAT MAKES YOU THINK I AM NOT VERY AGGRESSIVE
you don't argue with me.
WHY DO YOU THINK I DON'T ARGUE WITH YOU
you are afraid of me.
DOES IT PLEASE YOU TO BELIEVE I AM AFRAID OF YOU
my father is afraid of everybody.
.
.
.

ELIZA might be called a *script-* or *key-word*-driven system in which any knowledge which the program has access to is embedded in the input text and the script. In some sense, the dialogue supported by this particular version of ELIZA resembles the dialogue between a patient and a particular kind of psychotherapist.

The program searches the input sentence for the presence of one or more key words. Associated with each key word is a set of decomposition rules which specify how the input sentence is to be decomposed and a set of reconstruction rules which specify how the constituent parts are to be reconstructed to produce the output. This is best illustrated by example; assume the input is the sentence

YOU ARE VERY HELPFUL

and that the only key word found is YOU. The first step is to perform the substitution

I for YOU, resulting in

$$\text{I ARE VERY HELPFUL}$$

If the decomposition rules associated with the key word YOU are

$$D_1: \quad (0 \text{ I REMIND YOU OF } 0)$$
$$D_2: \quad (0 \text{ I ARE } 0)$$
$$D_3: \quad (0 \text{ YOU } 0)$$
$$D_4: \quad (0)$$

where 0 represents an arbitrary string, then only D_2 matches the input string, resulting in the following sentence constituents:

$$(1) \text{ empty} \quad (2) \text{ I} \quad (3) \text{ ARE} \quad (4) \text{ VERY HELPFUL}$$

If the first reconstruction rule (there may be several, selected at random for variety)

$K = $ keyword
$D_i = i$th decomposition rule
$R_{i,j} = j$th reconstruction rule associated with ith decomposition rule.

List Structure: $\quad (K((D_1)(R_{1,1})(R_{1,2}) \ldots (R_{1,m_1}))$
$\qquad\qquad\qquad ((D_2)(R_{2,1})(R_{2,2}) \ldots (R_{2,m_2}))$
$$\vdots$$
$\qquad\qquad\qquad ((D_n)(R_{n,1})(R_{n,2}) \ldots (R_{n,m_n})))$

Tree Structure:

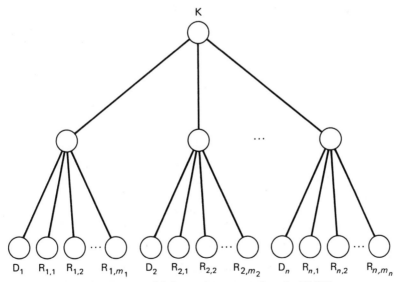

Fig. 12.5 Two possible internal representations for ELIZA.

associated with D_2 and the key word YOU is

WHAT MAKES YOU THINK I AM (4)

then substitution of the fourth constitutent of the input into the reconstruction rule results in the output

WHAT MAKES YOU THINK I AM VERY HELPFUL

The decomposition rule D_4 assures that if none of the previous decomposition rules apply, the last one will always match. Associated with this rule might be a noncommittal response.

The key words, decomposition rules, and reconstruction rules may be represented by a variety of data structures, two of which are shown in Figure 12.5. One of the characteristics of ELIZA is that it is straightforward to program (particularly in SNOBOL with its sophisticated pattern-matching and substitution operations) and fun to use. It also points out that one must be careful when claiming "comprehension" for a computer program. ELIZA is based on a simple but powerful pattern matching scheme, from which it derives most of its ability. How this relates to actual "understanding" of the input text raises some interesting questions.

12.2 GAMES AS AN APPROACH TO ARTIFICIAL INTELLIGENCE

An early approach to machine intelligence was through the medium of games. Games are an intellectual pastime of man and as such are designed to test skills of planning, problem-solving, creativity, and thought. They should be ideal vehicles to explore the hardware manifestations of these skills. The question with which we shall be most concerned is, How do you program a computer to play a game? For purposes of this discussion, we shall restrict ourselves to a certain class of games: the board games. Included in this class are the simple games such as tic-tac-toe and nim and the more intellectually challenging ones such as chess, checkers, and go. All these games share certain common characteristics:

1. The environment with which we are dealing is highly structured; we are given an initial position of pieces on a board of a particular configuration, a set of rules for transforming any legal configuration into another, and a clearly defined termination condition.
2. The environment provides a simple yet rich structure in which to explore machine learning, problem-solving, planning, and creativity.
3. The basics of a board game are easily programmed.

Let us, therefore, consider a very simple game: Last-One-Loses (abbreviated LOL). The game is played by two players, say A and B. A pile of N markers (poker chips, stones, matchsticks, . . .) is placed between the two players; player A goes first and may remove 1, 2, or 3 of the markers until one player is forced to remove the last marker from the pile. This player loses the game—hence the name. LOL is a variation on the game of nim. For purposes of discussion, assume $N = 5$.

   In general, board games may be represented as a tree structure in which the nodes of the tree contain the board configuration and the arcs connecting the nodes represent the legal moves of the game. The root node represents the initial board configuration. The tree shown in Figure 12.6 is the game tree for LOL with $N = 5$. Square

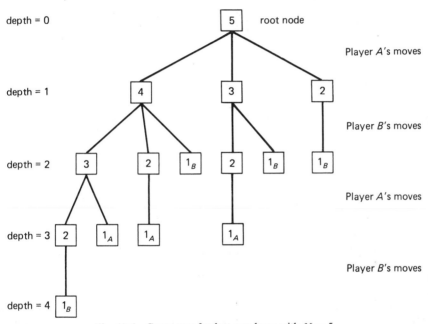

Fig. 12.6   Game tree for last-one-loses with $N = 5$.

boxes represent the nodes, and each node contains an indication of the number of markers left on the board after the sequence of moves leading to the node. Shown down the left margin of the figure is the *depth* of the nodes in the tree; the root node is conventionally assigned a depth of 0. Those nodes containing a letter are winning board configurations for the player indicated and are the *terminal nodes* of the tree. The entire tree represents a set of strategies for each player; in fact, careful examination of Figure 12.6 shows that player *B* has a winning strategy. In the face of any move by player *A*, player *B* can always win the game.

EXERCISE 12.3: Develop an informal algorithm for searching a given game tree for a winning strategy for either player. Determine if a winning strategy exists for either player in the following trees:

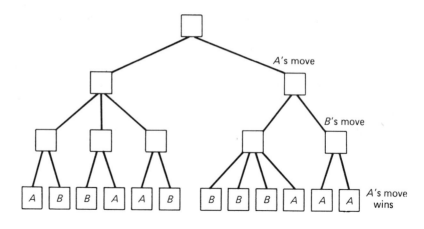

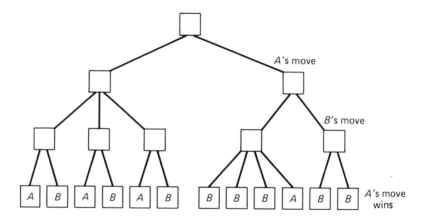

In those cases where it is possible to generate the entire game tree emanating from the root node (the tree in which each node eventually leads to an explicitly indicated node satisfying the termination criteria for the game), the existence of a winning strategy for one player depends on the player being able to achieve positions that lead to a win, independently of any move on his opponent's part. Once this is done, the strategy obtained governs the play of the game, and, consequently, the game loses some of its interest. Every child learns how to play tic-tac-toe reasonably early; thereafter the fun in playing rests in finding someone who doesn't know the strategy. The major difference between these simple games and games of high intellectual interest rests in the size of the game tree. The entire tree for LOL with $N = 5$ consists of 15 nodes; on the other hand, the number of nodes in the game tree for chess has been estimated to be on the order of 10^{120}.† While it is fairly easy to imagine the program

---

†The number of atoms in the visible universe is on the order of 10^{73}. For an interesting discussion on "large" numbers, see W. Ross Ashby, "Introductory Remarks at a Panel Discussion," in M. D. Mesarovic, *Views on General Systems Theory*, Wiley, New York, 1964.

written to play LOL by exhaustively searching the game tree, the program to play chess by the same exhaustive method is clearly outside the realm of the imagination. If each node in the tree could be generated in $\frac{1}{3}$ nanosecond, it would still take approximately 10^{102} centuries to completely generate the tree. What, then, are we to do?

12.2.1 Minimax Search

It is apparent that there are two limitations governing the generation of the tree: space and time. A possible solution would be to generate only a small portion of the game tree emanating from a given board configuration, produce a move on the basis of whatever information can be obtained from this subtree, and await our opponent's reply to this move. This process could then be repeated until the game terminates. To produce a "good" move, we must make two assumptions:

1. Our opponent is as intelligent as we are and is out to "get" us; that is, he will always make the best move available to him. Note that this assumption may not always be valid; one could conceive of an opponent deliberately making bad moves in order to lull her opponent into a false sense of complacency.
2. A measure exists which is an estimate of the "worth" of a given board position. This measure is positive for a "good" position for one player; the more positive the value, the better the move. Negative values are good for the other player (note the assumed symmetry in the function). Such a function might be an estimate of how close a given position is to a win.

These assumptions are known as the *minimax assumptions*. Consider the portion of the game tree shown in Figure 12.7; in this figure, nodes are labeled as $N_{i,j}$, where i is the

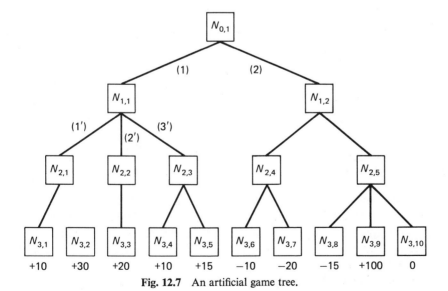

Fig. 12.7   An artificial game tree.

depth of the node in the tree and j is a running index at that depth. To facilitate discussion, arcs (which represent moves) emanating from certain nodes have been labeled 1, 2, 1', 2', etc. Values obtained from the measure function are shown below the nodes at level 3. Given only the information shown in the figure, and assuming that as player A you are an intelligent, rational game player, which move (1 or 2) would you choose?

To choose a move, we must evaluate nodes $N_{1,1}$ and $N_{1,2}$. We would then choose that move which results in the position (node) with the higher value. Presumably, the values at the bottom of the tree are some indication of the consequences of arriving at a particular node at this depth. The strategy is then to look ahead in the game tree, evaluate the resulting board configurations, and use this information to choose a move from the root node. Our line of reasoning might go something like this: If we choose the move to $N_{1,1}$, our opponent would be faced with a choice of move 1', 2', or 3'. If he chooses 1', node $N_{2,1}$ is worth $+30$ to us since we can move to node $N_{3,2}$; if 2' is chosen, node $N_{2,2}$ is worth $+20$ since we have no choice but to move to node $N_{3,3}$. Finally, if our opponent chooses 3', node $N_{2,3}$ is worth $+15$ since we can move to $N_{3,5}$. However, our opponent has the ultimate choice of move at level 1, and presumably, his strategy is to place us in the worst possible position, which in this case is node $N_{2,3}$ since it is worth the least to us. Therefore, if we choose move 1, node $N_{1,1}$ is worth $+15$. Note that to get this value, we start at the bottom of the tree and back values up to parent nodes. Whenever we have control of the game (our turn to move), we back up the maximum value among the descendant nodes. Whenever the opponent has control, we back up the minimum value among the descendant nodes. This strategy is consistent with the minimax assumptions.

EXERCISE 12.4: What value is backed up to node $N_{1,2}$ in Figure 12.7 and which move (1 or 2) should ultimately be chosen?

The procedure just described is called the *minimax search procedure* for the obvious reasons. Playing the game using this procedure is now fairly straightforward: When it is our turn to move, we generate the tree emanating from the current board position to a depth which depends on the time and resources we have available, evaluate the nodes at the bottom of the tree using the measure function, make the minimax move, and sit back and await our opponent's reply. Perhaps our opponent is using the same algorithm to make his moves. The game progresses until one player wins or a tie is reached.

EXERCISE 12.5: Within the framework developed thus far, how might a winning position for either player be reflected in the measure function?

The function measuring the worth of a node is called a *heuristic function*; heuristic has Greek origins and means "serving to discover." Many of the problems in artificial intelligence are of some complexity and generally have no analytic solution; that is, one cannot write down an algorithm which is guaranteed to find the "best" solution. Very often this is because the processes which are being modeled (or programmed) are not understood in any detail. One is therefore forced to employ a collection of "tricks" or heuristics, which work most of the time and which tend to produce both reasonable and acceptable results. Those programs which utilize heuristics are known as heuristic programs. In the case of the game-playing processes under discussion, the evaluation function which measures the "goodness" or worth of a given node is a heuristic function since in most cases it is not known how realistic the values which it produces are. One attempts to formulate the function using whatever knowledge of the game is available and whatever may be derived from an analysis of known strategies. Thus, the important features of game positions and their relationships to strategic decisions are determined, and the function is constructed to reflect these features.

Obviously, the ability to play a game well is intimately connected to the power of the heuristic function chosen. In addition, the depth of search in the tree is an important factor: It is sometimes possible to trade off depth of search versus the "goodness" of the heuristic function. Of course, if one had a perfect heuristic function, one would never have to search at all (why?).

The size of the tree to be searched is still a major problem. If each node in the tree has exactly 5 successors, then there are 5 nodes on the first level, 5×5 on the second, and finally 5^n on the nth level. The total number of nodes that must be generated and evaluated is then

$$N = 1 + 5 + 5^2 + \cdots + 5^n$$

This series may be easily summed, and we obtain

$$N = \frac{5^{n+1} - 1}{4}$$

Even for modest values of n, this gets large rather rapidly. For $n = 7$, $N = 97,656$. If each node could be generated and evaluated in 1 millisecond, it would take more than 97 seconds to search the tree; while this is much better than before, it is obvious that tree search by exhaustive enumeration is a rather time-consuming process. One might very well want to cut down on the number of nodes that were generated while still retaining the minimax procedure.

12.2.2 Tree Generation Methods

Implicit in the generation of the trees shown in Figures 12.6 and 12.7 has been a procedure known as *breadth-first* generation. Informally, this procedure may be stated as follows:

1. Begin with the root node.
2. Generate all the successors of the root node.
3. Generate all the successors to these nodes.
4. Continue by generating all the successors to nodes at depth i before generating successors to nodes at depth $i + 1$.

It is easy to see why this procedure is called breadth-first. Each level of the tree, as defined by the depth of that level, is completely generated before the next level generation begins. Breadth-first generation is graphically illustrated in Figure 12.8. In this figure, numbers contained in the nodes indicate the order in which nodes were generated. Numbers down the side indicate the depth level. If the game tree is large, normally breadth-first generation terminates after all the nodes at some predetermined depth have been generated. The minimax procedure is then applied to the resulting tree, and a move is chosen.

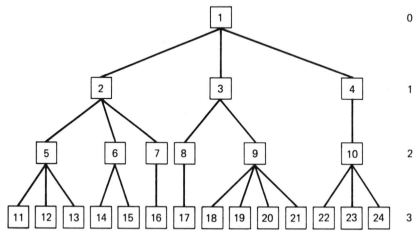

Fig. 12.8   Illustration of breadth-first tree generation.

The informal outline above suggests that the inductive technique be applied to the problem. First, if the level of the tree to be generated is 1, all we need to do is generate the descendants of the root. Assuming that the tree has been generated to a depth of i in the desired way, how can we obtain the tree of level $i + 1$? By imposing a list structure on the nodes of level i, as shown in Figure 12.9, the problem becomes trivial. Without specifying further the details of the physical data structure, Algorithm 12.1 will when given a *level_list* create a new *level_list* which contains all the descendants of the nodes on the previous level. It accomplishes this by repeatedly calling the procedure *gen_desc*, which generates all descendants of a node p, links them together,

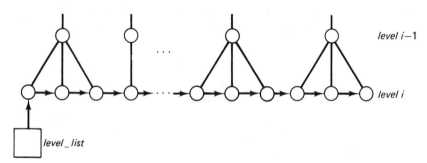

Fig. 12.9   Level_list for breadth-first generation.

and places them on the end of the *next_level* list. After termination of the **while** itera-tion, this list becomes the new *level_list*.

   Algorithm 12.1 (Induction part of breadth-first generation algorithm)

> **procedure** *breadth_induc(level_list; level_list)*
> **begin** /*induction step*/
> $p \leftarrow$ *first(level_list)*; *next_level* $\leftarrow$ **null**;
>   **while** $(p \neq$ **null**)
>   **begin**
>   *gen_desc(p, next_level; next_level)*;
> $p \leftarrow$ *next(nodes(p))*;
>   **end**;
>   *level_list* $\leftarrow$ *next_level*
> **end** /*induction*/

   EXERCISE 12.6: Describe a data structure in detail which could be used to implement the breadth-first generation algorithm. [Hint: For this particular problem there is no need to maintain *level_list* as a separate linked list. Actually, the list can be represented as a sequential structure sharing the nodes of the tree if the tree is represented properly (reread Sections 9.1 and 9.2 on representation for static trees).]

   As an alternative to breadth-first generation, consider the situation shown in Figure 12.10, where the tree is the same as in Figure 12.8. Again, the numbers asso-ciated with nodes indicate the order in which the nodes were generated. As the name implies, the *depth-first* procedure generates the first successor to a node, then its first successor, etc., until the depth bound is reached. The method then backs up one level, generates the next successor on this level, etc., until the entire tree has been generated.

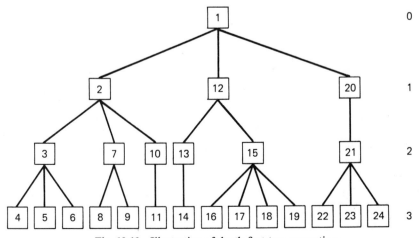

Fig. 12.10   Illustration of depth-first tree generation.

Whereas for the breadth-first generation of a tree, induction was an obvious technique and no other technique was apparent (see Exercise 6 at end of Chapter 11), for depth-first generation the principle of recursion leads us to a concise algorithm. Given the root of the game tree and the task to generate a tree of l levels, we first generate the first descendant of the root and apply the procedure recursively to generate a subtree of $l - 1$ levels; we repeat this procedure for the remaining descendants of the root. Again, in Algorithm 12.2 we do not assume any particular physical data structure and use the "access" procedure *gen_desc2* which will generate the ith descendant of a root, return a pointer to it in *des*, and do any necessary linking.

Algorithm 12.2 (Depth-first generation of a tree)

> **procedure** *depth_gen* (*root, levelind;*)
> **begin** /*depth*/
>   **if** *levelind* = 0 **then terminate**;
> $i \leftarrow 1$; *gen desc2(root, i; des)*;
>   **while** (*des* $\neq$ **null**)
>   **begin** /*build subtree*/
>   *depth_gen(des, levelind* $-$ 1;);
> $i \leftarrow i + 1$; *gen_desc2(root, i; des)*
>   **end** /*build*/
> **end** /*depth*/

Although on the surface Algorithm 12.2 differs considerably from Algorithm 12.1, internal execution is remarkably similar. Were the mechanism supporting recursion made explicit, the only difference would be the order in which nodes are saved for further processing. Normally, there would be no reason for choosing one method over the other. In actual practice, there is one reason for choosing depth-first over breadth-first, as we shall see in the next section.

EXERCISE 12.7: Describe a data structure in detail which could be used to implement the depth-first generation algorithm.

12.2.3 The Alpha-Beta Search Procedure

Our stated goal is to cut down on the number of nodes in the game tree which must be generated and evaluated. One procedure by which this might be accomplished is to interleave the processes of node generation and minimax evaluation. As an example, consider the portion of the game tree shown in Figure 12.11, assuming it is our turn to move. Furthermore, assume for the sake of argument that we already know the value of the nodes as indicated in Figure 12.11. Clearly, node $N_{1,1}$ is worth $+20$ to us using the minimax criteria. However, careful examination of Figure 12.11 yields one important observation. Assume we have generated and evaluated node $N_{2,1}$. Next, suppose we generate node $N_{2,2}$ and node $N_{3,4}$, followed by evaluation of node $N_{3,4}$ to $+60$. We know, without generating $N_{3,5}$ or $N_{3,6}$, that our opponent will

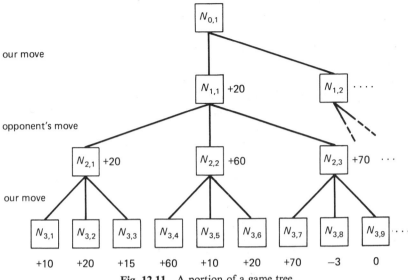

Fig. 12.11   A portion of a game tree.

never prefer the move to node $N_{2,2}$ over the move to node $N_{2,1}$; specifically, the values associated with nodes $N_{3,5}$ and $N_{3'6}$ can have no effect on our opponent's choice of move. These nodes do not have to be generated or evaluated, although the breadth-first generation algorithm automatically generates them. Suppose now we generate the tree using the depth-first search algorithm but evaluate each terminal node as it is generated and pass the resulting value back up the tree using standard minimax.

Before discussing the *alpha-beta search* procedure (as it will be called), let us quickly develop the algorithm for the minimax search. This can be accomplished by using Algorithm 12.2 and requiring it to return the minimax value of the subtree it builds (plus an indicator showing which move leads to it). Starting with a root, we then keep track of the maximum (or minimum if it's our opponent's move) of these values as we call the procedure recursively for the values of all the descendants. That is, as an input parameter we must have an indicator as to whose move it is. In Algorithm 12.3, the procedure *gen_move* is defined to generate the *i*th descendant of a node which will depend on whose move it is.

You will note that the two blocks of code in the second **if** statement are nearly identical and differ only in the comparison. Only for pedagogic reasons did we duplicate the code; in the SNOBOL implementation later on we shall coalesce them.

Let us now return to the problem of how to reduce the complexity of the tree generation process. We introduce two variables *alpha* and *beta* which will be used as criteria for cutting off further generations of subtrees on a given level. *alpha* will be used in determining whether to stop generating subtrees when computing the minimum value on a level and *beta* while computing the maximum. Since the actions for each case are symmetric, only the "beta" case will be discussed (maximization of "our" moves).

Algorithm 12.3 (Minimax search procedure)

```
procedure minimax(root, levelind, ourmove; val, move)
begin /*minimax*/
    if levelind = 0 then [val ← heuristic(root); terminate];
    if ourmove then begin /*our move*/ i ← 1; max ← −∞; mo ← 0;
                        gen_move(root, i, ourmove; des);
                        while (des ≠ null)
                        begin /*get minimax of subtree*/
                            minimax(des, levelind − 1, ¬ourmove; val, move);
                            if val > max then [max ← val; mo ← i];
                            i ← i + 1;
                            gen_move(root, i, ourmove; des)
                        end; /*get*/
                        val ← max; move ← mo
                    end /*our*/
                    else begin /*opponents move*/
                        i ← 1; min ← ∞; mo ← 0;
                        gen_move(root, i, ourmove; des);
                        while (des ≠ null)
                        begin /*get minimax*/
                            minimax(des, levelind − 1, ¬ourmove; val, move);
                            if val < min then [min ← val; mo ← i];
                            i ← i + 1;
                            gen_move(root, i, ourmove; des)
                        end; /*get*/
                        val ← min; move ← mo
                    end /*opponents*/
end /*minimax*/
```

The input to the *alpha_beta* procedure will be the same as for the *minimax* procedure with the addition of the variables *alpha* and *beta*. The statements parallel those of Algorithm 12.3 until the line

if *val* > *max* **then** . . .

In the new procedure, we now insert the check

if *val* > *beta* **then** [*max* ← *val;* **terminate**];

which causes execution of the iteration to terminate if a cutoff is appropriate. If *beta*

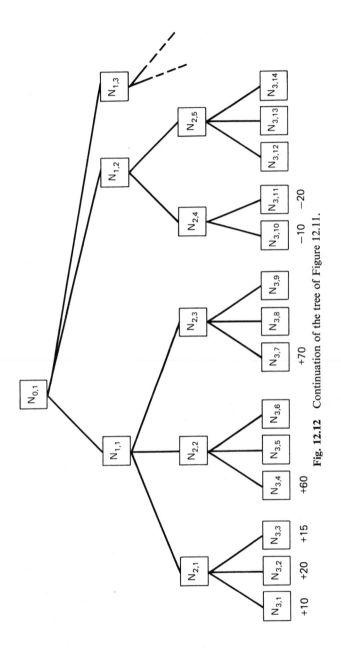

Fig. 12.12   Continuation of the tree of Figure 12.11.

(β) is greater than *val*, we update *alpha* (α) if necessary by

$$\textbf{if } val > alpha \textbf{ then } alpha \leftarrow val;$$

and then continue as in Algorithm 12.3. For this scheme to work properly we call *alpha_beta* initially with $-\infty$ ($+\infty$) as the value for alpha (beta). In future calls to *alpha_beta*, the variables *alpha* and *beta* will take on the values they have been assigned as a result of previous calls. (Note: *alpha* and *beta* are not output parameters; thus they cannot be modified through side effects.)

EXERCISE 12.8: Make the changes outlined above to Algorithm 12.3. Call the new procedure:

procedure *alpha_beta(root, levelind, ourmove, alpha, beta; val, move)*

Example 12.1

Execution of the *alpha_beta* procedure on the tree in Figure 12.11 will result in the following steps, assuming it is "our" turn to move:

1. Generate nodes $N_{1,1}$, $N_{2,1}$, $N_{3,1}$; evaluate $N_{3,1}$; as we maximize over the values returned as a result of generating and evaluating nodes $N_{3,2}$ and $N_{3,3}$, none will exceed the initial value of *beta* (∞). The local changes to *alpha* have no effect since the nodes to which *alpha* is passed are terminal. The minimax value returned to $N_{2,1}$ is $+20$.
2. When going from level 1 to level 2 in the tree, we are minimizing since it is the opponent's move; once the value 20 is obtained for $N_{2,1}$, *beta* is changed to the minimum of the old *beta* (∞) and *val* (20), which is 20. Generating $N_{2,2}$, we then call recursively with a value of 20 for *beta*, which will cause a β-cutoff after $N_{3,4}$ has been generated.
3. *beta* is not changed, and after generating $N_{2,3}$ again a β-cutoff will occur after $N_{3,7}$ has been generated.
4. The value of $N_{2,1}$, 20, is returned, causing *alpha* to be updated to 20.
5. See Exercises 12.9 and 12.10. ■

EXERCISE 12.9: Continue the analysis of node generation for the tree in Figure 12.12 (which is an extension of the tree in Figure 12.11) and determine all α- and β-cutoffs.

It can be shown that the α-β procedure always results in the same decision that would have been reached by minimax but sometimes with considerable savings in terms of the number of nodes that must be generated and evaluated. Many other procedures exist for streamlining search in game trees; these methods have important consequences in operations research and artificial intelligence.

EXERCISE 12.10: Analyze the game tree on page 451 and determine all α-, β-cutoffs for player *A*. Which move is ultimately chosen? Values shown at the bottom of the tree are obtained from the heuristic function. How much of a savings does the α-β procedure afford over the standard minimax procedure?

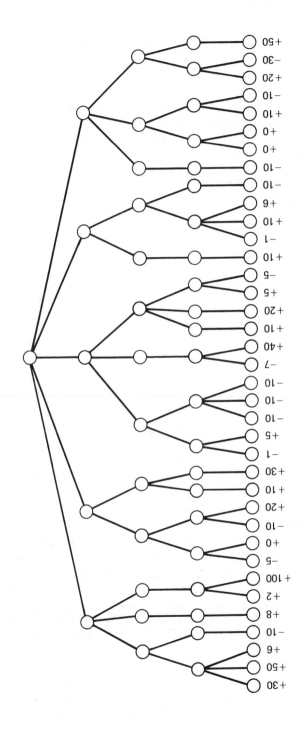

12.3 A KALAH PLAYING PROGRAM: AN EXAMPLE

As an illustration of the techniques discussed above, we shall develop a SNOBOL program to play the game of Kalah. Kalah is a version of one of the oldest known games—Mancala; boards of the type used for playing Kalah have been found carved in the stonework of Egyptian temples built over 3000 years ago. The game is sufficiently rich that there is no known optimal strategy for playing the game, yet the rules are remarkably simple to state.

12.3.1 The Rules of Kalah

Kalah is a game for two players. The board construction varies across several versions of the game. Figure 12.13 shows the construction of a modern Kalah board.

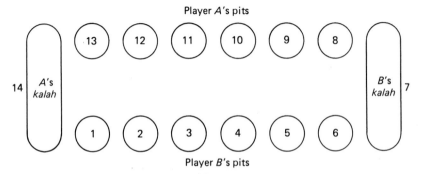

Fig. 12.13   The Kalah board.

Each circle represents a holder (a paper cup, depression in the ground, etc.) for the pieces. Each player has six holders known as his pits and a special holder known as the *kalah*. A number of indistinguishable pieces are provided (smooth round stones are sometimes used). The pits have been numbered for reference purposes; we furthermore assume that the two players are labeled *A* and *B*.

Each pit initially contains *n* stones (*n* = 3 is a good number, but experienced players agree that *n* = 6 is a more interesting game). The kalahs are initially empty; for *n* = 3, the initial board configuration is shown in Figure 12.14.

Fig. 12.14   Kalah board configuration for *n* = 3.

One player is designated to start the game, and play then alternates. Each player, during his turn, chooses a pit on his side of the board, removes all the markers, and distributes them (one in each consecutive pit) in a counterclockwise direction. The only pit ever passed during this distribution of markers is the opponent's kalah. Once a stone is placed in a kalah, it remains there for the duration of the game. There are two simple rules governing the above play:

1. If the last stone lands in your own kalah, you have another turn (for simplicity, we shall omit this rule in the subsequent program).
2. If the last stone lands in an empty pit on your side opposite a nonempty pit on the opponent's side, you capture all the stones in the opponent's pit and place them, along with the stone making the capture, in your own kalah. Capture by this rule ends your turn.

The game ends when all the pits on one side of the board are empty; the player with the most stones in his kalah wins the game.

12.3.2 The Kalah Program

We have already seen how the alternative moves in one play of a game may be represented in a tree structure. For illustrative purposes, the continuation move in Kalah will be ignored in the program to be developed. The nodes of the game tree must contain all the relevant information:

1. The board configuration at this node;
2. The value of the heuristic function at this node, or the minimax (backed-up) value from lower in the tree; and
3. The pointers to the nodes representing each legal position (node) that can be reached from this node; in the case of Kalah, a maximum of six moves is possible from any given board configuration.

Considerations such as these lead to a choice of data structure for representing the node itself and the board configuration. In this case, we shall assume a node structure as shown in Figure 12.15. The board configuration may be easily represented as a linear array (vector), as shown in Figure 12.16.

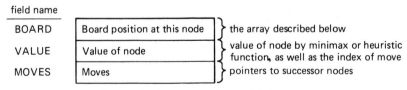

field name		
BOARD	Board position at this node	the array described below
VALUE	Value of node	value of node by minimax or heuristic function, as well as the index of move
MOVES	Moves	pointers to successor nodes

Fig. 12.15 Node structure for Kalah.

EXERCISE 12.11: The above choice for the physical structures to represent the node and board configuration was rather arbitrary. For example, a linked circular list might be more convenient for representing the board structure. Discuss the advantages and disadvantages of the linear array, linked circular list, and doubly linked lists for representing the Kalah board. What about the node structure? Are there more convenient representations?

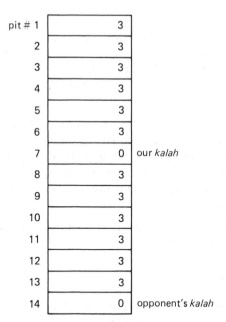

Fig. 12.16   Board configuration.

For the game of Kalah, the form of the heuristic function is nearly self-evident. At any given point in the game, a strong indication as to who has the better position is given by the relative number of stones in the respective kalahs. Although this is certainly not the only criterion, it will suffice for us since it is quite indicative of relative strengths, particularly toward the end of the game. Formally, we define the heuristic function as

$$heuristic(root) := board(root)(7) - board(root)(14)$$

In implementing a program for the Kalah game in SNOBOL we shall utilize Algorithm 12.3 and the data structures outlined above. In the problem statement in Figure 12.17, we have included a statement for the utility procedure *gen_move*. The refinement for module I of Figure 12.17 is given by Algorithm 12.3 except that we wish to coalesce the nearly identical blocks of code. To achieve this, we make *ourmove* a variable with values 0 and 1 instead of **t** and **f** and introduce a 2-tuple, *b*, which will contain the unevaluated expressions:

$$val > mm$$
$$val < mm$$

where *mm* stands for either the current minimum or maximum. The appropriate computation is then selected by the current value of *ourmove*.

Module II generates the *j*th move from a given board position by creating a new board which initially is a copy of the board in the root node. This copy is modified by distributing the stones from the *j*th ($j + 7$ if it is our opponent's move) pit according

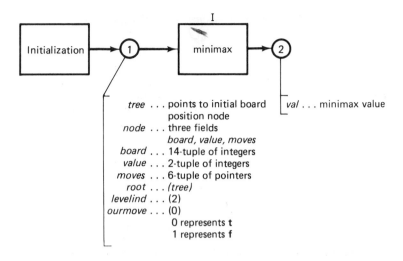

tree ... points to initial board
        position node
node ... three fields
        board, value, moves
board ... 14-tuple of integers
value ... 2-tuple of integers
moves ... 6-tuple of pointers
root ... *(tree)*
levelind ... (2)
ourmove ... (0)
        0 represents **t**
        1 represents **f**

val ... minimax value

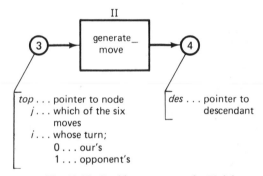

top ... pointer to node
  j ... which of the six
        moves
  i ... whose turn;
        0 ... our's
        1 ... opponent's

des ... pointer to
        descendant

Fig. 12.17   Problem statement for Kalah game.

to the rules of Kalah, checks for and performs the appropriate action if a capture occurs, and returns a pointer to a node containing the new board with **null** in the *value* and *move* fields. Although it is not really necessary to build the game tree, we shall link the proper *move* field of the root node to the new node. The recursion mechanism will keep track of nodes as long as a procedure has not returned with a minimax value. After that point there is no apparent reason to keep the just evaluated subtree around (which will happen if we have linked it to its father). However, since a complete game consists of a series of alternate moves, the minimax searches for subsequent moves can be optimized if the game tree is saved. Hence, we shall keep the game tree as one result of the minimax search. The function *gen_move* is straightforward, and we shall not give an algorithm for it, although it is somewhat clumsy due to the primitive physical data structure selected. It could be improved considerably with better data structures (see Exercise 12.11).

Purpose: Produce the *j*th descendant node of the node pointed to by TOP. The *j*th node corresponds to the choice of pit *j* or pit *j* + 7 (depending on the value of *i*, which keeps track of whose move it is) and the subsequent distribution of stones according to the rules.

> *Communication:*

global variable referenced: None.
formal parameters: TOP . . . . a pointer to a NODE;
                              J . . . . index of pit in BOARD(TOP) which
                                                         is to be emptied;
                              I . . . . 0 if our move,
                                                         1 if opponents move;
local variables: N . . . . index of starting pit;
                              K . . . . index of opponent's kalah;
                              PEBN. . . . . number of markers to be distributed;
                              CTR, T, NEW . . . temporaries.

GENMOVE returns a pointer to a new NODE (if it exists; **null** otherwise) which has been linked to TOP; entrypoint is NEXT.

> *Program:*

```
:::::::::          BEGIN OF GENMOVE
NEXT       NEW = COPY(BOARD(TOP))                                              29
:::::::::          INITIALIZATION BLOCK
::                 N DENOTES INDEX OF PIT
           N = J + 1 :: 7                                                      30
::                 K DENOTES INDEX OF OPPONENTS KALAH
           K = 14 - 1 :: 7                                                     31
::                 PEBN IS NUMBER OF MARKERS IN PIT N
           PEBN = NE(NEW<N>,0) NEW<N>                    :F(RETURN)            32
           NEW<N> = 0 ; CTR = 1;                                              33
:::::::::          END OF INITIALIZATION
:::::::::          DISTRIBUTION OF PEBBLES LOOP
LOOP       N = N + 1                                                          36
::                 SKIP OPPONENTS KALAH
           EQ(N,K)                                       :S(LOOP)             37
           NEW<N> = NEW<N> + 1                           :F(TURN)             38
           CTR = NE(CTR,PEBN) CTR + 1                    :F(END1)S(LOOP)      39
TURN       N = 0                                         :(LOOP)              40
:::::::::          END OF LOOP
:::::::::          CHECK FOR SPECIAL CASES BLOCK
::                 DID WE END UP IN PIT OF MOVER?
END1       GT(N - 7 :: 1,0) LT(N - 7 :: 1,7)             :S(CHECK)            41
SET        GENMOVE = NODE(NEW,,ARRAY('6'))                                    42
           T = MOVES(TOP)                                                     43
           T<J> = GENMOVE                                :(RETURN)            44
::                 WERE THERE PEBBLES IN PIT?
CHECK      EQ(NEW<N>,0)                                  :F(SET)              45
::                 DID OPPOSING PIT CONTAIN PEBBLES?
           EQ(NEW<14 - N>,0)                             :S(SET)              46
::                 MODIFY BOARD ACCORDING TO CAPTURE
           NEW<7 :: 1 + 7> = NEW<14 - N> + NEW<7 :: 1 + 7> + 1               47
           NEW<14 - N> = 0                                                    48
           NEW<N> = 0                                    :(SET)              49
:::::::::          END OF SPECIAL
:::::::::          END OF GENMOVE
```

The only difference between Algorithm 12.3 and the SNOBOL implementation of module I (below) lies in the criterion to terminate move generation. In the SNOBOL version, since only six moves are possible on the Kalah board, exactly six moves are generated. Those for which there are no pebbles in the corresponding pit are simply skipped, resulting in a **null** pointer in the corresponding location in NEXT.

Purpose: Generate game tree and return minimax value.
Communication:

global variables referenced:	B . . . . two-tuple of unevaluated expressions;
functions called:	GENMOVE . . . as given before;
	MINIMAX . . . recursive;
formal parameters:	TOP . . . . pointer to root NODE;
	LEVEL . . . . distance to level of terminal nodes;
	MOVE . . . . 0 our move,
	1 opponents move;
local variables:	MM, JM, BT, I, DES, VAL.

MINIMAX returns the "minimax" value of the TOP node and as a side effect builds the game tree; the VALUE field of a node contains as a string the minimax value plus the index of the pit which leads to it; entrypoint is MIMAX.

Program:

```
::::::::::            BEGINNING OF MINIMAX
::::::::::            INITIALIZATION BLOCK
::                    MM DENOTES CURRENT MINIMUM(MAXIMUM) VALUE ON
::                    A GIVEN LEVEL
MIMAX     MM = -1000 + 2000 :: MOVE                                      13
          JM = 1                                                        14
          EQ(LEVEL,0)                              :F(BEGIN)            15
::::::::::            TERMINATION ACTION
::                    EVALUATE HEURISTIC FUNCTION
          BT = BOARD(TOP)                                               16
          MINIMAX = BT<7> - BT<14>                                      17
          VALUE(TOP) = MINIMAX                     :(RETURN)            18
::::::::::            END OF TERMINAL CONDITION
::::::::::            OPTIMIZATION LOOP ON ONE LEVEL
BEGIN     I = 1                                                         19
START     DES = GENMOVE(TOP,I,MOVE)                                     20
          IDENT(DES)                               :S(SKIP)            21
::                    DETERMINE NODE VALUE
          VAL = MINIMAX(DES,LEVEL - 1,REMDR(MOVE + 1,2))                22
::                    UPDATE CURRENT OPTIMUM
          EVAL(B<MOVE>)                            :F(SKIP)            23
          MM = VAL                                                     24
          JM = I                                                       25
SKIP      I = NE(I,6) I + 1                        :S(START)           26
::::::::::            END OF OPTIMIZATION LOOP
          VALUE(TOP) = MM ' ' JM                                       27
          MINIMAX = MM                             :(RETURN)           28
::::::::::            END OF MINIMAX
```

It remains only to write the main program, and the Kalah game-playing program will be complete.

Purpose: Generate first move in the game of Kalah using minimax search.
Communication:

global variables introduced:	B	as before;
	TREE	pointer to root NODE of game tree;
functions called:	MINIMAX . . .	as before;
DATA structure introduced:	NODE	tree node with three fields:
	BOARD . .	14-tuple of integers representing board;
	VALUE . . .	string of: minimax value ' ' move index;
	MOVES . . .	6-tuple of pointers to descendants.

Program:

```
::              DEFINE FUNCTIONS AND DATA STRUCTURES
          DEFINE('MINIMAX(TOP,LEVEL,MOVE)MM,JM,BT,I,DES,VAL','MIMAX')
          DEFINE('GENMOVE(TOP,J,I)N,K,PEBN,CTR,NEW,T','NEXT')
          DATA('NODE(BOARD,VALUE,MOVES)')
::              INITIALIZE STRUCTURES
          INITBD = ARRAY('14','3')
          INITBD<7> = 0
          INITBD<14> = 0
          TREE = NODE(INITBD,,ARRAY('6'))
          B = ARRAY('0:1')
          B<0> = ::GT(VAL,MM)
          B<1> = ::LT(VAL,MM)
::              GET MOVE
          MINIMAX(TREE,2,0)
          OUTPUT = VALUE(TREE)                          :(END)

                    .
              .   ROUTINES DEFINED ABOVE
                    .
END
```

EXERCISE 12.12: Modify the Kalah program to include the continuation rule.

EXERCISE 12.13: Modify the Kalah program to include the alpha-beta search procedure. Does this procedure produce substantial improvement in performance?

EXERCISE 12.14: Modify the Kalah program to play an interactive game: This will include adding sufficient output information so that players will be aware of the current board configuration, accepting moves, providing the rules of the game if necessary, etc. The output information provided in the program as defined is not sufficient; in general, any usable program must contain enough interactive information arranged in an aesthetically pleasing form.

12.4 OTHER ASPECTS OF ARTIFICIAL INTELLIGENCE

In this chapter, we have been concerned, to a great degree, with game playing and its related aspects. This does not imply that game playing is a major portion of recent work in artificial intelligence. As pointed out in the introduction, current work in artificial intelligence covers a broad range of areas. Included in this work are questions pertaining to natural-language understanding and question-answering systems, automatic theorem-proving, execution and creation of plans for carrying out a series of actions, perception, pattern recognition, automatic analysis of complex visual scenes, construction of belief systems, semantics, aesthetics, etc. Implicit in this work is an attempt to understand complex processes and representation of knowledge; this may be viewed as the basic goal of artificial intelligence.

The remainder of this section is devoted to an exercise in robotics; the purpose of this exercise is to provide a reasonably simple framework from which to view the areas described above. We leave it to the reader to consult the literature and define those problems which may be of interest.

Computers as symbol-manipulators can operate on models which represent an approximation of complex real-world environments. One example might be the planning processor for a robot which carries out tasks in a room with a number of physical objects. The exercises developed below involve the construction and manipulation of an extremely idealized environment. One important aspect of artificial intelligence is the search for generality; the game-playing programs developed earlier in this chapter were very specific programs. After the program was completed, we had simply a program for playing Kalah (LOL). While the techniques developed were general, each game must be programmed anew; new heuristic functions must be developed, and the general approach is not very satisfying. The construction of a robot environment and the programs controlling the robot's "life" are something very different; only rarely do situations arise which are exact copies of previous situations and in which specific rules may be applied. These programs must be sufficiently general to cope with a wide variety of situations only remotely similar to past experiences.

The two entities which must be represented in the program are the robot and its environment. The environment contains objects with which the robot must interact; therefore, the characteristics of the objects in the environment are of importance and must be represented in the structure developed. Usually, characteristics such as these are stored in an *attribute-value* list; each object has an attribute-value list which contains the attributes of importance to the object and their associated values. For example, one attribute-value pair might specify the (x, y)-coordinates of the location of that object in the environment. In addition to the specific characteristics of the objects in the environment, the global organization of the environment itself must also be represented. For example, one possible environment might be that shown in Figure 12.18. In this case, an 8×7 array of subareas might be an adequate representation of the environment. The name in each array location would point to a list containing the attribute-value pairs for the object occupying that square. While this representation might be adequate for limited applications, it is a relatively static structure, and modifications to the environment's global organization become rather difficult. What would happen to this representation if we decided that an L-shaped room or some other

WALL	WALL	WALL	WALL	WALL	WALL	WALL
	CHAIR				TABLE	WALL
						WALL
ROBOT			CHAIR			WALL
		CHAIR	TABLE	CHAIR		WALL
			CHAIR			WALL
			TABLE		LAMP	WALL
WALL	WALL	WALL	WALL	WALL	WALL	WALL

Fig. 12.18   A possible robot environment.

nonrectangular shape was required? Since this exercise is goal independent, we should look for some more general representation of an environment.

EXERCISE 12.15: Develop a representation of the environment in terms of a node-like structure which is easily modifiable, which contains all the information required for the representation of objects in the environment, and which will be easily manipulatable (e.g., objects can be easily located and moved, etc.).

Each object appearing in the robot's environment will be represented in the following form:

$$\text{OBJECT NAME}/\text{attribute}_1,\text{value}_1/ \ldots /\text{attribute}_n,\text{value}_n/$$

A possible interpretation and coding of the attribute-value pairs is

Attribute	Value	
POS (position)	$I_1,J_1; \ldots I_n,J_n$	Where each pair I_k, J_k specifies the row and column coordinates (respectively) of one of the positions of the object
MOV (movable)	YES NO	Specifies whether the object is movable or fixed in position
MASS	ZERO LIGHT HEAVY	
DIR (direction)	NORTH WEST SOUTH EAST	Specifies the direction that the ROBOT is facing

Using these encodings, the environment of Figure 12.18 can be represented as

CHAIR/POS,2,2;4,4;5,3;5,5;6,4/MOV,YES/MASS,LIGHT/
WALL/POS,1,1;1,2;1,3;...8,6;8,7/MOV,NO/MASS,HEAVY/
ROBOT/POS,4,1/DIR,EAST/

and so on.

EXERCISE 12.16: Write a SNOBOL program which will construct the environment data structure (whatever your choice was from Exercise 12.15) from the information on the attribute-value list described above. The program should print out a map of the environment, similar to Figure 12.18. Complete the attribute-value description of the environment and use this as data for your program. Justify your choice of data structure for the environment.

We wish to control the movement of the robot within the given environment by a set of simple commands. Depending on your choice of data structure, it may be convenient to treat the robot as simply another object in the environment with a special set of attributes; for other structures, it may be more convenient to consider it to be a separate entity altogether. In either case, some of the commands will have a prerequisite set of conditions which must be satisfied before they can be carried out; each command will cause a set of resultant changes in the environment. For each command, a function must be written which will execute the command; these commands form the set of low-level primitives in the system. If the associated prerequisites (the *preconditions*) are satisfied, execution of a command involves updating the model of the environment and the object attributes on the attribute-value list. Otherwise, the cause of the failure to execute a command must be printed and the next command accepted. Thus, the system will be highly interactive and highly modularized; each command function may be developed independently. The set of commands are

Command	Prerequisites	Result
TURNLEFT	None	The robot's direction will be changed one unit counterclockwise.
TURNRIGHT	None	The robot's direction will be changed one unit clockwise.
MOV	Square adjacent to the robot in the direction it is facing has no mass in it.	The robot's previous position is deleted, and its new position is entered in the updated environment.
PUSH	The robot is adjacent to an object which is movable and whose mass must be light; the position (in the direction the robot is facing) in front of the object to be pushed must have no mass attached to it.	Update the environment map and the attribute-value pairs for the robot and the object pushed.

These functions involve referencing both the object attribute-value lists and the environment. For example, MOV can reference the position and direction of the robot under POS and DIR in the attribute-value list. This information can be used to determine the object occupying the position immediately in front of the robot. The mass of this object can be obtained from the attribute-value list, and if it is zero, the prerequisite to MOV is satisfied. Execution of the command MOV then involves updating the map to represent the movement of the robot one step forward as well as POS in the attribute-value list.

EXERCISE 12.17: Write a set of SNOBOL functions to implement the above commands; commands may appear in sequence followed by at least one blank [i.e., there may be more than one command per card (line)]. Devise a series of commands operating on the environment of Figure 12.18 which will thoroughly test your routines. After each command is executed, the command should be output; when the robot changes position, the environment should be output. When the final command is executed, the attribute-value list for each object should also be output.

EXERCISE 12.18: Initialize the position of the robot to 4, 1 facing EAST, and write a function involving a series of commands to push a chair (which is guaranteed to be somewhere in the environment) as far EAST as possible. Since this program should work for a set of environments satisfying the above condition, the robot should locate the chair by failure of a MOV command before pushing it (if it pushed blank space, the robot might fall on its face).

EXERCISE 12.19: Initialize the position of the robot to 7, 1, and write a general function whose goal is to have the robot reach the EAST side of the room as quickly as possible. This function should not be able to access the model of the environment directly (the robot is blind). The speed of the robot will be measured by the number of commands that must be executed before success. This number should be part of the final output.

EXERCISE 12.20: Augment the list of commands for the robot with generally useful functions. For example, FIND(object) might search the environment for a particular object and position the robot next to this object according to some specification.

Using this environment for the robot, or extending the environment in consistent ways, it should be possible to think of nontrivial problems for the robot to solve; routines could be added to the above set of programs to accomplish these actions. For example, write a set of routines which would allow you to converse with the robot in a restricted subset of English. Commands given in English would then be translated into a series of robot commands to accomplish the task. Add a general problem-solving capability to the robot; use it to solve problems of your own choosing; for example, consider a specialized chess-playing robot which pushes pieces around on a chessboard, playing against you. You should begin to get a feel for the general problems of importance in the realm of artificial intelligence.

12.5 CONCLUSIONS

The major focus of this chapter has been on a very narrow aspect of artificial intelligence: tree-searching methods in game playing. The techniques presented here can be extended in a variety of ways to produce very powerful search mechanisms; they have been applied to a variety of board games with varying results, depending on the complexity of the game and the specific evaluation function used. They are not, however, sufficient by themselves in many cases. For the very simple games, such as last-one-loses and tic-tac-toe, they are useful in determining a winning strategy for the game (if one exists), but one would not normally use them to play these games once the strategy is known. (Why not? Try writing an expert tic-tac-toe program with and without tree search processes.) For games of a complexity comparable to Kalah, they work well enough by themselves to result in "expert" programs, i.e., programs which almost never lose. One of the characteristics of Kalah is that there does not appear to be much of a long-range strategy involved in playing the game.

Other games do not share these characteristics; on a complexity continuum, probably in the next level are games similar to checkers. Here the play of the game is based on various offensive and defensive strategies that may change as the game progresses. By concentrating on the development of good evaluation functions, which take into account more global characteristics of the board, it is possible to produce programs which play near championship-level games. Such is not the case for chess, however; programs based solely on tree-searching methods do not play very interesting (or very good) chess. It has been necessary to augment tree searching with global strategy modules which attempt to set the long-range strategic goals and which are sensitive to strategy shifts on the part of the opponent.

As a representative of a game in which tree-searching methods have not resulted in any significant programs at all, we have go. This game is an extremely complex one, in which global strategies play the important role and where the evaluation of a given board position is a very subtle process. Thus far, go has resisted all attempts at developing "interesting" programs (i.e., those that play an interesting, nontrivial game). Work is continuing on many of these games, usually focusing on methods for capturing the specialized kinds of knowledge that humans use.

The other areas of artificial intelligence touched on here are addressing similar interesting questions, and we leave it to the reader to consult the references as entry points into the literature in the various areas.

The question which remains unanswered from the introduction is, Can a machine think? This question was addressed by Alan Turing in 1950. Turing proposed a test which could be used to decide if a properly programmed machine could "think." The test, in the form of a game, consists of two players, A and B, and a human interrogator H. H is set the task of determining which of A or B is the human and which is the machine by posing a series of questions that A and B must answer. If, after asking questions (which may be as difficult and complex as H wishes), H is unable to resolve the question, then the machine must have played the game as well as the human. Note that H is isolated from both A and B; all responses are via some neutral medium. Turing's test has come under some criticism in recent years because it is highly subjective. Other tests have been proposed based on the ability of a machine to survive in a hostile environment, on its ability to learn from experience, etc. Again, these tests are, for the most part, subjective, and it has been proposed that we accept the premise "The machine thinks" if it can carry out tasks which we would normally ascribe to human beings and which require some degree of intelligence. We have come full circle; what do you think?

References

Turing's test was first proposed in 1950 in a provocative article:

A. M. TURING, "Computing Machinery and Intelligence," *Mind, 59* (1950), pp. 433–460.

It has been reprinted many times; see

Z. W. PYLYSHYN, *Perspectives on the Computer Revolution*, Prentice-Hall, Englewood Cliffs, N.J., 1970, pp. 224–245

or

E. A. FEIGENBAUM and J. FELDMAN (eds.), *Computers and Thought*, McGraw-Hill, New York, 1963.

The game of last-one-loses and several variations, along with a discussion of simple machines which learn to play them, is discussed in

H. D. BLOCK, "Learning in Some Simple Non-Biological Systems," *American Scientist* (March 1965), pp. 59–79.

There is much interest in the areas of artificial intelligence and operations research concerning tree structures and efficient means for searching trees. The minimax procedure, alpha-beta search, and pruning methods are discussed in

J. SLAGLE, *Artificial Intelligence: The Heuristic Programming Approach*, McGraw-Hill, New York, 1971

and

N. NILSSON, *Problem-Solving Methods in Artificial Intelligence*, McGraw-Hill, New York, 1971.

Nilsson's discussion is quite technical, while Slagle discusses many of the problem areas of artificial intelligence under investigation during the 1960s.

A comparison of various search methods, including minimax and the alpha-beta variation on minimax, is found in

J. R. SLAGLE and J. K. DIXON, "Experiments with Some Programs that Search Game Trees," *Journal of the ACM, 16*(2) (April 1969), pp. 189–207.

This paper is doubly interesting since the vehicle for the comparison is the game of Kalah.

The rules and board structure for the game of Kalah as used in this chapter may be found in

S. SACKSON, *A Gamut of Games*, Random House, New York, 1969

and a discussion of a program for playing Kalah is presented in

A. G. BELL, "Kalah on Atlas," in *Machine Intelligence 3* (D. Michie ed.), Elsevier, Amsterdam, 1968, p. 181.

A discussion of the historical development of artificial intelligence and the kinds of problems comprising this area may be found in

ALLEN NEWELL, "Artificial Intelligence and the Concept of Mind," in *Computer Models of Thought and Language* (R. Schank and K. Colby, eds.), W. H. Freeman, San Francisco, 1973.

This book also contains other chapters devoted to the broad spectrum of problems confronting research in artificial intelligence.

The functional limitation of computers is always a controversial issue, particularly from the artificial intelligence point of view. See

H. L. DREYFUS, *What Computers Can't Do*, Harper & Row, New York, 1972.

There exists a vast literature in the field of artificial intelligence; the references listed above should provide a starting point for further exploration. Broad surveys of the area may be found in

P. C. JACKSON, *Introduction to Artificial Intelligence*, Petrocelli/Charter, New York, 1975.
E. B. HUNT, *Artificial Intelligence*, Academic Press, New York, 1975.
R. C. SCHANK and K. M. COLBY, *Computer Models of Thought and Language*, W. H. Freeman, San Francisco, 1973.
D. G. BOBROW and A. COLLINS, *Representation and Understanding: Studies in Cognitive Science*, Academic Press, New York, 1975.

For chess buffs, the Special Interest Group on Artificial Intelligence (SIGART) of the Association for Computing Machinery publishes a newsletter which features from time to time the results of chess games played by the various chess programs currently being developed.

The development of a very interesting checkers-playing program is described in

A. SAMUEL, "Some Studies in Machine Learning Using Checkers" in Feigenbaum and Feldman, *op. cit.*

and

A. SAMUEL, "Some Studies in Machine Learning Using Checkers, II, Recent Progress," *IBM Journal of Research & Development* (Nov. 1967), pp. 601–617.

Exercises

1 Discuss the utility of Turing's test as a reliable method for determining whether a machine "thinks" or not. What level of performance would it take to convince you that a computer is "thinking?" Is this level realistic?

2 Discuss the meaning of the application of the term *to think* with regard to properly programmed computers. In your opinion, what aspects of human behavior are beyond the realm of computer simulation?

3 Many of the simple board games make interesting programming projects. Choose one of them [see Sackson (in the references) for ideas] and design a complete game-playing program. Note that the power of these programs is often dependent on the effort involved in generating a good heuristic function.

4 The game-playing procedures based on minimax and alpha-beta algorithms are, in a sense, exhaustive algorithms. Even though the alpha-beta procedure may result in substantially fewer nodes being generated, there is still very little direction in the node generation phase

and no evidence at all of a higher-level strategy. Discuss alternatives to these procedures, particularly methods for developing high-level strategies governing the long-term play of the game.

5 Many simple puzzles are also amenable to solution by using the techniques discussed in this chapter. For example, the sliding block puzzle known as the "15" puzzle has been used [see Nilsson (in the references)] to illustrate the tree generation methods discussed here. There are many similar puzzles available on the market which have like characteristics. The solution to these puzzles is simply a string of moves which when applied to the starting configuration of the puzzle will result in some desired "goal" state. Show how the techniques discussed here could be modified to solve these kinds of puzzles. As an example, consider the Tower of Hanoi problem or the "15" puzzle; the traveling salesman problem is another possibility. Are perfect solutions guaranteed in the latter example?

6 Under what conditions is the alpha-beta procedure most efficient in terms of the number of nodes cut off? Discuss alternative methods (if any) for increasing the probability that the alpha-beta procedure is almost maximally efficient.

7 Complete the Kalah-playing program and configure it to play an interactive game. Can you improve upon the heuristic function used here? In general, game-playing programs can be configured to play against each other, using different heuristic functions or strategies. In this way, many games may be played in a reasonably short time and the results recorded. Marginally better heuristic functions should be detected by marginally better won/lost records.

8 The Kalah-playing program described here is relatively inefficient in its search procedure, since each time it is the machine's turn, it generates the entire tree from scratch. On the other hand, only two moves have taken place since the last time it was the machine's move. It might be more efficient (particularly if the depth of the tree generated is greater than 2) to retain the tree and start the next generation phase with a partially constructed tree. Modify the Kalah program to remember the tree; does this improve the efficiency of the program?

9 Assume that the game tree is a *full* tree of degree k, i.e., each node has k descendants, and of depth j; further assume that we measure the work T in terms of calls to *gen_move*. What is the complexity of the *minimax* procedure? And what is the best-case complexity of the *alpha_beta* procedure?

10 The evaluation function in the Kalah program described in this chapter used a very simple evaluation function. If we label the pits as shown in Figure 12.13 and call them p_i, for $i = 1$ to 14, then the function may be written as $e = p_7 - p_{14}$. A more general function might take into account the contents of the other pits as well; one could write a function such as

$$e = \sum_{i=1}^{14} w_i p_i$$

where the w_i are multiplicative weights, whose value represents the importance of a particular pit. Our original function can be put in this framework by noting that $w_7 = 1$, $w_{14} = -1$, and all other weights are 0. Write a Kalah program which will play against itself but use different evaluation functions on alternate moves. This is equivalent to having two separate programs which take the place of player A and player B. Can you vary the weights on the evaluation function so as to improve on our simple function? How might you have each program systematically and automatically vary the weights so as to generate the best evaluation function for the game?

11 Implement an ELIZA-type program in SNOBOL. Write a script which will support a dialogue in some area familiar to you (note that this is probably the most difficult part of the exercise) and try it out on some of your acquaintances. What are their reactions?

Index